Philological and Historical Commentary on
Ammianus Marcellinus XXVI

Philological and Historical Commentary on Ammianus Marcellinus XXVI

By

J. den Boeft, J.W. Drijvers,
D. den Hengst and H.C. Teitler

BRILL

LEIDEN • BOSTON
2008

This book is printed on acid-free paper.

A Cataloging-in-Publication record for this book is available from the Library of Congress.

ISBN: 978 90 04 16212 9

Copyright 2008 by Koninklijke Brill NV, Leiden, The Netherlands.
Koninklijke Brill NV incorporates the imprints Brill, Hotei Publishing,
IDC Publishers, Martinus Nijhoff Publishers and VSP.

All rights reserved. No part of this publication may be reproduced, translated, stored in
a retrieval system, or transmitted in any form or by any means, electronic, mechanical,
photocopying, recording or otherwise, without prior written permission from the publisher.

Authorization to photocopy items for internal or personal use is granted by Koninklijke Brill NV
provided that the appropriate fees are paid directly to The Copyright Clearance Center,
222 Rosewood Drive, Suite 910, Danvers, MA 01923, USA.
Fees are subject to change.

PRINTED IN THE NETHERLANDS

CONTENTS

Preface VII
Introduction IX
A note on chronology XV
Legenda XXVII

Commentary on Chapter 1 1
Commentary on Chapter 2 37
Commentary on Chapter 3 59
Commentary on Chapter 4 75
Commentary on Chapter 5 93
Commentary on Chapter 6 125
Commentary on Chapter 7 177
Commentary on Chapter 8 213
Commentary on Chapter 9 241
Commentary on Chapter 10 263

Bibliography 307
Indices 327

PREFACE

On the occasion of the publication of our commentary on Book 25 of the *Res Gestae*, the last of the 'Julianic' books, we organized an international conference on 'Ammianus after Julian'. We hope that the papers of this conference, which were recently published, will prove to be interesting for all scholars who are engaged in the study of Late Antiquity. To us the conference brought fresh inspiration at the start of our work on the last hexad of the books in which Ammianus describes the reign of the Pannonian emperors. We now present the commentary on the first of these 'post-Julianic' books, in which the author's gloomy interpretation of the entire period makes itself already clearly felt.

Thanks are due to friends and colleagues who have helped us with their advice, to Ines van de Wetering, who corrected our English, and to the Fondation Hardt at Vandoeuvres (CH), where two of us enjoyed a period of peaceful study. The publishing house Koninklijke Brill N.V. prepared the publication of this volume with professional care.

J. den Boeft
J.W. Drijvers
D. den Hengst
H.C. Teitler

INTRODUCTION

Book 26 of the *Res Gestae* is the first of the hexad which deals with the rule of the Pannonian emperors Valentinian and Valens. The preceding six books, in which the emperor Julian was the protagonist, covered a period of four years, from the pronunciamiento in Paris to the death of Julian's successor Jovian. The contents of Books 26–31 cover a much longer period, from Valentinian's designation as Augustus until the aftermath of the disaster at Adrianople, more than fourteen years. This implies a considerable difference in design. More than before the historian will concentrate on highlights and leave out petty details. However, this does not imply the absence of all minutiae or anecdotes. On the contrary, if such details illustrate what the author finds significant for his account, he does not eschew them. For instance, in Book 26 he reports a pithy remark of a member of the consistorium in chapter 2, and he dwells on the beggarly 'incognito' appearance of the usurper *in spe* Procopius in chapter 6.

Another characteristic of the hexad is Ammianus' authorial presence. In the earlier books his presence was at times quite manifest, but as an eyewitness or a participant rather than as a historian. The Persian siege of Amida and the hazardous escape of the young officer in Book 19, and Julian's Persian expedition are the most conspicuous examples. The last explicit mention of his personal presence occurs at the end of Book 25, when during their retreat from Persia Jovian and his men reached Antioch, and it may well be that this was, in fact, the last time Ammianus was on the spot. In Books 26–31 the author regularly adds historiographical notes and, above all, outspoken moral judgments to his reports. Right at the start of Book 26 one is confronted by a specimen of the former type. The author lectures his readers on the essence of historiography and chides them in advance for any silly expectations they might entertain. Many have assumed that the opening sections just referred to mean that the author's decision to describe the period of Valentinian and Valens was an afterthought, but this is improbable. It is more likely that a description of this period was essential for Ammianus' project, because it would provide a clear contrast with the brief rule of Julian. In this case the sections in question unequivocally express that, precisely by carrying on his history according to plan he was taking the risk that this would turn out to be a wasted effort because of the lack of discerning readers.

In any case, Julian is not forgotten in the third extant hexad of the *Res Gestae*. His name occurs ten times in Book 26, admittedly in a number of cases in a purely factual sense, for instance when some official is said to have been appointed by him, but there are also examples of Julian's friends becoming the victims of the new regime. Moreover, the general quality and conduct of the central characters compare unfavourably with all that Julian stood for.

The first part of the book describes the start of the new reign. As was the case after Julian's death, the civil and military authorities were confronted with the sudden need to find a successor to Jovian, who had died unexpectedly on 17 February 364. They unanimously chose Valentinian, whom they obviously regarded as a capable ruler, even accepting a risky interval of ten days before the candidate, who was on duty in Ancyra, arrived in Nicaea for the inaugural ceremony. Right at the beginning of his reign Valentinian makes two momentous decisions: he appoints his younger brother Valens as his co-ruler with the full title of Augustus, and subsequently he divides the empire into an eastern and a western part, assuming responsibility for the latter part himself. Remarkably, the historian does not mention Valentinian's considerations which led to this decision nor does he offer any comment himself. Instead, he focuses on the immediate dangers facing the new emperors. Valentinian had to go to Gaul in order to lead military actions against Alamannic invasions. After his arrival, he received the alarming news of a usurper's coup in Constantinople. However, precise details were lacking. He had no idea of the situation of his brother, nor of the seriousness of the matter. In a panic reaction he decided to travel immediately to the East to take matters in hand, but his staff convinced him that the campaigns in Gaul absolutely required his presence there.

From a narrative point of view the structure of Ammianus' account is excellent. The first time Procopius' usurpation is mentioned coincides with the anxious uncertainty of the western ruler. This will stir the reader's curiosity. Postponing the account of the campaigns against the Alamans to Book 27, Ammianus spends the rest of Book 26 on an episodic description of the affair, of which the very first stage, up to and including the usurpation scene itself, emphasizes its farcical aspects; the author revels in a satirical sketch of the immediate sequel of events, but then he realizes that the reader will have difficulty believing that such a ridiculous start subsequently grew to such dangerous proportions. He therefore tries to counter such scepticism with a number of historical precedents. Procopius soon succeeded in strenghthening his position, by taking some shrewd measures, but also helped by a few lucky coincidences, such as the presence of the widow of Constantius II and her small daughter, which even persuaded him to pretend that he was a relative of that emperor. He was able to gather enough military forces and profited from the general discontent with the harsh regime of Valens and his men. Some notable successes in Bithynia were a further asset to his enterprise. There was one serious flaw: the absence of truly competent military leaders of the highest rank. The few generals who seemed to have chosen his side let him down when he needed them most. Nevertheless, not all would have been lost, if Procopius had shown more determination and used the opportunities which were there for the taking. His hesitation, which was partly the result of financial problems, caused his downfall and execution. In a brief tailpiece one of his subordinates took his place, but he soon met with the same end.

Ammianus' description of the entire coup leaves much to be desired. It consists of a series of vivid individual episodes, such as the remarkable scene in which Procopius on the battlefield itself persuaded his opponents' soldiers to refrain from fighting and to join forces against the Pannonians, the successful siege of the strategic port of Cyzicus and Valens' hazardous escape from a tricky situation, but the overall strategies are less than clear, and the military actions and battles are merely touched upon, so that the reader is even kept in the dark about the number of massive clashes on the battlefields. As to the chronology of the events: if Ammianus' account had been the only source for Procopius' usurpation, our only knowledge would be that it started at some moment before 1 November 365 and ended during the spring of 366.

As was already noted briefly above, in Book 26, the first of the post-Julianic books, the memory of Julian lingers on in a number of details. This presence is even more marked in the implicit comparisons with the three protagonists of the book. Valentinian made a promising start, when in his inaugural address to the soldiers he showed a degree of authority which was not expected. Later, his decision to leave for Gaul in order to lead the military reaction against the Alamans' attacks testified to prudent determination. On the other hand, choosing his brother Valens as the eastern Augustus was open to question, and the brothers' witch hunt against Julian's supporters was an ugly omen. Valentinian's impulsive and ill-considered reaction to the threat posed by Procopius did not do him credit either. The rise of Valens to the position of Augustus brings to mind the appointment of Julian as the Caesar of Constantius II. In that case the better man had to content himself with a subordinate position; here it was almost the other way round but for the fact that, actually, the younger Augustus played second fiddle to his elder brother, as Ammianus emphasizes no less than four times. The first stages of Valens' rule brought out his cruelty, which was encouraged by the wrong advisors, as well as his pusillanimous anxieties during Procopius' coup, which at a moment of despair even prompted him to give up his emperorship. Whereas Valentinian was in principle not unfit to rule, as Jovian had been, but pulled in the wrong direction by his vices, Valens simply lacked the qualities needed for his task. However, according to Ammianus' account Procopius cut the worst figure. In his case the comparison with Julian is practically explicit. He constantly refers to his relationship with Julian, and several moments of his 'pronunciamiento' at Constantinople bear a certain likeness to Julian's rise to power in Paris. At the same time these similarities bring out the gap between the real and the counterfeit: in Paris Julian was taken by surprise, but in the end he managed to cope convincingly with the situation. Procopius, however, was entirely manipulated by the actions of others at the decisive moment. Although he subsequently grew into his part, he lacked the qualities of true leadership, and this finally caused his downfall.

Apart from looking back to the times of Julian, the reader is also invited to look forward and to take notice of some deplorable aspects of the Pannonians' rule, which bode ill for the future. The reader witnesses the first signs of the dangerous threats to which the empire would gradually be exposed, and the appalling violation of justice during the trials of people who had incurred the wrath of the authorities. This was a sinister harbinger of even worse experiences in the years to come. In this respect chapter 3 is remarkable, which describes the term of office of the *praefectus urbis Romae* Apronianus. Within the structure of the book it is an anachronistic 'Fremdkörper', because this period belongs to the reign of Julian. Presumably, the author could not find an appropriate place in Book 25, but the present position makes it possible to stress that before the Pannonian rule deplorable instances of injustice did indeed occur, but that such excesses were being curbed, in contrast to the ever-increasing lawlessness under Valentinian and Valens. The bloody inquisitions after the collapse of Procopius' revolt, which inspired more fear than any wartime operations, foreshadowed this in a horrible way.

The book ends with the description of a tsunami which had no precedent in myth or ancient history, and caused catastrophic disasters in many parts of the Mediterranean. Ammianus mentions the precise date, 21 July 365, 'when the usurper was still alive'. Actually, his usurpation had not even started then, but the historian's phrase seems to betray his assumption that the tsunami had taken place at some time during the usurpation. This implies that Ammianus did not present it as an omen announcing Procopius' insurrection – which would have been absurd after the account of his final demise –, but as foreshadowing the ever increasing atmosphere of menace and terror, which in the years to come would emerge both from inside and outside the Roman world. As to the latter, the characterization of the tsunami as a horrific force spreading terror throughout the entire world (10.15: *horrendi terrores per omnem orbis ambitum grassati sunt subito*) corresponds exactly with the phrase at the beginning of the list of peoples invading the Roman Empire in 4.5: *per universum orbem Romanum bellicum canentibus bucinis*. The reader is led to expect the historian's report to be pervaded with anxiety and gloom. The loss of Julian was truly a disaster.

Ammianus wrote Book 26 in 390 at the earliest, as appears from a phrase in section 14 of the fifth chapter, but probably a few years later, after the death of Valentinian II, the last scion of the Pannonian dynasty in 392. Several more or less clear parallels with other extant historiographical and panegyrical texts show, that he either used the same material as these authors or, less frequently, a work of such an author. Themistius' seventh oration, in praise of Valens, in which the menace posed by Procopius is played down and the usurper depicted in somewhat ridiculous colours, could be a case in point. However, here he may also have agreed with the official view of the regime, albeit in a far more satirical style. In any case, he heartily disliked the revolt and its perpetrator, even calling the actual punishment of the culprits an entirely correct measure, which only inspired disapproval because of the glaring instances of sheer injustice. Book 26 has its weaknesses, above all where chronology and the precise details of the events are concerned, but in many other respects Ammianus demonstrates the same power of expression and characterization which the reader of the preceding books had come to expect.

A NOTE ON CHRONOLOGY

Reiche, 1889, 5–18 and Heering, 1927, 12–30, 69–70 also give chronological overviews of the events described in Book 26. Cf. further Seeck, 1906a, 516–519; 1919, 214–229 and Barnes, 1998, 247–250.

The death at Dadastana of Julian's successor Jovian, related in the final chapter of Book 25, occurred on 17 February 364 (25.10.12 [q.v.], Eutr. 10.18.2, Socr. *HE* 3.26.5). After an interregnum of ten days (*diebus...decem nullus imperii tenuit gubernacula*, 26.1.5) Valentinian ascended the throne. While on duty in Ancyra he had been elected by the highest civil and military officials, who were in Nicaea at the time (26.1.3–5). The designated emperor was summoned to come to Nicaea. After his arrival, he at first refused to be seen and to appear in public, because he wanted to avoid the intercalary day of February, i.e. 24 February (*Qui cum venisset accitus...nec videri die secundo nec prodire in medium voluit bissextum vitans Februarii mensis, tunc illucescens*, 26.1.7), a day which was regarded by some to be unfavourable for beginning great enterprises (*die parum apto ad inchoandas rerum magnitudines, ut quidam existimant*, 26.2.1). It was only after this day had passed (*Elapso die*, 26.2.1; *cum...tandem finita nocte lux advenisset*, 26.2.2) that Valentinian stepped forward, was proclaimed emperor (*rector pronuntiatur imperii*, 26.2.2) and then held a speech in his new capacity (*mox principali habitu circumdatus et corona Augustusque nuncupatus...praemeditata dicere iam parabat*, 26.2.3; 26.2.6–11). Since, as the term *bissextus* implies, 24 February was counted twice, Valentinian's *dies imperii* was on 25 February 364 (cf. Socr. *HE* 4.1.1 κοινῇ ψήφῳ Οὐαλεντινιανὸν ἀνακηρύττουσι βασιλέα, τῇ πέμπτῃ καὶ εἰκάδι τοῦ αὐτοῦ Φεβρουαρίου μηνὸς and see for more details the notes ad 26.1.5 *quia nullo* and 26.1.7 *bissextum*).

After the description of the election and inauguration of Valentinian in the first two chapters of Book 26, Ammianus inserts in chapter 3 an episode, viz. the prefecture of Apronianus, which chronologically belongs to the reigns of Julian and Jovian (see the introduction to chapter 3 and the note ad 26.3.1 *Apronianus*). In 26.4.1 he resumes his narrative (*At in Bithynia Valentinianus princeps, ut praediximus, declaratus*) and relates that the new emperor gave orders to leave Nicaea on the next day but one, i.e. on 27 February 364 (*dato in perendinum diem signo proficiscendi*). From Nicaea the army marched in a hurry to Nicomedia and arrived there presumably on 28 February (*Nicomediam itineribus citis ingressus*, 26.4.2). In Nicomedia, on the first of March 364, Valentinian appointed his brother Valens as *tribunus stabuli* (*kalendis Martiis Valentem fratrem stabulo suo cum tribunatus dignitate praefecit*, ibid.). Within a month the emperor arrived in Constantinople and promoted his brother to an even higher position by making him co-emperor with the title Augustus (*inde...cum venisset Constantinopolim...quintum kalendas Apriles...Valentem...Augustum pronuntiavit*, 26.4.3). The date for Valens' *dies imperii* as given by Ammianus, 28 March (which happened to be Palm Sunday), is the same as in Socr. *HE* 4.1.4: προσλαμβάνει τὸν ἀδελφὸν Οὐάλεντα, μετὰ τριάκοντα ἡμέρας τῆς αὐτοῦ ἀνακηρύξεως (in the note ad 26.4.3 *quintum kalendas* divergent dates are listed). Apparently, soon afterwards the imperial brothers fell seriously ill, but recovered (*Quibus ita nullo interturbante perfectis constricti rapidis febribus imperatores ambo diu spe vivendi firmata*, 26.4.4).

So far the chronological order of events is relatively easy to reconstruct. Ammianus' wording in 26.4.5 and 26.5.1, however, causes problems. Although it is stated in 26.4.5 that *Hoc tempore*, i.e. in the early part of 364, savage tribes carried out raids and invasions throughout the Roman world (*Hoc tempore velut per universum orbem Romanum bellicum canentibus bucinis excitae gentes saevissimae limites sibi proximos persultabant*), it is evident that the barbarian raids and invasions subsequently listed (26.4.5-6) belong to a much longer period, viz. the years between 364 and 378. As to the statement in 26.5.1 that Valentinian and Valens crossed through Thrace and reached Naissus after they had spent a quiet winter (*Acta...tranquillius hieme concordissimi principes...percursis Thraciis Naissum advenerunt*), it is especially the reference to the winter which causes surprise: the 'winter' here merely consists of the months of April and May, since Valens had received the status of Augustus on 28 March 364 (26.4.3), and the imperial brothers were in Naissus on 2 June at the latest (*Cod. Theod.* 14.3.3).

Thanks to the subscriptions added to some constitutions in the Theodosian Code we are reasonably well informed about the movements of Valentinian and Valens in Thrace on their way from Constantinople, which they must have left after 17 April, to Naissus and its suburb Mediana (references and more details in the notes ad 26.5.1 *percursis Thraciis* and *in suburbano*). From Naissus and its vicinity the emperors went to Sirmium, where their presence is attested on 5 July 364 (*Consult.* 9.6). How long exactly they stayed in

Sirmium, and whether they departed from there at the same time, is not known. On 29 July 364 both emperors were still in Sirmium (*Cod. Theod.* 5.15.15). After their stay in this town their ways parted (they were never to see each other again; for the theme of "divisio regni" see the note ad 26.5.2 *in orientem*). Valentinian headed for Milan, Valens returned to Constantinople (*Et post haec cum ambo fratres Sirmium introissent...Valentinianus Mediolanum, Constantinopolim Valens discessit*, 26.5.4). They apparently were in no hurry to reach these destinations. Valentinian's presence in Milan is not securely attested before 9 November 364 (*Cod. Theod.* 11.30.34), but he may have reached the city already late in October. Alamannic ambassadors travelled to his court in the last months of the year (*legatis eorum missis ad comitatum*, 26.5.7, q.v.). Valens was in Constantinople on 16 December 364 at the latest (*Cod. Theod.* 8.11.1), but he probably arrived there much earlier (more details in the note ad 26.5.4 *Et post haec*).

On 1 January 365 the Pannonian brothers entered their first consulship, Valentinian in Milan, Valens in Constantinople (*agentes...in memoratis urbibus principes sumpsere primitus trabeas consulares*, 26.5.6). The whole of the following year brought heavy losses to the Roman state (*omnis...hic annus dispendiis gravibus rem Romanam afflixit*, 26.5.6), caused by a foreign war and a civil war, viz. the war with the Alamans after they had invaded Roman territory (*Alamanni...perrupere Germaniae limites*, 26.5.7) and the usurpation of Procopius (*in oriente Procopius in res surrexerat novas*, 26.5.8), not to mention a natural catastrophe, viz. the tsunami which ravaged various regions adjacent to the Mediterranean (26.10.15–19).

While Ammianus gives the exact date of the tsunami, 21 July 365 (*diem duodecimum kalendas Augustas consule Valentiniano primum cum fratre*, 26.10.15), a date confirmed by *Consul. Constant.* a. 365 (= *Chron. Min.* II 240) and the Syrian index to Athanasius' Festal Letters (nr. 37, Martin-Albert, 1985, 268–269), he is less informative and sometimes even confusingly unclear with respect to the chronology of the Alamannic war and Procopius' usurpation. In 26.5.8 Ammianus does say that news about Procopius' usurpation reached Valentinian when he was about to arrive in Paris around 1 November, but he nowhere relates that Procopius made his rebellion manifest on 28 September 365, a date which we owe to *Consul. Constant.* a. 365 and Theophan. p. 55 De Boor. He does imply in 26.5.8 that Valentinian was also informed around the first of November about developments in the Alamannic war, but the wording he uses to convey this message is, to say the least, rather cryptic: *Et circa id tempus aut non multo posterius in oriente Procopius in res surrexerat novas. quae prope kalendas Novembres venturo Valentiniano Parisios uno eodemque nuntiata sunt die.* In fact, as is argued in the note ad loc., without knowledge of the data provided in Book 27 it is almost impossible to understand fully what Ammianus says about the Alamans in Book 26 (cf. the notes ad 26.5.7 *Alamanni* and *cum legatis*). For instance, it is only in 27.1.1 (*statim...post kalendas Ianuarias*) that the reader becomes aware of the date of the Alamannic invasion mentioned in 26.5.7 (*Alamanni...perrupere Germaniae limites*), i.e. early in January 365. This is undoubtedly due to the way in which Ammianus organizes his material. It is important to realize that Ammianus, for reasons explained in 26.5.15 (*competenti loco singula digeremus nunc partem in oriente gestorum, deinde bella barbarica narraturi, quoniam pleraque et in occidentali et in eoo orbe isdem mensibus sunt actitata*), only starts his full account of the Alamannic war in 27.1.1, and only mentions the Alamans in 26.5.7–9 in order to show why Valentinian decided not to help his brother against Procopius (26.5.9–13).

Valentinian, presented around 1 November 365 both with the news about Procopius' rebellion in the East and about setbacks on the western front (26.5.8), ordered his general Dagalaifus to confront the Alamans (*Alamannis...occursurum Dagalaifum pergere mature praecepit*, 26.5.9, q.v.). As becomes clear in Book 27, Dagalaifus was shortly afterwards recalled from the front to enter the consulship of 366 on 1 January; he was replaced by Iovinus (27.2.1). As to the dangerous situation in the East, after intensive deliberations (26.5.9–13) Valentinian decided to remain in the West (*statuit...nusquam...extra confinia moveri Gallorum*, 26.5.13). From Paris, where he still was on 10 and 12 December 365 (*Cod. Theod.* 10.19.3, 8.1.11), the emperor moved to Rheims (*ad usque Remos progressus*, 26.5.14). When precisely he arrived there is not known, but certainly before 7 April 366 (*Cod. Theod.* 8.7.9).

From 26.6.1 onwards Procopius' usurpation, which chronologically falls into two parts, and Valens' measures against it occupy centre stage (dates and other details are often lacking). The usurper capitalized on the absence from Constantinople of the legitimate emperor to start his rebellion (*dimoto...longius principe Procopius...aleam periculorum omnium iecit abrupte et...facinus adoritur audacissimum*, 26.6.12). Valens had left his eastern capital in order to go to Syria after the winter (*consumpta hieme festinans ad Syriam Valens*, 26.6.11, q.v.), i.e. at the end of March or the beginning of April 365. At some point in time during his journey (the text and the interpretation of *iam...fines Bithynorum ingressus* in 26.6.11 is disputed; see the note ad loc.), he was informed by his generals that the Goths had agreed to make preparations for an invasion of the border region of Thrace (*docetur relationibus ducum gentem Gothorum...conspirantem in unum ad pervadenda parari collimitia Thraciarum*, 26.6.11). On hearing this he ordered a sufficient force of cavalry and infantry to be sent to the places threatened by the barbarians, in order not to interrupt his own march in the direction of Syria (*hoc...cognito, ut impraepedite ipse pergeret, quo tendebat, sufficiens equitum adiumentum et peditum mitti iussit ad loca, in quibus barbarici timebantur excursus*, ibid.). Meanwhile Procopius, who had disappeared from sight during Jovian's short reign (*e medio se conspectu discrevit*, 26.6.3; see the note ad loc. for a different view), hid in Chalcedon (pace Zosimus 4.4.3, cited ibid.) and made secret excursions from there to Constantinople (*ad Calchedonos agrum pervenit. ubi...apud fidissimum amicorum delitescebat...Constantinopolim, quantum fieri poterat, clanculo saepe intermeans*, 26.6.4–5).

On 28 September 365 (*Consul. Constant.* a. 365; Theophan. p. 55 De Boor) Procopius had himself proclaimed as emperor (26.6.12–18), taking advantage of the presence in Constantinople of the Divitenses and Tungricani Iuniores who were on their way to Thrace (*Divitenses Tungricanosque Iuniores ad procinctum urgentem per Thracias inter alios celerare dispositos et Constantinopoli moraturos sollemniter biduum*, 26.6.12) and proved willing to join the usurper (26.6.12–13). News of Procopius' usurpation reached Valens shortly afterwards, early in October 365 presumably, when he was about to leave his summer residence in Cappadocia to continue his journey to Syria now that the heat in Cilicia had become less oppressive (*vaporatis aestibus Ciliciae iam lenitis*, 26.7.2). He was persuaded by Sophronius, the bearer of the message, to return and take matters in hand while they were still unsettled, and so he went to Galatia (*Sophronius...Valentem a Caesarea Cappadocum iam profecturum, ut...ad Antiochiae percurreret sedes, ...avertit Galatiam res adhuc trepidas arrepturum*, 26.7.2, with the notes). Via Ancyra (see the note ad 26.7.3 *Qui dum*) he subsequently went to Nicomedia in Bithynia (*Valens Nicomediam pergit*, 26.8.2) and from there to Chalcedon, which he besieged (*exindeque profectus oppugnationi Calchedonos...insistebat*, ibid.). Before reaching Bithynia, however, on his way back through Galatia (*revertens per Gallograeciam*, 26.7.13), he had a nervous breakdown, which almost made him cast aside his imperial robes. After his recovery he sent two army units, the Iovii and Victores, to go on ahead and attack the rebel camp (*agmina duo praeire iussisset, quibus nomina sunt Iovii atque Victores, castra perduellium irrupturos*, ibid.).

While Valens was making his hurried march from Cappadocia to Bithynia during the last months of 365 (*Qui dum itineribus properat magnis*, 26.7.3), Procopius was frenetically busy to improve his position (*attentissima cura Procopius in dies agitabatur* [Günther, *agitabat* mss.] *et noctes*, ibid.). He brought Thrace under his power, replaced unsympathetic officials with men of his own choice and won over more troops (26.7.4–10). However, his attempt to win support from the troops in Illyricum failed (26.7.11–12). He had more luck in Bithynia, where he personally took the field (that he had left Constantinople is not explicitly stated). Whilst returning with the Divitenses and a mixed rabble of deserters from a visit to Nicaea, to which place he had gone shortly before (*a Nicaea regressus, quo nuper advenerat*, 26.7.14), he met, near Mygdum-on-the-Sangarius, the Iovii and Victores sent by Valens and won them over by a speech (26.7.14–17). Other successes were to follow. The tribune Rumitalca captured for Procopius Helenopolis and Nicaea (*Rumitalca...permeato...cum militibus mari ad Drepanum ante, nunc Helenopolim venit exindeque Nicaeam spe celerius occupavit*, 26.8.1), withstood an attempt of Valens' general Vadomarius to drive him out of Nicaea and even forced Valens himself to give up the siege of Chalcedon and to leave Bithynia to the usurper (26.8.2–3, q.v.).

Valens now returned speedily to Ancyra (*Unde cum Ancyram Valens citis itineribus revertisset*, 26.8.4), to spend the winter of 365/6 there (he was back at the front in the spring of 366: *aperto iam vere*, 26.9.1) and to wait for reinforcements to arrive from the East (*comperissetque Lupicinum ab oriente cum catervis adventare non contemnendis*, 26.8.4). In the meantime he left it to his officers to continue the war. Near Dadastana his general Arintheus met some enemy soldiers under the command of the despicable Hyperechius, who was arrested by his own men (26.8.4–5). Valens' *comes domesticorum* Serenianus was less successful: he failed to hold on to Cyzicus for the legitimate emperor (26.8.7–10). Procopius hurried to the newly won city and pardoned all who had opposed him except Serenianus, who was put in irons and removed to Nicaea (*Hoc Marte Cyzico reserata Procopius ad eam propere festinavit veniaque universis, qui repugnavere, donatis Serenianum solum iniectis vinculis iussit duci Nicaeam servandum artissime*, 26.8.11). Immediately afterwards (*statimque*, 26.8.12) Procopius made young Hormisdas *proconsul* of Asia; some time later, seemingly in the spring of 366 (cf. the note ad 26.8.12 *escensa navi* and the introduction to 26.9.5–7), this Hormisdas and his wife escaped when on the point of being seized by soldiers whom Valens had sent through lonely places of Phrygia (*per devia Phrygiae*, 26.8.12). The usurper further ordered the house of Arbitio to be plundered, because he no longer believed that this experienced general would come over to his side; hitherto (*antea*) he had spared the house (26.8.13).

In 26.9.1 Ammianus concludes his description of the end of the first phase of Procopius' rebellion with the words: *Haec adulta hieme Valentiniano et Valente consulibus agebantur*. In general, the course of events between 28 September 365 and the end of 365 is more or less clear, but dates and other details are more often than not lacking in Ammianus' account. This applies even more to the second phase of the revolt. Significantly, the date of Procopius' capture and execution on 27 May 366 is not mentioned (we owe it to *Consul. Const.* a. 366). It is also significant that Valens' moves in Asia Minor can only be understood properly if one follows Seeck and assumes that Procopius had divided his troops in two (cf. the introduction to chapter 9 and the introductory note to 26.9.5–7).

After the beginning of the spring of 366 (*translato…in Gratianum, adhuc privatum, et Dagalaifum amplissimo magistratu, aperto iam vere,* 26.9.1), Valens called his forces into action again and marched from Ancyra to Pessinus, joined by Lupicinus and his strong army of auxiliaries (*suscitatis viribus Valens iuncto sibi Lupicino cum robustis auxiliis Pessinunta signa propere tulit,* ibid.). The emperor reinforced Pessinus with defensive works and/or a garrison, and advanced along the rough paths skirting the foothills of mount Olympus towards Lydia (*quo praesidiis tutius communito…praeter radices Olympi montis excelsi tramitesque fragosos ire tendebat ad Lydiam* [mss. Lyciam], 26.9.2, with the notes), intending to attack Procopius' general Gomoarius there (*ibi Gomoarium aggressurus,* ibid., q.v.). On his way he came up against widespread and obstinate resistance (*cui pertinaci conspiratione multorum…resistebatur,* 26.9.3). His position became critical (*nutanti negotio,* 26.9.4), and even his own troops could no longer be trusted (*multis ad perfidiam inclinatis,* 26.9.5), but after Valens had persuaded the former consul Arbitio to come to his assistance and this old general had used his influence with the soldiers, the tide turned (26.9.4–5). Arbitio's successful intervention caused Gomoarius to go over to Valens with his troops (*quibus cognitis Gomoarius…ad castra imperatoris…transivit,* 26.9.6, q.v.). According to Zosimus (4.8.1–2) this took place at Thyatira, in the middle of a battle.

Zosimus (ibid.) further states that, apart from Gomoarius, Hormisdas was in command of Procopius' troops at Thyatira. Zosimus is silent about his fate after the battle; Ammianus on the other hand seems to have referred to it in advance in 26.8.12, when he reported that Hormisdas and his wife escaped the soldiers of Valens who tried to capture him. (On account of *Cod. Theod.* 4.12.6 it is sometimes argued that Valens himself was in Thyatira on 4 April 366, but that necessitates the emendation of *Triveris* into *Thyatirae* in the subscription to the constitution, which is palaeographically questionable).

Valens, heartened by the elimination of one half of Procopius' army, now marched via Sardis (Zos. 4.8.3) to Phrygia (*Qua succensus alacritate Valens castra promovit ad Phrygiam*, 26.9.7), where he encountered Procopius near Nacolia (*prope Nacoliam collatis manibus*, (ibid.; whether a real battle ensued, is not clear; see the note ad 26.9.7 *iam pila*). The result was disastrous for the usurper: at the critical moment his general Agilo changed sides (26.9.7). Procopius himself fled, together with two companions, Florentius and Barchalba (26.9.8). On the following day these men turned traitor and handed Procopius over to Valens (*maiore...noctis parte consumpta, cum a vespertino ortu luna praelucens in diem metum augeret...Procopius...subito a comitibus suis artius vinctus relato iam die ductus ad castra imperatori offertur*, 26.9.9), who beheaded him at once (*statim...abscisa cervice*, ibid.). This happened on 27 May 366 (*et ipso anno idem hostis publicus et predo intra Frygiam salutarem et in Nacoliensium campo ab Aug. Valente oppressus atque extinctus est die VI kl. Iun, Consul. Const.* a. 366; see for divergent dates the note ad 26.9.9 *subito*). Florentius and Barchalba, who had brought Procopius in, were also executed, at once and without the pros and cons being weighed up (*confestim non pensata ratione sunt interfecti*, 26.9.10), also presumably on 27 May.

Thus ended Procopius' usurpation. The subsequent attempt of his relative Marcellus to become emperor was nipped in the bud. After he had heard of Procopius' fate (*Isdem fere diebus...proditione militum et interitu Procopii cognito*, 26.10.1), this Marcellus, commander in Nicaea, killed Valens' *comes domesticorum* Serenianus (who had been sent in chains to Nicaea after the fall of Cyzicus, 26.8.11). He then took possession of Chalcedon (*occupata celeri cursu Calchedone*, 26.10.3), but, before he could continue his adventure, he was captured and killed by soldiers sent by the *magister militum per Illyricum* Equitius. Equitius, who had left his defensive position on the pass of Succi, was besieging pro-Procopian Philippopolis at the time (26.10.4–5). It took a while before he got hold of the city: the inhabitants only surrendered when they were shown the head of Procopius which was being taken to Gaul (26.10.6). They and others paid a heavy penalty for supporting the usurper's cause: *saevitum est in multos acrius, quam errata flagitaverant vel delicta, maximeque in Philippoleos defensores* (26.10.6, q.v.).

A NOTE ON CHRONOLOGY XXIII

In Book 27 Ammianus mentions Procopius again. In 27.2.10 he tells us that the usurper's head was shown to Valentinian in Paris. Whether Valentinian really was in Paris when the head arrived, is disputed, as is the date of the head's arrival (see the note ad 26.10.6 *maximeque*). In Book 26 we encounter similar problems. We therefore want to warn the reader: some of the dates presented in the reconstruction above and in the following diagram are reasonably certain, others are no more than educated guesses.

364

17 February	Jovian dies at Dadastana (25.10.12, Eutr. 10.18.2, Socr. *HE* 3.26.5)
17–25 February	Interregnum (26.1.5)
24 February	Intercalary day (26.1.7)
25 February	Valentinian proclaimed *Augustus* in Nicaea (26.2.2–3, Socr. *HE* 4.1.1)
27 February	Valentinian leaves Nicaea (26.4.1)
1 March	In Nicomedia Valentinian appoints his brother Valens as *tribunus stabuli* (*kalendis Martiis*, 26.4.2)
28 March	In Constantinople Valentinian proclaims Valens co-emperor with the title Augustus (*quintum kalendas Apriles*, 26.4.3)
17 April	Terminus post quem for the departure of both emperors from Constantinople (*Cod. Theod.* 13.01.05); their journey through Thrace (26.5.1–4) leads via Adrianople, Philippopolis, Bona Mansio and Serdica
2 June	Valentinian and Valens in Naissus (*Cod. Theod.* 14.3.3)
5 July	Valentinian and Valens in Sirmium (*Consult.* 9.6)
29 July	Terminus post quem for the departure of both emperors from Sirmium (*Cod. Theod.* 5.15.15). After their stay in this town their ways part (26.5.4)
9 November	Valentinian's presence in Milan attested (*Cod. Theod.* 11.30.34)
November/December	Alamannic ambassadors travel to Milan (26.5.7)
16 December	Valens' presence in Constantinople attested (*Cod. Theod.* 8.11.1)

365

1 January	Valentinian and Valens enter their first consulship (*principes sumpsere primitus trabeas consulares*, 26.5.6)

Early in January	Alamans invade Gaul (*Alamanni...perrupere Germaniae limites*, 26.5.7, *statim...post kalendas Ianuarias*, 27.1.1)
March/April	Valens leaves Constantinople in order to go to Syria (*consumpta hieme festinans ad Syriam Valens*, 26.6.11); on his way he sends troops back because of an imminent invasion of the Goths (26.6.11)
21 July	A tsunami ravages various regions adjacent to the Mediterranean (*diem duodecimum kalendas Augustas consule Valentiniano primum cum fratre*, 26.10.15, *Consul. Constant.* a. 365 [= *Chron. Min.* II 240], Syrian index to Athanasius' Festal Letters, nr. 37, Martin-Albert, 1985, 268–269)
28 September	Procopius makes his usurpation manifest (*Consul. Constant.* a. 365, Theophan. p. 55 De Boor)
October	Valens informed about Procopius' usurpation (26.7.2)
October/November	Valens marches from Caesarea in Cappadocia through Galatia to Nicomedia and Chalcedon (26.7.2, 26.8.2); he besieges Chalcedon in vain (26.8.2–3); he returns to Ancyra (26.8.4)
Circa 1 November	Valentinian on his way to Paris hears of Procopius' rebellion and of setbacks in the Alamannic war (*quae prope kalendas Novembres venturo Valentiniano Parisios uno eodemque nuntiata sunt die*, 26.5.8)
November	Valentinian sends his general Dagalaifus to confront the Alamans (26.5.9)
November/December	Operations of Procopius in Bithynia. He wins over the Iovii and Victores near Mygdum (26.7.14). His tribune Rumitalca takes Helenopolis and Nicaea and drives Valens away from Chalcedon (26.8.1–3). Encounter of Valens' general Arintheus with Hyperechius (26.8.4–5). Procopius gets hold of Cyzicus (26.8.6–11). He makes Hormisdas proconsul of Asia (26.8.12) and orders Arbitio's house to be plundered (26.8.13)
10–12 December	Valentinian in Paris (*Cod. Theod.* 10.19.3, 8.1.11)

366

1 January	Gratian and Dagalaifus enter their consulship (26.9.1, 27.2.1)
7 April	Valentinian in Rheims (*Cod. Theod.* 8.7.9)
Spring	*Aperto iam vere* (26.9.1) Valens takes the field again. Together with Lupicinus he marches from Ancyra to Pessinus and from there via mount

	Olympus towards Lydia (26.9.1–2). Battle at Thyatira (Zos. 4.8.1–2). Gomoarius, influenced by Arbitio's pleading in favour of Valens' case (26.9.4–5), defects from Procopius (26.9.6). Escape of Hormisdas (26.8.12)
26 May	'Battle' at Nacolia (26.9.7)
27 May	Procopius beheaded (26.9.9, *Consul. Const.* a. 366). Execution of Florentius and Barchalba (26.9.10)
June/July	Marcellus' coup. Death of Serenianus. Equitius besieges Philippolis. Marcellus executed. Procopius' severed head sent to Gaul. Philippolis surrenders. Procopius' followers punished (26.10.1–8)

LEGENDA

1. The lemmata are taken from W. Seyfarth's Teubner-edition (Leipzig 1978), with one alteration: consonantial u is always printed as v (*venit* instead of *uenit*).

2. For references to Greek authors we follow the abbreviations and indications of books and chapters in H.G. Liddell and R. Scott, *A Greek-English Lexicon*. Passages in Latin authors are indicated according to the system of the *Oxford Latin Dictionary*. For later and Christian authors we follow the *Thesaurus Linguae Latinae*.
   Some exceptions to these rules:

   – In the case of Caesar, Sallust and Tacitus the division of the chapters into sections in the Teubner-editions has been taken into account.
   – Seneca's *Dialogi* are referred to with the title of the individual works.
   – For the *Panegyrici Latini* Mynors' OCT-edition has been used.
   – Strabo is quoted from Radt's edition (*Strabons Geographica mit Übersetzung und Kommentar herausgegeben von Stefan Radt*, 4 vols., Göttingen 2002–2005).
   – The Letters of Julian are quoted from Bidez' edition in the Budé-series.
   – Eunapius' *History* is quoted from Blockley's edition (*The Fragmentary Classicising Historians of the Later Roman Empire*, vol. II, Liverpool 1983).
   – Iohannes Antiochenus is quoted from Roberto's edition (*Iohannis Antiocheni Fragmenta ex Historia chronica*, Introduzione, edizione critica e traduzione a cura di Umberto Roberto [Texte und Untersuchungen zur Geschichte der altchristlichen Literatur 154], Berlin–New York 2005).

3. As to secondary literature the following rules are observed:

   – References to the six volumes of De Jonge's commentaries and to our commentaries on Books 20, 21, 22, 23, 24 and 25 are usually given with 'see (the note) ad...' or 'q.v.'.
   – Books or articles are normally referred to with the name of

the author(s), the year of publication and the page(s). The full titles can be found in the bibliography; e.g. Hagendahl, 1921, 64 refers to H. Hagendahl, *Studia Ammianea*, Uppsala 1921, page 64.
- Quotations from existing translations and secondary literature are given between double inverted commas ("..."). Our own explanations of words or phrases in Greek and Latin texts are given between single inverted commas ('...').
- Occasionally reference is made to commentaries on other authors, e.g. Austin's on Vergil and Koestermann's on Tacitus, or to well-known editions like those in the Budé-series. As a rule these works are omitted from the bibliography.
- The volumes of the Groningen Commentaries on Apuleius are indicated by *GCA* and the year of publication.
- Of the following books, which are referred to regularly, only the name of the author and the page(s) are given:

Barnes	T.D. Barnes, *Ammianus Marcellinus and the Representation of Historical Reality*, Ithaca–London 1998.
Blomgren	S. Blomgren, *De sermone Ammiani Marcellini quaestiones variae*, Diss. Uppsala 1937.
Ehrismann	H. Ehrismann, *De temporum et modorum usu Ammianeo*, Diss. Argentorati 1886.
Fesser	H. Fesser, *Sprachliche Beobachtungen zu Ammianus Marcellinus*, Diss. Breslau 1932.
Harmon	A.M. Harmon, *The Clausula in Ammianus Marcellinus* (Transactions of the Connecticut Academy of Arts and Sciences 16, 117–245), New Haven 1910.
Jones	A.H.M. Jones, *The Later Roman Empire 284–602. A Social Economic and Administrative Survey*, Oxford 1964 (repr. 1986).
Kühner-Stegmann	R. Kühner and C. Stegmann, *Ausführliche Grammatik der lateinischen Sprache*, II Satzlehre, 2 vols., Hannover 1955[4], 1976[5].
Leumann	M. Leumann, *Lateinische Laut- und Formenlehre*, Munich 1977.
Marié	M.-A. Marié, *Ammien Marcellin, Histoire V (Livres XXVI–XXVIII)*, Paris 1984.
Matthews	J.F. Matthews, *The Roman Empire of Ammianus*, London 1989.

Paschoud	F. Paschoud, *Zosime, Histoire Nouvelle, II*² (*Livre IV*), Paris 1979.
Sabbah	G. Sabbah, *La méthode d'Ammien Marcellin. Recherches sur la construction du discours historique dans les Res Gestae*, Paris 1978.
Seager	R. Seager, *Ammianus Marcellinus. Seven studies in his Language and Thought*, Columbia 1986.
Szantyr	J.B. Hofmann and A. Szantyr, *Lateinische Syntax und Stilistik*, Munich 1965 (repr. 1972).
Wagner-Erfurdt	J.A. Wagner, *Ammiani Marcellini quae supersunt, cum notis integris Frid. Lindenbrogii, Henr. et Hadr. Valesiorum et Iac. Gronovii, quibus Thom. Reinesii quasdam et suas adiecit, editionem absolvit Car. Gottl. Aug. Erfurdt*, 3 vols., Leipzig 1808 (repr. in 2 vols, Hildesheim 1975).

The following translations are often referred to with the name of the translator only:

Caltabiano	M. Caltabiano, *Ammiano Marcellino. Storie*, Milan 1998.
Hamilton	W. Hamilton and A. Wallace-Hadrill, *Ammianus Marcellinus: the Later Roman Empire (AD 354–378)*, Harmondsworth 1986.
Rolfe	J.C. Rolfe, *Ammianus Marcellinus*, with an English translation, 3 vols., London-Cambridge Mass. 1935–1939 (repr. 1971–1972).
Selem	A. Selem, *Le Storie di Ammiano Marcellino. Testo e Traduzione*, Turin 1965 (repr. 1973)
Seyfarth	W. Seyfarth, *Ammianus Marcellinus, Römische Geschichte. Lateinisch und Deutsch und mit einem Kommentar versehen*, IV, Berlin 1986³.
Veh	O. Veh, *Ammianus Marcellinus. Das römische Weltreich vor dem Untergang*, übersetzt von Otto Veh, eingeleitet und erlaütert von G. Wirth, Zurich–Munich 1974.
Viansino	G. Viansino, *Ammiano Marcellino. Storie*, 3 vols., Milan 2001–2002.

4. In cases where this is helpful for the reader or relevant for the interpretation the cursus is indicated as follows:

– *revocávit in státum*: cursus planus
– *sublátius éminens*: cursus tardus
– *fécit et vectigáles*: cursus velox

CHAPTER 1

Introduction

Ammianus opens Book 26 with a programmatic statement, marking a new departure after Books 15–25, in which Julian as Caesar and Augustus dominated the narrative. He tells his readers that there had been good reasons for him not to write the history of his own times. This would spare him the dangers involved in writing history and inept criticisms of people who would blame him for omitting details which they considered important. Ammianus dismisses this type of criticism out of hand. According to him it only shows that those criticasters are unaware of the elementary rule of historiography, which dictates that the historian must restrict himself to people and events which have determined the course of history. Both the dangers of writing contemporary history and the requirement to confine oneself to *digna memoratu* are topoi in programmatic statements of ancient historians. What makes Ammianus' introduction stand out among them is the vehemence and the haughtiness with which he rejects the anticipated criticisms.

Ammianus' opening statement has been interpreted by a majority of scholars as evidence that the historian had intended to end his work with the death of Julian and the end of the Persian expedition. There would have been several reasons for him to do so. The death of Julian meant the disappearance from the scene of Ammianus' central character. There is no doubt that recording the achievements of Julian as Caesar and Augustus was Ammianus' main objective in writing his *Res Gestae*. Julian's death also marked the end of the Constantinian dynasty. According to these scholars the historian waited until the death of Valentinian II, the last member of the next dynasty, in 392 before starting on the history of the Valentinians. Plausible as this may be, the opening statement of 26.1 cannot be used as evidence that Ammianus changed his plan and made a fresh start at a later date, as its contents may be summarized as follows: 'There were good reasons for me to end my work with the death of Julian (however, I decided to carry on)'.

Ammianus had introduced the history of Julian's career with a similar statement in 15.1. The two passages are closely related, and the earlier statement must be kept in mind when reading the present introduction. Since the preface to the *Res Gestae* as a whole has been lost, the few remaining declarations of intent by the author, to which the closing statement or *sphragis* in 31.16.9 also belongs, have received much attention. The most recent studies about the programmatic statements in 15.1 and 26.1 are Fornara, 1990, Blockley, 2001 and Paschoud, 2005. The earlier study by Samberger, 1969 is still of great value.

Sections 3–7 are devoted to the election of Valentinian as Jovian's successor. There were other candidates, but Ammianus leaves the reader in no doubt that Valentinian was the one best equipped for the task. Since Valentinian had to come from Ancyra to Nicaea, where the main body of the army was stationed, ten days went by during which the Empire was without an emperor. Even after arriving in Nicaea, Valentinian waited a full day before presenting himself to the troops. The reason was that he did not want the intercalary day, or *dies bissextus*, to be his *dies imperii*, because in the eyes of some that day was inauspicious.

This induces Ammianus to write one of his learned digressions, in which he sets out to provide the reader with the necessary background to understand the question of the leap year. There is no doubt that Solinus is his main source, who in his turn probably used Suetonius' treatise *On the Year*. Other traces of that influential study are to be found in Censorinus and Macrobius. The Roman calendar, before Caesar's introduction of the solar year in 45 B.C., is a notoriousy difficult subject. Unfortunately, the historian is not at his best in this digression. Apart from one or two glaring errors, his language betrays his diffidence in treating the problem. He does not say anything of substance, and cloaks his lack of comprehension in hazy phrases. He ends, surprisingly, with a confession of his faith in Rome's eternity.

1.1 *Dictis impensiore cura rerum ordinibus ad usque memoriae confinia proprioris* With these words Amm. recalls what he had written at the beginning of the Julianic books in 15.1.1: *residua, quae secuturus aperiet textus, pro virium captu limatius absolvemus*. It is important to realize that *limatius* ('with greater care') is not only a stylistic term but also connected with research, as is evident from 15.13.2 *Constantinus enim cum limatius superstitionum quaereret sectas*. See Sabbah 44 and n. 68. The words *impensiore cura*, for which see the note ad 20.8.1, imply that Amm. has kept the promise that he would write *pro virium captu limatius*. *Dictis...rerum ordinibus* is the counterpart of *ordine casuum exposito diversorum* in 15.1.1. For *rerum ordines* see the first note ad 20.1.1.

Samberger, 1969, 379 makes an important distinction between two shades of meaning in this expression, viz. "zeitliche Abfolge" and "innerer Zusammenhang" of the events described, the latter notion becoming dominant in the last six books, where the annalistic ordering of events is less pronounced than in the preceding twelve. See for this the note ad 26.5.15. A similar observation had already been made by Thompson, 1947, 25.

For *confinium* see the note ad 25.6.4 *prope confinia noctis*. In Amm. the word indicates the dividing line between two periods in 17.7.7 *inter vitae mortisque confinia*. In the other instances it designates the lower limit of a new period, as in *prope lucis confinia*. To decide the exact meaning of the prepositional phrase introduced by *ad usque*, a textual problem must first be eliminated. Samberger, 1969, 371–374 has been the first to defend V's reading *proprioris*. All editors, including Gelenius, had preferred *propioris*, the reading of the other mss. According to Samberger the prepositional phrase might be interpreted as "soweit meine ganz persönliche Erinnerung reichte." After the Persian campaign Amm. had left the army, and for that reason had less direct access to information than when he was an eyewitness of the events. The period which was 'more specifically his own' had thereby come to an end. Samberger has been followed by Seyfarth in the Teubner-edition and by Marié in the Budé-edition. The comparative *proprior* is extremely rare, but it does occur, see Neue-Wagener, 1892, 206–207 and TLL X 2. 2093. 43–45, where Mar. Victorin. *adv. Arium* 4.8.l. 23, Hil. *in psalm.* 118 samech 4 and Heges. 3.3.2 are mentioned. In classical texts a circumscription with *magis* is preferred. In the mss. *propior-proprior* and *propius-proprius* are often confused; TLL X 2.1952. 31–33 and X 2. 2026.33. There are two examples of this in Amm. himself: 16.7.2 *ut erat vanidicus et amenti proprior*, and 20.11.28 (q.v.) *ostendit aspectum flammeo propriorem*, both of which are evidently wrong. Therefore not too much weight should be attached to the reading of V in the present passage. The problem is discussed in detail by Paschoud, 2005, who concludes on p. 112: "Ob Ammian die Form *proprior* überhaupt benutzt hat, scheint mir nach dem bisher Gesagten schon aus rein formellen Gründen höchst fraglich." One might add that an emphasis on the author's personal experience would not sit well with *a notioribus* in the immediate sequel, since the context shows that *notiora* refers to knowledge shared by Amm. and his readers. There are no parallels either for *propior* or for *proprior memoria*.

The expression *propior memoria* is comparable to *aequalis nobis memoria* in 31.14.8: *Haec super Valente dixisse sufficiet, quae vera esse aequalis nobis memoria plene testatur* ("This is a sufficient account of Valens, and it is amply confirmed by the evidence of my contemporaries", tr. Hamilton). Other examples of *propior* in a temporal sense are Cic. *Div.* 2.22 *abeamus a fabulis, propiora videamus* and Tac. *Dial.* 21.7 *quamquam propioribus temporibus natus sit.* Contemporary historians like Eutropius and Sulpicius Severus use the expression *nostra memoria* in comparable programmatic statements: Sulp. Sev. *Chron.* 1.1.1 *res a mundi exordio...usque ad nostram memoriam,* Eutr. *pr. Res Romanas...ab urbe condita ad nostram memoriam.*

convenerat iam referre a notioribus pedem Solinus had written in his dedicatory letter to Adventus (§3): *exquisitis enim aliquot voluminibus studuisse me inpendio fateor, ut et a notioribus referrem pedem et remotis largius inmorarer.* Given the fact that Amm. was familiar with Solinus' work (see e.g. the notes ad 22.15.7), and that he used this author in his digression on the *dies bissextus* in §8–14 below, it is likely that Amm. borrowed the expression from him, without any regard for the context in which he had used it. In 27.4.14 we find *pedem referre* in the conclusion of a digression: *his ita digestis pedem referamus ad coepta.* As regards *iam*, it seems best to take it with *referre pedem* as "marking the beginning of an action extending into the future" (OLD s.v. 1). It may be compared to expressions like 20.03.12 *verum ad instituta iam revertamur*.

Much depends on the interpretation of the verb form *convenerat*. The meaning of the verb is not in dispute. Ammianus uses *convenerat* twice in the phrase *quibus (ita), ut convenerat, ordinatis* (23.1.5 and 24.4.23, q.v.), in the sense: 'as was fitting', where the pluperfect is probably chosen to create a *cursus velox*. In two instances he uses the verb in the same meaning in statements about his own work: 21.6.1 *Replicare nunc convenit tempora* and 31.14.8 *illud autem praeteriri non convenit*.

The next question is more difficult to decide: is *convenerat* a factual statement about an existing state of affairs in the past: 'it had been fitting (but is no longer)' or is it an irrealis: 'it would have been fitting'? Those who opt for the former alternative read the statement as a declaration by Amm. that he had originally ended his history with the death of Julian and the conclusion of the Persian campaign, and that Books 26–31 were a later addition. "At first he had not wished to deal at all with events which were so closely contemporary as the reigns of Valentinian and Valens, but he changed his mind for a reason which he does not tell us", Thompson writes (1947, 108; see also 1966, 147–148). Demandt, 1965, 63 and Blockley,

1975, 12–16 are of the same opinion. According to Syme Amm.'s design was to end with the death of Julian "with a brief epilogue on the brief reign of Jovian" (1968, 7). Rosen, 1982, 73 speaks of a "Neubeginn". Paschoud, 2005, 115, after some hesitation, also favours this interpretation of *convenerat*.

Indeed, Amm. would have had excellent reasons for doing so: Julian had been the author's hero, a righteous emperor and a great military commander, to whom he had devoted a large part of his work; his death, moreover, marked the end of the Constantinian dynasty; Julian's Persian campaign was the last military event in which the *miles* Ammianus was personally involved; the peace treaty with Sapor II, however humiliating in the eyes of Amm., ended decades of hostilities between the Roman and Sasanid Empires, and introduced what turned out to be a long period of stability and peaceful coexistence.

Another reason to stop before the Valentinian dynasty could have been that it was not without risk for a historian to write about members of the ruling dynasty. Paschoud, 2005, 107 aptly adduces a passage from the Historia Augusta in which Pescennius Niger is quoted as saying (*PN* 11.6): *nam viventes laudare inrisio est, maxime imperatores, a quibus speratur, qui timentur, qui praestare publice possunt, qui possunt necare, qui proscribere*. He proceeds to compare the passage under discussion with statements in Eutropius (10.18.3), Festus (30.1), Jerome (*Chron. pr.* p. 7.3–9 Helm) and the Historia Augusta (*Car.* 15.10), which have in common that the authors (with the exception of Festus) decline to describe the ruling emperor or dynasty, because this would require the more elevated style of a panegyric. A similar *recusatio* is to be found in Amm.'s *sphragis* (31.16.9): *scribant reliqua potiores aetate doctrinis florentes. quos id, si libuerit, aggressuros procudere linguas ad maiores moneo stilos*. This reason to avoid writing about the Valentinians would have disappeared with the death of Valentinian II in 392 (Naudé, 1984, who interprets the statement in 26.1.1 in the same way, does not subscribe to this conclusion regarding the date of composition of the later books, but prefers the 380s). Thus Amm.'s programmatic statement would provide us with a *terminus post quem* for the books 26–31.

A weakness of this interpretation is that its defenders tend to read *convenerat* as a declaration of intent on the part of the author. Demandt, 1965, 63 e.g. paraphrases it as follows: "Ammian sagt hier, dass er ursprünglich mit dem Tode Jovians in Buch XXV sein Werk zu beenden gedachte." *Convenerat*, however, cannot be made to mean "I had already determined" (Rolfe) or "J'étais désormais résolu" (Marié in her Introduction to volume V of the Budé-edition, n. 2; in her translation she writes "il eût convenu"), but only 'it had been (or 'it was') fitting', which leaves the question unanswered whether the author acted in accordance with this statement. Apart from this reservation the interpretation of the sentence as presented above cannot be rejected out of hand. It is, however, by no means the only feasible one. The alternative reading of *convenerat* as a past irrealis ('it would have been fitting') also deserves careful consideration. The use of the indicative is unexceptional, since impersonal *convenit* belongs to "die Ausdrücke des Sollens, Müssens, Könnens, Dürfens u. ä." (Szantyr 327; cf. Ehrismann 41), in which this use of the indicative is the rule. Cf. e.g. the use of *oportuerat* in 26.9.10 *amplas eius memorabilis facti oportuerat deferri mercedes*. In the immediate sequel we read *non decuerat*, which is an indicative pluperfect of the same type. Amm. uses the subjunctive *convenisset* only once, in 24.1.3 *armorumque speciem diffundendi ex industria vel attenuandi perquam scientissimus, ut, ubi convenisset* (Heraeus, *venisset* V) *plures aestimarentur aut pauci*, where the subjunctive is iterative. This use of the indicative could be explained by the following paraphrase: 'When I had finished the history of Julian, it had been fitting that I would put an end to my work.' The fact that Amm. obviously carried on leads to the re-interpretation: 'it would have been fitting for me to stop (but I decided otherwise)'. *Iam*, as usual, marks the transition from one stage to the next ('at that moment').

The reasons why it would be fitting to abstain from writing more recent history are given by Amm. in the double *ut*-clause that follows: by doing so, he would have avoided the dangers inherent in the writing of contemporary history, and he would have spared himself the carping of incompetent critics (*examinatores intempestivos*) for leaving out certain important facts. The word *intempestivos* leads us back to 15.1.1. There, at the beginning of the history of Julian, which was to be more detailed than the preceding period, Amm. defended himself beforehand against *obtrectatores longi, ut putant, operis*, and argued that *brevitas* is desirable only when it does away with irrelevant delays (*moras rumpens intempestivas*). The statement in 26.1 may be called a mirror image of 15.1. There the author anticipated unjustified criticism of his detailed description of Julian's reign; here, ironically, he expects to be chided for leaving out details wrongly supposed to be important. Read in this way the two programmatic statements embrace what was no doubt intended to be the *pièce de résistance* of Amm.'s work, the *Res Gestae Iuliani*. For that reason we are inclined to subscribe to the cautious conclusion of Fornara, 1990, 170: "It is imperative to observe...that this ruling theory (viz. that 26.1 means a fresh start on the part of Amm.), whether probable or not, derives support neither from the logic of the passage in 26.1, taken as a whole, nor from any of its component parts." Matthews 205 holds a similar view: "the preface to Book 26 declares no more than the author's realisation that he is now approaching the generally more controversial field of contemporary history, without implying that what follows should be read as an amendment to any 'original' plan." In his opinion the narrative about the usurpation of Procopius was part of the integral plan, and he prefers to see "a single design running to Book 31". There is a striking parallel in Polybius who, before he presents his description of the Roman constitution, anticipates criticism from his Roman readers: 6.11.3–7 οὐκ ἀγνοῶ δὲ διότι τοῖς ἐξ αὐτῆς τῆς πολιτείας ὁρμωμένοις ἐλλιπεστέραν φανησόμεθα ποιεῖσθαι τὴν ἐξήγησιν, ἔνια παραλιπόντες τῶν κατὰ μέρος...οὐ τὸ λεγόμενον θαυμάσουσιν ἀλλὰ τὸ παραλειπόμενον ἐπιζητήσουσιν, οὐδὲ κατὰ πρόθεσιν ὑπολήψονται τὸν γράφοντα παραλιπεῖν τὰς μικρὰς διαφοράς, ἀλλὰ κατ' ἄγνοιαν παρασιωπᾶν τὰς ἀρχὰς καὶ τὰ συνέχοντα τῶν πραγμάτων. καὶ ῥηθέντα μὲν οὐκ ἂν ἐθαύμαζον ὡς ὄντα μικρὰ καὶ πάρεργα, παραλειπόμενα δ' ἐπιζητοῦσιν ὡς ἀναγκαῖα, βουλόμενοι δοκεῖν αὐτοὶ πλέον εἰδέναι τῶν συγγραφέων. ("I am quite aware that to those who have been born and bred under the Roman Republic my account of it will seem somewhat imperfect owing to the omission of certain details...they will not be struck by the extent of the information I give but will demand in addition all I have omitted: they will not think that the author has purposely omitted small peculiarities, but that owing to ignorance he has been silent regarding the origins of many things and some points of capital importance. Had I mentioned them, they would not have been impressed by my doing so, regarding them as small and trivial points, but as they are omitted they will demand their inclusion as if they were vital matters, through a desire themselves to appear better informed than the author", tr. Paton).

Sabbah 49 n. 92 has drawn attention to a very personal statement made by Eunapius, when he had reached the times of Julian, which also marks a new stage in his work (*fr.* 15): Τὰ μὲν οὖν ἀπὸ τῆς Δεξίππου συγγραφῆς ἐς τοὺς Ἰουλιανοῦ καθήκοντα καιροὺς ὡς ἐνῆν μάλιστα διὰ τῶν ἀναγκαίων ἐπιτρέχουσιν ἱκανῶς ἐν τοῖς ἔμπροσθεν δεδήλωται· φέρεται δὲ ἐντεῦθεν ὁ λόγος ἐφ' ὅνπερ ἐφέρετο ἐξ ἀρχῆς, καὶ ἀναγκάζει γε τοῖς ἔργοις ἐνδιατρίβειν ὥσπερ τι πρὸς αὐτὸν ἐρωτικὸν πεπονθότας ("In the preceding chapters the history from the end of Dexippus' work to the time of Julian has been summarised as adequately as possible, with a concentration on the most important events. Henceforth my narrative centres on the one who was its object from the beginning, and, feeling the love that I do for him, I am compelled to turn my attention to his achievements", tr. Blockley). Note the contrast between the brevity of the preceding work (διὰ τῶν ἀναγκαίων ἐπιτρέχουσιν) and the more detailed description of Julian's reign (τοῖς ἔργοις ἐνδιατρίβειν). One might add that after the death of Julian Eunapius again marks a transition (*fr.* 30): Περὶ μὲν οὖν τῶν παλαιοτέρων καὶ ὅσα πρὸ ἡμῶν ἀνάγκη συγχωρεῖν τοῖς γράψασιν ἢ τοῖς περὶ ἐκείνων λόγοις ἐς ἡμᾶς κατὰ μνήμην ἄγραφον ἐς διαδοχὴν περιφερομένοις καὶ καθήκουσιν· ὅσα δὲ ἐφ' ἡμῶν αὐτῶν γέγονεν, ἀλήθειαν τιμῶντι, καθά φησι ὁ Πλάτων, παραδοτέον τοῖς ἐντυγχάνουσιν ("In the case of persons and events before our generation, we must defer to the written authorities or to the reports about them which memory passes down to us via an oral tradition. But contemporary events we must hand down to posterity with due regard for truth, as Plato says", tr. Blockley).

ut et pericula declinentur veritati saepe contigua et examinatores contexendi operis deinde non perferamus intempestivos Despite the fact that both V and Gelenius read *veritatis,* there can be little doubt that *veritati* is correct. *Contiguus* without its complement in the dative is pointless, as Marié's translation shows: "les risques qui menacent la vérité, souvent tout proches". Avoiding recent history would have had a double advantage for the author: it would have spared him the dangers inherent in speaking the truth as well as untimely criticisms. The sentence is badly out of balance, because Amm. leaves the *pericula veritati contigua* unspecified, and describes the envisaged criticisms at great length. For the *pericula* we may think of the usual practice of historians to stop before the ruling dynasty, as discussed above, but as a historiographical topos it is much older. Sallust speaks about malevolent critics in *Cat.* 3.2 *quia plerique quae delicta reprehenderis malevolentia et invidia dicta putant.* Livy hints at the dangers of recent history in section 5 of his preface: *omnis expers curae, quae scribentis animum etsi non flectere a vero, sollicitum tamen efficere posset.* Horace's characterisation of Asinius Pollio's history of the Civil War is unforgettable: (*Carm.* 2.1.6–8) *periculosae plenum opus aleae, / tractas et incedis per ignis / suppositos cineri doloso.* Cf. also Tac. *Ann.* 4.33.4 *antiquis scriptoribus rarus obtrectator...at multorum, qui Tiberio regente poenam vel infamias subiere, posteri manent, utque familiae ipsae iam exstinctae sint, reperies qui ob similitudinem morum aliena malefacta sibi obiectari putent*, pointedly followed by the *leçon par l'exemple* of Cremutius Cordus. In its most succinct form the topos is found in Plin. *Ep.* 5.8.12 *vetera et scripta aliis? parata inquisitio, sed onerosa collatio. intacta et nova? graves offensae, levis gratia.*

More specifically, Thompson, 1947, ch. 7 has emphasized that Amm. was not free to write what he wanted under the regime of Theodosius, and that the emperor "kept a watchful eye on the contents of the historical works which appeared under his government" (110); Amm.'s freedom of speech would have been particularly restricted when writing about religious affairs and about the father of the emperor, Theodosius the Elder (92), who is eulogized by Amm. on every possible occasion, but whose trial and execution he does not discuss. That Amm. could not write with complete freedom may, perhaps, be surmised from 29.3.1 *quisquis igitur dicta considerat, perpendat etiam cetera, quae tacentur* or 28.1.2 *ac licet ab hoc textu cruento gestorum exquisite narrando iustus me retraheret metus*, although the author continues to say that he will tell the relevant facts *praesentis temporis modestia fretus*. In 27.9.4 he states explicitly that he is free to speak his mind: *et quoniam adest liber locus dicendi, quae sentimus, aperte loquemur.*

Matthews, 204 and 510 n. 1 is justifiably sceptical on this account. He prefers to think that the *pericula* refer to the criticisms of the *examinatores intempestivi*. The explicit divisio *ut et – et*, however, is a strong argument to keep the two notions apart.

Veritas, in the sense of historical truth, was of extreme importance to Amm., perhaps even "an obsession and a passion" (Syme, 1968, 94). See for this notion Ensslin, 1923, 11–12; Syme, 1968, 94–96; Blockley, 1975, 96–97, Sabbah 19–21 and above all Blockley 2001. In this study Blockley concludes (p. 20) "that Ammianus thought of historical truth in two ways: as the determinant in establishing the facts and as the aim of the historian in interpreting these facts." Sabbah makes the useful distinction between *veritas* as the ultimate goal of the historian and *fides*, "veracité", the indispensable requirement for him to attain this goal. Amm. also mentions *veritas* as the ultimate goal of the historian in 15.1.1 *Utcumque potui veritatem scrutari*, and in the sphragis (31.16.9) *opus veritatem professum numquam, ut arbitror, sciens silentio ausus corrumpere vel mendacio*. On this last passage see G. Kelly, 2007.

The noun *examinator* is, apart from in the present passage, used only once in the *Res Gestae*: 21.16.3 *examinator meritorum nonnumquam subscruposus*. It has the connotation of carefulness, as in the case of the cognate adverb, 25.7.7 *dum deliberatur examinatius*, q.v. Here the adjective *intempestivus* gives it an unpleasant ring: these people make an inappropriate use of their critical faculties. For *intempestivus* see the note ad 22.7.3 *per ostentationem intempestivam*. There is a curious parallel for *examinator intempestivus* in Diodorus Siculus, who reports that the historian Timaeus was nicknamed Ἐπιτίμαιος ('Criticaster') for his misplaced carpings: 5.1.3 Τίμαιος μὲν οὖν...διὰ τὰς ἀκαίρους καὶ μακρὰς ἐπιτιμήσεις εὐλόγως διαβάλλεται, καὶ διὰ τὴν ὑπερβολὴν τῆς ἐπιτιμήσεως Ἐπιτίμαιος ὑπό τινων ὠνομάσθη.

In 15.11.16 Amm. looks back and writes *et quoniam ad has partes opere contexto pervenimus*. Here, with reference to what he is going to write, he uses the gerundive. For this use of the gerundive as a passive future participle see the note ad 22.15.3 *mox ostendendis aliis*.

From *deinde* 'from now on', 'henceforth' (cf. 15.1.3 *immunemque se deinde fore ab omni mortalitatis incommodo fidenter existimans*) one might infer that Amm. had indeed been faced with adverse criticism of his work, possibly in the course of public *recitationes*; Thompson, 1947, 11.

strepentes ut laesos The verb *strepere* might be called a t.t. for noisy protests; it has a deprecatory ring. In 17.11.1 it is used of Julian's adversaries at the court of Constantius *talia sine modo strepentes insulse: "in odium venit cum victoriis suis capella, non homo"*. Cf. also 21.1.13 *et quia vanities aliquotiens plebeia strepit haec imperite mussando*, 22.6.2 *principem ipsum et praefectos praetorio gracularum more strepentes interpellabant incondite*, and above all 28.1.15, where Amm. defends himself against a similar criticism, viz. that of negligence in chronological matters: *et quoniam existimo forsitan aliquos haec lecturos exquisite scrutando notare strepentes id actum esse prius, non illud aut ea, quae viderint, praetermissa, hactenus faciendum est satis, quod non omnia narratu sunt digna, quae per squalidas transiere personas*.

quod locutus est imperator in cena Modern historians too have their qualms about such topics, as is evident from the title of the opening chapter of Demandt's *Privatleben der römischen Kaiser*: "Ein unseriöses Thema?".

quam ob causam gregarii milites coerciti sunt apud signa There is a note on *gregarius* ad 25.2.2 *munifici...gregario*. For *coercere = punire* cf. 22.4.6 *cum scriptum sit antiquitatibus Spartanum militem coercitum acriter*. *Apud signa* is a vulgarism according to Löfstedt, 1911, 252-253. See the note ad 21.4.5 *arte*.

et quod non decuerat in descriptione multiplici regionum super exiguis silere castellis Thompson, 1947, 117–118 makes the interesting observation that these words show that Amm.'s readers paid careful attention to his geographical digressions, since they were an integral part of the historical narrative. They would probably have been amazed to read what is said in the preface of Hamilton's translation, that the digressions "would be frankly tedious for the modern reader."

Amm. uses *decere* in an auctorial remark (27.2.11). After mentioning a number of minor battles in Gaul he writes: *quae superfluum est explicare, cum neque operae pretium aliquid eorum habuere proventus nec historiam producere per minutias ignobiles decet.* For *multiplex* see the note ad 21.6.6 *multiplicisque*. Here it must mean 'detailed', as in Quint. *Inst.* 4.5.3 (partitio) *si nimium sit multiplex, fugiet memoriam iudicis.*

ad urbani praetoris officium The praetors entered office on 1 January with an installation ceremony; cf. Plin. *Ep.* 1.5.11 *paucos post dies ipse me Regulus convenit in praetoris officio*; with the commentary of Sherwin-White. Although hardly anything is known about the *officium praetoris*, it seems that friends and clients came to the praetor's house and accompanied him to his seat of office. See also HA *H* 9.7.

On the function of the praetor urbanus in Late Antiquity see Chastagnol, 1958 and Roda, 1977. *Officium* is used in a similar meaning in 22.7.1: *Allapso itaque kalendarum Ianuariarum die cum Mamertini et Nevittae nomina suscepissent paginae consulares, humilior princeps visus est in officio pedibus gradiendo cum honoratis,* q.v.

similia plurima praeceptis historiae dissonantia discurrere per negotiorum celsitudines assuetae For *discurrere* used metaphorically in the sense of *tractare* see TLL V 1.1367.71 sqq. and 30.7.1 *actus eius discurrere per epilogos breves. Rerum celsitudines* is a clear example of the gen. inversus. Amm. uses *celsitudo* in its literal sense of mountains in 15.10.6, 23.6.28 and 27.4.6. Viansino, 1985, 218 aptly remarks: *translate (usurpant Christiani auctores)*, which is confirmed by TLL III 771. 61 sqq. For the contents of the sentence cf. Tac. *Ann.* 13.31.1 *pauca memoria digna evenere, nisi cui libeat laudandis fundamentis et trabibus, quis molem amphitheatri apud campum Martis Caesar exstruxerat, volumina implere, cum ex dignitate populi Romani repertum sit res inlustres annalibus, talia diurnis urbis actis mandare.* The most striking parallel is Hdn. 2.15.6–7 τῆς μὲν οὖν ὁδοιπορίας τοὺς σταθμούς, καὶ τὰ καθ' ἑκάστην πόλιν αὐτῷ λεχθέντα, καὶ σημεῖα θεία προνοίᾳ δόξαντα πολλάκις φανῆναι, χωρία τε ἕκαστα καὶ παρατάξεις, καὶ τὸν τῶν ἑκατέρωθεν πεσόντων ἀριθμὸν στρατιωτῶν ἐν ταῖς μάχαις, ἱστορίας τε πολλοὶ συγγραφεῖς καὶ ποιηταὶ μέτρῳ πλατύτερον συνέταξαν...τὰ κορυφαιότατα τοίνυν καὶ συντέλειαν ἔχοντα τῶν κατὰ μέρος πεπραγμένων Σεβήρῳ ἐν τοῖς ἑξῆς διηγήσομαι ("Many historians and poets, who have made the life of Severus the theme of their entire work, have given more detailed treatment to the stages of his march, his speeches at each city, the frequent manifestations that were interpreted as signs of divine providence, the topography of each place, the disposition of the forces and the number of soldiers on either side that fell in battle...I shall narrate only the most important and conclusive of Severus' actions separately, in chronological order", tr. Whittaker).

Amm. is very clear about the task of the historian. He must tell the truth about men and events which influenced the course of history, leaving out petty details. This last requirement is a well known topos in historical literature (Avenarius, 1956, 128, Herkommer, 1968, 155; Canfora, 1972, 71–87; Sabbah 25–26; Den Hengst, 1981, 44–47), cf. Lucianus *Hist. Conscr.* 27 about historians who omit important facts, but, because they do not have the expertise to distinguish between what needs to be said and what should be passed over in silence, concentrate on trivia, thereby slowing down the pace of the narrative (cf. *moras...tempestivas* in 15.1.1): εἰσὶ γάρ τινες, οἳ τὰ μεγάλα μὲν τῶν πεπραγμένων καὶ ἀξιομνημόνευτα παραλείπουσιν ἢ παραθέουσιν, ὑπὸ δὲ ἰδιωτείας καὶ ἀπειροκαλίας καὶ ἀγνοίας τῶν λεκτέων ἢ σιωπητέων τὰ μικρότατα πάνυ λιπαρῶς καὶ φιλοπόνως ἑρμηνεύουσιν ἐμβραδύνοντες. No author insists more forcefully on the duty of the historian to restrict himself to *digna memoratu* than Ammianus. See e.g. 27.2.11 *nec historiam producere per minutias ignobiles decet*; 28.1.15, quoted above ad *strepentes*, 31.5.10 *sufficiet enim veritate nullo velata mendacio ipsas rerum digerere summitates* and the passages quoted in Sabbah 25–26. Concentration on important events is what distinguishes historiography from biography, so it is supposed that with this remark Amm. criticizes authors and readers of imperial biographies like the ones written by Marius Maximus or the Historia Augusta. See his disdainful remark in 28.4.14: *Quidam detestantes ut venena doctrinas Iuvenalem et Marium Maximum curatiore studio legunt*. One should not conclude from this that Amm. rejected biographical elements, but he rejected the emphasis on petty details; Matthews 459; also Demandt, 1965, 99–100. It is highly ironical (and no doubt intended to be so) that the closest parallels to the present passage are found in the Historia Augusta: In *Gd* 21.3 the anonymous author heaps scorn on the biographer Cordus in the following terms: *haec de Gordiano iuniore digna memoratu comperimus: non enim nobis talia dicenda sunt, quae Iunius Cordus ridicule ac stulte composuit de voluptatibus domesticis ceterisque infimis rebus. quae qui velit scire, ipsum legat Cordum, qui dicit, et quos servos habuerit unusquisque principum et quos amicos et quot paenulas quotve clamydes, quorum etiam scientia nulli rei prodest, si quidem ea debeant in historia poni ab historiografis, quae aut fugienda sint aut sequenda.* And again in *Q* 6.3–4: *sed haec scire quid prodest? cum et Livius et Sallustius taceant res leves de his, quorum vitas arripuerunt. non enim scimus, quales mulos Clodius habuerit aut mulas Titus Annius Milo, aut utrum Tusco equo sederit Catilina an Sardo, vel quali in clamide Pompeius usus fuerit purpura.* There is general consensus among students of the HA that this Cordus is a product of the author's fantasy, who is criticized for doing exactly what the author himself loves to do, i.e. indulge in all kinds of banalities or *frivola*. In Mommsen's famous phrase (1890, 272): "der Biograph hat…in diesem pseudo-Cordus sich zugleich einen Gewährsmann und einen Prügelknaben geschaffen." This raises the much debated question whether the author of the HA knew (and parodied) Amm. Since the relationship between the historian and the biographer can only have been a one-way traffic from historian to biographer, this need not detain us here.

The question has been posed by Vogt, 1963, 806 and Paschoud, 2005, 113 whether Ammianus practiced what he preached. Vogt praises Amm. for his "Fähigkeit, interessante Einzelzüge scharf zu erfassen und wirksam im Bild festzuhalten" (p. 807) and lists a long series of detailed descriptions, thumbnail sketches and little anecdotes which together constitute Amm.'s unique narrative style. Is this attention to detail, this effort to provide *evidentia* really compatible with his pledge to restrict himself to *rerum celsitudines*? Paschoud says that some of the anecdotes Amm. tells us could not possibly belong to that category. In Vogt's opinion these details often nourish the reader's imagination and enhance his understanding of the past: "Dort freilich, wo das Einzelne etwas Allgemeines zu repräsentieren scheint oder durch seine Absonderlichkeit herausragt, nimmt er es in die grosse Darstellung auf" (p. 809). Indeed, there is a difference between a 'petit fait significatif' and a mechanical enumeration of events, people and places which happen to be known, but do not contribute to the readers' understanding of the situation described.

quas si scitari voluerit quispiam, individua illa corpuscula volitantia per inane, atomos, ut nos appellamus, numerari posse sperabit The wording seems to have been inspired by Cic. *Fin.* 1.17 *ille atomos quas appellat, id est corpora individua propter soliditatem, censet in infinito inani…ferri.* For the expression *ut nos appellamus* and similar phrases referring to Amm.'s Greekness, see Den Boeft, 1992, 12. The same thought is expressed in 14.11.34 *quae omnia si scire quisquam velit, quam varia sint et assidua, harenarum numerum idem iam desipiens et montium pondera scrutari putabit.*

1.2 *haec quidam veterum formidantes cognitiones actuum variorum stilis uberioribus explicatas non edidere superstites, ut in quadam ad Cornelium Nepotem epistula Tullius quoque, testis reverendus, affirmat* It seems best to interpret *haec* as referring both to the *pericula* and to the criticisms Amm. has enumerated at such length. Which ancient authors (cf. 15.9.2 *scriptores veteres*) Cicero had in mind cannot be ascertained. From the period after Cicero we have the example of T. Labienus, about whom Sen. *Contr.* 10 *pr.* 8 writes: *Memini aliquando, cum recitaret historiam, magnam partem illum libri convolvisse et dixisse: haec, quae transeo, post mortem meam legentur.* The Elder Pliny gave his heir the instruction to publish his historical work *A fine Aufidi Bassi* after his death: (*Nat. pr.* 20) *ubi sit ea, quaeres? iam pridem peracta sancitur et alioqui statutum erat heredi mandare, ne quid ambitioni dedisse vita iudicaretur* ("Where is this work? you will inquire. The draft has long been finished and is in safe keeping; and in any case it was my resolve to entrust it to my heir, to prevent it being thought that my lifetime bestowed anything on ambition", tr. Rackham). Josephus, in a polemic against the historian Justus, accuses him of keeping his history under cover until the persons who could judge its contents were dead: *Vit.* 359–360 εἰ δὲ θαρρεῖς ἄμεινον ἁπάντων συγγεγραφέναι, διὰ τί ζώντων Οὐεσπασιανοῦ καὶ Τίτου τῶν αὐτοκρατόρων τῶν τὸν πόλεμον κατεργασαμένων καὶ βασιλέως Ἀγρίππα περιόντος ἔτι...τὴν ἱστορίαν οὐκ ἔφερες εἰς μέσον; ...νῦν δ', ὅτ' ἐκεῖνοι μὲν οὐκέτ' εἰσὶν μεθ' ἡμῶν, ἐλεγχθῆναι δ' οὐ νομίζεις, τεθάρρηκας ("But, if you are so confident that your history excells all others, why did you not publish it in the lifetime of the Emperors Vespasian and Titus, who conducted the war, and while King Agrippa...was still among us? ...But not until now, when those persons are no longer with us, and you think you cannot be confuted, have you ventured to publish it", tr. Thackeray).

For *cognitiones* see the note ad 25.4.7, where it is interpreted as referring to Julian's various intellectual accomplishments. In 15.1.1 *cognitioni gestorum* it means 'knowledge of historical events'. August. *C.D.* 10.32 uses the expression *cognitio historialis.* The phrase *cognitiones actuum* is without parallel. Amm. uses *actus* regularly for (parts of) his own work, e.g. 14.1.8 *ut in Gordianorum actibus...rettulimus*, 21.8.1 *cuius in actibus Magnenti meminimus*, q.v., so *cognitio(nes) actuum* looks like a variation on *cognitio(nes) gestorum*. The addition *stilis ube-*

rioribus explicatas is concessive. These ancient authors did not publish their books, despite the fact that they were finished works, written in a rich style. For *superstes* = *vivus* see the note ad 21.7.5 *eo enim* and Hor. *Epod.* 1.5 with Mankin's note.

As stated ad 23.5.11 *philosophis...quorum reverenda tunc erat auctoritas* the adjective is forceful. It expresses Amm.'s deep respect for Cicero, whom he quotes more often than any other author. See the note ad 21.16.13 and Sabbah 72–75; Matthews 466, 483 n. 44, Fornara, 1992, 425, 428 and Blockley, 1998, 309–312. For Cicero's letters to Nepos see the note ad 21.16.13. It is quite conceivable that the two had corresponded about historiography. Nepos had a high opinion of Cicero's potential qualities as a historian: *ille enim fuit unus, qui potuerit et etiam debuerit historiam digna voce pronuntiare (fr. 3)*. Possibly he invited Cicero to do just that, and Cicero pointed out the risks involved in writing recent history.

proinde inscitia vulgari contempta ad residua narranda pergamus This is a surprising conclusion. According to TLL X 2.1806.9 *proinde* is often used by Ammianus and Augustine to introduce the consequences of a preceding statement. Cf. e.g. 26.2.7 ('you have chosen me as your emperor') *proinde pacatis auribus accipite, quaeso, simplicioribus verbis, quod conducere arbitror in commune*. At first sight it would seem more logical, after the reference to the ancient writers who, fearful of dangers and criticisms, had decided not to publish their work in their lifetime, if the author had decided to end his work there and then. There are two possible solutions for this problem: Amm. uses *proinde* here without real connective force, as he does at the end of the digression on the leap year in section 14, where *proinde pergamus ad reliqua* is only loosely connected with the preceding sentence; alternatively, *proinde* introduces the consequence of Amm.'s statement that it is just as impossible to incorporate all *minutiae* in his work as it is to count the atoms; in that case the immediately preceding sentence *haec quidam...affirmat* must be seen as a parenthesis. The latter interpretation is more attractive, since it links *proinde* to *inscitia vulgari contempta*. This does not refer to the ignorance regarding historical facts on the part of Amm.s' readers, as Paschoud, 2005, 116 suggests, but to their ignorance of the *praecepta historiae*: 'let us therefore pay no attention to this widespread ignorance and continue'.

There is no parallel for *inscitia vulgaris* except in the digression on earthquakes 17.7.9 *ad ipsius enim veritatis arcana non modo haec nostra vulgaris inscitia, sed ne sempiterna quidem lucubrationibus longis nondum exhausta physicorum iurgia penetrarunt*. As the addition of *nostra* in that passage makes clear, the phrase does not have the derogatory ring the translators give it. The ignorance of the layman is opposed to the long and inconclusive discussions of the experts, as in Gel. 2.28.11 *non modo his communibus hominum sensibus opinionibusque compertum, sed ne inter physicas quidem philosophias satis constitit*, which is Amm.'s model (Mary, 2004, 174 n. 13). As Ensslin, 1923, 15, says about the present passage, Amm. "fühlt sich dabei als Fachmann". Thompson, 1947, 88 is certainly right in discerning "a distinct aggressiveness in the apologies for omitting details". Amm. seems to have been stung by the inept criticisms levelled at his work by people who did not realize that the historian has to be selective with regard to the mass of available facts. His tone is haughty rather than derogatory, and in that respect resembles that of Tacitus when he criticizes the historians of the early principate in the opening chapter of his *Histories*: *veritas pluribus modis infracta, primum inscitia rei publicae ut alienae, mox libidine adsentandi aut rursus odio adversus dominantes: ita neutris cura posteritatis inter infensos vel obnoxios* (1.1.6).

1.3 *Hac volubilium casuum diritate exitu luctuoso finita* With this phrase Amm. returns to his historical narrative. The abl. abs. *hac diritate finita* refers to the dramatic events narrated in Book 25 with a complete disregard for the programmatic statement in the preceding passage. Fortune had been fickle indeed, bringing first victory on the battlefield, then the death of a respected and competent emperor, and finally a short-lived successor, who signed a peace treaty that in the eyes of Amm. was a disgrace. For comparable sentences at the beginning of a new book cf. 22.1.1 *Dum haec in diversa parte terrarum fortunae struunt volubiles casus* with the note. *Casuum diritas* is the equivalent of *casus diri*, with which we may compare Cic. *Tusc*. 3.29 *si qua invecta diritas casu foret* and Sil. 2.650 *diros urbis casus*.

obituque intervallato brevi tempore principum The suffix *-que* is best taken explicatively, with *obitu intervallato* in apposition to *exitu*. According to TLL VII 1.2292.58 the verb *intervallare* is a secondary derivation from *intervallatus*, itself derived from *intervallum*. Gel. 17.12.5 and Amm. 29.2.26 and 31.11.6 have the expression *intervallata febris* ('intermittent fever'). Amm. uses the gerund in 27.11.2 *intervallando potestates assiduas*, 'assuming at intervals'. It is impossible to decide, whether Amm. is thinking of the deaths of Constantius II (3 November 361), Julian (in the night of 26/27 June 363) and Jovian (17 February 364), or only of Julian and Jovian, so there is no compelling need to insert *trium* before *brevi*, as Hadrianus Valesius proposed.

corpore curato defuncti missoque Constantinopolim, ut inter Augustorum reliquias conderetur For *corpus curare* in the sense of 'to embalm' see the note ad 25.5.1. Like his predecessors Constantine I (Eus. *VC* 4.58–60, 70.2, with Cameron-Hall, 1999, 337–338) and Constantius II (see the note ad 21.16.20 *Constantinopolim*), Jovian was buried in the Church of the Holy Apostles in Constantinople. Julian was first buried in Tarsus but later, pace Woods, 2006, also transferred to Constantinople; see 25.9.12, 10.5 with the relevant notes. Add to the literature cited there Asutay-Effenberger/Effenberger, 2006, 59–65.

progresso Nicaeam versus exercitu, quae in Bithynia mater est urbium Jovian and his troops had been on their way to Constantinople when the emperor suddenly died in Dadastana (25.10.12). After this tragic event the emperor's retinue continued its march to Nicaea. Lenski, 2002, 22 n. 52, has drawn attention to the fact that Nicaea capitalized on Valentinian's nomination as emperor; it became the capital of Bithynia under Valentinian as two laws, preserved in the Acts of the Council of Chalcedon, indicate; *Actio* XIV.27–30 = Schwartz *ACO* I.3.61. Normally Nicomedia had the status of capital of Bithynia, but sometimes Nicaea and Nicomedia held the title of *mater urbium* simultaneously; see the note ad 22.9.5 *per Nicaeam*.

potestatum civilium militiaeque rectores This is an unusual way to designate civil and military officials, the phrase *potestatum rectores* being without parallel. One would have expected something like 21.16.2 *sed cunctae castrenses et ordinariae potestates* or *potestates civiles militiaeque rectores*. It is, however, a minor irregularity that does not necessitate an emendation. Unfortunately, Amm. does not mention those present at the meeting, but presumably at least four of the people who had deliberated about Julian's succession were there. They are mentioned by name in 25.5.2–3, q.v.: Salutius, Arintheus, Victor and Dagalaifus. All of them continued their careers under Valentinian and Valens. Possibly Nevitta, also mentioned in 25.5.2, was present as well, but of his career after the election of Jovian nothing is known. See further below, ad 26.1.5 *Valentinianus*.

magnitudine curarum astricti V has *magnitudineque*, which Blomgren defends unconvincingly. Petschenig's ⟨*ae*⟩*que* is, like most of his conjectures, ingenious, but the adverb is otiose. The suffix is probably a thoughtless repetition of *-que* after the preceding *militiae*.

moderatorem quaeritabant diu exploratum et gravem According to Zos. 3.36.1-2 (and Zon. 13.14.16) Salutius was offered the throne but he declined, after which it was offered to his son; he, however, was considered by his father too young and not up to the job: Βουλῆς δὲ ὑπὲρ τοῦ τίνα δέοι προστῆναι πολιτεύματος προτεθείσης, πολλοὶ μὲν καὶ περὶ πολλῶν ἐγίνοντο λόγοι τῷ στρατοπέδῳ καὶ τοῖς τὰς ἡγεμονίας ἔχουσι, πάντων δὲ ἡ ψῆφος εἰς ἕνα συνῄει Σαλούστιον τὸν τῆς αὐλῆς ὕπαρχον· τοῦ δὲ τὸ γῆρας προϊσχομένου καὶ διὰ τοῦτο φήσαντος οὐχ οἷός τε ἔσεσθαι πεπονηκόσιν ἀρκέσειν τοῖς πράγμασι, τὸν παῖδα γοῦν ᾔτησαν εἰς τὴν τῶν ὅλων ἀρχὴν ἐλθεῖν. Τοῦ δὲ καὶ νέον εἶναι καὶ οὐδὲ ἄλλως ἐπιτήδειον πρὸς τοσαύτης ἀρχῆς ὄγκον εἰπόντος κτλ. Amm., who does not mention Salutius as a candidate for Jovian's succession, does tell us that he was offered the throne after Julian's death, which in their turn Zosimus and Zonaras omit to mention. See the elaborate note ad 25.5.3 *nulla variante* for this discrepancy (add to the literature Lenski, 2002, 20). As is suggested there, it is likely that Salutius was offered the throne on both occasions. Amm. uses the word *moderator* for all sorts of 'rulers'; see the note ad 20.8.14 *residuos*.

1.4 *Et rumore tenus obscuris paucorum susurris nomen praestringebatur Equitii, scholae primae Scutariorum etiamtum tribuni* Note the threefold restriction *rumore tenus, obscuris susurris* (for which compare 26.6.18 *leni paucorum susurro*) and *praestringebatur* ('was touched upon'). Amm. goes out of his way to show that Equitius was not a serious candidate. *Obscuris* may well be a case of enallage; cf. 14.7.4 *a militibus obscurissimis* and 18.5.5 *Sabinianus...imbellis et ignavus et ab impetranda magisterii dignitate per obscuritatem adhuc longe discretus*. Seyfarth, despite V's *aequitii*, prints *Equitii*, a spelling which is found in the greater part of the epigraphical and papyrological evidence cited in *PLRE* I, Equitius 2 (but not in e.g. ILS 4147 *d.n. Gratiano Aug. ter et [Fl.] Aequitio conss.*). He was a Pannonian, and probably nominated tribune of the *schola scutariorum prima* by Jovian; Woods, 1997, 278. He was *magister militum per Illyricum* from 365 until Valentinian's death in 375. He was consul in 374 together with Gratian, 30.3.1, cf. Bagnall et al., 1987, 282-283. He probably owed his brilliant career to his support for the nomination of Valentinian and to being a loyal supporter of the emperor; he kept the soldiers under control until Valentinian's arrival in Nicaea (26.1.6); he arrested Procopius' envoys when they attempted to infiltrate Illyricum (26.7.11), and he besieged Philippopolis which supported the usurper (26.10.4-6). Further references to him by Amm.: 26.5.3, 10, 11; 29.6.3, 12; 30.6.2. He played a decisive role in the nomination of Valentinian II, on which Amm. is silent; Zos. 4.19.1; *epit.* 45.10. The unnamed Illyrian official in Lib. *Or.* 24.12 is possibly to be identified with Equitius; Bagnall et al., 1987, 283. For the *schola Scutariorum* see the note ad 20.2.5 *Gentilium Scutariorum* and ad 25.10.9 *Quibus compertis*. There are notes on *tribunus* ad 22.11.2 *Romanus quin*, 23.3.9 *tribuno Constantiniano*, and 24.3.1 *paucissimos trucidasse*. For tribunes in general in Amm. see Castillo, 2004. For tribunes of the *scholae* see Woods, 1997 and Barlow/Brennan, 2001.

qui cum potiorum auctoritate displicuisset ut asper et subagrestis Amm. uses *displicere* without its usual complement in the dative also in 20.4.16 *nihil visuri, quia displicet, transalpinum* and 30.2.2 *deleri penitus suadebat Armeniam, si id displicuisset, aliud poscens*, so there is no compelling reason to doubt the ablative *auctoritate*. The ablative expresses the reason why Equitius was rejected: 'because of the authoritative judgment of the higher officers', who thought him rude and boorish. For *auctoritas* see the note ad 22.14.7 *secreta librorum* and cf. 15.9.8 *ut auctoritas Pythagorae decrevit*, 16.1.5 *ut Tulliana docet auctoritas* and 27.4.3 *Homeri perennis auctoritas docet*. Rudeness and lack of culture are stereotypes which Amm. applies to many Pannonians. The emperor Valens has a boorish character (*subagrestis ingenii*; 31.14.5), is a man from the countryside (*subrusticum hominem*; 29.1.11) and is called *inconsummatus et rudis* (31.14.8), *imperator rudis* (27.5.8). Valentinian uses a boorish expression (*subagresti verbo*; 29.3.6). The Dalmatian Ursatius, *magister officiorum* under Valentinian, is characterized with the words *Delmatae crudo* (26.4.4) and *iracundo quodam et saevo* (26.5.7). For the stereotype of the uncultured Pannonian see also Chrys. *oppugn.* 1.7 (= PG 47.328–329); Jul. *Mis.* 348c–d; *epit.* 40.10; Aur. Vict. *Caes.* 40.17. See in general Lenski, 2002, 86–88, who draws attention to the fact that the Pannonian was not only characterized as uncultured but also as cruel. Amm. presents several instances of this: 26.6.8 (Petronius); 26.10.2 (Serenianus); 28.1.12 (Leo); 28.1.38 (Maximinus). Extreme cruelty is also ascribed to Valentinian (e.g. 30.8.2–3) and Valens (e.g. 29.1.18–22, 38; 2.10).

translata est suffragatio levis in Ianuarium, Ioviani affinem, curantem summitatem necessitatum castrensium per Illyricum Most translators interpret *levis* as 'unimportant', but Rolfe writes "fickle favour" and Caltabiano "il favore volubile", which is attractive at first sight, but does not sit well with the rather technical noun *suffragatio*. Probably Amm. only wants to indicate that Ianuarius too did not have strong support. This passage is the only source for Ianuarius (*PLRE* I, Ianuarius 5). According to the *PLRE* his function was either that of *magister militum per Illyricum* or *comes rei militaris*. According to Demandt, 1970, 586, however, his function was "wohl eher als *actuarius* in hohem Rang, d.h. als Quartiermeister...aufzufassen".

1.5 *quia procul iacebat* This is very idiomatic Latin for 'to be away from the action'; TLL VII 1.27.34 "de exulibus i.q. in terra aliena afflictum vivere", quoting i.a. Cic. *Sest. 7 socerum...in alienis terris iacentem, quem in maiorum suorum vestigiis stare oportebat; Att.* 11.6.2 *Brundisii iacere in omnis partis est molestum;* Ov. *Tr.* 3.3.13 *lassus in extremis iaceo populisque locisque*; cf. Hagendahl, 1922, 86–87.

Valentinianus nulla discordante sententia numinis aspiratione caelestis electus est Amm. may have been critical of Valentinian in many respects, but he describes his election as emperor in the most positive terms; see Teitler 2007. For *nulla discordante sententia* cf. the note ad 25.5.3 *nulla variante* and see Marié's introduction to volume V of the Budé-edition, p. 19–21. The phrase *numinis aspiratione caelestis* (cf. the note ad 25.8.3 *favore superi*; add to the literature mentioned there Davies, 2004, 265–268) had even been used by Amm. to describe the protection given to Julian by Eusebia: 15.2.8 *aspiratione superni numinis Eusebia suffragante regina*. Another view is voiced by Leppin, 2007, 34–42, who considers Amm's description far less positive and sees it full of ironic elements (the words *nulla discordante sententia*, for instance, would betray that there was no real enthusiasm for Valentinian's election). This view, interesting as it is, seems to be an over-interpretation of Amm.'s account which should be taken at face value for its historical information and hence as more positive with regard to Valentinian's election.

Valentinian (*PLRE* I, Valentinianus 7) had probably attracted attention because he was the son of the distinguished commander Gratianus (30.7.2), who had i.a. been *comes Africae* and *comes Britanniae*: *Cuius meritis Valentinianus ab ineunte adolescentia commendabilis* (30.7.4). In this respect he resembled Jovian, whose father Varronianus was also a great military leader (25.5.4). There are more similarities between the two: both came from the Balkans and both were representatives of the military middle ranks. However, there are also differences. Jovian was *commendabilis* because of his father's qualities and career, whereas Valentinian was not only commendable because of his background but also had qualities of his own; 30.7.4 *contextu suarum quoque suffragante virtutum*. Another difference between the two is that Jovian's election was not undisputed (see the note ad

25.5.4 *nondum pensatis*), whereas Valentinian was unanimously chosen by the consistory of military and civilian leaders.

According to several sources Salutius proposed Valentinian as emperor; Malalas *Chron.* 13.338; *Chron. Pasch.* a. 364; Zon. 13.14.18. Philost. *HE* 8.8 has the interesting information that Valentinian's election was due to a letter sent from Galatia by Datianus, which received the support of a certain Secundus who is generally identified with Salutius. Salutius definitely had an important hand in Valentinian's election, as is evident for instance from 26.2.1 (with relevant notes). That Datianus played a role is not unlikely. He had been very influential during Constantius' reign, and had been a supporter of Jovian; *PLRE* I, Datianus 1. He had followed Jovian's court to Ancyra and remained there for the winter, where he had probably become acquainted with Valentinian. According to Olariu, 2005, 354 Datianus may have considered Valentinian the perfect candidate to succeed Jovian: he had a military background, he lacked a strong faction to support him and he was not well educated which made him compliant. Tomlin, 1973, 28 had already mentioned Datianus as an important referee for Valentinian's candidature. As may be inferred from their careers under Valentinian and Valens, a large group of military and civil officials supported Valentinian's election. Among them were Victor, Arintheus and Dagalaifus (see for them the notes ad 26.5.2), but also the Pannonians Equitius and Leo (26.1.6, q.v.). Others who, according to Tomlin, 1973, 28 had endorsed the election of Valentinian were Caesarius and the Illyrians Ursatius and Viventius; all three made significant promotions soon after Valentinian had become emperor. Caesarius (*PLRE* I, Caesarius 1), who was *comes rei privatae* in 363–364, became *praefectus urbi* of Constantinople and opposed Procopius' usurpation (26.7.4). Ursatius and Viventius were appointed to investigate the cause of the sudden illnesses of Valentinian and Valens; 26.4.4 with relevant note. Ursatius was *magister officiorum*, but his career apparently ended there, probably because he was blamed for the Alaman invasion of 365; 26.5.7, q.v. Viventius was appointed prefect of Rome in 366–367 and *praefectus praetorio Galliarum* in 368–371. For further information on Ursatius and Viventius see the note *Ursatio officiorum* ad 26.4.4.

Valentinian already had considerable military experience when he became emperor. He had served as tribune in Gaul, but was dismissed from service by Constantius for undermining operations (16.11.6–7). Apparently he was allowed to enter the military again, since he was an officer in Mesopotamia, probably in 360/1 (Philost. *HE* 7.7) and *comes et tribunus cornutorum* in 362 (Philost. *HE* 7.7; cf.

Oros. *hist.* 7.32.2; Thdt. *HE* 3.16). Christian authors report that he was banished by Julian because of his Christian conviction: Rufin. *hist.* 2.2; Socr. *HE* 4.1.8; Soz. *HE* 6.6.3–6; Philost. *HE* 7.7, 8.5; Thdt. *HE* 3.16; Oros. *hist.* 7.32.2. He is said to have been recalled from exile by Jovian (Philost. *HE* 8.5; cf. Zon. 13.15.4), under whom he continued his military career. The reliability of the Christian account of Valentinian's banishment is generally disputed by modern scholars; e.g. Heering, 1927, 8–10; Woods, 1998; Lenski, 2002a; see also Raimondi, 2001, 32–40. During Jovian's reign he barely survived a mutiny of soldiers in Gaul (25.10.6–7 with relevant notes) and was made commander of the *schola secunda Scutariorum*, for which see the notes ad 20.2.5 *Gentilium Scutariorum* and 25.10.9 *Quibus compertis*. He had already been mentioned by Amm. in 15.5.36 and 16.11.6. Valentinian was born in 321 (30.6.6) and thus was 43 when he was raised to the throne. He was a native of Cibala (30.6.6; Lib. *Or.* 20.25; Zos. 3.36.2; Philost. *HE* 8.16). The date on which Valentinian was elected was probably 19 or 20 February (see note below).

relictusque apud Ancyram For this use of *apud* see the note ad 14.11.21 *apud Antiochiam*. Ancyra is some 220 Roman miles – the average of 203 miles given by *Itin. Burdig.* 573.4–575.4 and 239 miles given by the *Tab. Peut.* IX.2–IX.4 – that is some 325 km from Nicaea. Valentinian must have remained there after Jovian left to march on to Constantinople in the first half of February. There is a note on Ancyra ad 25.10.11 *Et cum*. According to Malalas *Chron.* 13.338 Valentinian, when nominated emperor, had to be fetched from Salabria; see Raimondi, 2001, 211–218 ('Appendice seconda').

quia nullo renitente hoc e republica videbatur, missis, qui eum venire ocius admonerent, diebusque decem nullus imperii tenuit gubernacula Again Amm. emphasizes that Valentinian was unanimously elected. The *quia*-clause explains why delegates were sent to Ancyra to invite Valentinian to come to Nicaea, not why there was an 'interregnum' of ten days; one would therefore expect *missi sunt* as the main verb. V's text *missis...diebusque decem nullus...tenuit* is a slight anacolouthon, of which Amm. is occasionally guilty (see e.g. the note ad 25.7.3 *custodibusque*), but only in long and complicated sentences. It seems best therefore, pace Pighi, 1935, 81, to follow Petschenig, 1892, 520 and read *missi sunt* and *diebusque*. For *ocius* see the note ad 20.1.3

The ten days are the period between Jovian's death in the early hours of 17 February and Valentinian's official accession to the throne. *Art. pass.* 70 incorrectly mentions a period of forty days during which the Roman Empire was without a sovereign.

The chronology of the events in this period, which also included the *dies bissextus*, is not easy to reconstruct. Essential is the establishment of the dates of Valentinian's *dies imperii* and the *dies bissextus*. Three sources allow us to establish that the date of Valentinian's acclamation as emperor was 25 February. It is stated explicitly in Socr. *HE* 4.1.1: κοινῇ ψήφῳ Οὐαλεντινιανὸν ἀνακηρύττουσι βασιλέα τῇ πέμπτῃ καὶ εἰκάδι τοῦ αὐτοῦ Φεβρουαρίου μηνός. Both Amm. (30.6.6 *imperii* (anno) *minus centum dies secundo et decimo*) and the *Epitome* (45.1 *Valentinianus imperavit annos duodecim minus diebus centum*) inform us that Valentinian died 100 days short of the 12th anniversary of his reign. Knowing that he died on 17 November (Socr. *HE* 4.31.6; *Consul. Constant.* a. 375 = *Chron. Min.* I. 242) 375, this would mean, by counting backwards, that his *dies imperii* was on 25 February. The date of the *dies bissextus* is also of importance to establish Valentinian's *dies imperii*. The year 364 was an intercalary year. In such a year *a.d. VI Kal. Mart.* was counted twice and was called *a.d. bis VI Kal. Mart.* The extra day could either be intercalated before *a.d. VI Kal. Mart.* as Cens. 20.10: *ut post Terminalia* [i.e. 23 February] *intercalaretur*) and Macrobius (*Sat.* 1.14.6 *id est ante quinque ultimos Februarii mensis dies*) suggest, or after, as Celsus says (*Dig.* 50.16.98 *posterior dies intercalatur, non prior*). In the first case the intercalary day would be 24 February and in the second 25 February. Because Amm. 26.2.1–2 reports that Valentinian was made emperor on the day after the *dies bissextus*, some scholars have concluded that the *dies imperii* was on 26 February; e.g. Seeck, 1919, 214, *PLRE* I, Flavius Valentinianus 7 and Curran, 1998, 81. However, Celsus also reports that *a.d. VI Kal. Mart.* and *a.d. bis VI Kal. Mart.* were juristically counted as one: *id biduum pro uno die habetur* (*Dig.* 50.16.98). That would mean that, as the term *dies bissextus* implies, 24 February was counted twice; see Heering, 1927, 13–15 and in particular Tomlin, 1973, Appendix 2. Following this line of reasoning Valentinian's *dies imperii* was on 25 February, which is in keeping with the information provided by Socrates, the *Epitome* and Ammianus himself. This date is preferred by e.g. Heering, 1927, 15 ("So halte ich den 25. Februar als Tag des Regierungsantrits Valentinians für gesichert"); Tomlin, 1973, 468 ("So we may speak of Valentinian's *dies imperii* as 25th February"); Kienast, 1996², 327; Lenski, 2002, 22. Raimondi, 2001, 63 leaves the matter undecided ("solo dopo un intervallo di una decina di giorni, il 25 o il 26 febbraio, l'esercito fu convocato per eleggere Flavio Valentiniano").

Counting 17 February as the first day and 25 February as the last day of the ten-day period, Amm.'s calculation is correct, provided that 24 February is counted twice.

The ten days, during which the empire was without a ruler, can be reconstructed as follows: Jovian died in the early morning of 17 February; it is not reported when the council assembled to discuss the matter of his succession, but it seems that this was not before 19 February, since the electors first travelled to Nicaea; at the earliest on 19 February, but more likely on 20 February, Valentinian was elected; after the council had elected Valentinian a courier was sent to Ancyra, who presumably reached his destination by 22 February; the distance between Nicaea and Ancyra is some 325 km (see above ad *relictusque*); on the same day (22 February) Valentinian probably set out for his journey to Nicaea, which he reached in the evening or night of 24 February; the following day was the *dies bissextus*, the second 24 February, and the next day, i.e. 25 February, he was officially inaugurated as emperor. See for this reconstruction of events Tomlin, 1973, 469.

Gubernaculum is used by Amm. only in one other instance, viz. in the context of the rule of Adrastia/Nemesis, the daughter of Iustitia; *illi fabulosa vetustas...praetendere gubernaculum dedit eique subdidit rotam, ut universitatem regere per elementa discurrens omnia non ignoretur* (14.11.26). In a speech to the troops Constantius describes himself as a helmsman steering the ship of state, 21.13.10 *clavos pro fluctuum motibus erigens vel inclinans*, q.v. Cf. also 26.6.3 *clavos summae rei gerendae*. As Michael, 1874, 27 points out, Cic. *Sest.* 20 *gubernacula rei publicae tenere* may have provided the model.

quod tunc venisse extis Romae inspectis haruspex edixerat Marcus Petschenig, 1892, 520 gives two parallels for *venire* = *evenire* in V: 26.9.4 *neque secus venit* and 29.1.26 *hoc quoque venerat triste*, so it seems advisable to accept *venisse*. Instead of a perfect infinitive one would expect a future infinitive here. À la rigueur, the perfect infinitive may be explained in the following manner: the *haruspex* had announced that a period of ten days without an emperor had passed. Given the distance from Nicaea to Rome, confirmation of the prophecy would have come much later. For *edicere* in a comparable context see 21.2.2 *horrore medio noctis imago quaedam visa splendidior hos ei versus heroos modo non vigilanti aperte edixit*. A similar incident is reported in 15.5.34, where the people of Rome cried out "*Silvanus devictus est*", even before Silvanus' revolt had started. Gel. 15.18 has the following story: a priest from Patavium saw in his mind the battle of Pharsalus when it was actually taking place and announced the victory of Caesar. Cf. Plut. *Caes.* 47, who mentions Livy as his source. One may also think of Apollonius of Tyana, who, while at Ephesus, witnessed the murder of Domitian at Rome, for which see the note ad 25.3.23 *medio noctis.* For haruspices see Briquel, 1998 and Haack, 2002.

ne quid novaretur contrarium placitis neve armatorum mobilitas saepe versabilis ad praesentium quendam inclinaret The election of Jovian, during which the disorderly behaviour of a few had influenced the procedure before it had run its normal course, had taught the *rectores* a lesson (25.5.4 *nondum pensatis sententiis tumultuantibus paucis...Iovianus eligitur imperator,* q.v.). For *novare* see the note ad 20.8.7 *si quid.* The soldiers (see for *armati* the note ad 20.4.22) are inconstant (*mobiles*) and easily swayed (*versabiles*); cf. 15.5.30 *Bracchiati...atque Cornuti ubertate mercedis ad momentum omne versabiles* and 20.4.21 *veritique versabilis perfidiam militis,* q.v. In that respect they resemble barbarians, like the vassals of the Persian king, 14.3.1 *mente quadam versabili hostiliter eum saepe incessunt et in nos arma moventem aliquotiens iuvant* or the Huns, 31.2.11 *per indutias infidi inconstantes, ad omnem auram incidentis spei novae perquam mobiles, totum furori incitatissimo tribuentes.*

With *praesentium quendam* Amm. refers to *quidam spe vana sufflati* in section 3.

Equitius et cum eo Leo. For Equitius see the note ad 26.1.4. Leo (*PLRE* I, Leo 1) was apparently *numerarius* of Dagalaifus in 364 and *notarius* in 370 (28.1.12; Teitler, 1985, 146). He succeeded Remigius as *magister officiorum* in 371/2 and carried out that office until 375/6 (30.2.10). He schemed to become *PPO Italiae* (30.5.10). Gratian probably dismissed him; Symm. *Or.* 4.10. Amm. accuses him of cruelty and brutality; 28.1.12 *Leonem notarium, postea officiorum magistrum, bustuarium quendam latronem Pannonium efflantem ferino rictu crudelitatem, etiam ipsum nihilo minus humani sanguinis avidissimum;* also 30.5.10.

Dagalaifo The first time Dagalaifus (*PLRE* I, Dagalaifus+A. Lippold in *Gnomon* 46 [1974] 272) is mentioned in the *Res Gestae* is 21.8.1 *Dagalaifus* (q.v.); see also the notes ad 24.1.2 *agmina vero,* 25.5.2 *Nevitta* and 25.8.9 *oblati magisterii.* Amm. prefers an unofficial formulation of his function to his official title *magister equitum.* In this book he is mentioned again in 26.4.1, 5.2, 5.9, 9.1.

exitialis See the note above for Leo's conduct.

exercitus universi iudicium...formantes The process of choosing an emperor went through three stages: the *electio*, the *commendatio* and the *acclamatio*; Heim, 1990, 161. The process of making Valentinian emperor was only in its first stage, the *electio*; the *commendatio* and the *acclamatio* by the army took place a few days later; see 26.2.3–11. The words *exercitus universi iudicium*, therefore, probably do not refer to the whole army, but only to the principal civil and military leaders (*potestatum civilium militaeque rectores*; 26.1.3) who had unanimously elected Valentinian. There seems to be no compelling reason to change V's *formantes* into *firmantes*. Although the civil and military leaders have reached a decision, there is still time and the need to influence the 'shape' of the soldiers' feelings. For this meaning of *formare* cf. 21.1.1 *formandis in futura consiliis* with the note.

quantum facere nitique poterant This expression is found only in Amm. He uses it also in 19.8.1 and 24.4.15.

1.7 *Qui cum venisset accitus, implendique negotii...praesagiis, ut opinari dabatur, vel somniorum assiduitate nec videri die secundo nec prodire in medium voluit* Valentinian arrived in Nicaea on the evening of 24 February; see the note ad 26.1.5 *quia nullo renitente*. Some word(s) must have dropped out after *negotii*. It is only possible to guess their content, if one has first decided whether the *praesagia* that follow were related to *implendi negotii*, the task that awaited Valentinian, or to his decision not to appear in public. Both Paschoud, 1992, 70 n. 16 and Weber, 2000, 223 in his translation opt for the latter interpretation. Signs and dreams, however, were not needed to know that the next day was the *bissextus* and, moreover, Valentinian's reason not to appear in public is explicitly given in the *quod*-clause. It is therefore highly probable that the signs and dreams were related to Valentinian's elevation to the throne. If that is accepted, Petschenig's *praescius* is a wonderfully economical solution (1892,520). For *ut opinari dabatur* see the note ad 24.8.5. The expression implies that the preceding statement is based on conjecture, since in 31.13.12 it is followed by: *neque enim vidisse se quisquam vel praesto fuisse asseveravit*. Wagner correctly glosses *videri* as *conveniri*. Pace Paschoud, 1992, 71 and Jouanaud, 2004, 178, no criticism of Valentinian's conduct is implied. It has nothing to do with *superstitio*. On the contrary, Amm. probably would have thought Valentinian's behaviour prudent.

bissextum vitans Februarii mensis, tunc illucescens, quod aliquotiens rei Romanae fuisse norat infaustum Bissextus is the intercalary day, introduced by Caesar when he reformed the calendar: *bissextus est post annos quattuor unus dies adiectus*; Isid. *Orig.* 6.17.25. It is called *bissextus* because 24 February – *ante diem sextum Kalendas Martias* – was doubled, Macr. *Sat.* 1.14.6, August. *Trin.* 4.4, *Dig.* 4.4.3.3; Bickerman, 1968, 47. According to Augustine superstitious people avoided this day, or even the whole leap year: *non plantem hoc anno vineam quia bissextus est, Ep.* 55.7. For monarchs 24 February may have had an ominous ring, because it was the day of the *Regifugium*, which was wrongly interpreted by Ovid as the day on which king Tarquinius was forced to leave Rome: *Nunc mihi dicenda est regis fuga: traxit ab illa/sextus ab extremo nomina mense dies* (*Fast.* 2.685–686). Actually, it refers to the flight of *rex sacrorum* from the Forum after performing the traditional rites on that day; cf. Forsythe, 2005, 136.

cuius notitiam certam designabo For Amm.'s introductory and concluding expressions see Emmett, 1981. The phrase *notitia certa* is less common than one would expect. In fact, the only parallel seems to be Cels. *pr.* p. 8, l. 22. *Cujus autem rei non est certa notitia, ejus opinio certum reperire remedium non potest.* For the meaning 'certain', 'indubitable' cf. 29.1.20 *quae...opertis susurris audierat, an vera essent, excutere tumore principis supersidens pro veris accipiebat et certis.*

Valentinian waits a day before he presents himself as emperor. **1.8–14** "Ammianus cleverly reproduces the delay in his text by inserting a careful account of the origin and vicissitudes of the bissextile day" is Matthews' perceptive observation on p. 189. Whether the short digression deserves the predicate "careful" is another matter. The main sources for the intercalary day or *bissextus* are Sol. 1. 34–47, Cens. 20. 1–10 and Macr. *Sat.* 1.12.38–14.15. They are conveniently collected and discussed in Michels, 1967, 148–159. The discussions have so much in common, that it is not rash to suppose a common source, for which Suetonius' lost *De anno* would be the ideal candidate. They are not easy to read and really difficult to summarize. Small wonder then, that Amm. tends to cloud the more complicated issues with circumlocutions and vague phrases. He skips the technical parts and culls his *flosculi* where he finds them, without regard for their context. On the ornate style of Amm.'s digressions see Den Hengst, 1992, 44–45.

1.8 *Spatium anni vertentis id esse periti mundani motus et siderum definiunt veteres* In *anni vertentis* the participle is dominant: 'the cycle of the year'; cf. Macr. *Sat.* 1.14.4 (solis annus) *quem peragit dum ad id signum se denuo vertit ex quo digressus est, unde annus vertens vocatur.* It is a normal expression, cf. Vitr. 9.1.6 *sol...perficit spatium vertentis anni,* Nep. *Ages.* 4.4 *quod iter Xerxes anno vertente confecerat.* Cic. *Rep.* 6.24 *ille vere vertens annus* (the 'Great Year'). On 'cataphoric' or preparatory *is* see the note ad 22.3.4 *cum id.* Astronomy is called *consideratio mundani motus et siderum* in 22.16.17 and astronomers *peritos mundanae rationis* in 25.10.3. In 23.6.33 we are told that the *magi* had received instruction from the Brahmans concerning *rationes mundani motus et siderum.*

Meton et Euctemon et Hipparchus et Archimedes Amm.'s work resonates with great names of the past. They are ornamental, meant to dignify his history, or to maintain the memory of these great men; Fornara, 1992, 421, 426. Apart from this passage, he does so, for instance, in 21.14.5 where he mentions Hermes Termaximus, Apollonius of Tyana and Plotinus as experts on guardian spirits, without having read their works; see the notes ad loc. The same is true for 22.8.10 (q.v.) where he mentions Eratosthenes, Hecataeus and Ptolemy as geographers who had provided information on the circumference of the Black Sea, whereas in fact Hecataeus and Ptolemy had not. This passage shows a similar example of name-dropping; it does not prove that Amm. knew the works of these men, let alone that he used them as sources for this excursus; Den Hengst, 1992, 42–43.

Two of the four are named by Vitruvius (9.6.3) as belonging to the seven famous astronomers of antiquity: *Quorum inventa secuti siderum ad ortus et occasus tempestatum significatus Eudoxus, Euctemon, Callippus, Meto, Philippus, Hipparchus, Aratus ceterique ex astrologia parapegmatorum disciplinis invenerunt et eas posteris explicatas reliquerunt.*

The Athenian Meton (2nd half of the fifth century B.C.) was responsible for the 19-year cycle introduced in Athens in 432 B.C. This cycle was meant to synchronize the solar year and the lunar months because a biennial cycle and an eight-year cycle did not work; Gem. 8.50–56; D.S. 12.36.2–3; Bickerman, 1968, 28–29. For Meton see further Hübner, 2000. Euctemon, astronomer and meteorologist, was a contemporary of Meton and co-responsible for the 19-year cycle; Hübner, 1998; Van der Waerden, 1988, 79–82. Hipparchus was an astronomer and geographer from the second half of the second century B.C. The only surviving astronomical work by Hipparchus is a critical commentary on the way in which Eudoxus and Aratus describe and arrange the constellations and stars: Τῶν Ἀράτου καὶ Εὐδόξου Φαινομένων ἐξηγήσεως βίβλια τρία. Most of what we know about Hipparchus' astronomical work comes from Ptolemy's *Almagest*. He was a careful observer and more of a practical than a theoretical astronomer. Most of what we know of his geographical work, which was mainly directed against Eratosthenes, comes from Strabo; Hübner, 1998a; Van der Waerden, 1988, 173 ff. Archimedes (c. 287–212/1) is mainly known as a mathematician and inventor. Born in Syracuse as the son of the astronomer Phidias, Archimedes also did some astronomical work. All his writings in this field of research are lost except for a method to find the diameter of the sun, preserved in his Ψαμμίτης ('Sand-reckoner') and a (corrupt) passage presenting the distances of the heavenly bodies; Hippol. *Haer*. 41.18 ff. Folkerts, 1996; Van der Waerden, 1988, 158–163.

cum sol perenni rerum sublimium lege polo percurso signifero The expression *res sublimes* is found only here. It is the equivalent of τὰ μετέωρα, whose movements are eternal and unchangeable. Cf. *motibus sempiternis* in §13. For *signifer polus* Valesius compares Luc. 3.253–254 *Aethiopumque solum, quod non premeretur ab ulla/signiferi regione poli*.

quem zodiacum sermo Graecus appellat The annual course of the sun through the fixed stars is divided into twelve equal parts according to the number of lunar months in a solar year. The zodiacal year starts with Aries, sign of the vernal equinox; when the sun entered Cancer it was summer; the sign of Libra marked autumn, and that of Capricorn winter; Bickerman, 1968, 56–57. For *sermo Graecus* see the note ad section 1 *quas si*.

ad eundem redierit cardinem The *cardo* is "one of the four turning points in the year (i.e. the solstices and equinoxes)"; *OLD* s.v. 4c. Vitr. 9.1.6, less specifically, speaks about *signum*: (sol) *cum redit ad id signum, unde coeperit, perficit spatium vertentis anni*.

ut, verbo tenus, si a secunda particula elatus Arietis ad eam dimensione redierit terminata Amm. gives this example because the zodiacal year began and ended with Aries. *Particula* has the technical meaning of 'degree' (of the Ecliptic); *TLL* X 1.510.12–20. Amm., surprisingly, takes the second instead of the first *particula* as his starting-point, possibly to demonstrate, as Wagner suggests ad loc., that it stands "pro quovis determinato initio anni". Amm. may have been familiar with the source of Macr. *comm*. 2.11.13: *annum solis non solum a kalendis Ianuariis usque ad easdem vocamus, sed et a sequente post kalendas die usque ad eundem diem et a quocumque cuiuslibet mensis die usque in diem eundem reditus annus vocatur.* For *verbo tenus*, 'so to speak' cf. 30.4.17 *si vero advena quisquam inusitatum sibi antea Marcianum verbo tenus quaesierit oratorem* ("nommé, disons, Marcianus", tr. Sabbah). It emphasizes that the example is arbitrarily chosen. For *dimensio* see the note ad 20.3.4.

1.9 *anni intervallum verissimum* The exact length of the year is 365 days and five hours, forty-eight minutes and forty-six seconds; Bickerman, 1968, 10. As a result, at the end of the sixteenth century the difference between the Julian calendar and the solar year had amounted to about ten days. This induced Pope Gregory XIII to omit ten days in 1582 – 5 October became 15 October – and to suggest that three intercalary days should be left out every four hundred years. For *intervallum* 'length' cf. Vitr. 9.1.6 (sol) *xii mensibus xii signorum intervalla pervagando*.

ad usque meridiem...plenam A strange expression, *meridies* being a point in time, not a period of time. It is formed by analogy with *plenus dies, plenus annus, OLD* s.v. 11. Normally, *meridies* is masculine. For exceptions to the rule see TLL VIII 839.69–72. The Greeks and Romans adopted the system of twelve hours to the day and twelve to the night from the Babylonians. The length of an hour varied according to the latitude and the season. Bickerman, 1968, 14–15.

1.10 *ne igitur haec computatio variantibus annorum principiis...scientiam omnem squalida diversitate confundat* The language is becoming vague, and it is difficult to understand what exactly is meant by *scientia*. Of course it would be highly impractical if one year would begin at noon, the next at six o'clock in the afternoon and so on, but one can hardly say that this would "confuse all science" (Rolfe). *Squalidus* is one of Amm.'s favourite adjectives. See the note ad 21.14.2 *quod interdum*. Here it must mean, that the irregularity (*diversitas*) would be incomprehensible. Cf. the important statement in 26.5.15, where Amm. announces that he intends to let thematic coherence prevail over strict chronology: *competenti loco singula digeremus nunc partem in oriente gestorum, deinde bella barbarica narraturi...ne, dum ex loco subinde saltuatim redire festinamus in locum, omnia confundentes squaliditate maxima rerum ordines implicemus.*

et quodam post horam sextam diei, alio post sextam excurso nocturnam The abl. abs. *quodam...alio...excurso* refers to the end of each year.

This is surprising after *annorum principiis*. Damsté, 1930, 9 saw the irregularity and proposed the elegant solution *exorso*. One cannot exclude, however, that Amm. simply made a mistake. *Ut quodam*, proposed by Petschenig, 1892, 520, would certainly be more logical than *et quodam*, since it would provide the reason why the years would start at a different time of the day, 'since one year would end (or, if one follows Damsté, begin) at noon and the next at midnight'. Again, however, one hesitates to draw the conclusion that the text must be altered. As the sequel will show, Amm. does not have a firm grip on his material.

et autumnalis mensis inveniatur quandoque vernalis This is nonsense. If each year would last 365 days and six hours, the correspondence between the calendar and the solar year would be perfect, or almost (see above the note ad *anni intervallum*). Amm. has slightly modified a phrase he had found in his source. Sol. 1.44: *nonnunquam accidebat, ut menses qui fuerant transacti hieme, modo aestivum modo autumnale tempus inciderent* ('It happened from time to time that months that had (originally) fallen in winter came to be part now of summer, now of autumn'), with which cf. Suet. *Jul.* 40.1: *fastos correxit iam pridem vitio pontificum per intercalandi licentiam adeo turbatos, ut neque messium feriae aestate neque vindemiarum autumno conpeterent*. That confusion was the consequence, not of the disturbance which would be caused by starting every New Year's Day six hours later than the preceding one, but of the arbitrariness with which the priests decided where the intercalations would be inserted, a subject to which Amm. will turn in § 12.

placuit senas illas horas…in unius diei noctisque adiectae transire mensarum The use of intransitive *transire* instead of e.g. *transferre* may be compared with the tendancy to use the passive infinitive after impersonal verbs, for which see the note ad 24.6.2 *eadem loca*.

hocque alte considerato eruditis concinentibus multis For *alte* 'deeply' cf. the note ad 20.5.2 *dum alte* and 21.14.5 *alteque monstrare*. It is not clear which experts, if any, Amm. had in mind. Pliny *Nat.* 18.211 mentions the Alexandrian astronomer Sosigenes as Caesar's adviser: *Sosigene perito scientiae eius adhibito*.

effectum est, ad unum distinctumque exitum circumversio cursus annui revoluta nec vaga sit nec incerta Blomgren 159 rejects Gelenius' *ut*, but in view of 25.8.15 *unde effectum est, ut*, quoted by himself, this is not likely. In Amm. *distinctus* most often means 'adorned', as in 21.1.4 *ambitioso diademate utebatur lapidum fulgore distincto*, 23.3.6, 26.6.15 and 27.10.11. Here and in 15.9.2 *distincte docebimus et aperte* it means 'definite', 'precise'. *Circumversio annui revoluta cursus* is a verbose equivalent of *annus vertens* in §8. The adjectives *vaga* and *incerta* anticipate what Amm. is going to say in §12 about the confusion that reigned before Caesar's reform, when the priests inserted the intercalary days at unpredictable moments (*incerta*), which differed from year to year (*vaga*). Amm. may have found the phrase in his source; cf. Macr. *Sat.* 1.14.2 *Sed postea C. Caesar omnem hanc inconstantiam temporum vagam adhuc et incertam in ordinem statae definitionis coegit.*

nulloque errore deinceps obumbrata ratio caelestis appareat For *obumbrare* in its literal meaning 'to darken' cf. 24.8.3 *dies et astrorum noctu micantium facies obumbratur*; here it is a well-chosen metaphor. One may doubt whether *ratio caelestis* refers to the eternal laws that govern the heavenly bodies, "le système céleste" (Marié), as in Apul. *Mun.* pr. *dicemus de omni hac caelesti ratione*, or whether it is used in the more limited sense of "the reckoning of the sun's course" (Rolfe; cf. Caltabiano and Seyfarth). In view of the following remark about the months, the latter alternative seems preferable. Amm. probably had Sol. 1. 39 in mind: *quandoquidem appareret solis meatum non ante CCCLXV diem...zodiacum conficere decursum.*

et menses tempora retineant praestituta See the note ad §10 *et autumnalis* and Sol. 1.45 *quo pacto...menses de cetero* ('for the future') *statuta ordinis sui tempora detinerent.* Cf. for *praestituta* the second part of the note ad 25.10.3 *vel certe.*

1.12 *haec nondum extentis fusius regnis diu ignoravere Romani* Amm. is not very precise in his anaphoric expressions. In this case we must suppose that *haec* refers to the reckoning of the sun's course (*caelestis ratio*). The statement, that the Romans were ignorant in this field because they were not yet rulers of the world, probably means that they had not yet come into contact with the Egyptians and the Greeks, who were far more knowledgeable. The use of *regnis*, instead of e.g. *imperio*, is without parallel. Probably, in Amm.'s view, the period indicated coincides with the Republic, since, as he will say in the next section, it was Octavianus Augustus who redressed the disorder. In his bird's-eye view of Roman history in 14.6.4, Rome's adolescence and maturity, preceding the old age (*senium*) of the principate, are the periods of conquest.

perque saecula multa obscuris difficultatibus implicati tunc magis errorum profunda caligine fluctuabant, cum in sacerdotes potestatem transtulissent intercalandi Caesar's measures, including the introduction of the *bissextus* are not difficult to understand. The history of the Roman calendar during the Republic is an entirely different matter. Amm. deliberately avoids it. The first half of the sentence is based on Sol. 1.34 (cursus anni ratio), *quae a rerum origine profunda caligine tegebatur.* The second comes straight from Sol. 1.43 *translata in pontifices intercalandi potestate.* Note that the context of the two borrowed phrases, welded together by *tunc magis*, is completely different.

The *sacerdotes* had to see to it that the same sacrifices took place in the the same seasons; Cic. *Leg.* 2.29: *Quod ad tempus ut sacrificiorum libamenta serventur fetusque pecorum, quae dicta in lege sunt, diligenter habenda ratio intercalandi est; quod institutum perite a Numa posteriorum pontificum neglegentia dissolutum est.* Not surprisingly, intercalation could be exploited for political and financial reasons, as the correspondence of Cicero shows; cf. Cic. *Fam.* 7.2.4, 8.6.5, *Att.* 5.9.2. For more examples see Bickerman, 1968, 45–46. The most amusing illustration is Cic. *Ver.* 2.129 *quae cum iste* (Verres; in the provinces the governors were responsible for the intercalations) *cognosset novus astrologus, qui non tam caeli rationem quam caelati argenti duceret, eximi iubet non diem ex mense, sed ex anno unum dimidiatumque mensem hoc modo ut quo die verbi causa esse oporteret Idus Ianuarias, in eum diem Kalendas Martias proscribi iuberet.* According to Davies, 2004, 254 n. 86 and 260 this is the only criticism of Roman priests in the *Res Gestae.*

qui licenter gratificantes publicanorum vel litigantium commodis ad arbitrium suum subtrahebant tempora vel augebant Cf. Suet. *Jul.* 40.1 quoted above ad §10 *et autumnalis.* Amm. hardly modifies his source: Sol. 1.43 *qui plerumque gratificantes rationibus publicanorum pro libidine sua subtrahebant tempora vel augebant*, only adding the interests of people engaged in a lawsuit (*litigantes*). In the words of Macr. *Sat.* 1.14.1: *per gratiam sacerdotum, qui publicanis proferri vel imminui consulto anni dies volebant, modo auctio, modo retractio dierum proveniebat.*

hocque ex coepto emerserunt alia plurima, quae fallebant, quorum meminisse nunc supervacuum puto This is easily the emptiest sentence of the digression. What is Amm. thinking of? The answer must be found in his source material. After the words quoted in the section above, Macrobius goes on to say that the priests, instead of controlling the calendar by precise intercalation, only created more confusion:

1.13

1.14.1 *sub specie observationis emergebat* (!) *maior confusionis occasio.* This idea, so it seems, lies at the base of Amm.'s sentence. If this is correct, *hoc ex coepto* refers to the mandate given to the priests to intercalate, and *alia plurima, quae fallebant* renders *maior confusionis occasio*. For Amm.'s concluding phrase cf. 20.11.30 *suppetunt aliae multae opiniones et variae, quas dinumerare nunc est supervacuum*, q.v.

quibus abolitis Octavianus Augustus Graecos secutus This is no longer just vague, it is plainly wrong. It was common knowledge, that the introduction of the Egyptian solar calendar including the *bissextus* was the work of Julius Caesar in his capacity of *pontifex maximus*; Macr. *Sat.* 1.14.3 *post hoc imitatus Aegyptios, solos divinarum rerum omnium conscios, ad numerum solis, qui diebus trecentis sexaginta quinque et quadrante cursum conficit, annum dirigere contendit*. The mistake may already have been present in Amm.'s source (in fact the ms. H of Solinus reads Augustus Caesar), but that is hardly an excuse. The addition *Graecos secutus* is revealing, since Macrobius explicitly (and correctly) mentions the Egyptians as Caesar's teachers. Amm. either changed his source deliberately, or took his cue from passages like Sol. 1.42, where Solinus mentions the Greek eight-year cycle and goes on to say (1.43) *quod cum initio Romani probassent* e.q.s., and Macr. *Sat.* 1.13.8 (in the same context) *necessario et intercalarem mensem instituerunt more Graecorum*. In either case it betrays Amm.'s cultural chauvinism. We may compare 15.9.2 *Timagenes, et diligentia Graecus et lingua*, for which see Barnes 96–98. In Lucan 10.187 Caesar boasts: *nec meus Eudoxi vincetur fastibus annus*.

Augustus did make a minor adjustment to the calendar: because after the death of Caesar the priests inserted an extra day every third instead of every fourth year, in 9 B.C. the calendar was three days ahead of the solar year; to correct this, Augustus ordered that there would be no intercalary years in the coming twelve years; Suet. *Aug.* 31.2; Plin. *Nat.* 18.211; Sol. 1.46–47; Macr. *Sat.* 1.14.13–15; Brind'Amour, 1983, 11–15.

hanc inconstantiam correcta turbatione composuit From Sol. 1.45: (C. Caesar) *hanc inconstantiam, incisa temporum turbatione, composuit*.

mensuum For this form of the gen. plural see the note ad 17.1.12.

duodecim siderum domicilia The zodiac, for which see the note in §8 of this chapter. *Domicilium* is an astronomical t.t. See the note ad 20.3.2 *in domicilio*.

quam rationem bissexti probatam etiam victura cum saeculis Roma adiumento numinis divini fundavit Amm. embellishes Solinus' matter of fact conclusion: 1.47 *ex qua disciplina* ('on the basis of these considerations') *omnium postea temporum fundata ratio est.* In Solinus' sentence *ratio* certainly has its basic meaning 'reckoning', 'computation'. It is advisable to attribute the same meaning to Amm.'s text, as does Seyfarth: "Diese Berechnung des Schalttags". For *probare* cf. Sol. 1.43 quoted above § 13 *quibus abolitis*. Rome 'accepted this computation' and 'made it the basis' (for all future time). Solinus' *omnium temporum* inspired Amm.'s confession of faith *etiam victura cum saeculis*, with which we may compare 14.6.3 *victura, dum erunt homines, Roma.* For the concept of *Roma aeterna* see the note ad 21.12.24 *urbi praefecit* (and add to the literature quoted there Brodka, 1998, 56–90, esp. 88–90; Edwards, 1996, 86–88). *Etiam* seems to reflect Solinus' *omnium temporum ratio*: just as the *ratio bissexti* will be valid forever, so too Rome will live forever. Amm. often uses *numen* in a henotheistic sense; see the note ad 25.8.3 *favore superi* and add to the literature mentioned there Davies, 2004, 265–268. Amm uses *fundare* often of human steadfastness, as in 20.4.15 *Et ille mente fundata*. The present passage may be compared to 25.7.5; see the note ad *et Persae*.

1.14

proinde pergamus ad reliqua For *proinde* see above ad § 2 *proinde inscitia*. At the end of his digression on the Black Sea Amm. uses the same phrase to resume his historical narrative; 22.8.48 with the note *prolati aliquantorsum*.

CHAPTER 2

Introduction

This chapter describes the inauguration ceremony of the new emperor Valentinian and his first speech to the soldiers. Salutius had seen to it that very strict measures were taken to prevent would-be pretenders from taking advantage of the imperial vacancy before the ceremony. Everything went according to plan until Valentinian got ready to speak. At that moment a unanimous protest began: the soldiers wanted the immediate appointment of an imperial partner for the new emperor. Valentinian acted swiftly by giving the ringleaders a good dressing-down and then delivering his speech, in which he agreed to the need for a partner, making it perfectly clear, however, that he reserved the choice of this person for himself. Valentinian won the day with his authoritative demeanour and all protests stopped.

It is important to note that Ammianus twice mentions that the speech was not improvised, but prepared. This implies that according to him the appointment of a second in command had already been planned, possibly in consultation with Salutius and the other members of the staff, but that the candidate could not be named, either because Valentinian had not made up his mind or, more likely, because he had decided for himself to choose his brother, but wanted to make sure that this choice would be accepted by the staff.

Elapso die parum apto ad inchoandas rerum magnitudines, ut quidam existimant This is Amm.'s only instance of *elabi* denoting the passing of time. See the list in TLL V 2.318.7–18, e.g. *Cod. Theod.* 7.4.17 (4 April 377) *priusquam annus elabatur*, 13.9.6 (17 March 412) *si...legitimum tempus fuerit elabsum*. Strictly speaking, the intercalary day had not yet fully passed, since its evening is only drawing near: *propinquante...vespera*. See for examples of *parum* as wellnigh the equivalent of *haud* the note ad 23.6.82 *parum alienis*, and for Amm.'s predilection for *magnitudo* with gen. (inversus) the note ad 24.3.9 *cum non*. In the present text 'important affairs' is an apt rendering of *rerum magnitudines*. The day referred to is the intercalary day of February, mentioned in 26.1.7 (*bissextum...Februarii mensis*), i.e. February 24, 364, which, as Amm.'s Valentinian knew, had several

2.1

times been unlucky for the Roman state (*quod aliquotiens rei Romanae fuisse norat infaustum*, 26.1.7); see the note ad 26.1.5 *quia nullo*.

As to the parenthetical phrase *ut quidam existimant*, such *ut quidam*-phrases with a *verbum sentiendi* or *declarandi* as predicate occur in many prose authors. In these cases the author explicitly presents a certain opinion or piece of information as being derived from others and, in spite of, perhaps, not being shared by everyone, as worthy of reporting. Scepticism is not implied, pace Camus, 1967, 170. If an author doubts the value of what 'some people think (or write)', this is clearly expressed, e.g. Cic. *Phil.* 1.29 *ut quidam nimis creduli suspicantur*, Quint. *Inst.* 12.5.1 *instrumenta, non artis, ut quidam putaverunt, sed ipsius oratoris*, Amm. 25.3.15 *non, ut quidam opinantur, afflictus*, 31.10.5 *ut quidam laudes extollendo principis iactitarunt*.

propinquante iam vespera monitu praefecti Salutii sub exitii denuntiatione statutum est prompta consensione cunctorum Both masc. *vesper* and fem. *vespera* occur from early Latin onwards; see Neue-Wagener I 855–856 and Kühner-Holzweissig, 1912², 481. In Amm. the instances of *vespera* are more than twice those of *vesper*. In most cases *vesper(a)* is used in phrases denoting that the evening is falling. The present phrase also occurs in 20.6.5 and 27.2.6. However, it is the content which is remarkable, not any formal aspect. The highest civil authority among the *potestatum civilium militiaeque rectores* of 26.1.3, who had opted for Valentinian as successor to Jovian (26.1.5), was the praetorian prefect Salutius, i.e. Saturninius Secundus Salutius (*PLRE* I, Secundus 3), for whom see the notes ad 22.3.1, 23.5.6 and 25.5.3 *nulla variante*; in this book he is mentioned again in 26.5.5 and 26.7.4 (q.v.); for his office see the notes ad 21.6.5 *Anatolio*, 23.5.6 *quem praefectus* and 25.3.14 *Salutius*; add to the literature cited there Coşkun, 2004. Salutius must have heard of the unruly night which preceded Julian's accession (*nocte vero coeptante in apertum erupere discidium*, 20.4.14), but he left it surprisingly late (*propinquante iam vespera*) to urge his fellow members of the staff to take the prudent measure described by Amm. Could this mean that he had only then received reliable intelligence about the dangerous possibility of a coup?

According to Zos. 3.36.1 and Zon. 13.14.15–16 the imperial throne had been offered first to this Salutius after Jovian's death, and only after Salutius had refused was Valentinian chosen (see the note ad 26.1.3 *moderatorem*). Amm. is silent on this and also on what is said about Salutius in other sources, by Philostorgius, who has Σεκοῦνδος join Datianus (*PLRE* I, Datianus 1 +J.F. Matthews, *CR* 24 [1974], 102) in recommending Valentinian (*HE* 8.8 συνεφἀψαμένου δὲ τῇ πράξει Σεκούνδου τε τοῦ ἐπάρχου) and by Malalas, who, followed by the *Chronicon Paschale*, makes the praetorian prefect primarily responsible for Valentinian's elevation. In *Chron. Pasch.* a. 364 we read that Σαλούστιος, after he had brought Valentinian from Selymbria, said to the army and the senate: 'No one will make an emperor for Roman affairs like him' (ὁ δὲ ἔπαρχος τῶν πραιτωρίων Σαλούστιος πέμψας ἤνεγκεν αὐτὸν ἀπὸ Σηλυβρίας, καὶ εἶπεν τῷ στρατῷ καὶ τῇ συγκλήτῳ ὅτι οὐδεὶς ποιεῖ βασιλέα εἰς τὰ Ῥωμαίων ὡς αὐτός, tr. Whitby and Whitby, adapted), while Malalas, who is often the source of the *Chronicon Paschale* (cf. Whitby and Whitby, 1981, xvi), moreover says: καὶ ἐστέφθη βασιλεὺς ὑπὸ Σαλουστίου τοῦ ἐπάρχου τῶν πραιτωρίων, ἐπιλεξαμένου αὐτὸν καὶ καταναγκάσαντος αὐτὸν βασιλεῦσαι (*Chron.* 13.337). The decisive role attributed to Salutius with respect to Valentinian's elevation is not implausible in itself, given the fact that the prefect really was a man of prime importance (cf. Alföldi, 1952, 11–12), but there are two elements in the accounts of Malalas and the *Chronicon* which should be regarded with extreme scepticism, and which make a reader suspicious as to the reliability of the rest, viz. the mentioning of the senate, which is totally anomalous in this context, and the claim that Salutius recalled Valentinian from Σαλαμβρία (Malalas) / Σηλυβρία (*Chron. Pasch.*), presumably Selymbria in Thrace. The latter is in flat contradiction of Amm.'s statement that Valentinian was stationed in Ancyra when he was called to the throne (26.1.5), and that he had served as a tribune under Jovian (25.10.6). It is part of the dubious story that the Christian Valentinian had been exiled from the army for defending his faith before Julian; its spuriousness, long ago recognized, has recently been demonstrated again by Lenski, 2002a, who convincingly rejects the arguments to the contrary of Woods, 1995 and 1998. See for the early career of Valentinian also Nixon, 1998.

Once again Amm. stresses the unanimity among the highest military and civil authorities (cf. 26.1.5 *nulla discordante sententia*). From the lemma *monitus* in TLL VIII 1421.41–1422.58 it can be inferred that the 'advice' or 'warning' is usually given by persons in authority, such as gods, prophets, kings or military commanders. This is Amm.'s only instance of *denuntiatio*, which according to TLL V 1.551.11 is "saepe cum minandi notione coniuncta". Caes. *Civ.* 3.9.2 is illustrative: *cum neque pollicitationibus neque denuntiatione periculi permovere posset*. Salutius had no difficulty at all in convincing his colleagues to act unanimously: the present text is a clear case of *promptus* used to indicate "quaecumque sine labore vel sine mora fiunt" (TLL X 2.1886.4).

ne potioris quisquam auctoritatis vel suspectus altiora conari procederet postridie mane Petschenig, 1892, 520 ingeniously conjectures *ut* for V's *vel*, which would produce just one category instead of two being banned from the field where the ceremonial inauguration of Valentinian was scheduled for the following morning. It is, however, not at all necessary to smoothe the text. The seriousness of the measure is emphasized by the partial overlap of the two groups. The first consists of those who had an elevated grade in the hierarchy, like the *potestatum civilium militiaeque rectores* in 26.1.3 (q.v.), but did not have higher ambitions themselves. In spite of this the soldiers might, in their unpredictable capriciousness, suddenly begin to hail such a man. Cf. for *potioris...auctoritatis* the note ad 19.3.1 *auctoritatis*: to his regret Ursicinus depended on the command of another person (viz. the *magister equitum per Orientem* Sabinianus) *auctoritatis tunc in regendo milite potioris*. See for *potior*, 'of greater power', the note ad 22.9.17 *inimico potiori* and cf. also the note ad 26.1.4 *qui cum potiorum*. The second category consists of persons of all ranks, whose ambitions presented a risk. One can only speculate as to the identity of these men. Apart from Salutius (see above), there were, according to Zos. 3.36.1-2, many other possible rivals for Valentinian (πολλοὶ μὲν καὶ περὶ πολλῶν ἐγίνοντο λόγοι, cf. *multorum* in 26.2.2), among them Salutius' son, who was, however, too young and not suitable (τὸν παῖδα γοῦν ᾔτησαν εἰς τὴν τῶν ὅλων ἀρχὴν ἐλθεῖν.Τοῦ δὲ καὶ νέον εἶναι καὶ οὐδὲ ἄλλως ἐπιτήδειον πρὸς τοσαύτης ἀρχῆς ὄγκον εἰπόντος κτλ.). Of the others only Equitius, tribune of the *schola prima Scutariorum* (26.1.4), and Jovian's relative Ianuarius (ibid.) are known by name. However, the latter can be ruled out because he was in Illyricum, and of Equitius it is said in 26.1.6 that he supported Valentinian. The time denoted by *postridie mane* is February 25, early in the morning.

Other passages in which Amm. uses phrases consisting of *altiora* in combination with a verb to denote unacceptable ambitions are: 22.11.2 (*agitare*), 15.5.4 and 16.6.2 (*coeptare*), 14.7.19 and 14.11.2 (*meditari*), 22.8.18 (*spirare*). See also the notes ad 22.3.12 *Eusebium* and 22.11.2 *agitasse*; cf. also *altius anhelabat* (18.4.2). The verb *procedere* here means 'to appear in public'; see the note ad 20.4.19 *nec procedere*. Possibly the connotation of appearing 'in an official capacity' (see TLL X 2.1497.6-26) is also present here.

2.2 *cumque multorum taedio, quos votorum inanitas cruciabat, tandem finita nocte lux advenisset* In 26.1.3 only 'some' (*quidam*) of the leading civil and military authorities were 'puffed up with vain aspirations' (*spe vana sufflati*) themselves, but now they have grown in number to become 'many', a fact which worried those officials who stuck to the choice of Valentinian; cf. also Zos. 3.36.1 περὶ πολλῶν ἐγίνοντο λόγοι, 'many candidates were discussed'. The text quoted in the lemma is not easy to explain. It is possible to interpret *multorum* as a gen. subiectivus: for many, who were fed up with being tormented by their vain aspirations, daybreak had come as a relief. There is one other example of *taedium* with gen. subiectivus in Amm.: *non sine taedio praesentium* (28.4.13). The translators are obviously convinced of this interpretation of *multorum*, but they fail to do justice to *taedio*: cf. e.g. "Zum Ärger vieler" (Seyfarth), "con pena di molti" (Caltabiano). Amm.'s other eight instances of *taedium* all denote "the state of being tired or weary of" (OLD s.v. 1) someone or something. It is combined with a gen. obiectivus in six of these cases, three of which concern human beings: 18.4.5 *horum et similium taedio*, 22.5.5 *Iudaeorum fetentium et tumultuantium saepe taedio percitus*, 22.15.24 (about the hippopotamus and its hunters) *insectantis multitudinis taedio*. An interpretation in this vein is also possible in the present text. Being fed up with all these prospective usurpers and the futile wishes which tormented them, Salutius *cum suis* had been eagerly looking forward (*tandem*) to daybreak.

The relative clause is remarkable for the following reason: as Matthews 273 notes, "Ausonius is one of the more intriguing omissions from Ammianus' history"; yet, as is noted by Fletcher, 1937, 395, here he clearly alludes to a phrase in Ausonius' speech of thanksgiving for his consulship in 379: *sunt quos votorum cruciat inanitas* (*Grat. act.* 3.15); there are no other parallels for this phrase, in which *votorum* is a gen. inversus: 'futile wishes', in the eyes of Salutius and his men.

in unum quaesito milite omni The phrase *in unum quaerere* is an idiosyncrasy of Amm., who also uses it in 15.7.7, 18.6.12, 26.7.9, 27.5.2, 28.2.13, 29.1.23, 31.4.9. For the strength of Julian's army see the note ad 23.3.5.

progressus Valentinianus in campum As is noted ad 20.5.1, *campus* is a military term for an open space used for parades, exercises and assemblies, cf. 20.9.6, 21.2.1, 21.13.9 and 27.6.5; TLL III 214.83–215.3. From the words *comitiorum specie* it can be deduced that Amm. possibly alludes here to the *campus Martius* in Rome, which, if we may believe HA *Tac.* 7.2, was the place where the emperor Tacitus mounted a tribunal when he had been elected successor to Aurelian (*inde itum ad Campum Martium. ibi comitiale tribunal ascendit*). Cf. Lact. *mort. pers.* 32.5 and see Alföldi, 1980³, 172 and Kolb, 2001, 93.

permissusque tribunal ascendere celsius structum The mounting of a *tribunal* is a traditional element in Amm.'s description of *adlocutiones*; see the introductory note to chapter 20.5 and the notes ad 20.9.6 *tribunali*, 21.13.9 *tribunali* and 24.3.3 *constructo*. At first sight it seems strange that the nominee for the emperorship is 'allowed' to mount the official platform. However, as yet he is only the commander of a *schola*, who, as an exception to the severe general ban, has been given this privilege. The height of the platform is also emphasized in 15.8.4 *tribunali ad altiorem suggestum erecto*, 19.11.8 *celsoque aggere in speciem tribunalis erecto*, 21.13.9 *tribunali celso insistens*.

comitiorum specie voluntate praesentium secundissima ut vir serius rector pronuntiatur imperii To many readers the first word will come as a surprise: Amm. suddenly reaches back to the elections of the Roman Republic to describe a scene which belongs to an entirely different political system; it is the only instance of *comitia* in the *Res Gestae*. Compare, however, the following passage in Symmachus' first *Laudatio in Valentinianum seniorem Augustum*, which refers to exactly the same situation as the one which Amm. is describing: *aderat exercitus ex omni robore Romanae pubis electus. digna plane comitia tanti imperii principatu! decernebant liberi, cui deberent esse subiecti* (Symm. *Or.* 1.9). One can hardly doubt that Amm. alludes to this passage, though with the telling addition of *specie*: the meeting had only the outward appearance of *comitia*. There is no reason to regard this correction as aggressive or cynical, as in *specie sapientiae stolidum* (17.9.3) or *specie humanitatis* (25.8.1). Such a meaning would not suit the context. It is more likely that the phrase here is used as a pure comparison, as in *corniculantis lunae specie* (22.14.7) or *gradientium collium specie* (24.6.8, q.v.), and that the historian makes a quiet and elegant addition to panegyrical terminology. See for comparable cases of such a use of *comitia* Symm. *Or.* 3.3 and 5, 4.2 and 7 and for the general impact of Symmachus' panegyrical orations on Amm. Sabbah 332–346. Cf. also Ausonius' juggling with the term in ch. 9 of his speech of thanksgiving for the consulship which the emperor had bestowed on him. He winds up with a remarkable rhetorical question: *quae comitia pleniora umquam fuerunt quam quibus praestitit deus consilium, imperator obsequium?*, "What elections have ever been more adequately attended than these, where God furnished the design, and the Emperor gave it effect?" (tr. Evelyn White).

As to *comitiorum specie*, the translation in Pabst, 1997, 14 is too bad to believe: "nach der typischen Art der *comitia*", "so, wie es bei *comitia* nun einmal auszusehen pflegt". The author does not adduce any parallel for this highly unlikely meaning of *species*, which is needed to support her argument that "der spätantike Historiker bei *comitia* an die Heerescomitien des 4. Jh., nicht an die traditionelle Volksversammlungen denkt". Her attempt, however, to prove the existence of these "Heerescomitien" (1997, 9–13) is not convincing. Cf. for this Kolb, 2001, 216–218 and for a correct interpretation of *comitiorum specie* Del Chicca's note ad loc.

This is the only example in Amm. of the superlative *secundissimus*, which stresses the absence of any resistance against Valentinian's rise to the emperorship. Cf. for *voluntate praesentium secundissima* Orosius' *consensu militum imperator creatus est* (*hist.* 7.32.1) and Socrates' κοινῇ ψήφῳ in *HE* 4.1.1. The date of the *acclamatio* is dealt with in the note ad 26.1.5 *quia nullo*. See for the various stages in the process of choosing a new emperor, '*electio*', '*commendatio*' and '*acclamatio*', Heim, 1990.

The use of the adj. *serius* to characterize a person is not common. Amm. uses it only here. Sozomenus has a similar qualification: Ἐπεὶ δὲ εἰς Νίκαιαν τῆς Βιθυνίας ἀφίκετο ἡ στρατιά, ἀναγορεύουσι βασιλέα Οὐαλεντινιανόν, ἄνδρα ἀγαθὸν καὶ τῆς ἡγεμονίας ἄξιον (*HE* 6.6.2). See for *rector* as a general term to denote any high authority the note ad 20.1.1. The only other passage in which Amm. combines it with *imperii* is 29.2.14.

mox principali habitu circumdatus et corona Augustusque nuncupatus cum **2.3** *laudibus amplis, quas novitatis potuit excitare dulcedo, praemeditata dicere iam parabat* Cf. for the imperial attire 15.8.10 *amictu principali*, 25.5.5 *indumentis circumdatus principalibus* (q.v.), 29.2.9 *principalia indumenta*, and for the *corona* or *diadema* (this term in 26.4.3) as belonging to the imperial insignia the notes ad 21.1.4 *ambitioso* and *assumpta*. See also Kolb, 2001, 105–107. For Malalas' statement that ἐστέφθη βασιλεὺς ὑπὸ Σαλουστίου τοῦ ἐπάρχου τῶν πραιτωρίων see above, ad §1 *propinquante*. Cf. for *nuncupatus* 23.6.5 *Augusta nuncupatio* (q.v.), 30.10.5 (about Valentinian II) *Augustus nuncupatur more sollemni*. In 26.5.1 *unus nuncupatione praelatus* refers to the present text.

The official hailing of Valentinian as the new emperor was accompanied by the praises which the 'attractiveness of a new situation' provoked. For such praises one can compare the way in which, according to HA *T* 7.4, the newly created emperor Tacitus was acclaimed in A.D. 275: *"felicissime Tacite Auguste, dii te servent"*, *et reliqua quae solent dici*, or the cheers which according to Constantinus Porphyrogenitus were addressed to the emperor Leo in A.D. 457: "Λέων αὔγουστε, σὺ νικᾷς, σὺ εὐσεβής, σὺ σεβαστός· ὁ Θεός σε ἔδωκεν, ὁ Θεός σε φυλάξει· ἀεὶ νικᾷς· πολλοὺς χρόνους Λέων βασιλεύσει· χριστιανὸν βασίλειον ὁ Θεὸς περιφρουρήσει" (*Cer.* 1.411 Reiske). Amm. uses *novitas* in a pejorative sense in 17.2.2 *rei novitate perculsus*, 21.6.5 *novitatis metu*. The latter case is interesting in that, as in the present text, *novitas* refers to the change in government. However, here the soldiers delight in the change. Amm. gives a comparable psychological explanation in 26.6.17: the initial tepidness towards the usurper Procopius *accendebatur tamen insita plerisque vulgarium novitatis repentina iucunditate*. Demandt, 2004, 808 cites both 26.6.17 and the present text as clear examples of "Lebensweisheit" in the *Res Gestae*.

See for the passive sense of deponentia the notes ad 21.5.1 *professa* and 22.6.4 *spe*, and for *praemeditari* Flobert, 1975, 358. The sentence quoted in the lemma ends with a pattern which can also be found in other narrative texts, e.g. Liv. 3.28.7 *Iam se...Aequi parabant*, Apul. *Met.* 10.18 *iamque...domuitionem parabat*. In such cases the reader is led to expect that something will interfere with the situation; cf. also Amm. 26.8.3 *discedere iam parabat*.

Whether or not Valentinian was raised on a shield during the coronation ceremony, as was Julian in 360 (20.4.17, q.v.), and as were other late-antique and Byzantine emperors (cf. Teitler, 2002), is disputed. Philostorgius' explicit mentioning of this element, κατ' αὐτὴν τὴν ἀναγόρευσιν ἐπὶ τῆς ἀσπίδος ἐποχούμενον τὸν βασιλέα (*HE* 8.8), is rejected by Straub, 1939, 218 n. 96, but accepted by e.g. Ensslin, 1941, 17 n. 64 and 1942, 284. In fact, Straub's argument ("Da Ammian von einer Schilderhebung nichts berichtet, sind die späteren Zeugnisse nicht glaubwürdig") is not very cogent, considering Amm.'s silence on other issues (see e.g. the note ad 26.2.1 *propinquante*).

eoque, ut expeditius loqueretur, brachium exsertante obmurmuratio gravis exoritur This is a delicately sketched detail, which could well betray the hand of an eyewitness, either the author himself or one of his informants. In order to speak according to the rules, Valentinian thrusts out his arm from the imperial robe. This is not merely a natural gesture, it is also prescribed in rhetorical textbooks as part of the *actio* or *pronuntiatio*: *bracchium procerius proiectum* ('stretched full length') *quasi quoddam telum orationis* (Cic. *de Orat.* 3.220), *Bracchii moderata proiectio...decet* (Quint. *Inst.* 11.3.84), *Quid brachia? Ut eorum sit moderata proiectio* (Fortunat. *rhet.* 1.30), *manus in contentionibus fusa porrectius* (Mart. Cap. 5.543). Cf. also the detailed advice in Quint. *Inst.* 11.3.89–120, and see further Martin, 1974, 354–355 and Aldrete, 1999, 3–43. Therefore when Valentinian freed his arm from his cloak, the soldiers knew that he was going to hold a speech, and concluded that the ceremonial investiture was over. This was not at all to their liking: in their eyes the ceremony was incomplete, and so they proceeded to murmur in protest; this had to be taken seriously. Cf. Soz. *HE* 6.6.8 κεκραγότων τῶν στρατιωτῶν.

This is one of only three instances of the rare noun *obmurmuratio* in TLL IX 2.118.79–84. In TLL VI 2.2300.50 the present instance of *gravis* is registered in a long list of cases in which it characterizes a sound produced by the human voice or by animals; cf. OLD s.v. 9 "low in pitch, deep". This is quite reasonable, but it can perhaps also be interpreted as "not to be taken lightly, grave, serious" (OLD s.v. 14a).

concrepantibus centuriis et manipulis cohortiumque omnium plebe urgentium destinate confestim imperatorem alterum declarari Amm. does his best to convey the unanimity and the urgency of the common soldiers' protest. He begins with an abl. abs. with the participle, which expresses a loud noise, in the first position, the Head following in the form of the three traditional, but out of date army units placed in the pattern of the "Gesetz der wachsenden Glieder", and *plebe*, which explicitly denotes the 'rank and file', at the end. The combination *centuriae, manipuli, cohortes* also occurs in 17.13.25, 21.13.9 (see the note ad *omnes centuriae*), 23.5.15. See for *plebs* the notes ad 20.6.6 *ad quam*, 24.8.2 *cum reverti*, 25.2.1 *imae*. The protesters stubbornly (*destinate*) press for the immediate appointment of a second person of imperial rank. Thus it becomes clear at the end of the phrase that *concrepantibus* did not indicate indiscriminate shouting, but the loud uttering of a well-defined demand. Perhaps Amm. even means to say that the soldiers literally cried out *imperator(em) alter(um)*: see the note ad 20.4.14 *Augustum Iulianum*. The soldiers' demand for a second emperor cannot have come as a big surprise. A joint emperorship was of course not new in Roman history (cf. e.g. Kolb, 2001, 27–31), and the success of Julian's government as Caesar in Gaul must have been still fresh in everyone's memory. Moreover, the army had learnt from recent experience, as Amm. explains in the next section (q.v.), where he alludes to the sudden death of both Julian and Jovian with the words *fragilitatem…sublimium fortunarum*. We can only speculate about the name of a possible candidate of the soldiers, but it may safely be said that it was not Valentinian's brother Valens (cf. *alienum* in section 9).

The term *imperator* does not necessarily mean 'emperor'; it denotes the Caesar in 14.1.7 (Gallus), and 15.8.21, 16.5.11, 17.8.3 and 20.4.8 (Julian); cf. also Béranger, 1976, 56. See for *destinate* as a synonym of *pertinaciter* the notes ad 17.2.2 *destinatis* and 25.5.3 *honoratior*.

2.4 *quod licet nonnulli existimarunt paucis corruptis ad gratiam fieri despectorum* See for Amm.'s predilection for *licet* as a concessive conjunction the note ad 20.6.9 *licet*. Some members of the staff considered what they observed to be merely the sound and fury of a handful of soldiers who had been bribed to do a favour to men who felt frustrated in their ambitions, i.e. the many, *quos votorum inanitas cruciabat* of § 2. See for such a case of bought sympathy 26.6.18 *leni paucorum susurro pretio illectorum*. Earlier authors usually wrote *in gratiam* with gen. to express 'to do a favour to', e.g. Liv. 28.21.4 *ducis*, Plin. *Pan.* 7.4 *uxoris*, Tac. *Hist.* 3.78.2 *Muciani*. Amm. has *ad gratiam* also in 18.5.2, 21.12.24, 26.10.7, 27.9.10. Capable high-ranking military men who found that their achievements were underrated could become a potential risk. The two most famous examples in the *Res Gestae* are Silvanus and Ursicinus; in 15.5.28 the former complained that he and his colleague *ita fuisse despectos* e.q.s., and the latter brought about the immediate end of his career by his outburst in front of the committee which inquired into the causes of the fall of Amida: *me despicit imperator* (20.2.4).

ex eo tamen id frustra creditum videbatur, quod non emercati, sed consoni totius multitudinis paria volentis clamores audiebantur documento recenti fragilitatem pertimescentis sublimium fortunarum The imperfect *videbatur* expresses that at the moment itself the opinion of the *nonnulli* proved to be wrong, if one realized that the protest was prompted by the sincere worries of the soldiers, who, within a period of eight months, had experienced the sudden deaths of two emperors without a colleague who could take over immediately. Cf. 26.1.3 *obituque intervallato brevi tempore principum* (q.v.) and Zos. 4.1.2 τοῦ δὲ στρατοπέδου καὶ τῶν ἄλλως πρὸς αὐτὸν ἐπιτηδείως ἐχόντων ἑλέσθαι κοινωνὸν τῆς βασιλείας παρακαλούντων, ὅπως εἴ τις τοῖς πράγμασι συμβαίη περίστασις, ἔχοιεν τὸν ἀντιληψόμενον καὶ μὴ ταὐτὰ πάθοιεν οἷς ἐπὶ τῆς Ἰουλιανοῦ πεπόνθασι τελευτῆς, "here the army as well as his friends urged him to choose a colleague, so that if ever a crisis occurred he would have an assistant and they would not suffer as they did on Julian's death" (tr. Ridley, adapted).

Both *emercati* and *consoni* are nom. pl. and belong to *clamores*. One could hear that the cries had not been procured by bribery, since they clearly testified to general unanimity. See for deponential *emercari* the note ad 22.9.12 *adeo ut* and for its use in a passive sense the note ad 21.6.8 *cultu ambitioso* and Flobert, 1975, 372. Cf. for *consoni* 15.8.21 *consonis laudibus* and 22.2.4 *consonis plausibus*. As in these cases, the situation reported in the present text shows that the noise was not chaotic, but harmonious.

The phrase *documento recenti* also occurs in 14.7.6 and 26.5.11; see also 31.4.8 *recenti documento*. It refers to a precedent from which a lesson can and should be learned; see Sabbah 380–382. Amm. uses *fragilitas* only here, where it is possibly vaguely reminiscent of Cic. *Marc.* 22 *naturae communis fragilitatem extimesco*; cf. also Cic. *Tusc.* 5.3. See for the use of *fortuna* with an adjective meaning 'high' to denote the imperial dignity the note ad 20.10.1 *celsiore*. Comparable phrases are dealt with in the note ad 20.5.3 *quoniam Caesarem*. The plural is used in a generalizing sense in 30.5.16 about the appearance of comets: *ruinas fortunarum indicantia celsarum* and in Sapor's letter to Constantius: *celsiores fortunas idem loqui decet atque sentire* (17.5.4). In the latter case *celsiores fortunas* obviously denotes the persons in such a position; see the note ad loc. This is the case in the present text too: the soldiers are worried, because they remember the sudden deaths of Julian and Jovian.

dein ex susurris immaniter strepentis exercitus cieri tumultus violentior apparebat This is a difficult sentence. At first sight the reader is inclined to combine *ex* and *apparebat*: 'from the noise it could be gathered that etc.'; cf. for the combination Cic. *Fin.* 2.58 *ea faciatis e quibus appareat* etc., HA *PN* 3.1 *ex eo apparuit quod*. However, *apparere e(x)* is, in fact, quite rare, and, moreover, one fails to understand the combination of *susurris* and *immaniter strepentis*. Amm.'s other instances of *susurrus* denote a rather soft sound and in view of 15.5.6 *strepebat immaniter*, 20.4.21 *strepituque immani* and 31.7.8 *immaniter fremens*, there cannot be any doubt that the soldiers produced a loud noise. Possibly Amm. hints at the variations in the sounds, as in 16.12.43 *clamor...a tenui susurro exoriens paulatimque adolescens*. However, for such an explanation it is perhaps more plausible to interpret *ex* as denoting 'change' (see OLD s.v. *ex* 13, TLL V 2.1101.26sqq.), as in Verg. *A.* 10.221 *nymphasque e navibus* (see

Harrison ad loc.), Amm. 24.3.4 *ex immensis opibus egentissima est* (q.v.). In that case the text could be rendered as 'next it became clear that a more violent uprising of the army was being stirred up, because it had changed from murmuring to huge shouting'. See for *tumultus* denoting 'mutiny' or 'uprising' the note ad 21.11.2 *iuvante*, and cf. 25.10.9 *concitorem tumultus*.

et confidentia militis erumpentis interdum ad perniciosa facinora timebatur See for *confidentia* in a negative sense the note ad 20.5.4 *cum dispersa* and cf. also the note ad 20.4.18 *capiti Iuliani*. Such an 'arrogant audacity' sometimes burst forth into "acts of outrage" (Hamilton) and was therefore a cause of fear. See for a comparable use of *erumpere* the notes ad 20.4.14 *in apertum* and 22.1.3 *forsitan*.

2.5 *quod Valentinianus magis prae cunctis ne fieret extimescens* See for the combination of *prae* (with abl.) as a "Vergleichspartikel" and a comparative Szantyr 112 and the list in TLL X 2.375.34–57. Did Valentinian fear the outbreak of a mutiny more 'than all others' (Rolfe, Seyfarth, Caltabiano) or 'than anything' (Marié, Hamilton, Viansino)? Since there seems to be no need to state explicitly that mutiny was the worst possible scenario, the former interpretation, in which *cunctis* is regarded as abl. pl. masc., is a shade more likely: Valentinian's newly gained imperial dignity implied that his responsibility now exceeded that of all others.

elata propere dextera vi principis fiducia pleni ausus increpare quosdam ut seditiosos et pertinaces cogitata nullis interpellantibus absolvebat This is an elaborate version of Philostorgius *HE* 8.8 τῇ χειρὶ μὲν σιγᾶν αὐτοὺς ἐπιτρέπει, ἀτρέμα δὲ καὶ βασιλικῷ τῷ φρονήματι ἔφη. In contrast to Clark and Seyfarth, Marié prints V's *prospere*. This adverb usually accompanies verbs denoting a process or a (series of) event(s), such as *evenire, gerere, succedere*, to express the successful development of situations. This does not suit the lifting of an arm, and therefore Marié translates "d'un geste de bon augure", which would have been expressed by e.g. *fauste*. In fact, the conjecture of Price and Bentley fits the context excellently: Valentinian quickly raises his right arm (see above the note ad §3 *eoque*; contemporary readers may have been reminded of the raised hand as an "iconic gesture of supreme power" on official portraits, such as medaillons, of an emperor. See for this Brilliant, 1963, 208–211, especially fig. 4.124, which pictures Valentinian and Valens) and with the power (*vi*) of a fully confident emperor he has the nerve to begin his speech by scolding some (*quosdam*) of the soldiers for their headstrong drive towards mutiny. This also testifies to psychological insight: instead of a general rebuke he singles out only a number of men who continue to show the wrong behaviour, and thus opens the way for the others to return to disciplined conduct. Although there are no clear parallels in Amm. for this use of *vi*, Valesius' modestly argued emendation is convincing. In classical Latin *plenus* was usually combined with a genitive, as e.g. in *alacres et fiduciae pleni* (Caes. *Gal.* 7.76.5), *pleno fiduciae bonae consilio* (V. Max. 3.7.9), *plenus fiduciae* (Sen. *Ep.* 111.2). For *princeps* see the relevant note ad 20.4.12.

Valentinian then went on to complete the speech which he had prepared in his mind (*cogitata* repeats *praemeditata* in §3) without any further interruptions. In contrast to *nullo interpellante* (21.12.9, q.v.) *interpellare* has its usual sense here. Amm.'s choice of the verb *cogitare* testifies to his familiarity with rhetorical terminology: see TLL III 1468.19–46 for *cogitare* as a rhetorical t.t. and especially Quintilian's chapter on *cogitatio* (*Inst.* 10.6). Neri, 1985, 170 rightly notes the importance of the fact that the soldiers' unrest had not caused any changes in Valentinian's speech. He said precisely what he had prepared beforehand.

In the church histories of Sozomen (6.6.8), Theodoret (4.6.2) and Philostorgius (8.8) Valentinian's speech to the soldiers is summarized in the following terms: it belonged to your competence to choose me as emperor; now its is my task, not yours, to make decisions. This blunt and clear-cut demonstration of authority differs considerably from Ammianus' version of the speech, in which a series of circumlocutory phrases intends to persuade the soldiers to leave the choice of a second in command to the speaker. Ammianus' version seems more probable in view of the circumstances.

2. 6–10

Exsulto, provinciarum fortissimi defensores, et prae me fero semperque laturus sum Amm. contrives a brilliant variation of the *captatio benevolentiae* pattern to begin Valentinian's speech with. The very first word strikes a note of uninhibited joy; see for *exsultare* the notes ad 23.5.8 *exsultantius* and 25.3.15 *quam reposcenti*. The appellativum is reminiscent of 15.8.5 *optimi rei publicae defensores* in Constantius' speech on the occasion of the official declaration of Julian as Caesar, and of 17.13.26 *Romanae rei fidissimi defensores*, in another speech of Constantius, and appeals to their patriotic service to the cause of the Roman empire. The safety and well-being of the provinces are a recurring theme in the *Res Gestae*. Some examples: 20.5.3 (in

2.6

Julian's speech to the soldiers after the usurpation at Paris) *mecum pro statu provinciarum vitam saepius obiecistis* (q.v.), 21.5.8 (at the end of Julian's speech to the soldiers on the eve of the campaign against Constantius) *indemnitas provinciarum et salus exemplis virtutum pervulgatae* (q.v.), 21.16.17, in the necrology of Constantius, where the late emperor is chided because *nec provinciarum indemnitati prospexit* (21.16.17, q.v.). See also the extensive note ad 25.4.15 *inter quae*. The combination of rejoicing at something and a statement that one intends to "parade" this (OLD s.v. *prae* 3b) can also be found in 22.10.4, where a saying of Julian is quoted: *gaudebam plane praeque me ferebam*, and 24.3.7, at the end of a speech of Julian to his soldiers: *praeque me fero et laetor*.

nec speranti nec appetenti moderamina orbis Romani mihi ut potissimo omnium vestras detulisse virtutes The first four words are perhaps again a tasteful correction by the historian of a passage in Symmachus' panegyric, viz. the *excusatio* implied in *cur in medium invitus existi, cur diu obluctatus, cur sero mollitus es?* (*Or*. 1.10). Symmachus' words formed the starting point for Béranger's famous article on "le refus du pouvoir", first published in 1948, for which see the note ad 20.4.15 *universis*. Cf. for this topic also Dovere, 1996 and Huttner, 2004. In Valentinian's speech the denial of any aspirations on his part is more appropriate. Apart from 28.1.6 *provinciae moderamina* and the present text, the plural of *moderamen* occurs only in poetry; see also Hagendahl, 1921, 35 on *moderamen* as a primarily poetical word. The nearest parallel is *moderamina mundi* (Claud. *carm. min*. 30.46). As Heus ad loc. explains, *mundus* denotes the Roman empire. Amm. keeps to the more prosaic *orbis Romanus*. See for this phrase the notes ad 21.13.13 *aequitate* and 25.9.7 *Tu hoc loco*. The superlative *potissimus* is here used to denote a person who is regarded as the best choice to carry out a specific task. The only parallel in Amm. is 28.1.52 *potissimum exsecutorem atrocis rei*; cf. also 19.6.5 *id potissimum...tandem elegimus*, 21.13.7 *id elegit potissimum*. After *omnium* the reader expects the sentence to end with something like *delata esse*. Instead the Agens is explicitly stated in the syntactical function of subject. This unexpected end emphasizes the speaker's acknowledgement that he owes his emperorship to the soldiers. In the note ad 21.13.11 *quem obruere* it is said that in the present text the plural *virtutes* denotes the shared quality of individual soldiers. Wagner suggests that this is a case of abstractum pro concreto: "vos tam egregie meritos", presumably as *provinciarum defensores*. See Szantyr 746–747 (section g) and Fedeli ad Prop. 3.5.4, who i.a. mentions *error...Herculis* (Prop.

1.20.15–16) and *nostra sitis* (03.5.4) as the poetic equivalents of *Hercules errans* and *nos sitientes* respectively.

quod erat igitur in manu positum vestra Cf. Soz. *HE* 6.6.8 τὸ μὲν ἑλέσθαι με, ἔφη, ἄρχειν ὑμῶν, ὦ ἄνδρες στρατιῶται, ἐν ὑμῖν ἦν, Thdt. *HE* 4.6.2 ὑμέτερον ἦν, ὦ στρατιῶται, βασιλέως οὐκ ὄντος, ἐμοὶ δοῦναι τῆς βασιλείας τὰς ἡνίας, Philost. *HE* 8.8 βασιλέα μὲν ἐμὲ ποιεῖν ἐξ ἰδιώτου ἡ ὑμετέρα ψῆφος τὸ κῦρος ἐπεῖχεν. In his speech at the beginning of the campaign against Constantius II Julian also states that his rise to *Augustum...culmen* had been brought about *auctoritate vestri iudicii* (21.5.5, q.v.).

2.7

nondum electo imperii formatore The Head of this abl. abs. consists of a puzzling phrase, which the translators interpret as the equivalent of 'emperor', which seems quite justified, especially in view of Thdt. *HE* 4.6.2 βασιλέως οὐκ ὄντος. Marié and Caltabiano try to come close to *formatore* with "maître d'oeuvre impérial" and "l'ordinatore dell'impero" respectively. In 18.6.6 Amm. uses the phrase in the plural. Having reported that Ursicinus and his staff, who had been recalled to the court of Constantius II and were travelling to Italy, were suddenly directed back to Mesopotamia, he interprets this change of plan as being contrived *per molestos formatores imperii*, by which he means the court clique. See De Jonge's note ad loc. For the present text TLL VI 1.1089.52–55 provides only two parallels: Tert. *Apol.* 34 and "Comput. a. 452 chron. I p. 153, 69". This brief chronological list, in which 452 A.D. is the last date, can be found in *MGH auct. ant.* IX p. 149–153. In both cases *formator imperii* denotes the first Augustus.

There is perhaps a connection with 21.1.1 (about Julian in the first phase of his sole emperorship) *formandis in futura consiliis*, if Seyfarth would after all be right in printing V's *formandis*. Cf. also Tac. *Ann.* 13.4.2 (about Nero) *tum formam futuri principatus praescripsit* with Koestermann's note.

utiliter gloriose complestis ascito honorum verticem eo Although conceding that *et* could easily have been lost after *-er*, Blomgren 16 prefers the asyndeton *utiliter gloriose*. There seem to be no other instances of this combination, which expresses that the interest of the commonwealth went hand in hand with the glory won by the soldiers. Apart from *complestis cognostis* (26.2.7), *nostis* (15.8.8, 17.13.28, 20.5.4, 25.3.18) and *ornastis* (20.5.6) are the only examples of this contracted verbal form in Amm.; cf. also Neue-Wagener 3.481. See for *complere*, 'to carry out', the note ad 25.9.1 *mandata*, and for *asciscere* the notes ad 20.4.22 *asciti* and 23.5.1 *Ascitis*. As in 27.1.2 *promptissimo ascito societatem*, Seyfarth's refusal to add *ad* or *in* is inspired by Pighi, 1935, 116, who advocates a similar course in 15.11.17, where, however, there are more textual problems; see the note ad loc. (*Ararim quem*). The most curious example of this editorial conservatism à outrance is 20.8.14 *eos latus imperatoris ascisci*; see the note ad loc.

quem ab ineunte adolescentia ad hanc usque aetatis maturitatem splendide integreque vixisse experiundo cognostis The rare phrase *ab ineunte adolescentia* is repeated in Valentinian's necrology, 30.7.4 (he was born in 321, as can be deduced from 30.6.6, where Amm., speaking of Valentinian's death on November 17, 375, says: *animam...efflavit aetatis quinquagesimo anno et quinto*); *maturitas aetatis* also occurs rarely, e.g. in Cic. *Fam.* 6.18.4, where the young son of Cicero's addressee is deemed to derive some benefit from the Orator, *etsi abest maturitas aetatis*, and in Plin. *Pan.* 4.7, where *aetatis indeflexa maturitas* is ascribed to Trajan. In his speech on the eve of the campaign against Constantius II, Julian also refers to his familiarity with military life: *vobis inter ipsa iuventae rudimenta permixtus* (21.5.3, q.v.). Of the two adverbs *splendide* characterizes his career and *integre* his unblemished moral conduct. It is reminiscent of Horace's famous *integer vitae* (*Carm.* 1.22.1). In Valentinian's own mouth these adverbs sound natural enough, but when the future emperor figured earlier in Amm.'s narrative, his role was not very glorious (16.11.6–7, 25.10.6–9). For Valentinian's early career see the literature cited ad 26.2.1 *propinquante*.

proinde pacatis auribus accipite, quaeso, simplicioribus verbis, quod conducere arbitror in commune See for *proinde* the first note ad 24.6.4, and for the urgency expressed by *quaeso* the note ad 20.4.16 *quaeso*. As is noted ad 25.4.13 *exhortatum*, the adj. *simplex* here means 'straightforward', 'without hidden meanings'; cf. Tac. *Hist.* 1.15.4 *ego ac tu simplicissime inter nos loquimur*. Since *simplicibus* (see 26.5.10) would also result in a cursus planus, the comparative denotes a high degree of honesty. See also the notes ad 21.6.9 *simplicioris* and 21.16.18 *Christianam religionem*. The phrase *conducere* ('to be profitable') *in commune* is dealt with in the last note ad 21.5.7.

2.8 *adhiberi oportere in omnes casus socia potestate collegam contemplatione poscente multiplici* The speaker goes out of his way to express his agreement with the soldiers' wish. The appointment of a partner is requisite (*oportere*) 'for all eventualities', as 'multiple reflections' show. Instead of the *imperator alter* demanded by the soldiers Valentinian uses a phrase which is reminiscent of Tac. *Ann.* 3.56.2 (Augustus) *Marcum deinde Agrippam socium eius potestatis...delegit*, and which returns in a comparable form in two other passages about the Pannonian dynasty: 27.6.16 *pari potestate collegam* and 30.7.7 *post Gratianum filium in societatem suae potestatis assumptum*. See, however, also a similar phrase in 27.12.16. As is noted ad 21.6.6 *multiplicisque*, Amm. greatly favours this adjective.

nec ambigo nec repugno curarum acervos et mutationes varias accidentium ipse quoque ut homo formidans See for *ambigere*, 'to doubt', with a.c.i. OLD s.v. 2 and the notes ad *ambigebat* (16.12.35) and *cum ambigi nequeat* (17.5.14). There seem to be no other examples of this construction in the case of *repugnare*. See for *acervus* with the gen. plur. of non-concrete entities OLD s.v. 2, and 14.1.5 *in his malorum...acervis* and 28.1.24 *acervi...aerumnarum*, and for *accidentium* the first note ad 20.4.20 and the note ad 23.1.2 *accidentium*. Cf. for *ut homo* expressing that a human being is liable to weaknesses and mistakes Cic. *Att.* 13.21.5 *possum falli ut homo*, Hier. *adv. Rufin.* 3.36 *si errasti ut homo*, August. *cura mort.* 9 *contristantur ut homines*; cf. also the list in TLL VI 3.2879.74–2880.18.

res quoque minimae convalescunt This obviously derives from Sal. *Jug.* 10.6 *concordia parvae res crescunt*, but in view of the context Seneca's report that Marcus Agrippa used to avow that he owed much to this saying (*Ep.* 94.46) may have been Amm.'s main point of reference. See for other reflections of the famous quotation Otto, 1890, 418. This is the only instance in Amm. of *convalescere*.

si patientia vestra cum aequitate consentiens id mihi, quod mearum est partium, concesserit libens As in the case of *quod erat in manu positum vestra* in 26.2.7 (q.v.), the church historians offer striking parallels: Soz. *HE* 6.6.8 ὃ νῦν ἐξαιτεῖτε οὐκ ἐν ὑμῖν ἀλλ' ἐν ἐμοί· καὶ χρὴ τοὺς μὲν ἀρχομένους ὑμᾶς ἡσυχίαν ἄγειν, ἐμὲ δὲ ὡς βασιλέα τὰ πρακτέα σκοπεῖν, Thdt. *HE* 4.6.2 ἐμὸν λοιπὸν καὶ οὐχ ὑμέτερον τὸ περὶ τῶν κοινῶν διασκοπεῖσθαι πραγμάτων, Philost. *HE* 8.8 τὸ πρακτέον σκοπεῖν καὶ διευθετεῖν οὐχὶ τῶν βασιλευομένων, τοῦ δὲ βασιλεύοντος ἡ κρίσις ὑπάρχει.

In the *Res Gestae* the instances of (*im*)*patientia* and *impatiens* in a strictly moral sense are rare. In 22.9.10 and 16 Julian's 'patience' with men who are making a nuisance of themselves is described and Brandt, 1999, 330 proposes to interpret the present case in a comparable way. However, it seems far more likely that *patientia* here refers to the readiness to wait in contrast to the more frequent cases in which *impatiens* is combined with *differendi* (31.10.7), *morarum* (14.10.3, 19.6.7, 21.10.2, 28.1.9), *otii* (22.12.2), *quietis* (28.3.4). Soldiers are particularly prone to such impatience. Julian twice ascribes *aequitas* to his army: 21.5.5 and 23.5.23, presumably hinting at the justness of his cause. In the present text the term seems rather to denote 'reasonableness'; see the note ad 25.5.7 *quodsi gravis*. See for *mearum est partium* TLL X 1.464.7 sqq. (*partes* denotes "cuiuslibet agentis officium") and OLD s.v. *pars* 10d ("it is in my province").

2.9 Having expressed his approval of the soldiers' wish and having argued that the choice of an imperial partner fell within his authority, Valentinian now comes up with the profile of the candidate he is looking for. This profile is very carefully worded, and no fewer than four more or less adapted quotations from Cicero have been woven into the text. All in all, the speaker's ideal candidate is a second Julian. Readers who were well aware of the outcome will have noticed the contrast between this ideal and Valens.

dabit enim, ut spero, fortuna consiliorum adiutrix bonorum, quantum efficere et consequi possum In Cicero's oeuvre the parenthesis *ut spero* occurs wellnigh eighty times. The phrase *fortuna consiliorum adiutrix bonorum* is part of a quotation from a letter of Cicero to Nepos in 21.16.13 (q.v.), where the word order is slightly different. The *quantum...possum* phrase is taken from Cic. *Q. fr.* 1.1.38 *quantum efficere et consequi possumus*.

diligenter scrutanti moribus temperatum V has *crutantibus temperatum*; obviously an *s* should be added at the beginning of the first word. See for *scrutari* the note ad 25.5.2 *de parte*. Petschenig, 1893, 317 argues that the plural *scrutantibus* does not tally with *quantum...possum* and should therefore be emended to *scrutanti*. The syllable *bus* could be the remnant of *moribus* in view of two passages in which Julian is characterized: presenting him to the army as the new Caesar, Constantius II refers to his *temperati mores* (15.8.10, q.v.), which had already been mentioned by the author in 14.11.28. The phrase also occurs in Cic. *Fam.* 12.27 and V. Max. 3.8.2 *ext.* Valentinian is therefore looking for a partner à la Julian, a man who has his behaviour (*moribus*) under control, "un collega equilibrato" (Caltabiano).

ut enim sapientes definiunt As the same phrase in 25.4.1 clearly indicates, *sapientes* means 'philosophers'. This is also the case in 29.2.18, 30.8.4 and 14. In fact, what follows derives partly from Cic. *Q. fr.* 1.1.19, as Valesius already noted, partly from Cic. *Amic.* 85, as Lindenbrog saw. Presumably, Amm. found a vague attribution to highly regarded experts more appropriate for the occasion than direct references to Cicero.

non modo in imperio, ubi pericula maxima sunt et creberrima, verum etiam in privatis cotidianisque rationibus This is an adaptation of the beginning of § 19 in Cicero's first letter to his brother Quintus, in which he gives advice regarding the continuation of his proconsulship in Asia. Having mentioned a number of much needed conditions and qualities, he then continues in § 19 with: *quae cum honesta sint in his privatis cottidianisque rationibus, in tanto imperio, tam depravatis moribus, tam corruptrice provincia divina videantur necesse est*, "Such conduct would be creditable enough in our private, everyday lives, but with so wide an authority, amid such a falling-off in moral standards and in a province so rich in temptations, it must surely appear superhuman" (tr. Shackleton Bailey). There is a marked difference in the pattern of the texts: whereas Cicero's text is construed after the manner of an a fortiori argument, Amm. completely changes the order, which can be regarded as an example of psychological insight; Cicero addresses himself to a member of the elite and appeals to his feeling for the fact that a rule which applies to all human relations should be heeded even more in the risky position he was in; Amm.'s Valentinian is speaking to soldiers, who, being used to hierarchical structures, would not be surprised at the demands of inner cohesion required at the top; they are now implicitly encouraged to strive after such a cohesion also at their own level.

alienum ad amicitiam, cum iudicaverit quisquam prudens, adiungere sibi debebit, non cum adiunxerit, iudicare This is an adaptation of the 'rule' in Cic. *Amic.* 85 *Quocirca – dicendum est enim saepius –, cum iudicaris, diligere oportet, non, cum dilexeris, iudicare*. Lindenbrog ad loc. lists a number of parallels, which can also be found in the note ad *Amic.* 85 in Seyffert-Müller; P. Rutilius Lupus is perhaps the closest: *Theophrastus dicitur dixisse: prudentis esse officium, amicitiam probatam appetere, non, appetitam probare* (Rut. Lup. 1.6, see also Brooks ad loc.). The most striking word in Valentinian's version is *alienum*. This term will have been enough for the wise among the listeners (and readers). It would soon appear that the new emperor had not chosen a 'stranger'. See what is reported in ch. 4.

2.10 *haec cum spe laetiorum polliceor* Although shorter, the end of Valentinian's brief speech has the same pattern as the final sections of Julian's speech on the occasion of the invasion into Persian territory (23.5.22–23): a promise by the speaker is followed by an exhortation. Here *haec* refers to the appointment of a good partner and *laetiorum* to a better future in general, after the hardships of the katabasis from Persia. See for a comparable meaning 27.10.3 *inopina rei Romanae spes laetiorum affulsit.*

firmitatem factorum retinentes et fidem The alliteration is mentioned in Hagendahl, 1924, 166. It could not figure in the long list in Petschenig, 1897, 556–560, which only contains cases in which three words in direct succession begin with the same letter, e.g. *fortiter fecisse firmatur* (17.6.3).

dum hiberna patitur quies The speaker makes light of the fact that they still have to march from Nicaea to Constantinople, some 150 km. In fact, the rest given to the soldiers was rather short, for after his accession Valentinian gave orders to march on the next day but one (*dato in perendinum diem signo proficiscendi*, 26.4.1).

ob nuncupationem augustam debita protinus accepturi For some unknown reason editors here print *augustam* with a small initial letter, whereas they use the capital in *Augusta nuncupatio* (23.6.5, q.v.). The meaning is the same in both cases: 'the official nomination as Augustus'. For the customary accession donative of 5 *solidi* and 1 lb. of silver given to the soldiers see the note ad 20.4.18 *quinos omnibus.*

2.11 *Finita oratione, quam auctoritas erexerat inopina, flexit imperator in suam sententiam universos* The first part of the sentence looks like a contamination of *Hac oratione...flexit imperator* and *Finita oratione...flexisse imperatorem apparebat.* Valentinian's ascendancy came as a surprise, presumably for the soldiers, but perhaps in a certain way also for the staff who had put all their money on this successor to the emperorship. The choice of the verb *erigere* is somewhat puzzling. One would have understood that the speech had 'roused' or 'stimulated' the audience, but here the speech is the Patiens (*quam*). Possibly the verb is here used as a rhetorical t.t. Characterizing a speaker in the grand style, Quint. *Inst.* 12.10.62 i.a. says: *amplificationibus extollet orationem et in superlationem quoque erigetur.* Gel. 1.11.10–16 tells a wonderful story about the great orator Gaius Gracchus: he used a flute-player to help him find the proper tone in the various parts of his speeches. Gellius refers to Cic. *de Orat.* 3.225, which he paraphrases in his own words: the flute-player was there *ut sonis tum placidis tum citatis aut demissam iacentemque orationem eius erigeret aut ferocientem saevientemque cohiberet* (Gel. 1.11.15), "in order that with notes now soft, now shrill, he might animate his oratory when it was becoming weak and feeble, or check it when too violent and passionate" (tr. Rolfe). Cf. also Plin. *Ep.* 9.26.2 *Debet enim orator erigi attolli,* "The orator ought in fact to be roused and heated" (tr. Radice). So one could tentatively translate Amm.'s words with: 'Having finished the speech, which his ascendancy had raised to a high level of pathos'.

Unanimous approval after a speech of an emperor is found more often in the *Res Gestae.* See the introductory note ad 20.5.8 and the notes ad 21.5.9 *hoc sermone* and 21.13.16 *Omnes post.*

consiliique eius viam secuti, qui paulo ante flagrantissimis vocibus aliud postulabant The metaphor *consilii via,* "la via tracciata nel suo progetto" (tr. Viansino) also occurs in 21.5.6 and 22.12.8. It may have been borrowed from Livy, who uses it six times, twice (5.5.11, 24.45.7) combined with *sequi.* The great variety of metaphorical uses of *flagrans* documented in TLL VI 1.847.78–848.31 makes Amm.'s bold combination with *vocibus* slightly less conspicuous. With the 'other course' (*aliud*) demanded by the soldiers Amm. refers to *confestim imperatorem alterum declarari* (§ 3), specifically to *confestim.* This is indeed no mean difference.

circumsaeptum aquilis et vexillis agminibusque diversorum ordinum ambitiose stipatum iamque terribilem duxerunt in regiam Pictures of an emperor surrounded by the military paraphernalia and the representatives of the various ranks occur more often in the *Res Gestae,* e.g. 16.10.4 *stipatusque agminibus formidandis,* 20.5.1 *signis aquilisque circumdatus et vexillis saeptusque tutius armatarum cohortium globis,* 22.2.4 *stipatusque armatorum et togatorum agminibus velut acie ducebatur instructa.* Cf. also 19.6.11 *Persarum regem armatorum centum milibus circumsaeptum.* In Valentinian's case all this happened 'in grand style', *ambitiose.* See for Amm.'s predilection for *ambitiosus* the note ad 14.7.6 *domum ambitiosam.* Taken together, these texts show that the plea of Petschenig, 1892, 520–521 for V's *circumspectum* is less than felicitous. Amm. indeed uses the p.p.p. of *circumspicere,* e.g. 18.10.1 *Craugasii Nisibeni cuiusdam…fama potentiaque circumspecti* ('prominent'), but it does not suit the scene sketched in the present text.

After the stereotyped phrases *iamque terribilem* catches the eye. Although conceding that the phrase could simply express that Valentinian had gained respect by his authoritative words, Paschoud, 1992, 72–73 regards this as perhaps a "perfide prolepse", which prefigures Amm.'s characterization of Valentinian as a "monstre de cruauté" later on. This seems far-fetched. In all other instances in Amm. of *terribilis* the word functions within its direct context. As to important persons, in the section on justice in Julian's necrology the emperor is said to have been *sine crudelitate terribilis* (25.4.8), because he took circumstances into account. The Moor Firmus was *terribili vultu Theodosi praestrictus* (29.5.15). There is no reason to assume that either Julian or Theodosius the Elder was attacked by Amm. in some hidden way. In fact, for Paschoud's idea *iam tum* would have been needed as a clear sign for the reader that the author intended to return to this later. In contrast, mere *iam* expresses that Valentinian inspired fear and awe at an earlier moment than those present in Nicaea had expected. See for a discussion in a wider perspective Teitler, 2007.

Regia denotes the emperor's accommodation. It can therefore mean 'palace', as in 21.10.1 (in Sirmium; see the note ad *duxit in regiam*) and 25.10.2 (in Antioch; see the note ad *Maximiani*). However, there was no palace in Nicaea. Here, as in 19.6.7, it means the emperor's 'headquarters' in the camp.

CHAPTER 3

Introduction

One of the ways in which Ammianus expresses his respect for Rome – *urbs venerabilis*, as he calls it in 14.6.5 – is his record of the urban prefecture. In the remaining books of the *Res Gestae* all *praefecti urbis* from 353 until 372 are individually reviewed. The descriptions of their terms of office are not evenly distributed over the *Res Gestae*. In Books 14–19 six urban prefects are discussed, whereas in Books 20–25 there is only one very brief note on the prefecture of Maximus in 21.12.24, who was in office during the first months of Julian's reign as Augustus. The main reason for this unevenness is that the reign of Julian is discussed in much greater detail than that of his predecessor Constantius. Books 14–19 cover a period of seven years (353–359), 20–25 of four (360–363). Consequently the passages on the urban prefects are wider apart. That, however, does not explain why the prefecture of Apronianus – the subject of this chapter – is narrated in Book 26, after the description of Valentinian's election as emperor. Apronianus had received the nomination from Julian, during the emperor's stay in Syria, as we are told in 23.1.4, probably in January 363. The first mention of his successor, Symmachus dates from April 364, so the second half of Apronianus' prefecture practically coincided with the reign of Jovian. A plausible explanation why Ammianus decided to postpone the description of Apronianus' prefecture to Book 26 would be that he gave precedence to coherence over strict chronology. It seems likely that he did not want to break up his account of the Persian campaign, including the peace treaty with Persia and the death of Jovian which followed shortly after.

Ammianus' accounts of the urban prefectures vary in length from a few lines to complete chapters. Recurring elements are the character of the prefect, his level of education and his behaviour in dealing with the Roman populace. The prefects were responsible for the provisioning of food for the city. Almost all of them were confronted with revolts caused by scarcity of food and wine, so much so that, when such riots did not occur, Ammianus mentions this. This is the case in the present chapter, which concludes with the statement that during Apronianus' prefecture there was plenty of food. Another important task of the prefect was jurisdiction. This is the aspect singled out for treatment by Ammianus in his discussion of Apronianus' tenure of office. The chapter is dominated by the account of Apronianus' vigorous fight against the crime of *veneficium*, which includes both poisoning and magic. Ammianus emphasizes repeatedly that such cases were rare in the days of Julian, and that the few that did occur, were dealt with swiftly and harshly. The reasons for his insistence on this point seem to be twofold. Firstly, as Sabbah has suggested, he defends Julian against criticisms that during his reign magical practices had increased, secondly the reader is prepared for the terrible accounts in Books 28 and 29 of the persecutions of people, both guilty and innocent, on similar charges under Valentinian and Valens. Julian may have no active role to play in Book 26, but he is still very much present as a foil to his successors.

We have greatly profited in writing our commentary on this chapter from Pia van de Wiel's doctoral thesis on Ammianus' treatment of the urban prefects *Hoofdstukken uit de geschiedenis van Rome in Ammianus Marcellinus' Res Gestae*, Amsterdam 1989.

3.1 *Dum haec in oriente volubiles fatorum explicant sortes* A standard transition formula as in 22.1.1 (q.v.), but emphasizing the diversity of the events in the East. The combination of *fatum* and *sors*, indicating the individual portion allotted by fate, is found in authors like Lucan (9.1046 *o sors durissima fati!*) and Apuleius (*Pl.* 1.12 *quare nec omnia ad fati sortem arbitratur esse referenda*). Amm. has *fatorum sors* in 14.11.19 *Pandente itaque viam fatorum sorte tristissima*, 28.4.22 and 31.16.8. This is the only instance with *sortes* in the plural, possibly on account of the variety of the developments, such as the Persian expedition and the deaths of Julian and Jovian. For *volubilis* see again the note ad 22.1.1. The word *oriens* here must refer to the East in general, and not, as in 20.1.1 *perque orientem* (q.v.), merely to the *dioecesis Orientis*.

Amm. uses the verb *explicare* in different shades of meaning. Its primary meaning 'to uncoil' is found in its literal sense in 19.8.8 *explicato fune ingenti*, and metaphorically (TLL V 2. 1728.1–20), 'to unroll', here and in Sen. *Nat.* 2.32.4 *alia ratione fatorum series explicatur*. With *acies* as its object it means 'to deploy' in 14.2.6 *acies explicare*, and with an abstract object 'to spread', as in 22.7.10 *timore eius adventus...latius explicato*. It is the equivalent of *expedire* in 16.12.36 *telaque dexteris explicantes*. Most frequently *explicare* is used in the meaning 'to explain', 'to expose', as e.g. in 26.1.2 *cognitiones actuum variorum stilis uberibus explicatas* and 31.16.9 *Haec...pro virium explicavi mensura.* Finally, in 23.4.6 (q.v.), *quaterni altrinsecus iuvenes repagula, quibus incorporati sunt funes, explicantes* it must mean 'to turn', 'to rotate'.

Apronianus regens urbem aeternam In 23.1.4 (q.v.) Amm. had reported the nomination by Julian of the *praefectus urbi* L. Turcius Apronianus *signo* Asterius (*PLRE* I, Apronianus 10): *et Apronianum Romae decrevit esse praefectum.* For the office of PVR see the note ad 21.10.6 *multo post* (add to the literature cited there Chastagnol, 1997). For an attempt to connect the fragmentary evidence of *CIL* 9.2461 and 10.6441 with Apronianus Asterius see Gaggiotti, 1985–1986.

In 23.3.3 Amm. also referred to Apronianus, in terms which are a skilful variation of the wording here: *praefecturam regente Aproniano in urbe conflagravit aeterna* (sc. the temple of Apollo on the Palatine at Rome; the burning down of this temple is dated by Amm., *ibid.*, to March 19, 363). Apart from the present chapter we hear of the prefect again in 27.3.3, where Amm. reports that he was succeeded by Symmachus (*PLRE* I, Symmachus 3): *Symmachus Aproniano successit* – this must have been early in 364 (the first law addressed to Symmachus as PVR, *Cod. Theod.* 7.4.10, dates from April 22, 364). For the designation of Rome as *urbs aeterna* see the notes ad 21.12.24 *urbi praefecit* and 26.1.14 *quam rationem.*

iudex integer et severus The word *iudex* in Amm. is often used in the sense of 'official' (see the note ad 20.5.7 *civilis...iudex*), but here it probably has its usual meaning of 'judge', since Amm. describes in this chapter primarily the juridical activities of Apronianus. Cf. Chastagnol, 1960, 84: "Le préfet urbain du IVe siècle est essentiellement un juge; il passe au tribunal la meilleure partie de son temps". The adjective *integer* is the opposite of *corruptus.* Cf. Cic. *Clu.* 49 *integrum consilium, iudici corrupti nulla suspicio* and Tac. *Ann.* 3.34.3 *corruptos saepe pravitatibus uxorum maritos: num ergo omnes caelibes integros?* Amm. may have had Cic. *Ver.* 1.30 in mind: *duos severissimos atque integerrimos iudices.*

CIL 6.1768 = *ILS* 1229 is dedicated to *Aproniano...omni virtute praestanti*, which formula, found on the base of a statue in honour of Apronianus, does not surprise. The praise for Apronianus' honest severity in our historian, however, has caused wonder: "we are astonished to discover that the conduct of which Ammianus approves is the very same sort of trial for magic, with its bloody end, for which Valentinian and his friends have been so violently abused" (Alföldi, 1952, 70).

inter curarum praecipua, quibus haec praefectura saepe sollicitatur The noun *cura* in this gen. inversus refers both to the tasks of the urban prefect and to his worries, underlined by the verb *sollicitatur*. A fuller designation of the office of PVR is found only in 27.6.2 (*in praefectura enim urbana*) and 27.9.8 (*praefecturam urbis*). *Praefectura* without further qualification to designate *praefectura urbana* is used by Amm. almost as often as for its alternative, the praetorian prefecture (the full expression *praefectura praetoriana* occurs seven times).

One of the *curarum praecipua* a PVR had to cope with, was the maintenance of law and order in cases of revolt by the populace, which were often provoked by a shortage of food and wine, cf. 14.6.1, 15.7.2–3, 17.11.5, 19.10.1–4, 27.3.4, 27.3.8–10 (see Palanque, 1931 and Kohns, 1961 for hunger riots in Rome, and in general Gregory, 1983 (1984), Herz, 1988, Garnsey, 1998 and Garnsey-Humfress, 2001, 107–131; for the *plebs* in Late Antiquity Seyfarth, 1969 and Kneppe, 1979). During Apronianus' prefecture, however, nothing of the sort occurred and there even was an abundance of victuals (§ 6, q.v.). Instead, Apronianus had to act as judge in some cases of magic, and it is to these that Amm. refers in this and the following sections.

opera curabat enixa For this expression see the note ad 22.12.5 *in praeparandis*.

veneficos, qui tunc rarescebant The only other certain instance of the verb *rarescere* in the *Res Gestae* is 22.15.25 *efficit, ut rarescant mortiferae pestes*, q.v. In the classical period *rarescere* is used with some frequency (5 instances) by Lucretius in the meaning 'to become rarefied'. Vergil uses it once: *A.* 3.411 *angusti rarescent claustra Pelori*; see Williams' note ad loc. It occurs in several Christian authors, e.g. Tert. *Apol.* 20.3 *iustitia rarescit, iniquitas increbrescit*. Amm. again emphasizes that there were few *venefici* during the reign of Julian by the words *paucorum discrimine* in the present section, and *nulli vel admodum pauci* in section 4. This may suffice to reject conjectures like *crebrescebant* (Bentley) or *clarescebant* (Petschenig, 1893, 495). Note that *rarescebant* has lost its inchoative force, in conformity with the general tendency in Late Latin, for which see Szantyr 298.

The only mention of the charge of *veneficium* in the preceding books is found in 19.12.14, as an instance of the fanatical zeal with which Paulus 'the Chain' pursued his adversaries: *nam si qui remedia quartanae vel doloris alterius collo gestaret sive per monumentum transisse vesperi malevolorum argueretur indiciis, ut veneficus sepulchrorumque hor-*

rores et errantium ibidem animarum ludibria colligens vana pronuntiatus reus capitis interibat. Amm. hastens to add that, in spite of his condemnation of Paulus, he is all in favour of stern measures in order to protect the person of the emperor: *Et inquisitum in haec negotia fortius nemo, qui quidem recte sapiat, reprehendet. nec enim abnuimus salutem legitimi principis, propugnatoris bonorum et defensoris, unde salus quaeritur aliis, consociato studio muniri debere cunctorum* (19.12.17).

The crime of *veneficium* covers both poisoning and the use of magical practices like incantation. Lotz, 2005, 33 points out that *venenum* has a wider meaning than the Greek φάρμακον: "Im Lateinischen kann *venenum* als Synekdoche für die gesamte magische Praxis stehen". It is not always possible to infer from the wording used by Amm. which of the two is meant, but one can safely say that magical practices are at issue in the majority of the cases he mentions.

A law against magical practices is already attested in the Twelve Tables (8.8–9, cf. Bruns-Gradenwitz, 1909, 30–31), and there is also Sulla's *lex Cornelia de sicariis et veneficis* (ibid., 92), if indeed the Cornelian law dealt with magic and not simply with poisoning (see on this the different views of Fögen, 1997, 58–60, Lotz, 2005, 75 and, most recently, Rives, 2006). However, Amm. no doubt refers not to these, but to the relevant fourth-century laws which have come down to us via the Theodosian Code, especially those under the heading *De maleficis et mathematicis et ceteris similibus* (9.16.1 ff.). For instance in a law of Constantine (*Cod. Theod.* 9.16.3) we read: *eorum est scientia punienda et severissimis merito legibus vindicanda, qui magicis adcincti artibus aut contra hominum moliti salutem aut pudicos ad libidinem deflexisse animos detegentur*, while Constantius II threatened among others *malefici* with capital punishment should they attempt to put their wicked doctrines into practice (*Cod. Theod.* 9.16.4). Cf. further *Cod. Theod.* 9.16.5 (cited in the next note) and 9.16.6 *Si quis magus vel magicis contaminibus adsuetus, qui maleficus vulgi consuetudine nuncupatur...in comitatu meo vel Caesaris fuerit deprehensus, praesidio dignitatis cruciatus et tormenta non fugiat. si convictus ad proprium facinus detegentibus repugnaverit pernegando, sit eculeo deditus ungulisque sulcantibus latera perferat poenas proprio dignas facinore* (both these laws were also issued by Constantius II).

Sabbah 498 plausibly suggests that Julian's adversaries had blamed him posthumously for the increase of magical practices as a consequence of his alleged *pravae artes* (21.1.7 *malevoli praenoscendi futura pravas artes assignant*) and that Amm. in this chapter defends Julian's memory. In the later books, more specifically in chs. 28.1 and 29.2, *veneficium*, along with crimes of a sexual nature, is an important issue, and its ruthless repression casts a slur on the reigns of Valentinian and Valens.

ut...captos postque agitatas quaestiones nocuisse quibusdam apertissime confutatos indicatis consciis morte multaret This is, even for Amm., a remarkable accumulation of participles, in which the successive stages of arrest, interrogation, confession and execution are swiftly enumerated. The expression *quaestiones agitare* is used in the meaning 'to start a judicial inquiry' in 22.3.1 *Salutio...summam quaestionum agitandarum...commisit*, q.v., and 25.10.13 *super neutrius morte quaestionem comperimus agitatam*. In other cases it denotes interrogation, usually with torture, as here, 15.6.1 *quaestiones agitabantur ex more et vinculis catenisque plures ut noxii plectebantur* and 26.10.9 *cruentae quaestiones*. *Apertissime* is added to insist on the fairness of the conviction. For *confutare = convincere* see TLL IV 271.34–50.

As to *morte multaret* (and *capitali animadversione damnavit* in § 3), in the fourth century the death sentence seems to have been the normal penalty for those who were found guilty of magic, as can be deduced from laws of Constantius II, *Cod. Theod.* 9.16.4 *supplicium capitis feret gladio ultore prostratus, quicumque* (i.e. among others *quos maleficos ob facinorum magnitudinem vulgus appellat*) *iussis obsequium denegaverit* and 9.16.5 *multi magicis artibus ausi elementa turbare vitas insontium labefactare non dubitant...hos...feralis pestis absumat*. Whether decapitation was *de rigueur*, as in 26.3.3 *abscisa cervice consumptus est* and *Cod. Theod.* 9.16.4, is disputed. Cf. on this Fögen, 1997, 46–47 with n. 63. See for the death penalty in Amm. Arce, 1974; in general Latte, 1940 and Grodzynski, 1984.

paucorum discrimine reliquos, si qui laterent, formidine parium exturbaret Apronianus follows the example of Julian, of whom it is said in 25.4.8 *paucorum discrimine vitia cohibebat*. TLL V 2.2093.37–40 is probably right in bringing the present use of *exturbare* under the heading "notione locali debilitata". The few who had escaped trial (*si qui laterent*) were deterred from further wrongdoing.

3.2 *efficaciter* 'Energetically', cf. *magna...industria* in this same section. For the adverb cf. 21.12.22 *congrua instantium sollicitudinum moli ipse quoque agitans efficaciter* with the note.

Iuliani promotus arbitrio agentis etiamtum per Syrias There are notes on *promovere*, 'to advance to a higher rank' ad 20.2.5 *immodico* and 20.9.5 *praefectum*. For the date of Apronianus' appointment by Julian, viz.

the first days of January 363, see the note ad 23.1.4 *imperator*. Shortly afterwards Apronianus probably received in person Julian's *constitutio de postulando*, issued at Antioch on January 17, 363 and addressed to him. See for this Bisschoff-Nörr, 1963, 40. For the plural in *per Syrias* see the note ad 22.10.1 *quibus abundant*, where it is stated that Amm. can use *Syriae* in a rather wide sense, viz. of 'the eastern provinces in general'. When Apronianus was appointed by Julian he was in the East, as one of the envoys sent to the emperor by the senate (23.1.4). Chastagnol, 1960, 192 observes that the nomination of a *praefectus urbi*, who was not in Rome at the moment of his appointment, was quite exceptional (for another example see 21.12.24). Rolfe's translation "after appointment of Julian, when he was still living in Syria" wrongly suggests that *etiamtum agentis* refers to Apronianus.

artibus se nefariis appetitum Amm. uses many different expressions for magical practices, *artes vetitae* (14.7.7), – *pravae* (21.1.7, 28.1.14), – *secretae* (23.6.78, 29.1.7, 30.5.11), – *malae* (26.3.4), – *noxiae* (28.1.26) and – *interdictae* (29.2.2). Cf. the list in the note ad 21.1.7 *malevoli* (where – *venenatus* should be omitted, because the cases mentioned concern poisoning). Fögen 1997, 22 n. 7 notes the following expressions in the imperial constitutions: – *odiosae*, – *clandestinae*, – *dolosae* and – *malignae*, to which *nefariae* may be added: *Cod. Theod.* 9.16.7 *ne quis deinceps nocturnis temporibus aut nefarias preces aut magicos apparatus aut sacrificia funesta celebrare conetur*.

Apronianus was, of course, not unique in ascribing a disease to unnatural causes. The Roman lady Anepsia accused Aginatius of having practiced magic in order to seduce her: 28.1.50 *appetitam se nefariis artibus vim in domo Aginati perpessam asseveravit*. In 26.4.4 Amm. reports that Valentinian and Valens thought that their illness was caused by sorcery. Cf. also Lib. *Or.* 36.15, with Bonner, 1932 and Sandwell, 2005, Tac. *Ann.* 4.22.3, *CIL* 8.2756 = *CE* 1604 (cf. *AE* 1998.1585), *Cod. Theod.* 9.16.5, with Seyfarth-Kudlien, 1960.

magna quaeritabat industria As De Jonge points out ad 14.7.7, the verb occurs frequently in Plautus, rarely in the classical period, and emerges again in post-classical authors like Apuleius. Parallels from contemporary sources are Hier. *Malchi* 3 *manuum labore victum quaeritans* and August. *Conf.* 1.18.29 *homo eloquentiae famam quaeritans*.

unde quibusdam atrox visus est in amphitheatrali curriculo undatim coeunte aliquotiens plebe causas dispiciens criminum maximorum This is the only instance of *atrox* in connection with a person in Amm., who uses it regularly with abstract nouns like *proelium, res*, or *facinus*. Tacitus is much less reserved in this respect. He qualifies i.a. Vitellius (*Hist.* 2.63.1), Agrippina (*Ann.* 4.52.2), Poppaea (*Ann.* 14.61.2) and Nero (*Ann.* 15.36.4) as *atrox*.

The unanimity with which modern editors prefer V's *curriculo* to *circulo* (SB) is surprising. *In curriculo* can only be understood in a temporal sense: "during the races" (Rolfe), "beim Wettrennen" (Seyfarth), for which, however, the amphitheatre is not the right place. Marié prints *curriculo*, but seems to translate *circulo*: "dans l'enceinte circulaire de l'amphithéatre". The alternative reading *circulo* is also found in 31.10.19, where we are told that Commodus killed a hundred lions *in amphitheatrali circulo*, that is to say in the arena of the amphitheatre. The same expression is used in ps. Acro's note on Hor. *Ep.* 1.1.6, who paraphrases *extrema harena* with *sub circulo Amphitheatri*.

Chastagnol, 1960, 251–252, referring to Symm. *rel.* 23.9 *ad circi secretarium* (cf. Vera ad loc.), may be right in stating that an urban prefect used to sit in a separate council chamber when administering justice, but that is not what Amm. suggests here. His words convey the idea that Apronianus investigated offences at the amphitheatre in open court, in the middle of a crowd – which was precisely what a law of Constantine, *Cod. Theod.* 1.16.6 of 1 November 331, commended to provincial governors, in order to prevent bribery: *praesides publicas notiones exerceant frequentatis per examina tribunalibus, nec civiles controversias audituri secretariis sese abscondant* ("the governors shall conduct public trials with their tribunals crowded by throngs of people throughout the trials, and when they are about to hear civil controversies, they shall not hide themselves in their private council chambers", tr. Pharr), and what, as Valesius pointed out, in A.D. 415 the *praefectus Augustalis* Orestes did (*PLRE* II, Orestes 1), when he tried and punished one of the supporters of Cyrillus, patriarch of Alexandria, publicly in the theatre (Ὀρέστου τοῦ τῆς Ἀλεξανδρείας ἐπάρχου πολιτείαν ἐν τῷ θεάτρῳ ποιοῦντος, Socr. *HE* 7.13.6).

The adverb *undatim* is rare. Pliny uses it for the wavy markings of citrus wood, *Nat.* 13.96 (*mensae*) *sunt et undatim crispae* or marble, *Nat.* 36.55 *Augusteum undatim crispum*. A remarkable parallel is quoted by Valesius: Oros. *hist.* 6.21.13 *ita omnes ad experientiam belli decisionemve foederis undatim gentes commovebantur*.

3.3 *post huiusmodi vindicata complura* Amm. uses the '*ab urbe condita*-construction' with greater frequency even than Livy and Tacitus, see the note ad 22.2.2 *post exemptos*.

Hilarinum aurigam Like his predecessor Leontius (*PLRE* I, Leontius 22), urban prefect in 355–356, Apronianus had to cope with troubles concerning a charioteer. Leontius had quelled a riot in the city following the arrest of the *auriga* Philoromus (15.7.2). Whether or not this Philoromus had anything to do with *veneficium*, like the *auriga* of the present text, is not stated, but another charioteer, also mentioned by name by Amm., certainly had: in 28.1.27 it is said that in 368 a certain Auchenius was supported by some men of senatorial rank (among them the future *urbi praefectus* Tarracius Bassus, *PLRE* I, Bassus 21), who were his accomplices in *veneficium*. See for the connection between charioteers and *veneficium* further 28.4.25 and 29.3.5.

To administer drugs to horses, whether to incite or to curb them (cf. *in curriculis equos debilitare incitare tardare*, Arn. 1.43), must have been as common in ancient hippodromes as it is now. The step from drugs to magic was apparently easily made, as is clear from literary texts (apart from Amm. e.g. Lib. *Or.* 36.15, Hier. *Hilar.* 11 p. 96 Bastiaensen *aemulo suo habente maleficum, qui daemoniacis quibusdam imprecationibus et huius impediret equos et illius concitaret ad cursum*, 'his rival having at his disposal a magician, who with devilish imprecations curbed someone's horses and incited those of another'), imperial constitutions (*Cod. Theod.* 9.16.11), and especially many curse tablets on lead (e.g. *ILS* 8753–8754, cf. Audollent, 1904, lxxxix–xc and Gager, 1992, 44–74) and papyrus (e.g. *PMag* 4.2211–2216, 7.390–394). For some Greek defixiones with respect to horses, not included in the special corpora see Jordan, 1985, 184–185, 187, 192. Cf. also Jordan, 2002 and see in general on *veneficium* at the hippodrome Barb, 1963, 119–120, Pavis d'Escurac, 1987 and Clerc, 1995, 164–166. The condemnation of Hilarinus is wrongly dated to 364 by Dickie, 2003, 296. Cf. also Jordan, 2002 and see in general on *veneficium* at the hippodrome Barb, 1963, 119–120; Pavis d'Escurac, 1987; Clerc, 1995, 164–166; Dickie, 2001, 293–298.

convictum atque confessum A Sallustianism: *Cat.* 52.36 *convicti confessique sint*. Hagendahl, 1924, 163–168 has a list of similar binary expressions with alliteration in Amm.

filium suum venefico tradidisse docendum The classical construction of *tradere* with predicative gerund is also found in 16.12.60 *tradidere se vinciendos* and 24.1.2 *cornu vero laevum...Arintheo tradidit et Hormisdae ducendum*.

68 COMMENTARY

secretiora quaedam legibus interdicta Note Amm's veiled terms. He avoids the terms *magus, magicus*, which are freely used in law texts, reserving it for the Persian Magi only (23.6.32, q.v.).

ut nullo conscio adminiculis iuvaretur internis This use of *internus = domesticus* is not registered in TLL. It belongs to the category "pertinet ad familiaritatem, fere i.q. proximus", VII 1.2237.35.

capitali animadversione damnavit This is a variation on Amm.'s usual expression for the death penalty, viz. *capitale supplicium*, which is found eight times in the *Res Gestae*. In 29.1.43 Amm. writes *capitali est poena affectus*. See for the death penalty for magical practices the notes ad § 1 *veneficos* and *ut...captos*.

laxius retinente carnifice subito lapsus confugit ad ritus Christiani sacrarium Cf. Liv. 9.10.7 *cum apparitor verecundia maiestatis Postumi laxe vinciret*. For *labi = effugere* see the note ad 24.6.13 *perrupissetque*. In TLL VII 2.788.58–59 it is acutely observed that this use is most often found with the perfect participle *lapsus*, because *effugere* lacks such a participle. The attempt of Hilarinus to escape death by taking refuge in a Christian chapel was as fruitless as that of the usurper Silvanus in Cologne in A.D. 355 (15.5.31). It is disputed whether at this time the state had acknowledged that Christian churches could grant asylum. Although the existence of a Constantinian law *de his qui ad ecclesias confugiunt* is assumed by e.g. Demandt, 1989, 71, no such law is passed down to us (the first existing constitution under this heading in the Theodosian Code is of the year 392, *Cod. Theod.* 9.45.1), and other scholars are sceptical. Cf. Langenfeld, 1977, 107–209 (contra Wenger, 1950, 840–844) and Manfredini, 1986, 43–44. See in general Ducloux, 1994.

abscisa cervice The same expression is found in 14.11.23 and 28.1.16.

3.4 *verum* There is a note about *verum* ad 21.12.10, where it has adversative sense. Here it marks the transition from the details of Hilarinus' escape to Amm.'s main point, Apronianus' energetic action against *venefici*. Other instances of 'resumptive' *verum* are 20.3.12 *verum ad instituta iam revertamur*, 25.3.5 *verum principe volitante inter prima discrimina proeliorum exsiluit...armatura*, 25.4.19 *Verum tamen cum haec essent, aestimari poterat* eqs.

tum etiam ut coercenda mox cavebantur In the phrase *tum etiam*, *etiam* has either temporal or additive force; TLL V 2.930.80–84 and 942.43–55. In the former case it normally refers to the past, meaning 'at that time...still'. Apart from Tac. *Ann.* 3.61.1 *oleae, quae tum etiam maneat*, the examples quoted under this heading in the TLL are taken from Amm., e.g. 20.3.11 (*luna*) *in eodem* (*signo*) *tum etiam agens*, q.v. In spite of the word order, *mox* is best taken with *coercenda*. In Julian's time swift measures were taken in order to suppress these undesirable practices.

vigori publico insultarunt 'The strong arm of the law' is the meaning suggested by *Cod. Theod.* 14.6.3 *ut, qui in usurpatione fuerit, austeritatem vigoris publici ferre cogatur*, as well as the following instances from Christian authors: Cypr. *epist.* 3.1 *pro episcopatus vigore et cathedrae auctoritate* and August. *Ep.* 108.6 *ecclesiasticum vigorem*. In 14.7.8 *modo non reclamante publico vigore* the meaning is more likely to be "though the strength of the public opinion almost resulted in a demonstration" (Hamilton). For *insultare* 'to demonstrate contempt', cf. 27.1.6 *Herulorum Batavorumque vexillum direptum, quod insultando tripudiantes barbari crebro sublatum altius ostendebant* and 27.12.4 *ut arbitrio se monstraret insultare nostrorum*.

tempore secuto longaeva impunitas nutrivit immania The explicit comparison of the *mores* during Julian's reign with the moral corruption under his successors reveals Amm.'s intention to uphold Julian's reputation. A similar use of *nutrire* is found in 28.3.2 *fusis variis gentibus et fugatis, quas insolentia nutriente securitate aggredi Romanas res inflammabat*. For *immanis* as one of Amm.'s favourite adjectives see the note ad 21.11.1 *ausa indicans*.

quidam senator "This Senator he does not name, but the reference is so open and so insulting that the Senator in question could not have failed to recognize it, and Ammianus must have had ample protection against any retaliation which he could have attempted" (Thompson, 1947, 88).

usque eo grassante licentia A daring personification, possibly inspired by Tac. *Hist.* 1.37.5 *minore avaritia ac licentia grassatus esset T. Vinius, si ipse imperasset*. Cf. 19.4.3 *huiusmodi grassante pernicie*, 28.6.21 *eo usque iniquitate grassante*, 29.5.8 *iniquitate grassante licentius*.

servumque suum modo non per syngrapham arcanis piacularibus inducendum commisisse doctori malarum artium confutatus The impudence of the anonymous senator is emphasized by the words *modo non per syngrapham*, 'almost in a formal contract'. For *modo non* see the note ad 21.2.2 *hos ei versus*. A *syngrapha* is a binding agreement in writing; Gaius *Inst.* 3.134 *litterarum obligatio fieri videtur chirografis et syngrafis, id est si quis debere se aut daturum se scribat*. The adjective *piacularis* means "needing to be expiated" (OLD). Cf. TLL X 1.2068.19–38, where Apul. *apol.* 45.6 is quoted: *quinam testes huic piaculari sacro* (during which Apuleius allegedly had bewitched a boy) *adfuerint*. For *inducere* "to initiate" (OLD 8b) see TLL VII 1.1236.73–1237.19. This is the only instance of *inducere* with a complement in the dative. The normal complement is *in*+acc. Note the parallelism with the case of Hilarinus' son: *filium suum venefico tradidisse docendum secretiora* ≈ *servum suum arcanis piacularibus inducendum commisisse doctori malarum artium*.

supplicium redimeret opima mercede For *redimere* 'to buy off', cf. Cic. *Ver.* 3.49 *qui se…omnia sua pericula redempturum esse dicebat*. V's *optima mercede*, retained by Marié, is a prime example of a *lectio facilior*. For *opima merces* cf. Liv. 21.43.7 *in hanc tam opimam mercedem* and Apul. *Met.* 2.13 *non parvas stipes, immo vero mercedes opimas iam consecutus*.

3.5 *hoc genere, quo iactatum est, absolutus* For *hoc genere, quo = eo modo, quo* cf. TLL VI 1905.20 sqq. Seyfarth prints Gelenius' *iactatum* instead of V's *iactum*. At first sight this does not seem necessary, since *iacere* in the meaning 'to utter' is well-attested; TLL VII 1.41. 39 sqq., e.g. Liv. 5.15.5 *quod primo velut temere iactum sperni*, Tac. *Ann.* 11.18.3 *nimia et incertum an falso iacta*. An example from Amm. himself is 26.8.2 *e muris probra in eum iaciebantur et irrisive compellabatur ut sabaiarius*. In all these cases, however, single words or remarks are the subject of the verb, whereas in the present text we are dealing with rumour (cf. the preceding *fama vulgarat*). The verb for that is *iactare*: 15.5.4 *ut iactavere rumores incerti*, 16.11.13 *illud tamen rumore tenus ubique iactabatur*, so *iactatum* is to be preferred to *iactum*. Petschenig, 1893, 495, rejected both forms, because *quo iac(ta)tum est* would be a pointless repetition of *fama vulgarat*. Instead he proposed *dictum est*. This would undeniably be more logical, but Amm. always (14 instances) refers to what he has said previously with the phrase *ut dictum est*. It seems best therefore to accept the slight irregularity and to write *ut iactatum est*.

cum vitae pudere deberet et culpae, non abolendae incubuit maculae There is a tone of real indignation in this passage. *Vitae et culpae* is an effective hendiadys. Cf. [Quint.] *Decl.* 12.14 *gravior in dies facti paenitentia est, pudet vitae, lucem ac sidera intueri non audeo.* For *incumbere* with gerundive cf. Flor. *Epit.* 3.16.2 *rogandis Gracchorum legibus ita vehementer incubuit* eqs.

phalerato insidens discurrensque per silices There are no parallels for substantivized *phaleratus* without *equus*. It seems best therefore to follow Gelenius and all later editors and to add the missing noun either before *phalerato* or after *insidens*, despite Meurig-Davies' plea to accept V's reading (1949, 189). For the *phalera(e)* or breastplate, an ornament for horses as well as a military decoration, see the note ad 20.4.18 *equi phalera*. The vignette of the arrogant senator is strongly reminiscent of Amm.'s first Roman digression, 14.6.16 *quidam per ampla spatia urbis subversasque silices sine periculi metu properantes equos velut publicos signatis quod dicitur calcibus agitant* (q.v.). One wonders if Amm.'s indignation at the sight of the anonymous senator has inspired this satirical vignette.

multa post se nunc usque trahit agmina servulorum Cf. again the more detailed description in 14.6.17 of the retinue of the ostentatious rich. Expressions like *nunc usque* referring to the author's own time are not very frequent. Cf. e.g. 14.2.13 *Paleas..., ubi conduntur nunc usque commeatus distribui militibus...assueti*, 22.11.10 *qui deviare a religione compulsi pertulere cruciabiles poenas ad usque gloriosam mortem intemerata fide progressi et nunc martyres appellantur*, 27.7.5 *quorum memoriam apud Mediolanum colentes nunc usque Christiani locum, ubi sepulti sunt, Ad Innocentes appellant* and 31.7.16 *ut indicant nunc usque albentes ossibus campi*. New names of cities, regions or nations are often introduced by *nunc*, e. g. 14.8.7 *Commagena, nunc Euphratensis*, 22.15.2 *Arabas, quos Saracenos nunc appellamus*. Most comparisons between past and present are found in the Roman digressions (14.6 and 28.4), for which see Den Hengst, 2007. Needless to say, the comparisons are invariably to the disadvantage of the present.

per novum quoddam insigne curiosius spectari affectans The senator and Duilius resemble each other in their craving for attention from the public. Duilius, however, had earned their admiration in return for his victory over the Carthaginians, whereas the senator had only his criminal record to be proud of. *Insigne* probably does not refer to any outward sign of the senator's merits, but to his deeds: 'some unheard of achievement'. The note ad 25.9.7 *nullis ante actae vitae insignibus...cognitum* stated that parallels for this use of *insigne* are difficult to find. This may well be one. The translation of Marié "ambitionnant d'être avidement contemplé pour une particularité inédite" is puzzling. For *affectare*, clearly in a deprecatory sense, see ad 25.4.18 *popularitatis*, and for *curiosius* 'with passionate interest', see the note ad 20.11.9.

ut Duilium accipimus veterem Amm. likes to introduce his historical parallels in this way; cf. 25.4.17 *Marci illius similis Caesaris, in quem id accipimus dictum*, 31.13.13 *simili clade Caesarem accipimus Decium...equi lapsu prostratum*. C. Duilius, consul in 260 B.C. (Broughton, 1951, 205), celebrated in 259 Rome's first naval triumph after his victory over the Carthaginians in the battle off Mylae, in which the Romans used boarding-bridges (for which see Wallinga, 1956). To commemorate his victory a column, adorned with the beaks (*rostra*) of captured ships, was erected in the Forum Romanum (Quint. *Inst.* 1.7.12, Plin. *Nat.* 34.20). Parts of the inscriptions on this column are still extant (*ILS* 55 and 56). We read there i.a. about the custom to which Amm. alludes here: *H]uic per[miss]um est u[t ab e]pulis do[mum cum tibici]ne e[t f]unali rediret* (*ILS* 55). Note, however, the difference between *permissum est* (cf. Liv. *per.* 17.2 *ei perpetuus quoque honos habitus est, ut revertenti a cena tibicine canente funale praeferretur*) and Amm.'s *sibi sumpsisse*. Among the authors from whom Amm. heard the version of the story he transmits (*accipimus*), may have been Cicero, whose wording (*sumpserat, licentiae*) is close to that of Amm.: *C. Duellium M. f. qui Poenos classe primus vicerat, redeuntem a cena senem saepe videbam puer; delectabatur cereo funali et tibicine, quae sibi nullo exemplo privatus sumpserat; tantum licentiae dabat gloria* (*Sen.* 44; cf. Powell, who reads *devicerat*, ad loc.). Note, however, that in Amm.'s version the *funalis cereus* is missing. See further Flor. 1.18.10, V. Max. 3.6.4 (on Amm. and Valerius Maximus there is now Rohrbacher, 2005) and *Vir. ill.* 38.4.

tibicine lenius praecinente The adverb *lenius* is probably an embellishment added by Amm. himself. It means 'melodiously', 'sweetly', as in Gel. 4.13.1 *ischia cum maxime doleant, tum, si modulis lenibus tibicen incinat, minui dolores* ("when gouty pains in the hips are most severe, they are relieved if a flute-player plays soothing measures", tr. Rolfe). The infix *prae-* obviously has local meaning: 'while leading the way', as in 24.6.10 *velut pedis anapaesti praecinentibus modulis lenius procede-*

bant, q.v. Elsewhere *praecinere* means to 'predict', as in 25.3.19 *fide fatidica praecinente*.

Sub hoc tamen Aproniano ita iugiter copia necessariorum exuberavit, ut nulla saltim levia murmura super inopia victui congruentium orerentur In transitional phrases like this *tamen* has become a purely connective particle. See the note ad 20.5.1. For *iugiter* 'continually', 'all the time'; see the note ad 20.3.1 *intermicabant iugiter* and for this use of *saltim* (*saltem*) 'not even –', 'however –' cf. 20.5.9 *ne turbandae dispositioni consultae tempus saltem breve concederetur*, 21.16.6 *ut nec... saltem suspicione tenus posset redargui*. *Inopia victui congruentium* is a somewhat tortured phrase for 'a food shortage'. Amm.'s usual expression for 'provisions' is *victu(i) congrua* (16.4.4, 16.12.12, 24.5.12 [q.v.], 29.5.15, 31.5.1).

3.6

As *praefectus urbi* Apronianus was not only the supreme judicial authority in Rome (see above, ad § 1 *inter curarum*), but he was also responsible for the water and food supply of the city (cf. Chastagnol, 1960, 296–334; Jones 695–705). Regarding the supply of pork during his prefecture we are informed by a regulation of Julian directed at him, *Cod. Theod.* 14.4.3, and by edicts of Apronianus himself, recorded in *CIL* 6.1770 and 6.1771. See for this in the first place Sirks, 1991, 361–387, esp. 370–375. As is noted ad 21.12.24 *hoc administrante*, Amm. more often (cf. further 27.3.3, 27.3.11, 29.6.17–19) refers to a prefect's tenure which was not afflicted by disorders related to the food supply.

quod assidue Romae contingit A list of instances is given in 26.3.1 *inter curarum*.

CHAPTER 4

Introduction

After the report on Roman affairs, the author returns in this chapter to Nicaea, where Valentinian had been hailed as Augustus. He now had to appoint an imperial partner, and in a meeting of the *consistorium* he tries to elicit the name of a candidate from those present. This only results in a shrewd remark by the *magister equitum* Dagalaifus, which showed that he had read the new emperor's intention, viz. to have the staff put forward the name of his brother Valens. Having waited a few weeks he finally appointed Valens, with the agreement of everyone.

When all seemed well the two brothers fell severely ill, and after regaining their health they ordered a criminal investigation into the causes of their illness, which they ascribed to magic. Their objective was to blacken the reputation of Julian's friends. However, this affair came to nothing.

The final part of the chapter consists of a brief catalogue of raids and invasions by barbarian tribes in several regions of the Roman empire. In fact, it is a survey of all attacks during the entire reign of the Pannonian brothers (364–378), but within the context the suggestion is that the trouble began in early 364.

At in Bithynia Valentinianus princeps, ut praediximus, declaratus The particle *at* does not occur frequently in the *Res Gestae*: 33 times, once every seventeen pages in Seyfarth's Teubneriana. In thirteen cases it denotes the change to another situation, in a different part of the empire. Not surprisingly, seven of these cases can be found in Books 26–31, for which the author explicitly announces such changes in 26.5.15. With *ut praediximus* Amm. returns to the narrative about Valentinian, which he had interrupted by describing Apronianus' prefecture of Rome in ch. 3. For some unknown reason Amm. does not mention Nicaea, *quae in Bithynia mater est urbium* (26.1.3, q.v.), but the region (see the note on Bithynia ad 22.8.16) as the place where Valentinian's inauguration, described in 26.2.3, took place.

4.1

Shortly after Valentinian had been acclaimed emperor at Nicaea, some embassies arrived, which brought to him, presumably still in Nicaea, golden crowns originally intended for Jovian: Ὅτι Βαλεντινιανοῦ ἀνάρρησις ἐν Νικαίᾳ τῆς Βιθυνίας γίγνεται, πρεσβεῖαί τε, ὅσαι συνεπεφοιτήκεσαν ἐπὶ τοῦτον (Jovian) τοὺς χρυσοῦς ἔχουσαι στεφάνους, πρὸς ἐκεῖνον (Valentinian) ἀνεφέροντο. According to Eunapius, to whom we owe this information (*fr.* 31), Valentinian was rather curt in his reaction, which may be explained by the fact that the emperor was in a hurry (cf. *dato in perendinum diem signo proficiscendi* in the section under discussion and *itineribus citis* in § 2): καὶ πρὸς πάσας ἀπεφαίνετο μὲν οὐδέν, ἐπιτρέχων ῥᾳδίως οὑτωσὶ καὶ συντόμως, ἐπηγγέλλετο δὲ ἅπασιν ὡς ποιήσων αὐτίκα μάλα ("to all he revealed nothing, so quickly and summarily did he deal with them, and he declared to all that he would very quickly take action", tr. Blockley). Blockley ad loc. gives a different explanation: "Eunapius, in drawing the implicit and rather unfair contrast between the terse Valentinian and the expansive Julian in the same situation (*fr.* 24), reveals the cultivated easterner's distaste for the brusque Illyrian soldier".

in perendinum diem This is the only instance in Amm. of this rare chronological phrase ('for the day after tomorrow'). Valentinian was eager to continue the march to Constantinople, but he obviously found it necessary to consult his staff first, before the army left Nicaea. Valentinian was inaugurated as emperor on 25 February (see the note *quia nullo* ad 26.1.5), so the departure from Nicaea took place on 27 February.

convocatis primoribus The term *primores* occurs only in two other places in the *Res Gestae*: 16.12.69, where it denotes those fighting in the front rank (see the note ad loc.) and 29.5.22, where the leaders of the archers are mentioned. Only in the present text does it refer to the general staff. The *primores* were probably the same men who had agreed on the election of Valentinian; see for them the note *Valentinianus nulla discordante* ad 26.1.5. It seems reasonable to assume that the meeting took place on the day between Valentinian's inauguration and the departure to Constantinople, the 26th of February. Lenski, 2002, 23, however, suggests that the assembly was held on the same day as Valentinian's proclamation.

quasi tota consilia quam sibi placentia secuturus Basically, *quasi* is a comparative particle: 15.5.18 *Constantio icto quasi fulmine fati* (when he heard about Silvanus' usurpation), 20.5.2 Julian rouses his soldiers *quasi lituis verbis*, 24.6.11 during a battle Julian *quasi conturmalis strenuus properabat*. In 14.11.14 *Lucillianus quasi domesticorum comes* it denotes a function, in 31.10.4 *haec quasi vicini cernentes* a geographical fact, in both cases as an explanation of what is reported. Often the comparison has an ironical intention: 15.3.9 (an official) *quasi pinnis elatus ad comitatum principis advolavit*, 28.4.21 the only friendships appreciated by Roman aristocrats are those between gamblers, *quasi gloriosis quaesitae sudoribus*. As to future actions, Julian may have seriously expected that merely to begin the siege of Pirisabora would be enough: *quasi sola formidine oppidanos a propugnandi studio summoturus* (24.2.9); when Valentinian and Valens *quasi mox separandi* (26.5.1), viz. to go to their own half of the empire, proceeded to divide up the *comites*, there can be no doubt about the reality of this intention. However, when the Armenian king Pap was invited to come to Valens' court *quasi futurus particeps* (30.1.4) in discussions about the state of the eastern empire, this was a treacherous pretext. In other cases too there is a distinct suggestion of hypocrisy. In all probability, the present text is also an instance of make-believe.

In his bilingual edition Seyfarth followed Valesius' emendation *tuta*, but he now returns to V. One would like to learn what *tota consilia* means, but if it happens to be something like "consigli dati da tutti" (Viansino), it is entirely unconvincing. See the relevant discussion in the note ad 25.4.11 *praetenturae*. Wirz, 1877, 628 refers to Sal. *Cat.* 41.2 *tuta consilia* and Liv. 22.38.13 *apparebat tuta celeribus consiliis praepositurum*. See for *quam* as shorthand for *magis* or *potius quam* Szantyr 593–594 and the note ad 20.7.18 *multis acceptis*.

percunctabatur, quemnam ad imperii consortium oporteret assumi "Mit *quisnam*...fragt man dringender als mit *quis*" (Kühner-Stegmann 2.656). This is true for classical Latin, but in Amm. *-nam* has lost much of its urgency. It does not occur very frequently either: only a dozen times. In some cases it is perhaps possible to detect some pressing doubt, e.g. 15.5.10 *ambigens diu, quidnam id esset*, but in 21.13.3 *speculaturos, quonam rex erumperet* this is far less likely, and in 18.10.3 *percontando, cuiusnam coniux esset* even improbable. It is therefore prudent not to attach too much importance to *-nam* in the present text.

The phrase *imperii consortium* is quite rare, in fact Tac. *Ann.* 14.11.1, where Agrippina is being accused posthumously of having aspired to *consortium imperii*, seems the only direct parallel. See Koestermann ad loc. Cf. also HA *V* 3.8 *sibique consortem fecit* (Marcus Aurelius gave Lucius Verus a share in his imperial power), *Cl* 10.6 *de fratre Quintillo, quem consortem habere volebat imperii*, Aur. Vict. *Caes.* 28.1 *sumpto in consortio Philippo filio*. These parallels show that in the present text more than a position as Caesar is meant. Such a position was given to Julian by Constantius II, who said to his soldiers: *in Caesaris adhibere potestatem exopto* (15.8.8), and after the usurpation at Paris, *gesta omnia Constantius improbans Caesaris potestatem sufficere Iuliano censebat* (20.9.6). Claudius Mamertinus corrected this in the panegyric which he addressed to Julian: *Quid enim aliud a te consortis imperatoris alienavit animum nisi gloriae tuae splendor?*, 'What else than your brilliant glory alienated your imperial colleague from you?' (*Pan.* 3.3.1). See on Valentinian's decision to appoint his imperial partner not as a Caesar, but as an Augustus the note ad 26.4.3 *universorum*.

silentibusque cunctis Dagalaifus tunc equestris militiae rector respondit fidentius See for Dagalaifus the note ad 26.1.6 *Dagalaifo*. Amm. prefers an unofficial formulation of his function to his official title *magister equitum* (used in 26.1.6). When other members of the staff were too embarrassed to react, he had the guts (*fidenter*) to delineate the alternative solutions in the barest terms. See for *fidenter* denoting a justified confidence or courage the note ad 20.8.19 *et super*.

"Si tuos amas", inquit, "imperator optime, habes fratrem, si rem publicam, quaere quem vestigas" Lindenbrog is rightly praised by Valesius for having detected the parallel in Cedrenus: εἰ τοὺς σοὺς φιλεῖς, ἔχεις ἀδελφόν· εἰ δὲ τὴν πολιτείαν, σκόπησον ὅτῳ ἂν τὴν ἁλουργίδα περιβαλεῖς (*Chron.* 1.541). The setting is different (it takes place at Constantinople, Dagalaifus is a senator and, strictly speaking, no specific meeting of an official body is mentioned), but the similarity is striking, and this applies even more to the version of Leo Gramm., *Chron.* p. 97 Bonn, which is identical, with the addition of κράτιστε αὐτοκράτορ after φιλεῖς. These parallels can only mean that Amm. has borrowed the pithy anecdote from a written source which (in)directly also reached the Byzantine historians. Bleckmann, 1995, 89–91 considers it likely that the story goes back to a common source, i.e., according to him, the annals of Nicomachus Flavianus; however, see for this identification the sceptical remarks of Burgess, 2005, 168–169. One is at a loss to explain why Seyfarth in his Teubneriana retracts his former acceptance of Lindenbrog's obvious correction *vestias*. The absence of the imperial robe is indeed remarkable. Perhaps *publicam* caused the loss of any explicit mention of *purpura*.

We do not know how the members of the *consistorium* or the staff addressed the emperor during the meetings. It is, however, beyond doubt that *imperator optime* is very polite: it is used three times in

Nazarius' panegyric of Constantine (*Pan.* 4.4.5, 4.9.5, 4.16.4) and twice by Ausonius in his thanksgiving speech (*Grat. act.* 2.6, 6.29).

Without referring to Cedrenus and Leo Grammaticus, Paschoud, 1992, 74 regards the anecdote as straining the imagination. No general would have dared to be so insolent. Bleckmann, 1995, 90 agrees. In its 'literal' form it is indeed "incroyable" (Paschoud), but if one interprets the words ascribed to Dagalaifus as a summary or the gist of a far more subtly worded contribution to the discussion or, to use Paschoud's own words, as "toute une discussion en une formule prégnante", the anecdote is less 'unbelievable'. However, the most important aspect of the anecdote is that Valentinian did not get what he wanted, viz. the consistorium's proposal to nominate Valens.

quo dicto asperatus ille, sed tacitus et occultans, quae cogitabat The only other instance of *asperatus* in Amm. is 30.2.7 *ultraque solitum asperatus* (about Sapor). It is a strong word to denote anger. Valentinian was furious, because all members of the staff had seen what he was up to. As will become clear in the description of his reign, he fell easily victim to fits of rage (cf. 30.8.2 *in acerbitatem naturae calore propensior*, his death of apoplexy in a fit of anger in 30.6.3 and Amm.'s general reflections in 27.7.4; see also Tomlin, 1973, 36–38), but as yet he was not in a position to allow himself any demonstration of this weakness. Since there are no indications that Dagalaifus' career was ever in jeopardy, *quae cogitabat* can only mean Valentinian's purpose to appoint his brother.

Nicomediam itineribus citis ingressus. See the notes ad 22.8.5 *Hylam* for Nicomedia and 20.8.21 *venit* for various phrases to express speedy marches. Valentinian certainly was in a hurry, covering the sixty odd km from Nicea to Nicomedia in two days, arriving there on February 28.

kalendis Martiis Valentem fratrem stabulo suo cum tribunatus dignitate praefecit Valens' name is here mentioned for the first time in the *Res Gestae*. On March 1, 364 he was appointed *tribunus stabuli*, for which function see the note ad 20.4.3 *stabuli tunc tribunus*. The career of Valens before he became emperor was insignificant; according to Zos. 4.4.1 he had led an inactive life and according to Amm. 31.14.5 he was *nec bellicis nec liberalibus studiis eruditus*. His only military post seems to have been that of *protector domesticus*; Socr. *HE* 4.1.8 (ἐν τοῖς οἰκείοις τοῦ βασιλέως ἐστρατεύετο); Joh. Antioch. *fr.* 179 Müller = 271 Roberto. According to Thdt. *HE* 4.6.3 Valens, staying at Pannonia at the time, was sent for when his brother became emperor (ὁ δὲ τὸν ἀδελφὸν ἐκ Πανονίας μεταπεμψάμενος), but, as Lenski, 2002, 52–53 argues, Theodoret must be wrong, since Valens' appointment to the function of *tribunus stabuli* was too soon after Valentinian's proclamation five days earlier for him to have made the journey from his home in Pannonia to Nicomedia. It is therefore better to assume that Valens was already serving in the army as *protector domesticus* when his brother appointed him tribune of the imperial stable on March 1, 364. Woods, 1998, 474–477, according to whom Valens was instrumental to Valentinian's election as emperor, thinks that Valens was already *tribunus stabuli* and had been appointed as such by Jovian; this fanciful conjecture is rightly rejected by Lenski, 2002a, 257 and 274.

With *suo* Amm. probably wants to express Valens' specific task in the immediate proximity of the emperor, "while he waited in the wings to be appointed" (Lenski, 2002, 23).

4.3 *indeque cum venisset Constantinopolim* It may have taken some three days to travel the 90 km from Nicomedia to Constantinople. Assuming that the emperor left Nicomedia the day after Valens' nomination as *tribunus stabuli*, i.e. on 2 March, he probably arrived at the eastern capital on the evening of 4 March or on 5 March. The march from Nicomedia to Constantinople was no doubt also made *itineribus citis*, for Socr. *HE* 4.1.4 (cf. Soz. *HE* 6.6.9) writes that Valentinian arrived forthwith in Constantinople: εὐθὺς ἐπὶ τὴν Κωνσταντινούπολιν γενόμενος. During Valentinian's stay there, envoys from Antioch (and no doubt from other cities as well) brought him a crown: Lib. *Ep.* 1186.1.

multa secum ipse diu volvens et magnitudine urgentium negotiorum iam se superari considerans The first five words are a conflation of two phrases in Sallust: *multa ipse secum volvens* (*Cat.* 32.1) and *secum ipse diu volvens* (*Jug.* 113.1). Pointing to these two texts, Wirz, 1877, 635–636 rightly concludes that V's *divolvens* should definitely be emended to *diu volvens*.

From time to time Amm. mentions the many tasks, problems and worries which an emperor has to cope with. See the note ad 25.10.4 *Moratum*, in which it is shown that, according to Amm., Julian proved equal to all difficulties, in contrast to Jovian, who wellnigh collapsed under the load. Valentinian also feels hard-pressed and is already losing his grip on the huge problems (*magnitudine negotiorum*). His anxiety is *mutatis mutandis* comparable to the worries of Constantius

II: *id...urgente malorum impendentium mole confessus est proximis succumbere tot necessitatibus tamque crebris unum se, quod numquam fecerat, aperte demonstrans* (15.8.2).

nihil morandum ratus Note the close connection with the immediately preceding words *iam se superari considerans*: Valentinian thinks that he is on the brink of collapsing, so that any further delay in providing himself with an imperial partner must be avoided.

quintum kalendas Apriles productum eundem Valentem in suburbanum The sources give several dates for Valens' *dies imperii*. According to Socr. *HE* 4.1.4 Valens was made emperor thirty days after Valentinian's *dies imperii* (προσλαμβάνει τὸν ἀδελφὸν Οὐάλεντα, μετὰ τριάκοντα ἡμέρας τῆς αὐτοῦ ἀνακηρύξεως), i.e. on 28 March. *Consul. Constant.* a. 364 has 29 March (*Ipso anno levatus est Valens Aug. Constantinopolim in miliario VII in tribunali a fratre suo Valentiniano die IIII k. Apr.*); see also *Chron. Pasch.* a. 364 (29 March). *Art. pass.* 70 reports that Valens was made emperor thirty-two days after Valentinian's *dies imperii*, i.e. at 30 March. According to Malalas, *Chron.* 13.338, Valens was made emperor on 1 April. In general the date of 28 March is preferred; e.g. Tomlin, 1973, 57; Kienast, 1996², 330; Lenski, 2002, 24. There seems to have been an explicit Christian aspect to the reign of the new emperors from the beginning, because 28 March in 364 was Palm Sunday and Valens' *dies imperii* will therefore have coincided with the festivities for the beginning of the Holy Week, such as a procession into Constantinople; McLynn, 2004, 251; Hunt, 2007, 76; T.D. Barnes, *CR* 55 (2005) 639 remarks that the choice of Palm Sunday to raise Valens to the purple was "surely a deliberate choice and a central aspect of the occasion, though one which Ammianus Marcellinus naturally declined to mention." See for *producere*, "to bring before a public meeting" (OLD s.v. 2a), the note ad 21.5.7 *producturo*, and for *eundem*, 'just mentioned', the note ad 15.5.19 *Ursicinum* and Szantyr 188.

The last time Amm. mentions his personal presence in the East is 25.10.1 *Antiochiam venimus*. Does this mean that he remained there when Jovian travelled on? See the final part of the note ad 25.10.1 *His hoc modo* for some reflections. The present text betrays perhaps that he did not witness the ceremony on March 28, 364 himself. Otherwise he would, presumably, at least have mentioned the name of the suburban place, seven miles south-west from Constantinople astride the Via Egnatia: Ἕβδομον, in Latin *Septimum*. Nearby was a large field, called Κάμπος, on which stood a *tribunal*, mentioned in

Consul. Constant. a. 364.3: *in tribunali.* Henricus Valesius refers to a passage in Claudian's *In Rufinum*, book 2: *planities vicina* (349) and *sublime tribunal* (382). In his sixth panegyric speech, which according to Leppin-Portmann, 1998, 113 should be dated to late 364, Themistius says that Valens had embellished the place where he had been invested with the imperial purple κρηπῖδι καὶ βήματι καὶ ἀνδριάσι (*Or.* 6. 83 a). Hadrianus Valesius has a long and learned historical note on the place, which became the standard site where Eastern and, later, Byzantine emperors were proclaimed. See further Dagron, 1974, 87–88, 100–102 and Mango, 1985.

universorum sententiis concinentibus – nec enim audebat quisquam refragari – Augustum pronuntiavit See for the metaphoric use of *concinere* to express unanimity the note ad 20.4.1 *perfugae*. Note the contrast to the unanimous choice of Valentinian: *nulla discordante sententia* (26.1.5, q.v.) is not negatively explained, as in the present parenthesis. With *enim* Amm. appeals to the healthy judgment of his readers: what else could you expect? Curiously, there is only one precise parallel for the present instance of *pronuntiare*: *epit.* 42.16 (Julianus) *a militibus Gallicanis Augustus pronuntiatur.*

Valentinian's choice of his brother was prompted by several considerations. He avoided any problems which might have arisen, had he chosen as a candidate either one of the former *palatini* of Constantius II or one of Julian's former supporters. Moreover, in that case it would have been vital to define the precise position of the emperor's brother. However, there were personal reasons too. Amm. reports that Valentinian was attached to his brother: *in Augustum collegium fratrem Valentem ascivit ut germanitate, ita concordia sibi iunctissimum* (30.7.4), and privileged him among his relatives: *necessitudinibus suis nihil indulgens, quas aut in otio reprimebat aut mediocriter honoravit absque fratre, quem temporis compulsus angustiis in amplitudinis suae societatem assumpsit* (30.9.2). According to Zos. 4.1.2 Valentinian had considered other candidates before finally choosing Valens: ἐκ πάντων ὧν ἔλαβε κατὰ νοῦν Οὐάλεντα τὸν ἀδελφὸν αἱρεῖται, πιστότατον αὐτῷ πάντων ἡγησάμενος ἔσεσθαι. The decision to appoint him as an Augustus and not as a Caesar may have been inspired by Constantius' experiences with both Gallus and Julian. See also Symmachus' praise of Valentinian's decision in *Or.* 1.12, which begins with these words: *Hinc plerique principum, quos secundos creaverant, quasi aemulos mox timebant.* See further Heering, 1927, 16–18, Pabst, 1989, 208–214, Kolb, 2001, 104–105, Lenski, 2002, 24–25. In 27.6.16 Amm. remarks that in appointing both Valens and

Gratian as Augusti, Valentinian deviates from tradition. Only Marcus Aurelius *Verum adoptivum fratrem absque diminutione aliqua auctoritatis imperatoriae socium fecit.* Valesius ad loc. tries to explain away this somewhat dubious remark.

See further on Valens' investiture *epit.* 45.4, Rufin. *hist.* 11.2, Socr. *HE* 4.1.4, Soz. *HE* 6.6.9, Thdt. *HE* 4.6.3, Philost. *HE* 8.8, Theoph. p. 54 De Boor. According to Them. *Or.* 6. 82 d Valens considered Constantinople as μητέρα...τῆς βασιλείας.

decoreque imperatorii cultus ornatum et tempora diademate redimitum in eodem vehiculo secum reduxit Cf. 16.6.1 *decora cultus imperatorii.* Here the *diadema* is specifically singled out from the imperial attire. At the time of Julian's 'usurpation' in Paris the soldiers regarded it as the imperial distinction par excellence: *iubebatur diadema proferre* (20.4.17, q.v.). See also the notes ad 21.1.4 *ambitioso* and 26.2.3 *mox principali.* The privilege of joining the emperor in his carriage is dealt with in the note ad 22.9.13 *ascitumque.* Valentinian took his brother back (*re-*) to the city.

participem quidem legitimum potestatis, sed in modum apparitoris morigerum, ut progrediens aperiet textus In the majority of Amm.'s fourteen instances of *legitimus* it is used to describe an emperor or Caesar, denoted as *princeps*: 15.8.21, 19.12.17, 25.5.3, 26.9.10, 27.5.1, 30.10.1. In 30.10.5 Valentinian jr. is *imperator legitime declaratus,* a phrase which is the starting point of the argumentation in Szidat, 1989. Since the adj. *morigerus* is normally used to characterize people, it is better not to take it with *modum.* It should rather be regarded as a direct qualification of Valens, emphasizing his obedient demeanour towards his brother. The use of *apparitor,* 'servant', 'attendant', has a 'previous history' in the *Res Gestae.* When Constantius summoned the Caesar Gallus, he reminded him of the fact that Diocletian and his colleague had been obeyed by their Caesars *ut apparitores* (14.11.10). Julian himself wrote to Constantius that, having been appointed Caesar, he behaved *ut apparitor fidus* (20.8.6, q.v.); cf. also 16.7.3. Thus the present text expresses that Valens, in spite of his official position as an Augustus, behaved as a compliant Caesar. Other phrases denoting Valens' real position are 26.5.1 *honore specie tenus adiunctus,* 26.5.4 *ut potiori placuerat* and 27.4.1 *ut consulto placuerat fratri, cuius regebatur arbitrio.* Understandably, Symmachus in his speech on Valentinian's *quinquennalia* in 369 had to be less blunt. He called Valens *Augustum pari iure* (*Or.* 1.11). According to Tritle, 1994, 142, "Ammianus' characterization of Valens' 'submissiveness' to his brother should not be accepted too readily, as it appears to reflect Ammianus' anti-Valensian bias".

For *progrediens aperiet textus* cf. *quos* ('new commotions') *docebit orationis progrediens textus* (18.4.7, q.v.). TLL X 2.1774.22–25 mentions Cic. *Inv.* 2.10 and *Rep.* 1.62 as the only other instances of this use of *progredi.*

4.4 *Quibus ita nullo interturbante perfectis* Nobody caused any trouble by interfering in the proceedings which led to the investiture of Valens. Amm. mentions this as a clear contrast to the events which he will report next: problems at the court (§4) and reverses in several regions of the empire (§5–6). The comparatively rare verb *interturbare* occurs once in Plautus and once in Terentius and after that in late Latin. The present phrase also occurs in 18.2.5 and 31.12.12.

constricti rapidis febribus imperatores ambo diu spe vivendi firmata This differs from Zos. 4.1.1, who only mentions that Valentinian fell ill somewhere on his journey from Nicaea to Constantinople: νόσου δὲ κατὰ τὴν ὁδὸν ἐνσκηψάσης αὐτῷ. Paschoud n. 106 regards Zosimus' entire version of Valentinian's journey from Nicaea as "contradictoire", adding "la version d'Ammien est évidemment préférable". See for *constrictus*, 'in the shackles of', the note ad 20.4.19 *cura constrictus*. Amm. does not specify the illness in question, but restricts himself to the symptom 'serious fever'. Cf. for *rapida febris* Gel. 12.5.2, 18.10.2, 20.1.26. To which part of the sentence does *diu* belong? Blomgren 116 argues that it should be combined with *constricti*, adding a German translation of the first six words of the lemma: "wurden beide Kaiser von einem langwierigen hitzigen Fieber befallen". Rolfe, Seyfarth and Hamilton agree. Rightly, it seems, especially when compared with various solutions of the Italian translators and Marié's deplorable "un solide espoir de longévité", which does not suit the context at all. See for the 'final' position of *diu* 15.5.10 *haerens et ambigens diu*, 16.7.3 *Caesarem obsessum apud Senonas diu*, 17.12.10 *signum exspectantibus diu*, 23.5.11 *perseverantium diu*. Thus the seriousness of the illness is emphasized by three words, *constricti, rapidis, diu*: they were very ill. The phrase *spe vivendi firmata* is the positive counterpart of *exigua ac prope nulla vivendi spe* (20.8.21) and *spe deinceps vivendi absumpta* (25.3.9).

ut erant in inquirendis rebus graviores quam in componendis This is Amm.'s first truly negative remark about the new regime. See for the 'causal' function of *ut* Szantyr 635 and OLD s.v. 21 ("inasmuch as"). Both *inquirere* and *componere* are here used as a juridical t.t. See for the latter Heumann-Seckel s.v. 5: "einen Streit durch Vergleich schlichten, beilegen", and the note ad 21.16.18 *in qua*. Like Constantius in his church policy, the Pannonian brothers exerted their influence in criminal investigations rather than in reconciliations. Translators tend to be imprecise in their handling of *graviores*. Marié's "ils montraient plus d'autorité" (viz. for the wrong priority) clearly is a step in the right direction (cf. OLD s.v. *gravis* 13), but may sound too positive; 'let themselves be felt more strongly' is perhaps preferable. The entire phrase conveys an ominous anticipation of Amm.'s reports on ugly lawsuits in 28.1, 29.1 and 2.

suspectas morborum causas investigandas acerrime Ursatio officiorum magistro, Delmatae crudo, et Viventio Sisciano quaestori tunc commiserunt This tallies with Zos. 4.1.1 ὑποψία μὲν αὐτὸν εἰσῄει ψευδὴς ὡς ἔκ τινος γοητείας ὑπὸ τῶν Ἰουλιανοῦ φίλων αὐτῷ σκευωρηθείσης νοσοίη, κατηγορίαι δὲ κατά τινων ἦσαν ἐπιφανῶν. Ursatius (*PLRE* I, Ursacius 3) is mentioned only here and in 26.5.7, where it is said that he offended Alamannic envoys by his rudeness: *tractatique asperius ab Ursatio tunc magistro officiorum iracundo quodam et saevo*; see also the note ad 26.1.5 *Valentinianus*. Viventius (*PLRE* I, Viventius) hailed from Siscia in Pannonia (see Talbert, 2000, 21 D4). In 27.3.11 Amm. calls him *ex quaesitore palatii*; for his function, which was created by Constantine, see Vera, 1986; Loguercio, 1986; Harries, 1988. The main task of this official was to draft imperial constitutions. As *praefectus urbis Romae* in 365–367 he was unable to suppress the riots between supporters of Damasus and Ursinus over the episcopacy of Rome (27.3.11–12; cf. Chastagnol, 1962, 170–171). He was *praefectus praetorio Galliarum* in 368–371. He died before 384; see Symm. *rel.* 30.3 *Viventius clarissimae et illustris memoriae vir*. In 27.3.11 he is called *integer et prudens Pannonius* by Amm., who obviously found this phrase less suitable for the present context.

ut loquebatur pertinax rumor, invidiam cientes Iuliani memoriae principis amicisque eius tamquam clandestinis praestigiis laesi See Sabbah 397–398 on the historian's handling of rumours as a "moyen de l'insinuation" and on the degrees of uncertainty. The latter subject is also discussed in the note ad 25.6.6 *audierant*. Among the various qualifications of rumours *pertinax*, which also occurs in 16.6.3 and 30.5.7, suggests at least an element of truth in the idea that the real objectives of the investigations were to besmirch Julian's memory and to attack his friends. It is improbable that with *tamquam* the author wants to give vent to any general scepticism concerning the potential evil which magic might cause. Fear for the effects of magic was widespread. In the present text *tamquam* primarily expresses that Valentinian and Valens themselves ascribed their illness to magic. See for a discussion of this function of *tamquam* the relevant note ad 24.4.11 and Szantyr 597 (section c). In 14.11.23 and 17.5.11 Seyfarth prints *praestrigiis*, but here and in 28.4.22 *praestigiis*, a form caused by dissimilation; see Leumann 292. Only in the present case is the 'trickery' of the magical kind; cf. for this Lact. *Inst.* 4.15.4 *praestrigiis magicis*, 5.3.11 *de fraude ac praestrigiis artis magicae*.

Without paying particular attention to the disease Zosimus devotes his entire chapter 4.2 to the two emperors' general hostility towards Julian's friends. Zosimus refers especially to Valentinian's hatred of Julian's teacher and friend Maximus of Ephesus (*PLRE* I, Maximus 21; mentioned by Amm. in 22.7.3, q.v., 25.3.23 and 29.1.42), who, he says in 4.2.2, had accused Valentinian of impiety during Julian's reign. See on this Paschoud's n. 108 and Banchich, 1998, 372–373.

sed hoc evanuit facile ne verbo quidem tenus insidiarum indicio ullo reperto
In contrast to Amm.'s 'triumphant' words Zosimus' version is matter of fact: ἃς ἀγχινοίᾳ τε καὶ φρονήσει διέλυεν ὁ τῆς αὐλῆς ὕπαρχος· ἦν δὲ ἔτι Σαλούστιος 'these accusations were rebutted with cleverness and prudence by Salutius, who still was *praefectus praetorio*' (4.1.1). If Zosimus' information is correct here, it is tempting to assume that Amm. deliberately omitted the fact that at this early stage of the new regime a stalwart of Julian's reign was still quite influential. The verb *evanescere* denotes the complete disappearance of a person or thing (TLL V 2.995.74: "i.q. in nihilum redigi"); cf. *evanuit pertinax calumniandi propositum* (22.6.4), *sed evanuit cogitatum hoc casu* (30.1.12). In the present text the addition of *facile* is remarkable, since this adverb usually qualifies something which is being actively done. It seems to suggest that precisely those who carried out the investigation lent a hand to remove it from the agenda. The curious phrase *ne verbo quidem tenus* could be taken literally: no rumour or statement by anyone became available, but perhaps it functions 'proverbially' to emphasize the complete absence of any evidence whatsoever. There are, however, no parallels for this. For *reperire* as t.t. in criminal investigation cf. *cumque nihil quaestiones repperirent assiduae* (29.3.7), *ne vestigia quidem ulla delatorum reperta sunt criminum* (29.3.8).

In these sections barbarian raids and invasions in no less than seven 4.5–6 regions of the Roman Empire are listed. Tomlin, 1979 shows that at least some of these attacks did not take place in the early period of the Pannonian emperors' reign. In fact, as he points out, the list is "an outline of the complicated military history" between 364 and 378. *Hoc tempore* (§5), according to him, denotes the entire period, not merely (the early part of) the year 364. Unfortunately, his gallant effort to defend the author had already been undermined by Sabbah 274–276, who pointed to a similarity with a passage near the end of Libanius' *Funeral Oration over Julian*. Having mentioned a notable worsening of the situation in various sections of contemporary society after Julian's death, Libanius then continues with: Σκύθαι δὲ καὶ Σαυρομάται καὶ Κελτοὶ καὶ πᾶν ὅσον βάρβαρον ἠγάπα ζῆν ἐν σπονδαῖς, αὖθις τὰ ξίφη θήξαντες ἐπιστρατεύουσι, διαπλέουσιν, ἀπειλοῦσι, δρῶσι, διώκοντες αἱροῦσι, διωκόμενοι κρατοῦσιν, ὥσπερ οἰκέται πονηροὶ δεσπότου τετελευτηκότος ὀρφανοῖς ἐπανιστάμενοι ("Goths, Sarmatians and Celts, and every barbarian tribe that thought itself lucky to live in peace, have whetted their swords once again: they are descending upon us again, crossing the rivers, threatening, acting: if they pursue us, they take us captive, if pursued, they beat us, like wicked slaves who, on their master's death, rise up against his orphaned children", *Or.* 18.290, tr. Norman). Sabbah concludes: "la logique du chapitre d'Ammien apparaît liée à son intention polémique". Even if one judges that he is reasoning along too straight lines and if one also reflects that after all the division of chapters is due to Valesius and not to Amm., nevertheless, considering the entire context, 'at this time' can only refer to the early part of 364, indicating that precursors of the events of later years were already visible. Most of the problems with peoples crossing the Roman borders go back to at least the reigns of Constantius II and Julian, and are not specific to the reigns of Valentinian I and Valens.

It should be noted that Zosimus also reports that, as soon as the news of Julian's death reached them, barbarian tribes prepared an invasion of Roman territory: Τῶν δὲ ὑπὲρ τὸν Ῥῆνον βαρβάρων, ἕως μὲν Ἰουλιανὸς περιῆν, τὸ Ῥωμαίων ὄνομα δεδιότων, ἀγαπώντων τε εἰ μηδεὶς αὐτοῖς κατὰ χώραν μένουσιν ἐνοχλοίη, τῆς τούτου τελευτῆς ἀγγελθείσης ἀπανέστησαν αὐτίκα τῶν οἰκείων ἠθῶν καὶ πρὸς τὸν κατὰ Ῥωμαίων παρεσκευάζοντο πόλεμον ('While Julian lived the barbarians beyond the Rhine feared the Roman name and were contented if nobody bothered them on their own territory, but as soon as they heard of Julian's death they immediately left their normal abode and prepared for a war with the Romans', 4.3.4). Cf. also

30.7.5 *Gallias petit Alamannicis patentes excursibus reviviscentibus erectius cognito principis Iuliani interitu, quem post Constantem solum omnium formidabant.* See for the chronological problems involved the notes ad 26.5.7 *Alamanni* and 26.5.8 *Et circa.*

4.5 *velut per universum orbem Romanum bellicum canentibus bucinis excitae gentes saevissimae limites sibi proximos persultabant* 'Throughout the entire Roman Empire' (see for *orbem Romanum* the notes ad 21.13.13 *aequitate*, 25.9.7 *Tu hoc loco*) is hyperbolic in view of what follows. Spain, Italy, Egypt, Greece and Asia Minor are not concerned. As to *velut...bellicum canentibus bucinis*, the transferred use of such expressions occurs already in Cic. *Phil.* 7.3 *bellicum me cecinisse dicunt.* Cf. also Amm. 16.8.11 *inflabant itidem has malorum civilium bucinas potentes* and the attempts at emendation of 16.12.1. Although Roman individuals and troops are quite often guilty of *saevitia*, "foreigners bear the brunt" (Seager 55), especially foreign tribes. See for *persultare* denoting the overrunning of Roman territory by barbarians the note ad 20.5.4 *cladis immensitas* and cf. TLL X 1.1774 "speciatim de gentibus, exercitibus, qui insultando, populando sim. regiones hostium persultant". Evidently, it has a ring of arrogant provocation.

Gallias Raetiasque simul Alamanni populabantur After Constantius' and Julian's campaigns against various Alamannic tribes and the settlements they had concluded with their kings (14.10, 15.4.1, 16.11–12.66, 17.1–3, 17.8–10, 18.2, 20.10, 21.3–4) the Alamans renewed their invasions into Roman territory. The Alamannic crossing of the Rhine frontier demanded serious military attention from the Romans and Valentinian himself; 26.5.12–14, 27.1–2, 27.10, 28.2.1–10, 28.5.8–15, 29.4, 30.3. For the Alamans see the literature cited ad 21.3.1 *Alamannos*, to which can be added Fuchs, 1997 and Drinkwater, 2007. For Raetia see the note ad 21.3.1 *confines Raetiis.*

Sarmatae Pannonias et Quadi Constantius had campaigned against the Sarmatians and Quadi (17.12–13, q.v., 19.11) but they invaded Roman territory again during the reigns of Valentinian and Valens; see 29.6.15–16. For the Sarmatians and Quadi see the note ad 22.5.5 *o Marcomanni*; add to the literature Sulimirski, 1970. For Pannonia see the notes ad 21.5.13 *in Pannonias* and ad 21.10.6 *Pannoniae secundae.* Add to the literature Hajnóczi, 1995. Note that *Quadi* is trisyllabic, as in 30.5.11 *opportune Quados.*

Picti Saxonesque et Scotti et Attacotti Britannos aerumnis vexavere continuis The elder Theodosius, father of Theodosius I, put a stop to the raids of these peoples; 27.8, 28.3; Tomlin, 1974. Problems with the Scots and Picts – see on them the note ad 20.1.1 – go back to the year 360. For the Attacotti, who are probably Irish people who migrated to Britain, see Rance, 2001. For the Saxons in the context of fourth-century British history, see Bartholomew, 1984. According to Tomlin, 1979 this passage is a preview of the barbarian invasions about which Amm. reports later in his narrative, in particular 27.8 and 28.3; cf., however, Bartholomew, 1984, 174–177.

aerumnis vexavere continuis See for Amm.'s notable predilection for *aerumna* the note ad 20.7.7 *post aerumnas.*

Austoriani Mauricaeque aliae gentes Africam solito acrius incursabant For the problems in Africa see 27.9.1–2, 28.6, 29.5. Cf. e.g. Romanelli, 1959, 565–594; Demandt, 1968; Drijvers 2007.

Thracias et diripiebant praedatorii globi Gothorum The copula *et* has puzzled philologists. Petschenig, 1893, 495 deleted it as "unerklärlich". Bickel, *Göttingische gelehrte Anzeigen* 180 (1918) 295 disagrees; he interprets *et* as expressing the fact that the Gothic invasion of Thrace, which posed a threat to Constantinople itself, is a climax in the list. Blomgren 97 adheres to this view, which is not convincing, if only for the reason that the real climax is reached with the Persian king's claim to Armenia in §6. Heraeus had hypothesized another solution, viz. the loss of *Moesias* after *et.* Clark's idea is similar, but he prints a lacuna. This seems the best solution, although Bickel's rejection of *Moesias* because of 27.4.12, where *Mysia*, i.e. Moesia inferior, is mentioned as a part of Thrace, is too 'technical' for the present, less precise, survey. In any case, it is likely that after the use of *et* and *-que* in the preceding clauses here, too, *et* linked some geographic entity to *Thracias*; see for the plural the note ad 20.8.1 *Thracias* and for *praedatorii globi* the relevant note ad 14.6.16. The adj. occurs already in classical Latin, but is not frequently used. Amm. has seven instances.

For Amm.'s account of the wars with the Goths, see 27.5, 31.3–4, 31.6–9, 31.11–13, 31.15–16.8. On the Gothic wars see e.g. Lenski, 2002, chaps. 3 and 7. This is the second time that Amm. mentions the Goths; the first time was in 22.7.8 *Gothos saepe fallaces et perfidos*; see the note ad loc. Amm. has a digression on Thrace in 27.4.

4.6 *Persarum rex manus Armeniis iniectabat eos in suam dicionem ex integro vocare vi nimia properans* The Persian king is Sapor II; see for him the note ad 20.6.1 *truculentus rex*. There is a note on Armenia ad 20.11.1 *Armeniae*.

The full story of Sapor's conquest of Armenia can be found in 27.12; cf. 27.12.1 *iniectabat Armeniae manum*. See further the note ad 25.7.12 *quibus exitiale*. TLL V 1.962.4–61 registers the verbs which are combined with *ad, in* and *sub dicionem*. Amm.'s instances are *concedere* (28.3.7), *redigere* (21.10.3, 26.8.3), *trahere* (23.6.55), *transire* (25.8.14, 27.4.11), *venire* (15.11.5, 18.6.15, 20.11.7); *vocare* in the present text is the only example in the TLL list. As to *vi nimia*, in 27.12.2 it is said that the king at first proceeded *per artes fallendo diversas*, followed in 27.12.3 by *per exquisitas periuriisque mixtas illecebras*. See the note ad 25.7.4 *ferro properans*, for *properare* with the meaning 'to be eager'.

sed iniuste, causando, quod post Ioviani excessum, cum quo foedera firmarat et pacem, nihil obstare debebit, quo minus ea recuperaret, quae antea ad maiores suos pertinuisse monstrabat In contrast to 25.5.3 *eoque causante*, which concerns an excuse for not accepting a task, *causari* in the present text means "to plead as a reason" (OLD s.v. 2), as in 28.6.4 *Huius necem ulcisci…causantes* and Suet. *Cal.* 23.3 *causatus…, quod hic ingressum se turbatius mare non esset secutus*.

The clause about Armenia in the peace settlement of 363 was not clear cut. In 25.7.12 (q.v.) Amm. had mentioned that it included the condition that the Romans would not come to the help of Arsaces, should he need military assistance against the Persians; this would give Sapor a free hand to invade Armenia. If the Romans were indeed to abstain from military intervention in Armenia in case the Persians invaded that kingdom, Amm.'s *iniuste* is hard to explain. It could be an emotional comment, as in the case of his remark in 25.7.12 *quibus exitiale aliud accessit et impium* (q.v.); Seager, 1996, 277. However, considering Amm.'s remark in 27.12.1 that Sapor breached the agreement of 363 by invading Armenia (*Rex vero Persidis…calcata fide sub Ioviano pactorum iniectabat Armeniae manum, ut eam velut placitorum abolita firmitate dicioni iungeret suae*), it seems that the Persian invasion of Armenia was not in keeping with the settlement of 363. Also, Valens' conflict with Sapor over the status of Armenia (30.2) does not suggest that the Romans had given the Persians a free hand in Armenia. It is more likely, as Blockley, 1992, 29 suggests, that "the Romans had agreed to Armenian independence and not to a free hand in the country";

see also Chrysos, 1993, 182–183, who thinks it inconceivable that Jovian would have agreed not to intervene militarily in case of a Persian invasion of Armenia, and argues that the 363 agreement included a clause with respect to the neutral status of Armenia. According to Seager, 1996, 284 the agreement did not include a clause prohibiting Persia from invading Armenia; as a consequence it felt free to do so. In the opinion of Rome the agreement did not state that Persia was explicitly allowed to invade Armenia; it was therefore prohibited from doing so. Winter/Dignas, 2001, 159 argue that the 363 agreement had "einen provisorischen Charakter" and that its clauses should not be considered as "definitiv". From the Roman perspective the term *iniuste* in this passage seems therefore a correct qualification of Sapor's interference in Armenia, and the information Amm. provides in 25.7.12 should be regarded as the author's own emotional comment. Only in 387 was the conflict over Armenia terminated by a division of the kingdom; the western part came under Roman influence and the – larger – eastern part under that of the Sasanians. See Blockley, 1992, 42–43; Winter/Dignas, 2001, 113–114; Mazza, 2003.

With 'after Jovian's decease' Sapor probably argues that the death of the emperor with whom he had concluded the treaty, did not vitiate its legitimacy and his rights. Cf. for (*non*) *obstare quo minus* Cic. *N.D.* 1.95 *Quid autem obstat quo minus sit beatus?*, Sal. *Cat.* 51.37 *neque illis superbia obstabat, quo minus aliena instituta…imitarentur.* See for the indic. fut. instead of the imperfect subjunctive in *quod*-clauses the note ad 20.8.10 *quod.* Other examples are 25.2.7 *oportebit* and 25.4.12 *desistent.* The king considered Armenia to be a Persian hereditary possession: this is an example of *pertinere ad*, "to belong by right to" (OLD s.v. 6, see also TLL X 1.1800.66 sqq.). The other example in Amm. is *admonitus iurisdictionem eo die ad alterum pertinere* (22.7.2). The indicative *monstrabat* could be interpreted as a note by the author, but is perhaps rather an instance of the indicative in subordinate clauses of oratio obliqua; see the note ad 20.4.12 *ubi potestas.*

CHAPTER 5

Introduction

The first part of this chapter is devoted to the implementation of a momentous decision of Valentinian, which as such is not explained by the author and not even explicitly mentioned, viz. to divide the Empire in a western and eastern zone, each under the guidance of an emperor. At Naissus the generals and their troops were divided between Valentinian and Valens, and shortly afterwards the same happened at Sirmium with the court personnel. After this the emperors travelled to their respective residences, Milan and Constantinople. However, Valentinian found himself confronted with Alamannic invasions into Gaul, which required his personal presence, and in the East Procopius' revolt began.

Ammianus postpones dealing fully with the campaigns against the Alamanni, but this postponement is only announced at the very end of the chapter. This implies considerable problems of a chronological nature, which can only be solved satisfactorily by taking the facts mentioned at the beginning of Book 27 into account. Procopius' usurpation will be dealt with extensively in chapters 6–9 of Book 26, but sections 9–13 of the present chapter provide a foretaste, with the description of Valentinian's anxious reaction to the bad, but at first very vague, news from the East. He is inclined to make his way to the scene of the disaster himself, but his advisers manage to persuade him that his presence in Gaul is indispensable. Ammianus' lively report of Valentinian's anxiety and indecision has no comparable parallel in other sources. From a narrative point of view it is cleverly contrived: precisely Valentinian's lack of exact information and the fears resulting from this make the reader look forward to what the historian will report on this potentially dangerous development.

Acta igitur tranquillius hieme This is a very surprising statement. The phrase *hiemem agere* occurs ten times in the *Res Gestae*, but here the 'winter' merely consists of the months of April and May, since Valens had received the status of Augustus on March 28, 364 (26.4.3) and the brothers were at Naissus on June 2; see for this the note below on *percursis Thraciis*.

5.1

Moreover, they had suffered from a long illness (26.4.4) and had subsequently launched a criminal investigation into its causes. Then there were the barbarian invasions, mentioned immediately before in 26.4.5–6. These facts do not harmonize with "Der Winter verging ruhig", in Seyfarth's correct rendering. See for *igitur* the notes ad 25.1.18 *pulsis igitur* and 26.7.1 *Igitur*, and for the use of the comparative the notes ad 20.4.17 *sublatius* and 23.6.53 *quos*.

concordissimi principes, unus nuncupatione praelatus, alter honori specie tenus adiunctus The brothers lived "in perfect harmony" (Rolfe): with the rare superlative of *concors* Amm. reflects one of the ideological catchwords of the Pannonians' rule. Cf. the opening words of an inscription to commemorate the construction, under Valentinian and Valens, of a camp near the Danube *disponente Equitio* (i.e. the *comes rei militaris*, later *magister militum per Illyricum* of 26.5.3 and 11): *imperatores Caesares dd. nn. Valentinianus [e]t Valens fratres concordissimi victores maximi ac triumphatores [s]emperque Augusti* (*ILS* 762). See also Them. *Or.* 6.75 d: the subjects of the Roman empire are not protected by soldiers, but βασιλεῦσιν ἀρτίοιν ἀμφοῖν, ὁλοκλήροιν δυοῖν καθάπερ ἑνί, 'by emperors who are both perfect and form a complete pair as if it was one person', and Symm. *Or.* 1.13: if sun and moon shared power in the same way as Valentinian and Valens, *isdem curriculis utrumque sidus emergeret*. So the perfect harmony is founded on complete parity. Precisely on this point Amm. deviates from the official picture. He does not dispute the brothers' evident unanimity, but ascribes it to personal feelings (cf. 30.7.4 *in Augustum collegium fratrem Valentem ascivit ut germanitate, ita concordia sibi iunctissimum*) and Valens' loyal subordination. In the present text this is expressed in a phrase which can only have been borrowed from Ausonius' speech of thanksgiving (see the note ad 26.2.2 *cumque*); in ch. 3 he rejoices that he was *cum clarissimo collega meo honore coniunctus, nuncupatione praelatus* (Auson. *Grat. act.* 3.13). This phrase, which expresses the relative positions of the two consuls, obviously struck Amm. as excellently adaptable to those of the two emperors. It also shows that the emendation *honori*, proposed by Mommsen and Petschenig, 1893, 495, is wrong. The latter's argument is that *honori* = *principatui*. However, even if one could find a parallel for this, which is unlikely, Valens was not 'associated' with the emperorship, but with his brother: 'in honour only outwardly coupled'. Note the subtle change of *coniunctus* to *adiunctus*: as 'emperor' Valens is only 'added to' or 'associated with' his brother. The juxtaposition of two ablativi sing. (*honore specie*) does not cause any confusion, because the second one forms a unity with *tenus*. The phrase *specie tenus* occurs six times in Amm.

Lenski, 2000b, 32 aptly refers to another text of Ausonius, which is highly relevant to the ideological harmony of the Pannonian ruling family, viz. the *Versus Paschales*, a poem of 31 dactylic hexameters, section IV in Green's edition. The middle part of this poem, vss. 6–23, consists of a prayer, in which the specific acts and the unity of the Trinity are developed. In the third and final part the heavenly Trinity is mirrored on earth by the Pannonian dynasty, in which Valentinian *numine partitur regnum neque dividit unum* (27). See for detailed, but divergent interpretations Charlet, 1984, 259–273 and Green's introduction and commentary on the poem.

percursis Thraciis Naissum advenerunt Thanks to the subscriptions of some constitutions in the Theodosian Code we are reasonably well informed about the movements of Valentinian and Valens in Thrace on their way to Naissus in 364. They must have left Constantinople after April 17, since *Cod. Theod.* 13.1.5 was issued in the eastern capital on that day. The first known stop on the via Egnatia was Adrianople, modern Edirne. Their presence there on May 13 is firmly attested by *Cod. Theod.* 8.4.8, 11.7.9 and 12.1.58, but in all probability they arrived in this city earlier, for, as Pergami, 1993, 29 rightly argues, there is no reason not to accept the date of the ms. in *Cod. Theod.* 7.1.5 *dat. III Kal. Mai.* (i.e. 29 April) *Hadrianop(oli)*. Next the emperors visited Philippopolis (for which town, modern Plovdiv, see the notes ad 21.10.3 *vicinae* and 22.2.2 *emensa*), for *Cod. Theod.* 15.1.11 must have been issued there on May 25 – in view of the fact that Philippopolis is mentioned in *Cod. Theod.* 8.5.19 and 6.37.1 as the place where these laws were issued, the word *Philippis* of the ms. in 15.1.11 of the Theodosian Code should be emended to *Philippopoli*. From Philippopolis the journey went to Serdica, modern Sofia (cf. the note ad 21.10.3 *vicinae*), as is shown by *Cod. Theod.* 12.12.3: *dat. III Kal. Iun.* (i.e. 30 May) *Serdicae*. On their way they passed a halt on the cursus publicus at Bona Mansio (mentioned also in *Itin. Burdig.* 567), some 40 miles from Philippopolis – this can be deduced from the subscription of *Cod. Theod.* 7.4.12 *dat. VI Kal. Iun.* ([ms. Ian.], i.e. 27 May) *Bonamansione* (cf. *Cod. Theod.* 14.2.1). Naissus was reached on 2 June at the latest, as is clear from *Cod. Theod.* 14.3.3 *dat. IIII Non. Iun. Naissi* (cf. Pergami, 1993, 48–49). Their presence there until at least June 13 is attested by *Cod. Theod.* 11.1.8 *dat. Id. Iun. Naissi* (but see the next note). There is a note on Naissus, modern Nish, ad 21.10.5 *imperator* (add to the literature cited there Petrović, 1993 and Duval, 1997, 131–132).

in suburbano, quod appellatum Mediana a civitate tertio lapide disparatur
Excavations at Mediana near Naissus, the suburb (see for *suburbanum* the note ad 20.4.12 *in suburbanis*) which is mentioned by Procop. *Aed.* 4.4.3 (p. 123.2 Haury-Wirth) among the forts provided with new walls by Justinian, have brought to light several villas, which could have been used by the imperial brothers as residences during their stay (cf. Gušić, 1993 and Duval, 1997, 131–132). In one of them an altar was discovered, dedicated by the *tribunus Batavorum* Aurelius Ampelius to Iuppiter Optimus Maximus, for which see Mirković, 1982.

The suggestion of Gothofredus to take *Med.* in *Cod. Theod.* 15.1.13 *dat. XIII Kal. Iul. Med.* as an abbreviation of *Medianae* (and not, as is mostly done in similar cases, of *Mediolani*) is attractive (it is accepted by e.g. Tomlin, 1973, 76 n. 24 and Barnes 248 with n. 5, but rejected by Pergami, 1993, 62, who conjectures *Naissi* instead of *Med.*). If correct, it would provide a terminus post quem, viz. 19 June (and not 13 June, for which see the previous note), for the departure of the emperors from the vicinity of Naissus to Sirmium, where their presence is attested on 5 July (*Consult.* 9.6; cf. the note ad §4 *Et post haec*). An analogous case is found in *Cod. Theod.* 1.6.2 *dat. VI Id. Iun.* (i.e. 8 June) *Med.* If in this constitution *Med.* is also to be taken as *Med(ianae)*, one has to assume that Valentinian and Valens stayed alternately in Mediana and Naissus, which is perfectly conceivable in view of the distance of only three miles between Naissus and its suburb. However, one has to admit that in view of the notoriously corrupt state of the subscriptions in the Theodosian Code certainty cannot be reached. To interpret *Med.* as *Medianae* in *Cod. Theod.* 8.5.17, 10.1.8, 11.30.32 and 11.36.15, for instance, is of no help. Cf. Pergami, 1993, 7–8 and 16.

It is an idiosyncrasy of Amm. to indicate distances with the verb *disparare* in combination with the abl. *lapide* (15.11.18, 18.7.9, 24.1.3, 25.7.8, 29.6.7, 30.10.4), *mansione* (16.12.70) and *miliario* (21.9.6, 24.2.3) and an ordinal.

quasi mox separandi partiti sunt comites In contrast to Clark and Seyfarth, Marié prints V's *separando*. Her rendering "dans la perspective de leur prochaine séparation" does not clarify the syntactical status of *separando*. It could be taken as an abl. gerundii which is the equivalent of the part. praes.; see for this the note ad 20.4.22 *diu tacendo*. This does, however, not result in a convincing interpretation. As a part. fut. pass., Gelenius' *separandi* combines far better with *mox* and offers no great difficulties. In order to interpret it correctly, one has to start by explaining *partiti sunt*. The verb occurs for the first time as a deponens in Cic. *Inv.* 1.32 *qui ita partitur*; the oldest example of passive *partiri* is Andr. *trag.* 3–4 *praeda per participes aequiter partita est*. See for further information TLL X 1.521.82–522.38. Of Amm.'s three instances *partiti munera* (20.11.22) and *partiti* (26.5.3, with or without Harmon's addition *sunt*) are certainly deponential and passive respectively. Regarding the present text both are possible: if *partiti sunt* is passive, *comites* is subject; these were divided 'in order to be (physically) separated'. Regarded as deponential, it has *principes* as subject and *comites* as direct object. This seems preferable, since it is the intended separation of the brothers which leads to the partition. In this case *separandi* should be interpreted as reflexive (see for this the note ad 25.8.9 *properare*): they were going to take leave of one another, which they did at Sirmium, as is clear from §4. As to *comites*, from the catalogue of names in the next sections it appears that both *magistri equitum* and *comites rei militaris* must be meant (cf. the notes ad 20.4.18 *postea comes* and 21.9.5 *rem curabat*).

Iovinus…dudum promotus a Iuliano per Gallias magister armorum See for *promovere*, 'to advance to a higher rank' the note ad 20.2.5 *immodico*, and for its construction with double accusative the note ad 20.9.5 *praefectum*. Iovinus (*PLRE* I, Iovinus 6), who appears a number of times in the *Res Gestae*, had risen to prominence as a general under Julian. See the relevant notes ad 21.8.3, his first appearance, and 25.8.11, where Amm., as in the present text, uses for his function of *magister equitum per Gallias* the unofficial designation *armorum magister per Gallias* (more examples of this habit in the note ad loc.). Before obtaining this post he had been *magister equitum per Illyricum* (22.3.1). Although initially the emperor Jovian had wanted to replace Iovinus (25.8.11), he later confirmed him in his job in Gaul (25.10.9). Under Valentinian the general operated successfully against the Alamanni and as a reward was made consul in 367 (27.2.10). For the function of magister equitum see the notes ad 20.1.2 *ire* and 25.8.9 *oblatis*.

It is sometimes assumed that Valentinian promoted Iovinus from *magister equitum per Gallias* to *magister equitum praesentalis* at Naissus or Mediana, and that under Valentinian, since the emperor himself was campaigning in Gaul, the function of *magister equitum per Gallias* ceased to exist (so e.g. Ensslin, 1931, 146 and Tomlin, 1973, 474–

478). However, as Demandt, 1970, 589 argues, there are insufficient grounds for this assumption and "es ist schwer einzusehen, weshalb Ammian die 'Beförderung' Iovinus' verschwiegen haben sollte, wenn sie stattgefunden hätte".

et Dagalaifus, quem militiae rectorem provexerat Iovianus For 'to advance to a higher rank' Amm. also uses *provehere* (see OLD s.v. 4b). Like *promovere* it is constructed with a double acc. in 14.7.9, 16.6.2 and 20.9.5. That it was Jovian who promoted Dagalaifus to *militiae rector*, i.e. *magister equitum* (cf. 26.1.6 *Dagalaifo magistro equitum*, q.v., and 26.4.1 *Dagalaifus tunc equestris militiae rector*) is stated only here. As in the case of Iovinus (see the previous note), scholars disagree about the precise function of Dagalaifus under Valentinian. The authors of the *PLRE*, for example, apparently following Ensslin, 1931, 123, think that "he was probably *magister peditum* rather than *magister equitum*". However, there is no direct evidence for this, and the only argument cited is rather weak: "since his successor was apparently Severus 10". It is better to assume, with Demandt, 1970, 591–592, that Dagalaifus kept the post of *magister equitum* which he already occupied under Jovian.

in orientem vero secuturus Valentem ordinatus est Victor ipse quoque iudicio principis ante dicti provectus By mentioning the fact that Iovinus, the *magister armorum* of Gaul, was assigned to the staff of Valentinian (*Valentiniano...Iovinus evenit*), Amm. had implicitly indicated which part of the empire each of the imperial brothers was to obtain. Here he becomes explicit: Valens was to rule the eastern part – as in 26.3.1 (q.v.), *oriens* must refer to the East in general. Zos. 4.3.1 gives a more detailed overview of the division: ἐδόκει τῷ Οὐαλεντινιανῷ, διελομένῳ πρὸς τὸν ἀδελφὸν τὴν ἀρχήν, ἐπιτρέψαι μὲν αὐτῷ τὴν ἑῴαν ἄχρις Αἰγύπτου καὶ Βιθυνίας καὶ Θρᾴκης, λαβόντα δὲ τὰς ἐν Ἰλλυριοῖς πόλεις αὐτὸν εἰς Ἰταλίαν διαβῆναι καὶ τὰς ἐν ταύτῃ πόλεις ἔχειν ὑφ' ἑαυτῷ μετὰ τῶν ὑπὲρ τὰς Ἄλπεις ἐθνῶν Ἰβηρίας τε καὶ τῆς Βρεττανικῆς νήσου καὶ Λιβύης ἁπάσης ('Having shared the empire with Valens, Valentinian deemed it most prudent to place under his brother's care the East as far as Egypt, Bithynia, and Thrace, and to take charge of Illyricum himself. From thence he designed to proceed to Italy, and to retain in his own possession all the cities there and the provinces beyond the Alps, with Spain, Britain, and Africa'). See on this passage, apart from Paschoud n. 110, Lenski, 2002, 26–27, who in nn. 79 and 80 cites other sources with details about the division, viz. Ruf. Fest. 13, Greg. Nyss. *Eun.* 1.143, Iord. *Rom.* 307, Philost. *HE* 8.8, Rufin. *hist.*

11.2, Soz. *HE* 6.6.9, Symm. *Or.* 1.14, 3.11, Synes. *Ep.* 66, Them. *Or.* 6.74 b, 6.82a–b, 7.92 a, Thdt. *HE* 4.6.3, 5.1.2, Theoph. p. 54 De Boor and Zon. 13.15. For the theme of "divisio regni" in general see Pabst, 1986.

Valentinian's decision to take the West must have surprised his contemporaries. As has often been observed (e.g. by Alföldi, 1952, 50 and Tomlin, 1973, 63), in the course of the fourth century the centre of gravity of the empire had continually been pushed eastwards. It is not altogether clear why Valentinian reversed this trend and left the eastern part of the empire, and with it the dangers which threatened Rome from the side of Goths and Persians, in the care of his brother. The reason Socrates in *HE* 4.2.1 gives for his choice is rather vague: εἷλκε γὰρ αὐτὸν (sc. Valentinian) ἐκεῖ (i.e. to the West) ἡ τῶν πραγμάτων φροντίς ('the care for the problems there'). Symmachus, in his speech before the emperor in 369, is more concrete: the western part of the empire threatened to collapse (*sedem quodammodo in ea parte posuisti, qua totius rei publicae ruina vergebat, Or.* 1.15), and one had to put one's shoulder to the wheel (*maximeque hoc in Galliis delegisti, quod hic non licet otiari, Or.* 1.16). In view of the war against the Alamans this sounds reasonable enough (cf. Leo Gramm. *Chron.* p. 97 Bonn: ἐθνῶν τινων ἐπανάστασιν ἐνταῦθα μαθών). One should keep in mind, however, that Symmachus did not write his speech in 364, when Valentinian had to make his choice, but a couple of years later, after several campaigning seasons in Gaul. As to 30.7.5 (in the necrology of Valentinian), taken by some scholars, e.g. Raimondi, 2001, 91, as further evidence of the "esplicita connessione tra scelta dell'Occidente e lotta contro i barbari", this passage is not as unambiguous as is sometimes thought. In the first place, the text is not without problems. Seyfarth, assuming a lacuna after *urbes* (which is itself a conjecture for V's *turbines*), reads: *igitur Valentinianus post periculorum molestias plures, dum esset privatus, emensas imperitare exorsus, ut arces prope flumina sitas et urbes...et Gallias petit Alamannicis patentes excursibus reviviscentibus erectius cognito principis Iuliani interitu.* In the second place, even if one accepts, as does Raimondi, Heraeus' conjecture *muniret* and reads *ut arces prope flumina sitas et urbes muniret* (Sabbah, following Petschenig, prints *viseret*), it is questionable whether this should be taken to mean that in the summer of 364 Valentinian chose the West in order to fortify strongholds and cities in Gaul. Granted, the emperor went to Gaul, but that was not before October 365 (see for this date the note ad 26.5.8 *Et circa*). To sum up, the sources for Valentinian's decision to choose the West are not as explicit as one would wish, and leave room for speculation, e.g. of Piganiol, 1972², 171: "Il avait sans doute observé le dangereux esprit séparatiste des Gaules".

As to Victor, it is disputed by whom this prominent general had been promoted, in other words, whether the *princ(eps) ante dict(us)* of the present text was Jovian (so e.g. *PLRE* I, Victor 4 and Paschoud n. 36) or Julian (so e.g. Demandt, 1970, 581-584). For the following reasons the latter interpretation seems preferable. In the first place, it tallies with the testimony of Zosimus, who in 3.13.3 says that Julian, before he invaded Persia, made Victor *magister peditum* (τοῦ μὲν πεζοῦ Βίκτορα στρατηγὸν καταστησάμενος). Secondly, it is more natural to assume that in this section Amm. refers twice to Julian (*promotus a Iuliano, iudicio principis ante dicti provectus*) and twice to Jovian (*quem...provexerat Iovianus, a Ioviano...promotus*) rather than thrice to Jovian and only once to Julian (put differently, abab is to be preferred to abbb). Under Valens Victor served as *magister equitum* (references in the *PLRE* and ad 24.1.2 *agmina*). See for *ordinare*, 'to appoint', the note ad 20.9.8 *Anatolium*.

cui iunctus est Arintheus According to Philost. *HE* 8.8 Arintheus (*PLRE* I, Arinthaeus) had supported Valentinian's election as emperor (cf. the note ad 26.1.5 *Valentinianus*). As in 25.5.2 *Arintheus et Victor et e palatio Constanti residui* (q.v.) and 27.5.9 *missique vicissim Victor et Arintheus*, Amm. mentions him and his colleague Victor in the same breath. While Victor operated under Valens as *magister equitum*, Arintheus served as *magister peditum* (27.5.4).

Lupicinus enim, pridie a Ioviano pari modo promotus, magister equitum partes tuebatur eoas In the editions of Henricus Valesius and Wagner-Erfurdt the second comma is not put after *promotus*, but after *equitum*, which is correct from a syntactical point of view, but neglects the rhythmical pattern which caused modern authors to print it after *promotus*. Amm.'s use of the 'empathic' particle *enim* is comparable to 25.3.9 (q.v.), where the seriously wounded Julian learns that the place where the battle took place was called 'Phrygia': *hic enim obiturum se praescripta audierat sorte*. As in the present text, the reader had not yet received the relevant information. The particle indicates the viewpoint of the Agens of *iunctus est* (sc. Valens), who did not need to appoint a *magister equitum per orientem*, and could be paraphrased as 'for the reader should know (that)'. For Lupicinus (*PLRE* I, Lupicinus 6, cf. the note ad 20.1.2 *ire...Lupícinum*), the promotion by Jovian had meant a comeback, since under Julian he had fallen into disfavour (cf. the note ad 20.9.9 *timebatur Lupicinus*). He supported Valens against Procopius (26.8.4, 9.1).

As in 21.2.4 *a quo iam pridie occulte desciverat* (see the note ad loc.), V's *pridie* is defended by Fletcher, 1937, 395 and 1939, 242 as a late Latin synonym of *pridem*. Clark prints *pridem* in both cases, Fontaine follows suit in 21.2.4, but in the present text Marié prefers *pridie*. However, the scepticism expressed in TLL X 2.1232.34–53, which is prompted by the confusion of *pridem* and *pridie* in the manuscript tradition of various authors, seems justified. Clark is probably right.

See for Amm.'s great predilection for the predominantly poetic adj. *eous* Hagendahl, 1921, 71 and for his use of *partes* and *tractus* with the meaning 'provinces', 'regions' the notes ad 18.4.2 *ad tuendas partes* and 20.3.1 *per eoos tractus*.

tunc et Equitius Illyriciano praeponitur exercitui, nondum magister, sed comes   5.3
A tribune of the *schola prima Scutariorum*, Equitius (*PLRE* I, Equitius 2) had been one of the candidates for the imperial throne after Jovian's death (26.1.4, q.v.). Not deemed worthy of the emperorship, he subsequently supported the nomination of his fellow Pannonian Valentinian (26.1.6) and apparently owed his promotion to the post of *comes* (*rei militaris per Illyricum*) to this. He was soon to be advanced to a still higher function: *eodem Equitio aucto magisterii dignitate*, 26.5.11 (q.v.).

et Serenianus olim sacramento digressus recinctus est ut Pannonius sociatusque Valenti domesticorum praefuit scholae See the note ad 20.2.5 *digredi* and the final section of the note ad 25.5.4 *erat enim* for various phrases denoting retirement. The note ad 25.1.9 *abiecti* contains examples of phrases for 'releasing from military service'. In classical Latin *recingere* means "to ungird", "to unfasten" (OLD s.v.), but in the present text and in 31.12.1, Amm.'s only other instance, it obviously means that the retired person receives the official *cingulum*, 'belt', anew. Perhaps it is a Grecism. Wagner refers to Them. *Or.* 18.224 a, where Themistius praises the emperor Theodosius I, who did not permit the speaker's mind to become weary and inactive, but awakens it and οἷόν τινα εὐδόκιμον στρατιώτην ἀνακαλεῖται καὶ ἀναζώννυσιν, 'as if it was a soldier in good repute, recalls and regirds it'. See on the *cingulum* as a symbol of an official function the anecdote in 22.10.5 and the notes ad loc.

Like the Pannonian Equitius, who was characterized as *asper et subagrestis* in 26.1.4, Serenianus (*PLRE* I, Serenianus 2), another fellow countryman of the imperial brothers, had been described unfavourably in his first appearance in the *Res Gestae*: *Serenianus ex duce, cuius ignavia populatam in Phoenice Celsein ante rettulimus, pulsatae maiestatis imperii reus iure postulatus ac lege* (14.7.7). In 26.10.5 Amm. calls him *crudelem ut Phalarim*. As such he and the emperor whom he was to serve as *comes domesticorum* (see for this post the notes ad 20.4.21 *tribuni* and 25.5.4 *domesticorum*) were a good match (26.10.2). Why and when Serenianus had gone into the retirement from which he was recalled by Valentinian and Valens, is not known (Amm.'s *olim* here is rather vague), but we may safely assume that under Julian he had been *persona non grata*: in 354 Serenianus had, together with the *notarius* Pentadius and the *agens in rebus* Apodemius, assisted at the execution of Julian's half-brother Gallus (14.11.23) – Pentadius (*PLRE* I, Pentadius 2) and Apodemius (*PLRE* I, Apodemius 1) were tried for this by the tribunal at Chalcedon in 361 (22.3.5, 11).

With the exception of 20.8.11 *sociamur*, in Amm.'s eleven instances of *sociare* the verb is combined with a dat.; cf. Szantyr 115 and see the note ad 16.11.6 *Barbationi sociatus*: as in the present text, the phrase refers to a subordinate position.

quibus ita digestis Amm. uses *digerere* with various meanings. The present instance is comparable to *negotio plene digesto* (17.8.3, q.v.) and *reque digesta* (21.11.2, q.v.), where the verb means 'to settle', 'to organize'. As is foreshadowed at the end of §2 (*partiti sunt comites*), in sections 2 and 3 Amm. reports about the division of the military commanders: Valentinian took the *magistri militum* Iovinus and Dagalaifus and the *comes rei militaris* Equitius, while Valens got three *magistri militum*, Victor, Arintheus and Lupicinus, plus the *comes domesticorum* Serenianus. In sections 4 (*diviso palatio*) and 5 (*et orientem...Germanianus*) a few words are spent on the division of the civil officials.

Amm.'s report is not exhaustive. For instance, Serenianus' counterpart, the western *comes domesticorum*, is omitted – presumably this was Severus (*PLRE* I, Severus 10), mentioned as such in 27.8.2 and *Cod. Theod.* 6.24.2–3. Neither does Amm. comment upon the arrangement he reports. In this he differs from Zosimus, who in 4.2.3 i. a. says that the imperial brothers felt inclined to remove the provincial governors from their stations and replace them with others, and that in general they dismissed all those who had been appointed by Julian (οἱ μὲν οὖν ἄλλοι πάντες, ὅσοι παρὰ Ἰουλιανοῦ διοικήσεις ἐθνῶν ἢ ἀρχὰς ἄλλας ἔτυχον ἐπιτετραμμένοι, παρελύοντο τούτων). Zosimus adds that even the *praefectus praetorio* 'Saloustios' (*PLRE* I, Secundus 3; cf.

the note ad 26.2.1 *propinquante*) fell victim to this purge ('Εν οἷς καὶ Σαλούστιος ὁ τῆς αὐλῆς ὕπαρχος ἦν, 4.2.4) and that only Arintheus and Victor were allowed to keep their generalship (μόνου δὲ Ἀρινθαίου καὶ Βίκτορος αἷς εἶχον πρότερον στρατιωτικαῖς ἐπιμεινάντων ἡγεμονίαις, ibid.). At first sight this seems a valuable addition to Amm.'s account.

However, Zosimus is surely mistaken when he states that of the military commanders only Arintheus and Victor remained, since Iovinus and Dagalaifus, who were as prominent under Julian as the other two generals, also continued to serve under the new regime. Furthermore, it would seem that Zosimus is also wrong with respect to the dismissal at this time of Salutius Secundus ('Saloustios'). So, rightly, e.g. Paschoud n. 109 and Raimondi, 2001, 74–75; for a different view see e.g. *PLRE* I, Secundus 3, Elliott, 1983, 141–143 and Marié n. 24. It is true that we find a parallel in Malalas *Chron.* 13.338 εὐθέως διεδέξατο ("dismissed", tr. Jeffreys e.a.) τὸν αὐτὸν ἔπαρχον Σαλούστιον, cf. *Chron. Pasch.* a. 364, but, in the first place, Zosimus' and Malalas' words flatly contradict Amm., who states in 26.5.5 that Salutius continued to serve under Valens (*et orientem quidem regebat potestate praefecti Salutius*). Secondly, it would be very odd if shortly after his election Valentinian dismissed the prefect who had staunchly supported his candidature (cf. Philost. *HE* 8.8 and 26.2.1, q.v.). In the third place, Salutius is still attested as PPO in the Theodosian Code on April 17, 364 (*Cod. Theod.* 13.1.5) and September 9, 364 (*Cod. Theod.* 9.16.7). It is also true that at a certain point in time Salutius lost his office (temporarily, as can be deduced from Zos. 4.10.4, Eun. *VS* 7.5.9 and *ILS* 1255; see below), but this took place later, if Amm. 26.7.4 is to be believed (cf. Zos. 4.6.2) – the terminus post quem is July 4, 365, for *Cod. Theod.* 12.6.5 attests that at this date Salutius was still in function (cf. Pergami, 1993, 236–237). Finally, if Zosimus in 4.2.3 and Malalas are right, this would imply that within a very short period Salutius was twice cashiered and reappointed again. This seems unlikely and, moreover, does not tally with passages in Zosimus himself (4.10.4, cf. Eun. *VS* 7.5.9) and *ILS* 1255 (datable to 365–367), where it is said that Salutius occupied the office of praetorian prefect twice (and not: thrice), [Salutius] ἤδη δεύτερον ταύτην μεταχειρισάμενον τὴν ἀρχήν and *praef. praetorio iterum*, respectively. To sum up, Zos. 4.2.3 and Malalas *Chron.* 13.338 must have dated the later dismissal of Salutius wrongly to the beginning of Valentinian's and Valens' reign.

The fact that Zosimus' statements in 4.2.4 about Salutius, Victor and Arintheus are proved wrong does not necessarily mean that Zosimus is also totally mistaken in 4.2.3. He certainly exaggerates when he states that the Pannonian emperors replaced all Julian's personnel with men of their own choice (see for this also below, ad 26.5.5), but that they did push forward some of their confidants is clear from the fact that the Pannonians Equitius and Serenianus were promoted. In itself a change of personnel at the start of a new regime is not surprising. Another example can be found in 22.4: Julian's purge of Constantius' court clique. Cf. further for Julian Delmaire, 1997, 116–118.

et militares partiti sunt numeri These few words formed the basis of a once influential theory. Trying to explain the fact that in the *Notitia Dignitatum* many military units are listed as pairs, designated as *iuniores* and *seniores*, Hoffmann and, independent from him, Tomlin, 1972 argued that this should be related to the division of the army between Valentinian and Valens in 364. However, the publication of an inscription by Drew-Bear in 1977 proved this theory wrong. In the inscription, found at Nacolia in Phrygia and securely dated to 356 A.D., a *ducenarius* of the *numerus Ioviorum Cornutorum seniorum* is mentioned: therefore one may conclude that already in 356 the *Cornuti* and, by analogy, other units were divided in *seniores* and *iuniores*. More on this in Nicasie, 1998, 24–27. Blomgren 70 regards Harmon's addition c.c. *sunt* as plausible. See for the passive *partiti* the note ad 26.5.1 *quasi mox*.

5.4 After the survey of the highest military ranks Amm. turns to the top-ranking civilian authorities, first the court dignitaries (§4), next the three *praefecti praetorio* (§5) and finally the consulate (§6).

Et post haec cum ambo fratres Sirmium introissent, diviso palatio, ut potiori placuerat, Valentinianus Mediolanum, Constantinopolim Valens discessit After they had divided the army and its commanders (*post haec*), the Pannonian brothers left the vicinity of Naissus for Sirmium, modern Sremska Mitrovica, the capital of Pannonia Secunda – see for this town the note ad 21.9.5 *agensque apud Sirmium* (add to the literature cited there Popović, 1993 and Duval, 1997, 129–130). The terminus post quem for their departure from Naissus is 13 or 19 June 364 (see the note ad 26.5.1 *in suburbano*), their presence in Sirmium is first attested on July 5 (*Consult.* 9.6 dat. *III Non. Iul. Sirmio*).

In Sirmium the court officials were divided. Although Wagner proposed to take *palatio* in the sense of "urbibus, quibus pro sedibus domiciliisque uterque uterentur" (he was followed by e.g. Rolfe: "after sharing the places of residence", and Marié: "se partagèrent les résidences impériales"), *palatium* here, as in 25.5.2 (*Arintheus et Victor et e palatio Constanti residui de parte sua*), does not denote a building, but the court personnel (see the note ad 20.4.11 *ad comitatum*). Cf. Philost. *HE* 8.8 ἐν δὲ τῷ Σερμίῳ τὰ τῆς βασιλείας πρὸς αὐτὸν διανειμάμενος ὁπόσα εἰς κόσμον καὶ τὴν ἄλλην ἐτέλει θεραπείαν, τὸν μὲν (sc. Valentem) εἰς Κωνσταντινούπολιν ἀποπέμπει (sc. Valentinianus) ('in Sirmium Valentinian divided with his brother all the imperial ornaments and the court attendants, and then sent Valens back to Constantinople'). As to *ut potiori placuerat*, after the relevant phrases in 26.4.3, 26.5.1 and 26.5.2 this is the fourth expression to emphasize Valens' inferiority. See for *potior*, 'more powerful', the notes ad 19.3.1 *auctoritatis* and 20.4.4 *potioris*.

How long exactly Valentinian and Valens stayed in Sirmium, and whether both departed from this town at the same time, is not known. After they had parted, the imperial brothers were never to see each other again. On 29 July 364 they were still in Sirmium (*Cod. Theod.* 5.15.15 *dat IIII Kal. Aug. Sirmio*). We find Valentinian in Emona (Ljubljana) on 28 August (*Cod. Theod.* 12.13.2 *dat. V Kal. Sept. Emonae*). He was apparently in no hurry to reach Milan (not Rome, as Soz. *HE* 6.7.8 would have it), for on his way to this city he stayed some time in Aquileia (from at least 7 September, *Cod. Theod.* 12.12.4, till September 19 [so i.a. Pergami, 1993, 87–88] or 29, *Cod. Theod.* 8.5.21), Altinum (*Cod. Theod.* 9.30.1 d.d. 30 September and *Cod. Theod.* 14.21.1 of 8 October) and Verona (*Cod. Theod.* 11.31.1 of 15 October). As Lenski, 2002, 27 acutely observes, "the imperial ceremonies of accession and *adventus*, both inextricably intertwined in the fourth century, dictated the august pace of this grand procession" (see his n. 84 for references to three Aquileia medaillons bearing the legend FELIX ADVENTUS AUG N). Valentinian's presence in Milan on 9 November 364 is securely attested (*Cod. Theod.* 11.30.34 *dat V Id. Nov. Med(iolano)*), but he may have reached the city already late in October (cf. *Cod. Theod.* 11.2.2, probably to be dated to 23 October 364, with Pergami, 1993, 102). Milan had been an imperial residence before – it had, for instance, served as winter quarters for Constantius II (cf. e.g. 14.10.16, 14.11.5, 15.1.2) –, but "da questo momento, e per tutto il regno di Valentiniano e della sua dinastia, Milano è la vera capitale dell'Occidente" (Sordi, 1991, 43). See for Milan further Cracco Ruggini, 1990 and the literature cited ad 25.8.9 *properare Mediolanum*.

About the stages of Valens' journey from Sirmium to Constantinople we are less well informed. We only hear of Valens' passing through Heraclea (Soz. *HE* 6.7.8), otherwise known as Perinthus (cf. the note ad 22.2.3 *Heracleam*), but when exactly is unknown. On 16 December at the latest he was in Constantinople (*Cod. Theod.* 8.11.1 *dat. XVII Kal. Ian. Const(antinopoli)*), but he probably arrived there much earlier. For the history of Constantinople in the fourth and fifth centuries Dagron, 1974 is still fundamental. Cf. further Berger, 2005. For Amm. on Constantinople see Kelly, 2003.

5.5 *et orientem quidem regebat potestate praefecti Salutius, Italiam vero cum Africa et Illyrico Mamertinus et Gallicas provincias Germanianus* It is argued above, ad 26.5.3 *quibus ita*, that Zosimus in 4.2.3 exaggerates when he states that the Pannonian emperors replaced all Julian's personnel with men of their own choice. Amm.'s words here provide, pace Elliott, 1983, 141–143, more proof against Zosimus: Salutius, Mamertinus and Germanianus, who had all three already served under Julian, kept their position. This is the more remarkable since "ein neuer Kaiser üblicherweise auch neue Prätorianerpräfekten [ernannte]" (Gutsfeld, 1998, 91 n. 110). See for the office of PPO the notes ad 21.6.5 *Anatolio*, 23.5.6 *quem praefectus* and 25.3.14 *Salutius*.

In the note ad 26.5.3 *quibus ita* (q.v.) it was already mentioned that under Valens Salutius Secundus administered the eastern prefecture. See for him (*PLRE* I, Secundus 3) also 26.2.1 and 26.7.4 with the relevant notes. As to Germanianus (*PLRE* I, Germanianus 4), it is noted ad 21.8.1 *Germaniano iusso vicem tueri Nebridii* (q.v.) that under Julian he first acted for a while as *vicarius* in Gaul and then, in 363, became PPO Galliarum as successor of Sallustius (*PLRE* I, Sallustius 5). Mamertinus (*PLRE* I, Mamertinus 2) had been appointed as *praefectus praetorio per Illyricum* by Julian in 361 (21.12.20, 25, q.v.). By 362 his territory included Italy (*ILS* 755, *Cod. Theod.* 8.5.12) and under Valentinian also Africa (*Cod. Theod.* 7.6.1). These data seem to confirm Amm.'s statement here that in the beginning of Valentinian's reign Mamertinus ruled as praetorian prefect *Italiam...cum Africa et Illyrico*. However, there is a problem, since *Cod. Theod.* 1.29.1, issued on 27 April 364, which deals with Illyrian matters and is addressed to a praetorian prefect, does not mention Mamertinus as addressee, but Probus, i.e. Sextus Claudius Petronius Probus (*PLRE* I, Probus 5), a man who held the praetorian prefecture four times (*ILS* 1267 and 1268) and who is mentioned several times by Amm., for the first time in 27.11.1. How to explain this? Some scholars, e.g. Seeck, 1919, 91–92, 232 and Pergami, 1993, 25–28 argue that the date of *Cod. Theod.* 1.29.1 must be wrong and that the constitution was issued in 368 instead of in 364. It is better, however, to accept the date of the cited law and assume with e.g. Jones, 1974, 390–391 and the authors of *PLRE* I that Mamertinus in 364 was temporarily replaced as PPO of Illyricum by Probus. See for this in the first place Cameron, 1985, 178–181 and cf. further Wirbelauer/Fleer, 1995, 199.

agentes igitur in memoratis urbibus principes sumpsere primitus trabeas con- **5.6** *sulares* The 'cities mentioned' are Milan (Valentinian) and Constantinople (Valens). The present text is, surprisingly, absent in Appendix 4 in Barnes 218–221: "Consular Dates in the *Res Gestae*". For the year 365 only 26.9.1 and 26.10.15 are mentioned. The date is January 1, 365 (cf. Bagnall e.a., 1987, 264–265). In all of Amm.'s fourteen instances *primitus* means 'for the first time'. The brothers held the consulship also in 368, 370 and 373, Valens moreover in 376 and 378. The *trabea* is the official robe of the consuls of late antiquity; see the final section of the note ad 21.10.8 *eum aperte* and the note ad 23.1.1 *ascito*.

omnisque hic annus dispendiis gravibus rem Romanam afflixit The noun *annus* often occurs as grammatical subject. In the majority of cases the phrase contains factual information, e.g. *Deinceps fuit annus quo ego consulatum petivi* (Cic. *Cael.* 10), *ab externis bellis quietus annus fuit* (Liv. 3.32.1), *quartus decimus annus est, Caesar, ex quo* (Tac. *Ann.*14.53.2), *cum Arbitionem consulem annus haberet et Lollianum* (Amm. 15.8.17). Cases in which *annus* is the Agens in the full sense of that term are less frequent. Some phrases which are comparable to the present text are: *labefactarat enim vehementer aratores iam superior annus* (Cic. *Ver.* 3.47), *Terrebat et proximus annus lugubris duorum consulum funeribus* (Liv. 27.40.7), *idem annus gravi igne urbem adfecit* (Tac. *Ann.* 6.45.1; cf. also 4.15.1). By ascribing an actively destructive force to the year 365 immediately after mentioning that the two emperors donned the consular robes, Amm. suggests a direct link between this consulate and the heavy losses inflicted on the Roman state. Cf. for *dispendiis* the note ad 20.6.9 *dispendio tamen fuit rei Romanae*.

Alamanni enim perrupere Germaniae limites The dates of the invasion **5.7** of the Alamans and of the contemptuous treatment inflicted by the Romans on their embassy, which according to Amm. triggered the Alamannic attack (*hac ex causa solito infestius moti…gentes immanissimas concitarunt*), are disputed, and the relevant scholarly debate is a little confusing (for example, Demandt, 1989 dates on p. 112 the arrival in Milan of the Alamannic ambassadors to 365, but on p. 233 of the same book he writes: "364 erschien eine alamannische Delegation in Mailand").

One cause of dissent is Amm.'s statement in 26.4.5 *Hoc tempore...Gallias Raetiasque simul Alamanni populabantur.* These words, in combination with Amm. 30.7.5, Lib. *Or.* 18.290 and Zos. 4.3.4 (the texts are quoted in the introductory note ad 26.4.5–6), suggest that immediately after the news of Julian's death had reached the West, that is, in the second half of 363 or early in 364, Alamans began to devastate Gaul and Raetia. Some scholars, among them Tillemont and Sievers (references in Heering, 1927, 26 and Lorenz, 1995, 74), accepted this, as did Demandt, 1989, 112: "Die Nachricht vom Tode Julians hatte die Alamannen zu Einfällen nach Gallien und Raetien verlockt (Amm. XXVI 4, 5)", and, admittedly, the possibility that Amm.'s suggestion is true cannot be excluded. However, there are some obstacles. In the first place, as Tomlin, 1979 pointed out, in 26.4.5–6 Amm. presents an outline of the military history of the entire period of Valentinian and Valens rather than a description of the manifold crises at its beginning. Secondly, if the Alamans already had opened hostilities in 363 or early in 364, it would be very surprising indeed to find them sending an embassy to Milan (where Valentinian arrived in October 364 at the earliest; see above, ad 26.5.4 *Et post haec*) and asking for the gifts they usually received (*certa et praestituta ex more munera*). Finally, Amm. in 26.5.6–7 explicitly says that it was in 365 (*hic annus*) that the Roman state had to endure heavy losses inflicted by the Alamans. In view of this it seems better to regard the story of an Alamannic attack immediately after Julian's death as an invention of pro-Julianic authors who wanted to contrast their hero favourably with his successors, and to date the first invasion of the Alamans to 365. We can be even more precise. In 27.1.1, where Amm. resumes the narrative of the warfare in the West which he had interrupted to describe Procopius' revolt, he reports that the Alamans attacked very early in 365: *statimque post kalendas Ianuarias* – Heering, 1927, 27 ("Im September/Oktober 365 überschritten sie die römischen Grenze und fielen in Gallien ein") and in his wake Gutmann, 1991, 12 ("Aus Ammian ergibt sich zwingend, daß ein alamannischer Vorstoß nicht bereits Anfang 365, sondern erst im September dieses Jahres stattfand") are wrong. They misinterpreted 26.5.8 *Et circa id tempus* and failed to "realize Ammian's literary disposition of his material" (Baynes, 1955, 320). More on this below in the note ad §8.

Note that Amm. says that the Alamans broke through the *Germaniae limites*, while in 27.1.1 he reports that they leapt across the

Gallicanos limites. In both cases he means the same. See for *limes* the notes ad 23.3.4 *vicino limite* and 25.6.11 *fama*.

hac ex causa solito infestius moti Although Amm.'s use of the abl. comparationis *solito* is somewhat stereotyped (see the notes ad 14.6.9 *solito altioribus* and 20.8.8 *solito saevius*), the phrase does imply that the Alamans' aggressiveness was a normal phenomenon, which was now intensified because of a specific motive.

cum legatis eorum missis ad comitatum certa et praestituta ex more munera praeberi deberent, minora et vilia sunt attributa If the context is taken into account, the envoys travelled to the court at Milan, where Valentinian resided from November (or perhaps October) 364 onwards (see the note ad 26.5.4 *Et post haec*). There is a short note on *comitatus* ad 20.4.11 *ad comitatum*; more information in Noethlichs, 1998 and Schlinkert, 1998, 138 n. 13. Since the Alamans invaded Gaul shortly after New Year 365 (*statimque post kalendas Ianuarias*, 27.1.1), their ambassadors must have come to Milan in the last months of 364, pace Heering, 1927, 27 ("so ist es unwahrscheinlich, daß diese Gesandschaft eher als im Frühjahr 365 vor dem Kaiser erschien"), Lorenz, 1995, 74 ("Im Verlauf dieses Jahres [i.e. 365], wahrscheinlich in den Sommermonaten, kam eine Delegation der Alamannen an den Mailänder Hof") and others who were misled by Ammianus' admittedly rather complicated compositional technique (see on this the note ad §8).

The nature of the *munera* which the Alamannic envoys expected to receive is not quite clear, but the gifts were, in view of the chronology, certainly not "New Year's gifts", as Drinkwater, 1996, 25 assumes. Perhaps the Alamans expected some sort of donative from the newly inaugurated emperor, who, for that matter, was himself the recipient of golden crowns from the cities in his empire (cf. the notes ad 26.4.1 *at in Bithynia* and 26.4.3 *indeque cum*), but, considering Amm.'s wording (*certa et praestituta ex more*), it is more likely that regular payments to appease the barbarians are meant, like the ones referred to in 24.3.4 (*auro quietem a barbaris redemptare*). See also 17.10.8 (*cum munerandus venisset ex more*, sc. Hortarius, king of the Alamans) and 21.6.8 (*cultu ambitioso indumentorum emercabantur et multiformibus donis*) with the note ad loc. (25.6.10, q.v., is, pace Marié, 1984, n. 52, of a different order). As is noted ad 24.3.4, Julian chided Constantine (*Caes.* 329 a), Constantius II (*Ep. ad Ath.* 280a–b, 286 a) and Silvanus (*On Kingship* 98 c–d) for having given subsidies to barbarians. If this can be taken as proof that Julian himself refrained from giving such gifts, the implication is that the Alamans tried to renew a practice once common (*ex more*), but interrupted under Julian (for a different view see Lorenz, 1995, 74, "eine Weiterzahlung dieser von Julian bewilligten 'Geschenke'", with n. 12).

quae illi suscepta furenter agentes ut indignissima proiecere In the first part of the note ad 22.14.1 *nulla probabili* it is pointed out that *suscipere* should not unquestioningly be regarded as a mere synonym of *accipere*. However, the present text is no doubt an instance of this. The adv. *furenter* is very rare; see TLL VI 1.1629.11-14.

tractatique asperius ab Ursatio tunc magistro officiorum iracundo quodam et saevo The Alamans' indignant rejection of the Roman gifts in its turn produced a harsh reaction on the part of Ursatius, the "raw Dalmatian" (26.4.4 [q.v.] in Hamilton's rendering), whose hot and savage temper could not stand such a scene. In his capacity of *magister officiorum* Ursatius was responsible for the reception of foreign ambassadors and the control of audiences at court (Clauss, 1980 [1981], 63-67; Lee, 1993, 40-48), but it is sometimes argued (e.g. by Gutmann, 1991, 11 and Lorenz, 1995, 75), that he cannot have acted on his own authority but must have been instructed by the emperor to provoke the Alamans in an insulting manner. Amm.'s characterization of the man (*iracundo quodam et saevo*) does, however, not support this suggestion. Neither does the fact that Ursatius soon after was replaced as MO by Remigius (cf. Clauss, 1980 [1981], 197: "Vielleicht hing seine Entlassung mit seiner Mitschuld an dem Alamanneneinfall zusammen").

As to *quodam*, this can be interpreted as an instance of *quidam* adding emphasis to the preceding adjective: see Kühner-Stegmann II 1.643, Szantyr 196, the discussion in the note ad 20.4.13 *fortuna quaedam*, and the note ad 25.5.8 *his ita*. Ursatius was a particularly hot-tempered man.

ut contumeliose despectas gentes immanissimas concitarunt With *ut* Amm. indicates that the envoys used the 'outrageous contempt' of the tribes which they represented as an argument to rouse them to action. See for *immanissimas* Amm.'s characterization of the Alamannic leader Vadomar: *immanissimus homo* (21.4.6, q.v.), and also Seager 4-7 and 14-15 on Amm.'s "obsession" with the word *immanis*. As De Jonge notes ad 14.10.1 *Alamannos* (q.v.), three Alammannic *gentes* or *populi* (14.10.14, 31.10.2) are mentioned by name in the *Res Gestae*, the Iuthungi (17.6.1), Bucinobantes (29.4.7) and Lentienses (31.10.2).

Et circa id tempus aut non multo posterius in oriente Procopius in res surrexerat novas. quae prope kalendas Novembres venturo Valentiniano Parisios uno eodemque nuntiata sunt die This section, of which the text is not quite certain (see below), together with its context drove many scholars to despair (cf. the review of preceding opinions in Lorenz, 1995, 84–91) and led to verdicts like Klein's: "Die Datierung ist wieder recht töricht" (1914, 27) and Heering's (1927, 27): "Ammian ist hier...unlogisch und widerspricht sich in demselben Satze". Such judgements are overhasty, but one has to admit that Amm. does not make it easy for his readers to understand him properly.

5.8

First some preliminary remarks. Procopius' usurpation became manifest on 28 September 365 (references in the note ad 26.6.14 *ubi excanduit*). Its description by Amm. covers the chapters 6–9 of Book 26. Modern studies include Solari, 1932; Solari, 1933; Hahn, 1958; Austin, 1972; Blockley, 1975, 55–61; Grattarola, 1986; Matthews 191–203; Wiebe, 1995, 3–85; Lenski, 2002, 68–115. Valentinian was still in Milan on 24 September (*Cod. Iust.* 11.62 [61].3 *d. viii k. Oct. Mediolani*), his presence in Paris on 18 October 365 is attested by *Cod. Theod.* 11.1.13 (*dat. xv kal. Nov. Parisis*), which means that Amm.'s statement that the emperor was to arrive in Paris around the first of November is, though not very precise, more or less correct. The preposition *prope* in phrases denoting a moment in time is entirely normal. However, in combination with a precise date it is rare: the list in TLL X 2.1961.33–55 does not contain a single example, and this is the only one in Amm.; 14.3.3 *prope Septembris initium* is the nearest parallel.

The main hindrance to the correct interpretation of this section, as Baynes, 1955 has shown, is caused by the way in which Amm. arranges his material. It is, pace e.g. Lorenz, 1995, 87ff., very important to realize that Amm., for reasons explained in 26.5.15 (*competenti loco singula digeremus, nunc partem in oriente gestorum, deinde bella barbarica narraturi, quoniam pleraque et in occidentali et in eoo orbe isdem mensibus sunt actitata*), starts his full account of the war against the Alamans not before 27.1.1, and only mentions the Alamans in 26.5.7–9 in order that Valentinian's decision not to help his brother against Procopius (26.5.9–13) might be understood. A related problem is the fact that in the chapter under discussion Amm. takes for granted information which he will only later supply. In other words, without knowledge of the data provided in Book 27 it is hardly possible to understand fully what Amm. means in 26.5.7–9. One example of this we already saw in the note ad *Alamanni perrupere* in §7 concerning the date of the Alamannic invasion: it is to 27.1.1

that we owe the information that the Alamans, provoked by Ursatius' behaviour (*ob causam expositam supra*), invaded Gaul *statimque post kalendas Ianuarias*, i.e. early in January 365. Another example is the following: it only becomes apparent in 27.1-2 that Dagalaifus, mentioned in 26.5.9 (q.v.) as the general ordered by Valentinian to meet the Alamanni, was not the first commander to do so. Charietto and Severianus had been Dagalaifus' predecessors, and Charietto and Severianus had suffered a crushing defeat. They themselves were killed and the standards of some of their *auxilia* were captured by the barbarians. Knowledge of this disaster is indispensable for the correct interpretation of 26.5.7-9 in general, and of the section under discussion in particular, as Baynes, 1955 and in his wake Tomlin, 1974, 492-498 rightly argued (for a different view see e.g. Demandt, 1968b, 341-344 and Lorenz, 1995, 84-91).

The only other example of the phrase *in res surrexerat novas* seems to be Amm.'s own *in res novas quendam medium surrexisse* (25.10.7). His statement that the news of Procopius' usurpation, which, as we saw, dates to 28 September 365, reached Valentinian in or near Paris around the first of November, that is, about a month later, is generally, and rightly, accepted as reliable. But is it really credible that it took about ten months for the news of the Alamannic invasion – which, as we saw, dates to January 365 – to travel to Paris and be reported to Valentinian on the same day as the news of the Procopian revolt (*quae...uno eodemque nuntiata sunt die*)? And are we really to believe Amm. when he says that the invasion of the Alamans (shortly after New Year) and the beginning of Procopius' revolution (at the end of September) took place at about the same time (*circa id tempus aut non multo posterius*)? The answer to these questions is a resounding no. However, instead of concluding that Amm. is making a mistake, one should conclude that the wrong questions have been asked. In what follows it is argued 1) that some phrases in Amm.'s text have been neglected or misunderstood (*omnisque annus* and *dispendiis gravibus* in §6, *Et* and *quae* in §8) and 2) that the assumption that Amm. in this section speaks merely about Procopius' revolt on the one hand and the Alamannic invasion of Gaul early in 365 on the other is false.

In 26.5.6 Amm. had stated that 'this whole year (i.e. 365) inflicted heavy losses on the Roman state' (*omnisque hic annus dispendiis gravibus rem Romanam afflixit*). Note the words *omnis* and *dispendiis gravibus*. The use of these words suggests that Amm. in the explanation (*enim*) he gives in 26.5.7 is thinking of more than the mere fact that the Alamans invaded Gaul after their envoys had been snubbed by Ursatius. Not the invasion alone caused a *dispendium grave*, but, presumably, other attacks during 'this whole year' as well, and, at any rate, the disastrous campaign of Charietto and Severianus, which did not occur immediately after the Alamannic invasion early in the year, but later in 365; the date can be deduced from the combined evidence of 27.2.1, where it is stated that Dagalaifus was sent from Paris against the Alamans after the news of the defeat of his predecessors had been received (*Qua clade…comperta…Dagalaifus a Parisiis mittitur*), and 26.5.9, where we learn that Valentinian, who was on his way to Paris *prope kalendas Novembres* (26.5.8), ordered Dagalaifus to go and meet the Alamans (*Et Alamannis quidem occursurum Dagalaifum pergere mature praecepit*).

It is of course regrettable that, if indeed Amm., in 26.5.7, was thinking primarily of Charietto's and Severianus' *clades*, he did not say so expressly. But the acceptance of this suggestion removes the stumbling blocks mentioned above, viz. how to interpret *circa id tempus aut non multo posterius* in the first part of the present section and *quae…uno eodemque nuntiata sunt die* in the second. A paraphrase of 26.5.6–8 may show this: 'This whole year of 365 inflicted heavy losses on the Roman state (§6). There was in the first place ⟨the calamitous defeat of Charietto and Severianus, which was the deplorable result of⟩ the Alamannic invasion earlier in the year caused by Ursatius' provocation (§7). And (*Et*) in the second place there was Procopius' revolt, about that time (that is, about the same time as Charietto's defeat) or not much later. Both these disasters were reported to Valentinian when he was about to arrive in Paris around the first of November (§8)'.

The interpretation given here helps to solve another problem. The text printed by Seyfarth *quae prope kalendas Novembres venturo Valentiniano Parisios uno eodemque nuntiata sunt die* is not quite certain. After *Valentiniano* V has *Parisios eodemque nuntiata*, in which *-que* has no function. Petschenig, 1897, 381 suggests *eo denique nuntiatae*, "um einen ganz erträglichen Sinn zu erhalten". It is a beautifully contrived 'economical' conjecture, but the fact that *eo…die* can only refer to 1 November poses a problem because of *prope*: Valentinian was to arrive in Paris 'around' this date. Petschenig would have needed a further conjecture, viz. the substitution of *prope* by *pridie*. Heraeus noted a small lacuna after *Parisios* in Gelenius' text, which he filled with *uno*. This has two advantages: the solitary position of *eodemque* is removed and *nuntiata* can be kept: *quae* is now not plur. fem., referring to *res…novas*, but neuter, referring to both the Alamannic aggression and Procopius' usurpation; see Blomgren 52.

5.9-14 This passage is highly interesting in that it is the only extensive account of Valentinian's reaction to the news of Procopius' revolt. Zos. 4.7.4 only notes his refusal to come to the rescue of a man 'who had failed to protect the part of the empire which had been entrusted to him'. Amm.'s report provides a vivid picture of Valentinian's grave worries, caused by the lack of clear and reliable information, and his indecision as to whether he should leave Gaul to cope directly with Procopius or stay to combat the Alamans. In the end, both the consistorium and envoys from Gallic cities persuaded him to give priority to the protection of Gaul.

The only other source for this specific episode is Symmachus' first *Oration*, sections 17 ff., where it is suggested that Valentinian's decision was the result of his own reflections. Sabbah 340 (cf. also 448) concludes: "l'opposition d'Ammien à la thèse officielle représentée par le panégyriste est profonde". In itself this observation is correct, but one can hardly imagine Symmachus sharing the version of the historian. In fact, this is an enlightening illustration of the differences between panegyrical rhetoric and historiography. Both have their specific functions and both Symmachus and Ammianus did what they ought to do within the rules of their respective professions. Cf. Lepore, 2000.

5.9 *Et Alamannis quidem occursurum Dagalaifum pergere mature praecepit* In the note ad 25.1.1 *Et hanc quidem* it is pointed out that *et...quidem* often functions to wind up an episode, after which *vero* or *autem* introduces a new development. In the present case Amm. uses this pattern to abandon the Alamannic threat for the time being and to concentrate on the usurpation of Procopius. In 27.1.1 Amm. will return to the Alamanni, and, as has already been stated in the note ad §8, in 27.2.1 he refers again, in a different context, to the mission of Dagalaifus: *Qua clade* (i.e. the defeat of Charietto and Severianus reported in 27.1.1–6) *cum ultimo maerore comperta correcturus sequius gesta Dagalaifus a Parisiis mittitur*. The fact that it is explicitly stated there, and that it is implied in the present text that Dagalaifus was sent by Valentinian from Paris, is decisive proof against the theory of some scholars that Amm. here and in 27.2.1 talks about two different campaigns. See on this Tomlin, 1973, 492–498 and for Dagalaifus the note ad 26.1.6 *Dagalaifo*.

See for *mature*, 'speedily', the note ad 21.3.3 *qui cum*. In all probability this adverb is to be taken with *pergere*, as in Rolfe's "Then Valentinian ordered Dagalaifus to go in haste to meet the Alamanni", and not, as Hamilton would have it, with *praecepit*: "He at once sent

Dagalaif to encounter the Alamanni" (for a similar case see 31.12.15 *assentientibus cunctis ire pignoris loco mature disponitur* and cf. TLL VIII 503.32–79). However, whatever the case may be, 27.2.1 makes it clear that Dagalaifus did not carry out the emperor's order quickly and was soon recalled (to enter the consulship of 366) and replaced by Iovinus (ibid.): *eoque diu cunctante causanteque diffusos per varia barbaros semet adoriri non posse accitoque paulo postea, ut cum Gratiano etiamtum privato susciperet insignia consulatus, Iovinus equitum magister accingitur.*

qui vastitatis propinquioribus locis longius discesserant incruenti The rare frequentativum *vastitare* also occurs in 16.4.4 and 18.2.7. In both cases Gelenius has the corresponding form of *vastare*. In view of Amm.'s predilection for frequentativa V's text cannot be regarded as suspect; see Blomgren 172–173. Note Amm.'s subtle belittling of the Alamans' exploits: they only dared to attack places near their own territory and then retreated a very long way (*longius*). With *longius discesserant* compare *diffusos per varia* in 27.2.1. The adj. *incruentus* occurs six times in the *Res Gestae*: in four cases it qualifies the comparatively 'mild' character or conduct of a person in authority, in 14.10.14 Constantius in a speech to his soldiers expounds that a moderate treatment of the Alamans will make it possible *ut incruenti* ("without bloodshed", tr. Rolfe) *mitigemus ferociae flatus*. In that phrase it is not made clear whose blood will not be shed, but in the present text *incruenti* clearly means "ohne Verluste" (Seyfarth), "sans subir de pertes" (Marié). This is precisely the exasperating aspect of the barbarian attack.

super appetitu vero Procopii, antequam adolesceret, reprimendo See for *appetitus* the note ad 24.4.10 *ut erat*. In the present text it can be regarded as a shorthand version of *rerum appetitu novarum* (20.4.16).

curis diducebatur ambiguis See the note ad 20.11.24 *imperator* for comparable phrases inspired by Verg. A. 5.720 *tum vero in curas animo diducitur omnis*. The present phrase is an amalgam of this verse and *curae ambiguae* in A. 8.580, which makes it very apt for the present context. Although the focus is on the revolt of Procopius in the eastern half of the empire, for the moment the author remains with Valentinian and his worries, which are caused by a lack of reliable information. He is not even aware of his brother's fortunes. For this reason Valentinian 'was in two minds': should he leave Gaul to face up to the dangerous situation in Illyricum or cope with the Alamannic threat?

ea potissimum ratione sollicitus, quod ignorabat, utrum Valente superstite an exstincto memoratus imperium affectarat It is quite understandable that the first reports about Procopius' revolt which reached Valentinian were rather vague, and that the western emperor was ignorant of the fate of his brother. Valentinian got the news of the usurpation from his general Equitius, who, in Illyricum at the time, was ill-informed himself, as Amm. explains in 26.5.10. Zosimus is no doubt right when he reports in 4.7.3 that Valens, as soon as he learned of Procopius' proclamation, wanted to inform his brother, but, since Valens' messengers had to come to the west from Caesarea in Galatia (26.7.2), their arrival must have occurred somewhat later than Equitius' communication.

TLL VIII 694.35 sqq. presents a list of instances in which *memoratus* is "i.q. supradictus"; lines 51–64 contain the cases where it occurs as a noun. Other examples of this in Amm. can be found in 29.1.5, 29.5.39, 31.4.10. In principle *affectare* is a vox media, which expresses that a person strives after something. However, it often occurs in contexts denoting a condemnable lust for power. See the notes ad 21.16.4 *doctrinarum* and 25.4.18 *popularitatis*.

5.10 *Equitius enim relatione Antoni tribuni accepta agentis in Dacia mediterranea militem* Equitius had been entrusted with the command of the army in Illyricum (26.5.3, q.v.). The t.t. *relatio* denotes an official dispatch to a higher authority; see the notes ad 16.11.7 *relatione* and 20.4.7 *ad relationem*. Cf. for *agentis...militem* 21.8.1 *cum Scutarios ageret*, 26.1.5 *agens scholam Scutariorum secundam* and OLD s.v. *agere* 13. Dacia mediterranea is one of Dacia's two provinces, as is explained in the note ad 21.5.6 *Daciarum*. These provinces were the most eastern of Valentinian's territory and therefore nearest to the city where Procopius was proclaimed emperor. The tribune Antonius (*PLRE* I, Antonius 3) is otherwise unknown. For *tribuni* cf. the note ad 26.1.4 *Et rumore*.

qui nihil praeter negotium ipsum auditum obscure significabat Amm. expresses the vagueness of Antonius' account in various ways: it only concerns the mere fact, "la vicenda in sé" (Viansino); no Agens of *auditum* is mentioned (Rolfe's "which he himself had heard" is evidently a slip); Antonius' words were far from clear: see for *obscure* as "fere i.q. ambigue, non plane, non evidenter" TLL IX 2.173.51–75, and cf. 15.5.10 *quid significatum esset obscurius*, 18.6.17 *haec consulto obscurius indicantem*. This is markedly different from Symm. *Or.* 1.17, where *pernices nuntii et fidae litterae* bring the bad news to Valentinian.

ipse quoque nondum liquida fide comperta simplicibus verbis principem gestorum conscium fecit The words *liquida fide comperta* are reminiscent of 17.1.4 *Quibus clara fide compertis* and 21.13.6 *nuntii..., quorum clara fide compertum est.* However, in contrast to the first of these two cases, in the present text *fide* is itself the Head of the abl. abs. One is tempted to assume the loss of *re* after *quoque*, but the text can be explained as it stands, if *fides* is taken in the sense of 'reliable account'; see for this the notes ad 23.5.9 *fidem* and 24.2.16 *sed fides*. For his dispatch to Valentinian Equitius availed himself of 'uncomplicated terminology', which probably means that he openly used words indicating rebellion or usurpation. There seem to be no parallels for *aliquem conscium facere*, 'to inform a person'.

Valentinianus eodem Equitio aucto magisterii dignitate repedare ad Illyricum festinabat See for the anaphoric use of *idem* the note ad 20.4.5 *cum isdem*, and for *augere* c. abl., 'to provide with', in phrases denoting promotion the notes ad 20.11.7 *dignitatibus* and 25.10.9 *Vitalianus*. From *comes*, i.e. *comes rei militaris per Illyricum* (cf. 26.5.3), Equitius was promoted to *magister*, i.e. *magister militum per Illyricum*. See for this function the note ad 20.2.1 *peditum magistrum*. Amm., who is not always precise in his military designations, speaks of Equitius as *per eas regiones militum rector* in 26.7.11 and calls him *per Illyricum eo tempore magistrum armorum* in 29.6.3. In inscriptions we find more technical terms. Cf. e.g. *ILS* 762 *disponente Equitio v.c. comite mag. equitum peditumque* and *ILS* 774 *ordinante viro clarissimo Equitio comite et utriusque militiae magistro.*

As to *Illyricum*, in the beginning of Valentinian's reign the civil authority over this diocese was wielded by Mamertinus (26.5.5, q.v.), but it would appear that meanwhile Vulcacius Rufinus had succeeded him (see for this *PLRE* I, Rufinus 25). There is a short note on *Illyricum* ad 20.1.1.

As is noted ad 24.4.30 *ad signa*, the verb *repedare* occurs both in archaic and late Latin. Gärtner, 1969, 370–371 defends *festinabat*, the correction in V, mainly on the basis of Amm.'s "Sprachgebrauch". Marié disagrees and, following Rolfe, prints *destinabat*, "décidait", but in this case it is very difficult, if not impossible, to explain the imperfect tense. In fact, *festinabat* does not mean that Valentinian was actually hurrying away, but that he 'was anxious' to go: see OLD s.v. 4b and the note ad 22.1.1 *avesque*. Moreover, Kellerbauer, 1873, 132 had put forward the decisive argument by noting that *ardens ad redeundum eius impetus* in §12 refers back to *repedare...festinabat.*

ne persultatis Thraciis perduellis iam formidatus invaderet hostili excursu Pannonias See for *persultare* the final part of the note ad 26.4.5 *velut per* and for Amm.'s use of *perduellis* to denote a usurper the note ad 20.8.21 *Iulianum ut perduellem*; cf. also TLL X 1.1293.19 sqq. Valentinian was by no means inclined to underrate Procopius: he had 'already' acquired the status of an adversary 'who inspired fear' (*iam formidatus*). As is noted ad 20.9.7 *recreatae*, Amm. often avails himself of the word *excursus* to denote a barbarian invasion. Since he is, in fact, a *hostis*, Procopius' potential attack has to be styled *hostilis*. An invasion into the Pannonian provinces would directly involve the western half of the empire and hit the very basis of Valentinian's power. For Thrace and Pannonia see above, the notes ad 26.4.5 *Sarmatae* and *Thracias*. The military commander in Thrace at the time was Iulius (*PLRE* I, Iulius 2), who, as appears in 26.7.5, was soon to be lured away from his post by Procopius and imprisoned in Constantinople.

documento enim recenti impendio terrebatur See for *documento...recenti* the second part of the note ad 26.2.4 *ex eo* and for *impendio* the note ad 20.7.1 *munimentum*: it occurs more than twenty times in the *Res Gestae*, but only here and in 30.2.1 *impendio conabatur* to qualify the finite form of a verb.

reputans paulo antea Iulianum contempto bellorum civilium ubique victore nec speratum ante nec exspectatum ab urbe in urbem incredibili velocitate transisse In the last six books of the *Res Gestae* Julian's 'posthumous presence' is a recurrent phenomenon. The great majority of Amm.'s instances of *reputare* consists of the various forms of the part. praes. The successes of Constantius II in civil warfare, in contrast to external conflicts, are regularly stressed by Amm.; he is, however, not the only author to do so: see the note ad 21.1.2 *utrumque*. Compared to V's *contempto rebellorum*, Gelenius' *contempto imperatore bellorum*, printed by Clark and Marié, is persuasive. The combination *speratum...exspectatum* does not occur as an example of 'Synonymenhäufung' in the list of verbs in Hagendahl's survey "De abundantia sermonis Ammianei" (1924, 183–187), perhaps rightly. In cases like Cic. *Ver.* 4.101 *quid speras, quid exspectas?* and ps. Cic. *epist. ad Oct.* 3 *Quid de hoc sperare aut exspectare oportebat?*, the two verbs seem to be synonymous, but Macr. *comm.* 2.12.3 *plantata sperandi exspectandive temperie* is different; cf. Armisen-Marchetti's rendering "un juste compromis d'espoir et de patience". The present text could well imply that some people had been 'looking forward to' Julian's arrival, whereas others had 'expected' it in a less cheerful mood. For a characterization of Julian's speedy eastbound march Amm. quotes himself; in 22.2.5 he wrote *ab urbe in urbem inopina velocitate transgressum*. See for Julian's speed the note ad 21.9.6 *ut fax*.

verum ardens ad redeundum eius impetus molliebatur consiliis proximorum 5.12
As is noted ad 25.6.15 *ardens*, there are very few instances of *ardere ad*. Cf. for *mollire*, "to lessen" (OLD s.v. 7) Liv. 3.35.7 *mollire impetum*. See the note ad 22.7.8 *suadentibus proximis* for *proximi* denoting the members of the consistorium. In this case Amm. refers to the members of Valentinian's consistorium, in 26.7.13 to those of his brother's, who, on the verge of renouncing the throne, reconsidered his decision *vetantibus proximis*.

ne interneciva minantibus barbaris exponeret Gallias neve hac causatione provincias desereret egentes adminiculis magnis See for Amm.'s use of *internecivus*, 'murderous', the note ad 20.4.10 *internecivas*. The term *causatio*, 'excuse', is treated in the note ad 18.6.5 *omni causatione*. Evidently, the members of the consistorium did not mince their words, calling Valentinian's ardent wish to 'return' (*repedare, redeundum*) to Milan (or, indeed, Pannonia) a desertion of Gaul. For literature on barbarians in late antiquity in general and in Amm. in particular see the note ad 20.4.1 *a barbaris*. Add to the works cited there Rugullis, 1992; Chauvot, 1998; Heather, 1999 and Guzmán Armario, 2002. For Amm.'s description of the various parts of Gaul see 15.11, where i.a. the following provinces are listed: secunda and prima Germania, Belgica prima and secunda, Sequani, Lugdunensis prima and secunda.

iisque legationes urbium accessere nobilium precantes, ne in rebus duris et dubiis impropugnatas eas relinqueret Clark, Seyfarth, Marié and Viansino all print *magnis, iisque*, Valesius' fine emendation of V's *maenisque*, the only drawback of which is the fact that against Amm.'s twenty instances of *eis* there is only one other case of *iis* (14.5.9). Cf. for *accedere* with dat., 'to join', 14.11.3 *isdemque residui regii accessere spadones*, 29.5.47 *hisque Iesalenses auxiliares accessere*. The apt alliterative combination *duris et dubiis* seems to be a creation of Amm. From TLL VII 1.698.29–33 it appears that apart from Gel. 1.6.4, where the text is not certain, the present text and 27.12.15, 29.6.10, 31.15.8 are the only passages in which *impropugnatus* occurs. In 15.11.7–12 Amm. lists 22 *urbes...splendidae Galliarum* (his wording in the present text is reminiscent of Ausonius' *ordo urbium nobi-*

lium). The most threatened of these cities will have sent *legationes* to the emperor.

metu ambitiosi nominis sui Germanis incusso See the notes ad 14.7.6 *Domum ambitiosam* and 20.5.1 *ambitiosius* for Amm's frequent use of *ambitiosus*. In a general sense it denotes that something is impressive, because its proportions are larger or its outward appearance more splendid than is ordinarily the case. It is i.a. used of buildings, e.g. *ambitiosum quondam apud Hierosolyma templum* (23.1.2, q.v.), clothes, e.g. *cultu ambitioso indumentorum* (21.6.8, q.v.), armed forces, e.g. *cum ambitiosis copiis* (24.5.7, q.v.). Amm.'s use of the word does not necessarily imply pejorative connotations, as is evident from the present text: the envoys from the Gallic cities meant to emphasize the salutary effect of Valentinian's impressive and frightening reputation in Germania.

5.13 *Tandem denique utilitate rei perpensius cogitata* See Hagendahl, 1924, 213 on the pleonastic combination *tandem denique*, which also occurs three times in Apuleius' *Metamorphoses*: 2.15, 3.22 and 10.14. In her note on the last case Zimmerman makes an interesting observation: "All three passages refer to a mental process, a self-conquest, which, it is implied, requires much effort and time. Consequently, the combination should not be regarded as an empty pleonasm in any of these passages." The present text is comparable to this: persuading Valentinian to reflect that he ought to give priority to the defence of Gaul had taken considerable time.

It is perhaps useful to explain the somewhat cryptic report on Damsté's suggestion in Seyfarth's app. crit.: Damsté, 1930, 10 proposes to assume that before *perpensius* a *p*, representing the abbreviation of *publicae*, has been lost. Miller, 1935, 55 regards this as a good suggestion. He may well be right: the phrase *utilitas rei publicae* is by no means rare, it occurs e.g. more than twenty times in Cicero's oeuvre. With this emendation the difficult problem as to what precisely is meant by *rei* would disappear.

Whether one should print *cogitata* or, in agreement with Marié, *excogitata* is in fact an academic problem. In the latter case the verb would not have its usual meaning "cogitando invenire" (TLL V 2.1274.74), 'to devise', as in 22.16.9 *excogitavit* (q.v.), but rather belong to the list of cases in which it is a synonym of *cogitare* (TLL V 2.1276.9–20). The proposal to read *recogitata* (Petschenig, 1897, 381) is less plausible, because it would be Amm.'s only instance of a rare verb.

Zosimus is totally silent on Valentinian's considerations as reported by Amm. Instead, he states in 4.7.4 that Valentinian refused to help his brother because he was annoyed with 'a man who was incapable of defending his part of the empire' (ἀνδρὶ πρὸς φυλακὴν οὐκ ἀρκέσαντι τῆς αὐτῷ παραδεδομένης ἀρχῆς). As Lepore, 2000, 587 points out, some modern scholars explained Valentinian's decision to remain in Gaul in yet another way. Cf. e.g. Seeck, 1920–1923²⁻⁴, V, 51: "Valentinian wollte neutral bleiben, vielleicht weil er so hoffen durfte, mit Procop, falls dieser Sieger blieb, noch ein Abkommen schliessen zu können, vielleicht auch nur, weil müssiges Abwarten seiner Natur am besten zusagte". As motives for Valentinian's behaviour these reasons seem less likely than the one given by Amm.

in multorum sententias flexus replicabat aliquotiens hostem suum fratrisque solius esse Procopium, Alamannos vero totius orbis Romani This emphasizes the effort needed to keep Valentinian on the right track. He was finally inclined to the course advocated by many and then kept repeating the magnificent principle that Procopius was merely a personal enemy, but the Alamans were a threat to the entire empire. As appears from Symm. *Or.* 1.18, this was the official version: *At tu rei publicae plus timebas et inter duas causas hinc intestinam, inde finitimam malebas potentia tua interim frui aemulum quam longa inpunitate vicinum,* 'but you were more apprehensive for the state and, when you were on the horns of a dilemma – on the one hand an internal conflict, on the other a war with a neighbouring tribe –, you preferred for the time being a rival enjoying a power that belonged to you to a neighbour remaining unpunished for a long time.' In the next chapter Symmachus ascribes a similar phrase to Valentinian himself: *hic communis hostis est, ille privatus; prima victoriae publicae, secunda vindictae meae causa est* (Symm. *Or.* 1.19). Bleckmann, 1995, 92 notes that Zonaras ascribes this praiseworthy principle to Claudius Gothicus: ὁ πρὸς τὸν τύραννον πόλεμος ἐμοὶ διαφέρει, ὁ δὲ πρὸς τοὺς βαρβάρους τῇ πολιτείᾳ, καὶ χρὴ τὸν τῆς πολιτείας προτιμηθῆναι, 'the war against the tyrant is my department, that against the barbarians is the task of the state, and the war of the state should be given priority.' (Zon. 12.26).

See for Amm.'s frequent use of *replicare* with the meaning 'to repeat' the note ad 20.9.6 *replicatoque*. As is stated in the note ad 20.6.9 *aliquotiens*, this adverb is a great favourite of Amm., who uses it mainly as a synonym of *saepe*.

122   COMMENTARY

5.14   *et ad usque Remos progressus* Valentinian, who had reached Paris in 365 *prope kalendas Novembres* (26.5.8), was still there on December 10 and 12 (*Cod. Theod.* 10.19.3, 8.1.11). When precisely he moved to Rheims is not known. His presence there on 7 April 366 is attested by *Cod. Theod.* 8.7.9.

sollicitusque super Africa, ne repente perrumperetur L'histoire se répète: less than four years before, in order to thwart the attempts of another usurper, Constantius II, *veritusque ne Africa absente eo perrumperetur* (21.7.2), had taken due measures; see for *perrumpere*, 'to invade', the note ad loc.

Neoterium postea consulem In his app. crit. Seyfarth has failed to note that in his edition of 1636 Henricus Valesius already prints *Neotherium* and in the note ad loc. correctly mentions 390 as the year of his consulate (cf. Bagnall et al., 1987, 314–315). This indicates that Amm. wrote Books 26–31 after 390. See for further indications for the time of writing Rosen, 1982, 34, Matthews 22–23 and the note ad *Serapeum* (22.16.12). For the rise in importance of imperial *notarii* during the fourth century see Teitler, 1985, 64 ff., for Neoterius *PLRE* I, Neoterius+J.F. Matthews in *CR* 24 (1974) 102 and Teitler, 1985, 298 n. 220

et Masaucionem domesticum protectorem Amm.'s passage here is the only source we have for this soldier (*PLRE* I, Masaucio). For his function see the note ad 21.16.20 *Iovianus*.

ea consideratione, quod ibi sub patre Cretione quondam comite educatus suspecta noverat loca We know less about the son, who was instructed by Valentinian to guard Africa against Procopius, than about the father (*PLRE* I, Cretio), who had been ordered in 361 by Constantius to guard this region against Julian (21.7.4). *Cod. Theod.* 7.1.4 of 27 June 349 (Seeck's date) was sent *ad Cretionem v.c. com.* and deals with military discipline, which justifies the conclusion that Cretio was *comes rei militaris* at the time (cf. for this function the note ad 20.4.18 *postea comes*), presumably, in view of his connection with Africa in 361, *comes rei militaris per Africam* (according to *PLRE* I the anonymous *comes rei miltaris per Africam* mentioned in *Cod. Theod.* 7.4.3 of 18 December 357 is perhaps to be identified with this Cretio too). If, indeed, Cretio was in Africa from at least 349 till 361 (after becoming emperor Julian will have dismissed this supporter of Constantius) and assuming that his son was with him during that period, there was plenty of time for Masaucio to get acqainted with the *suspecta...loca* there.

See for *consideratio*, 'reflection', the note ad 21.7.3 *cuncta* and for a similar combination with a *quod*-clause 26.9.3 *hac maxime consideratione... quod.*

hisque scutarium adiunxit Gaudentium olim sibi cognitum et fidelem Cf. 22.9.13 *iam inde a studiis cognitum Atticis.* In contrast to *fidus*, Amm. scarcely uses *fidelis*, only five times in all. Given the fact that Valentinian himself had been commander of a *schola Scutariorum* (26.1.5), it is not surprising that he knew Gaudentius (*PLRE* I, Gaudentius 4) well. See for this army corps the note ad 20.2.5 *Gentilium Scutariorum* and ad 25.10.9 *Quibus compertis.* As Nicasie, 1998, 47 observes, "members (sc. of the *scholae*) often were entrusted with special or secret missions, both diplomatic and military". As to the spelling of *scutarium*, it is not clear why Seyfarth here and in 27.10.16, 29.1.16 and 31.10.20 does not print the word with a capital letter, as in the other 23 times it occurs in Amm.

This section contains a programmatic statement concerning the treatment of events in West and East. In Book 20 the author had reported events in Julian's western surroundings and Constantius' actions and measures in the East alternately with frequent changeovers. He obviously found this method unsuitable for the changed situation of a structurally divided empire. Instead he decides to cover the developments in East and West in much larger separate units.

5.15

turbines exarsere maestissimi As is shown in the notes ad 24.8.5 *vis quaedam* and 25.10.7 *cuius fallaciis*, the majority of instances of the noun *turbo* in Amm. is used in a metaphorical sense. In the present text *maestus* means "maeroris efficiens, maerore dignus" (TLL VIII 49.7-34), "causing or associated with sorrow" (OLD s.v. 4): the storms in West and East caused great distress.

competenti loco singula digeremus The phrase *competenti loco* also occurs in 16.10.17 (*monstrabo*), 17.9.7 (*monstrabitur*), 30.7.4 (*docebimus*); cf. also 23.5.7 *digessimus tempore competenti.* In contrast to the present text none of these cases occurs in a programmatic context. See for *digerere*, 'to set out in orderly fashion', the note ad 25.10.3 *quae digerere.*

in eoo orbe isdem mensibus sunt actitata The eastern half of the empire is also denoted by *eous orbis* in 14.8.4, 20.8.8 (q.v.), 25.8.14 (q.v.) and

27.1.1. The 'same months' are September 365 to May 366. Amm.'s other four instances of the frequentative *actitare* are 14.9.8, 15.8.3, 28.1.17 and 47.

subinde saltuatim redire Amm. uses *subinde* most often with the meaning 'repeatedly', as is stated in the final part of the note ad 23.1.7 *subinde*. The only other occurrence of *saltuatim*, 'by leaps', in Amm. is 29.1.31, in an entirely different context. In a similar context, as Marié n. 60 points out, the word is used by Sisenna, quoted in Gel. 12.15.2: *Nos una aestate in Asia et Graecia gesta litteris idcirco continentia mandavimus, ne vellicatim aut saltuatim scribendo lectorum animos impediremus.*

ne squaliditate maxima rerum ordines implicemus This is a variation of the phrase (*ne*) *scientiam omnem squalida diversitate confundat* (26.1.10, q.v.). As a professional historian, Amm. loves *ordo*.

CHAPTER 6

Introduction

This chapter is devoted to the initial stage of Procopius' usurpation. It opens with a brief sketch of his character and promising career, which was further enhanced by Julian. The sudden death of this emperor spelt immediate danger for him: because of the rumour that the deceased had intended him to become his successor, he had every reason to fear the new emperor Jovian. Having gone into hiding far away, he was finally fed up with his exile and went to Chalcedon, from where he was able to observe the political and social climate in Constantinople. People of all ranks were disgusted by the cruel practices of the high-ranking Petronius, Valens' father-in-law, and prayed for a change of regime. However, as yet Procopius, like an animal of prey, could only wait for the right occasion.

Suddenly, as is reported in §11, the time was ripe. Valens had left the city for Syria, and some military contingents, destined to march to Thrace as reinforcements against the Gothic threat, stayed for two days in Constantinople. They proved ready to sell their support to Procopius, who was declared emperor in a meeting of a random crowd. He immediately visited the senate house, where he was confronted with the absence of all the important senators; he then hurried to the palace.

Ammianus' entire description is suffused with a spirit of deprecatory derision, especially from §11 onwards. The coup lacked a clear plan, sheer luck and coincidence marked its progress, and far from being a genuine leader, Procopius was pushed on by the whims of paid supporters. In short, it was an amateurish and haphazard affair. Yet this affair was soon to develop into an organized revolt, which posed serious problems to the imperial government. For this reason the author expects his readers to wonder how on earth such a ridiculous beginning could be followed by reasonably successful periods. In the final sections of the chapter he reacts to such questions by briefly mentioning four episodes in Roman history in which someone's sudden dash for power brought havoc to the commonwealth. It remains to be seen whether these historical parallels are convincing enough to prevent one from questioning Ammianus' report of the initial stage of Procopius' usurpation. However, in the absence of other coherent and detailed reports on the same scale, the reader is not in a position to contradict the historian, and he is thus only left with doubts about the correctness of the overall characterization of the events, regarding the text as tinged by "l'imagination satirique d'Ammien" (Sabbah 203; cf. also Matthews 193–195).

6.1 This section contains a brief survey of Procopius' career up to the reign of Julian, including a succinct characterization of his personality. Although refraining from strongly disapproving terms, Amm. pictures him as a sly and pushy type of man. His life and career are summarized in *PLRE* 1, Procopius 4+A. Lippold in *Gnomon* 46, 1974, 270 and Matthews 191–192. See also the relevant notes ad 17.14.3, 23.3.2, 25.9.12, and in particular the literature mentioned in the note ad 26.5.8 *Et circa*.

Insigni genere Procopius in Cilicia natus et educatus Comparable phrases about other men are 27.3.2 *humili genere in urbe natus*, 29.1.8 *claro genere in Galliis natus*, 29.2.5 *procerum genere natus*. The combination of *natus* and *educatus* can be found from Pl. *Rud.* 741 *Immo Athenis natus altusque educatusque Atticis* onwards. Some examples in Amm. are 17.10.10 *inter tributarios nati et educati*, 25.9.5 *in quibus nata erat et educata*. As appears from Them. *Or.* 7.86 c, Procopius hailed from the town Corycus on the Cilician coast; see Ruge, 1922, 1451–1452. The town was less famous than the nearby Corycian cave, in which the Giant Typhon hid Zeus after maiming him; see Apollod. 1.6.3. This mythological story is referred to when Procopius is called Τυφὼν ἀτεχνῶς ἐκ τοῦ Κιλικίου Κωρύκου by Themistius in the passage just referred to. See for literature on Cilicia the note ad 21.15.2 *Mobsucrenae*.

ea consideratione, qua propinquitate Iulianum postea principem contingebat The phrase *ea consideratione, qua* also occurs in 18.7.10; in both cases it is V's text, which is also accepted by Clark, Sabbah, Marié and Viansino. Obviously, these editors were not impressed by the argument of Löfstedt, 1907, 72–74, who notes that in 19.11.2, 26.5.14, 26.9.3 and 28.1.6 *consideratio* is followed by *quod*, and argues that the text of 18.7.10 and 26.6.1 should be emended following these examples. According to Löfstedt this is paleographically justified. Judging by their translations, the editors take *qua* to be syntactically equivalent to *quod*. Presumably, they interpret it as a case of attraction comparable to the phenomenon dealt with by Szantyr 566–567. As to the fact that Procopius was a relative of Julian Wagner notes:

"consobrinus fortasse, ut mater esset soror Basilinae matris Iuliani". Seeck, 1920, V, 46–47 and 443 elaborates on this: since any kinship with other members of the dynasty is never mentioned or alluded to, "kann jene Verwandtschaft nur durch die Mutter des Kaisers vermittelt sein". See further below the note ad *iamque summatibus* and Lenski, 2002, 69, and cf. Philost. *HE* 9.5 ὁ δὲ Προκόπιος οὗτος εἰς τὸ τοῦ Ἰουλιανοῦ γένος ἀνεφέρετο. In 23.3.2 Amm. himself had already mentioned the relationship between Procopius and Julian: *propinquo suo...Procopio*.

a primo gradu eluxit et ut vita moribusque castigatior, licet occultus erat et taciturnus, notarius diu perspicaciter militans et tribunus By way of introduction the first four words summarize his career as bright right from its beginning. See for *gradus* denoting a rank in the civil or military hierarchy TLL VI 2.2152.57 sqq. and the note ad 20.5.7 *ad potiorem*; cf. also 28.1.42 *ad gradus potestatum excelsos*. TLL V 2.425.30–38 contains a list of cases in which *elucere* is used about persons with the meaning "eminere, praestare, excellere"; cf. 15.13.2 about Musonianus: *sublimius, quam sperabatur, eluxit*.

After the brief introduction the development of Procopius' career is sketched in more detail. From Plautus onwards the combination of *vita* and *mores* is regularly used to indicate a person's perceptible conduct and way of life. Many examples can be found in Cicero and the *Historia Augusta*. The other occurrences in Amm. are 15.1.3 *formare vitam moresque*, 30.4.6 *vita, moribus frugalitateque spectati*. With *ut* the causal link between his blameless life and his successful career is expressed. Cf. for the rare *castigatior* 22.3.12 *monensque, ut castigatius viveret* (q.v.), 31.14.3 *ut castigatius agerent*. Procopius obviously stuck to a strict and rigorous lifestyle, but there was a drawback in his being *occultus...et taciturnus*. The latter adj. denotes the habit of keeping one's mouth shut, which can be praiseworthy, as in 21.13.4 *praeter optimates taciturnos et fidos* and 28.5.10 *per taciturnos quosdam et fidos*, where it characterizes reliable people who can keep a secret. In the present text, however, the combination with *occultus* clearly implies that it should be taken 'in malam partem'. See for *occultus* TLL IX 2.369.10–26 for instances where it means "fere i.q. non sincerus, non apertus, falsus". Some examples: Cic. *Fin.* 2.54 *occultus et tectus*, Tac. *Ann.* 4.52.3 (about Tiberius) *raram occulti pectoris vocem*. There was nothing reprehensible in Procopius' way of life, yet one felt that he had something up his sleeve; cf. also Them. *Or.* 7.90 b. TLL XI 1.1739. 7–22 provides examples of *perspicaciter* meaning "argute, diligenter"; cf. OLD s.v. *perspicax* b: with "a keen mental vision". See for *militare* denoting non-military functions the numerous examples in TLL VIII 968.59 sqq. and the notes ad 22.7.5 *si eis* and 26.6.5 *ubi quoniam*.

As Teitler, 1985, 19–21 demonstrates, there is a clear connection between the functions of *notarius* and *tribunus*: imperial *notarii* often had the rank of *tribunus*. In his capacity of *notarius* Procopius was sent as envoy to Persia in 358, as Amm. 17.14.3 reports: *Lucillianus missus est comes et Procopius tunc notarius*. See further Teitler, 1985, 162–163.

iamque summatibus proximus post Constanti obitum in rerum conversione velut imperatoris cognatus altius anhelabat adiunctus consortio comitum
In 361 Procopius' career had brought him close to the highest functions. See for *summates* the notes ad 19.1.6 *leni summatum* and 23.6.30 *quibus*. Amm.'s only other instance of *conversio* is 20.3.3 *utriusque sideris conversiones et motus* (q.v.). The present phrase derives from Cicero: *in conversione rerum ac perturbatione* (*Flac.* 94), *in tanta conversione et perturbatione omnium rerum* (*Phil.* 11.27). Note that Amm. leaves out *perturbatio*: the change, brought about by Julian's reign, was not a 'disorder'.

With *velut* Amm. expresses that Procopius himself used his relationship with Julian as a justification for his increasing ambitions; see OLD s.v. *velut* 6, but cf. also the note ad 20.9.5 *velut*. The word *cognatus* either denotes kinship in a general sense or, as a t.t., specifically refers to a relationship on the maternal side. Other examples of *altius anhelare* in Amm. are 16.12.46 (q.v.) about the Alamanni, 18.4.2, where excessive ambitions are ascribed to Ursicinus by the court clique, and 31.7.1 about two incompetent generals. A comparison of these cases shows that the phrase is definitely unfavourable.

The words *post Constanti obitum in rerum conversione velut imperatoris cognatus* make clear that Procopius became connected with the imperial house only after Julian had become emperor, Procopius was a relative of Julian, possibly a maternal cousin; *PLRE* I, Procopius 4. Other sources which refer to a relationship between Procopius and Julian: Lib. *Or.* 24.13; Eun. *fr.* 34.3; Zos. 3.35.2, 4.4.2, 7.1; Zon. 13.16; Philost. *HE* 9.5. In 26.6.18, 7.10, 16 and 9.3 a direct relationship with the Constantinian family is implied. However, it seems that Procopius had no clear Constantinian connections, but that he pretended such a relationship to give an air of legitimacy to his usurpation; Lenski, 2002, 69. Entering the *consortium comitum* probably means that Procopius' function can be compared to that of the *comites consistoriani*; Jones 506–507. For the *comites consistoriani* see also Noethlichs, 1998, 34–35 and Schlinkert, 1998.

et apparebat eum, si umquam potuisset, fore quietis publicae turbatorem For those who kept their eyes open it was evident that, given the opportunity, this man would some day disturb the peace of the commonwealth. Later on Amm. will characterize the rebel Firmus in similar terms: 29.5.21 and 45. See also the note ad 21.10.8, where Constantine is abused in a similar manner.

hunc Iulianus Persidem ingrediens consociato pari potestatis iure Sebastiano in Mesopotamia cum manu militum reliquerat valida This repeats 23.3.5 *triginta milia lectorum militum eidem commisit Procopio iuncto ad parilem potestatem Sebastiano comite.* See the note ad loc. for the number of soldiers, about which the sources are not unanimous. See for Sebastianus the note ad 23.3.5 *Sebastiano.* As to equality of rank see 23.3.5 *commisit Procopio iuncto ad parilem potestatem Sebastiano comite* (q.v.). Under Julian Procopius had made a significant career: from being *notarius* and *tribunus* he became *comes*, as can be concluded from the words *adiunctus consortio comitum* in the previous section. Cf. Wiebe, 1995, 8, who suggests that Procopius became *comes primi ordinis*: "Julian aber machte ihn zum *comes*, wohl zum *comes primi ordinis*, wie der Kontext bei Ammian vermuten lässt"; also Grattarola, 1986, 84. In this case he was also a member of the *consistorium* (Jones 333–334). For *comites primi ordinis*, see Scharf, 1994.

The fact that Procopius was put on an equal footing with the older, distinguished general Sebastianus, illustrates Julian's regard for his maternal cousin.

6.2

mandaratque, ut susurravit obscurior fama – nemo enim dicti auctor exstitit verus –, pro cognitorum ageret textu Catullus 80.5 *fama susurrat* is the first instance of a whispering rumour; see further OLD s.v. *susurro* and cf. also Prud. *c. Symm.* 2.920 *non memini, nec tale aliquid vel fama susurrat.* The lack of clarity and certainty regarding the content of rumours can also be found in Liv. 23.20.3 *obscurior fama*, 30.19.11 *obscura eius pugnae fama est*, Plin. *Ep.* 5.13.10 *obscurior fama.*

With *enim* the author appeals to the reader's understanding of this qualification of the information about Julian's 'nomination' of Procopius: the rumour was entirely anonymous. One is reminded of Trajan's rebuke of Pliny's acceptance of anonymous reports concerning Christians: *sine auctore vero propositi libelli.* Using such evidence was *et pessimi exempli nec saeculi nostri* (Plin. *Ep.* 10.97.2). The present text is comparable in that Amm. notes that the story in question could not be ascribed to any named person. The editors prefer Gelenius' *ageret* to V's *agere*, presumably because of the parallelism with *provideret.*

See for the paratactical structure without preceding *ut* Blomgren 157–159, Szantyr 528 sqq. and the note ad 20.5.9 *recturi*.

Amm. had already reported the rumour in 23.3.2 *dicitur...occulte paludamentum purpureum propinquo suo tradidisse Procopio mandasseque arripere fidentius principatum, si se interisse didicerit apud Parthos*, with relevant notes. The only other source which mentions that Julian had designated Procopius as his successor is Zos. 4.4.2, who says that Julian gave Procopius an imperial robe for reasons only known to the two of them; δοὺς αὐτῷ καὶ βασιλικὴν στολὴν ἔχειν δι' αἰτίαν πᾶσι τοῖς ἄλλοις ἠγνοημένην. Wiebe, 1995, 9–17, who thinks that Amm.'s story about the purple mantle being handed to Procopius is inspired by Hdn. 4.13.3, discusses in detail the passages in Amm. and his sources, which are concerned with Procopius being designated as Julian's successor. That it was a rumour is very clear from Amm.'s words in the next section: *falsoque rumore disperso inter abeuntis anhelitus animae eundem Iulianum verbo mandasse placere sibi Procopio clavos summae rei gerendae committi*; cf. Philost. *HE* 9.5 who reports that opinions circulated that the empire ought to be offered to Procopius; καὶ πολλοὶ ἀνεκινοῦντο λογισμοὶ τὴν βασιλείαν αὐτῷ περιάπτοντες, καὶ τοὺς λογισμοὺς καὶ λόγοι διέφερον ('and many opinions were batted around that the emperorship ought to be offered to him; and these thoughts were spread by words'). Neither Lib. *Or.* 18.273 nor *epit.* 43.4, quoted in the note ad 25.3.20 *super imperatore* (q.v.), states that Julian had designated Procopius as his successor. The rumour was either deliberately spread by adversaries of Procopius to put him in the position of a usurper, or invented by Procopius himself to give the impression that his usurpation was legitimate; Wiebe, 1995, 9–10; Lenski, 2002, 69–70.

See for the general meanings of *textus*, viz. 'train of events' and 'written text', the note ad 20.4.11 *quo textu*. The present instance is a variation of the former: Procopius should act 'in accordance with the developments of which he was informed'.

et, si subsidia rei Romanae languisse sensisset, imperatorem ipse se provideret ocius nuncupari The euphemistic formulation in the protasis of this conditional period approaches the 'oracular' style: 'if he recognized that the resources of the Roman state had lost their vigour'. Of course, this could only be the case after the disappearance of Julian, and precisely this disappearance would create such a situation.

Amm. has the classical combination of *providere* with an *ut*-clause in 16.4.4 and 27.12.7, and with a *ne*-clause in 16.3.3, 24.4.2, 26.1.6. The construction with an a.c.i. (with a passive inf.) also occurs in

28.1.53 and 28.6.8. As is noted ad 20.1.3 *festinaret ocius*, this adv. often occurs when orders are given or carried out.

qui iniuncta civiliter agens et caute This is Amm.'s only instance of the verb *iniungere*, 'to impose (a task)'. The manner in which Procopius performed his tasks left little to be desired: the first adverb expresses "moderation...in keeping to one's proper station or within the bounds of one's office" (Seager 22; see also the note ad 21.16.9 *acrius*), whereas *caute*, which like *cautus* occurs quite often in the *Res Gestae* (see Brandt, 1999, 386 n. 34), means that people act with careful prudence in military and political matters; see the notes ad 20.11.1 *quae dum* and 23.5.5 *posthabito*, and Seager 69–76. Procopius' conduct implies that as yet he hid his ambitions and bided his time.

6.3

Iuliani letaliter vulnerati funus et ad regenda communia comperit Iovianum evectum This news meant that Procopius had already lost considerable ground. Worse was to follow. There can be no doubt that *funus* means 'death' here: Julian's 'funeral' was in fact entrusted to Procopius; see 25.9.12–13 with the notes. Cf. 25.8.8 *Iovianum post eius obitum ad culmen augustum evectum* (q.v.) and the note ad 20.8.21 *eum ad.* TLL III 1977.60 sqq. presents a list of cases in which *commune* indicates the (affairs of the) state or the commonwealth. However, for this meaning the plural *communia* is rare; Sen. *Tranq.* 3.1 *communia privataque pro facultate administrans* is the nearest parallel. Valesius remarks ad loc.: "Et hic graecissat Marcellinus. Graeci enim τὰ κοινὰ dicunt rempublicam". If it is indeed a Grecism, it does not follow that this is due to Amm. Cf., for instance, Ov. *Met.* 12.7 *mille rates gentisque simul commune Pelasgae* with Bömer's note.

falsoque rumore disperso inter abeuntis anhelitus animae eundem Iulianum verbo mandasse placere sibi Procopio clavos summae rei gerendae committi The reader who remembers Amm.'s description of Julian's deathbed will not be surprised by *falso*; in 25.3.20 the dying emperor said: *super imperatore vero creando caute reticeo*; see the notes on the section. Amm. may well mean that the rumour was deliberately spread by Jovian's courtiers, in order to put Procopius in the position of a usurper.

With *abeuntis* Amm. possibly refers to *abeundi tempus e vita* (25.3.15) and *abeo* (25.3.18) in Julian's deathbed speech. V's *vero* was corrected to *verbo* by Madvig, 1884, 268, an excellent emendation in spite of his curious argument, which is a reaction against a rival conjecture *sero*: "sera non erat significatio voluntatis, si audiebatur et intelligebatur; brevissima fuit, quoniam vix loqui moriens imperator poterat". The addition of *verbo* to *mandasse* is not pleonastic or superfluous, but neither does it express brevity. In fact, it means that Julian was actually heard giving his order; cf. Sal. *Cat.* 44.6 *mandata verbis dat*, Cic. *Fam.* 10.8.5 *plura etiam verbo quam scriptura mandata dedimus*, HA *AC* 10.10 *verbo mandabo*, *Dig.* 36.1.38 *si verbo dicit*. Moreover, *verbo* implies that no written document was available.

Although the metaphor of the 'helm of state' is less frequent than one might have expected, it does occur a number of times in Latin literature; Cicero has eight examples, among which *clavum tanti imperii tenere et gubernacula rei publicae tractare* (*Sest.* 20); cf. also Liv. 4.3.16 *ad gubernacula rei publicae accedere*, Plin. *Ep.* 10.1.1 *virtutes tuos ad gubernacula rei publicae quam susceperas admovere*; cf. also Constantius' words in Amm. 21.13.10 *utque cautius navigandi magister clavos pro fluctuum motibus erigens vel inclinans* (q.v.). See for *summa res* 15.5.19, where it is stated that Ursicinus was called *orientis vorago invadendaeque summae rei...affectator*, in other words a dangerous potential usurper. A more difficult case occurs in 24.1.1: see the note ad *Iulianus summae rei*.

veritus, ne hac ex causa indemnatus occideretur, e medio se conspectu discrevit Cf. Lib. *Or.* 24.13 οἰκεῖός τε ὢν ἐτύγχανεν Ἰουλιανῷ καὶ δεδιὼς καὶ κρυπτόμενος καὶ ἀεὶ ληφθήσεσθαι προσδοκῶν κτλ. The term *indemnatus*, "not found guilty in a court of law" (OLD, s.v.), also occurs in classical Latin. There is only one other undisputed instance in Amm., viz. 15.2.5 about Ursicinus. The occurrences in 15.5.15 and 29.5.3 are dubious and conjectural respectively. From Pacuvius *trag.* 184 *Non tu te e conspectu hinc amolire?* onwards *e conspectu* in combination with verbs meaning 'to remove (oneself)' occurs throughout Latin literature, e.g. Cic. *Ver.* 5.88 *evolarat iam e conspectu*, Apul. *Met.* 6.10 *e conspectu perniciter abeunt*, Amm. 24.6.5 *evolant e conspectu quinque subito naves*. The entire phrase is an elaboration on *discessit* in 25.9.13.

In Book 25 Amm. had reported that Procopius was charged by Jovian to bring Julian's body to Tarsus and to bury it there. After he had fulfilled this assignment he disappeared; 25.9.12–13 with relevant notes. Zos. 4.4.3 has the unlikely story that Procopius, after the election of Jovian, rushed to the new emperor to hand him the imperial robe, said to be given to him by Julian. He begged Jovian to release him from his military duties and to be allowed to retire. Jovian granted this request and Procopius retired together with his wife and children to Caesarea in Cappadocia, where he had prosperous estates, and devoted his life to farming and private business. Ἐπεὶ δὲ ὁ δαίμων εἰς ἕτερόν τι τὴν τῶν πραγμάτων ἤγαγε τύχην καὶ μετὰ τὴν Ἰουλιανοῦ τελευτὴν Ἰοβιανὸς εἰς τὸν βασίλειον ἀναβέβηκε θρόνον, δραμὼν εὐθὺς ὁ Προκόπιος τὴν δεδομένην αὐτῷ βασιλικὴν ἐσθῆτα Ἰοβιανῷ παρέδωκεν, ὑπὸ τίνος τε εἴη λαβὼν ὡμολόγει, καὶ ἐξελιπάρει τὸν βασιλέα τῆς τε στρατείας αὐτὸν ἀνεῖναι καὶ ἐν ἡσυχίᾳ συγχωρῆσαι βιῶναι, γεωργίᾳ καὶ ἐπιμελείᾳ τῶν οἰκείων ἐγκαρτεροῦντα· καὶ τούτου τυχὼν ἐπὶ τὴν Καισάρειαν, ἣ Καππαδοκίας ἐστίν, ἅμα γυναικὶ καὶ τέκνοις ἐχώρει, ταύτην οἰκεῖν ἐγνωκὼς οἷα ἐν αὐτῇ τὰ τίμια κτήματα ἔχων. See Paschoud n. 114. Presumably, Jovian considered him as a serious rival for his position. The moment of Procopius' disappearance is not quite clear from the sources, but it is most likely that he went into hiding already during Jovian's reign, considering Amm.'s words in the next section: *cumque a Ioviano exploratius indagari latibula sua sentiret*; cf., however, Ensslin, 1957, 252 – followed by Wiebe, 1995, 6 – who argues that Procopius was threatened under Jovian, but was only forced to hide when Valentinian and Valens attempted to stir up hatred of the memory of Julian and his friends; 26.4.4 *ut loquebatur pertinax rumor, invidiam cientes Iuliani memoriae principis amicisque eius tamquam clandestinis praestigiis laesi.*

maxime post Ioviani territus necem, notariorum omnium primi, quem Iuliano perempto veluti dignum imperio paucis militibus nominatum novaque exinde coeptare suspectum cruciabiliter didicerat interfectum This is to some extent a literal repetition of the contents of the last part of 25.8.18: see the notes ad loc. Procopius' relationship with Julian, but also the rumour that he was named as Julian's successor by Julian himself, put him in serious danger, even more so after Jovian had put Iovianus to death, who, as Amm. mentions in this section as well as in 25.8.18, was considered worthy of imperial power by some. According to Amm. Jovian even considered Procopius such a serious rival for the throne, that he hastened to reach the peace agreement with the Persians in order to forestall a possible usurpation; 25.7.10–11 with notes; cf. 25.9.8 *dum extimescit*. See also Lenski, 2002, 71.

As to the dat. of the Agens *paucis militibus*, see the notes ad 18.4.7 *morantibus*, 20.3.10 *exortus* and 22.8.42 *eisque*. Revolutionary projects are indicated by *nova* in 21.13.1 (q.v.). The adv. *cruciabiliter* is by no means exaggerated with regard to the horrible way in which Iovianus was liquidated: *praeceps actus in puteum siccum obrutus est saxorum multitudine superiacta* (25.8.18).

In 25.9.13 Amm. reports very briefly that, after having taken care of Julian's burial in Tarsus, Procopius completely disappeared, thwart- **6.4** ing all endeavours of the authorities to arrest him, only to reappear suddenly, after a long time, in Constantinople, dressed in purple. The reader is now reasonably well informed of Procopius' wanderings and hardships.

et quia se quaeri industria didicerat magna Cf. 25.9.13 *studio quaesitus ingenti* (q.v.).

vitans gravioris invidiae pondus ad abdita longiusque remota discessit The remarkable metaphor of the 'weighty mass' of intense hatred seems to occur only in Amm.; the other cases are 14.11.3, where the eunuchs at the court try to crush Ursicinus by that weight, 16.12.29, where the Caesar Julian cautiously avoids it by an irreproachable conduct, 28.1.52, where even the cruel Maximinus is wary of the hatred which he would encounter should he execute a prominent member of the Roman patriciate. The combination of *abditus* and *remotus* can also be found in entirely different contexts in Sen. *Ot.* 5.2, where the author censures those who go to the lengths of a perilous sea voyage to become acquainted with *aliquid abditum et remotum*, Apul. *Met.* 4.18 *monumentum quoddam conspicamur procul a via remoto et abdito loco positum*, Dict. 6.14, where Ulixes, plagued by bad omina and nightmares, retires *in alia loca abdita remotaque*. Obviously, Amm. did not know in which remote and secret places Procopius was hiding before he reached Chalcedon; Lenski, 2002, 71.

cumque a Ioviano exploratius indagari latibula sua sentiret et formae vitae iam fuisset pertaesum See for *exploratius*, 'with great care', the relevant notes ad 18.6.21 and 21.12.20. In the note ad 17.13.16 *ad indagandum* De Jonge suggests that the verb there is a "a hunter's term". This is quite likely in view of the context, in which it is reported that Constantius' soldiers, having routed the Limigantes, next 'hunted down' all those who were hiding on the other side of a river: light-armed troops crossed and *occuparunt latibula*. For the present text this meaning or connotation of *indagare* is plausible too: Procopius compares himself to a beast which is being hounded. In itself this could prove that Seyfarth and Viansino are wrong in not acknowledging that V's *formae* should be emended to E's *ferinae*, printed by Clark and Marié. In fact, Amm. was directly inspired by Gel. 5.14.26 (in the famous story of Androclus and the lion) *Sed ubi me, inquit, vitae illius ferinae iam pertaesum est*. Obviously, this clinches the matter.

In 16.5.6, 22.4.1 (see the note ad *non ut*), 26.1.1, 30.8.8 *indagare* denotes (intellectual) research.

quippe a celsiore statu deiectus ad inferiora etiam edendi penuria in locis squalentibus stringebatur hominumque egebat colloquiis Cf. for *celsiore statu* 17.5.4 *celsiores fortunas* (q.v.), 21.16.1 *celsiores dignitates* (q.v.). Procopius "had fallen from a lofty position" (Hamilton). Procopius fell from the status of *comes* (26.6.1) and one of Julian's foremost commanders (and according to rumours his named successor) to a persona non grata. Although Gelenius' *inferiora* is no doubt the best correction of V's *inferi* one can think of, it is strangely vague and euphemistic, expressing something like 'the lower rungs of the social ladder'. The phrase *edendi penuria* is borrowed from Verg. A. 7.113; see Fordyce ad loc. See for *squalentibus locis* the notes ad 22.15.22 *inter arundines* and 23.6.60 *squalentia*, which make clear that Amm. means impenetrable areas outside the civilized world. The basic meaning of *stringere*, and the various contexts in which it occurs, are dealt with in the note ad 20.11.2 *suis rationibus*. Procopius was 'bound' by the pangs of hunger and could not manage without social contacts.

postremae necessitatis impulsu deviis itineribus ad Calchedonos agrum pervenit To express 'dire straits' Amm. uses *necessitas* with a superlative in a number of cases, e.g. 16.12.33 *ante necessitatem ultimam*, 19.8.8 *necessitate docente postrema*, 20.4.18 *trusus ad necessitatem extremam* (q.v.). See further Seager 58–60. The phrase *deviis itineribus* is reminiscent of Tac. *Ann.* 6.15.3 (about Tiberius) *deviis plerumque itineribus ambiens patriam* (i.e. Rome) *et declinans*, the more so since Procopius as yet had avoided the new Rome. For Chalcedon see the note ad 22.3.2. According to Zos. 4.5.1–2 soon after Valentinian and Valens were elected, they sent agents to arrest Procopius. The latter gave himself up and told them to take him where they wanted, on condition that he was first allowed to speak to his wife and see his children: Ἐπεὶ οὖν ἐνδεδώκασιν, ἑστίασιν αὐτοῖς παρεσκεύαζε, καὶ οἰνωθέντας ἰδὼν ἅμα τοῖς οἰκείοις ἅπασιν ἐπὶ τὸν Εὔξεινον ἔδραμε πόντον, ἐκεῖθέν τε νεὼς ἐπιβὰς ἐπὶ τὴν Ταυριανὴν διῄει Χερρόνησον· χρόνον δέ τινα διατρίψας αὐτόθι καὶ τοὺς οἰκήτορας θεασάμενος οὐδεμίαν ἐν αὐτοῖς ἔχοντας πίστιν, δεδιὼς μή ποτε τοῖς ἐπὶ ζήτησιν ἀφικνουμένοις αὐτοῦ παραδοθείη, παραπλέουσαν ἰδὼν ὁλκάδα καὶ ταύτῃ παραδοὺς ἑαυτὸν καὶ τοὺς οἰκείους τὴν Κωνσταντινούπολιν καταλαμβάνει νυκτὸς οὔσης ἔτι (4.5.2). "When they [the agents] consented, he prepared a feast for them and, as soon as they were drunk, escaped with his whole family to the Black Sea, where they embarked and crossed to the Tauric Chersonese. He stayed here some time, but seeing that the people were quite untrustworthy and fearing that they would betray him some day to his pursuers, he put himself and his family on board a passing merchant ship and arrived in the evening at Constantinople" (tr. Ridley).

6.5 *ubi quoniam ei illud firmius visum est receptaculum apud fidissimum amicorum delitescebat, Strategium quendam ex palatino milite senatorem* Amm.'s other instances of *receptaculum*, 'place of refuge', which already occurs in classical Latin, are 28.1.48, 29.5.25, 31.3.8, 31.6.6. The gen. part. *amicorum* implies that *fidissimum* has a comparative sense: Strategius was Procopius' most reliable friend. *PLRE* I Strategius 2 refers to Zos. 4.5.3, but there it is only stated that, while in Constantinople, Procopius stayed with an acquaintance whom he had been in close contact with before; no name is given. He should not be confused with the other Strategius (Musonianus) mentioned by Amm. in 15.13.2. As to Procopius' other supporters, Amm. names several of them: Araxius (26.7.6, 10.7), Hormisdas junior (26.8.12), Phronimius (26.7.4, 10.8), Euphrasius (26.7.4, 10.8), Hyperechius (26.8.5) and Marcellus (26.10.1 and 3). Amm. mentions furthermore Agilo and Gomoarius, who both deserted Procopius when they realized they were fighting a lost cause (26.7.4, 9.6–7). According to Wiebe, 1995, 48 ff.; Delmaire, 1997, 118–120; Lenski, 2002, 108–110 other supporters of Procopius not mentioned by Amm. were: Helpidius (Philost. *HE* 7.10; *PLRE* I, Helpidius 6), Eugenius (Zos. 4.5.3; *PLRE* I, Eugenius 4), Andronicus (Lib. *Or.* 62.58–60; *PLRE* I, Andronicus 3) and possibly Heraclius (Eun. *fr.* 34.3; *PLRE* I, Heraclius 4). Libanius may also have been associated with the revolt – e.g. Lib. *Or.* 1.163–165 with commentary Norman, 1965, 196–197. He was also accused of having composed a panegyric in honour of Procopius; whether he had done so is quite uncertain; Lenski, 2002, 108. Wiebe, 1995, 51–52 mentions bishop Eunomius as a possible supporter of Procopius' revolt; however, Philost. *HE* 9.6, the only source which connects Eunomius to Procopius, does not explicitly say that Eunomius favoured Procopius.

Many of Procopius' supporters, though not all, seem to have been pagan and former adherents of Julian. This has led some scholars to speculate that Procopius' revolt might be considered as a pagan reaction against the new Christian emperors; Solari, 1932, 145; Blockley, 1975, 56; Wiebe, 1995, esp. 54, 82–83. In particular Grattarola, 1986, 90–94 and Lenski, 2002, 110–111 have rightly objected to this. First of all, Procopius himself was a Christian, as e.g. appears from the ChiRo symbol on his coinage (Pearce, 1951, 193, 215, 240, 252). Moreover, not all of Procopius' supporters were pagan – there were also Christians among them –, and on Valens' side Christians fought as well as pagans. The fact that the sources, both Christian, such as the church historians, and pagan, such as Ammianus and Zosimus, do not present the revolt as a pagan reaction to the Christian rule of Valens and Valentinian, makes it highly unlikely that Procopius' revolt was also motivated by religious sentiments. More likely, the revolt was a reaction to the dissatisfaction with the rule of the Valentinian dynasty in general.

Since most supporters of Procopius seem to have been former adherents of Julian's (e.g. Lenski, 2002, 108–110), it is likely that Strategius had also favoured Julian's reign. Wiebe, 1995, 49 considers it possible that the two men had become acquainted at Julian's court and participated in the Persian campaign. Possibly Strategius' career had stalled when the Pannonians came to the throne. It is likely that he had held a bureaucratic position at the imperial court; see for palatine officials the note ad 21.16.3 *palatinas dignitates*. The words *palatino milite* probably do not refer to a military position at the palace as, for instance, several translations seem to imply ("soldier of the court" Rolfe; "Palastsoldaten", Seyfarth; "soldato palatino", Caltabiano) but to an administrative function. The later Roman bureaucracy was modelled on the army, and service was known as *militia* or *militia officialis*, and military titulature was common within the civil service. A law dating from 341, for instance, refers to accountants, secretaries and record keepers as *milites* (*Cod. Iust.* 10.69.1); cf. also *militans* in 26.6.1. See Jones 566; Kelly, 2004, 20–21, Speidel, 2006 and especially MacMullen, 1963, Chap. 3. It is more likely that Strategius became a senator of Constantinople as a civil court official than "aus der kaiserlichen Leibgarde" (Wiebe, 1995, 49). For the Constantinopolitan senate see the note ad 22.2.4 *verecundis senatus*; add to the literature mentioned there Vanderspoel, 1995, 61–66 and Heather, 1998, 184–191.

See for *ex*, 'former', with terms denoting military and political posts the note ad 25.10.7 ...*ex actuario*.

Constantinopolim, quantum fieri potuit, clanculo saepe intermeans The *Res Gestae* contains a variety of restrictive clauses introduced by *quantum*, 'insofar'. The one in the present text also occurs in 18.3.3, 21.9.2, 22.5.1. TLL VII 2222.47–55 lists only four instances of *intermeare*, two of them in Amm. The other one is 15.11.16 about the river Rhône, which flows into Lake Geneva *eamque intermeans nusquam aquis misceatur externis*. The meaning proposed in TLL, "i.q. meando penetrare", fits the present text excellently: it was, of course, too risky for Procopius to pay his frequent visits to Constantinople via any normal direct route, used by many travellers.

ut indicio eiusdem Strategii patuit, postquam saepius in factionis conscios inquisitum Amm. hastens to anticipate any questions of a reader who might wonder how he knew about Procopius' journeys, which nobody had witnessed (*clanculo*): this evidence became available in the course of the interrogations during the investigation of Procopius' putsch. See for *indicium* as a juridical t.t. denoting evidence gathered during investigations Cic. *Clu.* 39 *crimen...indicio Avilii comprobabatur*, Verg. *A.* 2.84 *infando indicio*, Tac. *Ann.* 11.35.3 *Titium Proculum...indicium offerentem*, Cod. Theod. 7.1.10 *pro praemio huius indicii*, Amm. 26.4.4 *ne verbo quidem tenus insidiarum indicio ullo reperto*; cf. further Heumann-Seckel s.v. and OLD s.v. 2b. Cf. for *inquirere in aliquem*, 'to search for grounds to indict a person', Cic. *Mur.* 45 *inquirere in competitores*, and for *factio*, 'clique', 'group of conspirators', the passages in which it is reported that Silvanus and Gordian III were brought down *factione iniquorum* (15.5.32) and *factione Philippi* (23.5.17) respectively. Procopius' supporters are denoted by *factio* in 26.7.8 and 26.8.10 *cum in factionis participes saeviretur*. This phrase and 26.10.6 *saevitum est in multos* could raise the question whether in the present text the slightly puzzling *saepius* ought to be emended to *saevius*. However, this form does not occur often, in Amm. only in 20.8.8, whereas *saepius* is quite common: Amm. has more than twenty instances. The gruesome story of the heavy-handed interrogations and ruthless executions of these people can be found in 26.10.9-14. See for the frequent ellipsis of forms of *esse* Blomgren 68-79; the present case (*inquisitum*) is dealt with on p. 71.

6.6 *ritu itaque sollertissimi cuiusdam speculatoris ignotus ob squalorem vultus et maciem* Cf. for *ritu* with gen. expressing a comparison 19.7.8 (the Persian king) *proeliatoris militis ritu prosiluit in confertos*, 22.8.42 (the Halani and their likes) *ferarum taetro ritu vescuntur*, 29.2.23 *histrionis ritu mutata repente persona*. Although the use of *quidam* to intensify a preceding adj. does not normally occur with a superlative, here it is the most likely explanation; after all one also finds phrases like *divina quaedam et inaudita auctoritas* (Cic. *Red. Pop.* 7). See further the note ad 20.4.13 *fortuna quaedam* and OLD s.v. *quidam*[1] 2. Amm. uses the adj. *sollers* in a laudatory sense in 17.2.3 *sollertissimus Caesar*, 24.7.2 *princeps sollertissimus* (q.v.), but also pejoratively ('crafty', 'wily'): 30.1.2 *male sollertes homines dispendiis saepe communibus pasti*, 31.12.9 *astu et ludificandi varietate nimium sollers*. The translators interpret *ignotus* as expressing that he was not recognized, e.g. "inaperçu" (Marié), "irreconoscibile" (Caltabiano). This is not incorrect in view of *ob*, but there may be more to it. The adj. is sometimes used to denote low-class people whom one does not pay attention to. This is the case in 14.1.6, where one of Gallus' devices to spy among the population was *ut homines quidam ignoti vilitate ipsa parum cavendi ad colligendos rumores per Antiochiae latera cuncta destinarentur* and 26.7.16 *pro ignotis* (q.v.). Cf. also Aeneas complaining about his predicament in Verg. A. 1.384: *ipse ignotus, egens*, 'a nobody, deprived of everything'. For his disguise Procopius paid particular attention to his face, which looked dirty and emaciated.

rumusculos colligebat tunc crebrescentes The deminutivum of *rumor* is *rumusculus*, as is noted by Prisc. *gramm.* II 105.5–6. It occurs three times in Cicero: *imperitorum hominum rumusculos aucupati* (*Clu.* 105), *Cassio...omnis rumusculos...aucupante* (*Leg.* 3.35), *Att.* 2.5, and seven times in Jerome, e.g. *ep.* 52.13 *cave ne hominum rumusculos aucuperis*. As appears from these examples, people are sometimes 'hunting after' (*aucupari*) or 'collecting' (*colligere*) rumours: *qui omnis rumorum et contionum ventos colligere consuesset* (Cic. *Clu.* 77), Amm. 14.1.6 *ad colligendos rumores*.

ut sunt acerba semper instantia This use of *ut* is described in OLD s.v. 20: "as accords with the way in which...by reference to a general tendency or characteristic": people tend to call the circumstances in which they have to live at that specific moment, harsh and disagreeable. Amm. often uses *instans* to denote what is happening in the actual situation which is described. See for this meaning *Rhet. Her.* 2.8 *tempora tria: praeteritum, instans, futurum*, Quint. *Inst.* 5.10.42 *praeteritum, instans, futurum*; cf. also Gel. 17.7.7. It often occurs in this sense in the grammatici, when they are dealing with tenses. See for a number of examples in Amm. the note ad 21.7.1 *rigore itaque*. The present text is the only instance of the substantivized neutr. plur.

incusantium multorum Valentem quasi cupiditate aliena rapiendi succensum One would have expected that the *ut*-clause in the preceding lemma implies that Amm. is inclined to take the accusations of 'many people' against Valens' administration with a pinch of salt. However, in the next section he immediately continues with a reference to Valens' *diritas*. The genitive *incusantium multorum* denotes the Agens of the rumours. The figurative use of *succensus*, 'inflamed (by a passion)' is poetic: *laudis succensus amore* (Verg. A. 7.496), *succensa cupidine* (Ov.

Met. 8.74), *dulcedine famae/succensus* (Juv. 7.39–40), *rabie succensa* (Claud. *IV Cons. Hon.* 243). Seizing the property of others was a passion of Sapor (18.10.2), but decidedly denounced by Procopius himself in 26.7.16. Other examples of *aliena rapere* occur in 26.10.11 and 30.8.9.

6.7 *cuius diritati adiectum erat incentivum exitiale socer Petronius* Valens was a frightful man, who inspired terror; cf. Hor. *Carm.* 3.6.36 *Hannibalemque dirum*. With this *diritas* the emperor was in the unenviable company of Gallus (14.7.3) and Sapor (18.10.4). Cf. 14.1.2 *cuius* (= Gallus) *acerbitati uxor grave accesserat incentivum*: Petronius played Constantia to Valens' Gallus. See for the remarkable conceit of a person being an *incentivum* the note ad 20.6.1 *incentivo Antonini*. Petronius (*PLRE* I, Petronius 3) was father of Valens' wife Domnica; Socr. *HE* 4.26.21, 5.1.3; Soz. *HE* 7.1.2. He may have come from Sirmium; Lenski, 2002, 53. It is not known whether he had had another official position apart from the command of the Martenses, and before he became *patricius*. His rank of *patricius* made him influential. He supported the appointment of Nebridius as PPO; 26.7.4. See also Lenski, 2002, 60–62.

ex praeposito Martensium militum promotus repentino saltu patricius Other 'saltatorial' promotions of men disliked by Amm. are Gallus (14.1.1 *ad principale culmen insperato cultu provectus*, where V's *cultu* should be emended to *saltu*, as is pointed out in the last part of the note ad 22.4.3 *ab egestate*) and Agilo (20.2.5 *Agilone ad eius* (= Ursicinus) *locum immodico saltu promoto*). The *Martenses seniores* were a *legio comitatensis* in the East; *Not. Dign. Or.* 7.40. *Praepositus militum* is a general term used by Amm. for a military commander; see the note ad 21.4.3 *viso praeposito*. It has been supposed that the unit under command of Petronius was not the legion of *Martenses* itself, but a detachment of the *Martenses* stationed at the frontier. Cf., however, Hoffmann, 1969–1970, vol. 1, 356–357, who argues that the legion itself is meant; Hoffmann even suggests that Petronius, as commander of this legion, may have participated in Julian's Persian expedition.

The term *patricius* does not denote a function, but is a honorific title, which was devised by Constantine: πρώτου ταύτην ἐπινοήσαντος τὴν τιμήν (Zos. 2.40.2). See for this title Ensslin, 1934; Jones 106, 528, 534, 1225 n. 28, and, in particular, Heil, 1966. See also Kübler, 1949, 2231–2232. *Cod. Theod.* 7.22.7 from April 365, concerning the recruitment of sons of veterans, was directed *ad Petronium patricium* and is the first piece of evidence that Petronius bore the title *patricius*, although he had probably received this title earlier.

animo deformis et habitu His ugly appearance mirrored his soul. As is noted ad 20.3.10 *cornutae habitu*, in Amm. the most usual meaning of *habitus* is 'clothes'; see e.g. 20.4.22 *fulgentem eum augusto habitu*, 26.2.3 *principali habitu circumdatus et corona* with the notes. However, in 14.1.6 *egentium habitu* the outward appearance in general is meant, and in 30.4.11 *vultus gravitate ad habitum composita tristiorem* specifically the look on the faces of the *iuris consulti* satirized by Amm. Since in the present text *habitu* is the counterpart of *animo*, it no doubt denotes either Petronius' face or, rather, his appearance. The translators interpret *habitu* in this way, e.g. "de coeur et d'aspect également répugnant" (Marié), "brutto nell'animo e nel corpo" (Viansino).

qui ad nudandos sine discretione cunctos immaniter flagrans nocentes pariter et insontes post exquisita tormenta quadrupli nexibus vinciebat Petronius' greed is again mentioned in 26.6.17 *Petronium, ut praediximus, divitias violenter augentem*. Cf. for *nudare*, 'to fleece', Hor. *Ep*. 1.18.21 *quem praeceps alea nudat*, Amm. 30.4.19 *nudatis litigatoribus*. Petronius turns the principle of justice 'without regard to persons' into the practice of injustice in gathering money. The emperor Valentinian had the same habit: 30.5.5 *propositum principis quaerendae undique pecuniae vias absque iustorum iniustorumque discretione scrutantis*. See also the note ad 17.1.1 *sine discretione*. TLL VI 1.847.32–34 notes only one other instance of *flagrare ad*: Greg. M. *Dial*. 1.5 *ad sola coelestia flagrabat*. Cf. also the note ad 26.5.12 *verum ardens*.

The combination guilty – innocent also occurs in 14.7.21 *nullo...discernente a societate noxiorum insontes*, 15.3.2 *sine innocentium sontiumque differentia*, 18.3.5 *vexatique multi nocentes sunt et innocentes*, 29.1.18 *nocentes innocentesque...perurgebat*. TLL V 2. 1821.83–1822.42 lists a remarkable number of cases in which *exquisitus* is used "cum nota vituperationis", e.g. Cic. *Off*. 3.100: *exquisita supplicia* awaited Regulus on his return to Carthage, Suet. *Tib*. 62.2: on Capri Tiberius had the condemned *post longa et exquisita tormenta* thrown into the sea. Other clear examples in Amm. are 15.1.3 *studio blanditiarum exquisito sublatus*, 19.11.3 *exquisitorum detestanda nomina titulorum*, "the abominable refinements of taxation" (tr. Hamilton), 27.12.3 *per exquisitas periuriisque mixtas illecebras*, 28.2.11 *exquisitis fallaciis abundantes*. See for *exquisitus* used in bonam partem the note ad 22.10.1 *exquisita docilitate*. In his *Ep*. 21 Basil of Caesarea reports that the world is full of men who demand payment and make accusations; like Amm. he mentions the 'much-discussed' fourfold: ἡ πολυθρύλλητος αὕτη τετραπλῆ. See also *P. Oxy.* 3393–3394 cited by Lenski, 2002, 292 n. 179. As to *quadrupli nexibus vinciebat*, one should probably imagine, that people were condemned to paying four times the amount of tax which they still owed to the treasury. The quadruple punishment (*poena quadrupli*) is not uncommon in Roman law, as appears from several laws in the *Codex Theodosianus* in which this punishment is mentioned, e.g. 2.33.2, 3.5.11, 3.10.1, 4.6.3, 10.24.1, 11.7.20, 13.5.29; see also Gaius, *Inst.* 4.4, 173 and *Inst. Iust.* 4.6.25–27. The offences for which quadruple punishment was applied almost all concerned extortion, illegitimately acquiring property and money, and financial embezzlements.

debita iam inde a temporibus principis Aureliani perscrutans et impendio maerens, si quemquam absolvisset indemnem Attentive readers will have noticed the contrast with the handling of overdue taxes during Julian's rule; see for this the note ad 25.4.15 *remissa debita*. Petronius' scrutiny of the relevant dossiers went back wellnigh a century: Aurelian was emperor from 270 to 275. With *impendio* Amm. emphasizes the misplaced passion with which Petronius did his job: he was thoroughly distraught when he had no convincing case against someone, whoever it might be; having to acquit a potential victim without inflicting any damage or harm on him was a mishap. The emperor Aurelian is also mentioned in 22.16.15, 30.8.8, 31.5.17. For his reign see Watson, 1999, Gilliam, 1972, 143–144 and Stertz, 1980, 509. Two laws from the year 365 seem to sustain the collecting of old debts; both laws refer to the collection of back taxes from delinquent landholders: *Cod. Theod.* 11.1.13 (18 October 365) and *Cod. Theod.* 12.6.10 = *Cod. Iust.* 10.72.3 (31 October 365). Although Amm. mentions that Petronius went back to the time of Aurelian to look up tax debts, this is hyperbolic rather than realistic, because it is hard to believe that tax records were still available that went that far back. He could definitely not go further back, because under the reign of Aurelian tax records were lost through fire; HA *A* 39.3 and Aur. Vict. *Caes.* 35.7. Records of tax revenues were apparently kept for a long time, as may be surmised from Procopius' remark that tax documents of Libya, written down in former times by the Romans (ἥπερ αὐτοὺς ἀπεγράψαντο ἐν τοῖς ἄνω χρόνοις Ῥωμαῖοι), were destroyed by the Vandal Geiseric (Procop. *Vand.* 2.8.25).

cuius morum intolerantiae haec quoque pernicies accedebat, quod, cum ditaretur luctibus alienis, erat inexorabilis et crudelis   TLL VII 2.25.80–26.4 lists this instance of *intolerantia*, the only one in Amm., among the cases in which it is the equivalent of "superbia, adrogantia, intemperantia". Suet. *Tib.* 51.1 reports that Tiberius' mother confronted her son with a dossier of Augustus *de acerbitate et intolerantia morum eius*. Translators tend to obscure the precise meaning of *cum*, but Viansino's "poiché si arrichiva" is correct: the fact that Petronius also enriched himself at the expense of his victims was the reason of his being 'relentless and cruel'. The combination of these adjectives also occurs in Ps. Quint. *Decl. XIX maiores* 10.19 *crudelis et inexorabilis*.

et in rapido corde rudissimus nec reddendae nec accipiendae rationis umquam capax   In his bilingual edition Seyfarth followed in the footsteps of Clark, who accepted the emendations of Haupt, 1876, 502 and Bentley respectively, and printed *intrepido corde durissimus*, rendering this by "Sein Herz war nicht zu rühren und völlig verhärtet". However, he repented and returned to V's text, which involves some difficult problems: a) *in corde* is quite rare, b) what does *rapidus* mean as a qualification of *cor*?, c) *rudissimus* could well be the only superlative of *rudis* in the entire history of ancient Latinity, d) Amm.'s instances of *rudis* all concern a lack of (elementary) schooling, which it is difficult to ascribe to Petronius. Marié's "avec ce coeur rapace" is a cheerful solution of a and b, but her "totalement inculte" for *rudissimus* does not suit the context at all. Viansino has resorted to *in rabido* and *crudissimus*: "ferocissimo nel suo cuore rabbioso". Although the superlative of *crudus* occurs very rarely, this does at least tally with Amm.'s usage: he uses *rabidus* in a more or less comparable way in the anecdote about Sophocles (25.4.2, q.v.) and *crudus* qualifies *natio* in 30.8.4 and *victor* in 31.8.8. As to *intrepido*, the adj. occurs a dozen times in Amm., the adv. *intrepide* twice. Most often it is used in a laudatory manner, and never with a clearly pejorative connotation. However, TLL VII 2.50.1–8 lists a number of cases in which *intrepidus* can be regarded as the equivalent of "male audax". Among these cases is the present text, in which Haupt's conjecture is accepted. In conclusion: certainty cannot be reached, but *intrepido corde durissimus* (or *crudissimus*) is the most likely text.

Note that Petronius was not merely unwilling, but simply "incapable of either speaking or listening to reason" (tr. Hamilton). This was the direct result of his principle to fleece *nocentes pariter et insontes* (§7).

invisior Cleandro, quem agentem sub imperatore Commodo praefecturam sublata vecordia diversas legimus vexasse fortunas M. Aurelius Cleander (*PIR*² A 1481) was a *libertus* of Marcus Aurelius. In 182 he became *cubicularius* of Commodus; D.C. 72.12.1; Hdn. 1.12.3; HA *C* 6.3. His position was very strong in the 180s but ultimately he fell out of favour with the emperor and was killed in 190. Although Amm.'s information, that Cleander was *praefectus praetorio*, finds a parallel in HA *C* 6.12–13, Dio and Herodian only mention that he had much power. Inscriptions give the title of *a pugione*, which implies that Cleander was directly responsible for the protection of Commodus, a function which must have given him considerable influence with the emperor, possibly even more than that of a praetorian prefect. He is said to have sold functions, to have been corrupt and to have enriched himself tremendously; D.C. 72.10.2, 12.3, 12.5; HA *C* 6.9–10. He was generally hated; HA *C* 7.1, *P* 3.7. See Hekster, 2002, 67–75.

Like Valentinian and Valens, Commodus is also often chided for his cruelty; 21.16.8 (q.v.) *Caligulae et Domitiani et Commodi immanitatem facile superabat* (about Constantius); also 31.10.18. Commodus is furthermore mentioned in 22.9.6 and 29.1.17. For Commodus, see the already mentioned Hekster, 2002. For Commodus in the *Res Gestae*, see Gilliam, 1972, 134–136 and Stertz, 1980, 505–506.

Wagner interprets *sublata vecordia* as "stulta superbia", which is plausible. Although *sublatus* does not necessarily occur in negative descriptions of a person's mental state, as is shown in the last part of the note ad 25.1.18 *in tentoria*, it can denote a swollen head, as in 29.2.7 *ea fiducia sublatior, quod* etc., 31.10.5 *sublati in superbiam*. The present instance of *vecordia* is the only one in the *Res Gestae*.

This is one of ten instances of *legimus*, in which the author refers to his reading experience. Only two of these concern Roman imperial history, 30.8.10 *quo vitio exarsisse principem legimus Hadrianum* and the present text, which clearly implies that Amm. used written sources for his information about Cleander, but in this case probably not Dio and Herodian; neither of them mentions, as Amm. does, that Cleander was praetorian prefect. It also means that Cleander did not figure *in actibus Commodi principis* (22.9.6, q.v.) in the lost part of the *Res Gestae*. See for Amm.'s references to Books 1–13 the note ad 21.8.1 *cuius in actibus*. The absence of an important person like Cleander in Commodus' entourage gives some idea of the scale of the lost books.

Concerning Cleander Amm.'s sources were evidently most unfavourable. The phrase *vexare fortunas* may have been borrowed from

Cic. *Ver.* 3.24 *ad fortunas aratorum vexandas* or *Sest.* 145 *eversa domus est, fortunae vexatae*. The social position and the fortune of those who were ruined, differed greatly: they obviously belonged to divergent strata of society (*diversas*).

et onerosior Plautiano, qui praefectus itidem sub Severo ultra mortale tumens C. Fulvius Plautianus (*PIR*² F 554) came from Africa, just as Septimius Severus to whom he may have been related; Birley, 1999, 97, 101 and, in particular, 221. At the latest in 197 he became praetorian prefect; D.C. 75.14.1. He exercised great influence at the imperial court and on the emperor himself. He became extremely rich, because Severus gave him a share of the possessions of the convicted; Hdn. 3.10.7. His daughter Plautilla married Caracalla; D.C. 75.14.5, 15.2; Hdn. 3.10.5, 7; HA *S* 14.8. He became consul in 203 (D.C. 78.13.1) and Septimius even seems to have wanted him as his successor (D.C. 75.15.2). At the court Julia Domna and Caracalla were his enemies and, after a failed coup, Plautianus was killed with the help of Caracalla at the beginning of 205; D.C. 76.2.5; Hdn. 3.12; HA *Cc* 1.7; Amm. 29.1.17 *alter* [Severus] *inopinabili impetu tempore aetatis extremo a Saturnino centurione consilio Plautiani praefecti in cubiculo iacens confoderetur, ni tulisset suppetias filius adolescens* (Caracalla). He is said to have made many victims (D.C. 75.14, 15) and he was brutal and feared (Hdn. 3.10.7; HA *Cc* 1.7). For Plautianus see Van Norren, 1953. Apart from the present reference, Septimius Severus (193–211) is mentioned six times in the *Res Gestae*: 22.15.1 (q.v.), 23.5.17 (q.v.), 24.6.1 (q.v.), 25.8.5, 26.8.15, 29.1.17; see Gilliam, 1972, 136–137 and Stertz, 1980, 506.

The word *itidem*, 'likewise', only concerns *praefectus*: like Cleander, the immensely powerful Plautianus was *praefectus praetorio*. Petschenig, 1892, 521 conjectured *mortalem*, in view of the parallel phrases *ultra hominem* (27.12.11, 31.10.19) and *ultra homines* (22.9.1, 26.8.13). Seyfarth was obviously convinced by Baehrens, 1925, 54 and Fletcher, 1930, 196, who both rejected the emendation because of *ultra mortalitatem* (28.4.12), presumably in view of the abstract character of the noun. Cf. also *ultra mortalem modum* (14.11.3 and 13). One cannot help thinking that Petschenig was right.

cuncta confuderat, ni gladio perisset ultore Cf. for *confundere*, 'to bring into disorder', 21.13.11 *confundendis rebus...inhaerebat*, 28.5.8 *rem Romanam...confundentes*. The sentence pattern with '*ni* de rupture' is discussed in the notes ad 20.11.18 *et Persae* and 25.6.9 *ni expeditiores*. See for the (quasi-)adjectival use of nouns Szantyr 157–158, for such use of nouns with the suffix *-tor* Kühner-Stegmann I 232 and of *ultor* in particular OLD s.v. c. Far more important, however, is the fact that the phrase *gladius ultor* occurs seven times in the *Codex Theodosianus*. Five of these instances can be found in texts dated between 342 and 356, during the reign of Constantius II: 2.1.1, 9.7.3, 9.16.4, 9.42.2, 16.10.4; the other two are 9.6.3 (397) and 9.34.10 (406). It is therefore reasonable to assume that Amm. borrowed the phrase from official language.

6.9 *haec lacrimosa, quae incitante Petronio sub Valente clausere multas paupertinas et nobiles domus* The remarkable sentence pattern is designed to emphasize the complete upheaval of Constantinople's society: with Petronius as instigator and Valens as the overall responsible ruler, the tearful events have themselves become the Agens. These events hit both the poor and the rich, and shut their houses. It is not clear what this closure means, a (temporary) sign of mourning or the definite end of these households. See for *paupertinus* the note ad 25.2.2 *quidquid*.

impendentiumque spes atrocior provincialium et militum paria gementium sensibus imis haerebant The present was terrible, but the prospects were even worse. See for *impendere* in a context of threatening evil the notes ad 20.8.15 *ne...desperatione* and 25.8.4 *Dum nos*. Although *spes* usually has a positive or a neutral sense (e.g. *spe celerius*), it can also be qualified by negative adjectives: Sal. *Cat.* 20.13 *mala res, spes multo asperior*, Liv. 22.48.5 *in mala iam spe*, Amm. 20.11.11 *spes nostrorum inferior* (q.v.). Not only in the eastern capital, but also among people from the provinces and the soldiery the same complaints could be heard, and all these troubles made a deep and lasting impression on them. This is a sweeping generalization, in which all precision concerning the identity of the *provinciales* and *milites* is lacking, as is a delineation of *paria*. See for *haerere* in phrases describing a lasting impression TLL VI 3.2494.7–38; some examples: Cic. *Cat.* 4.22 *in omnium gentium sermonibus ac mentibus semper haerebit*, *Phil.* 2.64 *tamen infixus animo haeret dolor*, Cypr. *Ep.* 58.11 *Haec, fratres dilectissimi, haereant cordibus vestris*.

et votis licet obscuris et tacitis permutatio status praesentis ope numinis summi concordi gemitu poscebatur With this somewhat contradictory phrase Amm. tries to sketch the general atmosphere of desperation. There seems to be a contradiction between prayers, which were not openly expressed (*obscuris et tacitis* is an instance of 'Synonymenhäufung'), and the unanimous appeal to God to bring about a change. Presumably Amm. means to say that people did not express themselves publicly in clear terms, but that an attentive observer like Procopius was able to get a good impression of their feelings when he listened to the lamentations in which all of them placed their hopes in God's help. See for comparable phrases denoting 'the present situation' the note ad 25.9.4 *detestantes*, and for henotheistic expressions like *numen summum* the notes ad 21.13.14 *favore* and 23.5.19 *adero ubique*. Of course, among the complainers of the present text there will have been many Christians, but already Tertullian noticed (and indeed exploited) the general use in pagan society of phrases like *Deus videt* or *Deus mihi reddet* (*Apol.* 17, *test.* 2), which prompted his famous words *O testimonium animae naturaliter christianae!* (*Apol.* 17.6). See also Camus, 1967, 134-136.

quae Procopius latenter accipiens Procopius was able to 'learn' (see OLD s.v. *accipere* 18) all this without anybody noticing it (*latenter*), since he was *ignotus ob squalorem vultus* (§6).

6.10

arbitratusque, ubi felicius acciderit fatum, negotio levi ad apicem summae potestatis assumi V's *adsiderit* being a non-existent verbal form, most editors have chosen Gelenius' *acciderit*. If this is right, it is best to take *felicius* as an adverb or a predicatively used adjective: 'when fate would turn out in a more happy form'. See for Amm.'s idiosyncratic *negotio levi*, "easily" (Hamilton), the note ad 20.10.2 *superavit*. Comparable phrases with *assumere* in Amm. are 14.11.29 *assumptus autem in amplissimum fortunae fastigium*, 15.8.3 *ad imperium placuit Iulianum assumi*, 26.4.1 *ad imperii consortium...assumi*, 31.5.17 *assumpto in imperium Claudio*. Cf. for *apex* denoting a high point in a hierarchy *ad apicem summae potestatis* (21.16.2; see the last part of the note ad *sed cunctae*).

subsidebat ut praedatrix bestia viso, quod capi poterat, protinus eruptura In 26.6.4 too Amm. had compared Procopius' life with that of a wild beast: *cumque a Ioviano exploratius indagari latibula sua sentiret et formae vitae iam fuisset pertaesum* (*formae* should be emended to *ferinae*; see note ad loc.).

See for *subsidere*, 'to lie in ambush', the note ad 24.4.29 *fallaces*. Blockley, 1975, 183-184 provides a list of Amm.'s numerous animal images. From this it appears that individuals and groups are compared twelve times to *bestia(e)*; cf. also Wiedemann, 1986 and Den Boeft, 2007, 296-297. Müller, 1873, 354 and Haupt, 1876,

502 want to change V's *poterat* to *poterit.* Only Haupt gives a reason: "nam *poterat* nequaquam ferri potest". This lapidary statement cannot be regarded as convincing, yet he may be right. In 14.11.6 V has *spe tamen, quod eum lenire poterat.* Here Seyfarth accepts the conjecture *poterit,* put forward by Kellerbauer, 1873, 82, who adduces a list of such instances of *quod* with indic. fut.; cf. also the note ad 20.8.10 *quod...libens.* The present case is, of course, different, because here *quod* is not a conjunction, but a relative pronoun. Nevertheless, here, too, the future is seen from the viewpoint of the Agens, in this case the *bestia,* ready to pounce (*eruptura*), as soon as it sees something it might catch. Clark tentatively suggests *potuerit* c.c., but this verbal form occurs only once more in the *Res Gestae*: 22.14.7.

6.11 *cui in haec, quae maturabat, ardenti fors hanc materiam dedit impendio tempestivam* This is V's text with the addition of *in* before *haec.* Referring to 14.10.16 *multitudo omnis ad quae imperator voluit promptior,* Müller, 1873, 354 proposed to substitute *haec* by *ad.* As is noted ad 25.6.15 *ardens,* Amm. indeed has a few instances of *ardere ad.* This prompted Kellerbauer, 1873, 133 to add *ad* before *haec.* Alternatively, he suggested to change *ardenti* to *audendi,* a worthwhile emendation in view of the parallels he adduces, especially 27.5.7 *Aderant...finiendi belli materiae tempestivae.* Kellerbauer was not aware of the fact that Bentley had written this conjecture in his personal copy of the *Res Gestae*; its only disadvantage is that it is further removed from V. Finally, Clark printed *in* in his edition, no doubt ascribing the loss of this preposition to haplography. The combination *ardere in* occurs in 22.3.11 *quem in Silvani necem et Galli effrenatius arsisse docuimus*; cf. Tac. *Hist.* 1.43.2 *Othonis...in caedem eius ardentis* (see Heubner ad loc.).

The phrase *impendio tempestivus* occurs five times in Amm.; see the note ad 25.3.15 *impendio.* Almost all Amm.'s instances of *fors* in the nominative occur in 'formulaic' phrases like *si copiam fors dedisset* (15.10.10), *si iuvisset fors* (16.11.9). The only parallel for the 'factuality' of *fors* in the present text is 31.9.2 *erectus prosperitate nimia, quam ei fors obtulit insperata.* See for *materia,* 'opportunity', the list in TLL VIII 464.53 sqq. The active role of 'chance' is, so to speak, programmatic: the present text sets the tone for Amm.'s report of Procopius' usurpation proper. He had neither a plan nor supporters, and the entire episode is characterized by coincidence and improvisation, with Procopius grasping the chances which offered themselves.

consumpta hieme festinans ad Syriam Valens In the year after his nomination, i.e. in 364 and the beginning of 365, Valens travelled through Thrace (26.5.1–5) or resided in Constantinople; Socr. *HE* 4.2.2. After the winter of 365, possibly after he had celebrated the first anniversary of his *dies imperii*, at the end of March or the beginning of April, the emperor headed for Antioch (26.7.2), because the Persians were threatening to break the truce of 363 according to Socr. *HE* 4.2.4; Soz. *HE* 6.7.10; Zos. 4.4.1; Philost. *HE* 9.5. Because Amm. only speaks of the Persian threat in 27.12.1 where he relates events of 368, it may not have been all that serious yet in 365. The emperor did not travel with great speed, as Amm. implies by using the word *festinans*. He only left Caesarea in Cappadocia in the beginning of October to set out for Antioch (see the note ad 26.7.2 *Valentem*). Assuming that he left Constantinople at the end of March or the beginning of April (pace Lenski, 2002, 77 who assumes that Valens left Constantinople in the late summer), his journey to Antioch – which he never reached because he had to return as a consequence of Procopius' revolt which broke out at 28 September – took more than six months.

Other phrases in Amm. in which the participle *consumptus* denotes the passing of time are: 26.9.9 *maiore itaque noctis parte consumpta*, 27.3.4 *consumptis aliquot annis*, 27.5.4 *aestate omni consumpta*, 29.1.4 *aestateque consumpta*.

iamque fines Bithynorum ingressus Seeck, 1920, V, 48 writes: "Nachdem er Bithynien schon durchzogen hatte". On p. 444 he accounts for this by explaining that *ingressus* should be emended to *egressus*. "Denn in die Grenzen Bithyniens trat Valens ein, sobald er den Bosporus überschritt, während hier schon das *iam* verrät, dass er bereits einen längeren Marsch hinter sich hatte." From a historical point of view Seeck's idea is quite plausible, but this does not imply that the emendation is correct. In the first place Amm.'s phrase can very well refer to the heartland of Bithynia: cf. 25.4.24 *a Persis ad usque Bithynos et litora Propontidos*, which suggests that the coastal parts were distinguished from the interior of Bithynia; secondly, *egredi* with acc. is indeed quite possible: it occurs regularly in classical Latin, e.g. in Tac. *Ann.* 2.64.3 *mox Rhescuporis egredi finis*, and Amm. has a few instances: *fluenta egreditur Nili* (22.15.27), *Antiochiam egressurus* (23.2.3). However, Amm. has no examples of *fines egredi*, but *fines ingressus* also occurs in 18.6.1 and 24.1.1; thirdly, Amm. may simply be wrong here.

docetur relationibus ducum gentem Gothorum ea tempestate intactam ideoque saevissimam conspirantem in unum ad pervadenda parari collimitia Thraciarum Since Constantine had struck a treaty with the Goths in 332 (Eus. *VC* 4.5; *Exc. Val.* 6.31; see Lenski, 2002, 122 ff. for the treaty), Romans and Goths lived in peaceful coexistence for some thirty years; Heather, 1991, 107–115. During these years there were economic, cultural and religious contacts between the two nations. There are a few indications of a deterioration of Romano-Gothic relations in the early 360s. According to Eunapius *fr.* 27.1 Julian had mentioned in a letter, that he foresaw that the Goths would become unquiet, and according to Libanius *Or.* 12.78 and 17.30 Julian anticipated a Gothic campaign at some point in the future. Amm. clearly speaks of Gothic preparations in 365 for the invasion of Thracia (*ad pervadenda parari collimitia Thraciarum*); earlier he had mentioned that the Goths were often deceitful and treacherous (22.7.8 with note *propinquos Gothos*). It seems that, particularly after Julian's death, the relationship between Romans and Goths deteriorated. According to Wolfram, 1988, 66 the Goths felt threatened, because they expected a Roman offensive at the Danubian frontier after the Roman disaster in Persia; as a consequence the Gothic tribes formed a confederation under the leadership of Athanaric. In general the Goths are considered the aggressors in the conflict – e.g. Heather, 1989b, 498–499 – but this is doubted by Lenski, 2002, 126–127, in whose opinion it was primarily Valens who went to war with the Goths "to boost his position as emperor". The worsening of the Romano-Gothic relationship eventually led to Valens' campaign against the Goths in 367–369 and ultimately to the Roman defeat at Adrianople in 378.

See for *relatio* denoting an official report to a higher authority the notes ad 20.4.7 *ad relationem* and 20.8.4 *relatu*. Some translators take *intactam* in a strictly military sense, e.g. Rolfe's "unassailed", others prefer a more general meaning, the most outspoken being Viansino with "senza rapporti con altri". The second interpretation seems attractive, because it tallies well with *ideoque saevissimam*: one is reminded of Caesar's famous explanation of the robust vigour of the Belgae: *propterea quod a cultu atque humanitate provinciae longissime absunt* (Caes. *Gal.* 1.1.2). The Goths were as yet savage and violent, because they had not become acquainted with the blessings of Graeco-Roman civilization. However, the use of *intactus* in 28.5.9 favours the military interpretation: during their history the Alamannic people, an *immanis…natio*, surmounted so many setbacks, *ut fuisse longis saeculis aestimetur intacta*. Their capacity to recover precluded attacks from outside. In both interpretations *ideoque saevissi-*

CHAPTER 6.12   151

mam entails the question what this means for the author's assessment of the Goths' mentality at the time of writing, some 25 years later. See for *conspirantem in unum* the note ad 17.10.2 *conspirantes*.

TLL III 1624.73–80 mentions only one instance of the rare noun *collimitium* in the singular, and only one example of the plural outside the *Res Gestae*. See the note on the first of its ten instances, 14.3.1 *collimitiis*, where it is stated that in Amm. it always means "Grenzgebiet"; see also the note ad 21.13.4 *collimitia*. See for *pervadere*, 'to force one's way aggressively into something', the note ad 20.10.2 *regionem*. Cf. for *parare*, 'to gather (military) forces', Caes. *Gal.* 3.23.2 *copias parare coeperunt*, Sal. *Jug.* 74.2 *Numidae ab Iugurtha pro tempore parati instructique*; see further OLD s.v. 5 and TLL X 1.419.66 sqq.

ut impraepedite ipse pergeret   From TLL VII 1.673.50–52 it appears that Amm.'s five instances of *impraepedite* are the only ones registered. See the note ad 21.10.5 *quo impraepedite*, where it is a conjecture. Valens was heading for Antioch; see the note above ad *consumpta hieme*.

equitum adiumentum et peditum   I. e. *Divitenses Tungricanosque Iuniores* as well as other unspecified troops mentioned in the next section.

dimoto itaque longius principe   Far away from Chalcedon and Constantinople, where Procopius was hiding.   6.12

aerumnis diuturnis attritus   See for *attritus*, 'worn out', the note ad 22.8.18 *attritis*; cf. also *angustiis formidandae paupertatis attriti* (29.1.21). Cf. Philost. *HE* 9.5 πολλοὺς ἐν ταλαιπωρίᾳ τόπους ἀμείψας.

vel atrocem mortem clementiorem ratus malis   Comparable phrases, though by no means similar in content, are Tac. *Agr.* 33.6 *honesta mors turpi vita potior*, Quint. *Decl.* 276.10 *sunt enim plerique qui mortem potiorem quam egestatem putent*.

aleam periculorum omnium iecit abrupte   Cf. 24.2.14 about Julian: *omnes aleae casus inter mutuas clades experiri festinans*; see the note ad loc. The metaphor of the present text is closer to the actual game of dice and is strongly reminiscent of the famous words ascribed to Julius Caesar: *iacta alea est* (Suet. *Jul.* 32). Its terseness is lost by the addition of the gen. qualitatis *periculorum omnium*. Remarkably, the metaphor is also used about Procopius in Lib. *Or.* 24.13 ἀνέρριψε τὸν κύβον and Philost. *HE* 9.5 τὸν ἔσχατον, φησί, ἀναρρίπτει κύβον. This must lead to the assumption of a common source, in which Procopius' throwing of the dice denoted a bold attempt to end his misery; see for the last term above, the note ad *aerumnis* in the same section. Only Amm. combines it with his approaching the soldiers who happened to pass through Constantinople. Libanius does not mention any specific moment, and Philostorgius places it at a different point of the developing situation, viz. Procopius' capture of Chalcedon, which in Amm.'s report takes place after his usurpation. See Sabbah 284 with n. 140 and Bleckmann, 2007, notes 34 and 35.

The present text is not listed in Blomgren's long section on the final position of adverbs (108 sqq.) in contrast to 28.1.56 *Aginatius ad supplicia duci pronuntiatur abrupte*. In the present case, which can be regarded as an example of the cursus planus, the position of *abrupte* also brings out the suddenness with which Procopius threw the dice.

et extrema iam perpeti nequaquam timens praeeunte perdita ratione facinus adoritur audacissimum Although agreeing that the addition of *et* by Petschenig, 1897, 381 can be defended by assuming that the loss of this copula was caused by haplography, Blomgren 37–38 argues that it is not indispensable, since the entire sentence quoted in the lemma "explicatiuum quendam praebeat sensum" of the preceding sentence *aleam...abrupte*. In contrast to Clark and Seyfarth this argument did not convince Marié. See the note ad 22.8.19 *extrema perpessae vicinitatis*. TLL X 2.597.79–81 persuasively lists the present text and 27.6.8 *parentis amorem...praeeuntem* and 28.4.34 *praeeunte nidoris indagine* ('the search for the rich smell of food functioning as guide') in the category of phrases in which *praeire* is used metaphorically about something which "ducem se praebet". Translators tend to render *perdita* with 'desperate', but this does not suit the context. Procopius' plan is morally wrong; cf. Seyfarth's "seiner verderblichen Berechnung". TLL X 1.1276.41–42 rightly lists the present text and 31.4.10 *perditis rationibus* among the instances of *perditus* as a synonym of "turpis" or "pravus". Cf. for *ratio*, 'consideration', 'plan', 20.11.18 *potior ratio* (q.v.), 23.2.2 *consultae rationes*, 24.4.9 *librata ratione*.

Divitenses Tungricanosque Iuniores...inter alios celerare dispositos Both legions were *legiones palatinae* (*Not. Dign. Occ.* 5.147 and 148), originally formed by Constantine. The full name of the Divitenses was *Legio II Italica Divitensis*; it was a detachment of *II Italica* – the legion of Noricum – and had been stationed at Divitia which was located on the right bank of the Rhine; *ILS* 2346 and 2777. The Tungricani took their name from the territory of the Tungri, where they were stationed; Jones 97–98. The *Notitia Dignitatum* only mentions the *seniores*, and it is thanks to Ammianus that we also know that there were *iuniores* of these legions. The latter served in the eastern provinces with Valens, whereas the former served in the western part of the empire under Valentinian. Matthews 190–191 suggests that *Divitenses iuniores* and *Tungricani iuniores* do not occur in the *Notitia Dignitatum* because they were either disbanded by Valens because of their support for Procopius or because they were annihilated in the battle of Adrianople. The legions of Divitenses and Tungricani serving under the command of Severianus in Gaul in 365 and mentioned by Ammianus in 27.1.2 were *seniores*; Hoffmann, 1969–1970, vol. 1, 120–121. The *Divitenses* (*iuniores*) are also mentioned in 26.7.14. Probably the other troops which Amm. refers to were cavalry and infantry units which had been raised for the expedition in Thrace: *transeuntes ad expeditionem per Thracias concitatae equitum peditumque turmae* (26.7.9).

ad procinctum urgentem See for *procinctus*, 'campaign', the notes ad 16.11.6 *procinctum* and 20.1.3 *festinaret*; cf. also 29.4.5 *urgente procinctu*.

Constantinopoli moraturos sollemniter biduum An attentive reader of the *Res Gestae* cannot but be reminded of what had happened in Paris five and a half years before; at the time it had been decided that the contingents which were to strengthen the Roman forces in the East, *per Parisios omnes transire* (20.4.11). There Julian entertained the officers at dinner and this triggered off his acclamation as Augustus. See for *sollemniter* as the equivalent of *ex more* the note ad 20.6.1 *transmisso*. The soldiers probably stayed for two days in Constantinople, to rest and prepare for the campaign.

per quosdam ex isdem numeris notos Cf. 20.4.12 about Julian: *princeps occurrit ex more laudans, quos agnoscebat*. See for *numeris* the note ad 20.1.3 *numerisque*. Who these acquaintances were remains in the dark, but in his capacity of *tribunus et notarius* and that of *comes* Procopius must have become acquainted with many military commanders. Some of them probably served with him when he was in command of the army in Mesopotamia during Julian's Persian expedition; Paschoud n. 115; Matthews 196.

qui pellecti spe praemiorum ingentium sub consecratione iuris iurandi promisere se quae vellet cuncta facturos Amm.'s only other instance of **6.13** *pellicere* is 14.11.11 *eum* (= Gallus)...*proficisci pellexit*. The considerable difference with Julian comes out clearly: Procopius can only win support by promising huge rewards. In return, his newly gained supporters swore a far-reaching oath. See for *consecratio* the note ad 25.7.14 *eaque iuris iurandi religionibus consecrata* and cf. also the note 25.9.4 *iuris iurandi*. According to Zos. 4.5.3 Procopius was financially backed by the immensely rich eunuch Eugenius (*PLRE* I, Eugenius 4), who had been dismissed from the imperial court: ἦν τις εὐνοῦχος Εὐγένιος ὄνομα, τῆς βασιλικῆς ἄρτι ἐκβεβλημένος αὐλῆς, ὑγιῶς δὲ πρὸς τοὺς κρατοῦντας οὐκ ἔχων. Τοῦτον οἰκειωσάμενος ὁ Προκόπιος, ἐπειδὴ καὶ κύριον εὗρεν ὄντα πλούτου παμπόλλου, φράζει τέως τίς εἴη καὶ κατὰ τίνα ἥκοι χρείαν καὶ ὅπως δέοι τοῖς πράγμασιν ἐπιθέσθαι· τοῦ δὲ κοινωνεῖν ἅπασι τοῖς ἐγχειρουμένοις ὁμολογήσαντος, καὶ ἔνθα [δ'] ἂν δεήσειε χρήματα χορηγεῖν, προοίμιον ἐποιήσαντο τῆς πράξεως τὸ διαφθεῖραι χρήμασι τὴν ἐν τῇ πόλει καθεσταμένην φρουράν, ἣν τάγματα στρατιωτῶν δύο ἐπλήρου. "There was a eunuch called Eugenius, lately expelled from the imperial palace and not at all favorably disposed towards the emperors. Finding he was very rich, Procopius won his friendship by identifying himself and explaining his arrival and plans. When the eunuch agreed to collaborate in all his undertakings and to lend him whatever money he needed, he took the first step in this venture by bribing the city guard, which consisted of two legions" (tr. Ridley). Eugenius had probably been *cubicularius* of Valens before he had lost his position; *PLRE* I, Eugenius 4. Zosimus' information about Constantinople's city guard consisting of two legions is incorrect. Constantinople did not have a guard, and it is most likely that with the legions the Divitenses and Tungricani are meant; Dagron, 1974, 108–113; Paschoud n. 115.

favorem quoque polliciti conturmalium, inter quos ipsi potiorem locum obtinebant in suadendo stipendiis excellentes et meritis Only Amm.'s five instances of *conturmalis*, 'brother in arms', are listed s.v. in TLL IV 809.14–17: 16.12.45 (q.v.), 17.1.2, 23.5.19, 24.6.11. The relative clause is admirably rendered by Hamilton: "with whom their long and meritorious service gave them commanding influence". See for *locus* denoting the position of "a person or thing in treatment or estimation", in one word: "status", OLD s.v. 18. The importance of esteem when giving advice is clearly worded in Cic. *de Orat.* 2.334 *in suadendo nihil est optabilius quam dignitas*; cf. also Cic. *Att.* 8.9.1, Quint. *Inst.* 3.8.15. Cf. for *stipendia*, 'years of service', 22.9.12 *stipendiorum numero*, Vell. 2.101.2 *sub initia stipendiorum meorum*, Tac. *Hist.* 3.75.1 *quinque et triginta stipendia in re publica fecerat*.

According to Veg. *mil.* 2.21 the centurions of the first of the ten cohorts which made up a legion were the most honourable and privileged. In particular the chief centurion, the *centurio primi pili*, held great authority. It is possible that Procopius had sought the support of the foremost centurions belonging to the Divitenses and Tungricani. Payment of soldiers in this period was for the most part in kind, although they received their annual stipend and donatives in cash; see the note *cuius iracundiae* ad 20.8.8. It has been estimated that the average stipend of a legionary soldier was some 1,800 *denarii* per annum; donatives were mostly 5 *solidi*; Elton, 1996, 121. Nevertheless, the average soldier did not exactly make a fortune and sometimes he did not even receive his annual pay (20.8.8 *cuius iracundiae nec dignitatum augmenta nec annuum merentis stipendium id quoque inopinum accessit*) which made him susceptible to promises of high rewards.

utque condictum est See for *condicere*, 'to agree upon', the note ad 20.1.1.

ubi excanduit radiis dies This was the day of 28 September; *Consul. Constant.* a. 365. Themistius, who was an eyewitness of the event, says that it was still night when Procopius started his coup: μεσούσης τῆς νυκτὸς (*Or.* 7.91a–b); μέχρι τῆς ἑσπέρας ἐκείνης (*Or.* 7.92 b). Zos. 4.5.5: νυκτὸς ἀωρί. *Consul. Constant.* a. 365 calls Procopius a *latro nocturnus*.

See for Amm.'s other instances of *excandescere* the notes ad 20.9.2 *hisque recitatis* and 22.16.23 *ad singulos*. The present text is paralleled by 21.10.2 *ubi lux excanduit tertia*, but it is more reminiscent of Sol. 53.26 *cumque flagrantioribus radiis excanduit dies*. However, as is explained in TLL V 2.1200.65–66 and 1201.66, the context is entirely different. Solinus notes that shellfish retreat into deeper water, when the heat of the sun increases.

idem Procopius diductus in cogitationes varias Anastasianas balneas petit a sorore Constantini cognominatas, ubi locata noverat signa See for comparable phrases denoting hesitation and indecision the notes ad 20.11.24 *imperator* and 26.5.9 *curis*. From the passage quoted in the lemma Dagron, 1974, 110 i.a. concludes "qu'il n'y a pas de casernes dans la ville, mais seulement des monuments publics que l'on transforme en cantonnements provisoires." See also Lenski, 2002, 72 n. 23.

Amm.'s explanation of *Anastasianas* is upheld in *PLRE* 1, Anastasia 1, in spite of Dagron, 1974, 90 n. 2, who is convinced that these *thermae* are named after one of Valens' two daughters: *PLRE* 1, Anastasia 2. Her sister was Carosa; Socr. *HE* 4.9.5 mentions them both and then adds: ὧν ἐπ' ὀνόματι καὶ δημόσια λουτρὰ ἐν τῇ Κωνσταντινουπόλει κατεσκευασμένα ὑπὸ Οὐάλεντος δείκνυται. Cf. also Theoph. p. 57 De Boor. The same information can be found in Soz. *HE* 6.9.3, *Chron. Pasch.* a. 364. *Not. Urb. Const.* 10.8 places Anastasia's *thermae* in the ninth region. If Socrates e.a. are right, one has to assume that within eighteen months after Valens' proclamation as Augustus public baths, large enough to accommodate two military contingents, had been built. Another explanation could be that the construction of the baths had started in the reign of Constantine, who named them after his (half-)sister Anastasia, but were only completed in the time of Valens, who rededicated them to his daughter, also named Anastasia; Lenski, 2002, 399 n. 32. Anastasia was the daughter of Constantius Chlorus and Theodora, and hence Constantine's halfsister. She was married to the senator Bassianus; Barnes, 1982, 37, 265. For Anastasia see also Chausson, 2002. The Divitenses and the Tungricani had placed their standards (*signa*) in the *thermae* where they were stationed.

doctusque per arcanorum conscios omnes in eius studium consensisse societate coita nocturna This is a clear case of *per* to indicate the direct Agens. See for this Szantyr 127 and for some other examples in Amm. the notes ad 22.8.12 *inter Ionas* and 23.6.24 *qua per*. The men 'privy to the secrets' are the same as *quosdam ex isdem numeris* in §12. Similar phrases in Amm. are 14.1.7 about walls, 15.2.5, 15.5.9, 27.10.10, 31.12.9 about confidants. Cf. for *consentire in,* 'to reach an agreement in order to realize an objective', 14.10.16 *consensit in pacem,* Tac. *Ann.* 15.61.4 *scelera, in quorum ultionem consenserat.* Already in classical Latin *studium* often occurs with the meaning 'support'; see OLD s.v. 5. TLL III 1420.19–40 provides a list of instances of *societatem coire,* in which phrase *coire* is transitive, e.g. Cic. *S. Rosc.* 87 *qui societatem coieris,* Nep. *Con.* 2.2 *cum Lacedaemoniis coierat societatem.* See for the time of night above, the note ad *ubi excanduit.*

According to Zos. 4.5.5 Procopius also rallied support from slaves and volunteers: Δούλους δὲ πρὸς τούτοις ὁπλίσαντες, καὶ σὺν οὐ πολλῷ πόνῳ πλῆθος οὐκ ὀλίγον συναγαγόντες οἷα πολλῶν ἐν τούτοις ἑαυτοὺς ἑκόντας ἐπιδιδόντων. See on the population's support the second part of the note ad 26.6.17 *Huic intimidius.*

fide salutis data libenter admissus constipatione vendibilium militum cum honore quidem, sed in modum tenebatur obsessi Procopius is not in control of the situation: it is the other way round. See for *fides*, 'guarantee, promise, assurance', OLD s.v. 2 and cf. Hirt. *Gal.* 8.23.2 *quem timor prohibebat cuiusquam fidei suam committere salutem*. The adv. *libenter* is not superfluous: the soldiers gladly gave their guarantee of safety to a sheep which they were going to shear. Like a real emperor, Procopius is encircled by a throng of military men; cf. the note ad 26.2.11 *circumsaeptum*. However, *constipatione* converts it into a caricature. This noun occurs in three other passages of the *Res Gestae*: 24.8.5, where it denotes a dense mass of wild donkeys, 29.1.3, where crowded jails are referred to, and 31.13.3, the battlefield at Adrianople. Such parallels suggest that Procopius was not so much surrounded by officers, but drowned in a crowd, which had only one objective: selling their loyalty to a man whom they were ready to pay homage to and at the same time holding on to him, as if he was being besieged. There seem to be no parallels for the metaphoric use (*in modum*) of *obsidere*, which verb can be used to denote the real situation of a person who is "surrounded in a hostile way" (OLD s.v. 4b), e.g. Cic. *Sest.* 84 *principem civitatis ferro opsessum*, Sal. *Jug.* 24.3 (Adherbal complains:) *socius et amicus populi Romani armis obsessus teneor*, Tac. *Ann.* 1.28.4 *quo usque filium imperatoris obsidebimus?*

ut praetoriani quondam post Pertinacis necem licitantem imperii praemia Iulianum susceperant This is the only time that Pertinax is mentioned in the surviving books of the *Res Gestae*. On March 28, 193 Pertinax, who had succeeded Commodus on the imperial throne three months before on December 31, 192, was murdered in his Roman palace by mutinous guards, who were unhappy with his attempts to redress the financial crisis and restore discipline. See for his short reign D.C. 73.1–10; Hdn. 2.1–5; HA *P*; Fluss, 1918; Kienast, 1996², 152–153. He was replaced by Didius Iulianus. Lindenbrog and Seyfarth refer to HA *DI* 2.6, where he is portrayed as *ingentia pollicentem* to the *praetoriani* in order to thwart the claims of Pertinax' father-in-law, the prefect of the city Sulpicianus. They would have done better to refer, with Marié, to the contemporary report of the same scene by Dio Cassius, who calls it disgraceful; both men were bidding against one another, Sulpicianus inside the camp, Iulianus outside (D.C. 74.11.3–6). However, in view of a remarkable parallel in § 16 (q.v.), another contemporary historian, Herodian, is perhaps Amm.'s most likely source; see Wiebe, 1995, 34–35. Wiebe questions the historical reliability of Amm.'s account: "Dass es Ammian hier weniger um historische Authentizität geht, bestätigt sich m.E. in der Tatsache, dass er sich bei der Schilderung des Auftretens Prokops ziemlich eng an den Bericht Herodians über die Erhebung des Didius Julianus anlehnt." Didius Iulianus' reign was also short; already on 1 June of the same year he was deposed and assassinated; see further Wotawa, 1905; Kienast, 1996², 154-155. See also Gilliam, 1972, 136 and Stertz, 1980, 506.

The precise meaning of *licitantem* is difficult to pinpoint. TLL VII 2.1373.6 sqq. distinguishes two meanings of the verb, which can be used about both the buyer and the seller. In the first case it means "pretium ponere", in the second 'to offer something for sale'. Curiously, the present text is put in the second category. It is more likely that the soldiers were ready to sell their support and that Iulianus was offering a price. It is true that the normal construction would have been *licitantem imperium*, 'bidding for the emperorship', but *praemia* for services rendered by soldiers occur regularly in the *Res Gestae*, and Amm. may have added the word here as an explicit reference to the price Iulianus was ready to pay. TLL X 2.720.28-44 is a list of cases in which *praemium* is combined with a genitive in various functions. In this way one could do justice to the meaning of *licitantem imperii praemia* with 'offering them rewards for helping him to win the emperorship'.

ipsi quoque Procopium infausti dominatus exordia molientem attenti ad omne compendium defenderunt Cf. Jovian's fear of Procopius whom he expected *novas res nullo renitente facile moliturum* (25.7.10, q.v.). The verb *moliri*, "to engineer" (OLD s.v. 1), is boldly used here with *exordia* as direct object. This is Amm.'s only instance of *dominatus*. However, it seems to have the same connotation as his two instances of *dominatio* (21.16.8 [q.v.] and 26.9.9), which both concern illegal power. From a comparative overview in TLL V 1.1878.1-13 it appears that from Sallust onwards *dominatio* is by far the more usual of the two synonyms. Amm. has a great predilection for the plural of *exordium* where actions on a larger scale are concerned, e.g. *Gallicani procinctus exordia* (17.8.1, cf. also 23.1.7), *rerum novarum exordiis* (20.8.3), *inter exordia ipsa coeptorum* (21.7.1), *immanium exordia concitare bellorum* (29.5.28); cf. also *inter exordia principatus* (21.1.4, 25.9.3), *inter imperandi exordia* (21.16.8). Procopius was organizing the start of his ill-starred tyranny.

The soldiers had a keen eye for every opportunity which might benefit their situation (*attenti ad omne compendium*). Precisely such feelings had caused Julian to warn Constantius in his letter after the events in Paris: watch out for men *ad compendia sua excitare secessiones principum suetos* (20.8.11).

CHAPTER 6.15   159

In the preceding sections Amm. has depicted the improvised preparations for Procopius' coup, which culminated in the disgraceful scene of bargaining with the soldiers. Now he turns from the shameful to the ridiculous aspects of the affair, beginning with a memorable description of the first appearance of the would-be emperor. This description is spiced up by a comparison with a domain which the author despised, the theatre. See for this Jenkins, 1987, who shows the negative tenor of Amm.'s theatrical metaphors. Curiously, the section was inspired by a phrase in Solinus' chapter on Sicily: *hic primum inventa comoedia: hic et cavillatio mimica in scaena stetit* (5.13). One cannot escape the impression that the remarkable *stetit* right at the beginning of Amm.'s sketch was borrowed from Solinus, to be used for an entirely different purpose.

In his 7th *Oration* Themistius, too, had emphasized the farcical aspects of Procopius' usurpation (91 a sqq.), actually calling it a κωμῳδία. Sabbah 363–364 argues that this passage was used as a source of information by Amm., who "doit peut-être l'idée maîtresse de sa stylisation théâtrale au témoignage déjà haut en couleur de l'orateur de Constantinople." This may be right, but Zos. 4.5.5 has a comparable idea: people left their houses and ἐθεῶντο Προκόπιον ὥσπερ ἀπὸ σκηνῆς βασιλέα σχεδιασθέντα, 'observed Procopius as an improvised emperor from the stage'. It therefore seems more likely that all three authors, each in his own way, reflect a written source which contained an official view of the affair. See for this idea Leppin, 2007, 41.

6.15

Stetit itaque subtabidus Amm. does not report the details of the transactions with the military units in the *thermae*, the results of which are evidently taken for granted. Instead, he introduces a new scene, focussing entirely on the outward appearance of Procopius. As is usual in later Latin, and different from earlier usage, *itaque* takes the second place in the sentence, in the present text preceded by the predicate. There is only one other example in Amm. of a sentence beginning with a finite form in the perfect tense followed by *itaque*: 16.12.49 *Exsiluit itaque subito ardens optimatium globus*. See for a general predilection for the predicate to be in first place in narrative texts Szantyr 403. In the present text the perfect, as the basic narrative tense for reporting events, expresses a further step in the account, in contrast to *stabat*, which would have been used if information about the background of the story were given.

Procopius was not in good shape, he looked 'a bit poorly'. See for the prefix *sub-* the note ad 21.16.3 *examinator* and Leumann 401, and for *tabidus*, 'emaciated', Luc. 6.737 *Hecate pallenti tabida forma*, "Hecate wan and wasted" (tr. S.H. Braund).

excitum putares ab inferis Summoning someone from the underworld occurs in various contexts. Some examples: Cic. *Ver.* 5.129 *quasi ego eius excitare ab inferis filium possem*, Liv. 40.56.6 *Demetrium excitatum ab inferis restitutumque credam mihi, si te...in locum eius substitutum relinquam*, HA *AC* 12.5 *utinam possem multos etiam ex inferis excitare*. In the present text Amm. may be referring to one of the forms of *prosopopoeia*, as in Cic. *Cael.* 33 *si...aliquis mihi ab inferis excitandus est* (see also the reference to this passage in Quint. *Inst.* 3.8.54). Quint. *Inst.* 12.10.61 notes that this rhetorical device specifically belongs to the grand style: *Hic orator et defunctos excitabit ut Appium Claudium*. However, in view of the final part of the section it is more likely that Amm. is thinking of a scene in a play; cf. 28.4.5 *si fabularum ritu ab inferis excitatus redisset ad nostra*. On the other hand, most translators assume that this phrase refers to mythology in general.

nusquam reperto paludamento tunica auro distincta ut regius minister indutus It was absolutely essential that a new emperor, legal or otherwise, showed himself as soon as possible in full attire. For the purple cloak as one of the imperial *insignia* see the notes ad 20.5.4 *specie tenus* and 22.9.10 *"purpureum sibi"*. The presence of an imperial robe was indispensable for a successful usurpation; Oros. *hist.* 7.40.6 *nam tyrannidem nemo nisi celeriter maturatam secrete invadit et publice armat, cuius summa est assumpto diademate ac purpura videri ante quam sciri.* Cf. the case of Jovian: *confestim indumentis circumdatus principalibus* (25.5.5, q.v.). This had not been easy; as is revealed in Jovian's necrology, it proved difficult to find an official robe with the right measurements for so tall a man (25.10.14). In Julian's case the absence of a proper *diadema* was a considerable problem; see the scene described in 20.4.17–18. Valentinian made his first public appearance *principali habitu circumdatus et corona* (26.2.3).

When Silvanus usurped power he got his purple vestment from military standards: *cultu purpureo a draconum et vexillorum insignibus ad tempus abstracto ad culmen imperiale surrexit* (15.5.16 with note De Jonge). The possession of purple cloth was dangerous. The anonymous commission of an *indumentum regale* at the purple factory in Tyre led to an investigation by the provincial governor and the subsequent torture of those employed in dyeing purple and of a Christian deacon (14.7.20, 9.7). Many people were imperilled because the *princeps apparitionis praefecturae praetorianae* Rufinus accused them of keeping a *velamen purpureum* stolen from Diocletian's tomb (16.8.4–6). In Aquitania a man was ruined because his table cloth contained so much of the colour purple that it resembled an emperor's garment (16.8.8). In 17.11.4 Amm. mentions an anecdote according to which even Pompey was playfully reproached for having a white bandage tied around his leg to cover a wound, as if this was a sign of his dictatorial aspirations. See the relevant notes ad loc. and cf. also the version of the same anecdote in V. Max. 6.2.7 *Favonius 'non refert' inquit 'qua in parte sit corporis diadema', exigui panni cavillatione regias ei vires exprobrans*, "Favonius said: 'It makes no odds on what part of your body you have the diadem', quibbling the tiny piece of cloth to reproach him with monarchical power" (tr. Shackleton Bailey). See on purple further the note ad 20.5.4 *specie tenus* and Steigerwald, 1990. Also Firmus, who revolted against Roman rule *c.* 370, is said to have worn a purple cloak: *visus est Firmus equo celsiori insidens sago puniceo perrectius panso* (29.5.48). Remarkably, Amm. does not refer to the diadem, the other sign of imperial authority since the days of Constantine; see the note ad 20.4.17 *iubebatur*. Blockley, 1975, 58 has drawn attention to the fact that in Amm. no usurper was properly dressed with the purple robe, whereas all legitimate emperors were dressed in a proper purple mantle when presented to the soldiers. By presenting usurpators as not fully dressed with the imperial regalia Amm. expressed his disapproval of anyone who illegitimately seizes power.

The absence of an imperial robe is a further indication of the improvised character of the usurpation. At the same time Amm.'s report belies the rumour about Julian which is mentioned in 23.3.2 *dicitur ante aras nullo arbitrorum admisso occulte paludamentum purpureum propinquo suo tradidisse Procopio* (q.v.). As is noted ad 21.5.12 *ad genua*, the term *paludamentum* as such does not denote the emperor's cloak, but in the present text this is clearly implied. Procopius contented himself with a gold-embroidered tunica, but this meant that the counterfeit emperor (Them. *Or.* 7.91 c παράσημος αὐτοκράτωρ) looked like an attendant of the imperial court, a *regius minister*. Cf. for *regius*, 'imperial', 21.16.20 *cum regia...pompa*, 25.10.14 *indumentum regium*, 30.4.2 *regiorum arbitrio spadonum*.

a calce in pubem in paedagogiani pueri speciem purpureis opertus tegminibus pedum hastatusque purpureum itidem pannulum laeva manu gestabat
Petschenig, 1897, 560 lists this among Amm.'s remarkable instances of allitteration. With sardonic delight Amm. becomes more specific: in fact, when one cast a glance at his legs, Procopius looked like one

of those apprentices, who were being trained in a *paedagogium* for service at court. Procopius wore purple shoes, as most translators assume, or purple gaiters, as Viansino suggests, perhaps rightly in view of 'from heel to private parts'. See for *paedagogiani pueri* Ensslin, 1942 and Balty, 1982 (with relevant illustrations). Cf. for purple 'covers of feet (or legs)' the anecdote in 22.9.11: showing his disregard of outward signs of distinction, Julian orders a querulous person to give purple shoes to his opponent.

Alföldi, 1980, 175 ff. uses precisely this section as a list of the various parts of an emperor's official "Dienstkostüm". Each of these parts bore a certain likeness to comparable elements of the court personnel's costumes. Alföldi regards Amm.'s description as a caricature and "nur das Zerrbild eines Herrschers", which is composed of authentic elements: "Die Attribute selbst sind nichtsdestoweniger authentisch" (175 n. 3). Evidently, this poses a problem. Had Amm. never seen (a picture of) an emperor in full attire in an urban and civil setting, or is his derision due to the fact that the absence of the truly essential parts, *corona* and *paludamentum*, made Procopius merely look like some courtier? The former explanation is unsatisfactory, and the latter may be nearer to the truth. See also Steigerwald, 1990, 218–219 and Kolb, 2001, 116–117.

Amm. uses the word *paedagogianus* only once more, in 29.3.3 *Adultus quidam ex his, quos paedagogianos appellant*. *Paedagogiani* were slaves who were being trained and educated in the household of the emperor and of the rich nobles by a *paedagogus*. The growing luxury at the imperial court manifested itself in the dress and the training of *pueri paedagogiani*; Plin. *Nat.* 33.40; Sen. *Ep.* 124, *De Vita beata* 17.2; Tert. *Apol.* 13.9. Augustus assigned them a special place, near his own, at the public spectacles; Suet. *Aug.* 44.2. Nero gave offence by causing free boys to be brought up as *paedagogi*; Suet. *Nero* 28.1. In palaces and other great houses the *paedagogiani* slept and lived in a separate apartment, which was called *paedagogium*; Plin. *Ep.* 7.27.13. In the later empire they carried out the menial services in the palace together with the *ministeriales* and *curae palatiorum*; Jones 571.

To understand the meaning of *hastatus* one has to turn to the list in TLL VI 3.2552.57–64 (s.v. *hasta*), which i.a. contains Amm. 16.12.39 *purpureum signum draconis, summitati hastae longioris aptatum* and Claud. *In Ruf.* 2.177 *purpureis undantes anguibus hastas* (see Levy's note ad loc.). Thus Procopius also looked like a *draconarius* (see on this function and its relation to the term *hastatus* the note ad 20.4.18 *Petulantium*). This could entail that *itidem* refers both to the purple *tegmina pedum* and *hastatus*, 'carrying a lance with a purple dragonlike banner (in his right hand)'. Procopius' patchy outfit is completed by a purple scrap of cloth, which he held in his left hand. As Alföldi, 1980, 152 shows, this was meant to be a *mappa*, the symbolic sign to open the public games with, which i.a. appears on coin portraits of emperors. Either Amm. did not know this usage or Procopius' *pannulus* was obviously makeshift. Again the first alternative is unlikely. Perhaps the author, *ut quondam miles*, found this attribute and its function a token of degeneration. An attentive reader may be reminded of Julian's sovereign remark about a private person, who had stitched a purple cloak for himself: this makes clear, *sine viribus maximis quid pannuli proficient leves* (22.9.11, q.v.).

ut in theatrali scaena simulacrum quoddam insigne per aulaeum vel mimicam cavillationem subito putares emersum As a climax of his description of the farcical appearance of the fake emperor Amm. adds a comparison with something which could occur during a performance in the theatre. Unfortunately, he expresses himself in phrases which are difficult to understand. It seems best to interpret *scaena* as 'stage' in the material sense of the word, as in 16.6.3 *velut aulaeo deposito scenae* (q.v.). Till, 1975, 80 refers to 31.1.3: the nightly appearance of the betrayed king Pap's *larvale simulacrum*, "l'apparition du spectre" (tr. Sabbah), frightened Valens. Interpreting *simulacrum* in the present text in the same vein would tally with *excitum...ab inferis*. However, Till adds that such a meaning only "unterschwellig mitschwingt" and that in Amm.'s phrase *simulacrum quoddam insigne* primarily "ein Schauspieler in prächtigem Gewand" is denoted. This actor appears *per aulaeum*, 'in front of the main curtain'. As to *mimicam cavillationem*, Till comes up with a complicated explanation: this phrase is the equivalent of *mimus* and this in its turn is the equivalent of *siparium*, 'a small screen as a piece of scenery', the counterpart of *aulaeum*; the two terms 'allegorically' indicate tragedy and mime. Eichele, 1984, 160 agrees with the two genres, but explains Amm.'s theatrical references in an entirely different, and more convincing, manner. He firmly rejects all hypotheses, that in Late Antiquity the *aulaeum* was not lowered at the start of a performance and pulled up at the end, but that a method, comparable to present-day usage, had been introduced. Amm.'s *simulacrum* appears at the end on the curtain, when it is pulled up. Eichele seems to imply that *mimicam cavillationem* simply means 'mime'. This may be too simplistic. Beacham, 1991, 171–175, sketches an ingenious mechanical system by which part of the *siparia* could be removed so that another scenery became visible. Tentatively combining elements from the various explanations, one might perhaps surmise that Amm. refers to high-level drama, at the end of which the curtain was pulled up and the figures painted or embroidered upon it, rose from the ground (Verg. *G.* 3.25 (ut) *purpurea intexti tollant aulaea Britanni*, Ov. *Met.* 3.111–112 *sic ubi tolluntur festis aulaea theatris, / surgere signa solent*), and to a mime in which 'a striking apparition' became manifest between the *siparia*. In the latter case one might think of a scene in a piece comparable to the *Phasma Catulli*, 'The Ghost by the Neronian mime-writer Catullus' (Juv. 8.186). In all probability the phrase *mimicam cavillationem* as such was borrowed from Solinus (see the introduction to this section), in the present text it possibly denotes the mechanical devices, dealt with by Beacham, which were used during the performance of a mime.

6.16 *ad hoc igitur dehonestamentum honorum omnium ludibriose sublatus* Amm. adapts a fine oxymoronic phrase of Sallust: *Fufidius, ancilla turpis, honorum omnium dehonestamentum* (Sal. *Hist.* 1.55.22: see McGushin's note ad loc. = 1.48.22 in his numbering). It is also used in HA *Cl* 5.4 *Gallus Antipater, ancilla honorum et historicorum dehonestamentum*, but Amm. remains much closer to the context of Sallust's phrase, which concerns the *cursus honorum* of the Roman Republic. He adds a further paradox with *ad...sublatus*: Procopius was raised to the degradation of all honours. It is the exact opposite of Julian's views: *Caesarem vestrum firmo iudicio ad potestatum omnium columen sustulistis* (20.5.3, q.v.), he said to his soldiers. Note the contrast between *firmo iudicio* and *ludibriose*, a rarely used adverb, which here once more emphasizes the fake and ridiculous character of the entire affair.

et ancillari adulatione beneficii allocutus auctores Sallust's disparaging *ancilla* inspired Amm. to sketch a noteworthy reversal of roles: with the servile flattery (*adulatione*) of a female (!) slave (*ancillari*) the so-called emperor addresses his soldiers, who, in fact, were his benefactors, 'those who had bestowed this favour on him'. Amm.'s *beneficii...auctores* may have been inspired by Auson. *Grat. act.* 7.34, where *auctore beneficii*, 'the person to whom I owe the consulship', refers to the emperor Gratian.

opesque pollicitus amplas et dignitates ob principatus primitias processit in publicum multitudine stipatus armorum Procopius' promises are diametrically opposed to the course which Julian charted in his first speech to the soldiers after the pronunciamiento at Paris: nobody was to be promoted *praeter merita* (20.5.7, q.v.). Even Jovian proceeded along a more responsible path: *perpensius, ut apparebat ex paucis, quos promoverat iudices, electurus* (25.10.15, q.v.). See for *dignitas* denoting an official function or rank 19.13.2 *adiecta comitis dignitate*, 20.4.20 *palatii decurio, qui ordo est dignitatis* (q.v.), 26.4.2 *tribunatus dignitate*, and for *primitiae*, 'beginning', the note ad 14.1.1 *primitiae*; the present phrase is paralleled in 28.6.7 *ob imperii primitias*. The phrase *procedere in publicum* means 'to come out into the streets', 'to appear in public'; cf. e.g. Liv. 34.5.7 *in publicum processerunt*, Amm. 14.7.10 *nec processit in publicum*. See for *stipatus* the note ad 26.2.11 *circumsaeptum*.

signisque sublatis erectius ire pergebat circumclausus horrendo fragore scutorum lugubre concrepantium In earlier authors *signis sublatis* denotes leaving a position to go elsewhere, e.g. Liv. 25.33.7 *signis repente sublatis Celtiberi abeunt*, Vell. 2.61.2 *sublatis signis ad Caesarem se contulerunt*. In the present text, however, the soldiers in question have no other places to go to, and the phrase rather expresses taking up the standards for a demonstrative march through the streets of Constantinople. TLL V 2.785.79–786.4 incorporates the present text and 15.5.11, 15.5.16, 28.1.22 (where it is a conjecture of C.F.W. Müller) and 30.7.5 as instances in which the adverb *erecte* is the equivalent of "audacter, fortiter, libere", but it may well express graphically how Procopius stopped moving clumsily and walked upright as if he truly was a leader. Amm. seems to be the only author using *circumclausus* instead of the usual *circumclusus*. The three other instances in the *Res Gestae* (15.11.3, 24.5.2, 25.6.5) are topographical. Here it expresses Procopius' real situation: he was entirely hemmed in by gloomy sounds. See for *lugubre* in combination with sounds the note ad 25.1.18 *armorumque*; consult also Kühner-Stegmann II 1.281.

According to Matthews 194 "Ammianus surely means us to recall his descriptions of how soldiers expressed their sentiments in parade-ground situations." Although we cannot be certain of what Amm. intended his readers to recall, the clashing of shields in this context is in stark contrast with the soldiers striking their shields against their knees as an expression of support because of Julian's elevation to Caesar (*horrendo fragore scuta genibus illidentes*, 15.8.15), the clashing of spears against their shields at his proclamation as Augustus (*hastis feriendo clipeos sonitu assurgens ingenti*, 20.5.8 with note), and when Julian informed his soldiers of his intention to march against Constantius (*contio...voces horrendas immani scutorum fragore miscebat*, 21.5.9). In this case the clashing of shields is not an expression of approval and support; the clashing was caused by the soldiers using their shields in order to protect Procopius and themselves against the possibility of being pelted by stones and tiles. Another instance of tile-throwing is given by Amm. in 27.3.8: the neighbours and friends of Rome's city prefect Lampadius chased off a mob which threatened to set fire to his house. For roof tiles as a weapon in urban conflicts, see Barry, 1996. For *scutum* see the note ad 21.2.1 *quatiens scutum*.

quae metuentes, ne a celsioribus tectis saxis vel tegularum fragmentis conflictarentur, densius ipsis galearum cristis aptabant The soldiers were fully aware that their march was not going to be a ticker tape parade. As was already noted by Henricus Valesius (his note occurs in the 1681 edition of his brother Hadrianus), Amm.'s description is strongly reminiscent of Herodian's report on Didius Iulianus being escorted to the palace: ἐν μέσοις αὐτοῖς ἔχοντες τὸν ἴδιον βασιλέα, ὑπέρ τε τῆς κεφαλῆς αἰωροῦντες τὰς ἀσπίδας καὶ τὰ δόρατα, μή που καὶ λίθων τις βολὴ ἀπὸ τῶν δωμάτων ἐπὶ τῇ πομπῇ γένοιτο (Hdn. 2.6.13). It can hardly be doubted that Amm. was inspired by this passage. Cf. for *aptare* with dat. meaning 'to fasten on', 'to join closely with', 16.12.24 *cuius vertici flammeus torulus* ('plume') *aptabatur*, Liv. 44.34.8 *aptare corpori arma*.

6.17 *Huic intimidius incedenti nec resistebat populus nec favebat* At first sight the use of anaphoric *hic*, referring to Procopius, is slightly surprising after the immediately preceding extensive description of the soldiers accompanying him in the streets of Constantinople. However, the author remains focussed on the protagonist, as e.g. in 18.3.2 *huic uxor erat Assyria nomine*, where *huic* refers to the general Barbatio, in whose house a swarm of bees had settled, a phenomenon about which he consulted experts in divination. After the report of their explanation the text continues with the quoted words. The next word, *intimidius*, is puzzling in that, according to TLL VII 2.16.62–65, it is the only instance of this adverb or adjective. CLCLT only contains a few instances in medieval authors. Petschenig, 1892, 521 also found it less suitable within the context and suggested *inter medios*. This brilliant conjecture may, however, well be superfluous. In the context 'without fear' can be regarded as a variation of *erectius* in the preceding section. Moreover, formally there is nothing wrong with *intimidius*, which is an example of *in*-privativum (Leumann 387), comparable to ἄφοβος, and can be regarded as a rare 'rival' of *impavidus* or *intrepidus*. The phrase, describing the absence of any resistance or enthusiasm on the part of the population, was in all probability inspired by Herodian's report on Didius Iulianus (see above the note ad §16 *quae metuentes*): μηδενὸς τῶν δημοτῶν μήτε ἀντιστῆναι τολμῶντος μήτε μὴν εὐφημοῦντος (Hdn. 2.6.13).

Zos. 4.5.5 seems to be more positive about the support of the population of Constantinople; see the note ad 26.6.14 *doctusque*. Libanius (*Or.* 19.15) reports that the Constantinopolitans welcomed Procopius: τὴν γὰρ αὖ μεγάλην πόλιν ἡδέως ὑποδεξαμένην τυράννου θράσος καὶ τὰ μὲν εἰποῦσαν, τὰ δὲ καὶ πράξασαν. Soz. *HE* 6.39.4 also reports that the inhabitants of Constantinople supported Procopius. In 26.7.1 Amm. mentions that Procopius was supported by dealers in dainties, servants and ex-servants in the palace, and veterans. According to Amm.'s narrative the higher echelons of the urban society did not favour Procopius. When Procopius went to the senate house the distinguished senators were absent, and only a few of low rank were there (26.6.18), and the *notarius* and later city-prefect Sophronius immediately travelled to Valens to inform him about the situation (26.7.2); see Wiebe, 1995, 62–63 and Grattarola, 1986, 91. Blockley, 1975, 59–60 argues that Amm. in his description of Procopius' supporters – corrupt soldiers, merchants, servants etc. – reveals his prejudices against the revolt, whereas Procopius, in fact, had considerable support from the inhabitants of Constantinople and also from distinguished military and civilian officials. With regard to Procopius' support in Constantinople Marxist scholars have interpreted the revolt as a conflict between social classes; e.g. Hahn, 1958, 211 characterizes Procopius' usurpation as "eine städtisch-plebejische und gleichzeitig bäuerliche Bewegung"; cf. Grattarola, 1986, 92 who argues that the support of petty merchants, (ex-)servants in the palace, veterans (26.7.1) and of the populace of various cities (26.8.2, 14) "non significa però che la ribellione debba essere interpretata come opera delle classi basse".

The hope of rewards (26.6.13 *pellecti spe praemiorum ingentium*) and the charm of novelty mentioned in this section were, according to Wiebe, 1995, 63 the main motives to back Procopius. According to Lenski, 2002, 111 "we might regard the revolt as a reaction to a variety of tensions – economic, cultural, dynastic, and political...". However, an even more important motive was probably the hatred directed at Petronius and the way in which he had enriched himself at the cost of the population. This motive is once again emphasized by Amm. in this section.

accendebatur tamen insita plerisque vulgarium novitatis repentina iucunditate See for *accendere* denoting the arousing of feelings the note ad 25.1.2 *hocque viso*. Depending on the circumstances an unexpected turn in the course of events (*novitas*) can be disturbing (17.2.2 *Hac Iulianus rei novitate perculsus*) and cause fear (21.6.5 *novitatis metu*) or denote something pleasant, as in 26.2.3 about the shouts of praise, *quas novitatis potuit excitare dulcedo* (q.v.). The present phrase is comparable, but *iucunditas* cannot be regarded as a synonym of *dulcedo*, because of *insita*. This implies that *iucunditate* does not belong to the list of instances in TLL VII 2.589.37–590.24, in which *iucunditas* is a synonym of *suavitas*, but should have been incorporated in the list of cases in which it is the equivalent of *laetitia* (TLL VII 2.590.25–60), although this list only contains references to the Bible and Christian authors. Blomgren 146 defends *repentina* as an example of enallage. See on this also the note ad 20.10.2 *scruposa*.

Petronium, ut praediximus, divitias violenter augentem omnes eadem mente detestabant The cruel methods by which Petronius enriched himself and the hatred which he generated are amply treated in 26.6.7–9; see above the various notes ad loc. By repeating this here Amm. emphasizes both his own disapproval of Petronius and the people's abhorrence of Valens' father-in-law. Bickel, *Göttingische gelehrte Anzeigen* 180 (1918) 277 criticizes Clark for printing *detestabantur*. He refers to 27.3.12 *conflictabant*, where Clark also prefers the passive form. However, the verb *conflictare* is far more often used non-deponentially. Flobert, 1975, 320 lists *detestabant* as the first instance of "activation" of *detestari*. There are, however, earlier cases of a passive meaning of the perf. participle, e.g. Hor. *Carm*. 1.1.24–25 *bellaque matribus / detestata*; see Flobert, 1975, 353.

qui sepulta iam dudum negotia et redivivas nebulas debitorum in diversos ordines excitabat The author's flowery expressions pose a few problems. In two other cases he uses *sepelire* in the sense "to consign to oblivion" (OLD s.v. 3): in 16.12.70 Constantius keeps silent about Julian's glorious deeds, *quae sepelierat penitus, ni* sqq., in 26.9.9 Procopius' execution *discordiarum civilium gliscentes turbines sepelivit et bella* (q.v.). See for other examples of this use of *sepelire* Housman ad Luc. 8.529, Woodman ad Vell. 2.129.4 and Ferri ad [Sen.] *Oct.* 523–524. There are, however, very few examples of the metaphoric use of *nebula* with gen. inversus. Amm. has one more instance: *per suspicionum nebulas aestimati quidam noxii* (14.1.4), where the 'hazy' character of the suspicions is indicated. One of the chapter headings of book 8 of Gellius' *Noctes Atticae* concerns a stupid grammarian who paraded *remotarum...quaestionum nebulas* (8.10). Petronius' 'awakening' (*excitavit*) of affairs which were dead and buried is an entirely acceptable expression, and presumably its combination with 'misty debts' is zeugmatic as is *redivivas*, which contrasts with *sepulta* and does not suit *nebulas* at all. Indicating the result of *excitavit*, it should be regarded as 'proleptic'; see Szantyr 413–414. With *diversos ordines* Amm., as in 26.6.9, probably refers to the poor, the rich, the provincials and the soldiers.

cum itaque tribunal idem escendisset Procopius et cunctis stupore defixis **6.18**
timeretur silentium triste Cf. Zos. 4.6.3 ἀνελθὼν δὲ εἰς τὸ πρὸ τῆς αὐλῆς βῆμα. With anaphoric *idem* Amm. emphasizes the renewed focus on Procopius. Understandably, those present were dumbfounded when they saw a man in an inept motley outfit climb onto the platform where sollemn ceremonies normally took place. Amm.'s phrasing may have been inspired by Liv. 3.47.6 *Primo stupor omnes admiratione rei tam atrocis defixit; silentium inde aliquamdiu tenuit*; cf. also Liv. 1.29.3 about the atmosphere at Alba Longa directly before its evacuation and destruction: *silentium triste ac tacita maestitia ita defixit omnium animos ut* etc. However, *stupore defixus* occurs more often, e.g. in Apul. Met. 11.14 *at ego stupore nimio defixus tacitus haerebam* (see also 3.22, 9.11 and 34). Haupt, 1876, 502 regards *timeretur* as inexplicable and conjectures *teneretur*. In view of Liv. 3.47.6, just quoted, Mommsen's *teneret* would be a better choice, but, in fact, there is nothing wrong with *timeretur*, as long as one neglects the explanation given by Blomgren 56: "ad *Procopius* referendum". The passive is caused by the focus on *silentium*, and if an Agens is wanted, 'Procopius' supporters' would be a better choice. The silence did not testify to sollemnity or respect, but was "lugubre" (Marié) or "infausto" (Caltabiano); cf. 22.9.15: Julian entering Antioch in the days of the lamentations during the Adonea *visum est triste*. The contrast with Julian's *adlocutio* and his acceptance of the imperial dignity in 20.5 is considerable; Julian is presented as a self-assured, fearless and confident man. The same is true of Valentinian's acceptance of power in 26.2.6–10. For *adlocutiones* and their standard topics see the introduction to the commentary on 20.5.

The tribunal was near the senate house and opposite the palace; *Not. Urb. Const.* 3.9 *tribunal purpureis gradibus exstructum in regio*. Imperial addresses or *adlocutiones* were given by the emperor (or usurper) standing on a tribunal, or at least on an elevated place. Amm. presents Procopius' coup d'état as a rather clumsy and not well-prepared affair, and as doomed to fail from the beginning. Possibly Amm.'s narrative is influenced by the rhetorical strategy of Valens' propaganda to dismiss Procopius' revolt as farcical; this should not lead us to underestimate the possibly sophisticated organization of the revolt; see Lenski, 2002, 73–74. Zosimus gives a somewhat different impression. Even though he compares Procopius with a king in a play (4.5.5), it becomes clear from his report that, even though the revolt came as a complete surprise to the Constantinopolitans, Procopius' attempt to assume the emperorship was apparently well prepared. On the very night of his proclamation and before mounting the tribunal he had the city prefect Caesarius and the praetorian prefect Nebridius arrested; Καὶ συλλαβὼν Καισάριον, ὃν ἔτυχον οἱ βασιλεῖς πόλεως ὕπαρχον καταστήσαντες, ἔτι δὲ καὶ Νευρίδιον, ᾧ τῆς αὐλῆς μετὰ Σαλούστιον παρέδωκαν τὴν ἀρχήν, γράφειν τὰ αὐτῷ δοκοῦντα τοῖς ὑπηκόοις ἠνάγκαζεν (Zos. 4.6.2–3); "So arresting Caesarius, whom the emperors had appointed prefect of the city, and Nebridius, Salustius' [in fact Salutius Secundus'] successor as praetorian prefect, he forced them to communicate his ideas to the subjects of the empire" (tr. Ridley, adapted). Amm. also mentions the arrest of Caesarius and Nebridius (26.7.5, q.v.).

procliviorem viam ad mortem, ut sperabat, existimans advenisse per artus tremore diffuso implicatior ad loquendum diu tacitus stetit Procopius expected the worst and thought that a downward path towards death had appeared. Cf. for *sperare*, 'to expect with fear', 14.7.5 (about lack of food) *affore iam sperabatur* (q.v.), 20.11.16 *exitium affore iam sperantes* (q.v.). The state of his nerves was easily visible: his entire body was shaking and he was unable to speak for quite some time. TLL VII 1.644.81–82 interprets the present case of *implicatus* as "fere i.q. *impeditus*".

pauca tamen interrupta et moribunda voce dicere iam exorsus, quibus stirpis propinquitatem imperatoriae praetendebat Cf. Cic. *Cael.* 59 about the dying Q. Metellus: *interruptis ac morientibus vocibus*, Tac. *Ann.* 1.65.1 *interruptae voces* (Goodyear ad loc.: "the broken utterances stem from broken spirits."). Procopius' voice sounded like that of a dying man. However, he did remember the one indispensable statement which he simply had to make: his relationship with the Constantinian dynasty. As is pointed out in the note ad 23.5.11 *etenim*, the verb *praetendere* tends to be used when statements are dubious. Cf. also 26.7.10 *necessitudinem praetendebat et Iuliani*, 31.14.2 *propinquitatem eius praetendens*. Remarkably, in 23.3.3 *propinquo suo...Procopio* (q.v.) Amm. does not express a comparable doubt.

Procopius was related to Julian, possibly through the latter's mother Basilina; see the note ad 26.6.1 *iamque summatibus*. He probably had no agnatic connections to the Constantinian family. Because there was still great affection for the dynasty of Constantine (Blockley, 1975, 61), Procopius, for the sake of his cause, pretended to have such a connection as Amm. also reports elsewhere. In 26.7.10 he mentions that Procopius carried Constantius' daughter around the soldiers, thereby claiming kinship with the late emperor; in the same section Amm. mentions that Faustina, Constantius' wife and mother of the child, was present when he received some of the imperial *insignia*, and in 26.9.3 he adds that Constantius' wife and little daughter accompanied Procopius on his military expeditions and even into the line of battle, in order to incite his soldiers to fight more bravely for the imperial family, to which he himself claimed to be connected. In 26.7.16 Procopius presents himself as the representative of the imperial house and the rightful heir to the throne; "*quin potius sequimini culminis summi prosapiam, non ut rapiat aliena, sed in integrum maiestatis avitae restituatur, arma iustissima commoventem.*"

leni paucorum susurro pretio illectorum, deinde tumultuariis succlamationibus plebis imperator appellatus incondite petit curiam raptim Amm. pulls out all the stops to disparage the *acclamatio*. It starts with the soft whisper of a paid claque, followed by haphazard shouts of approval by the mob, in which Procopius is declared emperor 'in a disorderly manner'. Then he races to the senate building. See for *tumultuarius*, 'haphazard', 'improvised', the notes ad 24.2.18 *His raptim* and 25.6.4 *quod tumultuaria*, and for *incondite*, "sine ordine, confuse" (TLL VII 1. 1002.58 sqq.) the note ad 22.6.2 *interpellabant*. In itself it is fully understandable that Procopius afterwards went straight to the senate to make sure of the support of that body, but he should have done so in a dignified manner, not 'in a rush': Amm.'s other eight cases of *raptim* all belong to descriptions of speedy military actions. The various elements of the lemma are all meant to bring out once more the 'amateurish' character of the coup.

Constantinople had two senate buildings, one at the Augusteion and another on the forum of Constantine; *Not. Urb. Const.* 3.8, 4.19; Dagron, 1974, 98–99, 138–139; Bauer, 1996, 148, 170; Berger, 2005, 446. See also the note ad 22.7.3 *Frequentabat*. Amm.'s *curia* undoubtedly refers to the first building, which was probably dedicated under Julian; Bauer, 1996, 149–150. This *curia*, the tribunal and the imperial palace, all situated close together, formed the political heart of Constantinople and were therefore a most appropriate place to start a rebellion. For the senate of Constantinople, which consisted of

2000 members since Constantius II had made it equivalent to the senate of Rome, see the note ad 22.2.4 *verecundis senatus*; add to the literature mentioned there Vanderspoel, 1995, 61–66 and Heather, 1998, 184–191.

ubi nullo clarissimorum, sed ignobilium paucitate inventa palatium pessimo pede festinatis passibus introiit In 28.1.27 *omnes clarissimi* Amm. uses a t.t., but here *clarissimus* seems to be used in a general sense, contrasting the truly distinguished and influential men with the *ignobiles*, whose role was unimportant. The existing distinctions of status within the senatorial order were legislatively formalized by Valentinian and Valens in 372 when three imperial grades were created: *clarissimi*, *spectabiles* and *illustres*; Jones 143–144, 528–529; Demandt, 1989, 281–282.

The remarkable alliteration in the last part of the lemma (see Petschenig, 1897, 560) stresses Procopius' ill-starred entrance into the imperial palace. Cf. for *pessimo pede* Apul. *Met.* 6.26 *pessumo pede domum nostram accessit* and see Häussler, 1968, 200–201 and Appendix I in *GCA* 1981, 275–278. Apart from the 'utterly unfavourable foot' Procopius did also wrong by 'racing' to the palace: he ought to have heeded Cicero's advice in *Off.* 1.131 *cavendum autem est ne…in festinationibus suscipiamus nimias celeritates*, because this will result in panting and a distorted face; see Dyck ad loc. For the imperial palace in the heart of Constantinople and dating from Constantine's reign, see Dagron, 1974, 92–97 and map on 536–537; Mango, 1985, 27, 33; Bauer, 1996, 149, 151; Berger, 2005, 437–438 Abb. 1.

6.19 The importance of this short section, which consists of only one sentence, can hardly be overrated. The author is fully aware that his readers will be surprised by his account of the initial phase of Procopius' coup. Some of them may still have lively memories of the affair, others will read the author's description of its dangerous developments in the next chapters. For this reason he explains that a ridiculous start more than once had momentous consequences. Those who are unfamiliar with the past tend to regard it as an unprecedented phenomenon, but the historiographer is able to demonstrate the benefits of his specialism. He can show that there is nothing new under the sun. In other words, the message functions as a hinge in a seemingly contrasting diptych: the beginning was ludicrous, but what followed was dangerous and even disastrous, and in this respect history repeated itself. See also Sabbah 396–397.

Mirantur quidam profecto irrisione digna principia incaute coepta et temere ad ingemiscendas erupisse rei publicae clades, ignari forsitan exemplorum accidisse primitus arbitrantes See on Amm.'s use of *profecto*, when expressing his personal convictions, the note ad 25.4.1 *Vir profecto*. Note that the author does not use *forsitan*, as in 28.1.15 *et quoniam existimo forsitan aliquos haec lecturos exquisite scrutando notare* sqq. In the present text he has not the slightest doubt that his readers will question the correctness of his report.

In judging Amm.'s report of the Procopius affair one should take good notice of *principia...coepta*: it is the initial stage of the usurpation which deserves to be ridiculed. From then on it clearly endangered the entire commonwealth. The historiographer's handling and interpretation of the evidence at his disposal may raise questions, but he cannot be blamed for overlooking its paradoxical nature. On the contrary, he himself concedes that there is a problem. This can, however, be solved by studying comparable precedents. See for the 'Synonymenhäufung' *incaute...et temere* the note ad 21.9.8 *"incaute"*. In the present case the combination summarizes once more the author's description of Procopius' coup up to this moment.

Other examples of *erumpere*, 'taking a (sudden) turn (to something far worse)' are 21.4.1 *in exitiale malum eruptura*, 27.7.4 *erupit ad perniciem plurimorum*, 28.3.3 *erupturum in periculum grave*. See for instances in other authors TLL V 2.841.3–59. The "lamentable disasters" (Rolfe) return in 30.7.10 *clades ingemiscendas Illyrici*.

In this section Amm. gives four examples of revolts which were disastrous for the state: one example from republican times and the other three from the imperial period of the first half of the third century AD. The instances from imperial times are remarkable not only because they are chronologically close to each other, but in particular because Amm. generally has a predilection for examples from the time of the Republic. The revolt of Andriscus resulted in the disappearance of the kingdom of Macedonia. Heliogabalus' coup ended the reign of Macrinus (217–218). The revolt of Maximinus Thrax ended the good reign of Severus Alexander (222–235); his rule (235–238) was unpopular and resulted e.g. in opposition against the usurper by the senators of Rome, who declared him a *hostis*, and in the revolt of the Gordiani (238). The reign of Gordian I and II only lasted twenty days.

6.20

Adramytenus Andriscus de genere quidam infimae sortis ad usque Pseudophilippi nomen evectus Cf. 14.6.25 *ex turba vero imae sortis*, 22.3.12

ab ima sorte ad usque iubendum imperatoria paene elatum, 28.1.42 *idque portendebat extollendos quosdam despicatissimae sortis ad gradus potestatum excelsos*, 29.2.1 *ipsa sortis infimitate ad omnia praeceps*. In all these cases *sors* denotes "social position" (OLD s.v. 9b). The author cannot stand people of low birth climbing the social ladder. This is the second time that Amm. mentions Andriscus. The first time was in 14.11.31 where he mentions how through Fortune's gift some people were raised to the highest ranks: *haec Adramytenum Andriscum in fullonio natum ad Pseudophilippi nomen evexit et Persei legitimum filium artem ferrariam ob quaerendum docuit victum*; see the note of De Jonge ad loc. Andriscus, pretender to the Macedonian throne, claimed to be Philip, Perseus' son by Laodice. He won control of Macedonia in 149/8, thereby provoking the so-called third Macedonian War in which he was crushed in the battle of Pydna (148) by Quintus Caecilius Metellus Macedonicus. Afterwards Macedonia was annexed as a Roman province. See for Andriscus Plb. 36.10; Liv. *per.* 48–50; D.S. 31. 40 a, Zon. 9.28; Green, 1990, 447–448.

This first of the four examples does not seem to be well chosen, because Procopius was *insigni genere...natus* (26.6.1, q.v.). However, Amm. would have reacted by pointing to the 'tertium comparationis', viz. the ridiculous character of the usurpation. See for *evectus* the note ad 20.8.21 *eum ad*.

sic Antiochiae Macrino imperatore agente ab Emesa Heliogabalus exsiluit Antoninus This is the only reference to the emperor M. Opellius Macrinus (11 April 217 – 8 June 218) in the *Res Gestae*. Macrinus, praetorian prefect of Caracalla, became emperor after the latter's death (in which he may have had a hand); Hdn. 4.12.5–13.8; HA *OM* 2.1–3, 5; 4.7. He remained in the east, where he was fighting the Parthians; HA *OM* 8.1. He was defeated at Nisibis, which caused unease among the soldiers; after this defeat and the subsequent conclusion of a peace treaty, he went to Antioch; Hdn. 4.15.9; HA *OM* 8.4. On 15 May 218 Heliogabalus revolted against him and the rebel army defeated Macrinus, who was deserted by many of his soldiers, outside Antioch on 8 June 218; Macrinus fled but was captured at Chalcedon (Hdn. 5.4.11; HA *OM* 10.1–3) and executed in Cappadocia; see *PIR*² O 108; Millar, 1993, 144–146; Kienast, 1996², 169–170. This is also the only time that Amm. mentions Heliogabalus; he came from Emesa, his name was Varius Avitus, but he was officially called M. Aurelius Antoninus; *PIR*¹ V 184; Kienast, 1996², 172–173. For Antioch see the notes ad 22.9.14 and 25.10.1; add to the literature mentioned there Cabouret, Gatier and Saliou,

2004. For Emesa, modern Homs, see De Jonge's note ad 14.7.18 and Millar, 1993, 300–309.

Note that in this example *exsiluit*, a rather bold metaphoric expression denoting Heliogabalus' sudden appearance from an unexpected place, is the essential term.

ita inopino impetu Maximini Alexander cum Mamaea matre confossus est Maximinus Thrax, emperor from 235 to 238, had been mentioned earlier by Amm. in 14.1.8 (with note De Jonge) as well as in the lost books as appears from Amm.'s information in that passage (*ut in Gordianorum actibus factitasse Maximini truculenti illius imperatoris rettulimus coniugem*). Maximinus, who was the first of the so-called 'soldier-emperors' (Aur. Vict. *Caes.* 25.1, *epit.* 25.1), revolted against Severus Alexander (222–235) in 235 at Mainz. The latter was killed and his mother Julia Mamaea was also murdered. See for Maximinus and his revolt Hdn. 6.8–9; HA *AS* 59.7–8, 61.4–7; HA *Max.* 7.4; Zos. 1.13.1–2; see also *PIR*² I 619; Kienast, 1996², 184–185; Sommer, 2004, 29–36. This is the only passage in the *Res Gestae* where Alexander Severus is mentioned; see for him *PIR*² A 1610; Cleve, 1982; Bertrand-Dagenbach, 1990; Kienast, 1996², 177–179. For Julia Mamaea see *PIR*² I 649; Kettenhofen, 1979, *passim*; Kienast, 1996², 180.

in Africa superior Gordianus in imperium raptus adventantium periculorum angoribus implicatus vitam laqueo spiritu intercluso profudit See for the Gordiani the note ad 14.1.8 *Gordianorum actibus*. The oldest of the three Gordiani was proconsul of Africa under Severus Alexander and Maximinus Thrax; HA *Gd* 5.1, 7.2; *epit.* 26.1. Protests against the reign of Maximinus led to his proclamation as Augustus by the populace of Africa in the beginning of 238; Hdn. 7.5; HA *Gd* 8.1–4; *epit.* 26.2. The Senate of Rome recognized him as emperor (Gordian I) and also recognized his son (Gordian II), who had been declared Augustus by his father. For Maximinus and his supporters, among them Capelianus, the governor of Numidia, this was unacceptable. Gordian II fell in battle against Capelianus. The elder Gordian, realising the hopelessness of his situation, hanged himself at the age of about 80 after having been emperor for only twenty days; Hdn. 7.9.1–4; HA *Gd* 15–16. See further *PIR*² A 833; Kienast, 1996², 188–190; Dietz, 1980, 5–7, 56–73. Rolfe incorrectly refers to Gordian's cenotaph in 23.5.7 (*hic Gordiani imperatoris longe conspicuum vidimus tumulum*); this was the tomb of Gordian III.

The phrase *periculorum angoribus implicatus* is perhaps borrowed from Cic. *Tusc.* 5.3 *suis angoribus et molestiis implicatos*. See also the note ad 20.1.1 *implicaret*. The word *laqueus* occurs regularly in phrases denoting suicide by hanging: *multique superstites bellorum infamiam laqueo finierunt* (Tac. *Ger.* 6.4), *statim me laqueo nexili suspendam* (Apul. *Met.* 5.16; see the note ad loc. in *GCA* 2004, 229–230), *laqueo vitam finivit* (HA *Gd* 16.3), Amm. 28.6.27 *innodato gutture laquei nexibus interiit*. The suicide by the former *magister officiorum* Remigius must have made a considerable impression on Amm., for he mentions it three times: *laqueus vitam...erupit* (15.5.36), *laqueo vitam elisit* (28.6.30), *innodato gutture laquei nexibus interiit* (30.2.12, repeating the phrase in 28.6.27).

CHAPTER 7

Introduction

After the sarcastic and disdainful description of Procopius' pronunciamiento in the preceding chapter, Ammianus turns to the manner in which the usurper sought to consolidate his position. Some low-ranking courtiers and military men, both in active service and retired, threw in their lot with the new emperor. Others left Constantinople and fled to the legitimate emperor Valens, who was on his way to Syria. One of them, Sophronius, persuaded Valens to return to Constantinople in order to stamp out the revolt in its initial stages. Valens is described as alarmed and dejected at the news of Procopius' coup (§ 1–2).

In the meantime Procopius devoted all his time and energy, and not a little ingenuity, to strenghthen his position. Fake messengers from East and West arrived in Constantinople with the news that Valentinian had died, and that nothing stood in the way of the new emperor. High officials, appointed by Valens, were thrown into jail and replaced by men loyal to Procopius. In his choice of military personnel Procopius was less successful, because the retired generals Gomoarius and Agilo, whom he recalled to active service, would betray him in the end, as Ammianus informs his readers in advance (§ 3–4).

The *comes* Iulius, commander of the troops in Thrace, was lured to the capital under false pretences and also put under arrest, by which means Procopius gained control over the strong military forces in that region. Ammianus stresses, that some of the people appointed by Procopius did not join him of their own free will. As always in civil disorders, people from the lowest social strata rose to the highest ranks, whereas scions of great families fell victim to the new regime (§§ 5–7).

Having filled the highest military and civil positions Procopius turned his attention to the army. Again luck was on his side. Cavalry and infantry regiments on their way to Thrace passed through Constantinople and were bribed to swear allegiance to Procopius. This looks suspiciously like a repetition of the story in chapter 6 about the Divitenses and the Tungricani, who on their way to Thrace passed through Constantinople, where Procopius bought their support. The relationship between the two reports will be discussed more fully in the introduction to §9. Procopius was greatly helped by the presence of Constantius' widow Faustina and her young daughter, who made visible the ties with the imperial family, on which Procopius based his claim to power (§8–10).

Next, Procopius tried to win support from the troops in Illyricum. Here, however, he met a formidable opponent in the person of Equitius, who killed his emissaries and effectively blocked all acccess to the Balkans. This was the first major setback for Procopius, who was now completely cut off from the western part of the empire (§11–12).

When Valens heard about Procopius' appointments in Constantinople and his increased military support, he was totally discouraged and even contemplated abdicating his power. His advisers, however, prevailed upon him to continue the struggle, and to dispatch a strong force against his enemy (§13–14).

The two armies met near Mygdus, but when the real battle was about to begin, Procopius intervened personally. He addressed the troops of Valens, and in a powerful speech reminded them of their sworn loyalty to the Constantinian dynasty. He called upon them to follow him as a member of the imperial familiy rather than a Pannonian upstart like Valens. The soldiers of Valens lowered their banners as a sign of surrender, and proclaimed Procopius' invincibility (§15–17).

In this chapter the reader witnesses Procopius growing into his part. In chapter six Ammianus had characterized his address to the troops at the pronunciamiento as servile flattery, whereas in his intervention at Mygdus Procopius displays real courage and authority. This change in his character and behaviour is not commented upon by Ammianus, who persists in his utter condemnation of the usurpation.

7.1 *Igitur cuppediarum vilium mercatores* The primary discourse function of *igitur* has been defined by Kroon, 1995, 100–101, as signalling the introduction of a main unit of discourse after a subsidiary unit. It may have a local rhetorical use (marking the conclusion in an argumentative sequence) or a text-organizational use (marking the transition to the main discourse line after a digression). The latter is the case here: after presenting a series of historical parallels, Amm. returns to the narrative of Procopius' revolt. Examples of this use of *igitur* in Amm. are numerous, e.g. at the beginning of the Constantius' necrology: 21.16.1 *Bonorum igitur vitiorumque eius differentia vere servata praecipua prima conveniet expediri* and at its end 21.16.20 *Pollinctum igitur corpus defuncti...Iovianus...prosequi pompa Constantinopolim usque iussus est.*

One wonders why 'dealers in cheap dainties' are singled out as Procopius' first followers. The answer may be, that one of Procopius' friends was Hyperechius (*PLRE* I, Hyperechius), who was given a military command over the troops in Dadastana (26.8.5 *cui ut amico Procopius auxilia ductanda commisit*, q.v.). This Hyperechius was *castrensis apparitor*, a servant on the household staff of the palace in Constantinople, whom Amm. contemptuously called *ventris ministrum et gutturis*. The equally contemptuous phrase *cuppediarum vilium mercatores* may refer to his colleagues. There is a note on *cuppediae*, 'dainties', at 25.2.2 *et imperator*. Amm. uses *vilis* of people as the opposite of *honestus*, e.g. 21.6.9 *aspectu vilis et lingua*, q.v. In his first 'Roman satire' Amm. says that the aristocrats considered everyone who was not born in Rome as a person of no account: 14.6.22 *vile esse, quidquid extra urbis pomerium nascitur*. The adjective also denotes behaviour which is *infra dignitatem*, as in 27.5.9 *indecorumque erat et vile ad eum imperatorem transire*. Used of food *vilis* means 'simple, cheap', as in 16.5.3 *munificis militis vili et fortuito cibo contentus* (cf. 25.4.4), further emphasizing the low social rank of the food merchants.

et, qui intra regiam apparebant aut parere desierant For *regia* as the equivalent of *palatium* see the note ad 26.10.1 *Serenianum*. The verb *apparere* here has the meaning of 'to serve', for which cf. the notes on *apparitor* ad 15.7.3 *ab omni* and 20.8.6 *ut apparitor*. For this meaning of *apparere* Lindenbrog aptly quotes Verg. A. 12.849–850 *saevique in limine regis/apparent* and Servius' note *apparent, id est, praesto sunt: unde etiam apparitores constat esse nominatos*. TLL II 267.62 sqq. lists a number of instances, also from classical authors, such as Cic. *Clu.* 147 *scribae...lictores...ceteri, quos apparere huic quaestioni video* and V. Max. 2.2.4 *proximo lictori ut sibi appareret imperavit*. Seyfarth's translation: "Leute, die einmal innerhalb des Palastes aufgetaucht waren, dann aber ihren Dienst aufgegeben hatten" is therefore wrong. Gardthausen, followed i.a. by Clark, preferred to read *apparere* instead of V's *parere*. There are, however, good reasons to keep V's reading. In Greek, when a compound verb has to be repeated it is often replaced by the verbum simplex, e.g. Pl. *Phdr.* 248 a αἱ δὲ ἄλλαι ψυχαί, ἡ μὲν...ὑπερῆρεν εἰς τὸν ἔξω τόπον...ἡ δὲ τοτὲ μὲν ἦρεν, τοτὲ δ' ἔδυ, Pl. *Phd.* 59 b ὁ Ἀπολλόδωρος...παρῆν...ἦν δὲ καὶ Κτήσιππος. Examples from tragedy are given in Kühner-Gerth, 1955, I 552. One might therefore be tempted to interpret this as a Grecism, but the phenomenon is not entirely unknown in Latin. Szantyr 300 in this context speaks about "die unterschiedslose Verwendung von Simpl. und Kompos. im nachklassischen Latein im Dienste der Variatio". See also Löfstedt, 1911, 58–59 on *(ap)parere* and Hagendahl, 1921, 110. Pighi, 1935, 63 has the following parallel: 15.2.5 *id sederat, ut... Ursicinus indemnatus occideretur, ut quondam Domitius Corbulo dicitur caesus.*

Hyperechius, mentioned above, belonged to these *apparitores*. Another court official who chose Procopius' side and is known by name is Helpidius (*PLRE* I, Helpidius 6); he had served i.a. as *comes rei privatae* under Julian. We already met one of those who *intra regiam...parere desierant* and later became collaborators of Procopius, viz. *Strategium quendam ex palatino milite senatorem* (26.6.5, q.v.). Another is mentioned by Zos. 4.5.3, the eunuch Eugenius (*PLRE* I, Eugenius 4; cf. the note ad 26.7.6 *aliique plures*).

quique coetu militarium nexi ad pacatiora iam vitae discesserant The phrase *coetu militarium nexi* to denote military men seems to be all Amm.'s own. Germanicus' indignant question in Tac. *Ann.* 1.42.2 *quod nomen huic coetui dabo? militesne appellem?* is indeed very different. In 26.7.4 Amm. gives the names of two such soldiers: *et administratio negotiorum castrensium Gomoario et Agiloni revocatis in sacramentum committitur.*

Ad pacatiora vitae is a variation on *ad tranquilliora vitae* (25.5.4, q.v.). For the different phrases used by Amm. for retirement see also the note ad 20.2.5 *digredi iussit*.

insoliti casus ambigua partim inviti, alii volentes asciscebantur For the construction of *asciscere/ascisci* see the notes ad 20.4.22 *asciti* and 26.2.7 *utiliter*. For the reasons given there it seems best to write *in insoliti*. The "extraordinary and hazardous adventure" (Hamilton) is the revolt of Procopius. Hamilton's translation brings out well the practical use of the gen. inversus as a means to join two attributes to one Head, as is also the case in 20.11.17 *post ambiguam proelii varietatem*. As there are no unequivocal instances in Amm. of mediopassive *ascisci*, 'to join', it seems best to interpret *asciscebantur* as a real passive. The ex-soldiers were willy-nilly enrolled in the revolt. In 26.9.8 we will meet the tribune Barchalba, *quem...necessitas in crimen traxerat, non voluntas*. Cf. section 6 below about some other creatures of Procopius: *quidam inviti, alii ultro semet offerentes cum praemiis*. The list of supporters given by Delmaire, 1997, 118–119 is not exhaustive.

Zos. 4.6.3 refers to Procopius' attempts to persuade people to choose his side by making generous promises: πληρώσας ἐλπίδων καὶ ἁδρῶν ὑποσχέσεων ἅπαντας.

nonnulli omnia tutiora praesentibus rati The same turn of phrase is found in Liv. 9.26.17 *adeo omnia tutiora, quam ut innocentiam suam purgarent, visa* and Curt. 5.12.18 *omnia tutiora parricidarum comitatu ratus. Praesentibus* must refer to the situation in which they found themselves in Constantinople.

e civitate occulte dilapsi For *(di)labi* in the sense of *effugere* cf. the note ad 26.3.3 *laxius retinente*. Them. *Or*. 7.91 d states that Procopius hermetically sealed Constantinople: λιμένες δὲ ἀνεφράγνυντο καὶ νεώρια, πολιορκία δὲ εἴσω τείχους περιειστήκει τὴν πόλιν ('harbours and dockyards were barricaded, the city was blockaded within its own walls'), which i.a. implies that the usurper tried to prevent anyone from leaving the city.

imperatoris castra petivere itineribus festinatis As De Jonge pointed out ad 16.8.1 *in castris Augusti*, Amm. uses *castra* in the meaning of *comitatus* as the equivalent of Greek στρατόπεδον in 14.5.9 *reversusque ad principis castra*, 18.5.6 *in castris Constantii* and here. Cf. TLL III 561.43-50. For *itineribus festinatis* and similar expressions see the note ad 20.8.21 *venit ad*.

Hos omnes Sophronius vivacissimo cursu praegressus tunc notarius, praefectus póstea Constantinopóleos Harmon 169 mentions 30.4.21 *Aésopi cavillatiónibus* as the only other cursus of this type in the *Res Gestae*. For *cursu* with an attribute denoting speed of travel cf. 16.12.36 *concito quam considerato* –, 16.12.45 – *celeri*, 16.12.59 *anhelo* – , 19.11.11 – *effuso*, 21.16.11 *incohibili* – , 23.3.1 – *propero*, 23.3.5 *praestricto* (q.v.), 29.6.13 – *ruenti*. This is the only instance of *vivax* in Amm. It is probably inspired by Gel. 5.2.4 about Alexander's horse Bucephalus: *e mediis hostibus regem vivacissimo cursu retulit*, which makes it even less probable that Amm. is thinking of the *cursus publicus*, as Seyfarth's translation "mit der Schnellpost" suggests. For this he prefers expressions like 14.11.19 *itineribus rectis per mutationem iumentorum emensis* or 15.1.2 *equorum permutatione veloci*.

In contrast to the ample information he provides about the prefects of Rome, Ammianus refers only sparingly to the eastern urban prefects (and to Constantinople in general; see Kelly, 2003). He names only three of them, viz. the Sophronius of the present text, a native of Caesarea in Cappadocia (*PLRE* I, Sophronius 3), and Caesarius and Phronimius, both mentioned in 26.7.4 (q.v.). Before becoming *praefectus urbis Constantinopolitanae*, a post which existed since 359 (cf. Jones 132, Dagron, 1974, 213 ff.), the former *notarius* Sophronius (see for his function Teitler, 1985, esp. 167 and 304 n. 296) held the post of *magister officiorum* (cf. Clauss, 1980 [1981], 190–191). For other possible steps in his career see Brauch, 2002, 53–60, 70, 73, 79–80, 89, who argues that Sophronius was vicar of Pontus before he became prefect of Constantinople and that he occupied the latter post twice. Cf. further Raimondi, 2006, 201–206, who stresses the importance of Sophronius as an official at Valens' court.

Valentem a Caesarea Cappadocum iam profecturum The emperor had left Constantinople for Syria in the spring of 365 (*consumpta hieme festinans ad Syriam*, 26.6.11, q.v.), but apparently spent the greater part of the summer in Cappadocian Caesarea, for which city see the note ad 20.9.1 *apud Caesaream*. Valens' presence there on the fourth of July is attested by *Cod. Theod.* 12.6.5 (*dat. iiii non. Iul. Caesarea*; there is no reason to reject the date of this law as transmitted by the ms., pace Lenski, 2002, 77 n. 53, who follows Seeck's proposal to change the date into Nov. 2, 365; see on this Pergami, 1993, 236–237). Sophronius will have informed the emperor about Procopius' proclamation, which occurred on 28 September 365 (see the note ad 26.6.14 *ubi excanduit*), early in October, in view of the fact that he travelled the roughly 750 km from Constantinople to Caesarea *vivacissimo cursu*. According to Zos. 4.7.3 it was ἐν τῇ κατὰ Φρυγίαν Γαλατίᾳ that Valens learned about Procopius' usurpation, but this must be a mistake. Zosimus presumably confused the moment when Valens first heard of the usurpation (in Caesarea) with the moment when the emperor received more details (in Galatia). Cf. below, ad 26.7.13 *fecissetque*.

ut vaporatis aestibus Ciliciae iam lenitis ad Antiochiae percurreret sedes For the heat of the summer in Cilicia Valesius compared Curt. 3.5.1 *et tunc aestas erat, cuius calor non aliam magis quam Ciliciae oram vapore solis accendit* and Hier. *epist.* 3.3 *cum me...fervido Cilicum terra fregisset aestu*. For *vaporatus* cf. 18.9.2 and 19.4.1, both about Amida.

If Sophronius indeed arrived in Caesarea in the beginning of October (see above), this neatly tallies with Amm.'s statement, that the emperor was about to leave this city when the oppressive heat in Cilicia had already somewhat diminished. See for Cilicia and

Antiochia the notes ad 21.15.2 *Mobsucrenas* (add to the literature cited there Mutafian, 1988) and 26.6.20 *sic Antiochiae*.

For *sedes* 'residence' cf. 16.10.20 *Cupiens itaque augustissima omnium sede morari diutius imperator* (Constantius at Rome), 18.4.7 *Samosatam, Commageni quondam regni clarissimam sedem*, 29.1.4 *et rex quidem Parthus hiemem Ctesiphonte acturus redit ad sedes*.

textu narrato gestorum As is explained in the note ad *quo textu* (20.4.11), *textus* can denote a 'written text', but also, as in the present case, a 'train of events'. Sabbah 363 may well be right in supposing that Amm.'s account of Procopius' revolt "repose très vraisemblablement sur un rapport officiel dont l'auteur pourrait être Sophronius".

spe dubia ut in talibus percitum et stupentem avertit Galatiam Cf. *Haec per eum annum spe dubia eventu tamen secundo per Gallias agebantur* (16.6.1). In the note ad 20.11.5 *dolore percitus* it is stated that *percitus* is normally combined with an abl. causae. That is the function of *spe dubia*, 'because he did not know what to expect', in the present sentence. The phrase is less common than one would expect. As part of a litotes it is found four times in Livy, e.g. 3.2.3 *haud dubia spe profectus famam nominis sui pacaturam Aequos*. Cic. has it just once: *Inv.* 2.27 *summae fuisse amentiae dubia spe inpulsum certum in periculum se committere*. The words *ut in talibus* 'as is normal in such circumstances', with which cf. 31.10.15 *ut in tali negotio*, seem to gloss over Valens' temporary loss of control. The situation is reminiscent of 21.3.1, where Julian's reaction is described when he hears about Vadomarius' treachery: *nuntio percitus inopino ad tristitiam versus est et maerorem*. A much more violent reaction on the part of Valens is described in section 13 below. According to Amm. the gravity of the situation only became clear to Valens when he was already on his way back to Constantinople and heard how Procopius had managed to consolidate his position. For the accusative of Goal with the name of a country or region see the note ad 23.2.7 *unde contractis*.

While Amm. says that Valens intended to go to Antioch but was persuaded by Sophronius to go to Galatia instead, Socr. *HE* 4.3.1, 5.2 and Soz. *HE* 6.7.10 claim that Valens did reach Antioch. The church historians must be mistaken. They may have been misled, as Lenski, 2002, 78 argues (referring to *Cod. Theod.* 7.22.7, Lib. *Ep.* 1499, 1505 and Thdt. *h. rel.* 13.15), by the fact that Valens probably had sent part of his army ahead to Syria, and that preparations had been made for the emperor's arrival in Antioch. For Galatia or Gallograecia (thus in 26.7.13) see the note ad 22.9.5 *ad Gallograeciae*. Add to the literature cited there Belke, 1994.

res adhuc trepidas arrepturum Again we are reminded of Julian's rise to power, when he decided to inform Constantius of his assumption of the title of Augustus: 20.8.3 *circumspectis itaque trepidis rerum novarum exordiis*.

7.3 *Qui dum itineribus properat magnis* The natural supposition, that Valens on his journey through Galatia called in at its capital before continuing his westbound march (for Ancyra see the note ad 22.9.8 *Ancyram rediit*), finds support in 26.8.4 (*Unde cum Ancyram Valens citis itineribus revertisset*). From there the emperor headed for Nicomedia in Bithynia and Chalcedon (26.8.2).

attentissima cura Procopius in dies agitabatur et noctes V's reading *agitabat noctes* was evidently regarded as a simple case of haplography by Valesius and accordingly emended to *agitabat et noctes*. Surprisingly, modern editors have followed Günther's *agitabatur* (1891, 68). Günther compared 29.1.11 *qui dum formidine successoris agitaretur in dies*. *Attentissima cura*, however, does not refer to worries or fears, but means 'with the utmost care', as in V. Max. 2.2.7 (tribuni plebis) *decreta patrum attentissima cura examinabant*. The expression *in dies et noctes*, 'day and night', is found also in 31.4.5.

subditivos quosdam ostentans, qui astutia confidenti partim ab oriente, alii e Gallis se venisse et Valentinianum obisse fingentes The rare adjective *subditivus* 'spurious', 'suppositious' is used also in 14.9.1, where Ursicinus risks becoming the victim of trumped up accusations, *cum accusatores quaesitoresque subditivos sibi consociatos ex isdem foveis cerneret emergentes*. In HA *AS* 5.3 Heliogabalus is called *subditivus*, because he called himself Antoninus without being related to the Antonini. *Astutia confidenti* is probably inspired by Cic. *Clu*. 183 *confidens astutia*. In Amm. *confidens* usually has negative connotations; see the note ad 20.4.18 *capiti Iuliani*.

On the subject of these so-called messengers Valesius quotes Them. *Or*. 7.91 d: τοὺς ἀγγέλους τοὺς ἐκ τῶν προαστείων κεκονιαμένους, τοὺς μὲν ἐξ Ἰλλυριῶν, τοὺς δὲ ἐξ Ἰταλίας, τοὺς δὲ ἐξ Ὠκεανοῦ τοῦ ἑσπερίου, ('the messengers from the suburbs covered in dust, some of them coming from Illyria, others from Italy or the western Ocean'). Amm.'s *ab oriente* is pleasantly short compared to the sequel of

Themistius' text *Or.* 7.91d–92a πρεσβεῖαι δὲ εἰσεκαλοῦντο εἰς τὰ βασίλεια Σύρων, Ἀσσυρίων, Αἰγυπτίων, Λιβύων, Ἰβήρων, ὥσπερ διαπτᾶσαι ἐξαίφνης ἐκ τῶν ἐσχάτων τῆς οἰκουμένης ('embassies from Syria, Assyria, Egypt, Libya and Hiberia were received in the palace, or so it seemed, as if they suddenly had come flying from the remotests parts of the world'). Possibly, the alleged emissaries from Gaul had in their possession coins with the head of Procopius and the mint mark CONST or SCONST (a mint mark of Arelate), clear imitations of Julian's coinage from Arles, suggesting that Procopius had western support. See for this Pearce, 1951, 215 with n. 18, Wiebe, 1995, 76. More on Procopius' coinage in the notes ad 26.6.5 *ubi quoniam* and 26.7.11 *aureos*.

cuncta patere novo et favorabili principi memorabant Cf. Tac. *Hist.* 4.81.3 *Vespasianus cuncta fortunae suae patere ratus nec quicquam ultra incredibile.* The adjective *favorabilis*, 'popular', 'beloved' is normally combined with an abl. causae, such as 14.11.3 *decore corporum favorabiles et aetate* or 26.10.5 *hoc favorabilis solo*, q.v. It is used absolutely in 29.3.5 *Athanasius favorabilis tunc auriga.* For *princeps* see the notes ad 20.2.1 *commilitium* and 20.4.8 *proiceret*.

et quia res novae petulanter arreptae celeritate muniri solent interdum For *et quia* in Amm. see the notes ad 20.4.6 and 25.10.17. Julian acted on the same principle: 21.5.1 *nihilque tam convenire conatibus subitis quam celeritatem sagaci praevidens mente.* See also the note ad 21.9.6 *ut fax.* For *petulanter* 'insolently', 'recklessly', cf. 17.13.28 *parique petulantia ruentes in agmina nobilium legionum Quados...attrivimus.* Amm. uses *munire* in the wider sense of 'to strengthen', 'to protect' also in 28.1.35 *ut Maximini muniretur auxilio* and 31.5.4 *At ille genuina praevidendi sollertia venturos muniens casus.* Cf. Cic. *dom.* 80 *iure munitam civitatem et libertatem*; Sal. *Jug.* 28.4 *quorum auctoritate quae deliquisset munita fore sperabat.* For *interdum* with *solere* cf. 18.3.8 *animalia ratione carentia salutem suam interdum alto tueri silentio solent.* It is common in all periods of Latin. Cf. Cic. *Ver.* 3.141 *ut solemus interdum in defensionibus dicere*, Ov. *Tr.* 2.141 *solet interdum fieri placabile numen*, Suet. *Tib.* 50.2 *ne consiliis, quibus tamen interdum et egere et uti solebat, regi videretur.*

7.4

ne quid formidandum omitteretur, confestim Nebridius...et Caesarius...in vincula compinguntur "That nothing might be neglected which could arouse fear" (Rolfe); Seyfarth's translation "um keinen Grund zur Besorgnis aufkommen zu lassen" is wrong. For the importance of new nominations after a revolt see Delmaire, 1997. Procopius obviously tried to intimidate wavering officials by the sudden arrest of these highly placed people. One is reminded of Seianus, who attacked the famous general Silius for similar reasons: Tac. *Ann.* 4.18.1 *quanto maiore mole procideret, plus formidinis in alios dispergebatur.* According to TLL III 2072.32–34, apart from Iust. 16.4.17 *Clearchus LX senatores conprehensos...in vincula conpingit* and *Vir. ill. 1.2*, Amm. is the only author to use the expression *in vincula compingere*, 'to put into irons' in 17.8.5, 28.1.8 and here. As is noted ad 24.5.10 *reliquos* (q.v.), *compingere* is combined with *in custodiam* in 26.10.5. The expressions seem to be synonymous, although one cannot rule out that the prisoners were really chained. According to *Cod. Theod.* 9.2.3 of 380 *nullus in carcerem, priusquam convincatur, omnino vinciatur*, which implies *a silentio*, as Chauvot, 2004, 33 rightly observes, that in actual practice this was not always the case. Imprisonment could last a considerable time, although as a rule the accused only stayed in jail temporarily, pending the final decision of the judge c.q. his execution. Detention as a legal penalty was exceptional. See Krause, 1996, 89–90, 336, 345–346 and the note ad 26.10.5 *unde post dies.*

Zosimus (4.6.2) names Caesarius before Nebridius (συλλαβὼν Καισάριον...ἔτι δὲ καὶ Νευρίδιον), and relates that the prisoners were kept apart, to prevent them from plotting together (ἐφύλαττε δὲ ἰδίᾳ ἕκαστον, τὸ μὴ κοινωνῆσαι σκέμματος αὐτοῖς ἀποκλείων). Themistius refrains from mentioning the names of 'the highest authorities except you (sc. Valens), put into prison like criminals' (ἀρχαὶ δὲ αἱ μέγισται μετά γε τὴν ὑμετέραν ἐν μοίρᾳ κακούργων ἦσαν συνειλημμέναι, *Or.* 7.91 b).

Nebridius in locum Saluti praefectus praetorio factione Petronii recens promotus Nebridius (*PLRE* I, Nebridius 1), who had been Julian's *quaestor sacri palatii* before becoming praetorian prefect of Gaul (20.9.5, q.v.), was dismissed after he had refused to follow Julian against Constantius, and lived in retirement in Tuscany during the rest of Julian's reign (21.5.11–12). Zos. 4.6.2 refers, like Amm., to his appointment as PPO Orientis in succession to Salutius (*PLRE* I, Secundus 3), but is silent about the influence of Petronius (*PLRE* I, Petronius 3): (Nebridius) ᾧ τῆς αὐλῆς μετὰ Σαλούστιον παρέδωκαν τὴν ἀρχήν (sc. the emperors Valentinian and Valens). He must have died soon after his imprisonment – Them. *Or.* 7.92 c τοῖν δὲ ἀρχόντοιν τοῖν κορυφαίοιν ὁ μὲν τεθνηκὼς ἠπιστεῖτο, ὁ δὲ οὐ τεθνηκὼς ἐπιστεύθη τεθνάναι ('As regards the two officials at the top, it was not believed that the one who had died was dead; on the contrary, it was thought that the other, who had not died, had passed away') is best taken, with e.g. Valesius and Leppin-Portmann, as a reference to Nebridius and Caesarius, respectively, and not to Procopius and Valens, as Vanderspoel, 1995, 164–165 suggests. For Salutius as *praefectus praetorio* under Valens see the note ad 26.5.3 *quibus ita* and 26.5.5 *et orientem*, for Petronius 26.6.7 with the relevant note. The notes ad 21.6.5 *Anatolio*, 23.5.6 *quem praefectus* and 25.3.14 *Salutius* deal with the office of PPO.

Caesarius Constantinopolitanae urbis praefectus Caesarius, ὃν ἔτυχον οἱ βασιλεῖς πόλεως ὕπαρχον καταστήσαντες ('whom the emperors Valentinian and Valens had made prefect of the city of Constantinople', Zos. 4.6.2; see for his office the note ad 26.7.2 *Sophronius*), had been *comes rei privatae* under Jovian (*PLRE* I, Caesarius 1). While his co-prisoner Nebridius soon died (see the previous note), Caesarius survived Procopius' revolt (Them. *Or.* 7.92 c, just quoted). Brauch, 2002, 48–53 even argues, that in 366 Caesarius was urban prefect of Constantinople for a second term. In Amm. he is not mentioned anymore.

iubetur civitatem curare solita potestate Phronimius TLL IV 1505.10–19 offers a few instances of *curare* in the sense of 'to administrate', most of them taken from Amm. See the note ad 23.6.14 *quas vitaxae*. As Amm. relates in 26.10.8, after Procopius' revolt had been quelled Phronimius (*PLRE* I, Phronimius) was sent for trial to Valentinian and exiled. As to the spelling of his name, Marié's *Phronemius* is the reading of Gelenius; V here reads *fronemus*, in 26.10.8 *fronemius*.

esseque magister officiorum Euphrasius Like Phronimius, Euphrasius (*PLRE* I, Eufrasius 2) was also sent for trial to Valentinian after Procopius' fall, but he was acquitted (26.10.8). For Euphrasius as *magister officiorum* see Clauss 1980 (1981), 105, 153.

ambo Galli institutis bonarum artium spectatissimi When Constantius presented Julian as the new Caesar to the troops, he recommended him for his lofty character, which had been perfected by his studies: 15.8.10 *praeclaram indolem bonis artibus institutam*. In a similar way Phronimius and Euphrasius are said to be greatly respected (*spectatissimi*) for their studies of the liberal arts (*institutis bonarum artium*). According to TLL VII 1.1995.81 there is a confusion here with *institutio*, which is the proper word for 'training', 'education'; cf. the definition of *humanitas* in Gel. 13.17.1 *'humanitatem' appellaverunt id propemodum, quod Graeci* παιδείαν *vocant, nos eruditionem institutionemque in bonas artis dicimus*. The few parallels adduced in TLL, e.g. Aur. Vict. *Caes.* 39.28 *Aureliani Probique instituto*, are all from the fourth century and after.

Phronimius and Euphrasius were both Gauls, which may account for the fact that as prisoners they were later sent to Valentinian in Gaul (26.10.8). According to Wiebe, 1995, 49 it also "dokumentiert...die Existenz konspirativer Verbindungslinien zwischen dem Usurpator und Gallien", but in view of the paucity of the evidence this is far from certain. Understandably, though *viri litterati*, Euphrasius and Phronimius are not referred to in Nellen, 1981[2], whose study about "die Rolle der gebildeten Beamtenschaft" mainly deals with the western part of the empire and only occasionally discusses officials in the East.

et administratio negotiorum castrensium Gomoario et Agiloni revocatis in sacramentum committitur Another expression denoting return to military service is *recingi*, for which see the note ad 26.5.3 *et Serenianus*. For the opposite see ad 25.1.9 *abiecti*. For Gomoarius (*PLRE* I, Gomoarius+A. Lippold in *Gnomon* 46 [1974] 270), who served under Constantius but was dismissed by Julian, see the relevant notes ad 20.9.5 and 21.8.1. Agilo (*PLRE* I, Agilo; cf. the note ad 20.2.5) seems to have retired after he had been a member of the commission of Chalcedon under Julian (22.3.1). As to *administratio negotiorum castrensium*, since Gomoarius had served as *magister equitum* and Agilo as *magister peditum*, one may assume that they held the same positions under Procopius; Demandt, 1970, 703.

inconsulte, ut docuit rerum exitus proditarum The reading of E *proditarum* was defended by Cornelissen, 1886, 285, V's reading being *proditar* (similarly, in section 11 below V has *poenar* for *poenarum*). The other mss. have *proditor*, which looks like a desperate remedy for V's *proditar*, but was printed by all editors before Clark. Cornelissen took *prodere* to be the equivalent of *tradere*, as in 22.8.25 *ut auctores prodidere nonnulli*. So did Günther, 1888, 45–46, but he rejected *proditarum* on the ground that Amm. could not use a perfect participle for a story which he intended to tell only in ch. 9. An answer to this might be, that Ammianus does not necessarily have his own account of the usurpation in mind, but is perhaps thinking of the reports of others. An alternative would be to take *prodere* in the sense of 'to betray' and to suppose that Amm. anticipates the betrayal by Gomoarius and Agilo in 26.9.6–7, where we actually read *Agilo rem excursu prodidit repentino* (although the text is uncertain). This would also tally perfectly with Amm.'s qualification of Gomoarius as an arch traitor in 21.8.1, q.v., (Julian appointed Nevitta as *magister armorum*) *Gomoarium proditorem antiquum timens, quem, cum Scutarios ageret, latenter prodidisse Veteranionem suum principem audiebat*. In other words, here again Procopius is implicitly shown to be inferior to Julian, who had given evidence of being a sound judge of men.

The sentence as a whole is a form of prolepsis, introduced by *ut docuit*, comparable to 16.12.13 where the outcome of the events shows that a *salutaris genius* had roused the fighting spirit of the soldiers: *ut exitus docuit, salutaris quidam genius praesens ad dimicandum eos, dum adesse potuit, incitabat*. Cf. also 17.13.5 *ad citeriorem venere fluminis ripam, ut exitus docuit, non iussa facturi, sed ne viderentur militis praesentiam formidasse* and 27.3.3 on the prefecture of Symmachus: *quo instante urbs sacratissima...ambitioso ponte exsultat atque firmissimo, quem condidit ipse et magna civium laetitia dedicavit ingratorum, ut res docuit apertissima*. Another type of prolepsis is found when the historian tells us about later events in the life of one of his characters, as e.g. in 15.2.7 *Indeque ad Iulianum recens perductum calumniarum vertitur machina, memorabilem postea principem* or 15.5.36 *idque scrutari iusserat artius interrogato Remigio ..., cui multo postea, Valentiniani temporibus, laqueus vitam...erupit*. A notorious example is 28.1.57, where Amm. promises to record the execution of his bête noire, Maximinus: *namque ut postea tempestive dicetur, ...idem Maximinus sub Gratiano intoleranter se efferens damnatorio iugulatus est ferro*, which he fails to do.

Iulius comes per Thracias copiis militaribus praesidens Amm. calls this Iulius (*PLRE* I, Iulius 2) *comes*, which probably means that he was *comes rei militaris* (see the note ad 20.4.18 *postea comes*). For the suggestion that "he may perhaps more likely have been *magister militum per Thraciam*" (Nicasie, 1998, 161 n. 171), there is no confirmation in the sources. Iulius later became notorious as the *magister militiae* who, after the battle of Adrianople, ordered the massacre of the Goths recently enlisted in the Roman army (31.16.8). For the strategic importance of Thrace cf. 26.5.11 *Valentinianus...ad Illyricum festinabat, ne persultatis Thraciis perduellis iam formidatus invaderet hostili excursu Pannonias*. Amm. uses *praesidere* more often for military commands, e.g. 27.1.2 (Severianus) *apud Cabyllona Divitensibus praesidebat et Tungricanis*; TLL X 2.881.10–17 quotes some parallels, i.a. Tac. *Ann.* 1.58.2 (Varus) *exercitui praesidebat*.

7.5

oppressurus rebelles, si comperisset conata, ex propinquis stationibus timebatur The syntax of this sentence is comparable to 30.10.1, which describes the tense situation after the death of Valentinian: *anceps rei timebatur eventus cohortibus Gallicanis, quae non semper dicatae legitimorum principum fidei velut imperiorum arbitrae ausurae novum quoddam in tempore sperabantur.* There *ausurae* must be interpreted as the elliptical future infinitive in a NcI-construction, just like *secuturae* in Tac. *Hist.* 2.74.1 *ceterae Illyrici legiones secuturae sperabantur.* In the present sentence, however, *oppressurus* must be taken as a predicative participle: Iulius was feared, because he would crush the rebellion as soon as he heard about it. The fact that he was close at hand made the danger even greater. The situation is reminiscent of Julian's preventive measures against Lupicinus as described in 20.9.9, but note the very different wording: *oppressurus rebelles* in the case of Iulius, whereas in the case of Lupicinus Amm. writes *erat...suspicio, quod, si haec trans mare didicisset, novarum rerum materias excitaret.*

As a noun *rebellis* appears for the first time in Tac. *Ann.* 1.40.1 *Eo in metu arguere Germanicum omnes, quod non ad superiorem exercitum pergeret, ubi obsequia et contra rebelles auxilium.*

The *stationes* here are clearly to be taken in the sense of 'military posts' (as e.g. in Caes. *Gal.* 4.32.2, 6.42.1), where *milites stationarii* (18.5.3, (q.v.), 21.3.6) or *stationarii* (19.6.7) were quartered as garrisons (cf. the note ad 20.4.9 *e stationibus*). One such Thracian *statio* was perhaps Nice, not far from Adrianople (*unde cum itinere edicto per tesseram Nicen venisset, quae statio ita cognominatur,* 31.11.2, cf. 31.12.3). However, one cannot rule out that Nice was merely a station of the *cursus publicus* (for *statio* in this sense see e.g. *ILS* 5905). See for *stationes* in general Nelis-Clément, 2006.

commentum excogitatum est validum For *commentum*, 'device', see the note ad 20.6.6. Amm. uses the adjective *validus* 'effective' with *consilium* in 19.9.8 *ille enim ingenio et usu rerum diuturno firmatus consiliis validis sufficiebat in cuncta.* Cf. also Apul. *Met.* 1.25 *prudentis condiscipuli valido consilio et nummis simul privatus* and 5.10 *consilium validum requiramus ambae.*

quasi iussu Valentis seria super barbaricis motibus tractaturus Nebridii litteris adhuc clausi violenter expressis accitus Constantinopolim strictius tenebátur This extremely condensed period well illustrates "der masslose Gebrauch der Part. bei den Spätlateinern" (Szantyr 384), who calls it "eine gelehrte Entwicklung, wobei jetzt bei manchen Konstruktionen griechischer Einfluss unverkennbar ist." For a more nuanced discussion of the participles in Amm. see Den Boeft, 1992, 14–16. *Quasi* is best taken as a "Partizipialkonjunktion" qualifying *tractaturus* and introducing a deceptive pretext. See the note on 26.4.1 *quasi tota*. The phrase *adhuc clausi* refers back to the preceding section where Amm. mentioned the arrest of Nebridius and Caesarius. The comparative *strictius* is chosen to produce a cursus velox. There is no parallel for *stricte tenere* 'to keep under close arrest'.

For the pretended 'movements of the barbarians' cf. 26.6.11 *gentem Gothorum...conspirantem in unum ad pervadenda parari collimitia Thraciarum*. While Amm. speaks of one letter to Iulius, extorted by violence from Nebridius, Zosimus' wording in 4.6.2 seems to imply that Nebridius wrote more than one letter, and that Caesarius did likewise: Καὶ συλλαβὼν Καισάριον...ἔτι δὲ καὶ Νευρίδιον...γράφειν τὰ αὐτῷ δοκοῦντα τοῖς ὑπηκόοις ἠνάγκαζεν· ('He had Caesarius and Nebridius arrested and forced them to write to their subordinates what seemed best to him [sc. Procopius])'. Unlike Amm. Zosimus does not mention that Iulius was lured to Constantinople. Zosimus is also in other respects not quite compatible with Amm., if only because that as *comes rei militaris* Iulius can hardly be styled 'ὑπήκοος' of the PPO Nebridius. One wonders further to whom and with what purpose other letters were sent, especially those pretending to have come from the urban prefect Caesarius.

hacque callida fraude bellatrices Thraciae gentes sine cruore acquisitae adminicula ausis tumultuariis maxima compararunt The wording *callida fraus*, with which cf. the characterisation of Cleopatra in 22.16.11 as *femina callida semper in fraudes*, in combination with the preceding *commentum validum* is a reluctant admission on Amm.'s part that the usurper had a few dangerous tricks up his sleeve. In a similar fashion he refers in 26.9.4 to Procopius taking advantage of the presence of Constantius' daughter and her mother Faustina with the words *has calliditatis argutias*. Although the noun *ausum*, as is observed in the note ad 21.11.1 *ausa indicans*, is a vox media, Amm.'s characterization of Procopius' revolt as *ausa tumultuaria* has prospective force, and leaves the reader in no doubt that this 'sloppily improvised undertaking' is doomed to failure.

On the warlike spirit of the Thracians see the note ad 21.12.22 *dispersum per Thracias*. For the rare phrase *sine cruore* see the note ad 20.11.7 *alienis sine*. Plin. *Nat.* 15.125 uses it in his description of the *ovatio*: (Tubertus), *qui primus omnium ovans ingressus urbem est, quoniam rem leniter sine cruore gesserat, myrto Veneris victricis coronatus incessit.* The verb *acquirere* is used with a human object also in Pub. *C. 43 Cum inimico ignoscis, amicos gratis conplures adquiris* and Sal. *Jug.* 13.6 *Romam legatos mittit, quis praecipit, primum uti veteres amicos muneribus expleant, deinde novos adquirant.* In the context of an (alleged) revolt *adminicula* is used in 14.9.4 *ut adminicula futurae molitioni pollicitos*. See also the note ad 20.4.9 and on *adminicula* as a synonym of *auxilia* or *copiae auxiliares* the note ad 21.12.21. As Lenski, 2002, 83 points out, with the acquisition of Thrace the mint of Heraclea fell into Procopius' hands, which from now on issued his coins (more on this ad § 11).

7.6 *Araxius exambita regia praetorio praefectus accessit velut Agilone genero suffragante* The verb *exambire* 'to solicit the favour of' might have been mentioned by Löfstedt, 1911, 94 as an instance of "Dekomposition", as he calls the tendency in Late Latin to make composita more expressive by adding a second prefix. Cf. for this phenomenon the note ad 25.7.8 *quo temporis*. The instances of *exambire* in TLL V 2. 1162.18–49, where *regiam exambire* is correctly paraphrased as *aulicos captare*, all date from the fourth century. *Regia* sounds rather grandiose for the abode and court of a usurper, but in 15.5.31 it is even used in connection with the short-lived usurper Silvanus *caesis custodibus regia penetrata Silvanum extractum...trucidarant*. For *regia* in the wider sense of 'court' cf. 19.1.10 *quo funere regia maesta et optimatibus universis cum parente subita clade perculsis* and Tac. *Ann.* 11.29.2 *Callistus prioris quoque regiae peritus*. The present text is, among many others, cited by Schlinkert, 1998, 138 n. 13 ("Die Begrifflichkeit, die das Phänomen "Hof" in der Spätantike erfaßt, ist sehr heterogen"). The expression *praetorio praefectus accessit*, 'he was appointed as PPO', seems to be without parallel. For *praetorium* in the meaning 'pretorian prefecture' see TLL X 2.1073.46–56. Elsewhere Amm. writes 15.13.2 (Musonianus) *ascendit ad praefecturam*; 20.9.5 *praefectum praetorio Nebridium tum quaestorem eiusdem Caesaris promoverat*, (q.v.); 20.9.8 *admissus est ad praefecturam Nebridius*; 28.1.41 *auctusque* (Maximinus) *praefectura praetoriana*.

The qualification *velut* probably means that Agilo was not openly behind Araxius (*PLRE* I, Araxius), but that the courtiers assumed this to be the case. For *suffragari* see the note ad 20.5.7 *alio quodam*. The name of Araxius' daughter, Agilo's wife, happens to be known: *PLRE* I, Vetiana. In 26.10.7 Amm. repeats that Nebridius' successor as PPO, Araxius, who during Constantius' reign had been i.a. governor of Palestine and *proconsul urbis Constantinopolitanae*, did not owe his appointment to any personal merit, but purely to court protection (*adeptus ambitu praefecturam*), adding that the intercession of Agilo saved him from the death penalty.

aliique plures ad aulae varios actus et administrandas provincias sunt admissi This is the only instance of *actus* in the sense of 'service', 'office' in the *Res Gestae*. Most frequently *actus* in the plural refers to Amm.'s own account of the reign of an emperor, as in 14.4.2 *in actibus principis Marci*. See further the note ad 21.7.2 *exploratorem actuum*. TLL I 452.76 has a few parallels, such as HA *Car* 6.2 *felix autem esset nostra res p., si, qualis Carus est aut plerique vestrum, plures haberem in actibus conlocatos* and August. *de nupt. et concup.* 1.2.2 *actibus publicis eisdemque militaribus occupato*.

Some of these officials are known by name, thanks to Amm. himself: the *cura palatii* Rumitalca (26.8.1, q.v.) and the *proconsul (Asiae)* Hormisdas (26.8.12, q.v.). Another is mentioned by Libanius: the governor of Bithynia and subsequently vicar of Thrace Andronicus (*Or.* 62.58–60, cf. *PLRE* I, Andronicus 3). Perhaps the eunuch Eugenius (*PLRE* I, Eugenius 4) also belongs to this category. Zos. 4.5.3–4 relates that under Valens he was expelled from the palace, where he must have served as *cubicularius*, and that he supported Procopius with money. No return gift is mentioned, but to assume that Eugenius was reinstated into his former position would not seem implausible. Mutatis mutandis the same holds good for the former *palatinus miles* Strategius (26.6.5, q.v.) and Helpidius (*PLRE* I, Helpidius 6). Philostorgius states that Helpidius, who had been i.a. *comes rerum privatarum* under Julian, collaborated with Procopius (*HE* 7.10), which may have brought him a function at court or a governorship in return.

quidam inviti, alii ultro semet offerentes cum praemiis Cf. 26.7.1 *insoliti casus ambigua partim inviti, alii volentes asciscebantur* with the note. For *praemium* 'bribe' see TLL X 2.718.83 sqq. "in petendis honoribus". Cf. Sal. *Jug.* 13.8 *pars spe, alii praemio inducti singulos ex senatu ambiundo nitebantur* e.q.s. In combination with its equivalent *merces* it is found in Sal. *Hist.* 3.48.5 *Quamquam omnes alii creati pro iure vostro* ('to protect your rights') *vim cunctam et imperia sua gratia aut spe aut praemiis in vos convortere* ('use against you') *meliusque habent mercede delinquere quam gratis recte facere*.

utque in certaminibus intestinis usu venire contingit, emergebant ex vulgari faece nonnulli desperatione consiliisque ductantibus caecis There are no parallels for the tautological *usu venire contingit*. It is clear that Amm. in principle condemns any revolt against the legitimate power of the emperor, on whom all subjects depend for their well-being: *nec enim abnuimus salutem legitimi principis, propugnatoris bonorum et defensoris, unde salus quaeritur aliis, consociato studio muniri debere cunctorum* (19.12.17). In the case of Procopius Matthews 201 speaks of Amm.'s

7.7

"categorical endorsement of legitimate power." The disturbance of the established social order, which an uprising entails, is viewed with unmistakable distaste by the historian. One of the few good qualities he attributes to Constantius II is his strict upholding of the hierarchy both in the civil service and in the army: *erga tribuendas celsiores dignitates impendio parcus nihil circa administrationum augmenta praeter pauca novari perpessus numquam erigens cornua militarium* (21.16.1, q.v.).

That civil disorder is a breeding ground for desperadoes, is a recurring theme in descriptions of the revolt of Catilina, whom Cicero calls *Cat.* 1.27 *principem coniurationis, evocatorem servorum et civium perditorum*. The expression *faex vulgaris* is probably borrowed from Sol. 1.82 *Menogenes e faece vulgari*. According to TLL V 1.2167.56–60 *ductare* with abstract Agens is found only in Amm. For *caecus* 'misguided' cf. e.g. 25.5.8 *his ita caeco quodam iudicio fortunae peractis* and Stat. *Th.* 2.489–490 *o caeca nocentum / consilia!*

contraque quidam orti splendide a culminibus summis ad usque mortes et exsilia corruebant Cf. Tac. *Agr.* 6. 1 *splendidis natalibus ortam; epit.* 32.1 *parentibus ortus splendidissimis*. The premature death of the Caesar Gallus inspired Amm. to lament at length the vicissitudes of life, where we find similar well-worn phrases: *alter insperatae praeficitur potestati, alius a summo culmine dignitatis excutitur* (14.11.33).

7.8 *Ubi per haec et similia factio firmiter videbatur esse composita* By *factio* Amm. means the 'clique' of officials appointed so far by Procopius. The term, for which see the note ad 26.6.5 *ut indicio*, is certainly deprecatory. In fact, Amm. had used it in section 4 for the following of Petronius, the hated father-in-law of Valens. Since these officials included both civil servants (Phronimius, Euphrasius, Araxius) and military commanders (Gomoarius, Agilo), one cannot say that "Ammianus explicitly distinguishes between the formation of an administrative establishment, which he calls 'factio' or 'party', and the assembling of military support" (Matthews 195). The opposition is rather between the civil and military authorities on the one hand and the military forces (*militum manus*) on the other. For *firmiter* see the note ad 17.2.1 *Quibus ut in tali re compositis firmiter*.

restabat, ut abundans cogeretur militum manus Other sources confirm that Procopius managed to raise a considerable force: Socr. *HE* 4.3.1 (πολλὴν συγκροτήσας ἐν βραχεῖ χρόνῳ δύναμιν), Eun. *VS* 7.5.2, Them. *Or.* 7.97 d and Zos. 4.6.4 (συνήει τε πλῆθος οὐκ εὐκαταφρόνητον αὐτῷ). Zosimus explains how legionaries and their officers were enticed to join the usurper (χρημάτων αὐτοῖς τε καὶ τοῖς τούτων ἡγουμένοις διαδοθέντων, 4.6.4; cf. 4.5.3-4, cited ad 26.6.13 *qui pellecti*), and states that Roman as well as non-Roman troops (*auxilia*, presumably) supported Procopius ('Ρωμαίων τε γὰρ τάγματα καὶ βαρβάρων αὐτῷ πλῆθος προσετίθετο, 4.7.1). Cf. also Amm. 26.7.14 *cum Divitensibus desertorumque plebe promiscua, quam dierum brevi spatio congregarat, Mygdum acceleravit* (sc. Procopius) and 26.7.15-17, about the way in which Procopius won over to his side the Iovii and Victores. Zosimus moreover relates that Procopius sent some distinguished envoys to a Gothic ruler on the other side of the Danube ("Ἤδη δὲ τῶν ἐπιφανῶν τινὰς ἔστελλε πρὸς τὸν ἔχοντα τὴν τῶν ὑπὲρ τὸν Ἴστρον Σκυθῶν ἐπικράτειαν, 4.7.2), who sent him ten thousand men in their bloom as allies (ὁ δὲ μυρίους ἀκμάζοντας ἔπεμπε συμμάχους αὐτῷ, ibid.), and that he approached still other barbarian tribes with the request to join his enterprise (καὶ ἄλλα δὲ βάρβαρα ἔθνη συνῄει μεθέξοντα τῆς ἐγχειρήσεως, ibid.). Cf. for the support Procopius received from the Goths 26.10.3 *Gothorum tria milia...ad auxilium transmissa Procopio* (note, for that matter, the difference with Zosimus' ten thousand) and Valens' reaction in 27.4.1: *arma concussit in Gothos ratione iusta permotus, quod auxilia misere Procopio civilia bella coeptanti*; see also 27.5.1.

et impetratum est facile id, quod in publicis turbamentis aliquotiens ausa ingentia vel iustis exorsa primordiis impedivit On Amm.'s use of preparatory or cataphoric *is* before AcI or clauses introduced by *ut* and *quod* see the note ad 22.3.4 *cum id*. As is remarked ad 25.7.12 *et Armeniae*, the rare *turbamentum* is probably taken from Sallust or Tacitus. *In publicis turbamentis* is a variation on *in certaminibus intestinis* in the preceding section. *Vel iustis exorsa primordiis* is an implicit condemnation of Procopius' coup d'état: even justifiable revolts had in the past failed to gain sufficient military support, yet Procopius managed to do so by sheer luck.

Amm.'s account of the stages of Procopius' usurpation is not very clear. In the present section the author seems to return to the pronunciamiento, since the events described here are very similar to those in 6.12-14. In chapter 6 we read that Valens ordered troops (*sufficiens equitum adiumentum et peditum*), among them (*inter alios*) the Divitenses and the Tungricani Iuniores, to be sent back to Thrace, because of the Gothic threat to that region. On their way to Thrace the troops were to stay in Constantinople for two days. During these days Procopius staged his revolt, after having bought, with huge sums

7.9

of money (*pellecti spe praemiorum ingentium*), the support of the leaders of the Divitenses and the Tungricani, who swore allegiance to him (*sub consecratione iuris iurandi*). In 7.9 we read that unspecified cavalry and infantry regiments, which were sent to Thrace (*ad expeditionem per Thracias concitatae equitum peditumque turmae*), passed through Constantinople (*transeuntes*) on their way. In Constantinople they swear allegiance (*sub exsecrationibus diris in verba iuravere Procopii*), eager for the promised riches (*promissis uberrimis inhiantes*). The verbal and factual similarities are so pronounced, that one is tempted to see in section 7.9 an abridged version of sections 6.12–14. Such an interpretation, however, raises insurmountable problems.

The first objection is an *argumentum*, admittedly *ex silentio*, but a powerful one. If in 7.9 Ammianus was referring to the extremely important events he had already narrated in such detail, it is inconceivable that he would not have signalled this return by a phrase like *ut dictum est*. Secondly, Ammianus introduces the story in 7.9 with the words *restabat, ut abundans cogeretur manus*. The choice of the phrase *restare ut* rules out that the event to be related in 7.9 is identical with an event related earlier. In the third place, the story in 7.9 is followed by a very important detail which is absent from 6.12–14, viz. the presence of Constantius' wife Faustina and her little daughter, which lends visible support to Procopius' claim to be a member of the imperial family. Again, if the event described in 7.9 was identical with the one in chapter 6.12–14, it is inconceivable that Ammianus would have left out this highly significant element in his description of the pronunciamiento. We may add two corollary arguments. Firstly, the soldiers in 7.9 are received in Constantinople *blande et liberaliter* (a clear reference to the Caesar Julian greeting his troops in Paris in 20.4.13; see below). Received by whom? By Procopius obviously. But in what capacity? As a fugitive, hiding from his persecutors or as the newly proclaimed emperor? The answer cannot be in doubt. Secondly, there is the difference between Procopius' attire, described with such sarcasm in 6.15, and the factual mention of *quaedam...habitus insignia principalis* in 7.10. It is hard to believe that the same garments are meant.

If 7.9 is not an abridged version of 6.12–14, how should we envisage the chain of events? The following reconstruction tries to do justice to the text of the two chapters: on his way to Antioch Valens orders his generals to send a detachment of his army to Thrace; they select the Divitenses, the Tungricani Iuniores and other troops for this assignment; after their arrival in Constantinople, the Divitenses and Tungricani raise Procopius to the purple; Procopius presents himself to the people and the senate of Constantinople; he appoints a number of people in high civil and military posts; what is still lacking is military power; then, by a stroke of luck, a fresh detachment, possibly the *alii* mentioned in 6.12, arrives in Constantinople; they are given a warm and generous welcome by Procopius; the newly arrived troops are assembled in the same place as the Divitenses and Tungricani; together they look like a real army; helped by the presence of Constantius' wife Faustina and her baby daughter, and of course by huge financial promises, Procopius wins their support.

transeuntes ad expeditionem per Thracias concitatae equitum peditumque turmae The verb *concitare*, on which *ad expeditionem* depends, has the connotation of urgency and speed (cf. *celerare dispositos* in 26.6.12), as is evident from 19.1.8, where the Chionitae go to great lengths to save the body of their prince: *gentes ad arma...concitarunt, quarum concursu ritu grandinis hunc inde convolantibus telis atrox committitur pugna*. Cf. also Liv. 10.28.6–7 *et quia lentior videbatur pedestris pugna, equitatum in pugnam concitat*. On *turma* see the note ad 23.3.4 *indicatur equestres*.

blandeque acceptae et liberaliter Again the reader is reminded of the events leading up to Julian's pronunciamiento in Paris. When the troops which had been ordered to join Constantius in the East passed through Paris, they were given a most friendly welcome by Julian. The similarity between the two occasions is emphasized by a verbal allusion: *blandeque acceptae et liberaliter* ≈ *qui liberaliter ita suscepti* (20.4.13).

cum essent omnes in unum quaesitae iamque exercitus species apparebat The combined efforts of Kellerbauer and Günther have resulted in this entirely convincing emendation of V's *cessent omnesque in unum sitae*. For the phrase *in unum quaerere* see the note ad 26.2.2. The alternation of subjunctive and indicative in *cum*-clauses is discussed in the note ad 22.1.2 *eratque ideo*. A similar case in a *quod*-clause is found in 21.7.3 *properaret* (q.v.). See Blomgren 56–58 for some highly dubious instances of the same alternation in *ut*-clauses. The phrase *species exercitus* is also found in Liv. 22.54.6 *iam aliqua species consularis exercitus erat* and Tac. *Hist.* 3.82.1 *vexilla...speciem hostilis exercitus fecerant*.

promissis uberrimis inhiantes sub exsecrationibus diris in verba iuravere Procopii There is a change of subject, possibly unnoticed by the author himself, from the *turmae* at the beginning of the sentence to the soldiers belonging to these units, as becomes clear with the participle *polliciti*. The scene is strongly reminiscent of 21.5.10 (q.v.), where the soldiers swear allegiance to Julian: *iussique universi in eius nomen iurare sollemniter gladiis cervicibus suis admotis sub exsecrationibus diris verbis iuravere conceptis omnes pro eo casus, quoad vitam profuderint, si id necessitas egerit, perlaturos*, but the difference between the two scenes is striking too. In 21.5.9 the army is motivated by its admiration for Julian, *magnum elatumque ducem et…fortunatum domitorem gentium appellans et regum*, whereas here the soldiers are solely driven by greed. For *inhiare* with dative, 'to covet', cf. 31.5.14 (vetustas) *nec ambitiosis mensis nec flagitiosis quaestibus inhiabat* and 31.16.4 *copiarum cumulis inhiantes*. As Michael, 1974, 33 noted, Amm. imitates Cic. *Tusc.* 5.19 *philosophiae promissum uberius*.

hanc polliciti pertinaciam, quod eum suis animis defensabunt The cataphoric use of *hic*, in this case introducing a *quod*-clause, is discussed ad 23.6.58 *his cedentes*. Amm. uses the intensivum *defensare* more often than any other author. It is found twice in Plautus, three times in Sallust and Tacitus, seven times in Amm. (14.5.8; 17.5.14; 19.6.6; 20.11.12, 14; 30.4.22). For the use of the indic. fut. in virtual indirect speech see the note ad 20.8.10 *quod…libens*.

The expression *suis animis defendere* or *defensare* seems to be unique. It cannot be compared to the sarcastic remark of the general Ursulus in 20.11.5 *en quibus animis urbes a milite defenduntur* eqs., where *animus* has the meaning 'courage', 'devotion'. Here the soldiers promise to defend the new emperor with their lives (*anima*), for which cf. 24.3.7 *contempturus animam* and 31.3.3 *animam effudit in proelio*. In a comparable scene in Petr. 117.5 the friends of Eumolpus swear an oath of allegiance like gladiators: *tamquam legitimi gladiatores domino corpora animasque religiosissime addicimus*. For a discussion of *animus* and *anima* in Amm. see the note ad 25.3.17 *animum tamquam*.

7.10 *inventa est enim occasio ad illiciendos eos pérqüam opportúna* Another stroke of luck for Procopius; cf. the note ad 26.6.11 *fors hanc*. The expression may be compared to 28.5.15 *Per hanc occasionem impendio tempestivam*. There is a note on *perquam* ad 20.6.9. The verb *illicere* is rare in Amm., and occurs mostly in a context of deceit (16.10.18 *venenum bibere per fraudem illexit*) or bribery (26.6.18 *paucorum susurro pretio illectorum*), which provides an argument to retain the original reading of V. Cf. also *aliaque ad illecebras aptantes* in the next section.

quod Constanti filiam parvulam, cuius recordatio colebatur, sinu ipse circumferens necessitudinem praetendebat et Iuliani In V the last words of the sentence are *et iul.* Blomgren 144 n. 1, notes that there are many parallels for the loss of similar word-endings in V, quoting as examples 28.1.57 *vorifor* (*Doryphorianum*, G) and 28.2.10 *valentini* (*Valentiniani*, G), and that Gelenius' *et Iuliani* may well represent the reading of the Hersfeldensis. With this reading the genitive *Constanti*, emphatically placed at the head of the sentence, as Blomgren observes, must be taken apo koinou with *filiam* and *necessitudinem*. Admittedly, this is a strained construction, because *Constanti* and *necessitudinem* are far apart. The reading proposed by Novák *eius praetendebat et Iuliani* is certainly more elegant, and superior both to Heraeus' *eiusdem* and Mommsen's *et eius* in that he takes V's *et iul.* into account. Since Amm. speaks without reservation about Procopius as a kinsman of Julian's in 23.3.2 (Iulianus) *dicitur...occulte paludamentum purpureum propinquo suo tradidisse Procopio* and 26.6.1 *ea consideratione, qua propinquitate Iulianum...contingebat*, the choice of the verb *praetendere* has probably been dictated by the mention of Constantius. For *necessitudo* 'family' see the note ad 20.8.21. For Procopius' alleged connection with the Constantinian dynasty see the notes ad 26.1.6 *iamque summatibus*, 26.6.18 *pauca tamen* and 26.7.16 *quin potius* and *non ut rapiat*.

That soldiers felt a strong dynastic loyalty is attested more than once. Some emperors (e.g. Septimius Severus, Elagabalus, Constantine) even invented blood relationships to predecessors who had been popular with the army in order to appeal to their soldiers. Both Constantine and Maxentius had the support of the army, because their fathers had been emperors; Demandt, 1989, 216–218. Examples are given by Lendon, 1997, 254. See also Lenski, 2002, 97–104 and Errington, 2006, Ch. 2 "Emperors and Dynasties". On Procopius' alleged connection with the Constantinian dynasty see the notes ad 26.6.1 *iamque summatibus* and 26.6.18 *pauca tamen*. The little girl (*PLRE* I, Constantia 2) was born posthumously and later became wife of Gratian (21.15.6, 29.6.7).

The expression *recordationem colere* is somewhat unfortunate, since *recordatio* means properly "(the faculty of) recollection" (OLD) rather than 'memory'. Elsewhere, in 27.7.5, Amm. has the usual expression: *quorum memoriam apud Mediolanum colentes nunc usque Christiani locum, ubi sepulti sunt, Ad Innocentes appellant*. Cf. Cic. *Red. Pop.* 24 *Quapropter memoriam vestri benefici colam benivolentia sempiterna*; Fron. *Aq.* 4.2 *fontium memoria cum sanctitate adhuc exstat et colitur*; Suet. *Nero* 57.2 *oravit, ut Neronis memoria coleretur*.

There may be some slight malice in the detail that Procopius himself (*ipse*) is said to have carried the child around in his arms to show it to the soldiers. (*In*) *sinu ferre* is normally said of the mother, e.g. Ov. *Met.* 9.338–339 (Dryope) *inque sinu puerum, qui nondum inpleverat annum, / dulce ferebat onus tepidique ope lactis alebat.* Amm. again refers to the fact that Procopius uses the wife and daughter of Constantius for his own ends in 26.9.3: *Constanti filiam parvulam cum matre Faustina et in agminibus et, cum prope in acie starent, lectica circumferens secum, ut pro imperiali germine, cui se quoque iunctum addebat, pugnarent audentius.*

adeptusque est aliud tempori congruum, quod Faustina matre puellae casu praesente quaedam acceperat habitus insignia principalis Amm. likes periphrastic expressions with *congruus*, such as 16.4.4 *victui congrua*, 'provisions', 20.6.1 *milite usuique congruis* ('necessities') *omnibus...munitam*, q.v. Here *tempori congruum* is the equivalent of *tempestivum*. Faustina (*PLRE* I, Faustina), Constantius' third and last wife, is only known from references in Amm. (apart from the present text, 21.6.4, 21.15.6, 26.9.3).

As has been noted in the introductory note to 7.9, the imperial adornment mentioned here can hardly have been identical to the ridiculous attire in which Procopius had presented himself to the troops in the Anastasian Baths. It is equally difficult to believe that it was just a coincidence that Faustina was present when Procopius received some of the imperial *insignia*, but Amm. refrains from saying explicitly that Constantius' widow supported Procopius. Instead, he stresses again the element of chance rather than planning with the word *casu*.

7.11 *adiungit his aliud veloci diligentia maturandi* This is the restored version of V's garbled text *vel occidi licentiam aturandi*. It is just conceivable that *veloci diligentia maturandi* is an instance of Amm.'s *abundantia sermonis*, as Blomgren 39 n. 1 maintains, meaning 'with swift and careful promptness of action'. Still, the purport of the sentence is not so much that Procopius issues his orders quickly and diligently, but rather, that this particular order had to be carried out speedily and with care. As the sequel will show, *diligentia* is hardly the right word for this ill-prepared attempt to secure Illyricum. Therefore *maturandum* ('which had to be carried out speedily') seems distinctly better than *maturandi*. For this meaning of *maturare* cf. the note ad 15.5.2 *Arbitione id maturari modis, quibus poterat, adigente*; 18.2.7 *Quae dum diligenti maturantur effectu*; 23.1.2 *negotiumque maturandum Alypio dederat*.

et electi quidam stoliditate praecipites ad capessendum Illyricum missi sunt The rare noun *stoliditas* is found again in what is probably Amm.'s most damning verdict on Valens: 29.2.14 *ibi tunc rectoris imperii caries tota stoliditatis apertius est profanata* ("This act of stupidity clearly revealed the utter rottenness of the emperor's rule", tr. Hamilton). As is observed in TLL X 2 414.8, *praeceps* suggests that these stupid fellows were driven to their death. There is no real parallel for *stoliditate praeceps*, but Tac. *Hist.* 4.15.2 *erat in Canninefatibus stolidae audaciae Brinno* comes close. For *capessere* = *occupare* cf. Verg. *A.* 4.346 *Italiam Lyciae iussere capessere sortes*.

Valentinian was put in charge of Illyricum when the imperial brothers divided the empire in 364 (cf. the note ad 26.5.2 *in orientem*). For *Illyricum* see ad 26.5.11 *Valentinianus*.

nullo praeter petulantiam adiumento confisi Amm. uses *petulantia* in the sense of 'recklessness', 'disregard for death' here and in 17.13.28 *calcatis obstinatis ad mortem animis conatos resistere Sarmatas...stravimus parique petulantia ruentes in agmina nobilium legionum Quados...attrivimus*. In 30.9.2 it refers to the wantonness at court: *tamquam retinaculis petulantiam frenarat aulae regalis*.

aureos scilicet nummos effigiatos in vultum novi principis aliaque ad illecebras aptantes Procopius' gold coins were issued at Constantinople (cf. Them. *Or.* 7.91 c–d θησαυροφυλάκια μὲν ἀνεπετάννυντο, 'the treasure-houses were opened'), Cyzicus (cf. 26.8.7 for the treasuries there) and Nicomedia. Cf. Pearce, 1951, 209, 239 and 250, respectively. There is a note on the *aureus solidus* or *solidus aureus* ad 20.4.18 *quinos*. The mints of the cities just mentioned also issued silver and bronze coins (Pearce, 1951, 213–215, 236, 239–241, 252), as did the mint of Heraclea (Pearce, 1951, 192–193). One of the most striking features of Procopius' coins, regardless of the material they were made of, is the fact that the usurper is depicted with a beard, clearly a reference to his relative Julian (the best introduction to Procopius' coinage is given by Wiebe, 1995, 73–81; cf. Lenski, 2002, 83, 96, 99–100). However, it is to other members of the Constantinian dynasty as well that his coins refer, for the legend most frequently found on the reverse, REPARATI-O FEL(icium) TEMP(orum), evokes Constantius' FEL. TEMP. REPARATIO (for which see Kent, 1967).

The only other instance of *effigiatus in* 'formed to resemble' is 14.6.9 *tunicaeque...effigiatae in species animalium multiformes*. As is observed ad 18.7.6 the verb *aptare* is found most frequently in post-classical Latin authors. Its shades of meaning are discussed in the notes ad 20.4.18 and 20.7.10. In this context *aliaque ad illecebras aptantes* seems to be shorthand for *aliaque ad illecebras aptas secum portantes*.

quos correptos Equitius...exstinxit genere diverso poenarum This laconic phrase marks the first real setback for Procopius, who, according to Amm., had so far gone from strength to strength by chance and cunning. In 26.5.11 (q.v.) Amm. related that Valentinian had appointed Equitius *magister (militum per Illyricum)*. See for the various sorts of punishment in Late Antiquity Latte, 1940 and Grodzynski, 1984; for the death penalty in Amm. Arce, 1974.

7.12 *per quos provinciae temptantur arctoae* For *temptare* in the meaning "to make an attempt on" (OLD) cf. 15.12.5 *Hae regiones...sub imperium venere Romanum primo temptatae per Fulvium*; 31.10.2 *Lentienses, Alamannicus populus...collimitia nostra temptabat* and Tac. *Hist.* 2.12.1 *Alpium, quibus temptandis adgrediendaeque provinciae Narbonensi...duces dederat*. On the poeticism *arctous* see the notes ad 19.11.3 and 21.13.1.

unum per ripensem Daciam As is explained in the note ad 21.5.6 *Daciarum* (q.v.), both *Dacia ripensis* and *Dacia mediterranea* were situated on the right bank of the Danube, their capitals being Ratiaria and Serdica, respectively – the notes of Rolfe and Seyfarth, who think that these provinces were separated by the Danube, are wrong.

alterum per Succos notissimum In his short digression on the Succi-pass in Book 21 Amm. i.a. sketches its location: *hinc vicinae mediterraneis Dacis et Serdicae, inde Thracias despectantes et Philippopolim* (21.10.3) and observes that it is an almost insurmountable barrier: *difficile scanditur etiam nullo vetante* (21.10.4). See the notes ad loc. and ad 21.10.2 *Succos*.

tertium per Macedonas, quem appellant Acontisma In his digression on Thrace Amm. again mentions the border passage between Thrace and Macedonia, 27.4.8 *per artas praecipitesque vias, quae cognominantur Acontisma*. Acontisma was a halt on the via Egnatia and is i.a. mentioned in an inscription of Trajan about the repair of this road (*AE* 1936.51 = 1993.1401). It lay some 13 to 14 kilometers from Neapolis, modern Kavala. For the location of the ancient site see Koukouli-Chrysanthaki, 1972. Cf. also Samartzidou, 1990.

hacque cautela vana persuasione rapiendi Illyrici destitutus usurpator indebitae potestatis magna perdidit instrumenta bellorum The phrase *vana persuasio* is found for the first time in Quint. *Inst.* 2.2.12 *hinc tumor et vana de se persuasio* and *Decl.* 314.17 *Nec tamen illa mihi vana quorundam videtur esse persuasio, qui credunt* eqs. It is used frequently by Christian authors, e.g. Lact. *Inst.* 1.11.39 *vana igitur persuasio est eorum qui nomen Iovis summo deo tribuunt*. The combination with a gerundive in the sense of 'the ill-considered plan to' seems to be unique.

The noun *usurpator* is not found before the fourth century and this may well be its first attestation. In *epist.* 6.30.10 to Valentinian II, published after 392, Ambrose writes *Nisi fallor, usurpator bellum infert, imperator ius suum tuetur.* August. *c. Maximin.* 1.747, dating from 428, gives the following definition: *raptor enim rei alienae usurpator est*, which tallies with the present text and with the proem to Iulius Severianus 1 (RLM, ed. Halm p. 355), who presents his work as an excerpt: *Forsitan me usurpatorem ardui operis adque inriti laboris, Desideri, fateare.* For *usurpator indebitae potestatis* cf. Ambr. *Noe* 21.75 *verecunda enim iustitia est, quia inverecunda iniquitas, quae usurpat indebita.*

In 26.5.11 (q.v.) and 26.7.13 (q.v.) Procopius, seen through the eyes of Valentinian and Valens respectively, is called *perduellis*. What is meant by *instrumenta bellorum* is made clear in 21.6.6 *Parabantur nihilo minus externorum atque civilium instrumenta bellorum*, where Amm. mentions troops, new recruits, clothing, siege engines, gold, silver, provisions and horses.

iamque revertens per Gallograeciam The news about the pronunciamiento of Procopius on Sept. 28 had decided Valens not to continue his journey to Antioch, but to return to Constantinople by way of Galatia (= Gallograecia), to face his opponent, as we have been told in section 2 of this chapter.

7.13

auditis apud Constantinopolim gestis diffidenter incedebat et trepide This must refer to the developments in Constantinople as described in sections 3–10, which had greatly strengthened Procopius' position. For *diffidenter et trepide* cf. 15.5.4 *barbarosque propellente iam sibi diffidentes et trepidantes.*

repentino pavore vias providendi turbante eo usque despónderat ánimum During his westward march (*incedebat*) Valens fell prey to sudden despair. The pluperfect *desponderat* is probably chosen instead of the perfect *despondit* to produce a regular cursus (tardus); see the note ad 24.4.29 *Exin profecto*. Amm. uses *via* as a metaphor for a train of thought several times, e.g. 21.5.6 *sequimini viam consilii mei salutarem*; 29.5.45 *per multas prudentesque sententiarum vias*; 31.16.1 *in varias consiliorum vias diducebantur*. In this situation Valens fails as a leader, whose task it is to show the way to his men; cf. Ambr. *epist. extra coll.* 14.40 *Providus ductor multas ostendit vias, ut qua vult unusquisque quam sibi adcommodam arbitratur incedat*. For *despondere* see the note ad 25.7.5 *animos ipsi*.

augustos amictus This expression is found only here and in 27.6.12 *"En", inquit, "habes, mi Gratiane, amictus, ut speravimus omnes, augustos"*.

fecissetque profecto, ni vetantibus proximis retractus a deformi proposito firmatusque meliorum sententiis agmina duo praeire iussisset Strictly speaking the protasis should have been *retractus firmatusque esset*. Riedl, 2002, 326 mentions this passage in a section on "Hinweise auf alternative Geschehensverläufe". The *proximi* are the members of the consistorium; see the notes ad 20.4.22 *asciti in* and 22.7.8 *suadentibus proximis*. That Valens was dispirited is confirmed by Zos. 4.7.3 ὁ δὲ βασιλεὺς Οὐάλης τὴν ἐπανάστασιν ἐν τῇ κατὰ Φρυγίαν Γαλατίᾳ πυθόμενος κατεπλάγη μὲν ἅμα τῇ ἀκοῇ καὶ ἐπίμπλατο ταραχῆς ('when the emperor Valens in Galatia heard about the insurrection, he was terrified by the news and panick-stricken.'). Cf. Socr. *HE* 4.3.2 Τοῦτο ἀπαγγελθὲν (i.e. the news of Procopius' usurpation and the collection of a large body of troops by the usurper) εἰς ἀγωνίαν μεγίστην τὸν βασιλέα κατέστησεν. It should be noted, however, that chronologically Zosimus' account is rather confused (cf. the note ad 26.7.2 *Valentem* and see in general Paschoud's notes 114ff.). According to both Zosimus and Eun. *fr.* 34.4 Arbitio played a leading role in encouraging the emperor: τὸν πρεσβύτην Ἀρβιτίονα...τὴν τοῦ βασιλέως ἄτακτον καὶ κυματώδη φορὰν εἰς ὁμαλὸν καὶ λεῖον καταστορέσαι τοῦ λογισμοῦ πάθος ("the old Arbitio...soothed the emperor's state of mind from erratic indecision to calm and orderly rationality", tr. Blockley). However, once again there is a chronological discrepancy between Amm. and Zosimus (cf. Paschoud n. 120 and Lenski, 2002, 77 n. 54): in the *Res Gestae* Arbitio only joins Valens later (26.9.4, cf. 26.8.13–14), and it is therefore doubtful whether it should be assumed that he already belonged to the *proximi* of the present text.

Amm. expresses his disapproval of Valens' attitude by speaking of his *deforme* propositum. See for this noun the note ad 20.5.4 *numquam a proposito*. It seems therefore better to interpret *meliorum* as 'of men better than himself', rather than "des meilleurs de ses conseillers" (Marié). As was to be expected, there is not a word of Valens' loss of heart in Themistius' seventh oration. On the contrary, in *Or.* 7.86 b Themistius abundantly praises the emperor's enduring steadfastness and courage.

quibus nomina sunt Iovii atque Victores, castra perduellium irrupturos See for these units and the question if they are rightly called *legiones* by Amm. (cf. § 15) the note ad 25.6.3 *legiones Ioviorum*. For the archaism *perduellis* see the note ad 26.5.11 *ne persultatis*.

a Nicaea regressus, quo nuper advenerat Marié n. 100 is probably right in supposing that *advenerat* implies a formal ceremony of *adventus*. See for this ceremony the note ad 21.10.1 *cum lumine*. To the literature cited there one may add Dufraigne, 1992 and Lehnen, 1997. There is information on Nicaea ad 22.9.5 *per Nicaeam*. Cf. further Strobel-Berger, 2001.

7.14

cum Divitensibus desertorumque plebe promiscua It seems likely that *Divitensibus* refers to Procopius' legionary soldiers, including the Tungricani Iuniores; see the note ad 26.6.12 *Divitenses*. As is stated in the note ad 20.6.6 *ad quam,* in Amm. the word *plebs* often refers to non-Roman peoples, so the *desertorum plebs promiscua* may refer to auxiliary troops, possibly identical with the *equitum peditumque turmae* of 26.7.9. For Procopius' army in general see the note ad 26.7.8 *restabat*, where Zosimus 4.7.1 is quoted, who mentions non-Roman troops in his army.

quam dierum brevi spatio congregarat This is an unparalleled expression. Normally *dierum* is qualified by a numeral, rarely by an adjective, e.g. Sen. *Nat.* 1 *pr.* 13 *paucissimorum dierum spatium*. This makes one pause at Gelenius' *dierum fere sex spatio*, which does not look like a conjecture. The speed, with which Procopius had assembled an army, is also commented on by Socr. *HE* 4.3.1, quoted ad 26.7.8 *restabat*.

Mygdum acceleravit, qui locus Sangario alluitur flumine Cf. 18.5.3 *qui locus Tigridis fluentis alluitur* and Plin. *Nat.* 6.11 *flumenque Sidenum, quo alluitur oppidum Polemonium*. Mygdum or Midum, *Mideo* on *Tab. Peut.* VIII 3, lay east of Nicaea on the road to Ancyra, „at or near Taşköprü" (French, 1981, 31); cf. further Ruge, 1932; Talbert, 2000, 52 F 4. The river Sangarius (Sakarya), for which see Strobel, 2001, is one of the rivers in Bithynia mentioned in 22.8.14 (q.v.).

7.15 *ubi cum legiones iam pugnaturae congrederentur* It seems best to take *iam* with the future participle and to interpret it as the equivalent of *iam iam*, just as we find it in e.g. Verg. *A.* 6.602–603 *quo super atra silex iam iam lapsura cadentique/imminet adsimilis*. The phrase may be compared to 21.15.3 (Constantius) *diuque cum anima colluctatus iam discessura abiit e vita*; 23.5.11 *quod et Maximiano antehac Caesari cum Narseo Persarum rege iam congressuro itidem leo et aper ingens trucidati simul oblati sunt*; 30.5.18 *quam aestimari dabatur Fortunam eius esse cum taetro habitu iam discessuram*. Ovid has a few parallels, e.g. *Ars* 2.69 *Iamque volaturus parvo dedit oscula nato* and *Rem.* 665 *Iamque vadaturus 'lectica prodeat' inquit*.

See for *legio* the last part of the note ad 25.1.7 *eodem die*.

inter reciprocantes missilia quasi procursatione hostem lacessens As Varro has it in *L.* 7.80 *reciproca est cum, unde quid profectum, redit eo*. Most often it refers to tidal movement or respiration, but Quadrigarius uses it in his description of the Gallic Goliath (*hist.* 12): *dux interea Gallorum vasta et ardua proceritate armisque auro praefulgentibus grandia ingrediens et manu telum reciprocans incedebat* in the Homeric sense of 'swaying to and fro'. Amm. probably means, that both parties actually exchanged a volley of arrows rather than javelins, as Elton, 1996,104 observes: "Since the interrruption was caused by Procopius rushing between the opposing battle lines the fire was probably from bows; javelins were generally thrown immediately before contact and Procopius could not have stopped fighting at this stage". For a similar situation cf. 29.5.25 *Mazicas in unum collectos invasit iam tela reciprocantes volitantia grandinis ritu*.

For *procursatio* see the note ad 24.4.15. The TLL X 2.1590.74-75 gives this definition of *procursatores*: "(milites) qui sive ante iustam pugnam hostes infestant sive explorandi munere funguntur." The former applies to the present passage.

solus prorupit in medium This display of boldness comes as a surprise after the profile of Procopius sketched by Amm. in the preceding chapters, in particular 26.6.18.

secundioris ductu fortunae The phrase *secundior fortuna* is as rare as *fortuna secunda* is common. In fact Amm. is the only author to use it, here and in 28.6.28 *hoc fortunae secundioris indicio*. Cf. also 16.12.18 "*perge, felicissime omnium Caesar, quo te fortuna prosperior ducit*" and 17.12.4 *ductu laetioris fortunae*.

velut agnitum quendam Vitalianum, quem si norat ambigitur, Latine salute data blande produxit The authors of *PLRE* I, Vitalianus 3 do not rule out the possibility that this Vitalianus is the same man as the *protector domesticus* mentioned in 25.10.9, but Marié n. 102 rightly observes that the addition of *quendam* makes this identification highly improbable. *Velut agnitum* is explained by *quem si norat ambigitur*. For the indicative in indirect questions see the note ad 20.11.5 *quales miseranda*. Procopius acts as if he recognizes an old comrade-in-arms. It is quite plausible, though, that among the Iovii and the Victores there were some who had served under Procopius during the Persian expedition. Interestingly, Amm. emphasizes the fact that Procopius greeted Vitalianus in Latin. This implies that Procopius normally spoke Greek, which is no surprise, since he was born in Cilicia (26.6.1). Of course, Latin was the official language of the Roman army. His ulterior motive may have been twofold: either he knew it was Vitalianus' first language, or he chose Latin because he wanted to remind Vitalianus of the Roman concept of *cana fides* and the Latin oath of allegiance he had sworn. For *producere* see the note ad 26.4.3 *quintum Kalendas*.

eumque porrecta dextera saviatus omnibus hinc inde attonitis According to Valesius, Procopius does not shake hands with Vitalianus or kiss his cheek, which is the interpretation of all translators, but blows handkisses. He adduces Tac. *Hist.* 1.36.3 as a parallel: *nec deerat Otho protendens manus adorare volgum, iacere oscula, et omnia serviliter pro dominatione*. There, however, *protendere manus* describes the *adoratio vulgi*; Otho stretches out his arms to the people in a gesture of respect, after which he blows them kisses. *Dexteram porrigere*, however, is a symbol of *fides*, as is evident from Cic. *Deiot.* 8 *per dexteram istam te oro quam regi Deiotaro hospes hospiti porrexisti, istam inquam dexteram non tam in bellis neque in proeliis quam in promissis et fide firmiorem*. One might add that blowing kisses is a gracious gesture to a crowd, but slightly ridiculous if directed at an old comrade-in-arms. In kissing Vitalianus Procopius may be imitating Julian, who, unlike his predecessor, used to kiss his friends; see for this the note ad 22.7.3 *exosculatum*. There is a note on *attonitus* ad 23.5.3 *populo venustate* and on *hinc inde* ad 20.6.5.

"en", inquit, "cana Romanorum exercituum fides et religionibus firmis iuramenta constricta! ..." In this dramatic speech Procopius, the *usurpator indebitae potestatis*, as he was called in §12, adopts a high moral tone, invoking Jupiter's prophecy of the *pax Augusta* and the

7.16

end of civil war in the first book of the Aeneid, lines 291–293 *aspera tum positis mitescent saecula bellis/cana Fides et Vesta, Remo cum fratre Quirinus/iura dabunt*. He turns the tables on his opponent Valens by insisting that the soldiers have sworn an oath of allegiance to Julian and his family (see for this aspect of the 'Kaisereid' Herrmann, 1968, 17, 43–45), so that they are bound to follow him, Julian's kinsman, not a Pannonian upstart like Valens. For the difference between a 'Kaisereid' or 'Treueid' and the 'Diensteid' or 'Fahneneid' see the note ad 21.5.7 *iuramento*.

The interjection *en*, on which see the notes ad 16.12.31 and 20.11.5, conveys the speaker's indignation, and was probably accompanied by a gesture to the troops. On the importance of oaths see the note ad 25.9.4 *iuris iurandi religionem*. The *iuramenta religionibus constricta* refer to the allegiance promised by the soldiers and confirmed by an oath. The present expression may be compared to 27.5.9 *asserebat Athanaricus sub timenda exsecratione iurandi se esse obstrictum* and 21.5.10 *quae secuti rectores omnesque principis proximi fidem simili religione firmarunt*. Normally *fides* is the object of *firmare*, whereas *constringere* has the person who takes the oath as its object. In the sentence under discussion the personification of *cana fides* explains *constricta*, and the element of *firmare* is represented by the adjective *firmis*.

placet, fortissimi viri, pro ignotis tot suorum consurrexisse mucrones Marié rightly interprets the whole sentence up to *vulneribus* as a rhetorical question, containing a proposition which the audience must reject, and followed by a preferable alternative introduced by *quin potius*. In his speech to present Gratian to the troops Valentinian chose the same form of address: *accipite igitur, quaeso, placidis mentibus, viri fortissimi, desiderium nostrum* (27.6.7). For the appellativa used by Julian see the note ad 23.5.16 *fortissimi milites*. The adjective *ignotus*, on which see the note ad 26.6.6 *ritu itaque*, is used contemptuously, as in 29.2.22 *Festus quidam Tridentinus ultimi sanguinis et ignoti*. The Latin in this sentence is highly suspicious, since *tot suorum mucrones* can only be interpreted as "the swords of so many of their supporters", as TLL IV 622.46 explains it, *suorum* referring to *pro ignotis*, i.e. Valentinian and Valens. If the text is correct, the use of the reflexive possessive pronoun *suorum* might be compared to that of *suus* treated in the note ad 20.5.4 *cum iactura*. One wonders whether Amm. had Liv. 10.13.4 *suis sociorumque viribus consurgere hostes ad bellum* in mind and wrote *tot sociorum surrexisse mucrones*, thereby emphasizing that both parties were in fact comrades-in-arms. The daring substitution of *mucrones* for 'men with their swords' may have been inspired by epic expressions like Verg. *A.* 9.749 *sublatum alte consurgit in ensem*; 12.729 *alte sublatum consurgit Turnus in ensem*. *Consurgere* in the sense of 'to prepare for battle' is found in 14.2.17 *eum in certamen alacriter consurgentem* and 16.12.46 *ad audendum exsertius consurgebant*.

utque Pannonius degener labefactans cuncta et proterens imperio, quod ne votis quidem concipere ausus est umquam, potiatur, ingemiscere nos vestris nostrisque vulneribus According to Austin, 1972, 189 insulting phrases like *Pannonius degener* "point very markedly towards use by the historian of source material that is biased in favour of Procopius." However, in view of the prejudice against Pannonians elsewhere in the *Res Gestae* and in the work of other ancient authors (cf. Balsdon, 1979, 66 and Lenski, 2002, 86–88), this reasoning is not cogent.

The metaphor *labefactare* (*rem publicam*) is common in Cicero, e.g. *Rab. Perd.* 3 *est boni consulis, cum cuncta auxilia rei publicae labefactari convellique videat, ferre opem patriae.* For *proterere* 'to trample' cf. 15.4.12 *cavendi immemores proterebant barbaram plebem*. Valens, according to Procopius, had not even dared to dream about becoming emperor, whereas he himself, a relative of Julian, was entitled to it by birth. Cf. Plin. *Pan.* 4.4, who confesses that he had not even dreamt of an emperor like Trajan: *numquam voto saltem concipere succurrit similem huic, quem videmus*.

In view of the fact that Valens is the legitimate emperor, *potiri* should have the meaning 'to be in the possession of', for which see the note ad 23.6.33 *cuius tranquillis*. Alternatively, and more in keeping with the purport of this speech, we may assume that Procopius turns the tables on his opponent and pictures Valens as the real usurper.

quin potius sequimini culminis summi prosapiam This is a high-flown description of the imperial family, comparable to Julian's reference to the Decii in 23.5.19 *memet vovisse sufficiet ut Curtii Muciique veteres et clara prosapia Deciorum*. See the notes ad 20.5.3 *quoniam Caesarem* and 21.6.4 *in culmine*. The phrase has an ominous ring for the reader who remembers section 7 of this chapter: *contraque quidam orti splendide a culminibus summis ad usque mortes et exsilia corruebant*.

non ut rapiat aliena, sed in integrum maiestatis avitae restituatur These words are found only in Gelenius' edition. "Ex conjectura, ut opinor, adjecta sunt" was Valesius' verdict, and Seyfarth, in his apparatus, marks them as an addition by Gelenius. Both scholars disregarded the possibility that Gelenius simply followed the Hersfeldensis. In fact it is unlikely that Gelenius would have added these words *suo Marte*, since the phrase *in integrum restituere* is nowhere else connected with an attribute in the genitive. He would in all probability have chosen a smoother wording like (ut) *maiestas avita in integrum restituatur*. The *ut*-clause depends on the following *commoventem*. Procopius' statement is a direct contradiction of the qualification *usurpator indebitae potestatis* given by Amm. himself (§ 12).

7.17 *Hac sermonis placiditate molliti omnes* The transformation of Procopius from a figure of ridicule into an authoritative leader is very striking. He has spoken like a real emperor. In speeches of Constantius and Julian to the troops their composure is commented upon repeatedly: 15.8.4 *haec sermone placido peroravit*; 16.12.8 *alloquitur genuina placiditate sermonis*; 25.3.21 *Post haec placide dicta*. See also the note 23.5.15 *talia ore*. For *mollire* cf. 20.8.9 *ante conspectum omnium steti molliri posse tumultum auctoritate ratus vel sermonibus blandis*, q.v.

signorum apicibus aquilisque summissis Lowering the banners is a sign of surrender; cf. Luc. 6.242-243 *pacem gladio si quaerit ab isto / Magnus, adorato summittat Caesare signa*; Vell. 2.85.5 *aegre summissis armis cessere victoriam*. A striking parallel from Zonaras 12.24 is mentioned by Valesius. When the armies of Gallienus and the usurpers Macrianus Senior and Macrianus Iunior were on the verge of joining battle, one of the standard-bearers of the Macriani stumbled and accidentally lowered his banner: ἰδόντες οὖν οἱ λοιποὶ ὅσοι τὰς σημαίας ἔφερον τὴν κλιθεῖσαν σημαίαν, καὶ ἀγνοήσαντες ὅπως ἐκείνη ἐκέκλιτο, ὑπέλαβον ἑκόντα τὸν ταύτην κατέχοντα ἐπικλῖναι αὐτὴν τῷ βασιλεῖ μεταθέμενον. καὶ αὐτίκα κἀκεῖνοι πάσας κεκλίκασι καὶ προσούδισαν καὶ τὸν Γαλιῆνον εὐφήμησαν ('when the other standard-bearers saw the lowered sign and did not know why it was lowered, they thought that the standard-bearer had lowered it on purpose, because he had chosen the side of the emperor. And suddenly they too lowered all the signs and dashed them to the ground and hailed Gallienus'). Similar stories are found in *Pan.* 2.36.3 and Oros. *hist.* 7.36.9-10.

pro terrifico fremitu, quem barbari dicunt barritum, nuncupatum imperatorem Before discussing the text of this much disputed sentence, we must try to determine the course of events. It is clear that the two armies are not joining battle, but that the troops sent by Valens to crush the revolt, are won over to Procopius' side and proclaim him emperor. That means the *barritus*, on which see the note ad 21.13.15, cannot have been raised, since it marks the start of a real armed encounter, as is stated expressly in Veg. *mil.* 3.18.9 *Clamor autem, quem barritum vocant, prius non debet attolli, quam acies utraque se iunxerit*. This eliminates the interpretations of those who propose to get rid of *pro* and want to read *perterrifico fremitu* (Heraeus), *protinus terrifico fremitu* (Thörnell) or *rupto terrifico fremitu* (Walter), since in all these versions the *barritus* is supposed to have been intoned. Moreover, with regard to Heraeus' *perterrifico* Hagendahl, 1921, 60 has pointed to the story of Androclus and the lion in Gel. 5.14.9 as Amm.'s probable model, where we read: *Is unus leo corporis impetu et vastitudine terrificoque fremitu et sonoro...animos oculosque omnium in sese converterat*, and concluded that *terrifico* should be left unchanged. It also eliminates the interpretation of Meurig-Davies, 1948 (1949), 190 who takes *pro* to mean "to the accompaniment of". With regard to the reading of V, Petschenig, 1892, 521 writes: "Was hier *pro* bedeuten soll, sucht man vergebens zu enträtseln." The obvious answer that *pro* means 'instead of' meets with the objection that in such cases Amm. always mentions the alternative, as e.g. in 14.10.14 *ut auxiliatores pro adversariis asciscamus*; 22.4.5 *pro victorialibus* (sc. triumphis) *epulares triumphi*; 22.4.6 *cum miles cantilenas meditaretur pro iubilo molliores*. It seems therefore, that we must either suppose a lacuna, in which the alternative would have been expressed, on the lines of 26.2.2 *Augustusque nuncupatus cum laudibus amplis*, or accept an elliptical expression in which *nuncupatum* means 'was hailed with jubilation', for which cf. εὐφήμησαν in the passage quoted from Zonaras above.

stipatumque de more consentientes in unum reduxerunt ad castra These are topical elements in the descriptions of speeches by an emperor to his troops, for which see the notes ad 20.5.1 *signis aquilisque* and 21.13.9 *stipatusque*. For *de more* cf. 14.5.5, 29.1.10 and 31.5.8 *vexillis de more sublatis*. The unanimity of the soldiers is another such topical element, which makes it all the more surprising in the context of a rebellion. See for this the note ad 20.4.14 *quo viso iterata magnitudine sonus Augustum appellavere consensione firmissima*.

testati more militiae Iovem invictum Procopium fore Constantius' speech in 17.13.34 gets a similar reception: (contio) *vocibus festis in laudes imperatoris assurgens deumque ex usu testata non posse Constantium vinci tentoria repetit laeta*. Note the element of praise for the emperor, which in our passage is either left out or implied in *nuncupatum imperatorem*. There is another difference: while Constantius' soldiers called a nameless *deum* to witness, the men of Procopius swore by

Jupiter, as Julian himself had done in 24.6.16: *Iovemque testatus est.* Maybe we should not attach too much importance to this difference, since an acclamation after a speech by Julian (24.1.1) is reported as follows: (exercitus) *principem superari non posse deum usitato clamore testati*. According to Jones, 1963, 24–25: "What little evidence there is suggests...that soldiers conformed more or less passively to the prevailing religion of the state whatever it might be for the time being", quoted in the note ad 21.2.4 *utque omnes*. Add to the literature cited there Tomlin, 1998 and Haensch, 2004. Julian is also acclaimed as an invincible leader after a speech in 21.5.9 (contio) *magnum elatumque ducem et, ut experta est, fortunatum domitorem gentium appellans et regum.*

CHAPTER 8

Introduction

In the first part of this chapter the successes of Procopius' party continue. Chalcedon, Helenopolis and Nicaea are captured, which means that the Procopians are in command of the situation in the Propontis. Valens' efforts to repair the damage turn against him, and he has to beat a hasty and hazardous retreat to his basis at Ancyra. However, in his much weakened position he still has one telling advantage: he can count on the support of some experienced generals, whereas Procopius' military leaders are a mixed bag of utterly unreliable generals, unqualified amateurs and ambitious officers. A good example of the latter group is Aliso, thanks to whose shrewdness and courage Cyzicus, another strategic town on the shore of the Propontis, is captured. This was the more important because large sums of money had been deposited at Cyzicus.

Remarkably, this enormous success heralds the beginning of the end for Procopius. His overconfidence sets Fortune's wheel in motion. Exasperated by yet another refusal of an important general, Arbitio, to join his party, he orders Arbitio's house to be plundered. Realizing the risk he had taken with this action, Procopius ought to have acted with determination and haste, because the general discontent with Valens' reign and the longing for change offered him excellent opportunities in Asia Minor. Instead, he hesitates at the cost of a decisive loss of momentum. The chapter ends with an ominous precedent of such a hesitation.

Huic perduellium prosperitati laetior accessit Amm.'s use of *perduellis* to denote a usurper is dealt with in the note ad 20.8.21 *Iulianum*. See also the note ad 26.5.11 *ne persultatis*. As in 26.7.13, the plural includes the usurper's party. Cf. for *prosperitas* denoting a particular success 24.6.16 *prosperitates similes* and see further the list in TLL X 2.2208.74 sqq.: "potius de singulis eventibus". Here it refers to the success at Mygdus mentioned in 26.7.15–17. Obviously Seyfarth, Marié and Viansino regard the addition of a word like *altera* or *alia* as superfluous. They may be right, but in that case a regular cursus is lacking. However, this is also the case if Mommsen's *altera*

8.1

or Clark's *alia* is added. One wonders whether assuming the loss of *successus* after *accessit* is feasible; cf. 31.10.11 *Hac laeti successus fiducia*.

Rumitalca enim tribunus in societatem Procopianorum ascitus et suscepta cura palatii Amm. is the only source of information on Rumitalca; see also section 3 below. The administrative duty of *cura palatii* was exercised by a tribune; see the note ad 22.3.7 *Saturninus*.

See for Amm.'s use of *asciscere* the notes ad 20.4.22 *asciti* and 26.2.7 *ascito*. In itself *societas*, 'partnership', 'alliance', is a neutral term, but in other contexts it can be used negatively, as in 21.13.13, where Constantius refers disparagingly to Julian's supporters: *ascitis in societatem superbam auxiliaribus paucis* (q.v.). See Leumann 325–326 for the use of the suffix *-anus* in "Bezeichnungen von Anhängern".

digesto mature consilio Cf. the note ad *Digesto itaque consilio* (24.7.1), where *digerere* also means 'to ponder', 'to devise'. Most translators take *mature* to express that Rumitalca took his time in devising his plan, e.g. "after careful preparation" (Hamilton), "après avoir mûrement établi son plan" (Marié). There are no parallels for this meaning of *mature*; TLL VIII 504.68–69 comes nearest by regarding the present instance as a unique case in which *mature* is "fere i.q. perfecte". However, why could it not have the same meaning as in Amm.'s six other cases, viz. 'swiftly'? See for this the note ad 21.3.3 *qui cum*. It suits the context, in which Rumitalca's speedy moves are briefly noted. Selem's "dopo aver rapidamente studiato il piano" and Caltabiano's "con rapide decisioni" are both feasible.

permeatoque cum militibus mari Until Gardthausen's emendation *permeatoque* (in his Teubneriana of 1875) scholars were obviously content with V's *permixtoque*. Presumably they interpreted it in the manner formulated by Wagner: "communicato *cum militibus*". There are, however, no parallels for such a meaning of *permiscere* and, moreover, *mari* without any addition makes a strange impression. Gardthausen's emendation is well supported by 21.13.2 *permeato flumine*, 23.6.11 *quibus angustiis permeatis*, 24.2.22 *permeato amne*, 31.11.6 *permeato Danubio*. In the present text the Propontis is crossed.

Apparently, Procopius had also acquired a naval force when he gained control of the Bosporus, as Lenski, 2002, 79 rightly observes. This naval force was used to besiege Cyzicus; see sections 8–10 below.

Drepanum ante, nunc Helenopolim Drepanum was named Helenopolis by Constantine the Great in honour of his mother Helena; see i.a. Eus. *VC* 4.61.1; Socr. *HE* 1.39.1; Soz. *HE* 2.2.5. Procop. *Aed.* 5.1.2–5 calls it Helena's birthplace. See Drijvers, 1992, 9–11 and Mango, 1994. Drepanum/Helenopolis was located on a promontory at the entrance of *Sinus Astacenus* (also named *Sinus Olbianus*) on which Nicomedia was situated; control of the city was therefore of strategic importance. Moreover, control of Drepanum/Helenopolis meant that troops could cross the sea to this city and from there have much faster access to Nicaea and the main route to Ancyra than by travelling all the way over land via Nicomedia.

Nicaeam For Nicaea see the note ad 22.9.5 *per Nicaeam*.

Vadomario misso, ex duce et rege Alamannorum See *PLRE* I, Vadomarius. He was a former king of the Alamans and an enemy of Rome; see the note ad 21.3.1 *Alamannos*. After having been captured by Julian in 361 (21.4.5, q.v.) he made a career in Roman service. He was appointed *dux Phoenices* (21.3.5) and under Valens he was not only sent to recover Nicaea (without success) but he was also ordered to ward off the Persians in 371: *contra has copias Traianus comes et Vadomarius ex rege Alamannorum cum agminibus perrexere pervalidis hoc observare principis iussu appositi, ut arcerent potiusquam lacesserent Persas* (29.1.2). See further Woods, 2000.

See for Ammianus' idiosyncratic use of *ex* for 'former' the note ad 25.10.7 *ex actuario*. Stroheker, 1961, 143 n. 72, later supported by Waas, 1971[2], 130, proposed to put *ex* directly before *rege*. Presumably, he assumed that *duce* was here a general term to denote a leading Roman military function, from which Vadomarius had not retired, as he had done from his Alamannic kingship; cf. 29.1.2 *ex rege Alamannorum*. However, why should *Alamannorum* not be combined with *duce* too? Cf. Caltabiano's "in passato comandante militare e re degli Alamanni".

Nicomediam See the note ad 22.8.5 *Hylam* for Nicomedia. According to Lenski, 2002, 78, n. 59 Valens' march may be marked by five milestones along the route from Dadastana to Nicaea. Lenski bases his information on French, 1988, 222, 227, 245, 250, 262.

oppugnationi Calchedonos magnis viribus insistebat Apparently the city of Chalcedon, opposite Constantinople on the other side of the Bosporus, had also come under the control of Procopius, although

Amm. does not mention this. In 26.6.5 (q.v.) Amm. had remarked that Chalcedon seemed to Procopius a safe refuge (*ei illud firmius est receptaculum*) from which Lenski, 2002, 78 n. 58 concluded that Procopius had probably won supporters in Chalcedon early on. For Chalcedon see the note ad 22.3.2.

See for *insistere* with dat., "to press on with" (OLD s.v. 6) Liv. 37.60.2 *cogitantique Fabio cui rei potissimum insisteret*, Tac. *Ann.* 2.21.2 (Germanicus asked) *insisterent caedibus*, Amm. 24.1.13 *agminibus cogendis insistens* (q.v.).

probra in eum iaciebantur et irrisive compellabatur ut sabaiarius Cf. 17.9.3 *Iulianum compellationibus incessebat et probris*, 23.2.4 *ira, quam ex compellationibus et probris conceperat*, 24.2.11 *probris atque conviciis ut male fidum incessebant et desertorem* (q.v.). See TLL III 2028.78–2029.26 for a list of instances in which *compellare* is "i.q. iniuriose alloqui, conviciari, increpare". The noun *compellatio* can have a comparable meaning. Curiously, Clark and Seyfarth have both been convinced by Novák's emendation of V's *iniuriase*. TLL VII 2. 423–426 mentions Schol. Juv. 4.13 and 13.33 as the only other instances of *irrisive* apart from the conjectures in Amm. 16.12.67 and the present text, where the obvious emendation is Gelenius' *iniuriose*, 'insultingly', to which Marié rightly returns. The adj. *iniuriosus* occurs in 31.14.6, where the emendation merely concerns the case ending.

See for the suffix *-arius* Leumann 297–298. The inhabitants of Chalcedon may have created this term of abuse by analogy with *vinarius*, 'wine-seller'. A *sabaiarius* is a drinker or maker of *sabaia*, a sort of beer made in Pannonia from barley or another grain, as Amm. explains in the next sentence. The word *sabaiarius*, for which Amm.'s source may have been an eyewitness, is clearly a term of abuse and labels Valens as a barbarian. In Graeco-Roman culture there was great contempt for drinking beer; it was the drink of "the other", of the barbarian, who is reported to have drunk it in great quantities, often until intoxication. By using *sabaia* and *sabaiarius* instead of one of the other expressions in Latin for beer and the drinkers of this liquid, the Chalcedonians are not only offensive towards Valens personally, but also to his Pannonian origin. It shows the contempt of the refined Greeks for the uneducated Pannonian emperor and his entourage, as well as the social divide between the two. Moreover, the episode shows the dissatisfaction of the local population with Valens, and perhaps the class prejudice of rich city dwellers towards imperial upstarts from scarcely urbanized and poor regions of the empire, such as Pannonia. According to Matthews

CHAPTER 8.3   217

199–200 it also demonstrates, that Procopius' power base consisted mainly of urban easterners. The episode at Chalcedon as well as the explicit use of the word *sabaiarius* is likely, as Dzino, 2005, 66 argues, to have complemented Ammianus' picture of Valens as a timid, cruel, uneducated, semi-barbarian rustic from Pannonia, who was ugly and crude, both in appearance and character. He is wrong, however, in characterizing Valens as a drunkard purely because he is called a *sabaiarius*. See on Valens as *sabaiarius* also Nelson, 2005, 30. Socr. *HE* 4.8.1 is less specific than Amm. and only reports that the Chalcedonians, who had sided with Procopius, had used insulting language towards Valens.

est autem sabaia ex hordeo vel frumento in liquorem conversis paupertinus in Illyrico potus Amm. assumes that his readers are not familiar with such a cheap and vulgar beverage (*paupertinus...potus*) as beer. Lindenbrog has a long note on the various words for 'beer' in antiquity and i.a. quotes the only other instance of the local Illyrian term, Hier. *in Is.* 7.19 *genus est potionis ex frugibus aquaque confectum, et vulgo in Dalmatiae Pannoniaeque provinciis, gentili barbaroque sermone appellatur sabaium*. He also refers to D.C. 49.36.3 about the Pannonians: ἀλλὰ τάς τε κριθὰς καὶ τοὺς κέγχρους καὶ ἐσθίουσιν ὁμοίως καὶ πίνουσιν, after having mentioned that the Pannonians have the most miserable existence of all mankind because they cultivate no olives and produce hardly any wine, and what they do produce is of wretched quality. Priscus *fr.* 11.2 (Blockley) mentions a barley beverage κάμον amongst the Pannonians.

In the present text *frumentum* presumably means 'wheat', as in Apul. *Met.* 6.10 *accepto frumento et hordeo et milio et papavero* etc. (see GCA 2004, 433), Plin. *Nat.* 18.151 *venti...nocent frumento et hordeo.* See further the list in TLL VI 1.1420.21–67.

In this section Amm.'s description of the events is rather succinct, so that the reader has some difficulty in understanding the details of the situation. Rumitalca c.s., who were besieged by Vadomarius at Nicaea, had apparently been able to break through the lines of the besiegers and to approach Valens and his troops from the rear. As a consequence Valens would have been trapped between Rumitalca's forces and the besieged in Chalcedon, had he not been able to get away to Ancyra with a manoeuvre around *Lacus Sunonensis*.

8.3

discedere iam parabat, cum Valens' lack of control of the situation comes out clearly in Amm.'s description, and this is emphasized by a timely use of a *cum inversum* structure, which highlights Rumitalca's successful tactics.

clausi apud Nicaeam Cf. for *clausi*, 'the besieged', 21.12.7 *erecti in audaciam clausi*.

munitorum magna parte prostrata As is noted ad 21.12.8 *munitores*, Amm. uses this term to denote the besiegers. In spite of the warning in TLL X 2.2228.12 that the somewhat drastic sounding verb *prosternere* in military contexts "saepius vergat in vim laxiorem perdendi, vincendi", Amm.'s instances usually imply a crushing or bloody defeat, e.g. 17.6.2 *prostravit acerrime multos*, 23.6.22 *Dareum Alexander...prostravit*, 24.2.8 *laniatu avium prostraverunt* (q.v.).

ductore fidentissimo Rumitalca See for the usual difference between *fidens* (in bonam partem) and *confidens* (in malam partem) the note ad 20.4.18 *capiti*. In the present case *fidentissimo* expresses that Rumitalca's confidence was fully justified.

patrassent conata See the note ad 24.2.1 *Quibus tali* for Amm.'s use of *patrare*, a verb often used by Tacitus.

rumore quodam praeverso...instantem vestigiis hostem per Sunonensem lacum et fluminis Galli sinuosos amfractus propere discedendo frustra sequentem lusisset In 16.11.14 the speed of the attackers beat the rumour (about their actions): *multitudo barbarica rumorem nimia velocitate praeversa*. Valens was fortunate enough to experience the contrary. Perhaps Amm. was inspired by Liv. 29.33.8 about Masinissa: *Verminam prope vestigiis instantem in alia atque alia flectendo itinera eludens*. Cf. for transitive *ludere*, 'to baffle', 27.12.11 *regis multiformes lusere conatus*.

The *Lacus Sunonensis* (modern Sapanca Gölü), also called *lacus Boana*, is located east of Nicomedia; Talbert, 2000, map 52 G3. Pliny in his *Ep.* 10.41 and 61 refers to the lake without mentioning its name. The main route from Chalcedon to Ancyra ran via Nicaea. By mentioning that Valens took a route just north of the lake, Amm. indicates that the emperor was forced to take a route which differed from the usual one. The Gallus river is possibly to be identified with the modern Mudurnu Suyu, which is located to the east of the *lacus Sunonensis* and flows out into the river Sangarius; Str. 12.3.7 (543C); Şahin, 1986, 125–128; cf. Talbert, 2000, map 86 A3. However, the Gallus/Mudurnu Suyu is not a winding river as Amm. says (at least not nowadays). It could therefore very well be that Amm. is mistaken and that he has confused the Gallus with the Sangarius river. The latter had many bends and it was probably by travelling along this river that Valens and his army reached Ancyra.

Unde cum Ancyram Valens citis itineribus revertisset In 26.7.2–3 and 13 Amm. reports that Valens had travelled as far as Caesarea in Cappadocia, but returned to Galatia when he heard of Procopius' revolt. In Galatia Ancyra was probably his main base (Lenski, 2002, 79), so that Amm.'s *revertisset* makes good sense. According to *Itin. Burdig.* 571.11–575.6 the distance from Chalcedon to Ancyra is 315 miles, i.e. some 466 km. There is a note on Ancyra ad 25.10.11 *Et cum.* As to *citis itineribus*, see the note ad 20.8.21 *venit ad* for Amm.'s various phrases expressing speedy marches.

Lupicinum ab oriente cum catervis adventare non contemnendis For Lupicinus (*PLRE* I, Flavius Lupicinus 6), *magister equitum* in Gaul under Constantius II and Julian when he was Caesar, see the notes ad 20.1.2 and 20.9.9. Jovian had appointed him *magister equitum* of the East, an office which he also held under Valens; 26.5.2 with note. He was consul in 367; Bagnall et al., 1987, 268–269. It is possible that Lupicinus returned with forces wich Valens had already sent ahead to Antioch; Lenski, 2002, 78–79.

In the note ad 16.2.6 *catervatim* De Jonge notes that *caterva* is especially used of barbarians or mercenary soldiers; see also OLD s.v. 2. It is doubtful that this holds true for Amm. Against eleven instances in which *caterva* denotes a group of enemy warriors, there are nine cases where soldiers on the Roman side are meant, without any disparaging connotation; cf. e.g. 15.3.1 *militarium catervae ab oriente perductae sunt*. In 20.7.14 *hostium nostrorumque catervis certantibus* soldiers on both sides are concerned and 14.6.17 *proeliorum periti rectores primo catervas densas opponunt et fortes* clearly shows that *caterva* is a vox media. The entire survey shows that in military contexts Amm. uses *caterva* as a non-technical word, which emphasizes the sheer quantity of the warriors; cf. 29.5.41 *pondere catervarum ingentium inclinati*. That is also the meaning of the word in non-military contexts, as in the author's famous exaggeration of the number of travelling bishops: *catervis antistitum iumentis publicis ultro citroque discurrentibus* (21.16.18, q.v.).

spe prosperorum erectior See for comparable phrases in Amm. the notes ad 23.5.8 *certiore iam spe* and 23.5.24 *speque prosperorum*.

Arintheum lectissimum ducem For Arintheus (*PLRE* I, Arinthaeus) see the note ad 26.5.2 *cui iunctus* but esp. the one ad 24.1.2 *Arintheo*. He served under three emperors: Julian, Jovian and Valens. Like his predecessors (see the note ad 25.10.9 *mittitur*) Valens fully trusted the prominent and loyal general Arintheus. Amm. mentions him a dozen times, but only here does he add the highly laudatory expression *lectissimum ducem*, which is a telling phrase in the context: military leadership of this quality was not available in Procopius' party.

8.5 This section culminates in a scene in which one of Procopius' first-rate supporters is thoroughly humiliated and cast aside. It has the appearance of a satirical exaggeration, yet it lays bare the Achilles' heel of Procopius' coup: a lack of competent military commanders. At the same time it is a tiny illustration of the author's self-referential characterization *ut miles quondam* in 31.16.9, the sphragis of the *Res Gestae*.

in qua statione perisse diximus Iovianum Jovian's death is reported in 25.10.12–13. It is not possible to determine for which reason Amm. refers explicitly to this event. Possibly he wanted to remind the reader that, in the final reckoning, the Pannonian era had got under way at Dadastana.

Hyperechium sibi oppositum repente vidit cum copiis antehac cellae castrensis apparitorem, id est ventris ministrum et gutturis, cui ut amico Procopius auxilia ductanda commisit This is the only time Amm. mentions Hyperechius, a native of Ancyra; see Pack, 1983, 200–201, Petit, 1983, 246, *PLRE* I Hyperechius. As one of Libanius' most popular students he received twelve letters from his teacher and is mentioned in twenty-seven others; Seeck, 1906, 182–183; Bradbury, 2004, 249–250. These letters are the main source of information for his life and career. He was anxious to make an administrative career, and Libanius wielded his influence to secure a position for him. Before becoming a *castrensianus* he was probably a *supernumerarius* on the staff of the governor of Galatia between 361–362 (Lib. *Ep.* 308) and enrolled among the *statuti* – i.e. established civil servants (Lib. *Ep.* 792). See further Petit, 1956, 162–165; Jones 571. His career failed to develop successfully, and Pack wonders whether his frustration drove him into the arms of Procopius.

Henricus Valesius was very suspicious of V's text; he regarded *recte* and *id…gutturis* as a gloss which had entered the text, and he therefore prints *cum copiis, antehac Castrensis apparitorem, cui, ut amico* etc. It can be doubted whether he was on the right track: the words *id...gutturis* seem quite apt, as Amm. is creating a satirical caricature of Hyperechius. See the note ad 26.7.1 *Igitur cuppediarum*. For this reason other scholars tried to emend *recte*, and editors have awarded the prize to Heraeus' *cellae*. Although clever, this suggestion suffers from the absence of any parallel for *cella castrensis*. There is perhaps room for another solution, in which part of Valesius' argument is used, viz. by considering only *recte* to be a marginal remark, affirming the correctness of a combination of words which at first sight might be surprising. See Reynolds-Wilson, 1991, 228–229. However, a crux is perhaps more in place. An *apparitor* was an official in the various offices of the civilian and military dignitaries; see the note ad 23.5.6 *apparitoris*. A *castrensis* was the quartermaster of the court or, in other words, the major-domo of the palace; see Jones 567. Hyperechius was therefore a member of the domestic staff of the imperial household. As a subordinate of the *castrensis*, who was responsible for food and drink (see Demandt, 1989, 242), Hyperechius was in fact a 'servant of belly and throat'. Such a person, who lacked any experience as a soldier, was given a military command by Procopius for the mere reason that he was a friend of his! One senses the former military professional's disdain for this form of amateurism. It is not known of how many soldiers the auxiliary troops in question consisted nor from which army units they came. As most auxiliary contingents in Late Antiquity they were probably light-armed troops; Nicasie, 1998, 192 ff.

et dedignatus hominem superare certamine despicabilem auctoritatis et celsi fiducia corporis ipsis hostibus iussit suum vincire rectorem Amm. now polishes off the would-be commander in a persuasively depicted scene, i.a. by two strong terms, which he uses only here, *dedignari* and the late Latin adj. *despicabilis*. It was beneath the dignity of the seasoned general Arintheus to combat a nonentity, and, merely by exploiting his personal authority and his imposing appearance, he ordered the enemy soldiers to arrest their leader. The words *celsi...corporis* are reminiscent of a phrase in Velleius' portrait of the young Tiberius: he i.a. excelled *celsitudine corporis* (Vell. 2.94.2). In his letter of condolence of 378 to Arintheus' widow Basilius referred to his physical force, which rivalled his spiritual qualities (*Ep.* 269.2). In 27.11.4 and 31.15.5 *iubere* also has a complement in the dat. This occurs already in classical Latin, e.g. Cat. 64.140 *non haec miserae sperare iubebas* (but see Fordyce ad loc.), Tac. *Ann.* 13.40.2

equites..., quibus iusserat (see Koestermann ad loc.), but becomes more frequent in late Latin; see Krebs-Schmalz, 1905, 802 and especially Löfstedt ad *Pereg. Aeth.* 5.9 (p. 151-152).

8.6 *Quae dum hoc modo procedunt* Cf. for *procedere*, 'to go on' (about events etc.), *cum haec ita procederent* (20.9.9), *haecque dum ita procedunt* (22.12.8 [q.v.] and 29.5.14).

Venustus quidam largitionum apparitor sub Valente multo ante Nicomediam missus, ut aurum susceptum stipendii nomine militibus per orientem diffusis viritim tribueret Presumably, *multo ante* implies 'before Procopius' coup'. Venustus, about whom nothing else is known apart from the information provided here by Amm., had two tasks: collecting the money and paying it to the individual soldiers in the eastern provinces. These soldiers were numerous, so that Venustus must have had a large amount of money with him. Cf. for *nomine* with gen., "under the heading of, by way of" (OLD s.v. 24), 14.4.4 *dotis nomine*, 16.5.14 *tributi nomine*, 18.2.18 *legationis nomine*. Payment to the soldiers was either in kind or in cash. The soldiers received rations (*annonae*), supplies, fodder and equipment (uniforms and armour); cash payments consisted of donatives, received on the accession of a Caesar or Augustus and at five-year intervals thereafter, and of an annual pay, the *stipendium*; Jones 623-630; Elton, 1996, 120-125; Southern/Dixon, 1996, 76-82. For *stipendium* see also the note ad 20.8.8 *cuius iracundiae*. We are reasonably well informed as to how payments in kind were distributed among the soldiers – see e.g. Jones 626-630 and Isaac, 1992[2], 285-291 – but we know far less about the distribution of cash payments. Payment of *stipendia* and *donativa* was the responsibility of the *sacrae largitiones*, led by the *comes sacrarum largitionum*; see the note ad 21.8.1 *Mamertino*. As *apparitor largitionum* – see the note ad 23.5.6 *apparitoris* for *apparitor* – Venustus was in the service of this official. Apparently, Venustus was sent to Nicomedia, which had a mint, to collect a large sum of gold and convey this to the East for the individual distribution among the troops. However, the outbreak of the revolt of Procopius prevented him from executing his assignment and he sought refuge in Cyzicus bringing with him the money which he had collected in Nicomedia. Jones 624 refers to this passage in Ammianus as evidence of the way in which the cash was distributed. Another example can be found in 28.6.12, where it is reported that Palladius was sent by Valentinian to pay the wages to the soldiers in various parts of Africa: *ideoque tribunus et notarius Palladius mittitur, ut et militi disperso per Africam praeberet stipendium debitum.* We probably should imagine that both Venustus and Palladius were heavily escorted by soldiers to protect the large sums of money they carried. *Oriens* can either refer to the *dioecesis Orientis* or the East in a wider sense, including the dioceses of *Pontica* and *Asiana*; see the note ad 20.1.1 *per Illyricum*. In this case it probably refers to the East in a broader sense.

hac tristitia cognita What does *hac tristitia* mean? The immediately preceding section does not contain any 'despondency', to which *hac* could refer. Probably the phrase indicates the events described in sections 1–3, which had led to Procopius' seizure of Bithynia; cf. for this OLD s.v. 1b: "a gloomy state of affairs", e.g. Petr. 117.7 *Accessisse huic tristitiae proximum naufragium*, where *huic tristitiae* summarizes the (fictional) mishaps which Eumolpus had suffered.

alienum pervidens tempus Cf. for *alienus*, 'inopportune', Caes. *Gal.* 4.34.2 *ad...committendum proelium alienum esse tempus arbitratus*, Cic. *Att.* 10.2.2 *sed et tempus alienum est*. TLL X 1.1870.14 sqq. shows that *pervidere* can be a synonym of *cognoscere* or *intellegere*, which suits the present text, where it is combined with a predicative acc. This is overlooked in the list in TLL X 2.1870.53–58. If Petschenig is right, there is one other instance of *pervidere* in Amm., viz. 16.12.33, where Clark and Galletier prefer *praevideret* for V's impossible *perviveret*, in contrast to Seyfarth and Viansino, who accept Petschenig's *pervideret*.

Cyzicum The former colony of Megara and metropolis of Hellespontus is described by Strabo 12.8.11 (575C–576C), who reports that it could compete with the first cities of Asia Minor with regard to size and beauty. Cyzicus was situated on the southwest coast of the Sea of Marmara and on its seaside it had two harbours. It had some great monuments, among them a temple for Zeus, which was magnificently restored by the emperor Hadrian after an earthquake and which accommodated the emperor's cult; Malalas, *Chron.* 11.279; Price, 1984, 146 ff.; Swain, 1996, 285 (with further literature). It had an important mint as well as a woollen mill; Soz. *HE* 5.15.7; Jones 436, 836. For Cyzicus see further Hasluck, 1910 and Akurgal, 1976. Apart from the mint the city was important for Procopius because it was the capital of Hellespontus, and possibly also for its harbours. Control over places which had a mint was of the utmost importance for propagandistic reasons and for the payment of the troops. Procopius controlled four mints – Constantinople, Herecleia, Cyzicus and Nicomedia – and in all four of them coins of his regime were minted; see the note ad 26.7.11 *aureos*.

8.7 *ubi forte Serenianus repertus domesticorum tunc comes missus ad thesauros tuendos* In Greek *forte Serenianus repertus* would have been expressed by Σερηνιανῷ ἐντυχών.

For Serenianus and his function see the note ad 26.5.3. He was no doubt sent to Cyzicus by Valens to secure its mint and to prevent it, as well as the bullion used for minting coins, from falling into the hands of Procopius.

urbem inexsuperabili moenium ambitu monumentis quoque veteribus cognitam The majority of instances in which *inex(s)uperabilis* qualifies a material object can be found in Livy. The phrase *moenium* or *murorum ambitus* hardly occurs outside the *Res Gestae*; the other instances are 18.6.10, 19.2.3, 24.6.13 (q.v.), 31.12.10, 31.15.3, 31.16.7. Some translators assume that *veteribus monumentis* denotes monuments, presumably buildings and the like; cf. e.g. "famous for its ancient monuments" (Hamilton), but in Amm.'s three earlier instances (22.16.13, 23.5.20 and 24.4.5) the phrase means 'historical sources or documents' (see the relevant notes ad loc.); *Hunorum gens monumentis veteribus leviter nota* (31.2.1) is an even closer parallel. This meaning suits the present context far better, as Seyfarth and Viansino saw; cf. the latter's "ben nota per le sue mura inespugnabili anche in base ad antiche testimonianze". Only in such a rendering does the text clearly make sense. Remains – dated to various periods – of the walls are extant; Hasluck, 1910, 6–10.

fretus tumultuario praesidio In the defence of Cyzicus personnel was the weak spot. See for *tumultuarius*, 'improvised', the notes ad 24.2.18 *His raptim* and 24.5.3 *vallatis*.

ad quam expugnandam Procopius, ut possessa Bithynia sibi etiam Hellespontum iungeret, validam destinaverat manum From Zos. 4.6.4–5 we learn that this force was led by Marcellus: πέμπει μὲν οὖν εἰς τὴν Βιθυνίαν μετὰ δυνάμεως Μάρκελλον ἐπὶ συλλήψει Σερηνιανοῦ καὶ τῶν σὺν αὐτῷ βασιλικῶν ἱππέων, ἐκ καραδοκίας τοῦ διαφθεῖραι. Συμφυγόντων ⟨δὲ⟩ αὐτῶν εἰς τὴν Κύζικον, τὴν μὲν πόλιν εἷλε Μάρκελλος ναυμαχίᾳ καὶ πεζῇ δυνάμει κρατήσας, Σερηνιανὸν δὲ διαφυγόντα καὶ εἰς τὴν Λυδίαν ἀναχωρήσαντα συλλαβὼν διεχρήσατο ("Accordingly, he sent Marcellus with a force to Bithynia against Serenianus and his imperial cavalry in the hope of destroying him. And when they fled to Cyzicus, Marcellus overwhelmed it through his superiority on both land and sea, and Serenianus, who had fled to Lydia, was caught and executed"; tr. Ridley). See for Serenianus' death 26.10.1 with the notes. Marcellus was *protector* (*domesticus*) and related to Procopius; 26.10.1 *protector Marcellus, eiusdem cognatus*. Having brought Constantinople and Thrace under his sway, Procopius next succeeded in gaining control of Bithynia, with its important cities Chalcedon, Nicomedia and Nicaea (26.8.3); in particular the control over Nicaea was of importance since it was the capital of Bithynia; see the note ad 26.1.3 *progresso Nicaeam*. By seizing Cyzicus Procopius also gained control over Hellespontus. *Hellespontus* was one of the ten provinces belonging to the diocese Asiana; *Not. Dign. Or.* 2.32.

See for *destinare ad*, 'to assign to a task', 14.1.6 *ut homines quidam ignoti...ad colligendos rumores...destinarentur*, 23.6.82 *ad iudicandum autem usu rerum spectati destinantur*. It should be noted that *possidere* does not only mean 'to possess', but also "i.q. occupare, sumere, in potestatem redigere" (TLL X 2.113.9–11), "to take control of" (OLD s.v. 3b); cf. *Chersonesoque omni armis possessa* (Liv. 38.16.4), *possessa per mare et navis maiore Italiae parte* (Tac. *Hist.* 2.12.1).

morabantur autem effectum sagittis et glandibus ceterisque iaculis obsidentium saepe globi confixi et propugnatorum sollertia claustrum per catenam ferream valde robustam ori portus insertum Predicate and direct object take the first positions in the sentence, because the focus is on the 'implementation' of Procopius' project. See for this meaning of *effectus* the note ad 20.8.5 *ut effectu*. The participles *confixi* and *insertum* are best interpreted as dominant: 'the fact that etc.' See for *globus* denoting a packed crowd of soldiers the notes ad 16.12.49 *globus* and 20.5.1 *armatarum*. The difficulty of the siege is emphasized by *saepe*. The term *claustrum* can denote a 'barrier', either natural or man-made. See for the former the note ad 20.11.24 *quod munimentum* (on mountain passes), and for the latter the note ad 25.8.14 *orientis* (on Nineveh). The present text is reminiscent of Verg. *G.* 2.161 *Lucrinoque addita claustra*. The phrase *ori...insertum* is curiously paralleled by V. Max. 8.7 *ext.* 1 about Demosthenes training his weak lungs: *ori insertis calculis* ('pebbles') *multum ac diu loqui solitus*. Hadrianus Valesius' emendation *insertum* is indispensable: otherwise the abl. *sollertiā* would have no function. Cf. the passages in Vegetius about the defence of a city against besiegers: *Adversum haec obsessos defendere consueverunt ballistae onagri scorpiones arcuballistae fustibali sagittarii fundae* (Veg. *mil.* 4. 22.1); *Sed ex alto destinata missibilia sive*

8.8

plumbatae vel lanceae, veruta vel spicula in subiectos vehementius cadunt (Veg. *mil.* 4.29.1). See also Veg. *mil.* 4.8.

ne rostratae irruerent naves hostiles Str. 12.8.11 (575C) already mentioned that Cyzicus had λιμένας δύο κλειστούς. Procopius besieged Cyzicus from both land and sea. The city eventually fell because the iron chain that prevented entrance to the port was broken and as a consequence the city lay open at the seaside and the naval force could enter the harbour.

The term *navis rostrata*, i.e. a ship with a battering ram, is a synonym for a warship. The rams, several of which have been found on the bottom of the Mediterranean, were made of bronze and had a triple point; hence the expressions *rostris tridentibus* (Verg. A. 5.143), *aere tridenti* (V. Fl. 1.668) and *trifidi...rostri* (Sil. 6.358). See further Reddé, 1986, 84–92 and Fig. 4. Apart from river fleets at e.g. the Rhine and the Danube (see for the latter Veg. *mil.* 4.46.9; Reddé, 1986, 288 ff.), the late Roman army had a number of standing fleets in various Mediterranean ports (e.g. Ravenna, Misenum, Aquileia, Arelate); Veg. *mil.* 4.31; *Not. Dign. Occ.* 38.8, 42.4, 7, 9, 11, 14. The *Notitia* does not record fleets in the East, but this must be an omission since other sources inform us about naval actions in the eastern Mediterranean; main naval ports in the eastern Mediterranean were Alexandria and Constantinople; Elton, 1996, 97–98. The Roman fleets consisted of warships – oared galleys with sails and a ram at the front – and ships for transport. John Lydus (*Mens.* 1.27) reports that in the time of Diocletian the total Roman naval force (sea and river fleets) consisted of 45.000 men. For the Roman naval fleet in the fourth century see Kienast, 1966, 124–133 and Reddé, 1986, 641–647. Amm. has little information on the Roman fleet; apart from this passage he mentions in 29.5.5 that Theodosius the Elder set out with a fleet from Arles to Africa.

This is one of the few instances in Amm. of actual warships operating at sea. In 27.4.10 Roman warships in the Propontis and the Bosporus are mentioned, and in 31.13.2 an infantry battle is compared to the collision of such ships: *collisae in modum rostratarum navium acies*.

8.9 *hanc post varios militum labores et ducum fatigatorum acerrimis proeliis Aliso quidam tribunus abscidit, exsertus bellator et prudens* Once more Amm. indicates that the siege of Cyzicus was a difficult and lengthy affair. In fact it could only be brought to a successful conclusion by a shrewd intervention of a first-rate officer. Cf. for *exsertus*, 'excellent',

27.10.16 *exsertus ita bellator*, and see the note ad 23.4.9 *hoc genere*. Amm.'s instances of *bellator* are usually in the plural, to denote soldiers in general, e.g. 19.9.9 *triginta perdidit milia bellatorum*. This passage in Amm. provides the only information we have for Aliso; *PLRE* I, Aliso+A. Lippold in *Gnomon* 46 (1974) 270. On account of his name Lippold suggests that Aliso was a German. For *tribunus* see the note ad 26.1.1 *Et rumore*.

testudinem hac specie superstruxit As is noted ad 20.7.2 *densitate opertus*, in Amm. *testudo* is not a fixed t.t., but functions in various descriptions of compact groups of soldiers protecting themselves with a 'tortoise-shell' of shields. The addition of the abl. qual. *hac specie* introduces the detailed description of such a 'structure' in the present case. This description bears an amazing likeness to Liv. 44.9, the report on the siege of Heracleum in 169 B.C., where a *testudo* of a comparable shape was formed after the example of a performance during horse races, which is described as follows: some sixty youths entered the arena and after some preliminary manoeuvres, *quadrato agmine facto, scutis super capita densatis, stantibus primis, secundis summissioribus, tertiis magis et quartis, postremis etiam genu nixis, fastigatam, sicut tecta aedificiorum sunt, testudinem faciebant*, "they would form in ranks, with shields close-set over their heads, the front rank erect, the second somewhat stooped, the third and fourth more so, and the rear rank down on their knees, so that they would form a 'tortoise' sloped like the roof of a house" (Liv. 44.9.6, tr. Schlesinger). Next, two armed men ran up along the sloping roof and skirmished with one another in a kind of circus act. This was imitated during the siege, at the lowest part of the wall, by soldiers, who, by climbing onto the *testudo*, reached the level of the defenders. As to those who formed the tortoiseshell, *nec ipsos tela ex muro missa subeuntes laeserunt, et testudini iniecta imbris in modum lubrico fastigio innoxia ad imum labebantur*, "the missiles hurled from the wall did not injure the men as they approached and those cast on the 'tortoise' slid harmlessly like rain down to the bottom of the slippery slope" (Liv. 44.9.9, tr. Schlesinger). It can only be concluded that Amm. imitated this passage. Granted, just enough remains of Plb. 28.11.2 to make clear that the Greek historian's description must have been used by Livy; cf. especially ὥστε τῇ τῶν ὅπλων πυκνότητι κεραμωτῷ καταρρύτῳ γίνεσθαι παραπλήσιον, "so that, owing to the density of the bucklers, it became like a tiled roof" (tr. Paton). Because Polybius restricts this roof construction to the first group (the only one left in the available text), it is unlikely that Amm. was inspired by the Greek historian. Livy is clearly the most probable model. See for soldiers on top of a *testudo* also Tac. *Hist.* 4.23.2 *invasere vallum...per testudinem suorum*. D.C. 49.30.3 even reports that a *testudo* could carry horses and wagons.

densetis cohaerentes supra capita scutis primi transtris instabant armati Cf. 14.2.10 *denseta scutorum compage* (q.v.), 24.2.14 *densetisque clipeis* (q.v.). TLL VII 1.2003.43 sqq. offers only a few examples of *instare* meaning "stare in aliquo loco"; the present text is listed among the instances in which this is coupled "cum colore minandi".

tertiis gradatim inclinatis summisse This is Amm.'s only instance of *gradatim*, "by successive degrees" (OLD s.v.). The adverb *submisse* (or *summisse*) usually means 'humbly': *mihi non nimis submisse supplicarat* (Cic. *Planc.* 12), *summisse ac humiliter* (Sen. *Ben.* 2.24.2), *aspere an leniter an etiam summisse loqui* (Quint. *Inst.* 6.5.5). The present text is a rare instance of its use in a 'physical' sense.

ita ut novissimi suffraginibus insidentes formam aedificii fornicati monstrarent This is slightly misleading: not only the last part of the group 'shows' the form of an arched building, but the entire group in its varied positions. *Suffrago* is an anatomical t.t. ('hock') for quadrupeds, which Amm. uses to denote the kneejoint of human beings in 19.6.2, 25.3.5 and 31.7.13, where these joints are cut through during or after battles. In the present text, however, Amm. would have done better by keeping close to Livy's *postremis etiam genu nixis* (44.9.6). Cf. for a 'vaulted building' 16.10.14 *speciosa celsitudine fornicatam* and especially 24.4.15 *testudine infigurabilium fornicum* (q.v.), brilliantly emended by Petschenig, 1892, 360 to *in figuram mobilium fornicum*.

quod machinae genus contra murales pugnas ideo figuratur hac specie, ut missilium ictus atque saxorum per decursus cadentium labiles instar imbrium evanescant Here *machina* does not mean "Belegerungswerke" (Seyfarth) or "macchinamento" (Viansino); it seems rather to denote a '(shrewdly contrived) formation', as a somewhat bold instance of *machina*, 'trickery', 'stratagem'; cf. the list in TLL VIII 12.26 sqq., which also contains 16.8.6 *totius machinae...auctorem* (q.v.) and 28.1.33 *machinas omnes*, "tutte le sue insidie" (Caltabiano). As is explained above, in the note ad *testudinem hac specie*, at Heracleum (169 B.C.) the *testudo* was used at a low point of the city wall, which clarifies Amm.'s *contra murales pugnas*. See for *figurare*, 'to shape', *figurantur hac specie* (23.4.14), *in stellae speciem figuratum* (25.2.6), *aciem rotundo habitu figuratam* (29.5.41). The text just quoted from Liv.

44.9.9 is quite helpful for the understanding of the second part of this passage: a comparison with *testudini iniecta imbris in modum lubrico fastigio innoxia ad imum labebantur* makes Amm.'s reworking visible; *missilium* and *saxorum* are instances of the gen. inversus: 'the missiles and stones which hit the tortoiseshell'; sliding downwards along the slippery slope they faded away (*evanescant*) like raindrops. Livy's *ad imum labebantur* has been reworded in *per decursus cadentium labiles*. Cf. for *labiles*, 'slippery', 22.8.48 *per infidum et labile solum* (caused by frost).

itaque coniectu telorum Aliso paulisper defensus ingenti corporis robore supposito stipite eandem catenam fortius bipenni concidens It is very difficult to pinpoint the precise function of the *testudo* described in §9. Obviously, the situation at Heracleum was very different: there it enabled attackers to reach the top of the walls. Who fired the missiles (*coniectu telorum*)? If this was done by the soldiers forming the tortoiseshell to protect Aliso for the short time he needed (*paulisper*) to break the chain, one fails to understand the objective of the formation and, moreover, how they could have managed to do this, if they did not have their arms and hands free? Amm.'s report would be more comprehensible, if the *testudo* protected Aliso against the enemy's missiles, and the men forming it provided cover on all sides, only leaving room directly in front of him, so that he could wield his axe. For this reason Petschenig and Mommsen suggested to add *a* before *coniectu*, an emendation which neither Seyfarth nor Marié regarded as worthy of mention in their respective app. crit., but which is nonetheless quite convincing; cf. 24.2.14 *densetisque clipeis ab ictu sagittarum defensus* (q.v.). The phrase *coniectus telorum* itself may have been borrowed from Livy; cf. *ad coniectum teli* (2.31.6), *ne primum quidem coniectum telorum tulerunt* (38.27.4). The same may be true concerning *corporis robore*: 9.17.13 *illo corporis robore*, 38.49.4 *robore corporum*, but such expressions occur also in e.g. Curtius Rufus, Valerius Maximus, Tacitus. Cf. for *eandem*, 'just mentioned', the note ad 20.4.5 *cum isdem*.

The lack of precise details makes it difficult to picture Aliso's action. Presumably at some point the chain was hoisted on board of the ships and a trunk put beneath it, so that Aliso could set to work with his axe more effectively.

hostili impetu patuit improtecta See for dat. -*u* of 4th declension nouns Leumann 442–443 and the note ad 19.1.6 *apparatu...instare*. As is noted ad 21.13.1 *improtectum*, this adi. only occurs in Gellius and Amm.

exstincto postea proterviae totius auctore This is a high-flown version of 'after Procopius' execution'. See for *exstinguere*, 'to kill', the final part of the note ad 19.2.15 *prostrati*. The last three words are an antonomasia of 'Procopius', in which *protervia* is a variation of the more usual *protervitas*. There are only two other instances of *protervia*, viz. Auson. *Mos.* 172 *capripedes agitat cum laeta protervia Panas*, "when the goat-footed Pans are seized with merry ribaldry" (tr. Evelyn White) and a phrase in the *Periocha Odussiae*, by some scholars ascribed to Ausonius, where it is stated about Melanthius that he *procorum proterviam semper armaverat* (22). This is not far from the present phrase, in which *protervia* means 'shameless enterprise'.

cum in factionis participes saeviretur Cf. 26.10.6 *saevitum est in multos* (q.v.). Apart from Procopius, Amm. mentions only three others by name who were killed because they had supported the revolt: Florentius and Barchalba (26.9.10), and Marcellus (26.10.5); the latter took the lead of the rebellion, after the death of Procopius. Others were treated more leniently: they were banished, like Araxius (26.10.7) and Phronimius (26.10.8); some were even pardoned like Euphrasius (26.10.8) and Aliso was allowed to keep his position in the army.

contemplatione facinoris clari See for *contemplatione* with gen. as a synonym of *causā* or *gratiā* TLL V 1.648.80–649.17. It is often found in juridical texts: see *Vocabularium Iurisprudentiae Romanae* I, Berlin 1903, 976–977. Such a function suits the present text, which refers to legal proceedings.

diu post in Isauria oppetit vastatoria manu confossus The adi. *vastatorius* only occurs in Amm.; in six of the nine cases it is combined with *manus*: see the note ad 18.6.9 *vastatoria(e) manu(s)*. The tribune Aliso may either have been killed in the suppression of an Isaurian uprising in 367/8, which is described by Amm. in 27.9.6–7, or he may have met his death in another revolt of the Isaurians which took place *c.* 376. On account of Amm.'s *diu post* it is more likely that his life ended in the latter conflict, which, by the way, is not described by Amm. but is mentioned by Zosimus (4.20.1–2; but cf. Paschoud n. 141 who questions the validity of Zosimus' information). See Lenski, 2002, 197–200, for the Isaurian revolts under Valens; for Ammianus on Isauria, see Hopwood, 1999.

CHAPTER 8.11   231

Hoc Marte Cyzico reserata See for *Mars* metonymically denoting 'warfare' or, as here, 'military operation' the notes ad 23.5.20 *devicta est* and 24.4.24 *extimabatur*, and for *reserare* denoting the conquest of a besieged city the note ad 20.6.5 *unde reseratam*. Apparently Procopius himself was not present at the siege of Cyzicus, but he rushed to the city after it had fallen.

8.11

veniaque universis, qui repugnavere, donatis Eunomius, bishop of Cyzicus, is said to have intervened and to have managed to get a pardon from Procopius for more prominent citizens of Cyzicus; Philost. *HE* 9.6: Ὅτι Προκοπίῳ ἔτι τῆς τυραννίδος ἐποχουμένῳ Εὐνόμιος πρὸς αὐτὸν ἐν Κυζίκῳ διάγοντα παραγίνεται. ἡ δὲ ἄφιξις λύσιν ἔπραττεν τῶν ἐν δεσμοῖς ὑπ' αὐτοῦ κατεχομένων· ὁ δεσμὸς δὲ τούτους ἐπίεζεν, ὅτιπερ ἔστεργον τὰ Οὐάλεντος. Cf. Suet. *Aug.* 51.1 (in a passage on Augustus' clemency) *venia et incolumitate donato*, *Dom.* 10.5 (about Domitian's cruelty) *duos solos...venia donatos*. See for Amm.'s predilection for *-ere* in the 3rd person plur. of the perfect tense the note ad 21.13.11 *quem obruere*, and for his use of the perfect in cases where one would have expected the pluperfect the notes ad 20.8.4 *qui ad* and 23.5.1 *Ascitis*.

Serenianum...servandum artissime Cf. 14.11.21 *cum ibi servaretur artissime*, 21.4.5 *arte custodiendum*. For Serenianus see the note ad 26.5.3.

The description of Procopius' success at Cyzicus, and his bright prospects as a consequence, is enhanced by an attractive vignette in which young Hormisdas (*PLRE* I, Hormisdas 3) and his impressive wife are succinctly portrayed without any precise factual details. In Amm.'s entire report on Procopius' coup the two are easily the most likeable of his supporters. However, at the same time the section forebodes the disastrous development of the affair.

8.12

Hormisdae maturo iuveni, Hormisdae regalis illius filio, potestatem proconsulis detulit et civilia more veterum et bella recturo With *maturo* Amm. adds a deft touch: the readers were familiar with Hormisdas (*PLRE* I, Hormisdas 2), who accompanied Constantius on his Roman visit (16.10.16), and Julian during the Persian campaign; by noting that the prince's son had reached maturity of age Amm. makes them realize that time had moved on and a new generation was entering the stage.

As a consequence of Diocletian's administrative reforms the traditional senatorial proconsulates were abolished except for a few, among them the proconsulate of Asia, the position with which Hormisdas was entrusted by Procopius. As proconsul Hormisdas stood outside the official hierarchy, and he could communicate with the emperor whilst bypassing the vicar of Asiana and even the PPO; Jones 47, 375; Demandt, 1989, 249. Apart from Asia the *insulae* and Hellespontus were also under the jurisdiction of the proconsul of Asia; *Not. Dign. Or.* 20. The control which Hormisdas had over both military and civil affairs is indeed *more veterum*, i.e. a return to the situation before Diocletian's reforms. However, this was done more out of necessity, because Procopius lacked support in the upper echelons of the army, than out of a desire to return to the old days and combine military and civil posts again; Lenski, 2002, 83. Not only Amm. but also Zos. 4.8.1 mentions that he was the son of the Persian of the same name; τοῦ Ὁρμίσδου τοῦ Πέρσου παιδὸς (ὁμώνυμος δὲ ἦν τῷ πατρί). The older Hormisdas, who had fled from Persia to the Roman Empire in 324, participated in Julian's Persian campaign and was a loyal supporter of Julian; see for him the note ad 24.1.2 *Arintheo*. See for *regalis*, 'prince', the note ad 16.10.16 *regalis Hormisdas*.

agens pro moribus lenius He acted 'in accordance with his usual conduct'; cf. Sal. *Jug.* 58.2 *sibi quisque pro moribus consulunt*. The adv. might create the impression that as yet the young man was too 'soft' for the task with which he had been entrusted, but it will soon appear that he certainly did not lack energy: *tanto vigore evasit*.

escensa navi, quam ad casus pararat ancipites When in early spring of 366 Valens marched against the forces of Procopius, Hormisdas seemed to be winning the battle – δόξαντος ἐν τῇ μάχῃ πλεονεκτεῖν (Zos. 4.8.1); see also Eun. *fr.* 34.8 – but was forced to escape when Gomoarius deserted to Valens. Apparently Hormisdas had reckoned with a possible defeat of Procopius and had prepared a flight plan.

sagittarum nube diffusa defensam Arrows are often shot in great numbers: *sagittarum creberrima nube* (19.2.8), *sagittarum undique volantium crebritate* (19.6.9), *sagittarum crebritate* (20.6.6), *sagittarum densitate* (20.7.2), *sagittarum enim nimbi crebrius volitantes* (20.7.6), *sagittarum volantium crebritate* (25.3.11) See on this topos especially the notes ad 19.6.9 and 20.6.6.

matronam opulentam et nobilem, cuius verecundia et destinatio gloriosa abruptis postea discriminibus maritum exemit See the treatment of this passage in Sabbah, 1992, 95, who stresses the remarkable "réciprocité de la *fides* conjugale". The name of Hormisdas' wife (*PLRE* I, Anonyma 26) is not known. The absence of any precise details makes it even impossible to establish whether the admirable lady was of Persian or Greco-Roman extraction. Note that of the four characteristics which she possessed two refer to her outward status and two to her personal virtues. The quartet should be incorporated in the 'dossier' of data illustrating the kind of people whom Amm. truly respected. See for the positive and negative forms of *destinatio*, 'determination', Seager 29 ff. and the note ad 20.11.7 *atque cum*. In order to make it perfectly clear that in the case of Hormisdas' wife the positive variety is meant, Amm. chose a highly laudatory qualification. See on his use of *gloria* and *gloriosus* Brandt, 1999, 366–381, who i.a. notes that only a quarter of Amm.'s instances occurs in a non-military context, e.g. Plato's *sapientia gloriosa* (22.16.22) and Hypatius, who as a result of his great virtues *maiorum claritudini gloriae fuit* (29.2.16).

As is noted ad 20.7.12 *diu cum*, TLL I 142,72–76 contains a list of cases in which Amm. uses *abruptus* about 'dangers' (*discrimina*, *pericula*). As to the 'steep dangers' from which Hormisdas was saved by his wife and how she brought this about, one can only speculate because of the lack of evidence. In fact, as Valesius saw, the only information about Hormisdas' later career is provided in Zos. 4.30.5, where it is reported that in 379 a group of Visigoths, serving in the Roman army, marched to their base in Egypt under his command, possibly as *comes rei militaris*. Along the way they misbehaved in a disgusting manner and came to blows with an Egyptian regiment at Philadelphia in Lydia.

Sections 13–15 introduce Procopius' change of fortune after his initial successes. In particular the fact that the experienced Arbitio chose Valens' side was a setback for Procopius among whose supporters there were no experienced and reliable generals. **8.13–15**

Ea victoria ultra homines sese Procopius efferens Cf. Zos. 4.7.1: Τούτῳ τῷ προτερήματι Προκόπιος ἐπαρθείς. The success was, of course, the capture of Cyzicus. Procopius had reached the goal mentioned in 26.8.7: *ut...sibi etiam Hellespontum iungeret*. However, his joy was excessive; see the note ad 22.9.1 *ultra homines* for similar phrases. In fact, his reaction put him in the same class as Sapor (27.12.11 *ultra hominem efferatus*) and Commodus (31.10.19 *ultra hominem exsultavit*). **8.13** *et ignorans, quod quivis beatus versa rota Fortunae ante vesperum potest esse miserrimus* Procopius was elated about his successes; as a consequence he suffered from *hubris* and ignored the fact that his fortune could change and that he could easily run out of luck. See for the use of *quod*-clauses instead of an a.c.i. in general Szantyr 576 and in the case of Amm. in particular Ehrismann 66–69. The essential information, needed to understand the object of Procopius' ignorance, was already gathered by Valesius. The first instance of the 'Wheel of Fortune' in Roman literature is Cic. *Pis.* 22 *fortunae rotam pertimescebat* (a passage criticized by Aper in Tac. *Dial.* 23.1). Tib. 1.5.70 *versatur celeri Fors levis orbe rotae* is the earliest occurrence in poetry; see Smith ad loc., who also mentions the 'Ball of Fortune', which "is largely confined to Greek authors", but does occur in Pac. *trag.* 366–367 about Fortuna: *saxoque instare in globoso praedicant volubilei*. See for further examples of the 'Wheel' Otto, 1890, 142, Robinson, 1946 and Häussler, 1968, 164. Amm. refers to it in two other passages: 14.11.26 (about Fortuna) *eique subdidit rotam*, 31.1.1 *Fortunae volucris rota*. For *Fortuna* see the notes ad 23.5.19 *at si fortuna* and 25.9.7 *Tu hoc loco*; add to the literature mentioned there Davies, 2004, 268–270, who also refers to this passage.

One of Varro's *Saturae Menippeae* was entitled *Nescis quid vesper vehat*. It dealt with the correct number of guests at a dinner and the topics suitable for conversation. See the comments in Cèbe, 1990, 1429–1447 and Krenkel, 2002, 601–616. Liv. 45.8.6 *nec praesenti credere fortunae, cum, quid vesper ferat incertum sit* is evidently a clearer parallel. It must have been a proverb; cf. Verg. *G.* 1.461: *quid vesper serus vehat*, will be shown by signs given by the Sun. The outcome of all this is, that Procopius was unaware not of some abstruse or profound wisdom, but of uncomplicated practical truths preserved in proverbs.

Arbitionis domum…iussit exinaniri mobilis census inaestimabilis plenam See for Arbitio the note ad 20.2.2. The location of his house is unknown. The last time Amm. had mentioned him was in 22.3.9 when he was in charge of the Chalcedon inquisitions. Afterwards he had probably gone into retirement. Amm. characterizes him as *ambiguus* and *praetumidus*. Procopius might have wanted his support for a combination of reasons. Not only was he one of the best generals of his time, but he was also successful in civil wars; *victoriarum civilium participem fortem* (22.3.9). Moreover, he had been a trusted commander of Constantius II and since Procopius was eager to connect himself to the predecessor of Julian to give an air of legitimacy to his usurpation (see the note ad 26.6.18 *quibus stirpis*), the support of Arbitio would enhance his claim to the throne. According to Blockley, 1975, 60 and Lenski, 2002, 79 Arbitio stayed aloof in the conflict between Procopius and Valens and only chose the side of the latter when Procopius, whom he called a *publicus grassator* (26.9.5), had looted his house and confiscated his estates; see 26.9.4–5 with notes. Cf., however, Zos. 4.7.3 where is said that it was Arbitio who urged Valens to take heart when he heard of Procopius' rebellion. This would imply that Arbitio was on Valens' side from the beginning.

Cf. for *exinanire*, 'to make empty', 17.2.1 *munimentis duobus, quae olim exinanita sunt* ('were deserted'), 24.3.5 *urbes exinanitae* ('plundered') and Cic. *Div. Caec.* 11 *Verres... domos exinanisse, fana spoliasse dicitur*, a passage quoted by Gel. 13.25.10. With an eye on 28.1.3 *mobili censu* Valesius contrived the undoubtedly correct emendation *mobilis census*; cf. also 28.6.26 *rem mobilem*. TLL VIII 1199.5–42 registers many instances of *mobilis* as a juridical t.t.: 'movable (property= census)'. TLL VII 1.814.9–10 lists the present text and 22.16.13 *bibliothecae...inaestimabiles* as cases in which *inaestimabilis* is the equivalent of "pretiosissimus". See for the latter case, however, the note ad loc. (*in quo duo*).

quod venire ad eum accitus aliquotiens distulit causatus incommoda senectutis et morbos Obviously to his disgust Procopius experienced *Arbitionem semper ambiguum* (22.3.9, q.v.). See for *causari*, 'to mention something as an excuse for not taking a particular action', the note ad 25.5.3 *eoque causante*. Arbitio agreed with Hor. *AP* 169 *multa senem circumveniunt incommoda*. Cf. for his age 26.9.5: *nam cum omnibus provectior natu et dignitate sublimior canitiem reverendam ostenderet*.

This section consists of one long period, the purport of which is slightly obscured, because one link in the 'chain' is only implicit. Summarized as briefly as possible, the period means: 'Although Procopius feared the consequences of the Arbitio affair ⟨and was badly in need of other support⟩, in spite of the ample opportunities offered by the situation, he failed to seize these.'

8.14

et licet hac ex causa praesumptor momentum pertimesceret grave With *hac...causa* Amm. means Procopius' failure to gain the support of one of the most respected generals of the time. He had every reason to fear that this had tipped the scales to his disadvantage. As appears from the lemma *praesumptor* in TLL X 2.975.17–976.43, this noun hardly occurs in non-Christian texts. Rejecting the meaning 'relying too much on one's own power' (as a reference to §13 *ultra homines sese...efferens*), TLL X 2.975.59 prefers to interpret it as expressing "actionem usurpandi". This decision is plausible: cf. §10 *proterviae totius auctore* (q.v.) and 26.7.12 *usurpator indebitae potestatis* (q.v.). As in 22.9.9 *causarum momenta...perpendens* (q.v.) and 24.2.14 *neutrubi inclinato momento*, in the present text *momentum* can be regarded as an instance of the metaphor of weighing: the impossibility to gain Arbitio's cooperation tipped the scales.

se in orientales provincias effundere Apparently the time was deemed ripe to invade the oriental provinces after his successes in Bithynia and Hellespontus, and because Valens had retreated to Ancyra. Usually *se effundere* in a topographical context has a mass of people as Agens: Liv. 26.5.5 (ut) *portis omnibus se effunderent*, Vell. 1.4.3 *magna vis Graecae iuventutis...in Asiam se effudit*, Amm. 17.12.4 *semet omnes effuderunt in fugam*. Cf., however, V. Max. 7.6.6 *cum effusurus se in nostras provincias Parthorum rex Phraates videretur*. As in the present text, the commander is mentioned as the representative of his forces.

avidas novitatem quandam visere taedio asperioris imperii The people in the eastern provinces, tired of the oppressive regime of Valens, were only too happy to welcome Procopius. However, he failed to use the momentum by staying in Asia during the winter.

See for *avidus* with inf. the note ad 22.6.1 *maximeque avidum* and for *novitas* denoting a change of government the note ad 21.6.5 *e Galliis*; cf. also 26.6.17 *novitatis repentina iucunditate* (q.v.). The people in the eastern provinces shared their aversion to Valens' 'oppressive' reign with the inhabitants of Constantinople (see 26.6.17).

erga alliciendas quasdam civitates Asiae legendosque eruendi peritos auri, ut sibi profuturos proeliis, quae magna exspectabat et crebra, segnius commoratus in modum acuti mucronis obtunsus est Amm.'s use of *erga* with a gerundive is somewhat idiosyncratic; his other instances are 16.10.17, 21.16.1, 30.5.3, 31.14.2. Bentley thought about adding 14.1.8 by changing *scrutandi* to *scrutanda*. Examples in other authors are few and far between, e.g. August. *doctr.* 1.30.31 about the good Samaritan: *erga illum recreandum atque curandum misericors exstitit*.

TLL V 2.844.51–58 lists the present text among the cases in which *eruere* is "per similitudinem" the equivalent of *extorquere*, e.g. Cic. *Att.* 10.14.1: both Pompey and Caesar were badly in need of money, *quae erui nusquam nisi ex privatorum bonis posset, CE* 1178.40

about a treacherous woman: *milia quom erueres auri de nomine nostro*. The conclusion would be that, in Amm.'s eyes, Procopius had every opportunity to gather a number of 'fund-raisers'. Hence Rolfe's "surrounding himself with men skilled in raising money" and Hamilton's "[to] recruit experienced fund-raisers". Other translators, however, regard *eruendi peritos auri* as a description of Thracian miners. No doubt the verb *eruere* can denote mining; see the examples in TLL V 2.844.38–47, e.g. Ov. *Am.* 3.8.53 *eruimus terra solidum pro frugibus aurum*, Sen. *Nat.* 5.15.3 *quae tanta necessitas...hominem...in fundum telluris intimae mersit, ut erueret aurum*. Cf. also Amm. 31.6.6 *sequendarum auri venarum periti*, according to Angliviel de la Beaumelle ad loc. a high-flown periphrasis for *metallarii*. These were "free men, bound to their place and trade by a hereditary tie" (Jones 838; see also notes 35 and 36 on p. 1351); "many of those had emigrated and taken up agricultural work" (Jones, *ib*.). In this case Amm. states that Procopius needed to trace these men in order to send them back to the Thracian goldmines. Cf. the translations of Marié ("à recruiter des hommes experts dans l'art d'extraire l'or"), Caltabiano ("per scegliere esperti nell'estrazione dell'oro") and Seyfarth ("Männer auszuwählen, die darin Erfahrung haben, Gold aufzustöbern"). This solution does seem plausible except when one considers the time needed to trace the expert miners, and then, for them, to procure with due speed enough gold to mint all the money which Procopius needed. However, this may precisely have caused the delay which according to Amm. 'blunted' his sword.

See for the sentence pattern in which adjectives are not added to a noun in the antecedent, but put in the relative clause Kühner-Stegmann 2.311–312, e.g. Tac. *Ann.* 6.31.1 *fretus bellis, quae secunda adversum circumiectas nationes exercuerat*. The figurative sense of *obtundere*, "to make blunt" (OLD s.v. 3), had long since developed into an overworked metaphor; some examples: Cic. *de Orat.* 3.93 *ingenia obtundi nolui*, Amm. 14.11.12 *utque solent...hebetari sensus hominum et obtundi*. The perf. part. *obtunsus* often functions as an adi.: Verg. *A.* 1.567 *non obtunsa adeo gestamus pectora Poeni*, V. Max. 7.3.2 (Brutus) *obtunsi se cordis esse simulavit*. However, in the present text Amm. persuasively revives the metaphor by adding *in modum acuti mucronis*: Procopius was a 'sharp sword', but he let it be blunted by his dawdling.

Strictly speaking, the full stop behind *obtunsum est* in § 14 is not correct. The entire § 15 consists of one comparative sentence introduced

8.15

by *ut*, 'as'. Procopius' usurpation is for the third time compared with a situation in the past. In 26.6.16 his first action is compared to that of Didius Iulianus, in 26.6.20 the relation between the initial phase and its further development is compared to four precedents. In the present text the historical precedent is ominous, causing the reader to expect the worst for Procopius.

ut quondam Pescennius Niger ad subveniendum spei rerum extremae a Romano populo saepe accitus, dum diu cunctatur in Syria This is the first and only time that L. Pescennius Niger is mentioned in the *Res Gestae*; see for him Kienast, 1996², 159–160; *PIR*¹ P 183. He was proclaimed emperor in Antioch probably in April 193 at the request of the inhabitants of Rome; Hdn. 2.7.8 καλούμενος καὶ βοηθήσων ἄπεισι Ῥωμαίοις δεομένοις; also Hdn. 2.8.4 οὐ φαῦλαι δὲ οὐδὲ κοῦφαι καλοῦσιν ἐλπίδες, ἀλλ' ὅ τε Ῥωμαίων δῆμος, ᾧ τὴν δεσποτείαν τῶν ἁπάντων ἔνειμαν θεοὶ καὶ τὴν βασιλείαν; D.C. 74.13.5; HA *PN* 2.2, 3.1. Herodian, who may have been Amm.'s source for this paragraph, describes Pescennius as indecisive and lacking perseverance; Hdn. 2.12.2; Hdn. 3.4.7 τέλει μὲν δὴ τοιούτῳ ὁ Νίγρος ἐχρήσατο, μελλήσεως καὶ βραδυτῆτος δοὺς δίκας. In 191 Pescennius had been appointed by Commodus to command the armies in Syria; HA *PN* 1.5. For Syria see the note ad 22.10.1 *quibus*.

Note the cumulation of reasons why Pescennius' help would have been fully justified: the situation was almost hopeless, he had 'often' been sent for, not by some criminal gang or revolutionary faction, but by 'the Roman people'.

a Severo superatus in sinu Issico, qui est in Cilicia, ubi Dareum Alexander fudit Hdn. 3.4.2–3 συνέρχεται δὴ ἑκατέρωθεν ὁ στρατὸς ἐς τὸ κατὰ τὸν Ἰσσικὸν καλούμενον κόλπον πεδίον πλατύτατόν τε καὶ ἐπιμηκέστατον... ἐκεῖ φασὶ καὶ Δαρεῖον Ἀλεξάνδρῳ τὴν ὑστάτην (sic) καὶ μεγίστην μάχην συμβαλόντα ἡττηθῆναί τε καὶ ἁλῶναι (*sic*); also Str. 14.5.19 (676C); D.C. 75.7.1. Septimius Severus is mentioned seven times in the *Res Gestae*, the last time in 26.6.8 (q.v.). For the Issic Gulf, now called Gulf of Iskenderun, see Talbert, 2000, map 67B3–C3; Str. 2.5.18 (121C), 24 (125C), 14.5.19 (676C); Mela 1.70; Beer, 1916. Darius (III) is also mentioned in 23.6.22 (q.v.) where Amm. refers to the battle of Gaugamela. For Amm.'s numerous references to words and deeds of Alexander see the notes ad 21.8.3 *id enim* and 24.4.27. The battle between Alexander and Darius at Issus took place in 333 B.C. The only reason for the introduction of this famous battle seems to be Amm.'s wish to show his historical knowledge.

fugatusque in suburbano quodam Antiochiae gregarii manu militis interiit Hdn. 3.4.6 ὁ δὲ Νίγρος ἵππῳ γενναίῳ ἐποχούμενος φεύγει μετ' ὀλίγων, ἔς τε τὴν Ἀντιόχειαν ἀφικνεῖται... καὶ ἔν τινι προαστείῳ κρυπτόμενος, εὑρεθείς τε ὑπὸ τῶν διωκόντων ἱππέων καὶ συλληφθεὶς τὴν κεφαλὴν ἀπετμήθη. Cf. HA *PN* 5.8 *apud Cyzicum circa paludem fugiens sauciatus, et sic ad Severum adductus atque statim mortuus.* Pescennius' death by the hand of a common soldier, a detail which is mentioned only by Amm., completes the ignominy of the anticlimax.

CHAPTER 9

Introduction

At the end of chapter 8 Ammianus indicated that Procopius would forfeit the victory that seemed to be within his reach; in chapter 9 he reports his downfall. During the spring of 366 Lupicinus, at the head of a strong contingent of troops, joined Valens, who subsequently went on the offensive. It is difficult to form a coherent picture of the events from Ammianus' report, as he leaves his readers in the dark about the chronology and other details concerning the confrontations between Valens' and Procopius' armies. Valens' moves can only be understood, if we start from the premise that Procopius had divided his troops, one half under the command of Gomoarius, the other under himself and Agilo, as Seeck had inferred from Zosimus' account of the revolt. Valens first directed his forces against the army corps in Lydia under Gomoarius. On his way there he met with stiff resistance, because Procopius had gained much support by parading Constantius' widow and her infant daughter as visual evidence that he belonged to the Constantinian dynasty (§ 1–3).

Valens' countermove was to persuade the old general Arbitio to come to his assistance. This produced the desired effect on Valens' troops, who had been wavering in their loyalty. When Gomoarius heard about Arbitio's successful intervention, he decided to change sides and went over to Valens with his troops (§ 4–6).

Greatly encouraged by the weakening of the forces of his adversary, Valens proceeded to attack the other half of Procopius' army near Nacolia in Phrygia. It is not possible to decide with certainty on the basis of Ammianus' account whether a real battle ensued. In any case, the encounter ended in disaster for Procopius, because his general Agilo, like Gomoarius, decided to betray him at the decisive moment (§ 6–7).

In despair Procopius together with two officers went into hiding, but after one night he was again betrayed and delivered by his companions into the hands of Valens, who summarily executed him and sent his head to his brother Valentinian in Gaul. Ammianus reports with indignation that the companions, who had handed Procopius over to Valens, were also executed (§ 8–10).

The last section (§ 11) contains a short elogium of Procopius, in which his age at he time of his death is mentioned and his outward appearance described. Although Ammianus had portrayed Procopius as a melancholy failure, he ends his description on a positive note: during his whole life he had shed no blood. This could not be said of his opponent.

9.1 *Haec adulta hieme Valentiniano et Valente consulibus agebantur* See the note ad 23.2.2 for *adultus* as the designation of the middle month of every season. The consular formula is exceptionally plain for Amm., who has a great variety of expressions at his disposal for the naming of the consuls at the beginning of the year, for which see the note ad 22.7.1 *cum Mamertini*. In 365 Valentinian and Valens were consuls for the first time; cf. 26.5.6 *principes sumpsere primitus trabeas consulares*; Bagnall et al., 1987, 264–265. With this expression Amm. refers to the happenings at the end of that year.

translato vero in Gratianum, adhuc privatum, et Dagalaifum amplissimo magistratu The particle *vero* marks the transition to a new stage in the narrative. See for this derived function of *vero* Kroon, 1995, 315–325. For *amplissimus magistratus* as a designation of the still very prestigious consulate see the note ad 21.6.5 *amplissimi suscepit*. For the consulship of Gratian and Dagalaifus see Bagnall et al., 1987, 266–267. For Dagalaifus see the notes ad 26.1.6 *Dagalaifo*, 26.4.1 *silentibusque* and 26.5.2 *et Dagalaifus*. This is the second time that Amm. mentions Gratian; the first time was in 21.15.6 (q.v.). Flavius Gratianus was born in Sirmium on 18 April 359 as the son of Valentinian and Marina Severa. He was only six, and as yet without imperial rank (*adhuc privatum*), when made consul and eight when proclaimed Augustus in 367. After his father's death in 375 he was the senior Augustus of the West. He died in 383. See *PLRE* I, Fl. Gratianus 2; Kienast, 1996², 333–334; Errington, 2006, *passim*.

aperto iam vere suscitatis viribus The phrase *aperto vere* appears to be unique, but spring is traditionally associated with the notion of 'opening'. Both Var. *L.* 6.4.33 *Quod ver omnia aperit, Aprilem* (dictum) and Ov. *Fast.* 4.89 *Aprilem memorant ab aperto tempore dictum* postulate a connection between the name of the month April and the verb *aperire*. This is the only instance of *suscitare*, 'to call into action', in Amm. He may have taken Vergil as his model, cf. e.g. *A.* 11.727–728 *Tyrrhenum genitor Tarchonem in proelia saeva / suscitat* and *A.* 9.462–463 *Turnus in arma viros, armis circumdatus ipse, / suscitat*.

CHAPTER 9.2   243

iuncto sibi Lupicino cum robustis auxiliis   See for Lupicinus the notes ad 26.5.2 and 26.8.4. The adjective is used of the strength of an army unit also in 31.7.12 *subsidialis robustissimus globus*. Cf. Cic. *Fam.* 7.3.2 *cum legionibus robustissimis*; Cic. *Phil.* 11.32 *robustus et victor exercitus*; Fron. *Str.* 2.3.3 *robustissimas copias in dextro cornu conlocatas habebat*. The *auxilia* must refer to the troops brought by Lupicinus from the East: *comperissetque Lupicinum ab oriente cum catervis adventare non contemnendis* (26.8.4).

Pessinunta...Phrygiae quondam, nunc Galatiae oppidum   For Pessinus see the note ad 22.9.5. It is identified with modern Ballihisar and is located some 130 km southwest of Ancyra. Strobel, 2000; Talbert, 2000, 62 G3. For Phrygia see Olshausen-Wittke, 2000; for Galatia see the note ad 26.7.2 *spe dubia*.

quo praesidiis tútius communíto, ne quid inopinum per eos emergeret tractus   The plural *praesidia* in Amm. refers either to a garrison, as in 23.6.3 *praesidiisque Macedonum pulsis*, or to fortresses, as in 25.7.8 *profecto venisset ad praesidia Corduenae* (q.v.), or to defensive works, as in 18.7.6 *ripas Euphratis castellis et praeacutis sudibus omnique praesidiorum genere communibant* (q.v.). In the present sentence both defensive works and military reinforcements are probably meant. For *tutius* cf. 20.5.1 *saeptusque tutius*, where, as here, V reads *totius*. See the notes ad 25.4.11 *praetenturae* and 26.4.1 *quasi tota* for this frequent confusion in V. The comparative *tutius* is much more common than *tuto*. It is without real comparative force here, and probably chosen to produce a cursus velox. The adjective *inopinus*, for which see the note ad 20.8.8 *cuius iracundiae*, regularly refers to surprise attacks, e.g. 23.3.5 *ne quid inopinum ex incauto latere oreretur*. For *tractus* as a synonym of *regio* see the note ad 16.3.1.

9.2

praeter radices Olympi montis excelsi tramitesque fragosos   There is a slight irregularity in the transition *praeter radices...tramitesque* and Novák's ⟨*per calles*⟩ *tramitesque* is certainly ingenious. However, one cannot rule out that Amm. intended the prepositional phrase as a kind of hendiadys meaning 'along the rough paths skirting the foothills of mount Olympus', so it seems prudent to leave the text unchanged. Amm. has a similar phrase in 21.10.4 *hincque et inde fragosis tramitibus impeditum* (q.v.). The *mons Olympus* is situated in Bithynia; its modern name is Ula Dagh; Ruge, 1939; Talbert, 2000, 52 E4.

ire tendebat ad Lyciam oscitantem ibi Gomoarium aggressurus The combination of *tendere* with infinitive is found for the first time in Lucr. 5.728 *astrologorum artem contra convincere tendit*; Szantyr 346. Here, as in 14.11.12; 27.8.3; 29.5.18 and 31.10.20, it is used as a simplex pro composito *contendere*, 'to hasten'. Seeck, 1920, V, 446, observed that according to Zos. 4.8.1–2 Gomoarius was in Thyatira in Lydia before he changed sides, and for that reason he proposed to read *Lydiam* instead of *Lyciam*. He was rightly followed by Paschoud n. 121, Marié and Lenski, 2002, 80 n. 71. As a matter of fact Procopius' revolt remained limited to Constantinople and the north-western part of Asia Minor (Bithynia, Hellespontus, part of Galatia) and parts of Thrace (see 26.10.6).

At the end of the winter or the beginning of the spring of 366 Valens started his offensive actions against Procopius from Ancyra, where he had returned in the autumn of 365 after an unsuccessful campaign in Bithynia (*Unde cum Ancyram Valens...revertisset*; 26.8.4). From Ancyra he went to Pessinus and thence westward along the slopes of *mons Olympus* to Lydia. Near Thyatira in Lydia he had a military encounter with Gomoarius (Zos. 4.8.1–2, cf. 26.9.6). It may have been Valens' intention to encounter Procopius himself since Eunapius *fr.* 34.6–7 reports: Παραλλάττουσι δὲ ἀλλήλους τῷ διαστήματι τῶν ὁδῶν ψευσθέντες ὅ τε Προκόπιος καὶ Οὐάλης ὁ βασιλεύς ("Procopius and the Emperor Valens, mistakenly taking different roads, missed each other"; tr. Blockley) and Ἐμβάλλουσι δὲ ὁ μὲν βασιλεὺς ἐς Λυδίαν ὁ δὲ Προκόπιος ἐς Φρυγίαν τὴν ἄνω ("The Emperor moved into Lydia, Procopius into Upper Phrygia", tr. Blockley); see also Lenski, 2002, 80.

Gomoarius is one of Amm.'s *bêtes noires*. In 21.8.1 he calls him *proditorem antiquum*, 'an arch-traitor'. The reason is probably that Gomoarius hated Julian, because he had been dismissed by him *ut contemptus in Galliis erat Iuliano infestus* (21.13.16). See also the note ad 26.7.4 *et administratio*. *Oscitantem* 'yawning' often has the connotation of dissolute living, as in Cic. *Mil.* 56 *adde inscitiam pransi poti oscitantis ducis* and Pers. 3.59 *oscitat hesternum* (vinum). Amm. has the same damning description of Ursicinus' successor Sabinianus in 18.6.8 *oscitante homunculo*.

9.3 *cui pertinaci conspiratione multorum hac maxime consideratione resistebatur, quod* The relative pronoun refers to Valens. As the qualifications *pertinaci* and *multorum* show, the term *conspiratio* does not refer to the revolt of Procopius as such, but rather to the stubborn unanimity of his numerous supporters. See for this meaning of *conspiratio* the note ad 24.5.11 *varietate munitionum.* The correction *maxime* for V's *maxima,* proposed by Petschenig, is wholly convincing in view of parallels like 14.10.16 *ea ratione maxime percita, quod*; 29.6.16 *eo maxime timore perculsi, quod* and 31.6.5 *eo maxime adiumento praeter genuinam erecti fiduciam, quod.*

hostis eius, ut ante relatum est Amm. refers to 26.7.10. The *hostis* is of course Procopius himself, not Gomoarius, as is suggested in Curran, 1998, 90: "Procopius' general had brought Constantia Postuma with him and was using her presence to sway popular support towards the usurper". As a rule, singular *hostis* is used collectively in the *Res Gestae.* Other exceptions are 29.5.4 *hostis implacabilis,* which, although the text is incomplete, must refer to the usurpator Firmus, and the gruesome story of the Saracene soldier in 31.16.6, who *interfecti hostis iugulo labra admovit effusumque cruorem exsuxit.*

Constanti filiam...circumferens secum This is the second time that Amm. refers to Procopius' policy of connecting himself to the Constantinian dynasty through Faustina and the infant daughter she had with Constantius II. For Faustina see the note ad 26.7.10 *adeptusque* and for her daughter Constantia Postuma the note ad 26.7.10 *quod Constanti.* Constantia married Gratian in 374; she died in 383 and was buried in Constantinople.

cum prope in acie starent Despite the fact that there is no parallel for *in acie stare* in Amm., the expression is so common that this is the most likely correction for V's *propin acies starent. Prope* is translated by "almost" (Rolfe), "presque" (Marié), or "quasi" (Selem). Seyfarth's "wenn es zum Gefecht ging" is probably based on the same interpretation. The alternative 'nearby', however, is far more likely in view of expressions like 14.7.5 *Theophilum prope astantem* (cf. 16.10.16) and 30.8.8 *ad comitum quendam prope astantem.* The subject of *starent* would be either 'the two armies', or, more likely, 'Procopius' men'. In both cases there would be a contrast between 'at a distance' (*in agminibus*) and 'close by' (*in acie*). In the historical precedent adduced below the baby king watches the battle from his cradle *post aciem.*

ut pro imperiali germine, cui se quoque iunctum addebat, pugnarent audentius, iras militum accendebat Another ornate phrase to denote membership of the imperial family like *culminis summi prosapiam* in 26.7.16. As TLL VI 1923.28 sqq. shows, *germen* in the sense "progenies sive suboles hominis" is found almost exclusively in fourth- and fifth-century texts. Cf. *Pan.* 7.2.5 *Qui non plebeio germine, sed imperatoria stirpe rem publicam propagatis* and Symm. *Or.* 1.3 *Meruisti quondam, inclute Gratiane, meruisti, ut de te sacra germina pullularent.* In the relative clause *cui* is best taken apo koinou with *iunctum* and *addebat*, 'to which he counted himself as a kinsman.' For the dynastic loyalty of the soldiers see the note ad 26.7.10 *quod Constanti.*

sicut aliquando dimicaturi Macedones cum Illyriis adhuc infantem in cunis locavere post aciem The story is told also by Iustinus and Nazarius, who according to Syme, 1988, 361 derived the passage directly from Pompeius Trogus. As Marié observes, a comparison of the texts shows that Iust. 7.2.8–11 was Amm.'s source: *Qui* (Macedones) *proelio pulsi rege suo in cunis prolato et pone aciem posito acrius certamen repetivere...miseratio eos infantis tenebat, quem, si victi forent, captivum de rege facturi videbantur* (Ilyrii). In *Pan.* 4.20.1 the name of the infant king is mentioned: *Illyrii quondam despicientes Aeropi regis infantiam Macedonas bello lacessiverunt.* Hdt. 8.137.1 mentions an Aeropus as brother of Perdiccas, the mythical founder of the Macedonian dynasty; there was also a Macedonian king by the name of Aeropus, who ruled c. 396–392 BC; Hdt. 8.139, Kaerst, 1894. Other Macedonian kings of this name are not known. A parallel, though not identical, case is to be found in Tac. *Hist.* 4.18.2 *Civilis...matrem suam sororesque, simul omnium coniuges parvosque liberos consistere a tergo iubet, hortamenta victoriae vel pulsis pudorem.* The word *regem* before *infantem* in Gelenius' edition is essential for the story, and may well have been in the Hersfeldensis.

cuius metu, ne traheretur captivus The gen. *cuius* indicates not the person who is feared, but the person for whom one is afraid. This is very rare, but cf. Hor. *Epod.* 9.37–38 *curam metumque Caesaris rerum iuvat/dulci Lyaeo solvere.* The combination of the genitive in this function with a *ne*-clause expressing the object of fear is unique.

adversos fortius oppresserunt For *adversus* in the sense of *adversarius* cf. TLL I 865.24–27, where parallels are quoted from Sallust (*Jug.* 97.5 *contra advorsos acerrume pugnantes*), Livy and Tacitus.

9.4 *Contra has calliditatis argutias sagaci opitulatione nutanti negotio consuluit imperator* For the gen. identitatis see the literature quoted in the note ad 22.12.7 *caerimoniarum ritus.* At two points in his report on Procopius' usurpation Amm. uses the qualification *callidus* or *calliditas*: when he describes how Procopius gained control over

Thrace in 26.7.5 and how he exploited the presence of Faustina and her little daughter. Although *callidus* and its derivatives may be used *in bonam partem*, there is hardly any doubt that in both cases the term has its usual negative connotation of craftiness. By contrast, Valens' countermeasure is called *sagax*, an exclusively positive qualification. *Opitulatio* is a rare noun, found only in late Latin texts; TLL IX 2.731.18 sqq. There can be little doubt that it was Procopius' high-handed treatment of Arbitio, as described in 26.8.13, rather than Valens' subtle diplomacy, which decided the old general to side with the legitimate emperor.

Up to this point, Procopius' usurpation was a success and Valens' position was becoming critical. Amm. uses the verb *nutare* to describe such a situation also in 16.12.12 *ergo quoniam negotiis difficillimis quoque saepe dispositio tempestiva prospexit et statum nutantium rerum... aliquotiens divina remedia repararunt* and 25.8.11 *auctoris sui nutantem adhuc statum*. Cf. Tac. *Ann.* 1.17.1 *novum et nutantem adhuc principem* and Suet. *Vesp.* 8.1 *afflictam nutantemque rem publicam*. For *negotium* see the note ad 21.6.8 *damna negotiis Romanis*.

Arbitionem...ad se venire hortatus est For Arbitio see the notes ad 20.2.2 and 26.8.13. He was certainly no favourite of Amm., who in 22.3.9 calls him *semper ambiguum et praetumidum*. Valens must have been well aware of his record in suppressing uprisings during the reign of Constantius; *ut decuit victoriarum civilium participem fortem* (ibid.). He had been consul in 355; Bagnall et al., 1987, 244–245; he was one of the main generals of Constantius II. This is the only source which mentions that Arbitio was already a *dux* under Constantine I and considering his advanced age this is quite possible. Amm. informs us that he was a military upstart and that he began his career as a common soldier; *a gregario ad magnum militiae culmen evectus* (16.6.1). The apex of his career was in the 350s, so he may have climbed the military ladder under Constantius in the 340s. Arbitio was not only a general and a man of great prestige, but he was also known for his loyalty to Constantius. For that reason he was of great value to Valens, because through him the emperor could establish a connection with the Constantinian dynasty; for the endeavours of Valentinian and Valens in this respect, see Lenski, 2002, 101–104. For the same reason Procopius had been eager to have him on his side; see 26.8.13 with note.

ut Constantiniani ducis verecundia truces animi lenirentur The *truces animi* are those of Procopius' men. For *trux / truculentus* see the note ad 20.6.1. The warlike spirit of Valens' men was already mentioned in 26.7.17 *acriter venerant pugnaturi*. In that situation the soldiers had been calmed down by Procopius' conciliatory words. Here Valens hopes, that the respect for the old general Arbitio will bring the rebels to their senses.

neque secus venit 'Which is exactly what happened'. For *venire* in the sense of *evenire* see the note ad 26.1.5 *quod tunc*.

9.5-7 Unfortunately, the information provided by Ammianus and Zosimus about the military encounters between Valens and Procopius is so fragmented and incomplete, that it is impossible to reconstruct in detail the chronology of the events which led to Procopius' defeat. It is of importance that, as Seeck, 1920, V, 54 had already suggested, the army of Procopius was divided into two: one army under the command of Gomoarius and another led by Procopius; see also Paschoud n. 121. The final encounter was at Nacolia in Phrygia probably on 26 May (see below the note ad 26.9.7 *Qua successus*) between the armies of Valens and Procopius; in this confrontation, described by Amm. 26.9.7 and Zos. 4.8.3, Procopius was finally defeated, due probably to the betrayal of Agilo. Some time before that, although the exact date is not known – Lenski's (2002, 80) date of early April is not firmly grounded – the battle of Thyatira, described by Zos. 4.8.1–2 (cf. Amm. 26.9.6) took place, between the armies of Valens and those commanded by Gomoarius and Hormisdas. In the midst of this encounter Gomoarius betrayed Procopius and went over to Valens' side with part of the army (Zos. 4.8.1–2; 26.9.6) and Hormisdas made his escape (26.8.12). Gomoarius went over to Valens because he had heard (*quibus cognitis*; 26.9.6) about Arbitio's success in persuading contingents of Procopius' army to take sides with Valens. It is not clear when Arbitio undertook his action; maybe during the battle of Thyatira itself, but according to Zosimus Arbitio managed to undermine the loyalty of Procopius' troops immediately before the battle; Zos. 4.7.4 μελλόντων δὲ ὅσον οὐδέπω τῶν στρατοπέδων εἰς χεῖρας ἰέναι, κατεστρατήγει τὴν τούτου προπέτειαν Ἀρβιτίων, ὑπαγόμενος ὅτι πλείστους τῶν συστρατευομένων, καὶ παρὰ τούτων ὅσα Προκόπιος ἐβουλεύετο προμανθάνων ("When the armies were about to join battle, this man outwitted the rash Procopius by winning over as many of his men as possible, from whom he learned his intentions"; tr. Ridley). Ammianus only says that Gomoarius decided to betray Procopius after he had heard of Arbitio's action (*quibus cognitis*, §6). There may have been earlier contacts between Arbitio and Gomoarius; cf. Lenski, 2002, 80 who seems to imply that Gomoarius was persuaded by Arbitio personally ("Gomoarius was easily persuaded by Arbitio, an old friend, to desert to Valens with all his men").

After the victory at Thyatira, Valens regrouped his army at Sardis and thence marched to Phrygia. According to Lenski, 2002, 80 n. 79 two milestones, dated between 364–367 and mentioning both Valens and Valentinian, testify to the emperor's route. For the inscriptions on the milestones see *AE* 1995, 1465 d and *AE* 1989, 699.

nam cum omnibus provectior natu et dignitate sublimior canitiem reverendam ostenderet Arbitio had used old age and ill health as an excuse to play for time when he was asked by Procopius to join him, *causatus incommoda senectutis et morbos*, 26.8.13 (q.v.). Now he is a trump card in the hands of Valens. *Provectus natu* is without parallel. It looks like a contamination of *aetate* or *annis provectus* and *maior (grandis) natu*. Cicero makes the following distinction in *Sen.* 10: *non admodum grandem natu, sed tamen iam aetate provectum*.

Arbitio is a retired general, so *dignitas* does not refer to one of the specific ranks, such as are discussed in the notes ad 19.1.3 *multiplici vertice* and 20.4.20 *qui ordo*, but to his prestige, in which respect he outshines all, including the emperor Valens. Amm. gives him the same respectful designation as the Roman senators of old in the first Roman digression, 14.6.6 *patrum reverenda cum auctoritate canities*.

multis ad perfidiam inclinatis This underlines *nutanti negotio* in the preceding section. Procopius' successes had their effect on Valens' men. Amm.'s wording again leaves no doubt as to his condemnation of Procopius' revolt. Soldiers who pledge allegiance to a usurper are guilty of treason, *perfidia*. Note that in Arbitio's conciliatory words to the troops the same act is euphemistically called *error*.

publicum grassatorem "Einen gemeingefährlichen Räuber" (Seyfarth). In this unique expression *publicus* is the equivalent of a gen. obiectivus, as in Suet. *Cal.* 28.1 *repente hostem publicum appellantes*. For *grassator* see the note ad 24.3.2.

orabat, ut se ac si parentem magis sequerentur felicissimis ductibus cognitum, quam profligato morem gererent nebuloni destituendo iam et casuro For *ac si* as an equivalent of *quasi* see the note ad 25.4.12 *dilectus artissime* and for *felicissimis ductibus cognitum* the note ad 21.5.9 *fortunatum domitorem*. As in 25.4.17 *superstitiosus magis quam sacrorum legitimus observator, magis...quam* means 'and not'. The qualification *profligatus nebulo*, 'a worthless and dissolute fellow', is a flagrant contradiction of Amm.'s own characterization of Procopius in 26.6.1 as *vita moribusque castigatior*, and as a melancholic in the short elogium at the end of this chapter. Amm. uses the noun *nebulo* again for the abject *delator* Heliodorus in 29.2.11. The expression *morem gerere* is found also in 17.5.7 *si morem gerere suadenti volueris recte* and 28.4.22 *his, quibus morem gerendo testati sunt*. On the basis of these three occurrences it is impossible to decide whether Amm. was aware, that the expression was used originally of the obedience of a wife to her husband or a son to his father, as is argued by Williams, 1958, 28–29. In any case this meaning is very apt here: instead of following a good-for-nothing the soldiers should obey their old father Arbitio like dutiful sons. The combination *destituendo iam et casuro*, 'soon to be abandoned and about to fall', illustrates well, that in late Latin the gerundive may be used as a kind of future passive participle. See the note ad 20.2.4 *opitulari*. A similar juxtaposition is found in 25.8.9 *res firmaturum ancipites et...opponendum*. For *iam* in the meaning 'at any moment' see the note ad 26.7.15 *ubi cum*.

9.6 *quibus cognitis Gomoarius cum elusis hostibus, unde venerat, redire posset innoxius* The result of Arbitio's intervention can be deduced from the reaction of Gomoarius. Apparently, the morale of Valens' troops had improved so much that Gomoarius, who had been sitting on the fence all the time, decided that Procopius' luck was running out. True to his reputation as a *proditor antiquus* (21.8.1), he acted accordingly. Although the movements of Gomoarius cannot be reconstructed on the basis of Amm.'s text, one gets the impression that his troops met the army of Valens, or a detachment of it, in the field. Gomoarius could have avoided an encounter, but preferred to let himself be taken prisoner. It is hard to believe that all this was accidental. More probably the old colleagues Arbitio and Gomoarius, who five years earlier had been ordered by Constantius to check Julian's advance together (21.13.16), arranged it secretly beforehand. *Unde venerat* is interpreted by Seeck, 1920, V, 54 as referring to Procopius' main force, from which Gomoarius had broken away. This is entirely possible, although Amm. does not seem to be aware of any division of Procopius' forces between the usurper himself, assisted by Agilo, and Gomoarius.

We know from Zosimus that the battle, during which Gomoarius betrayed Procopius was fought at Thyatira in Lydia (Talbert, 2000, 56 F4), where Valens opposed him and Hormisdas. The date of the battle is not certain (see the note ad 26.9.4 *Arbitionem*). Zos. 4.8.1–2 describes it as follows: Ἐπεὶ δὲ ἤλαυνον ἐπ' ἀλλήλους ὅ τε βασιλεὺς καὶ Προκόπιος, συναντῶσί πως σφίσιν εἰς Θυάτειρα τὰ στρατεύματα. μικροῦ δὲ ἐδέησεν ἡ Προκοπίου μερὶς ὑπερτέρα γενομένη τὴν τῶν πραγμάτων εἰς αὐτὸν μεταθεῖναι ῥοπήν, τοῦ Ὁρμίσδου τοῦ Πέρσου παιδὸς (ὁμώνυμος δὲ ἦν τῷ πατρὶ) δόξαντος ἐν τῇ μάχῃ πλεονεκτεῖν. Ἀλλὰ Γομάριος τῶν Προκοπίου στρατηγῶν ἅτερος, κοινωνῶν τῆς πράξεως ἅπασιν ὅσοι Προκοπίῳ συστρατευόμενοι τὰ βασιλέως ἐφρόνουν, ἐν αὐτῇ τῇ μάχῃ τὴν Αὐγούστου προσηγορίαν ἀναβοήσας ἅπαντας τοὺς σὺν αὐτῷ τὴν αὐτὴν ἀφιέναι φωνὴν ἔκ τινος ἐποίει συνθήματος, οὗ δὴ γενομένου μετεχώρουν ἅπαντες οἱ Προκοπίου στρατιῶται πρὸς Οὐάλεντα. ("The emperor and Procopius marched towards each other and the armies met at Thyatira. Procopius' side almost had the upper hand, which would have conferred control of the empire on him, and Hormisdas, son of the Persian of the same name, seemed to have overcome his opponents. Gomarius, another of Procopius' Magistri, had, however, taken into confidence all Procopius' men who were favourable to the emperor's cause. In the midst of the battle he shouted out the name Augustus and signalled all his men to do likewise, whereupon all Procopius' troops went over to Valens"; tr. Ridley). If Zosimus is to be believed, Gomoarius was instrumental in winning over many of Procopius' men for Valens at a moment when the troops of the usurper were close to victory. Gomoarius' demeanour was therefore a decisive factor in the defeat of Procopius. This seems to be confirmed by Philost. *HE* 9.5 who relates that Procopius, having engaged in battle with Valens, was overcome by the treachery of his generals Gomarius (and Agelius = Agilo): εἶτα μετ' οὐ πολὺν χρόνον πολέμῳ συρραγεὶς Οὐάλεντι, προδοσίᾳ τῶν αὐτοῦ στρατηγῶν Γομαρίου καὶ Ἀγελίου ἡττᾶται.

ad castra imperatoris opportunitate intervalli proximi captivi colore transivit The choice of the adjective *proximi*, instead of e.g. *minimi* is surprising. Elsewhere Amm. writes 16.12.19 *a superciliis Rheni haud longo intervallo distantem* or 20.6.9 *Nisibin…intervallo perquam longo discretam*, which is more correct. Could Verg. A. 5.320 have wrongfooted him (19.9.7 *ut ait poeta praeclarus, "longo proximus intervallo"*)? In the word group *proximi* is dominant: 'the opportunity offered by the proximity of the camp'. For the gen. cf. 31.12.2 *ad retinendas opportunitates angustiarum, quae prope erant.*

Color is used here in the sense of 'pretext'. In this meaning it is originally a rhetorical t.t. indicating "a method of interpreting the facts that was to the advantage of the speaker" (Winterbottom, 1974, xviii), as in Ov. *Tr.* 1.9b.27–28 *ut defendi nullo mea posse colore,/sic excusari crimina posse puto.* There are no parallels for this use of *color* in Amm., and there seem to be none at all for *color* with the genitive of a human being. In any case Gomoarius posed as a captive. There is no need to suppose that he changed his clothes, as TLL III 1721.45 suggests.

velut accursu multitudinis visae subito circumsaeptus This is Gomoarius' version of the events, from which Amm. distances himself by *velut*. For *accursus* see the note ad 24.4.2 *equitatus Persici*. The noun is normally used of a cavalry action, which is probably also the case here. *Visae subito* suggests a surprise attack. *Circumsaeptus* is ambiguous. It is used of the nocturnal arrest of Lucillianus in 21.9.7 *cum strepitu excitatus turbulento vidisset ignotorum hominum se circulo circumsaeptum*, but also of the emperor's guard of honour, as in 26.2.11 (Valentinianum) *circumsaeptum aquilis et vexillis agminibusque diversorum ordinum ambitiose stipatus*. Arrest or escort? The reader may decide for himself.

9.7 *Qua succensus alacritate Valens castra promovit ad Phrygiam* 'Fired by the enthusiasm about this (success)'. For the poeticism *succensus* see the note ad 26.6.6 *incusantium*, and in general on Amm.'s predilection for fire metaphors the note ad 21.11.1 *cursus eius*. Valens' despondency has disappeared after this first tangible success. *Qua alacritate* is the equivalent of *eius rei alacrite*. Zos. 4.8.3 is in accordance with the information given by Amm.: Ὁ δὲ μετὰ τὴν νίκην ταῖς Σάρδεσιν ἐπιδημήσας κἀκεῖθεν ἐπὶ Φρυγίαν ἐλάσας, εὑρὼν δὲ τὸν Προκόπιον ἐν Νακολείᾳ τῇ πόλει... ("After this victory, Valens moved to Sardis and thence into Phrygia, finding Procopius at Nacoleia..."; tr. Ridley). See also Socr. *HE* 4.5.2; Soz. *HE* 6.8.2; Joh. Ant. *fr.* 184.1 Müller = 276 Roberto; *Consul. Constant.* a. 366; *Chron. Pasch.* a. 366; Theoph. *Chron.* p. 55.29–33 De Boor; Lenski, 2002, 81 n. 80.

prope Nacoliam For Nacolia, see Olshausen-Wörrle, 2000 and Talbert, 2000, 62 E3. It is known that Procopius was executed by Valens on 27 May after the encounter at Nacolia (see below 26.9.9 *subito*). The engagement at Nacolia may have taken place on 26 May, since Amm. in section 9 speaks of one night that had passed (*maiore itaque noctis parte consumpta*) after Procopius had fled and before he was taken captive and executed. Kienast, 1996², 332 wrongly dates the battle at 27 May.

collatis manibus partium, dum in ancipiti...Agilo rem excursu prodidit repentino Garbled names and wrong word divisions are a frequent source of mistakes in V. In section 4 above *imperator et Arbitionem* had resulted in V's *imperatore tarbitiones*. Here *prope Nacoliam* was corrupted into *propensa colium*. The correct reading is found for the first time in Gelenius' edition, either by a brilliant conjecture or, far more likely, on the basis of the Hersfeldensis. Unfortunately, at this decisive point in the narrative the text is corrupt, possibly again on account of a name, Agilo, which led to the incomprehensible *in ancipitia culorum excursus*. There are several problems here: in the first place *partium* after *collatis manibus* is suspect, since there is no parallel for a gen. depending on *manibus* in this standard expression; in Gelenius' text the gen. *partium* depends on *dux*, which he reads instead of V's *dum*; that, however, results in the irregular cursus *collátis mánibus*; more seriously, a word defining the party is indispensable, as in Tac. *Hist.* 2.30.3 *duces partium Othonis* or Suet. *Vit.* 18.1 *ab Antonio Primo adversarum partium duce oppressus est*; and finally, the word order *partium dux in ancipiti Agilo* seems unacceptable. Therefore it seems best to retain V's *dum* and to accept a lacuna. Heraeus' suggestion *dum in ancipiti staret exitus proelii* is attractive in view of 20.6.5 *pugnabatur eventu ancipiti*.

For Agilo see the note ad 26.7.4 *et administratio*. Zosimus also (4.8.3) mentions Agilo's taking sides with Valens: κἀνταῦθα πάλιν Ἀγίλωνος τοῦ Προκοπίου στρατηγοῦ τὸ πρᾶγμα πρὸς τὸ τῷ βασιλεῖ λυσιτελοῦν διαθέντος, ἐνίκα κατὰ κράτος ὁ Οὐάλης ("And there again Agilo, another of Procopius' Magistri, collaborated with Valens who was victorious"; tr. Ridley).

Excursus is normally used for surprise attacks, e.g. 20.4.21 *diverso vagoque, ut in repentino solet, excursu* (q.v.); 24.5.12 *cum a vicina iam Ctesiphonte repentini excursus et alia formidarentur occulta* and 27.8.9 *per dolos occultiores et improvisos excursus*.

iam pila quatientes et gladios 'While they were already brandishing their spears and swords'. This is a surprising detail, because it seems to mean that a real battle had not started yet. *Pila quatere* is an extremely rare expression, the only other instance being Liv. 44.34.8 *quatere alii pila, alii micare gladiis*, where it is used of soldiers preparing for combat. *Gladios quatere* is completely without parallel and best understood as a zeugma. The preceding *collatis manibus* and *in ancipiti*, however, had suggested, that the two parties had already joined battle and that a critical stage had been reached. Marié is aware of the problem posed by *iam*, but smoothes it over by her translation "qui il y a un instant brandissaient leurs javelots et leurs épées". One is reminded of the scene in 26.7.15, where

Procopius prevents a real battle at the very last moment *cum legiones iam pugnaturae congrederentur.* According to Them. *Or.* 7.87 b ἅμα τῷ γενέσθαι ἐντὸς τῶν σῶν ὀφθαλμῶν ὑπὸ μάλης ἔκρυπτον τὰς ἀσπίδας ('as soon as they had come within your sight, they hid their shields under their armpits'), Agilo and his troops changed sides before the real battle had started.

ad imperatorem transeunt cum vexillis scuta perversa gestantes, quod defectionis signum est apertissimum The detail of the reversed shields is confirmed with some variation in Them. *Or.* 7.87 b quoted in the preceding note. *Cum vexillis* must be interpreted 'as well as their banners', as is evident from 26.7.17 *signorum apicibus aquilisque summissis. Perversus* as an equivalent of *inversus* or *conversus* is rare; TLL X 1.1863.49–51. Valesius quotes as similar tokens of surrender App. *BC* 2.6.42 οἱ δὲ ἐπέθεσαν ταῖς κεφαλαῖς τὰς ἀσπίδας, ὅπερ ἐστὶ σύμβολον ἑαυτοὺς παραδιδόντων ('they held their shields above their heads, which is a sign that they surrender themselves') and Oros. *hist.* 7.36.10 *Quo viso reliquae cohortes deditionem iam fieri priorum existimantes certatim sese ad Mascezil signis tradidere conversis.* Müller, 1905, 612 n. 15 adds HA *S.* 7.1 (Severus disarms the praetorians) *in Palatium...perrexit praelatis signis, quae praetorianis ademerat, supinis, non erectis.*

9.8 *Hoc praeter spem omnium viso Procopius salutis intercluso suffugio versus in pedes circumiectorum nemorum secreta petebat et montium* Procopius was obviously present at Nacolia and, presumably, had not witnessed Gomoarius' treason. This confirms the theory of Seeck, 1920, V, 54 that Procopius' army had been split in two, under the command of Gomoarius and Agilo. For *praeter spem omnium,* 'to the surprise of everybody', cf. 19.9.6 *Praeter spem itaque omnium digresso advena repentino.* V's *suffugio* has been convincingly defended by Hagendahl, 1924, 200–201, who compares 31.13.5 *ademptum esse omne evadendi suffugium* and Oros. *hist.* 2.19.13 *ad confugia salutis.* For *suffugium* see the note ad 21.12.11 *quos morte.* The expression *verti in pedes,* 'to take to flight', is found exclusively in Amm. (18.2.14; 27.2.3; 27.10.15; 28.5.6; 29.5.30; 31.13.7). For similar expressions see TLL X 1.1900.17–24. *Nemorum secreta* are remote places in the woods, as in Ov. *Met.* 1.593–594 *quodsi sola times latebras intrare ferarum, / praeside tuta deo nemorum secreta subibis.*

Florentio sequente Philost. *HE* 9.5 has a somewhat different story. He reports that Procopius, after the lost battle against Valens, retreated to Nicaea, and that on the next day Florentius (*PLRE* I, Florentius 4), who was in charge of the garrison of the city, seized Procopius and delivered him to Valens: καὶ φεύγων καταλαμβάνει τὴν Νίκαιαν. τῇ δὲ ἐπαύριον διανοηθεὶς ἐκεῖθεν ἀπαίρειν, ὑπὸ Φλωρεντίου, ὅς φρούραρχος ὑπ' αὐτοῦ τῆς πόλεως κατέστη, συλλαμβάνεται, καὶ δεσμώτην αὐτὸν ὁ συλλαβὼν πρὸς Οὐάλην ἄγει. This is improbable, because in 26.10.1 Amm. mentions that Marcellus was commander of Nicaea's garrison when he heard that Procopius was executed.

et Barchalba tribuno, quem per saevissima bella iam inde Constanti temporibus notum necessitas in crimen traxerat, non voluntas This man (*PLRE* I, Barchalba) is not known from other sources. One can only hazard a guess as to why Amm. provides these details about him. He may have known Barchalba personally. The name ('son of a dog') points to a Semitic origin and we may infer, that the fierce battles he had endured together with Procopius, had been on the Eastern front. *Bella saevissima* is the term Amm. used in 14.6.10 for the wars that brought Rome greatness, and in 30.1.22 for the wars Pyrrhus fought in Italy. *Iam inde* is followed either by a temporal conjunction like *ut*, as in 17.9.6 *iam inde, ut Iulianus illo est missus*, or a prepositional phrase with *ab*, like 26.6.7 *iam inde a temporibus principis Aureliani* (12 times). In the three cases where the preposition is missing in V (18.5.7; 28.5.11 and here) it can best be restored, pace Baehrens, 1925, 54 and Blomgren 42 n. 1. Amm.'s observation that Procopius and Barchalba were old comrades in arms, does not serve to condemn Barchalba's treachery, but is meant to explain why he had followed Procopius in his criminal undertaking. As *necessitas...non voluntas* (for which cf. Cic. *Off.* 3.4 [solitudinem] *quam mihi adfert necessitas non voluntas*) makes clear, Barchalba was one of the officers who supported the revolt against their will (*partim inviti*, 26.7.1). See for *tribunus* the note ad 26.1.4 *Et rumore*.

maiore itaque noctis parte consumpta, cum a vespertino ortu luna praelucens in diem metum augeret With 'resumptive' *itaque* Amm. returns to the narrative of Procopius' flight. The beautifully evocative phrase depicts the moon on her course from evening to dawn, as though leading the way with her light. Normally *praelucere* ('to shine on someone's path') refers to a welcome service, cf. 22.16.9 about the Pharos of Alexandria *turrim excelsam...praelucendi navibus nocturna suggerens ministeria*. Here the moon only increases Procopius' anxiety because its light made detection of his hiding place easier. Amm. may have been thinking of his own escape by night near Nisibis

9.9

in comparable circumstances 18.6.14 *terrebat autem nos plenilunium noctis.*

undique facultate evadendi exempta consiliorum inops Procopius The abl. abs. is a variation of *salutis intercluso suffugio* in the preceding section. The usual expression is *inops consilii*, as Amm. himself writes in 19.6.5 *Inopes nos consilii et, quid opponi deberet saevientibus, ambigentes.* Cf. Hagendahl, 1921, 73–98 on poetic plural.

ut in arduis necessitatibus solet On the varied expressions for 'dire straits' see the note ad 26.6.4 *postremae necessitatis.* Impersonal *solet* is found already in Cic. *Fam.* 9.16.7 *ut olim solebat* and Sal. *Jug.* 59.3 *uti...solet.*

cum Fortuna expostulabat luctuosa et gravi Fortune had clearly deserted Procopius, as Amm. had already intimated in 26.8.13 (q.v.). For Fortuna see the notes ad 23.5.19 *at si fortuna* and 25.9.7 *Tu hoc loco.* The verb *expostulare* is used of bitter complaints, cf. Cic. *Sul.* 44 *cur tacuisti, passus es, non mecum...questus es aut...iracundius aut vehementius expostulasti?* A similarly desperate complaint is found in Fro. *Amic.* 2.3.3 *saepe etiam expostulo cum deis immortalibus et eos ita iurgio compello* e.q.s. *Luctuosus* is a favourite with Cicero and Ammianus. Tacitus uses it for the destruction of the temple of Jupiter on the Capitol, *Hist.* 3.72.1 *Id facinus post conditam urbem luctuosissimum foedissimumque rei publicae populi Romani accidit.* In combination with *gravis* it occurs in Flor. 2.6.9 *illa gravis et luctuosa Punici belli vis atque tempestas.*

mersusque multiformibus curis For similar expressions see TLL VIII 2.835.3–17. There is a note on *multiformis* ad 21.6.8 *cultu ambitioso.*

subito a comitibus suis artius vinctus relato iam die ductus ad castra imperatori offertur reticens atque defixus Note the addition of *suis* adding pathos to the description. Hagendahl, 1921, 14 detected a Vergilianism here: *G.* 1.458 *at si, cum referetque diem condetque relatum* (where the subject is *sol*), so that the text must remain untouched. The tragicomedy of Procopius has come full circle. When he first presented himself to the people of Constantinople, they had been *stupore defixi*, while he himself had stared death in the face (*procliviorem viam ad mortem, ut sperabat, existimans advenisse*) not knowing what to say *implicatior ad loquendum diu tacitus stetit* (26.6.18, q.v.).

Amm.'s information is generally considered correct even though Socr. *HE* 4.5.3, Soz. *HE* 6.8.2, Nic. Call. 11.4 (= PG 146, 593) and Theoph. *Chron.* p. 55 De Boor report that Valens was able to take Procopius alive because Agilo and Gomoarius had delivered the usurper to him; Nicephorus even has the detail that they handed him over in chains. Zos. 4.8.3 only mentions that Procopius was captured, without giving the names of the men who delivered him to Valens. Procopius' capture, extradition and execution most probably happened on the same day, i.e. 27 May (366), as appears from *Consul. Constant.* a. 366 *et ipso anno idem hostis publicus et predo intra Frygiam salutarem et in Nacoliensium campo ab Aug. Valente oppressus atque extinctus est die VI kl. Iun*; cf. Kienast, 1996[2], 332, who, for obscure reasons, dates Procopius' death on 28 May. Cf. also Hier. *Chron.* a. 366 *Procopius...aput Frygiam salutarem extinctus et plurimi Procopianae partis caesi atque proscripti*. Socr. *HE* 4.9.8 mentions the end of May as the date for Procopius' execution. According to *Chron. Pasch.* a. 366 Procopius was arrested by Valentinian (*sic*) Augustus in Phrygia Salutaris, on the plain of Nacolia, in the month of Daisius, day 12 before the Kalends of July, i.e. 20 June; which must be wrong; Lenski, 2002, 81 n. 82.

statimque abscisa cervice discordiarum civilium gliscentes turbines sepelivit et bella Philost. *HE* 9.5 also mentions that Procopius was beheaded. Zos. 4.8.4 only reports that he was killed, but not in which way. Others have a more gruesome form of execution: two trees were bent down and each of Procopius' legs was fastened to one of them; then the trees were suddenly released, as a consequence of which the usurper was torn in two; Socr. *HE* 4.5.4 (καὶ οὕτως ὁ τύραννος διχοτομηθεὶς ἀπώλετο); see also Soz. *HE* 6.8.3; Joh. Ant. *fr.* 184.1 Müller = 276 Roberto; Theoph. *Chron.* p. 55 De Boor; Zon. 13.16. Seyfarth n. 114 in his bilingual edition remarks that this form of execution was a topos in myths and also occurs in HA *A* 7.4 (a soldier who had committed adultery with the wife of the man in whose house he was a lodger, was killed in this way), to which one may add Plut. *Alex.* 43.6.

Amm. does not waste one word on the tragic aspect of Procopius' death. The only thing that matters to him is that the disruption of the established order has come to an end. This is expressed in a highly wrought sentence rich in allusions to classical authors. For the archaism *gliscere* cf. Tac. *Ann.* 4.17.3 *neque aliud gliscentis discordiae remedium, quam si unus alterve maxime prompti subverterentur*. Amm. had used the metaphor of the whirlwind in 21.13.14 *Quid igitur superest, nisi ut turbinibus excitis occurramus succrescentis rabiem belli...oppressuri* (q.v.). It is found frequently in Cicero, e.g. *Pis.* 20 *in maximis turbinibus ac fluctibus rei publicae*. For *sepelire* in the sense of "to consign to oblivion" (OLD 3) cf. 16.12.70 *super Iuliani gloriosis actibus conticescens, quos sepelierat penitus, ni* eqs. Cf. Cic. *Phil.* 14.33 *vestra virtus neque oblivione eorum qui nunc sunt nec reticentia posterorum sepulta esse poterit*; Cic. *Man.* 30 *bellum exspectatione eius attenuatum atque imminutum est, adventu sublatum ac sepultum*. Cf. also the note ad 26.6.17 *qui sepulta*.

ad veteris Perpernae exemplum For *vetus* in this sense ("belonging to a past age"; OLD 5b) cf. 14.9.6 *Zenonem, illum veterem Stoicum*; 22.5.4 *Marci principis veteris dictum*. M. Perperna (or Perpenna) Veiento fought on the side of Sertorius since 77 BC. After several defeats against Pompey, he had Sertorius killed in 73 BC and seized his command over the Iberian peninsula. In 72 BC Perperna was executed by Pompey; Münzer, 1937. The story of Perperna is told most fully in Plut. *Pomp.* 20.3–4 τὸν δὲ Περπένναν ἀχθέντα πρὸς αὐτὸν ἀπέκτεινεν, *Sert.* 27.2–4 and App. *BC* 1.115.

post Sertorium, inter epulas obtruncatum dominatione paulisper potitus For prepositional phrases of this type see the note ad 22.2.2 *post exemptos*. The comma after *Sertorium* should be deleted. The incident is mentioned also by Vell. 2.30.1 *Tum M. Perpenna praetorius...Sertorium inter cenam Oscae interemit*. For *dominatio* referring to illegal power see the note ad 26.6.14 *ipsi quoque*. Amm. had earlier mentioned Sertorius in 24.6.7 *et miratur historia Rhodanum arma et loricam retinente Sertorio transnatatum* (q.v.). In the troublesome period after the deaths of Cinna and Sulla, Q. Sertorius (123–73 BC) managed to gain control over the Iberian peninsula and opposed the post-Sulla regime in Rome. His goal was to conquer Italy; however, he was defeated several times by armies of Pompey and in 73 BC he was killed by Perperna. See Schulten, 1923 and Konrad, 1994. Amm. mentions the murder of Sertorius again in 30.1.23 *verum excusabatur recens inusitatum facinus et pudendum necis exemplo Sertorianae*.

a frutectis, ubi latebat, extractus This detail is found only in App. *BC* 1.115: Περπέννας ὑπὸ θάμνῳ πόας ἐκρύφθη ('hid in a thicket'), δεδιὼς τοὺς οἰκείους μᾶλλον τῶν πολεμίων· λαβόντες δ' αὐτὸν ἱππέες τινες εἷλκον ἐς τὸν Πομπήιον...τέλος δ' ἦν τοῦτο τῷ περὶ Ἰβηρίαν πολέμῳ, τὸ καὶ Σερτωρίῳ τοῦ βίου γενόμενον. The fact that Perperna feared his own men more than his enemies may have seemed significant to Amm. in view of the perfidy of Procopius' friends, as well as Appianus' remark that Sertorius' death meant the end of the war.

oblatusque Pompeio eius iussu est interfectus Amm. does not mention Pompey's exemplary behaviour after the execution of Perperna, who had documents in his possession incriminating many leading personalities in Rome: Plut. *Pomp.* 20.4 φοβηθεὶς οὖν ὁ Πομπήϊος ταῦτα, μὴ μείζονας ἀναστήσῃ τῶν πεπαυμένων πολέμων, τόν τε Περπένναν ἀνεῖλε καὶ τὰς ἐπιστολὰς οὐδ' ἀναγνοὺς κατέκαυσεν ("Pompey, therefore, fearing that this might stir up greater wars than those now ended, put Perpenna to death and burned the letters without even reading them", tr. Perrin). Valens' vindictiveness after Procopius' revolt as described in 26.10.9–14 is in sharp contrast to Pompey's statesmanlike decision. Pompey is mentioned ten times by Amm. Seven times he is referred to as Pompeius (14.8.12, 16.7.10, 16.10.14, 17.11.4, q.v., 23.5.16, q.v., 26.9.9, 29.5.33), twice as Pompeius Magnus (14.11.32, 22.16.3, q.v.) and once as Gnaeus Pompeius (14.8.10).

Parique indignationis impetu…confestim non pensata ratione sunt interfecti **9.10**
Those authors, who incorrectly ascribe the betrayal of Procopius to the generals Agilo and Gomoarius (see the note ad 26.9.9 *subito a comitibus*), also mention that they, and not Florentius and Barchalba, were executed by being sawn in two. In reality Gomoarius' was probably spared after he took sides with Valens, and Agilo certainly survived his collaboration with Procopius as appears from 26.10.7; Lenski, 2002, 81 n. 83.

Amm. uses a more pointed expression than the usual *pari sorte* which he writes nine times. It emphasizes both the lack of discrimination and the rashness of the execution, repeated by *confestim* and *non pensata ratione*. Amm. uses *pensare* in the sense of 'to make up for', as in 14.11.22 *hominis enim salus beneficio nullo pensatur* or 'to ponder', as in 25.5.4 *nondum pensatis sententiis*. The phrase *pensata ratione* seems to be a contamination of *sententias*, c.q. *consilium pensare* (TLL X 1.1108.30–44; cf. 21.12.20 *id enim aequitate pensata statuerat placabilis imperator et clemens*) and *ratione pensare* (TLL X 1.1108.46–47; cf. Liv. 30.32.5 *cum oculis magis quam ratione pensarent vires*), meaning 'without weighing up the pros and cons'.

vel ipsa Iustitia iure caesos pronuntiaret Amm. loves such personifications of justice: 22.3.7 (cf. 28.6.1) *Ursuli vero necem…ipsa mihi videtur flesse Iustitia*; 22.10.6 (= 25.4.19) *vetus illa Iustitia*; 27.11.4 *vel ipsa repugnante Iustitia*; 31.15.7 *quod ipsa indicante Iustitia publicatum est*.

260   COMMENTARY

si rebellem et oppugnatorem internae quietis This second conditional clause is in accordance with the facts, so one would have expected something like *nunc autem* rather than *si*. Note, however, that the condemnation of Procopius represents the general feeling at that moment (*ut ferebatur*).

amplas eis memorabilis facti oportuerat deferri mercedes Amm. considers Valens' execution of Florentius and Barchalba to be an act of injustice. Although not in favour of Valens' reign, Amm. disliked even more any form of opposition against legitimate rule. Therefore, the lives of those who had handed over Procopius should have been spared and they should even have been honoured, because they had put an end to the disturbance of the public peace. Lindenbrog quotes a law of Arcadius and Honorius, issued in 397, to this effect *Cod. Theod.* 9.14.3.7 *Sane si quis ex his in exordio initae factionis studio verae laudis accensus ipse prodiderit factionem, et praemio a nobis et honore donabitur* and Sal. *Cat.* 30.6 *si quis indicavisset de coniuratione, quae contra rem publicam facta erat, praemium servo libertatem et sestertia centum, libero inpunitatem eius rei et sestertia ducenta*. The use of the indicative *oportuerat* is unexceptional, since impersonal *convenit* belongs to "die Ausdrücke des Sollens, Müssens, Könnens, Dürfens u. ä." (Szantyr 327; cf. Ehrismann 41), in which this use of the indicative is the rule. Note the difference between the imperfect *pronuntiaret*, indicating Iustitia's present opinion and *oportuerat* indicating what should have been done in the past.

9.11 *Excessit autem vita Procopius anno quadragesimo amplius mensibus decem* Since Procopius was executed on 27 May 366 (see the note ad 26.9.9 *subito a comitibus*), this means that he was born in July of 325. Cf. *PLRE* I, Procopius 4, which has the correct information that Procopius died aged forty on 27 May 366, but gives as his year of birth c. 326. Since Ammianus clearly mentions that Procopius died at the age of forty years and ten months, 325 is his most probable date of birth.

corpore non indecoro nec mediocris staturae, subaquilus humumque intuendo semper incedens This section is an elogium in miniature. Part of such an elogium is a physical description of the deceased ruler, since his *forma* reveals and reflects his character, according to ancient physiognomic tradition; see for this the note ad 21.16.19 *figura tali* and Sabbah 421 ff. The double negation with which the description opens sounds like a reluctant admission that Procopius was a fine figure of a man. *Subaquilus* ('darkish') is a conjecture by Heraeus, apparently chosen for its visual similarity to V's vox nihili *subcuitus*. The word is extremely rare: it occurs only once in a play on words, Pl. *Rud*. 422 *subvolturium – illud quidem 'subaquilum' volui dicere*, and once in HA *T* 30.15 as part of the description of queen Zenobia: *fuit vultu subaquilo, fusci coloris*. The conjecture seems completely arbitrary and unconnected to what follows. Admittedly, as is stated in the note ad *subniger* (22.16.19), compounds with *sub-* are a feature of physiognomic descriptions, but Sen. *Ep*. 90.13 *corpore incurvato et animo humum spectante* rather points in the direction of Gelenius' otherwise unattested *subcurvus*, which is preferable for paleographical reasons and confirmed by the portrait which Them. *Or*. 7.90 b draws of the usurper: ἀεὶ συγκεκυφώς, ἀεὶ συννεφής, ἐφελκόμενος τὰς ὀφρῦς, τὴν σιωπὴν ὥς τι σεμνὸν μετιών ('always bowed down, always gloomy, frowning, always veiling himself in quasi majestic silence'). As Sabbah 424 n. 73 saw, *humum intuendo* is the opposite of 21.16.19 *luce oculorum edita*, which depicts the majestic look of an emperor in direct communion with the gods. Other instances of people with downcast eyes are Petronius Probus in 29.6.9, who under the threat of war *oculos...vix attollens haerebat diu*, betraying his indecision in this way, or the schemer Terentius in 30.1.2 *demisse ambulans semperque submaestus, sed quoad vixerat, acer dissensionum instinctor*, who evidently walked with lowered eyes to conceal his evil intentions. In a more positive sense, downcast eyes are mentioned as a characteristic of provincial bishops, denoting their modesty in 27.3.15 *supercilia humum spectantia perpetuo numini verisque eius cultoribus ut puros commendant et verecundos*.

perque morum tristium latebras Matthews 201 rightly calls this "a marvellous phrase", but his translation (Procopius lived) "in the shadows of a sad nature" is too romantic. The phrase is a prime example of the gen. inversus, for which see the note ad 25.7.11 *hac perniciosa*. Amm. gives a double qualification to Procopius: 'by his sombre and close character'. This tallies with 26.6.1 *vita moribusque castigatior, licet occultus erat et taciturnus*.

illius similis Crassi, quem in vita semel risisse Lucilius affirmat et Tullius Amm. refers here to M. Licinius Crassus, grandfather of the triumvir and nicknamed Agelastus; Plin. *Nat*. 7.79 *Ferunt Crassum, avum Crassi in Parthis interempti, numquam risisse, ob id Agelastum vocatum*. The anecdote is told by Cicero in *Fin*. 5.92 *in eo M. Crasso, quem semel ait in vita risisse Lucilius* (*fr*. 1299/1300 Marx) and with a minor variation in *Tusc*. 3. 31. Macrobius adds an interesting commentary in *Sat.* 2.1.6 *neque ego sum nescius vos nec tristitiam nec nubilum vultum in bonis ducere, nec Crassum illum quem Cicero auctore Lucilio semel in vita risisse scribit magnopere mirari.* Jerome mentions the story three times, characteristically omitting Cicero, but directly referring to Lucilius, *adv. Rufin.* 1.30 *Crassum, quem semel in vita dicit risisse Lucilius;* cf. *epist.* 7.5 and 130.13. The full meaning of Lucilius' joke becomes clear from Tert. *anim.* 52.3 (people die from very different causes) *per risum, ut P. Crassus*: Crassus' only fit of laughter cost him his life; see Waszink's commentary ad loc. In 23.3.1 (q.v.) Amm. mentions the triumvir M. Licinius Crassus and his son Publius; the L. Licinius Crassus of 30.4.6 is the orator and consul of 95 BC; see Angliviel de la Beaumelle n. 251 ad loc. and Münzer, 1925.

This is the only time that Amm. mentions the satirist Lucilius; see for him e.g. Christes, 1999. For Cicero, to whom Amm. refers more often than to any other author, see the note ad 26.1.2 *haec quidam*.

et, quod est mirandum, quoad vixerat, incruentus Cf. Philost. *HE* 9.5 ἐγκρατὴς ἀναιμωτὶ τῆς βασιλείας γίνεται. This is a surprisingly positive conclusion of the description of Procopius' revolt, and in glaring contrast to the elogium of Valens, of whom Amm. says *in sanguinem saeviebat et dispendia locupletum* (31.14.5). The complimentary qualification *incruentus* is given to Helpidius in 21.6.9 and by implication to Julian 22.14.2 *Galli similis fratris licet incruentus* (q.v.) and Gratian 31.10.18 *ni vergens in ludibriosos actus natura laxantibus proximis semet ad vana studia Caesaris Commodi convertisset licet hic incruentus*. This positive evaluation, however, does not make Amm.'s condemnation of Procopius' revolt less severe. He would have agreed with Augustine's verdict *bon. coniug.* 14.16 *nec tyrannicae factionis perversitas laudabilis erit, si regia clementia tyrannus subditos tractet; nec vituperabilis ordo regiae potestatis, si rex crudelitate tyrannica saeviat* (quoted by Neri, 1997, 79).

CHAPTER 10

Introduction

This chapter deals with the last convulsions of Procopius' revolt and the reprisals that followed it. After the execution of the insurgent, the *protector* Marcellus, a relative of Procopius, took the lead. His first action was to kill Serenianus, one of Valens' closest associates. Ammianus, who heartily disliked this man because of his cruelty, applauds his execution. Marcellus' continuation of the revolt, however, was doomed right from the start. The support from the Goths, on whom he had based his hopes, never materialized, and he had reckoned without his host in the person of Equitius, the commander of Illyricum, who on his way to assist Valens, had laid siege to Philippopolis. As soon as Equitius heard that Marcellus had taken over from Procopius, he quickly and without effort outmanoeuvred him. Marcellus was kidnapped by special forces, tortured and killed (§ 1–5).

This was the starting signal for a spate of executions of people, who were accused of having sided with Procopius. The citizens of Philippopolis were the first to suffer for backing the wrong horse. Valens and his brother showed some leniency towards prominent supporters of Procopius like Araxius and Euphrasius (§6–8).

Others, however, were less fortunate. Sections 9–14 are a highly coloured and personal indictment of Valens' cruelty in pursuing the following of Procopius. This is something of a recurrent theme in Ammianus' work. The passage may be compared to his account of the reprisals after the revolts of Magnentius in 14.5, Silvanus in 15.6 and Theodorus in 29.1. In these three cases Ammianus insists, as he does here, that the emperors had the right, even the duty, to defend their position against usurpers, but that their excessive measures against their opponents caused more harm than the revolts themselves. The passage also shows striking similarities to Libanius' 24th Oration. It is especially noteworthy that in his complaint Libanius links the cruelty of the emperors to the natural disasters of the period, just as Ammianus places his description of the tsunami of the year 365 (§15–19) immediately after his account of the reprisals against the supporters of Procopius.

The description of the tsunami has received much attention in recent years, both as a splendid piece of writing in its own right, and because it offers valuable insights into the source material consulted by Ammianus, and the way in which he adapted it for his own purposes. There can be little doubt, that Ammianus wanted his readers to reflect upon the relation between this natural disaster and the political upheavals he had dealt with in Book 26 and was going to deal with in the rest of his work. For more background on this passage the reader is referred to the introduction to sections 15-19.

10.1 *Isdem fere diebus* I.e. shortly after Procopius had been killed on May 27, 366 (see for this date the note ad 26.9.9 *subito*). Cf. Zos. 4.8.3, where it is said that after the encounter of Nacolia not only Procopius, but Marcellus too was caught, οὐ πολλῷ...ὕστερον.

protector Marcellus, eiusdem cognatus See for *protector* the note ad 21.16.20 *Iovianus etiamtum protector domesticus*. What kind of family ties existed between Procopius and Marcellus (*PLRE* I, Marcellus 5), is not known, but they surely were one of the reasons why Marcellus deemed himself entitled to succeed Procopius. See for dynastic loyalty as a factor in the process of choosing a new emperor the note ad 26.7.10 *quod Constanti filiam*.

agens apud Nicaeam praesidium The commander of a garrison is called *praesidiorum praefectus* (24.2.21, q.v.) or *-magister* (24.4.26). His task *is agere (agitare) praesidium*; cf. 18.8.2 *praesidium per eos tractus agentes*; 29.5.27 *ad agitanda praesidia*. Nicaea, *quae in Bithynia mater est urbium* (26.1.3, q.v.), had been brought on Procopius' side again by the former tribune Rumitalca, at the time Procopius' *cura palatii* (26.8.1), after the usurper himself had left the city out of fear for the approaching Iovii and Victores (26.7.14). Vadomarius then tried to reconquer Nicaea for Valens (26.8.2), but his attempt apparently failed (cf. 26.8.3). Of Rumitalca nothing more is heard, and if we had only the *Res Gestae* at our disposal, the natural inference from the present text would be that Marcellus became commander in Nicaea and replaced Rumitalca. However, Philostorgius (*HE* 9.5) reports that Procopius appointed Florentius (*PLRE* I, Florentius 4) as commander of the troops stationed in Nicaea (φρούραρχος...τῆς πόλεως). Since there is no reason to reject this testimony, Marcellus must have become commander of the city only after Florentius had left Nicaea to follow Procopius (26.9.8).

proditione militum et interitu Procopii cognito Zosimus has a different report on these events. According to him, Marcellus had murdered Serenianus by order of Procopius, who welcomed the report of the execution, 4.7.1 Τούτῳ τῷ προτερήματι ('success') Προκόπιος ἐπαρθεὶς κτλ. The betrayal of Procopius by Florentius and Barchalba, reported in 26.9.9 (see the note ad *subito a comitibus*), directly led to the usurper's capture and subsequent death, but already Gomoarius (26.9.6) and Agilo had proved treacherous (*Agilo rem excursu prodidit repentino*, 26.9.7, q.v.).

Serenianum intra palatium clausum medio noctis horrore incautum adortus occidit On Valens' *comes domesticorum* Serenianus see the note ad 26.5.3. As has been reported in 26.8.11, Procopius had imprisoned him in Nicaea after the capture of Cyzicus. Once again Zosimus has a different story. According to him (4.6.5, quoted ad 26.8.7 *ad quam*), Serenianus was arrested and executed by Marcellus not in Nicaea, but during his flight from Cyzicus to Lydia.

Regrettably, TLL refers to the Onomasticon for the word *palatium*, which gradually looses its connection with the Roman hill of that name. One of the earliest instances of this shift in meaning is *Origo Const.* 5.20 *in Orientis partibus...Licinius omnes christianos a palatio iussit expelli.* It is also illustrated by Aur. Vict. *Caes.* 19.4 *apud palatium Romae* and 14.6 *Ipse* (Hadrianus), *uti beatis locupletibus mos, palatia exstruere*; Auson. 1. 25–27 Green *aurea et Augusti palatia iussus adire* (in Trier) /*Augustam subolem grammaticus docui*; *epit.* 40.10 *haud longe Sirmio eminet locus palatio ibidem constructo*; *Cod. Theod.* 15.1.35 (a. 396) *de palatiis aut praetoriis iudicum*; cf. Ziegler, 1949, 10–15 and Alessio, 2006.

Amm. uses *palatium* or *regia* for the residence of the Augustus (16.12.67 *in palatio Constanti*; cf. 15.1.2 *Mediolanum advenit ingressusque regiam* eqs.) or the Caesar (14.1.3 *per palatii pseudothyrum introducta*; cf. 14.1.6 *latenter intromissi per posticas in regiam*; 20.4.14 *fremituque ingenti omnes petiverunt palatium*; cf. 20.4.21 *occupavere volucriter regiam* and 26.6.18 *palatium pessimo pede festinatis passibus introiit*). In 15.5.31 *regia penetrata Silvanum extractum aedicula*, *regia* is used of the residence of the short-lived usurper and in 19.1.10 *quo funere regia maesta* it refers to the court of king Grumbates. For this meaning see also the note ad 26.7.6 *Araxius*. In Nisibis there is a *palatium* for the use of the emperor when on official journeys, which Jovian refuses to enter, 25.8.17 *ut ingressus palatio more succederet principum*. There *palatium* is the equivalent of *praetorium*, for which see De Jonge's notes ad 14.5.8 *comitatus* and the heading in *Cod. Theod.* 15.1.35 quoted above. This is also the case in the present passage and in 30.5.16 *apud Sirmium repentino fragore nubium fulmen excussum palatii et curiae partem incendit*. The terms are distinguished in 14.7.10 *praestrictis palatii ianuis contempto Caesare, quem videri decuerat, ad praetorium cum pompa sollemni perrexit*, where, as De Jonge observes, *praetorium* is the equivalent of *domus praetoria*, the official residence of the praetorian prefect. Finally, *palatium* can denote the court and its personnel rather than a building, as in 26.5.4 *Et post haec* (q.v.).

For *medio noctis horrore* see the note ad 21.2.2. There are notes on *incautus*, here used in its active sense, ad 21.10.4 and 23.3.5.

10.2 *nam si victoriae superfuisset incultis moribus homo et nocendi acerbitate conflagrans Valentique ob similitudinem morum et genitalis patriae vicinitatem acceptus* For *superesse* in the sense of *superstes esse* cf. 30.1.17 *si huic irrisioni superfuerit* ("if he survived these trickeries", Rolfe). Serenianus, a compatriot of the Pannonian emperors (26.5.3), shares the bad qualities Amm. attributes to them, viz. boorishness and cruelty, for which see the note ad 26.1.4 *qui cum*. The expression *incultis moribus* is a Sallustianism (*Jug.* 85.39), also found in Sol. 7.21; Fesser 22. Amm. calls him *crudelem ut Phalarim* in § 5.

There is a remarkable number of characters in Ammianus with a compulsive inclination towards harming other people: Gallus possesses *incitatum propositum ad nocendum* (14.7.4); Eusebius, Constantius' chamberlain, was *effusior ad nocendum* (14.11.2, = 30.8.3 about Valentinian); the old general Arbitio *inexplebili quodam laedendi proposito conscientiam polluebat* (15.2.4); Valens was *promptior ad nocendum* (26.10.12) and his brother Valentinian *ad acerbitatem proclivior* (28.6.22). The latter is called *trux suopte ingenio* in 29.3.2.

This is the only instance in Amm. of *conflagrare* in a metaphorical meaning. It is found already in Cic. *Ver.* 1.41 *invidia conflagravit*; TLL IV 234.52–65. The expression *genitalis patria* probably refers to Serenianus' birthplace, as in 22.9.2, where it is said of Julian *natus enim illic diligebat eam* (Constantinople) *ut genitalem patriam et colebat*. The adjective *acceptus* is rare in Amm. The only other instances are 26.10.8 (Phronimius) *ea re, quod divo Iuliano fuit acceptus* and 29.1.8 (Theodorus) *altis humilibusque iuxta acceptus*.

occultas voluntates principis introspiciens ad crudelitátem propensióris multas innocentium ediderat strages Amm. probably had Tac. *Ann.* 1.7.7 in mind: *ad introspiciendas etiam procerum voluntates*. The comparative *propensioris* is chosen to produce a cursus velox. Amm. again anticipates his report on the purges described in sections 9–14 of this chapter. For Amm.'s use of the terms *princeps* and *principatus* see the relevant notes ad 20.2.1, 20.4.8 and 20.4.12.

Quo interfecto idem Marcellus occupata celeri cursu Calchedone concrepantibus paucis, quos vilitas et desperatio trudebat in scelus, umbram principatus funesti capessit For anaphoric *idem* see the note ad 20.4.5 *cum isdem*. In the note ad 26.2.3 it is argued that *concrepantibus* does not denote indiscriminate shouting, but a well-defined demand. In view of 20.4.14 *Augustum Iulianum horrendis clamoribus concrepabant* it is not unlikely that a kind of acclamation is meant. The city of Chalcedon had fiercely opposed Valens' attempt to bring it under his control (26.8.2–3, q.v.), but apparently changed sides after Procopius' death, so that Marcellus had to gain possession of it anew.

10.3

Again Zosimus' version is different. According to him, Procopius had given an imperial robe to Marcellus, 4.8.4 εὑρὼν δὲ βασιλικήν τινα παρὰ Μαρκέλλῳ στολὴν ὑπὸ Προκοπίου δεδομένην αὐτῷ κτλ. As the description of Procopius' followers has made abundantly clear, such revolts attract desperadoes: *emergebant ex vulgari faece nonnulli desperatione consiliisque ductantibus caecis* (26.7.7). The disparaging phrase *umbra* ('a sham') *principatus* is also used with regard to Jovian; see the note ad 25.5.8 *docet Saporem*.

gemina ratione fallente Amm. uses *gemina ratione* several times in the meaning 'for a twofold reason', e.g. 15.10.7 *manesque eius ratione gemina religiose coluntur*. *Fallente* is added to make clear that Marcellus' considerations were misguided right from the start. In other authors the expression is rare and usually means 'in two ways', as in Plin. *Nat.* 33.81 *gemina ratione praedicunt*; Chalcid. *Comm.* 2.310 (p. 310.17W) *Possibilitas autem gemina ratione intellegitur*; Anon. *de mach. bell.* 10.1 *excipienti gemina ratione videtur afferre perniciem*.

Gothorum tria milia regibus iam lenitis ad auxilium transmissa Procopio Constantianam praetendenti necessitudinem The reading *transmissa* for V's *erant missa* is a brilliant emendation by Petschenig, 1892, 521–522, who noted that Gelenius had introduced the 'Verschlimmbesserung' *quae* before *ad societatem*. As a parallel for *transmissa* Petschenig quotes 25.10.9 (ut) *auctoresque seditionis ad comitatum vincti transmitterentur*. The last we heard about the Goths was, that they prepared for an invasion of Thrace; see the note ad 26.6.11 *docetur relationibus*. Zos. 4.7.2, quoted in the note ad 26.7.8 *restabat*, reports that Procopius had sent envoys to a Gothic ruler on the other side of the Danube, and in return had got ten thousand men as allies (note the difference in numbers: Amm., who in scholarly literature is given more credit, speaks of 3000 men). We know from Amm. himself that it was the Thervingian leader Athanaric (*PLRE* I, Athanaricus) who had provided Procopius with these auxiliary troops (*Athanaricus, Thervingorum iudex, in quem, ut ante relatum est, ob auxilia missa Procopio dudum Valens commoverat signa*, 31.3.4). In 27.4.1 and 27.5.1 Amm. also refers to the support given to Procopius by the Goths, as does Zosimus in 4.10.1: οὗτοι δὲ ἦσαν οὓς ὁ τῶν Σκυθῶν ἡγούμενος ἔτυχε Προκοπίῳ συμμάχους ἐκπέμψας. Cf. further Eun. *fr.* 37 ἀγγέλλεται τῶν Σκυθῶν στράτευμα πλησίον ἤδη που τυγχάνειν, οὓς ὁ Προκόπιος εἰς συμμαχίαν ἐξεκεκλήκει παρὰ τοῦ Σκυθῶν βασιλέως. ("it was announced [to Valens] that the levy of Scythians, which Procopius had summoned to his aid from the Scythian king, was now close at hand", tr. Blockley).

Amm. in 31.3.4, Zosimus in 4.7.2 and 4.10.1, and Eunapius in *fr.* 37 all make one Gothic leader responsible for the help sent to Procopius, but since Amm. here speaks of 'kings' in the plural, the conclusion must be that Athanaric was not the only Gothic chief who did so (see for a discussion of the terms *iudex* and *rex* to denote leaders of the Goths Heather, 1991, 97–98, who discerns "two distinct levels of leadership", r*eges* being subordinated to the *iudex*, at least among Athanaric's Thervingi). Amm. fails to explain why the kings of the Goths were by now (*iam*) more favourably disposed, but it is obvious that their respect for the founder of the Constantinian dynasty (*Constantinianam* should be read instead of *Constantianam*, see below), to which Procopius professed to belong, had decided them to join sides with him. It was with Constantine that in 332 the Goths had made a peace treaty (cf. the note ad 22.7.8 *propinquos Gothos*) and it is to this treaty that Amm. refers when in 27.5.1 he speaks about Valens' wish to know *quam ob causam gens amica Romanis foederibusque longae pacis obstricta tyranno dederat adminicula bellum principibus legitimis inferenti*. Eunapius also refers to the treaty (*fr.* 37): ὁ μὲν γὰρ ἔφασκε βασιλεῖ δεδωκέναι κατὰ συμμαχίαν καὶ ὅρκους· ("the Scythian king claimed that he had sent his men to the Emperor [i.e. Procopius] under the terms of the treaty", tr. Blockley).

It is relevant for a proper understanding of the present text to quote 27.5.1 at greater length. In Amm.'s account in Book 27 the Goths, in order to defend their sending of troops to Procopius, produced a letter of the usurper in which he asserted that he merely had assumed the sovereignty to which he was entitled as a close kinsman of the house of Constantine (*qui ut factum firma defensione purgarent, litteras eiusdem obtulere Procopii ut generis Constantiniani propinquo imperium sibi debitum sumpsisse commemorantis*). Note the words *generis*

Constantiniani. It would seem that these words alone suffice to prove that in the present text *Constantianam* is a scribal error for *Constantinianam*, but there is more. It is true that Procopius used the daughter and the widow of Constantius II to buttress his claims to the throne (26.7.10, 26.9.3), but, in the first place, Faustina and her daughter not only were wife and child of Constantine's son Constantius II, but they belonged eo ipso to the Constantinian dynasty, and, secondly, Procopius used the women for reasons of internal politics. It would have been rather odd, however, for the usurper to boast about his kinship with Constantius in his dealings with the Goths. After all, it was with Constantine, not with his son that they had made the peace treaty which "for over thirty years...dictated the nature of Gotho-Roman relations" (Heather, 1991, 107) and it was Constantine who had erected a statue to Athanaric's father in Constantinople (Them. Or. 15.190d–191a). Moreover, it was primarily through his being akin to Constantine's nephew Julian, not to his son Constantius, that Procopius could claim to belong to the *stirps imperatoria*, as is made abundantly clear in the *Res Gestae* and elsewhere (23.3.2, 26.6.1, 26.6.18 and 26.7.10 with the relevant notes). Cf. in this respect also Eunapius' *fr.* 37, where it is i.a. stated that the king of the Goths "justified his sending of assistance to Procopius on the ground of the latter's kinship with Julian" (ἐκείνου δὲ προστιθέντος τὸν Ἰουλιανόν, καὶ ὅτι διὰ τὴν ἐκείνου ἐδεδώκει συγγένειαν).

There is a note on *necessitudo* ad 20.8.21.

ad societatem suam parva mercede traduci posse existimabat Marcellus' confidence, that he would be able to bring the Goths over to his side, must have been based in the first place on the fact that he was a relative of Procopius (cf. 26.10.1 *eiusdem cognatus*).

quodque gesta in Illyrico etiamtum latebant Marié's translation "et d'autre part, en Illyricum, on ne savait pas encore ce qui s'était passé" is ambiguous at best. Marcellus must be understood as the complement of *latebant*. So, rightly, Hamilton: "he was as yet unaware of what had happened in Illyricum". Cf. 20.2.5 *quae scientiam eius latebant*. 'The events in Illyricum' most probably refer to Procopius' failed attempt to gain the support of the troops there, and the subsequent measures taken by Equitius, as reported in 26.7.11–12. For Illyricum see ad 26.5.11 *Valentinianus*.

Inter quae tam trepida A similar opening phrase introducing an important new development, is 22.2.1 *Inter quae tam suspensa*. One of the

10.4

reasons why the situation is so tense is that the parties involved lack information about each other's movements, a recurrent feature in the entire description of Procopius' revolt and its aftermath.

speculationibus fidis Equitius doctus conversam molem belli totius in Asiam Cf. 14.2.15 *horum adventum praedocti speculationibus fidis rectores militum*. The noun *speculatio* is not found before the end of the fourth century. Augustine uses it no fewer than 23 times, because it is the translation of Sion: *in psalm.* 50.22 *interpretatur enim Sion speculatio*. Ausonius uses it for the view from a villa in *Mos.* 326 *utque suis fruitur dives speculatio terris*. More in line with its meaning in Amm. ('reconnaissance') is Macrobius, who calls the Doloneia in the Iliad *speculatio nocturna* (*Sat.* 5.2.15). The phrase *moles belli* is probably derived from Livy, who uses it frequently in the sense of 'a huge war', e.g. Liv. 21.41.2 *minorem haud dubie molem belli*; cf. also Tac. *Hist.* 2.74.2 *in tanta mole belli*. Here it rather seems to mean "the centre of action" (Lenski, 2002, 81). Equitius was *per eas regiones* (i.e. Illyricum) *militum rector* (26.7.11). See for him further 26.1.4, 26.5.3 and 26.5.11 with the relevant notes.

degressus per Succos Philippopolim clausam praesidiis hostium, Eumolpiada veterem, reserare magna vi conabatur Having been informed that Procopius was completely occupied with the military operations in Asia, Equitius leaves his defensive position on the Succi-pass (cf. 26.7.12, q.v.) and moves eastwards. On Philippopolis/Eumolpias, the capital of the province Thracia, see the note ad 22.2.2 *emensa declivitate*. In §6 Amm. relates the subsequent fate of the *praesidia hostium* of Philippopolis. For *reserare* in a military context cf. Verg. *A.* 12.584 *urbem alii reserare iubent et pandere portas*. The juxtaposition of old and new names is found also in 14.8.7 *Commagena, nunc Euphratensis* and *Hierapoli, vetere Nino*; 22.2.2 *Philippopolim...Eumolpiada veterem* (q.v.); 22.8.14 *Bithyniae...quam veteres dixere Mygdoniam* (q.v.); 22.15.2 *Arabas, quos Saracenos nunc appellamus*; 23.5.16 *Massagetas, quos Alanos nunc appellamus* (cf. 31.2.12); 28.3.1 *Augusta...quam veteres appellavere Lundinium*. It is not always clear why Amm. gives such additions, but in the cases of Philippopolis, Hierapolis and Augusta the reason may be that Amm. wanted to help his readers in discerning these cities from others with the same name. See for Philippopolis in this respect Kolendo, 1992.

urbem admodum opportunam et impedituram eius appetitus For *opportunus*, 'strategically situated', see the note ad 20.7.16 *munimenti*. As in 24.4.10 *sed ut erat necessarius appetitus, ita effectu res difficillima* (q.v.), *appetitus* seems to mean 'plan', 'intention'; cf. the note ad 15.5.26.

si pone relicta adiumenta Valenti laturus...festinare ad Haemimontum cogeretur The abl. abs. *relicta* lacks a Head; this would have been *ea* (= Philippopoli). *Adminicula* goes with *laturus*. For *pone* see the note ad 20.11.22. *Haemimontus* with its capital Adrianopolis was one of the six provinces of the diocese Thracia (Rolfe's "a place on Mt. Haemus" is wrong). Cf. 27.4.11–12, Oberhummer, 1912 and the note ad 21.10.3 *vicinae*.

nondum enim apud Nacoliam gesta compererat See 26.9.7 for the events at Nacolia.

verum paulo postea cognita levi praesumptione Marcelli As is observed in TLL X 2. 969.5–7, *praesumptio* is a vox media, like its English derivative, but it is far more often used *in malam partem*, 'arrogance', than in the neutral meaning 'supposition'. There are countless instances of the word in its negative sense in Tertullian and Augustine; this is the only time it occurs in Amm. It refers to Marcellus' usurpation and has the connotation of illegitimacy and recklessness, which is emphasized by *levi*. In TLL X 2.972.32 it is compared to Anon. Vales. 12.64 *de praesumptione regni* ("with regard to his assumption of the rule", tr. Rolfe).

10.5

milites missi sunt audaces et prompti, qui eum raptum ut deditum noxae mancipium in custodiam compegerunt The combination of *audax* and *promptus*, 'bold' and 'resolute', is found from Sallust onward, e.g. *Cat.* 32.2 *quorum cognoverat promptam audaciam*; Tac. *Hist.* 1.48.4 *audax, callidus, promptus*; *Ann.* 1.57.1 *nam barbaris, quanto quis audacia promptus* (= 14.40.2), *tanto magis fidus rebusque motis potior habetur*. Amm. uses it in 17.12.8 *ne eos quidem prompta iuvit audacia*. For *rapere* used of a speedy arrest, cf. 15.7.2 *Philoromum enim aurigam rapi praeceptum* and 21.4.1 *eum vi incautum rapere festinabat* (q.v.). It is not known whether at the time of his arrest Marcellus was still in Chalcedon (cf. 26.10.3). The comparison *ut deditum noxae mancipium* must be taken with the following words. *Dedere noxae* is a juridical t.t., 'to hand over as compensation', cf. Gaius *Inst.* 4.75 *uti liceret patri dominove...noxae dedere*, here used less strictly in the sense of 'to hand over for punishment', as in Col. 1 *pr.* 3 *rem rusticam pessimo cuique servorum velut carnifici noxae dedimus*; TLL V 266.44–49. The phrase *in custodiam compingere* is a unique variation on *in vincula compingere*, for which see the note ad 26.7.4 *ne quid*.

unde post dies productus lateribus sulcatis acerrime pariaque perpessis consortibus Since there are no parallels for *post dies* without an attribute, we must assume that either a numeral or an adjective has been lost. Petschenig's *post dies ⟨paucos⟩ productus* is paleographically attractive and a common expression in Livy and Tacitus. Possibly even better is ⟨*paucos*⟩ *post dies*, which is found with greater frequency in Livy (22 times), Tacitus (5) and Suetonius (4). Amm.'s words perfectly illustrate the rule mentioned in the note ad 26.7.4 *ne quid* (q.v.), that accused people only stayed in prison temporarily, until the final decision of the judge c.q. their execution. Apart from Amm., who uses it three times (also in 14.9.5 and 28.1.10), the expression *latera sulcare* is found in Hier. *epist.* 1.3 *cum lividas carnes ungula cruenta pulsaret et sulcatis lateribus dolor quaereret veritatem* and *Cod. Theod.* 9.16.6 *si convictus ad proprium facinus detegentibus repugnaverit pernegando, sit eculeo deditus ungulisque sulcantibus latera perferat poenas proprio dignas facinore*. In Claud. *Rapt. Pros.* 2.340 the vulture feeding on Tityos' liver is called *sulcator lateris*. The mention of the *ungula* ('claw') in Jerome and the vulture's beak in Claudian, suggest that the flanks were lacerated by a hook. The expression *latera fodicare* (26.10.13, 29.1.28) must refer to the same treatment. All instances of *latera sulcare* or – *fodicare* are found in the context of judicial enquiries, where torture is practiced either in order to extort a confession or to compel the victim to name his accomplices. For the various forms of juridical torture see in general Ehrhardt, 1937, Vergote, 1972, 120–123, Grodzynski, 1984, MacMullen, 1986 and Harries, 1999, 122–134; for torture in the *Res Gestae* Angliviel de la Beaumelle, 1992. As a *protector*, Marcellus belonged to the *honestiores*. Some of his followers must have been *honestiores* too. Customarily such individuals were exempt from torture (Jones 519; Garnsey, 1970, 234–259), but there was at least one important exception to this rule: in cases of usurpations and other forms of high treason *honestiores* were also liable to torture. Cf. e.g. *Cod. Theod.* 9.5.1, Amm. 19.12.17 (with De Jonge's note) *a quaestionibus vel cruentis nullam Corneliae leges exemere fortunam*, and 26.10.9, where Amm. speaks about partisans of Procopius: *carnifex enim et unci et cruentae quaestiones sine discrimine ullo aetatum et dignitatum per fortunas omnes et ordines grassabantur*. Followers of other usurpers (Magnentius, Silvanus) suffered the same fate.

See for them 14.5.1-2, 15.6.1-4 and see further Chauvot, 2000. As to the purpose of torture, it is worth quoting Angliviel de la Beaumelle, 1992, 101: "Le droit pénal confère à la torture une double fonction: elle constitue un mode d'interrogatoire spécial (susceptible dans certains cas d'être imposé à des témoins) destiné à fournir la preuve fondamentale de la culpabilité qu'est l'aveu. Elle peut jouer d'autre part le rôle d'une peine autonome qui s'ajoute alors à la sanction principale".

interiit hoc favorabilis solo, quod abstulit Serenianum e medio For *favorabilis* ('deserving sympathy') cf. 17.13.25 *ore omnium favorabilis*, 23.5.15 *favorabilis studio concordi omnium* and 26.7.3. It is already found in Sen. *clem.* 1.10.2 (clementia) *gratum ac favorabilem reddidit*. This is the only instance of *auferre e medio* 'to eliminate' in Amm. It is not found before the fourth century. Cf. Ambros. *in psalm. cxviii*, 3 *si talis est qui emendari non queat, aufertur e medio, ne graviora committat; mortuus enim iam nescit errare*. Marcellus' death is reported, apart from by Ammianus and Zosimus (4.8.4), by Johannes Antiochenus: (Valens) ἀπέσφαξε δὲ καὶ τὸν Μάρκελλον καὶ πολλοὺς ἄλλους, ἐκ τῆς εἰς βασιλείαν ὑποψίας (*fr.* 184 Müller = 277 Roberto).

crudelem ut Phalarim et illi fidum, quia doctrinarum diritatem causis inanibus praetexebat Phalaris is known as the embodiment of cruelty since Pindar's *Pythian Ode* 1.96 in Greek and Cic. *Ver.* 4.73 *crudelissimus omnium tyrannorum Phalaris* in Latin literature. See Otto, 1890 (1962), 277. The mention of the tyrant aptly introduces the account of Valens' terrible reprisals after Procopius' revolt.

V reads *Falari mille et ille fidum*. Gelenius has *Falarim illi et illi*, which looks like a conjecture to produce a dative agreeing with *fidum*. The repetition of *ille* is puzzling. The only comparable phrase would be *ille vel ille*, used by Ovid in the sense of 'anyone, no matter who' in *Am.* 1.8.83-84 *Quin etiam discant oculi lacrimare coacti / et faciant udas ille vel ille genas* (also in *Ars* 1.227 and *Fast.* 5.188), for which, however, there is no parallel in Amm. or, for that matter, in any prose author.

In view of the fact that proper names are a constant source of corruption in V, we must consider the possibility that the name of Perillus is behind the repetition of *ille* or *illi*. The sculptor, who offered the monstrous bull to Phalaris, and ultimately perished in it himself, is often mentioned in the same breath as the tyrant and called as cruel as his master, e.g. Prop. 2.25.11-12 *nonne fuit satius duro servire tyranno / et gemere in tauro, saeve Perille, tuo?*; Ov. *Ars* 1.653-654 *Et Phalaris tauro violenti membra Perilli / torruit*; Ov. *Tr.* 5.1.53-54 *ipse Perilleo Phalaris permisit in aere/edere mugitus et bovis ore queri.* Plin. *Nat.* 34.89 *Perillum nemo laudet saeviorem Phalaride tyranno.* So behind *ut Falari mille et ille* we surmise *ut Phalarim vel Perillum.* Amm. likes such double comparisons, cf. 22.12.4 *ut Pygmaei vel Thiodamas;* 28.3.9 *ut Furius Camillus vel Cursor Papirius,* or even 28.4.9 *ut Semiramin Parthi vel Cleopatras Aegyptus aut Artemisiam Cares vel Zenobiam Palmyreni.*

That would leave us with *et fidum* without the incomprehensible reference *illi.* Amm. uses the adjective *fidus* in the meaning 'trustworthy', 'trusted' very often, both with a dative complement and without (e.g. 26.10.11 *ut familiaris suscipiebatur et fidus;* 31.12.9 *ut conscius arcanorum et fidus*). By whom then was Serenianus trusted? In the first place of course by his fellow-countryman Valens (see section 2; Rolfe's "loyal to Procopius" is at any rate wrong), whose henchman he would have become, had he lived (note that Serenianus played on the cruelty of his superior: *occultas voluntates principis introspiciens ad crudelitatem propensioris,* just as Perillus had done: Oros. *hist.* 1.20.3 *nam Perillus quidam aeris opifex adfectans tyranni amicitiam, aptum munus crudelitati illius ratus, taurum aeneum fecit*). But by leaving the reference unspecified Amm. also entitles us to think of what he had reported in 14.7.7. Serenianus had been found guilty of *laesa maiestas* involving magical practices. Nevertheless, Gallus had let him escape execution, *incertum qua potuit suffragatione absolvi aperte convictus,* cf. 14.11.23 *praestrigiis quibusdam absolutum.* The next clause explains how Serenianus, in spite of these magical practices, had retained the confidence of his superiors: "il voilait sous de vaines prétextes (*causis inanibus,* cf. *praestrigiis quibusdam*) une science maudite", tr. Marié (whose note ad loc. regrettably does not tally with her translation). Both *causae inanes* and *praetexere* are reminiscent of Vergil: *A.* 9.219 *causas nequiquam nectis inanis* and 4.172 *hoc praetexit nomine culpam* respectively. TLL X 2.1046.39–40 is uncertain whether to take *causis inanibus* as a dative or an abl. and opts for the wrong alternative. Finally *quia,* a conjecture of Heraeus for V's *a,* which provides a plausible causal link with the preceding *fidum.* Heraeus supposed a lacuna *cursus causa,* but this hypothesis is superfluous if we read *vel Perillum et fidum.* Instead of *quia* one might think of the copula *dum* and explain the corruption as the consequence of haplography. It must be admitted, however, that *fidum dum* would be a bad case of cacophony. Parallels for *dum* with imperfect indicative are given in the note ad 25.7.1 *Quae dum,* to which may be added 27.10.14, 28.1.34, 30.5.3, 31.5.6 and 31.13.8. These considerations would result in the following text: *crudelem ut Phalarim vel Perillum et fidum, dum* (or *quia*) *doctrinarum diritatem causis inanibus praetexebat,* 'cruel like Phalaris or Perillus and trusted as long as (or 'because') he cloaked his dreadful skills in vain pretexts'.

Doctrinarum diritatem must be taken as a gen. inversus, just like *casuum diritate* in 26.1.3. *Dirus* is a religious t.t. (TLL V 1268.67), denoting i.a. bad omens, incantations and other magical practices. Wagner was suspicious of the word *doctrinarum*, and indeed, its use to denote expertise in magic seems to be without parallel. Still, in 26.3.3 Hilarinus sends his son to a sorcerer *docendum secretiora quaedam* and in section 4 of that chapter Amm. speaks of a *doctor malarum artium*, so that there is no real reason to doubt *doctrinarum* in this context.

Exstirpatis occasu ducis funeribus belli 'Rooting out the casualties of war' is an awkward metaphor for 'bringing the war with its casualties to a definitive end'. Is the *dux* meant here Marcellus, as e.g. Rolfe supposes, or Procopius, as e.g. Wagner and Seyfarth suggest? The death of Marcellus is mentioned in the preceding section and forms the definitive end of the rebellion of Procopius. This speaks in favour of the first interpretation, as does the fact that Procopius' name is mentioned further on in the sentence. If Amm. had meant Procopius to be the *dux* in question, he would not have written *nisi capite viso Procopii*, but – *usurpatoris* or something similar. The phrase *funera belli* has a poetic ring, cf. Stat. *Th.* 4.620 *venturasque vices et funera belli* (also 9.756) and Claud. *Cons. Stil.* 3 *pr.* 17 *post funera belli*. After the *funera belli* will follow the horrors *post bellum*, which were even worse (*multo magis quam in proeliis formidanda*, §9). **10.6**

saevitum est in multos acrius, quam errata flagitaverant vel delicta The use of the impersonal passive *saevitum est* is in keeping with the rest of the chapter, in which Valens is not mentioned by name. The distinction between *errata* and *delicta*, for which cf. the tactful wording of Arbitio in 26.9.5 *milites vero secutos eius errorem*, will not be made during the oncoming trials. For *flagitare* with an abstract noun as subject, which Amm. uses freely, see TLL VI 844.29–52 and the note ad 20.10.1.

Amm. is not the only author who denounces Valens' brutal behaviour after Procopius' usurpation had been brought to an end. Zos. 4.8.4–5 (cf. 4.10.1) strikes a similar note: ἐπεξῄει πικρῶς ἅπασι, διερευνώμενος οὐ τοὺς συμπράξαντας τῇ τυραννίδι μόνον ἀλλὰ καὶ τοὺς τῆς βουλῆς κοινωνήσαντας ἢ ὅλως ἀκούσαντάς τι καὶ μὴ παραχρῆμα τὸ μελετώμενον ἀπαγγείλαντας. Πολὺς δὲ ἦν κατὰ πάντων σὺν οὐδεμιᾷ κρίσει δικαίᾳ χωρῶν, καὶ παρανάλωμα τῆς τοῦ βασιλέως ὀργῆς οἵ τε τοῦ νεωτερισμοῦ μετασχόντες καὶ οἱ κατὰ μηδὲν αἴτιοι διὰ συγγένειαν ἢ φιλίαν ἐγίνοντο ('he acted cruelly against all and sundry, commencing an inquiry not only into the actors in the revolt, but also into those who had been accessory to it or had only heard of it without immediately revealing what was devised. He thus acted with great severity towards all individuals, without regard to justice. Not only those who had conspired were sacrificed to the fury of the emperor, but also people, who were merely friends or relations of any of the conspirators, though themselves perfectly innocent'). Cf. further Hier. *Chron.* a. 366 *plurimi Procopianae partis caesi atque proscripti* and Eun. *fr.* 34.9, probably taken from a tirade against Valens' reprisals (so Blockley ad loc. and Lenski, 2002, 112 n. 277).

Contrasting opinions can be found, however, in Lib. *Or.* 1.171 ('Ἀλλ' ἐπάνειμι δὴ πρὸς τὸν Βάλεντα· ὃν ἔδειξε μὲν χρηστὸν τὸ μὴ τῷ τυράννῳ τοὺς τοῦ τυράννου φίλους ἐπαποκτεῖναι ("but to return to Valens – the fact that, after Procopius' death, he did not execute Procopius' friends too argued that he was a decent person", tr. Norman); cf. *Or.* 19.15, 20.25–26), Symmachus (*Or.* 1.21 *victoriae moderatus est*; 'Valens was reluctant to capitalize on his victory') and especially Themistius (*Or.* 7.93a–c, 95 c–d, 97 c–d, 98 a, 8.110d–111a, 11.148 b).

Modern scholars are divided on this question. Paschoud rejects the view of Themistius and the other orators completely: "il va sans dire que leurs affirmations n'ont aucun poids face au témoignage des historiens" (n. 122), but Lenski, 2002, though conceding that "he (i.e. Valens) fined, proscribed, exiled, tortured and executed a fair number" (112), is less severe: "the reprisals he took in the aftermath of the revolt were surprisingly mild compared to his iron-fisted policies leading up to it" (111), and "for all its rhetoric, however, Themistius's account probably has some basis in reality. Valens had every reason to promote concord, which, after such a rocky start, was possible only with a considerable measure of clemency" (112). Cf. also Grattarola, 1986, 102–103 and Wiebe, 1995, 56–61.

As to the number of those who were punished, it is impossible to establish the precise facts. Apart from the execution of Procopius and Marcellus (26.9.9, 10.5) and of Florentius and Barchalba, who were executed immediately after handing Procopius over to Valens (26.9.10), we only hear of the violent death of the former vicar of Thrace Andronicus (*PLRE* I, Andronicus 3), reported by Lib. *Or.* 62.59 (cf. *Or.* 1.171). The PPO Araxius was sent into exile (see the next section), as was Procopius' PVC Phronimius (the latter by Valentinian, 26.10.8). Helpidius (*PLRE* I, Helpidius 6) was imprisoned and saw his property confiscated (Philost. *HE* 7.10).

maximeque in Philippopoleos defensores, qui urbem seque ipsos non nisi capite viso Procopii, quod ad Gallias portabatur, aegerrime dediderunt For the siege of Philippopolis see §4. In 26.9.9 Amm. had reported that Procopius was beheaded immediately after he had fallen into the hands of Valens (*statimque abscisa cervice*). This took place on 27 May 366 (see the note ad 26.9.9 *subito*). Some time later Procopius' head was shown to Valentinian, who, according to Amm., was then in Paris: *Ei* (sc. Iovinus) *post haec redeunti Parisios post claritudinem recte gestorum imperator laetus occurrit brevique postea consulem designavit illo videlicet ad gaudii cumulum accedente, quod isdem diebus Procopii susceperat caput a Valente transmissum* (27.2.10). Whether Valentinian really was in Paris when Procopius' head arrived from the east, is disputed (Tomlin, 1973, 150 for instance argues in favour of Rheims instead of Paris as the emperor's residence at the time, in view of some constitutions in the Theodosian Code), as is the date of the head's arrival, some scholars opting for the end of June, others for the beginning of July or for some point in time between 14 June and 17 November (cf. Tomlin, ibid., Lorenz, 1985, 82–84 and Raimondi, 2001, 123, with the references). Whatever the date may have been, both the location of Philippopolis (cf. the note ad 26.5.1 *percursis Thraciis*) and Amm.'s wording in the present text suggest that Procopius' head was shown to the defenders of Philippopolis on the way out to Gaul, rather than that "the head had to be returned to the East to convince the defenders of Philippopolis to surrender", as McCormick, 1986, 41 n. 25 argues.

There is one other instance in Amm. of the maltreatment of a usurper's body (22.14.4, about Magnentius). However, to decapitate a defeated enemy and display in public his head stuck on a pole was a time-honoured practice among the Romans. Some examples: D.C. 73.10.2 (with respect to Pertinax in 193), D.C. 74.8.3 (Pescennius Niger in 194), Hdn. 3.8.1 and D.C. 75.7.3 (Albinus in 197), Hdn. 5.4.11 (Macrinus in 218), HA *Dd* 9.4 (Macrinus and his son in 218), Hdn. 7.1.10 (Quartinus in 235), Hdn. 8.6.5–6 (Maximinus and his son in 238), *Pan.* 4.31.4 and 12.18.3 (Maxentius in 312). See for the time of the Republic and the Early Empire Voisin, 1984, for subsequent centuries McCormick, 1986, 56–57, 60, 134, 180–181, 235.

Apart from Philippopolis we hear of one other city which was punished by Valens for its support of Procopius. In 31.1.4 Amm. relates that the walls of Chalcedon were torn down (cf. Socr. *HE* 4.8.1). Its inhabitants had derisively addressed the emperor as *sabaiarius* when he tried to get hold of it (26.8.2).

For *aegerrime*, 'with the utmost reluctance', cf. 15.3.6 *cum aegre homines dormisse sese praesentibus faterentur externis*; TLL I 944.45–56.

10.7 *ad gratiam tamen precantium coerciti sunt aliqui lenius* For *precari*, 'to mediate', cf. 15.3.11 *veniam Arbitione meruere precante* and for *coercere = punire* the note ad 26.1.1 *quam ob causam*. At first sight Amm. seems to qualify his condemnation of the judicial process after Procopius' revolt. Many fell victim to Valens' vindictiveness. However (*tamen*), in some cases the emperor acceded to mediation. It is of course acceptable that people in high places intercede for friends or relatives, and, indeed, it is expected of them. As Basil says in a letter to a provincial governor (*Ep.* 86.1) Οἶδα μεγίστην καὶ πρώτην σπουδὴν οὖσαν τῇ τιμιότητί σου πάντα τρόπον χαρίζεσθαι τῷ δικαίῳ, δευτέραν δὲ τὸ καὶ τοὺς φίλους εὐποιεῖν καὶ τῶν προσφευγόντων τῇ προστασίᾳ τῆς σῆς μεγαλονοίας ἀντιποιεῖσθαι ("I know that the first and greatest object of your Honour's zeal is to favour the cause of justice in every way, and the second, to benefit your friends and to take action in the interests of those who flee to the protection of your Magnanimity", tr. Deferrari). The many letters of Libanius, in which he puts in a word for friends who have to appear in court or before a high official, illustrate the practice. However, a closer look at the individuals concerned and the way in which Amm. presents the motives of Valens for his leniency shows that, in this section too, the author is critical of Valens' behaviour. These people were punished less severely neither for reasons of justice nor out of clemency, but *ad gratiam precantium*. The meaning of *ad gratiam* is illustrated by Amm.'s praise of Praetextatus in 27.9.10, which is given extra weight by a reference to Cicero (*Orat.* 34): *in examinandis vero litibus ante alios id impetravit, quod laudando Brutum Tullius refert, ut cum nihil ad gratiam faceret, omnia tamen grata viderentur esse, quae factitabat*. For the negative connotation of the phrase cf. also Liv. 9.30.1 (*lectio senatus*) *quae sine recti pravique discrimine ad gratiam ac libidinem facta esset*.

inter quos eminebat Araxius in ipso rerum exustarum ardore adeptus ambitu praefecturam Araxius had willingly joined sides with Procopius, indeed pulled strings to obtain the post of PPO under him, 26.7.6 *Araxius exambita regia praetorio praefectus accessit velut Agilone genero suffragante* (q.v.). The extravagant metaphor 'in the midst of the blaze of the conflagration' (with which cf. 20.4.8 *in ardore terribilium rerum* and Sallust's description of Africa, *Jug.* 19.6 *loca exusta solis ardoribus*) is added to accentuate the gravity of Araxius' treachery, since Procopius' revolt coincided with attacks on the Roman territory from all sides, 26.4.5 *velut per universum orbem Romanum bellum canentibus bucinis*. If anyone had deserved the death penalty, it was Araxius. We saw earlier that the tribune Aliso was spared because of his outstanding feat (*contemplatione facinoris clari*, 26.8.10) in the harbour of Cyzicus.

et Agilone intercedente genero supplicio insulari multatus breve post tempus evasit One would expect *et* to connect *adeptus* and *multatus*, or *qui* instead of *et* before *Agilone*, but one is forced to interpret *eminebat et evasit*, the perfect expressing, as usual, the main new development. As TLL VII 1.2039.59–70 shows, the adjective *insularis* is used almost exclusively by Amm. With the present phrase cf. 14.5.3 *capite vel multatione bonorum aut insulari solitudine damnabatur* and 15.7.2 *insulari poena multavit*. Although Agilo, like Araxius, had supported Procopius (26.7.4, q.v.), he deserted the usurper at Nacolia (26.9.7). Apparently he thus was pardoned (pace Socr. *HE* 4.5.3 and Soz. *HE* 6.8.3, who assert that he was executed by being sawn in half; see the note ad 26.9.10 *Parique*) and was able to intercede for his father-in-law. In view of the seriousness of Araxius' crime, the punishment will have been *deportatio*, not the milder *relegatio*. See for this form of punishment De Jonge's note ad 14.5.3 *insulari solitudine* and Vallejo Girvés, 1991. Araxius is not heard of again, neither is Agilo.

Euphrasius vero itemque Phronimius missi ad occiduas partes arbitrio obiecti sunt Valentiniani These gentlemen, under Procopius *praefectus urbis Constantinopolitanae* and *magister officiorum*, respectively, are characterised in 26.7.4 as *ambo Galli institutis bonarum artium spectatissimi*. The fact that they are from Gaul explains why they are sent to Valentinian for trial.

10.8

Phronimius Cherronesum deportatur Amm. uses the name Cherronesus for the NW-coast of the Hellespont (22.8.5) and for the Crimea. No doubt the latter is meant here. It was not a bad place of exile. Cf. 22.8.32 *coloniarum plena Graecarum; unde quieti sunt homines et sedati adhibentes vomeri curam et proventibus fructuariis victitantes*. By sending him to the Crimea, Valentinian returned Phronimius to that part of the empire whence he came, and where Valens was in charge. The verb *deportare* is a hapax in Amm. The substantive *deportatio* (see for this form of punishment the note ad §7 *Agilone*) only occurs in 29.3.7, in a context which has also to do with the aftermath of the Procopian revolt: the military tribunes Claudius (*PLRE* I, Claudius 4) and Sallustius (*PLRE* I, Sallustius 2), accused of having expressed sympathy with Procopius, were condemned by Valentinian, the latter to death, the former to exile; it was only after Valentinian's death that Claudius was released from his banishment (*nec Claudius nisi post eiusdem Valentiniani obitum deportationis maestitia liberatus*, 29.3.7).

inclementius in eodem punitus negotio ea re, quod divo Iuliano fuit acceptus, cuius memorandis virtutibus eius ambo fratres principes obtrectabant nec similes eius nec suppares Again, the reason why Euphrasius is acquitted, whereas Phronimius is sent into exile, has nothing to do with justice or clemency, but is the consequence of Valentinian's spiteful attitude towards the memory of Julian, which he shared with his brother: 26.4.4 *invidiam cientes Iuliani memoriae principis amicisque eius*. Lenski, 2002, 105–108 lists a number of men who had been close to Julian and were forced out of their posts by Valentinian and Valens shortly after Julian's death. Henricus Valesius saw the animosity of the imperial brothers against Julian also attested in some constitutions in the Theodosian Code "quibus leges a Iuliano latas abrogarunt". He apparently had in mind *Cod. Theod.* 5.13.3, 5.15.17, 7.7.2 and 8.1.11. However, there is nothing unusual in the wording of these constitutions. Differences of opinion existed, of course. *Cod. Theod.* 5.13.3, for instance, deals with Julian's attempt to restore confiscated property to pagan temples (cf. the note ad 25.4.15 *vectigalia*). Valentinian and Valens wanted to repeal this measure, but the law which they issued is, as far as we can judge, written in a matter-of-fact tone and does not betray a specific hostility: *Universa, quae ex patrimonio nostro per arbitrium divae memoriae Iuliani in possessionem sunt translata templorum, sollicitudine sinceritatis tuae cum omni iure ad rem privatam nostram redire mandamus* ("All property which was transferred from Our patrimony and placed in possession of temples by the authority of the Emperor Julian of sainted memory, We order to be restored with full legal title to Our privy purse, through the offices of Your Sincerity", tr. Pharr). Moreover, other constitutions of the imperial brothers explicitly approve of Julianic laws, *Cod. Theod.* 8.5.20 and 10.4.2 (*Divum Iulianum hoc competentissime decrevisse comperimus, ut...Quod adeo nos probamus, ut ratum esse iubeamus*).

The term *divus* to indicate deceased emperors was of course widely used during the period of paganism in the Roman empire. The practice was kept up in Christian times, as the present text and some other examples from the fourth century show: *divorumque veterum monumenta* (25.10.5, q.v.), *Constantio...divi Constantini maxi[m]i filio* (*ILS* 730; cf. Amici, 2000), *divus Iulianus*, *divo Ioviano* (*Cod. Theod.* 5.15.17), *divi Iuliani statuta* (*Cod. Theod.* 8.4.9), *divo Ioviano et Varroniano consul.* (*Cod. Theod.* 1.6.2, *ILS* 4938), *Stilichoni...comiti divi*

Theodosi Augusti in omnibus bellis (*ILS* 1277). See for Julian's consecration, ignored by Amm., the note ad 25.4.1 *Vir profecto* (add to the literature cited there Amici, 2002) and see in general for the phenomenon of deification in a Christian empire Bonamente, 1988 and Clauss, 1999, 196–215.

For *acceptus* see the note ad 26.10.2 *nam si*, for Julian's virtues 25.4.1–15 (q.v.). There are isolated instances of the combination of a relative and a demonstrative pronoun throughout the history of Latin, but the phenomenon becomes more frequent in its later stages. Szantyr 556–557 quotes Vulg. *Luc.* 3.16 *cuius non sum dignus solvere corrigiam calciamentorum* ('sandal strap') *eius* and a number of places in the *HA*. See also Löfstedt, 1907, 94–95. Although this is the only instance in Amm., it seems prudent to leave the text as it stands.

In Book 26 there is an unmistakable tendency to contrast the emperors Valentinian and Valens with Julian, and to convey the message, either explicitly, as here, or more often implicitly that Julian was by far superior to them. The qualification *nec similes eius nec suppares* sums it up in one scathing phrase. For *suppar*, 'almost equal', cf. Constantius' speech when he presented Julian as Caesar to the troops, 15.8.12 *in deferenda suppari potestate*. Cf. also August. *serm.* 239 (PL 38.1127) *Marcus et Lucas apostolorum non pares, sed suppares fuerunt*.

In sections 6–8 Amm. dealt with individuals who came off lightly after the defeat of Procopius. Now he is going to describe the excessive severity with which Valens took his revenge on others. The passage may be compared to Libanius *Or.* 24.13–14, in which the rhetor, like Amm., admits that the reigning emperors were justified in defending their position against usurpers like Procopius and Theodorus, but deplores the excessive cruelty with which they did so. Libanius even interprets this repression as a sign of the wrath of the gods, on a par with the barbaric invasions and the natural disasters of the period. It is obviously a subject that deeply concerned the historian. As Bleckmann, 1992, 271 observes, quoting as parallel passages 14.5, 15.6 and 29.1, "Immer wieder schildert der Geschichtsschreiber, wie wirkliche oder auch nur vermeintliche Anhänger von Usurpatoren verfolgt werden und wie in diesen Verfolgungen die legitimen Kaiser oft einen sehr viel grösseren Schaden anrichten als die Usurpatoren selbst." See also the discussion of Amm.'s attitude towards these matters in Matthews 202–203. The omission of these sections in Hamilton's translation is regrettable.

10.9 *His accedebant alia graviora et multo magis quam in proeliis formidanda* In view of the opening sentence of the next section *nam inter arma...leviora facit pericula*, it is best to take *quam in proeliis* both with *graviora* and *magis formidanda*: 'worse and much more frightening than (what happens) in battles'. Seyfarth's translation "Aber noch viel Schlimmeres kam hinzu, als man in einer Schlacht fürchten muss" neglects *et*.

carnifex enim et unci et cruentae quaestiones sine discrimine ullo aetatum et dignitatum per fortunas omnes et ordines grassabantur Not just the henchman, but also his frightening tools are the subject of *grassari*, suggesting an infernal machine set in motion against Valens' real or supposed enemies. The verb *grassari* is also used in section 15, the description of the tsunami, which may be called the physical analogon of the horrors to be reported here: *horrendi terrores per omnem orbis ambitum grassati sunt subito*; see also the note ad 26.3.4 *usque eo*. Similarly grim and impressionistic enumerations are found in 14.5.9 *intendebantur eculei* ("the rack was put in order", tr. Hamilton) *uncosque parabat carnifex et tormenta* and 29.1.23 *intenduntur eculei, expediuntur pondera plumbea cum fidiculis et verberibus, resultabant omnia truculentae vocis horroribus* e.q.s. For *cruentae quaestiones* cf. 29.1.35 *sub cruenta quaestione* and the note ad 26.3.1 *ut...captos*. Amm. is indignant about the fact that these cruel reprisals affected men and women, rich and poor, high and low, as did the harsh measures of Cleander, 26.6.8 *quem...diversas legimus vexasse fortunas* (q.v.), and Petronius, 26.6.17 (q.v.), whose actions were directed *in diversos ordines*. In Amm.'s opinion a judge must discriminate between people of different rank, as did Julian, who was *pro* ('in accordance with') *rerum hominum(que) distinctione sine crudelitate terribilis*, 25.4.8, q.v. On *dignitas* 'rank' see the note ad 20.4.20 *qui ordo*.

et pacis obtentu † itum detestandum agitabatur Despite many efforts to remedy V's *obtentuitum*, no fully satisfactory solution has yet been found. Although *obtentu* is a hapax in Amm., the phrase *pacis obtentu* ("under the mantle of peace", tr. Rolfe) is unexceptionable. Cf. Liv. 1.56.8 *sub eius obtentu cognominis*; Gel. 10.22.1 *obtentu philosophiae nominis*; August. *adult. coniug.* 1.7.7 *ne...obtentu continentiae perturbemus christiana coniugia*. The idea must be, as Wagner explains, that in a period of peace the laws, which had been silent during the armed conflict – *silent enim leges inter arma* (Cic. *Mil.* 11) – should reclaim their rights. Among the proposed conjectures Novák's *latrocinium* serves the context best, since in section 11 Amm. says that avarice was the main motive of the *delatores*. Moreover, as Novák has observed, the phrase *latrocinia agitare* is attested in Tac. *Ann.* 12.27.2 *Chattorum latrocinia agitantium*. The substitution of *latrocinium* for *iudicium*, the word one would expect, occurs in the form of a *correctio* in 14.9.5 *latrocinium illud esse non iudicium clamans* and, one might add, twice in Cicero: *Cat.* 1.27 *ut...latrocinium potius quam bellum nominaretur*; *S. Rosc.* 61 *confitere huc ea spe venisse quod putares hic latrocinium, non iudicium futurum*. Moreover, Cicero uses the phrase *latrocinium nefarium* four times (*Dom.* 107; *Phil.* 4.15; *Mur.* 84, *Ver.* 2.152) on which *latrocinium detestandum* may be a variation. Still, in the absence of a paleographical explanation for the genesis of the corruption, the crux must be kept.

infaustam victoriam exsecrantibus universis internecivo bello quovis graviorem Amm. conveys his personal indignation about the events by a series of highly expressive words. The oxymoron *infausta victoria* is unique. It may be significant that Amm. used the same adjective for Procopius' revolt in 26.6.14 *Procopium infausti dominatus exordia molientem*. The suppression of the revolt was just as unfortunate as its beginning. Amm. uses the phrase *internecivum bellum* also in his sarcastic characterization of Sabinianus: *lectissimus moderator belli internecivi* (18.7.7). Cf. Cic. *Dom.* 61 *acerbum bellum internecivomque*; Liv. 9.25.9 *perinde ac si internecivo bello certasset*.

nam inter arma et lituos condicionis aequatio leviora facit pericula The sentence explains the opening phrase of the preceding section. The combination of *arma* and *litui* gives it a poetic ring. Cf. Hor. *Carm.* 2.1.18–20 *iam litui strepunt / iam fulgor armorum fugacis / terret equos*; Man. 4.156 *arma procul lituosque volunt tristemque senectam*. With *condicionis aequatio* Marié aptly compares Sal. *Cat.* 59.1 *quo militibus exaequato periculo animus amplior esset*. The noun *aequatio* ('equalization') is a hapax in Amm.; cf. Liv. 8.4.3 *si societas aequatio iuris est* and Cic. *Off.* 2.73 *capitalis* ('pernicious') *oratio est ad aequationem bonorum pertinens, qua peste quae potest esse maior?*

10.10

et Martiae virtutis potestas aut absumit, quod occupat, aut nobilitat The text is practically that of V *aut ausum id quod*, if one takes into account V's habit of interchanging *b* and *u/v* and its frequent mistakes in the division of words. In his defence of V's text Petschenig, 1892, 522 pointed to 24.4.25 as a parallel. After the capture of Maozamalcha *quidquid impetus repperit, potestas iratorum absumpsit*. Still, one does not feel completely at ease with the text as it stands, because in Amm.

occupare is not used in the general sense of *vincere* or *potiri*, but either of the occupation of territory or the activities of a person. Marié translates *quod occupat* "les êtres qu'il habite", which attributes to *occupare* a meaning it does not seem to have.

"The force of martial valour" (Rolfe) is an unparalleled expression, indeed the phrase *virtutis potestas* is not found in any pagan work. Hagendahl, 1924, 200 mentions it as illustrating Amm.'s *abundantia sermonis*. Christian authors use it in theological discussions, where *potestas* is the equivalent of ἐξουσία. In Hilarius' treatise *De Trinitate* for instance it is found five times.

et mors, si acciderit, nullum ignominiae continet sensum finemque secum vivendi simul et dolendi perducit There are words here reminiscent of Cicero's speech in defense of Cluentius, in which the orator had to attack Oppianicus, who was dead and had been convicted for murder, in order to defend Cluentius: § 10 *cum illi in quem dicitur* (Oppianicus) *damnatio omne ignominiae periculum iam abstulerit, mors vero etiam doloris; huic autem* (Cluentius) *pro quo dicimus nihil possit offensionis accedere sine acerbissimo animi sensu ac molestia et sine summo dedecore vitae ac turpitudine.*

ubi vero consiliis impiis iura quidem praetenduntur et leges This complicated sentence hinges on the adverb *ibi*, which corresponds with *ubi* and introduces the main clause. The long subordinate clause introduced by *ubi* is in two parts, of which the second is marked by *autem*. Instead of using a neutral opposition to *inter arma*, e.g. *in iudiciis*, Amm. makes it clear from the start that justice is violated, the laws and the courts being used only as a pretence by people of evil intent. For *praetendere* in this sense cf. the note ad 23.5.11 *etenim ut*. The phrase *impia consilia* implies strong condemnation, cf. 21.16.13 *in perditis impiisque consiliis* (quoted from Cicero); 30.1.1 *cuius materiae impio conceptae consilio* (sc. to murder king Pap of Armenia); Liv. 40.23.8 *neque eum se esse qui ullius impii consilii* (sc. to murder a brother) *auctor futurus videri possit*.

et Catonianae vel Cassianae sententiae fuco perliti resíderint iúdices For Cato and Cassius as proverbially severe judges cf. Otto, 1890 (1962), 78 (Cato) and 77 (Cassius). Cato is quoted in 15.12.4 (drunkenness) *quam furoris voluntariam speciem esse Catoniana senteǹtia definivit*, in which *sententia* has the same meaning as in the present passage, viz. 'authoritative pronouncement'. He is further mentioned in 14.6.8 and 16.5.2. For Cassius cf. 22.9.9 *iudicibus Cassiis tristior et Lycurgis*,

CHAPTER 10.10 285

with the note. The magistrates of Amm.'s day adorn themselves with the reputation of these ancient judges, just like women use rouge to make up their faces. For *linere* and its derivatives cf. Lucr. 2.745 *nullo circum lita fuco*; Cic. *de Orat.* 3.199 *his tribus figuris insidere quidam venustatis non fuco inlitus, sed sanguine diffusus debet color* ("In each of these three forms there should be a kind of charming complexion, not as a result of rouge that has been laid on, but of blood that flows through them", tr. May/Wisse) and Auson. *Mos.* 309 *magico...noctua perlita fuco* ("that owl painted with colours of such magical power", tr. Evelyn White). For *residere* cf. 15.5.12 *cumque iudices resedissent* (Novák). *Resideint* is a convincing emendation by Heraeus of V's *residerendi*, superior both for paleographical and metrical reasons to Gelenius' *resident*. For the change from the indicative *praetenduntur* to the iterative subjunctive *residerint*, cf. Hagendahl, 1921, 124.

agatur autem, quod agitur, ad voluntatem praetumidae potestatis The phrase *agatur quod agitur* seems to denote human behaviour in general, as in Cicero's description of *decorum* in *Off.* 1.94 *agere quod agas considerate* and August. *Ep.* 194.10 *ut fide agatur, quod agitur.* The expression *ad voluntatem agere* must mean 'to do someone's bidding', formed after *ad voluntatem loqui* 'to play up to someone'; Cic. *Quinct.* 93 *Fatetur se non belle dicere, non ad voluntatem loqui posse*; Cic. *Amic.* 91 *levium hominum atque fallacium ad voluntatem loquentium omnia.* The qualification *praetumidus* is used of Arbitio in the context of the trial of Chalcedon, 22.3.9 *Arbitionem semper ambiguum et praetumidum* (q.v.). It is quite possible that Arbitio was again involved in the reprisals after the suppression of Procopius' revolt, but the *praetumida potestas* the judges tried to please was of course Valens.

et ex eius libidine incidentium vitae necisque momenta pensantur In view of 19.12.13 *cuius ex nutu, prope dixerim, pendebat incidentium omnium salus* there can be no doubt that Valesius' emendation of V's *incidentium* is wrong. For the absolute use of *incidere*, 'to run into trouble', see TLL VII 1.899 sqq. and Löfstedt, 1911, 339–340. Borleffs, 1930, 281 quotes as a parallel Lact. *mort. pers.* 37.1 *si quis inciderat, mari occulte mergebantur*, 'those who had fallen prey, were secretly drowned in the sea'. As in 22.9.9 *causarum momenta...perpendens*, the metaphor preserves the image of weighing on the scales. Michael, 1874, 27 pointed to Cic. *Mur.* 3 *diligentissime perpendenti momenta officiorum omnium* as a parallel.

ibi capitalis vertitur pernicies et abrupta A lapidary conclusion, although Amm.'s highly charged language risks becoming obscure. The unparalleled phrase *vertitur pernicies* is probably formed by analogy with *vertere (verti) in perniciem*, as in Liv. 39.48.1 *haec...in perniciem adulescenti verterunt* ('proved fatal'); Tac. *Ann.* 2.20.1 *astusque hostium in perniciem ipsis vertebat* ('he turned the wiles of the enemies against themselves'). Tacitus goes one step further and writes in *Ann.* 11.37.1 *ni caedem eius Narcissus properavisset, verterat pernicies in accusatorem* ('the threat of death would have turned against the accuser'). We find a similar use of *verti* in 15.2.7 *ad Iulianum recens perductum calumniarum vertitur machina*. In the present sentence we must suppose that ruin (*pernicies*) turns itself against (*vertitur*) those standing trial. *Capitalis* adds the notion that their life is at stake (cf. the note ad 26.3.3 *capitali animadversione*) and *abrupta* that the verdict will be carried out without delay; cf. 24.4.30 *in perniciem coegit abruptam*, q.v.

10.11 *nam ut quisque ea tempestate ob quamlibet valuerat causam* It seems best to take *valuerat* as an inchoativum, as in Tac. *Ann.* 13.46.2 *accepto aditu Poppaea primum per blandimenta et artes valescere*.

regio imperio prope accedens et aliena rapiendi aviditate exustus The addition of *imperio* after V's *regio* was proposed by Heraeus. The word may well have been lost because of the following *prope*. The phrase *regium imperium*, which is used by Sal. *Cat.* 6.7 to refer to the monarchy, is unique in Amm. If it is correct, Amm. says either that these individuals were close to the emperor, *regius* meaning 'imperial', as in 26.6.15 *regius minister* (q.v.), or he means, less specifically, "having almost royal authority" (Rolfe) in which case the adjective is used as in 25.2.2 *ex regio more*. The rare parallels for *prope accedere* with a dative complement ("to come near in quality, status etc.", OLD s.v. 12), e.g. Cic. *Fam.* 11.21.4 *me huic tuae virtuti proxime accedere*, are in favour of the second alternative. If Gelenius' *regiae*, printed by Marié, is correct, the noun would have to be interpreted as 'the court'. The participle *exustus*, used elsewhere for people burnt at the stake, is another instance of Amm.'s predilection for fire metaphors, for which see the note ad 26.9.7 *Qua succensus*.

licet aperte insontem arcessens ut familiaris suscipiebatur et fidus ditandus casibus alienis One is reminded of Valens' father-in-law Petronius, who, "consumed with sadistic eagerness to strip one and all of their possessions" (Hamilton), *nocentes pariter et insontes...quadrupli nexibus vinciebat* (26.6.7). Contrast the procedure under Apronianus in Rome, who punished only people whose guilt had been established beyond doubt, 26.3.1 *nocuisse quibusdam apertissime confutatos...morte multaret. Licet*, for which see the note ad 20.6.9, gives concessive force to *insontem*. The verb *suscipere* is almost the t.t. for a (friendly) reception by the emperor. Cf. e.g. 20.4.13 *qui liberaliter ita suscepti*; 20.9.6 *Leonas susceptus ut honoratus et prudens*; 22.7.3 (Maximus) *exosculatum susceptumque reverenter*; 28.3.9 *cumque gaudio susceptus et laudibus*. The gerundive *ditandus* serves as a passive future participle; see the notes ad 20.2.4 *opitulari* and 20.11.24 *alimentis destituendos*.

imperator enim promptior ad nocendum criminantibus patens et funereas delationes asciscens For the compulsive tendency to harm other people displayed by several characters in Amm. see the note ad 26.10.2 *nam si*. Valens is comparable to Constantius in his readiness to lend his ear to informers, cf. e.g. 18.3.6 (Barbatio) *sub Augusti patulis auribus multa garriebat et saeva*. The adjective *funereus*, 'deadly', is a poeticism (TLL VI 1582.43). In 29.5.46 the elder Theodosius calls the rebel Firmus *latronem funereum*. In 31.7.16 it is substantivized: *Romanos...funerea multa perpessos*. The verb *asciscere*, for which see the notes ad 20.4.22 *asciti in consistorium* and 20.11.1 *ascitum Arsacen*, has a stronger meaning than merely "listened" (Rolfe) or "admettait" (Marié). Valens actually invited informers to present their denunciations.

per suppliciorum diversitates effrenatius exsultavit The grim details will be given in the next section. Seager 43–49 discusses *effrenatus*, *exsultare* and related terms under the well-chosen heading "The Rhetoric of Excess". Again the reader is reminded of Constantius, who, like Valens, was justified in defending his position, but reprehensible in his cruelty: 19.12.18 *sed exsultare maestis casibus effrenate non decet, ne videantur licentia regi subiecti, non potestate*, followed, as here, by a reference to Cicero.

sententiae illius Tullianae ignarus docentis infelices esse eos, qui omnia sibi licere existimarunt The quotation cannot be traced to the remaining works of Cicero, so it is either from one of the lost works, or a very free paraphrase. The idea is repeated in a comparable context in 29.2.10, where Valens is attacked even more violently than in the present passage: *fremibundus et minax, cui nihil licere debuerat, quia omnia sibi licere etiam iniusta existimabat*. The perfect *existimarunt* must mean that these people learned the hard way that their former opinion was wrong.

10.13 *haec implacabilitas causae quidem piissimae, sed victoriae foedioris* Apart from Cassian. *inst.* 8.11 and the present passage TLL VII 1.626.70–73 mentions only two instances of *implacabilitas*, 'ruthlessness', both in Amm.: 14.1.5 *quidquid Caesaris implacabilitati sedisset, id...confestim urgebatur impleri* and 28.1.38 *implacabilitate ultra apposita iam pergente.* Amm. again adapts a text of Cicero, who in *Off.* 2.27 compared the behaviour of Sulla and Caesar after their victories in a civil war, and speaking about the latter uses the words *in causa impia, victoria etiam foediore* (sc. quam Sullae). Amm. contrasts Valens' *causa*, viz. the defence of his imperial power, which, as he emphasizes, was fully justified, *piissima*, with his monstrous behaviour after his victory over Procopius. It is interesting to note that he changes the sense of the comparative *foedioris*, which has its full force in Cicero, to something like 'exceptionally horrible'. Sabbah 340 suggests that Amm.'s *causae quidem piissimae* may be an implicit correction of Symmachus' exclamation *o mira inter vos similitudo pietatis!* in his panegyric on Valentinian (*Or.* 1.22). The fact that Amm. evidently makes use of a text by Cicero makes this less plausible.

innocentes tortoribus exposuit multos vel sub eculeo locavit incurvos aut ictu carnificis torvi substravit Amm. more than once points to the deplorable fact that in cases like this innocent people also fell victim. Cf. 14.5.2 *insontium caedibus fecit victoriam luctuosam* and 14.9.5–6 (about the followers of Magnentius); 15.3.2 *sine innocentium sontiumque differentia* (with respect to the friends of Gallus Caesar); 29.1.40 *sumptumque est de quibusdam...supplicium, dum quaeritur, an sumi deberet* (about the aftermath of the Theodorus affair), and see the introductory note to 26.10.9–14. Novák's conjecture *sub eculeo locavit* for V's *sub eculeo capit* makes excellent sense. The corruption was probably caused by haplography after which the scribe tried to make sense of the remaining *cavit*. The first member of this tricolon denotes torture in general, the second and third specific forms of punishment. The tools of the torturer's trade are enumerated in 29.1.23 *intenduntur eculei, expediuntur pondera plumbea cum fidiculis et verberibus*, ("the racks were made taut, the leaden weights were brought out along with the cords and the scourges", tr. Rolfe), which may be compared to Cic. *Phil.* 11. 7 *vincla, verbera, eculeum, tortorem carnificemque.* In most descriptions of the *eculeus* it is clear that the victim was forced to lie down on a horizontal wooden beam; cf. Curt. 6.10.10 *Tot conscii ne in eculeum quidem inpositi verum fatebuntur?* and V. Max. 6.8.1 *laceratus verberibus eculeoque inpositus, candentibus etiam lamminis ustus.* Hands and feet were tied with cords and the body was stretched out, cf. Hier. *epist.* 1.3 *cum eculeus corpus extenderet*; Sen. *Ep.* 67.3 *eculeo longior factus*. The treatment was regularly made even worse by scourging (*verbera*), lacerating the sides with iron claws (*unci, ungulae*) and burning with hot plates (*lamminae*). In the present text, however, the words *sub eculeo* and *incurvos*, with which cf. 28.1.19 *quamquam incurvus sub eculeo staret*, suggest a different use of the *eculeus*, plausibly compared by Vergote, 1972, 122 to the κύφων or pillory he describes in col. 116, quoting i.a. Plut. *Per.* 28.2 τοὺς τριηράρχους καὶ τοὺς ἐπιβάτας τῶν Σαμίων εἰς τὴν Μιλησίων ἀγορὰν καταγαγὼν καὶ σανίσι προσδήσας ("binding them to planks", tr. Stadter, 1989, 258) ἐφ' ἡμέρας δέκα κακῶς ἤδη διακειμένους προσέταξεν ἀνελεῖν. Cf. also the use of κύφων in a comparison by Chrys. *pan. Ign.* = PG 50, 590 ὥσπερ τις βαρύτατος τὸν αὐχένα τῆς ψυχῆς αὐτῶν ἐπίεζε καὶ κατέσπα διηνεκῶς.

With *substernere*, 'to expose to', cf. 14.11.32 (fortuna) *substravit... feritati Carthaginis Regulum*; and V. Max. 2.7.7 *dictatoriae se animadversioni substraverunt*. For the dative in *-u* see De Jonge ad 19.1.6 *apparatu*.

quibus, si pateretur natura, vel denas animas profundere praestabat in pugna Amm. returns to the starting point of this rhetorical outburst, *multo magis quam in proeliis formidanda* (§ 9). For the phrase *animam profundere* see TLL X 2.1744.24-30 and the note ad 23.6.44 *eosque ita*. It may have been borrowed from Cic. *Marc.* 31 *qui in acie cecidit, qui in causa animam profudit*. For the hyperbolical 'tenfold death' cf. 25.7.10 *et cum pugnari deciens expediret, ne horum quidquam dederetur* Compare also Hor. *Carm.* 3.9.15 *pro quo bis patiar mori* and the parallel passages from poetry quoted ad loc. by Nisbet and Rudd. Cicero even writes *mori miliens* (*Att.* 7.11.1 and 14.9.2). The indicative *praestabat* in the apodosis is in accordance with the grammatical rules, since *praestare* belongs to "die Ausdrücke des Sollens, Müssens, Könnens, Dürfens u. ä." (Szantyr 327; cf. Ehrismann 41).

quam lateribus fodicatis omni culpa immunis fortunis gementibus universis quasi laesae maiestatis luere poenas dilaniatis ante corporibus, quod omni est tristius morte For *latera fodicare* see the note ad § 5 *unde post* and *innocentes tortoribus* above. The phrase *(a) culpa immunis* is found only in Amm., here and in 14.5.6 *ut ab omni culpa immunibus parceretur. Immunis* is accusative as part of the AcI after *praestabat*. The abl. abs. *fortunis gementibus universis* is a variation on *per fortunas omnes et ordines* in section 9. For *fortunae* indicating social classes or people belonging to them cf. 14.9.8 *quaestione igitur per multiplices dilatata fortunas*; 17.5.4 *celsiores fortunas idem loqui decet atque sentire* and 26.6.8 *quem...diversas legimus vexasse fortunas* with the note. This seems to have been missed by Marié, who translates: "au milieu des lamentations unanimes sur leur infortune". On *quasi* see the note ad 26.4.1. Here it implies that the charge of *laesa maiestas* was unfounded (cf. the note ad §5 *unde post*). In his indignation Amm. repeats himself, for *dilaniatis ante corporibus* means exactly the same as *lateribus fodicatis*, as *Cod. Theod.* 9.12.1 shows, where it is said that a master is guilty of homicide if he kills his slave in this fashion: *si...dilaniaverit poenis publicis corpus ferarum vestigiis latera persecando* ("if he should lacerate his body by public punishments, that is by cutting through his sides with the claws of wild beasts", tr. Pharr). The concluding relative phrase is best taken with the whole sentence, not just with the immediately preceding words. Any death is better than to die after torture as a victim of a false accusation.

10.14 *exin cum superata luctibus ferocia deflagrasset* The number of victims was too great even when taking into account Valens' cruelty. For this use of *superare* cf. 19.4.1 (ubi) *cadaverum multitudo humandi officia superaret*. Metaphoric *deflagrare* is also found in Liv. 40.8.9 *deflagrare iras vestras...posse* and Tac. *Hist.* 2.29.2 *deflagrante paulatim seditione*.

proscriptiones et exsilia et quae leviora quibusdam videntur, quamquam sint aspera, viri pertulere summates From the death penalty Amm. turns to the less severe punishments. According to Heumann-Seckel s.v. *proscribere*, *proscriptio* is the equivalent of *publicatio* (*bonorum*), 'confiscation'. Proscription and exile are also distinguished in 14.5.3 *multatione bonorum aut insulari solitudine damnabatur*, 29.1.44 *post multationem bonorum exsulare praeceptus*, Arnob. 1.64 (reges vestri) *proscriptionibus, exilis, caedibus nudant nobilitatibus civitates* and *Cod. Theod.* 9.42.20 (ne) *supplicium exilii pariter et proscribtionis sustineant*. The only follower of Procopius whose property was confiscated is Helpidius (see ad 26.10.6 *saevitum est*). Araxius' exile is referred to in 26.10.7, that of Phronimius (by Valentinian) in 26.10.8. As to *leviora*, Sabbah 361 points to Them. *Or.* 7.98 d χαλεπωτέρα δὲ ἐλευθέρῳ λύπη τῆς διὰ τοῦ σώματος γινομένης ἢ διὰ τῆς αἰσχύνης ἐστί ('for a free man physical pain is easier to bear than loss of honour'). In the same context Sabbah suggests that the use of *quibusdam* implies that Amm. "pense ici à des personnes précises, qu'il pourrait nommer" (i.c. Themistius), but this is unwarranted, since Amm. uses *quidam* also in a less specific meaning, as in 16.12.63 *vacans quidam tribunus, cuius non suppetit nomen* or 17.12.12 *quorum alter Transiugitanorum Quadorumque parti, alter quibusdam Sarmatis praeerat.*

The phrase *summates viri*, 'men of the highest rank', is found in comedy, e.g. Pl. *Stich.* 492 *oratores populi summates viri*; it disappears in the classical period, but returns in an archaizing author like Gellius 6.3.7 *non pauci ex summatibus viris* (from Cato's speech *pro Rhodiensibus*), and is used freely by Amm., e.g. 14.6.12 *summatem virum*; 26.6.1 *iamque summatibus proximus.*

ut ditaretur alius, genere nobilis et forte meritis locupletior actus patrimonio praeceps Cf. *ditandus casibus alienis* in section 11. The type of victim Amm. has in mind was a nobleman, who happened to have acquired great wealth as a result of personal merit. For *actus patrimonio praeceps* phrases like Cic. *Caec.* 60 *si...aliquem de fundo praecipitem egeris*, or *Quinct.* 83 *a suis dis penatibus praeceps eiectus* may have provided the model.

trususque in exsilium consumebatur angore aut stipe precaria victitabat Cf. the very similar complaint in 14.1.4 about the victims of Gallus' cruelty: *quorum pars necati, alii puniti bonorum multatione actique laribus suis extorres nullo sibi relicto praeter querellas et lacrimas stipe collaticia victitabant.* The expression *stipe precaria* or *collaticia victitare*, 'to be reduced to beggary', seems to be all Amm.'s own.

nec modus ullus exitialibus malis impositus, quam diu principem et proximos opum satietas cepit et caedis This is an effective conclusion to an emotional indictment of Valens and his cronies – in 31.14.5 the emperor is called *magnarum opum intemperans appetitor* and *in crudelitatem proclivior*. Only after their greed and bloodthirst had been fully satisfied did they put an end to their judicial excesses.

Amm. concludes Book 26 with an impressive description of the tsunami. The basic facts about this phenomenon are the following: tsunamis are caused by a displacement in a seabed leading to the sudden raising or lowering of a large body of water. Following the initial disturbance to the sea surface, waves spread in all directions. Their speed of travel, depending on the sea depth, may reach 700 km per hour. The time interval between the arrival of successive wave crests may be as long as half an hour. When tsunamis approach the coast, the waves may reach a height of 20 to 30 metres above sea level and the speed of onrush may be in the order of 10 metres per second. The first of these waves is often preceded by an extraordinary

10.15–19

recession of water from the shore, which may commence several minutes or even half an hour beforehand.

The tsunami which hit the eastern part of the Mediterranean in 365 has been reported in many sources, ranging from Jerome's *Chronicon* (ca. 380) through the ninth-century Byzantine historians Theophanes and Georgius Monachus to Syrian chronicles from the thirteenth century. These sources were first collected in the seminal article by Jacques & Bousquet, 1984. Kelly, 2004 has demonstrated beyond reasonable doubt that Amm. knew and modified the common source of Theophanes and Georgius Monachus. Bleckmann, 2007 has studied the ancestry of these Byzantine sources and traced it back to fourth century church historians; according to him these sources were also used by Amm. in other parts of his history. On the basis of these findings it may be asserted, that Amm.'s account of the tsunami is not based on personal observation alone, but also on reports from other authors. This is important both for the assessment of the present passage and, in a wider sense, for our view of Amm.'s method in assembling the material for his history.

The oldest reports on the tsunami, those by Jerome and Amm., mention Sicily, the Adriatic and the coast of Egypt as areas hit by the tsunami. This has led geophysicists to posit an epicentre for the earthquake that caused the tsunami near the south coast of Crete, a region of great seismic activity. From Jerome onwards the earthquake and the ensuing tsunami were described as a universal disaster. As a consequence there has been a tendency among historians, archeologists and geophysicists to link roughly contemporaneous reports and traces of seismic activity from all quarters of the Mediterranean to this event. In the words of Waldherr, 1997, 171 "Die einzelnen Teildisziplinen neigten dabei dazu, manche thesenhaft bzw. hypothesenhaft formulierte Aussage der jeweils anderen Teilfächer als gesicherte Erkenntnis schnell zur Grundlage ihrer eigenen, weitergehenden Interpretationen werden zu lassen". Since the publication in 1984 of the article by Jacques & Bousquet scholars have become much more cautious in this respect.

From Amm.'s report we must conclude that it was the trough of the tsunami wave that first arrived on the coast (regrettably, he does not specify *which* coast). This caused the sea to withdraw, so that the sea bed became visible and people wandered around, catching fish and shellfish with their hands (§ 16–17). At this point his description is somewhat fanciful, but entirely plausible, as was strikingly confirmed during the Boxing Day tsunami of 2004. The sea then returned in enormous waves, destroying buildings and killing thousands of people. Ships were cast upon the shore, and after the waves had receded, bodies of drowned men and women were left lying around. In Alexandria even big ships landed on roof tops, and Amm. himself during one of his voyages saw a Laconian ship rotting with decay two miles inland near Mothone in Messenia (§ 17–19). Here again we can say that some details may be exaggerated, but that on the whole his account is in agreement with the facts as observed during a severe tsunami.

"Natur als Zeichensystem" is the telling title of the first section of Baudy's article on the literary repercussions of Procopius' revolt (1992, 47). In the ancient world natural calamities have always been interpreted as signs of divine anger or, in Roman terms, as a disruption of the *pax deorum*. In the troubled years following the death of Julian, when religious controversy had been exacerbated by the emperor's outspoken policies, when confidence was shaken by the disastrous ending of his Persian expedition, and all parts of the empire, now under a new dynasty, were under threat (26.4.5–6), a major natural disaster like the tsunami was observed and interpreted with anxiety from all sides. Jerome, the first author to mention it, connected it in his *Life of Hilarion* with the death of Julian and regarded it as a sign of God's wrath. In a very similar way Libanius in the *Epitaphios* (*Or.* 18) read the series of earthquakes following Julian's death as evidence of Earth's mourning for the loss of her hero. Compared with these extreme views, Amm. is more detached. It would be wrong, however, to think, as Ensslin, 1923, 91–92 did, that he did not regard the tsunami as a sign from heaven on the ground that he did not make its meaning explicit. Amm. presents the tsunami as an event of almost cosmic dimensions, inaugurating a return to primeval chaos. He uses his description as an impressive conclusion of Book 26, where it mirrors the threats and dangers that befell the Empire during the beginning of the reign of Valentinian and Valens. He differs from his contemporaries Jerome and Libanius, however, in that he does not press his point unequivocally, but leaves room for his readers to ponder the meaning of the disaster in the light of the events treated by him in his *Res Gestae*, up to and including the defeat at Adrianople in 378.

10.15 *Hoc novatore adhuc superstite* Surprisingly, Amm. writes as if he had mentioned Procopius in the preceding section. The phrase 'when the usurper was still alive' would have come naturally after the short *elogium* in 26.9.11, which begins with *excessit autem vita* and ends with *quoad vixerat incruentus*. A plausible explanation of the present state of the text would be, that the passage on the tsunami was originally intended to follow immediately after the report of Procopius' death, but that Amm. subsequently decided to give it a more prominent place in order to set the seal on Book 26 as a whole. As in 26.7.9 (q.v.) one gets the impression, that Amm. has not had the opportunity to add the final touches to his account of the revolt.

For *superstes* see the note ad 21.7.5 *eo enim*. Amm. had used the noun *novator* with its unmistakable negative connotations for Constantine in 21.10.8 *Constantini ut novatoris turbatorisque priscarum legum et moris antiquitus recepti* (q.v.). The date of the tsunami is given as 21 July 365, two months before Procopius' pronunciamiento on 28 September of that year (references in the note ad 26.6.14 *ubi excanduit*). It is, however, far from certain that Amm. knew the exact date of the pronunciamiento. Indeed, the vague phrase *circa id tempus aut non multo posterius in oriente Procopius in res surrexerat novas* (26.5.8) suggests otherwise. The only chronological data in the chapters dealing with Procopius' revolt are the moment when Valentinian was informed of the coup *prope kalendas Novembres* (of the year 365; ibid.) and the fact that the revolt continued during the spring of the next year, *adulto iam vere* (26.9.1). For this reason it would be rash to interpret Amm.'s description of the tsunami as an announcement of the revolt, as Baudy, 1992, 59 does. Moreover, if this had been Amm.'s intention, he would have placed the description before, not after the event.

In Libanius' 24th oration, for which see the introductory remarks to sections 9–14 above, the revolt of Procopius is interpreted as a sign of the wrath of the gods, because the death of Julian had not been avenged. Christian authors like Jerome, in his *vita Hilarionis* 29.1, and Sozomen connected the disaster to the reign of Julian. The latter begins his account of the tsunami with the words: 6.2.13 παρὰ πάντα τὸν χρόνον ταυτησὶ τῆς βασιλείας ἀγανακτῶν ὁ θεὸς ἐφαίνετο, καὶ παντοδαπαῖς συμφοραῖς ἐν πολλοῖς ἔθνεσιν ἐπέτριψε τὴν Ῥωμαίων ὑπήκοον ('during the whole period of his reign, God showed his wrath and afflicted with manifold disasters many nations in the provinces').

cuius actus multiplices docuimus et interitum The adjective, for which see the note ad 21.6.6 *multiplicisque*, refers to the detailed character of Amm.'s narrative on Procopius in Book 26. His death is reported in 26.9.9.

diem duodecimum kalendas Augustas consule Valentiniano primum cum fratre For the omission of *ante* cf. 17.7.2 *diem nonum kal. Septem-*

brium; 22.13.1 *diem undecimum kalendarum Novembrium* and 23.3.7 *diem sextum kalendas*. The only parallels to this usage quoted in TLL V 1.1034.19–24 are from the *HA*. The date is confirmed by *Consul. Constant.* a. 365 (= *Chron. Min.* II 240), in which it is mentioned in the same breath as Procopius' revolt: *Valentiniano et Valente Augg. his conss. mare ultra terminos suos egressum est die XII kal. Aug. et ipso anno latro nocturnus hostisque publicus intra urbem Constantinopolim apparuit die IIII kal. Oct.*, and also in the Syrian index to Athanasius' Festal Letters, nr. 37, Martin-Albert, 268–269. The date in *Chron. Pasch.* a. 365 (= *Chron. Min.* II 240) Τούτῳ τῷ ἔτει ἡ θάλασσα ἐκ τῶν ἰδίων ὅρων ἐξῆλθεν μηνὶ πανέμῳ πρὸ ιβ´ / καλανδῶν σεπτεμβρίων ('in that year the sea overstepped its own borders in the month Panemos on the twelfth day before the kalends of September') looks like a simple error. The fundamental skepticism of Baudy, 1992 with regard to this date, because it coincides suspiciously with the rising of Sirius and all this stands for in Egypt, is rejected by Mazza, 1994, 320; Waldherr, 1997, 193 n. 124 and Kelly, 2004, 146 n. 38. In addition to their considerations it is worth observing that, while an author like Amm. might have been tempted to introduce such a synchronization, it is hardly conceivable that consular lists would have been manipulated in this way.

horrendi terrores per omnem orbis ambitum grassati sunt subito, quales nec fabulae nec veridicae nobis antiquitates exponunt The lugubrious overtones of the opening words may be compared to the announcement of Valens' impending death in 31.1.3 (his victims) *per quietem stridendo carmina quaedam neniarum horrenda* ("shrieking horrible songs at night, in the form of dirges", tr. Rolfe) *multos diris terroribus agitabant*. The words *per omnem orbis ambitum* recall 26.4.5 *velut per universum orbem Romanum bellicum canentibus bucinis excitae gentes saevissimae limites sibi proximos persultabant*. In this way Amm. suggests the correspondence between historical and natural disasters.

The worldwide impact of the disaster of 365 is a much debated issue. Amm.'s *per omnem orbis ambitum* seems to be confirmed by other sources, such as Hier. *Chron.* a. 366: *Terrae motu per totum orbem facto mare litus egreditur et Siciliae multarumque insularum urbes innumerabiles populos oppressere* (Jerome dates the event inadvertently to 366, but it is undoubtedly identical with the disaster that concerns us here, in view of the words that follow: *Procopius, qui aput Constantinopolim tyrannidem invaserat, aput Frygiam salutarem exstinctus et plurimi Procopianae partis caesi atque proscripti*). Most scholars have followed Jacques and Bousquet, 1984, in accepting the testimony of Jerome as confirmation of Amm.'s report. That a tsunami as forceful as the one Amm. is about to describe would have damaged both Alexandria and Sicily is quite possible. The litany of disasters in Libanius' *Epitaphios, Or.* 18.292 has also been interpreted in this light: ἡ μέν γε Γῆ...τὸν ἄνδρα ἐτίμησεν ἀποσεισαμένη, καθάπερ ἵππος ἀναβάτην, πόλεις τόσας καὶ τόσας, ἐν Παλαιστίνῃ πολλάς, τὰς Λιβύων ἁπάσας. κεῖνται μὲν αἱ μέγισται Σικελίας, κεῖνται δὲ Ἑλλήνων πλὴν μιᾶς αἱ πᾶσαι ("Earth, at least, ...honoured our hero (i.e. Julian). Like a horse tossing its rider, she has destroyed ever so many cities – in Palestine, many, in Libya, all. The greatest cities of Sicily lie in ruins, as does every city in Greece except one", tr. Norman). It has been argued, however, by Henry, 1985, 59, that the earthquakes mentioned in this passage are anterior to the death of Julian, and that Libanius does not show any awareness of the tsunami of 365, which points to a date of publication before the summer of 365. Van Nuffelen, 2006 disagrees about the date of Libanius' speech, but does not deny that the tsunami of 365 has left no traces in *Or.* 18.

On the basis of records such as these, archeologists have explained destructions of buildings in regions as wide apart as Palestine and Spain as the effect of the disaster of 365. Recent studies, however, are much more cautious in this regard. For literature on the subject see Kelly, 2004, 144 with n. 20.

Fabulae refers to mythology; cf. 22.9.15 (Adonis) *amato Veneris, ut fabulae fingunt, apri dente ferali deleto*, whereas *veridicae antiquitates* are trustworthy accounts from ancient history, for which cf. the note ad 22.4.6 *cum scriptum sit*.

10.16 *paulo enim post lucis exortum densitate praevia fulgorum acrius vibratorum tremefacta concutitur omnis terreni stabilitas ponderis* The seemingly exact indication of the time when the earthquake and the ensuing tsunami occurred, raises the question where these phenomena were observed. Apart from two remarks at the end of the passage (§ 19), in which Alexandria and Mothone are specifically mentioned, Amm. does not provide any information on this matter. As the sequel will show, he presents a composite picture of the tsunami and its effects based on data from different quarters of the Mediterranean. It seems superfluous, therefore, to try to reconcile this indication with Theophanes p. 56 De Boor σεισμὸς δὲ μέγας γέγονε καθ' ὅλης τῆς γῆς...ἐν νυκτί, as Kelly, 2004, 144 n. 21 has tried to do. Note the similar introduction to his description of the earthquake which destroyed Nicaea in 358: 17.7.2 *Primo lucis exortu diem nonum kal. Septembrium*.

The gen. inversus after *densitas* occurs eleven times in Amm. "In solchen Verbindungen schwelgt die barocke spätere Sprache", Szantyr 152, who quotes 31.9.2 *per montium celsa silvarumque densitates* as an example. It is typical of the elevated style of the description of the tsunami. The abl. abs. *densitate praevia* is one of attendant circumstances ('preceded by'). Both Baudy, 1992, 50 "Kurz vor Sonnenuntergang (*sic*) bebte die ganze Erde unter heftigen Blitzschlägen" and Mary, 2004, 178 "la terre est ébranlée par un grand nombre de jets de foudre avant-coureurs" interpret *densitate* as an instrumental ablative. However, none of the four types of earthquake distinguished by Amm. in his digression in 17.7 is caused by thunderbolts.

In passages like this one Vergil is never far from the author's mind, cf. *A.* 8.524 *namque inproviso vibratus ab aethere fulgor*. Although the Agens of the participle *vibratorum* is suppressed, the verb suggests the anger of the gods. Mary, 2004, 178 aptly compares 17.7.3 (the earthquake of Nicaea) *velut numine summo fatales contorquente manubias* (thunderbolts). The comparative *acrius* is best understood as "more vigorously (than usual)".

Tremefacta concutitur is again an allusion to Vergil, the comparison of the capture and destruction of Troy (*Neptunia* (!) *Troia*) with a felled ash tree in *A.* 2.629 *et tremefacta comam concusso vertice nutat*. The compact phrase *omnis terreni stabilitas ponderis* ('the whole unshakable earth mass') combines the universal character of the disaster (*omnis*), its paradoxical nature (*concutitur stabilitas*) and the reason why the earth is supposed to be unshakeably fixed in the centre of the universe (*stabilitas ponderis*). As to the unnatural character of an earthquake, cf. e.g. Sen. *Prov.* 1.2 *ut terrarum gravissimum pondus sedeat immotum* and above all the opening chapter of Seneca's discussion of earthquakes, *Nat.* 6.1.4 *quid enim cuiquam satis tutum videri potest, si mundus ipse concutitur et partes eius solidissimae labant, si quod unum inmobile est in illo fixumque, ut cuncta in se intenta sustineat, fluctuatur, si quod proprium habet terra perdidit, stare?* The explanation for the earth's fixed position is that by their weight all things gravitate towards the centre of the universe, which is the middle of the earth. In the words of Cic. *Rep.* 6.17 (a passage with which Amm. was familiar, as was argued in the note ad 20.3.8 *circa terrenam*), *in eam* (terram) *feruntur omnia nutu suo pondera*.

It was common knowledge that tsunamis were caused by seismic activity. Thucydides concludes his description of the tsunami of 426 B.C. in the Sinus Maliacus with the words ἄνευ δὲ σεισμοῦ οὐκ ἄν μοι δοκεῖ τὸ τοιοῦτο ξυμβῆναι γενέσθαι (3.89.5) and the elder Pliny writes *Fiunt cum terrae motu et inundationes maris* (*Nat.* 2.200). On the other hand, it was equally known that earthquakes were local, not universal events, Sen. *Nat.* 6.6.3 *terrarum non universarum sed ex parte motus est.* The fact, however, that the tsunami affected widely distant regions, such as Sicily, the Adriatic and Egypt, may have induced Amm. to present the earthquake as universal. It is equally possible that Amm. has telescoped a great number of separate earthquakes into one major disaster. After all, the second half of the fourth century inaugurated a period of quite exceptional seismic activity, so much so that paleoseismologists have coined the acronym EBTP for it (Early Byzantine Tectonic Paroxysm); Stiros, 2001.

mareque dispulsum retro fluctibus evolutis abscessit The text has never been called into question, but *evolutis* is not above suspicion. The verb *evolvere* combined with *fluctus* does occur: Sen. *Herc. Oet.* 731–732 *utque evolutos frangit Ionio salo/opposita fluctus Leucas* ("when waves rolling in from the Ionian Sea break against the barrier of Leucas", tr. Fitch) and Curt. 4.2.7 (fretum) *Africo maxime obiectum crebros ex alto fluctus in litus evolventi.* ("exposed to the Afric wind, which rolls upon the shore wave on wave from the deep", tr. Rolfe). In both cases it refers to waves driven from sea to land, as one would expect. In the present passage, however, the movement is from land to sea, for which *revolvere* would be more natural. It is highly probable that *revolvere* is indeed the verb Amm. used, inspired, again, by Vergil, who describes ebb-tide as follows: *A.* 11.627–628 (pontus) *nunc rapidus retro atque aestu revoluta resorbens/saxa fugit* ("now it ebbs rapidly in retreat sucking back again the stones sent spinning by its tide", tr. Williams). Cf. also Sil. 15.237–238, where we find the following description of the outgoing tide: *verum ubi concessit pelagi revolubilis unda/et fluctus rapido fugiebat in aequora lapsu.* If indeed *fluctibus revolutis* is what Amm. wrote, it is clear that *retro* should be taken with *revolutis*, not, as TLL V 1.1395.7 suggests, with *dispulsum*.

ut retecta voragine profundorum species natantium multiformes limo cernebantur haerentes Cf. the description in Liv. 22.2.5 of Hannibal's men making their way through the marshes of the Arno *per praealtas fluvii ac profundas voragines hausti paene limo…signa sequebantur.* The expression *species natantium multiformes* for sea animals is a variation on 14.6.9 *species animalium multiformes.* Amm. took as his model Vergil's description of the effects of the plague in *G.* 3.541–543 *iam maris immensi prolem et genus omne natantum/litore in extremo ceu naufraga corpora fluctus / proluit* ('washes up'). *Limo* is probably dative, as in Luc. 9.343/4 (of a ship run aground on the Syrtes) *stant miseri nautae, terraeque haerente carina / litora nulla vident*; see also the end of the note ad 24.5.6 *vulnerato*.

Cernebantur is the reading of V; Gelenius has *cernerentur*. V's reading has been defended convincingly by Blomgren 56–57 on the grounds that it is *lectio difficilior*, and that the alternation of indicative and subjunctive in dependent clauses is a recurrent feature of Amm.'s language.

The phenomenon described here occurs when the trough of the wave signals the tsunami's arrival at a coast, in which case the water recedes and exposes the seafloor.

valliumque vastitates et montium tunc, ut opinari dabatur, suspicerent radios solis, quos primigenia rerum sub immensis gurgitibus amendavit
"Admodum poëtice, ut totus hic locus", Wagner, rightly. The alliteration, together with the use of the gen. inversus, the personification *vastitates suspicerent* and the periphrastic *primigenia rerum* are all part of the elevated register in which Amm. wrote this passage.

It is unlikely that the 'vast valleys and mountains' on the sea bed could be observed from the coast, even if the waves of the tsunami reached the height of the Boxing Day tsunami of 2004 (20 metres). This is confirmed by the phrase *ut opinari dabatur* (which occurs only in Amm.; see the notes ad 24.8.5 and 26.1.7). The expression implies that the preceding statement is based on conjecture, since in 31.13.12 it is followed by *neque enim vidisse se quisquam vel praesto fuisse asseveravit*. Amm. may have borrowed this element of his description from the common source of Theophanes p. 56 De Boor and Georgius Monachus 560–561 (Kelly, 2004, 150), who tell a story about sailors in the Adriatic, whose ship during the tsunami first came to rest on the sea bed, later to be refloated by the returning waters. One cannot rule out that the sailors in the Adriatic really saw the valleys and mountains on the sea bed. It is more likely, however, that Amm. was inspired by poetry. One is reminded of Ovid's description of the Flood, where, as in the present passage, the distinction between land and sea has been removed, and even towers are washed over and hidden from view, *Met*. 1.290–291 *pressaeque* ('submerged') *latent sub gurgite turres; / iamque mare et tellus nullum discrimen habebant*, or, alternatively, of the fall of Phaethon, *Met*. 2.263–264 *quod modo pontus erat, quosque altum texerat aequor, / exsistunt montes et sparsas Cycladas augent*, or again Ovid's description of the storm in which Ceyx was drowned: *Met*. 11.506 *suspicere inferno summum de gurgite caelum*.

The relative pronoun *quos* refers to *montium*, the most striking element in this sentence; cf. Ovid's *latent sub gurgite turres*, quoted above. The adjective *primigenius* occurs more often in Amm. than in any other author except Varro (TLL X 2. 1246.22). He uses it of the original names of towns in 14.8.6 *primigenia tamen nomina non amittunt*, the sources of rivers in 15.4.2 (the Rhine) *navigari ab ortu poterat primigenio* and 22.8.40 *Borysthenes a...primigeniis fontibus copiosus*, and birth, as in 29.1.16 *vitae terminis a primigenio ortu ascriptis* ("the span of life allotted to him at birth", tr. Hamilton) and 30.7. 1 *ab ortu primigenio patris*. In 14.6.17 *primigenios seminis fontes* is a discreet indication of the testicles. *Primigenia rerum* is a unique expression. In TLL X 2.1247.2–5 it is explained as a paraphrase of water, 'the firstborn of things', and compared to Cic. *N.D.* 1.25 *Thales...aquam dixit esse initium rerum*. This is attractive in a context in which earth and water may be called the protagonists, so there is no compelling need to add *natura*, as Mommsen and Novák have proposed. Champeaux, 1975, 935, n. 56, who wrote before the entry in TLL had been published, accepts the addition of *natura*, but is of the opinion that even without it *primigenia* would refer to Nature. On *amendare* see TLL I 1880.12–13: "significatio inde a IV saeculo...passim transit in vim abdendi, occultandi"; cf. also the notes ad 20.2.4 and 20.8.9.

10.17 *multis igitur navibus velut arida humo conexis* As Kelly, 2004, 153, n. 64 points out, in Latin *arida humus* refers to dry (e.g. desert) earth, never to dry land as opposed to sea. It is practically certain that Amm.'s *velut arida humo* renders ὡς ἐπὶ ξηρᾶς in the source of Georgius Monachus and Theophanes. TLL IV 165.42 sqq. does not mention the construction of *conectere* with ablative we find here, and contrary to what is suggested in 166.13, there are no parallels for *conexus* in the sense it has in this passage.

et licenter per exiguas undarum reliquias palantibus plurimis For *licenter* see the note ad 20.10.2 *inquietorum hominum*. With *palari* it occurs in 24.5.5 *cum pabulatoribus paucis licenter palantibus*, where the adverb conveys criticism of the soldiers' irresponsible behaviour. In the present passage it illustrates the astonishing naïveté of the people wandering about as if there were no cloud in the sky. This is confirmed by *cum minime speraretur* in section 18. Exactly the same happened during the terrible tsunami of 1755 in Lisbon, when curious people were attracted to the bay floor, and a large number of them were drowned by the wave crest that followed the trough only minutes later. During the Boxing Day tsunami of 2004 tourists in Thailand were seen wandering around the shoals and photographing the scene.

marini fremitus velut gravati repulsam versa vice consurgunt This is an impressive personification evoking the boom of the waves and the rage of the sea. It may be compared to the equally daring battle description in 25.1.18 (q.v.): *clipeorum sonitus et virorum armorumque lugubre sibilantium fragor...campos cruore et corporum strage contexit.* Amm. turns again to Vergil for inspiration, G. 2.159–160, where the poet addresses the Lago di Garda: *teque, /fluctibus et fremitu adsurgens Benace marino.* The verb *gravari* is here used in the sense of *aegre ferre*, for which see TLL VI 2314.6sqq. In 31.3.7 *gravati praedarum onere* it is passive. For *repulsa* see the note ad 25.1.3 *ad ultimum.* Amm. may have had in mind expressions like *dolor*, c.q. *ira repulsae*, as in Ov. Met. 3.395 *sed tamen haeret amor crescitque dolore repulsae* and Liv. 5.1.5 *ob iram repulsae*, but here he obviously plays with the etymological meaning of the word: 'beating off'. The sea is angry at having been sucked back, and now returns with a vengeance. For *consurgere* cf. Verg. A. 7. 529–530 *paulatim sese tollit mare et altius undas / erigit, inde imo consurgit ad aethera fundo.*

perque vada ferventia insulis et continentis terrae porrectis spatiis violenter illisi innumera quaedam in civitatibus et ubi reperta sunt aedificia complanarunt For *fervere*, 'to seethe', cf. Pac. trag. 416 *fervit aestu pelagus*; Lucr. 6.442 *mare fervere cogens.* The expression *continens* (*terra*) is found from Varro onwards; TLL IV 710.36. For *quidam* "in steigerndem Sinn" (Szantyr 196), see the notes ad 20.4.13 *fortuna quaedam* and 26.5.7 *tractatique asperius.* There is a note on *reperiri* 'to find oneself' ad 22.7.6 *ex negotio.* The verb *complanare* is used also in Amm.'s digression on earthquakes: 17.7.13 *climatiae...urbes, aedificia montesque complanant.*

proinde ut elementorum furente discordia involuta facies mundi miraculorum species ostendebat This is the only instance of *proinde ut*, 'just as if', in Amm. It is either ignored or smoothed over by translators ("so that", Rolfe; "and", Hamilton; "ainsi", Marié, "so", Seyfarth; "cosí", Selem). Probably it has to be taken apo koinou with the abl. abs. *furente discordia* and *involuta facies mundi...ostendebat* as the equivalent of *velut* or *quasi.* Compare the definition of the *narratio* in *Rhet. Her.* 1.3.4 *Narratio est rerum gestarum aut proinde ut gestarum expositio.*

The strife between the elements suggests a relapse into chaos, which Ovid describes as *rudis indigestaque moles / nec quicquam nisi pondus iners congestaque eodem / non bene iunctarum discordia semina rerum* in *Met.* 1.7–9. Cf. also Lucan's description of a storm 5.634–635 *extimuit natura chaos; rupisse videntur / concordes elementa moras* ("i.e. the laws which keep them in harmony", Haskins). This threat is made explicit by Jerome, *Hilar.* 29.1 *ea tempestate terrae motu totius orbis, qui post Iuliani mortem accidit, maria egressa sunt terminos suos, et quasi rursum deus diluvium minaretur vel in antiquum chaos redirent omnia, naves ad praerupta delatae montium pependerunt.*

The expression *facies mundi* occurs five times in Manilius. In other authors it is extremely rare; TLL VI 50.14–17. In the present context *involuta* is best interpreted as 'covered' (with water), for which meaning cf. Verg. A. 6.336 *obruit auster, aqua involvens navemque virosque* and V. Fl. 6.412 *fractas involvunt aequora puppes.* All these elements, water covering the face of the earth, are combined in the description of the world before the Creation in Genesis. Cf. Chrys. *Hom. 1–67 in Gen.* = PG 53, 33. Τοῦτο γὰρ ἦν τὸ καλύπτον τῆς γῆς τὸ πρόσωπον, τὸ σκότος λέγω, καὶ ἡ ἄβυσσος τῶν ὑδάτων and Zon. 1.13 τὸ ὕδωρ τὸ τῆς γῆς ἅπαν καλύπτον πρόσωπον ἐκέλευσεν ὁ θεὸς συναχθῆναι. It certainly looks as if Amm. knew this biblical representation of *chaos*, which is the term Augustine uses in *gen. c. Manich.* 1.5.9 *prima ergo materia facta est confusa et informis, unde omnia fierent quae distincta et formata sunt, quod credo a Graecis chaos appellari.*

For the interpretation "the face of the earth was changed" (Kelly, 2004, 153) no parallels can be found. *Miraculorum* is best taken as a gen. inversus with *species* "wonderful sights" (tr. Hamilton), "des spectacles prodigieux" (Marié).

10.18 *relapsa enim aequorum magnitudo, cum minime speraretur, milia multa necavit hominum et submersit* Both *relapsa* and *recurrentium* in the following sentence refer to the return of the waves after the reflux caused by the tsunami, described in section 16. For *aequorum magnitudo* see the note ad 22.8.30 *undarum magnitudo*. Amm. has many instances of *sperare* in its meaning 'to expect', as here, or even 'to fear', for which cf. 14.7.5 *ut inediae dispelleret metum, quae per multas difficilesque causas affore iam sperabatur* (q.v.). *Necavit et submersit* is best taken as a hendiadys 'killed by drowning'.

recurrentiumque aestuum incitata vertigine quaedam naves, postquam umentis substantiae consenuit tumor, pessumdatae visae sunt The first four words are a variation on *relapsa…aequorum magnitudo* above with added emphasis on the force and the towering height of the waves, *incitatus* combining the notions of speed and fierceness. In a speech to the troops Julian had compared the barbarians who had invaded Gaul with sweeping torrents inundating the province, 20.5.5 *velut incitatos torrentes hostes abruptius inundantes superastis. Vertigo* is used in its primary meaning 'whirl' in 18.8.9 *alii lacunarum hausti vertigine vorabantur*. Here and in 17.1.3 *ut primae vertiginis impetum declinarent* the meaning seems to be 'onslaught'. In 31.10.22 Amm. reports that the trusted general Frigeridus was given his notice on the eve of the battle of Adrianople *in ipsa vertigine pereuntium rerum* ("At the very moment when we were reeling under disasters", tr. Hamilton), borrowed from Luc. 8.16-7, as Hertz, 1874, 273 noted. For *umentis substantiae* cf. the digression on earthquakes 17.7.12 *ideoque Neptunum umentis substantiae potestatem Ennosigaeon et Sisichthona poetae veteres et theologi nuncuparunt*. Kelly, 2004, 142 n. 1 registered ten different words for water in the tsunami episode, not counting *primigenia rerum*. The metaphorical sense of *consenescere*, 'to lose force', is found also in 14.10.5 *tumor consenuit militum*. *Pessumdare* is used in its primary meaning 'to run aground'; TLL X 1. 1917.65–67.

exanimataque naufragiis corpora supina iacebant aut prona This seems to be based on Sol. 1. 95 *pudoris disciplinam etiam inter defuncta corpora natura discrevit: ac si quando cadavera necatorum fluctibus evehuntur, virorum supina, prona fluitant feminarum*.

ingentes aliae naves extrusae rabidis flatibus culminibus insidére tectórum, ut Alexandriae contigit It is amazing that Petschenig's proposal to read *fluctibus* for V's *flatibus*, – noted, but not accepted, by Clark – is not even deemed worthy of mention by Seyfarth, although it is obviously right. This is not a description of a storm, as in 16.10.3 *alium* (Caesar) *anhelante rabido flatu ventorum lenunculo se commisisse piscantis*, but of a tsunami, and although gales may force a ship ashore, they cannot lift it up to the roof of a house. *Rabidus* is used of a raging sea in [Tib.] 3.7.72 *rabidas...undas* and Sen. *Thy.* 361–362 *saevo rabidus freto/ventosi tumor Hadriae*. TLL V 2.2089.70–71 correctly points out that in the compound *extrudere* the prefix gives the sense of 'up', so the ships are both pushed out of the water and lifted up.

10.19

This is the only instance of *insidere* with *navis* as its subject (Vergil does use *sedere* for sailors in a harbour in *A.* 7.201 *fluminis intrastis ripas portuque sedetis*). In Greek καθίζω is used several times of ships, e.g. Plb. 20.5.7 ἐκάθισαν εἰς τὸ ξηρὸν αἱ νῆες αὐτοῦ. As Kelly, 2004, 151 suggests, here again Amm. may have followed the common source of Theophanes and Gregorius Monachus, who have forms of καθίζω in this context.

The perfect *insidi* is rare; TLL VII 1.1883.71–79. As regards the ending *-ére*, Hagendahl, 1923 has shown that in Amm. this form is more common than the ending in *-erunt* (53.9% against 32.3%; the remaining 13.8% being contracted forms of the type *trucidarunt*). Interestingly, 65.6% of the forms in *-erunt* are found in the last position in the colon, whereas the forms ending in *-ere* favour the penultimate position (62.5%). According to Hagendahl this proves that Amm. regularly takes the quantity of syllables into account, which is an important improvement on Harmon's basic study on the clausula in Amm., according to which (p. 187) syllable-quantity plays only a very minor part in his prose.

Alexandria is also mentioned by name as being hit by the tsunami in the Index to Athanasius' Festal Letters, Sozomen, Theophanes and Georgius Monachus. In Amm. Alexandria occurs 9 times, i.a. 22.16.15 (q.v.). Add to the literature cited there Haas, 1997.

et ad secundum lapidem fere procul a litore contortae sunt aliquae The verb *contorquere* is normally used of weapons; cf. 17.7.3 *velut numine summo fatales contorquente manubias* (thunderbolts); 31.15.12 (scorpio) *lapidem contorsit ingentem*. It would be rash to dismiss Amm.'s statement out of hand as being exaggerated. Jacques & Bousquet, 1984, 441 n. 73 refer to Str. 1.3.20, 61 C (λέγουσι) καὶ τῶν πεδίων ἔνια καὶ μέχρι εἴκοσι σταδίων ἐπικλυσθῆναι, καὶ τριήρη τινὰ ἐκ τῶν νεωρίων ἐξαρθεῖσαν ὑπερπεσεῖν τοῦ τείχους ('it is said that some of the plains were flooded for up to twenty stades, and that a triere was lifted out of the dockyard and thrown over its side') and quote spectacular parallels from recent times. In Aceh during the Boxing Day tsunami of 2004, the waves reached 1.5 km inland.

ut Laconicam prope Mothonen oppidum nos transeundo conspeximus diuturna carie fatiscentem Mothone or Methone is situated on the West coast of Messenia (see Meyer-Lafond, 2000), so it is likely that Amm. called in at its harbour in the course of a voyage to Italy. According to Henry, 1985, 43 "Les sites d'Épidaure (mentioned by Jerome) et Mothone sont particulièrement exposés, en temps normal, aux assauts de la mer, et évidemment très vulnérables en cas de conjoncture extraordinaire." With *Laconicam* supply *navem*. Mela mentions a *Laconica classis* in 2.26. Matthews 192 strikingly compared Amm.'s declaration that he personally had seen the effects of the tsunami to the signature on a painting. On the role and importance of autopsy in Amm.'s work see the perceptive remarks in Kelly, 2004, 155–159. At the end of his brilliant description of the tsunami Amm. salutes Vergil with an allusion to *A*. 1.123, where it is said that the ships of Aeneas' companions made water *rimisque fatiscunt*. By using the, at least in literary texts, equally rare *caries* and the addition of *diu-*

turna Amm. also evokes Ov. *Tr.* 5. 12. 27–28 *vertitur in taetram cariem / rimisque dehiscit, / siqua diu solitis cumba vacavit aquis.*

Kelly, 2004, 161–163 proposed to interpret the rotten ship near Mothone as a metaphor for the state. Amm. uses that well-worn metaphor twice in Book 26 (1.5 and 6.3, q.v.). He also calls Julian an experienced helmsman, *perito navigandi magistro*, in 25.5.7 and deplores the fact that the ship of state passed from his trusted hands into those of the immature Jovian in a poignant apostrophe to Fortuna in 25.9.7: *Tu hoc loco, Fortuna orbis Romani, merito incusaris, quae difflantibus procellis rem publicam excussa regimenta perito rei gerendae ductori consummando iuveni porrexisti* (q.v.). Still, a strictly allegorical interpretation risks being reductive and fails to do justice to the power of the image with which Amm. has chosen to conclude this impressive passage. If anything, the ship hurled inland and gradually falling apart evokes in the reader an awareness of the futility of human endeavour when confronted with the forces of nature, and of impotence before the menacing future that is hinted at in this book. Amm. leaves the interpretation of the disaster to his readers. In this way, as Mary, 2004, 184 perceived, he creates for his readers the same atmosphere of uncertainty and foreboding which the participants in the events must have felt.

BIBLIOGRAPHY

This is not an exhaustive or selective list of handbooks, monographs and articles pertaining to the study of Ammianus Marcellinus. It only registers all publications referred to in the commentary after the manner described in section 3 of the *Legenda*. As a rule *RE*-articles are cited after the date of the second 'Halbband'.

Akurgal, E., 'Kyzikos', in: R. Stillwell e.a. (eds.), *The Princeton Encyclopedia of Classical Sites*, Princeton 1976, 473–474.
Aldrete, G.S., *Gestures and Acclamations in Ancient Rome*, Baltimore–London 1999.
Alessio, S., '*Praetorium* e *palatium* come residenze di imperatori e governatori', *Latomus* 65 (2006) 679–689.
Alföldi, A., 'Insignien und Tracht der römischen Kaiser', *MDAI(R)* 50 (1935) 3–158 = *Die monarchische Repräsentation im römischen Kaiserreiche*, Darmstadt 1980³, 121–276, cited as Alföldi, 1980³.
Alföldi, A., *A Conflict of Ideas in the Late Roman Empire. The Clash between the Senate and Valentinian I*, Oxford 1952.
Amici, A., '*Divus Constantinus*: le testimonianze epigrafiche', *RSA* 30 (2000) 187–216.
Amici, A., 'La divinizzazione degli imperatori nel "*breviarium*" di Eutropio. Ancora sulla formula "*meruit inter divos referri*"', *GIF* 54 (2002) 29–51.
Angliviel de la Beaumelle, L., 'La torture dans les *Res Gestae* d'Ammien Marcellin', in: M. Cristol e.a. (eds.), *Institutions, société et vie politique dans l'empire romain au IVe siècle ap. J.-C.* (Actes de la table ronde autour de l'oeuvre d'André Chastagnol, Paris, 20–21 janvier 1989), Rome 1992, 91–113.
Angliviel de la Beaumelle, L., see also G. Sabbah.
Arce, J.J., 'El historiador Ammiano Marcelino y la peña de muerte', *HAnt* 4 (1974) 321–344.
Asutay-Effenberger, N., and A. Effenberger, *Die Porphyrsarkophage der oströmischen Kaiser. Versuch einer Bestandserfassung, Zeitbestimmung und Zuordnung*, Wiesbaden 2006.
Audollent, A., *Defixionum tabellae. Quotquot innotuerunt tam in Graecis Orientis quam in totius Occidentis partibus praeter Atticas in Corpore Inscriptionum Atticarum editas*, Paris 1904.
Austin, N.J.E., 'A Usurper's Claim to Legitimacy. Procopius in A.D. 365/6', *RSA* 2 (1972) 187–194.
Avenarius, G., *Lukians Schrift zur Geschichtsschreibung*, Diss. Frankfurt, Meisenheim 1956.
Baehrens, W.A., 'Bericht über die Literatur zu einigen wichtigen römischen Schriftstellern des 3. und 4. Jahrhunderts aus den Jahren 1910/1–1924, I. Ammianus Marcellinus', *JAW* 203 (1925) 46–90.

Bagnall, R.S., A. Cameron, S.R. Schwartz and K.A. Worp, *Consuls of the Later Roman Empire*, Atlanta 1987.
Balsdon, J.P.V.D., *Romans and Aliens*, London 1979.
Balty, J., '*Paedagogiani*-pages, de Rome à Byzance', in: L. Hadermann-Misguich and G. Raepsaet (eds.), *Rayonnement grec. Hommages à Charles Delvoye*, Brussels 1982, 299–312.
Banchich, T.M., 'Nestorius ἱεροφαντεῖν τεταγμένος', *Historia* 47 (1998) 360–374.
Barb, A.A., 'The Survival of Magic Arts', in: A. Momigliano (ed.), *The Conflict between Paganism and Christianity in the Fourth Century*, Oxford 1963, 100–125.
Barlow, J., and P. Brennan, '*Tribuni scholarum palatinarum* c. A.D. 353–64: Ammianus Marcellinus and the *Notitia Dignitatum*', *CQ* 51 (2001) 237–254.
Barnes, T.D., *The New Empire of Diocletian and Constantine*, Cambridge Mass. 1982.
Barnes, T.D., 'New Year 363 in Ammianus Marcellinus. Annalistic Technique and Historical Apologetics', in: J. den Boeft, D. den Hengst and H.C. Teitler (eds.), *Cognitio Gestorum. The Historiographic Art of Ammianus Marcellinus*, Amsterdam 1992, 1–8.
Barnes, T.D., *Ammianus Marcellinus and the Representation of Historical Reality*, Ithaca–London 1998.
Barry, W.D., 'Roof Tiles and Urban Violence in the Ancient World', *GRBS* 37 (1996) 55–74.
Bartholomew, P., 'Fourth Century Saxons', *Britannia* 15 (1984) 169–185.
Baudy, G.J., 'Die Wiederkehr des Typhon. Katastrophen-Topoi in nachjulianischer Rhetorik und Annalistik: Zu literarischen Reflexen des 21. Juli 365 nC.', *JbAC* 35 (1992) 47–82.
Bauer, F.A., *Stadt, Platz und Denkmal in der Spätantike. Untersuchungen zur Ausstattung des öffentlichen Raums in den spätantiken Städten Rom, Konstantinopel und Ephesos*, Mainz 1996.
Baynes, N.H., 'The Chronology of the Campaigns of Valentinian', in: N.H. Baynes, *Byzantine Studies and Other Essays*, London 1955, 317–320 (=*JRS* 18 [1928] 222–224).
Beacham, R.S., *The Roman Theatre and its Audience*, London 1991.
Beer, G., '*Issicus sinus*', *RE* 9 (1916) 2246.
Belke, K., 'Galatien in der Spätantike', in: E. Schwertheim (ed.), *Forschungen in Galatien*, Bonn 1994, 171–188.
Béranger, J., 'Le refus du pouvoir. Recherches sur l'aspect idéologique du principat', *MH* 5 (1948) 178–196 = *Principatus. Études de notions et d'histoire politiques dans l'Antiquité gréco-romaine*, F. Paschoud and P. Ducrey (eds.), Geneva 1975, 165–190.
Béranger, J., 'La terminologie impériale. Une application à Ammien Marcellin', *Mélanges d'histoire ancienne et d'archéologie offerts à Paul Collart*, Lausanne 1976, 47–60.
Berger, A., 'Konstantinopel', *RAC* 21 (2005) 435–483.
Berger, A., see also K. Strobel.

Bertrand-Dagenbach, C., *Alexandre Sévère et l'*Histoire Auguste (Collection Latomus 208), Brussels 1990.
Bickerman, E.J., *Chronology of the Ancient World*, London 1968.
Birley, A.R., *Septimius Severus. The African Emperor*, London–New York 1999 (= 1988).
Bischoff, B., and D. Nörr, *Eine unbekannte Konstitution Kaiser Julians (c. Iuliani de postulando)* (ABAW 58), Munich 1963.
Bleckmann, B., 'Bemerkungen zu den *Annales* des Nicomachus Flavianus', *Historia* 44 (1995) 83–99.
Bleckmann, B., 'Vom Tsunami von 365 zum Mimas-Orakel: Ammianus Marcelllinus als Zeithistoriker und die spätgriechische Tradition', in: J. den Boeft, J.W. Drijvers, D. den Hengst and H.C. Teitler (eds.), *Ammianus after Julian. The reign of Valentinian and Valens in Books 26–31 of the* Res Gestae, Leiden 2007, 7–31.
Blockley, R.C., *Ammianus Marcellinus. A Study of his Historiography and Political Thought*, Brussels 1975.
Blockley, R.C., 'Ammianus and Cicero: the Epilogue of the *History* as a Literary Statement', *Phoenix* 52 (1998) 305–314.
Blockley, R.C., 'Ammianus and Cicero on Truth in Historiography', *AHB* 15 (2001) 14–24.
Blomgren, S., *De sermone Ammiani Marcellini quaestiones variae*, Uppsala 1937.
Boeft, J. den, 'Ammianus graecissans?', in: J. den Boeft, D. den Hengst and H.C. Teitler (eds.), *Cognitio Gestorum. The Historiographic Art of Ammianus Marcellinus*, Amsterdam 1992, 9–18.
Boeft, J. den, '*Non consolandi gratia, sed probrose monendi* (*Res Gestae* 28.1.4). The Hazards of (Moral) Historiography', in: J. den Boeft, J.W. Drijvers, D. den Hengst and H.C. Teitler (eds.), *Ammianus after Julian. The reign of Valentinian and Valens in Books 26–31 of the* Res Gestae, Leiden 2007, 293–311.
Bonamente, G., 'Apoteosi e imperatori cristiani', in: G. Bonamente and A. Nestori (eds.), *I Cristiani e l'Impero nel IV secolo*, Macerata 1988, 107–142.
Bonner, C., 'Witchcraft in the Lecture Room of Libanius', *TAPhA* 63 (1932) 34–44.
Borleffs, J.G.P., 'An scripserit Lactantius libellum qui est *de Mortibus Persecutorum*', *Mnemosyne* 58 (1930) 223–292.
Bousquet, B., see F. Jacques.
Bradbury, S., *Selected Letters of Libanius from the Age of Constantius and Julian* (Translated Texts for Historians 41), Liverpool 2004.
Brandt, A., *Moralische Werte in den* Res gestae *des Ammianus Marcellinus* (Hypomnemata 122), Göttingen 1999.
Brauch, T., 'Notes on the Prefects of Constantinople AD 366–369', *Byzantion* 72 (2002) 42–104.
Brennan, P., see J. Barlow.
Brilliant, R., *Gesture and Rank in Roman Art. The Use of Gestures to Denote Status in Roman Sculpture and Coinage* (Memoirs of the Connecticut Academy of Arts & Sciences 14), New Haven 1963.

Brind'Amour, P., *Le calendrier romain. Recherches chronologiques*, Ottawa 1983.
Briquel, D., *Chrétiens et haruspices: la religion étrusque, dernier rempart du paganisme romain*, Paris 1998.
Brodka, D., *Die Romideologie in der römischen Literatur der Spätantike* (Europäische Hochschulschriften XV, 76), Frankfurt am Main 1998.
Broughton, T.R.S., *The Magistrates of the Roman Republic* I–II, New York 1951–1952; III, Atlanta 1986.
Burgess, R.W., 'A Common Source for Jerome, Eutropius, Festus, Ammianus, and the *Epitome de Caesaribus* between 358 and 378, along with Further Thoughts on the Date and Nature of the *Kaisergeschichte*', *CPh* 100 (2005) 166–195.
Cabouret, B., P.-L. Gatier and C. Saliou (eds.), *Antioche de Syrie. Histoire, images et traces de la ville antique* (Topoi. Orient-Occident, Suppl. 5), Lyon 2004.
Caltabiano, M., *Ammiano Marcellino. Storie*, Milan 1989.
Cameron, A., 'Polyonomy in the Late Roman Aristocracy: the Case of Petronius Probus', *JRS* 75 (1985) 164–182.
Cameron, Av., and S.G. Hall, *Eusebius. Life of Constantine*. Introduction, translation and commentary, Oxford 1999.
Camus, P.-M., *Ammien Marcellin. Témoin des courants culturels et religieux à la fin du IVe siècle*, Paris 1967.
Canfora, L., *Totalità e selezione nella storiografia classica*, Bari 1972.
Castillo, C., 'Tribunos militares en Ammianus Marcellinus', in: Y. Le Bohec and C. Wolff (eds.), *L'armée romaine de Dioclétien à Valentinien Ier*, Lyon–Paris 2004, 43–54.
Cèbe, J.-P., *Varron, Satires Ménippées*, IX, Paris 1990.
Champeaux, J., '*Primigenius* ou de l'originaire', *Latomus* 34 (1975) 909–985.
Charlet, J.-L., 'Théologie, politique et rhétorique. La célébration poétique de Pâques à la cour de Valentinien et d'Honorius, d'après Ausone (*Versus Paschales*) et Claudien (*De Salvatore*)', in: S. Costanza (ed.), *La poesia tardoantica: tra retorica, teologia e politica*, Messina 1984, 259–287.
Chastagnol, A., 'Observations sur le consulat suffect et la préture du Bas-Empire', *RH* 219 (1958) 221–253.
Chastagnol, A., *La préfecture urbaine à Rome sous le Bas-Empire*, Paris 1960.
Chastagnol, A., *Les fastes de la préfecture de Rome au Bas-Empire*, Paris 1962.
Chastagnol, A., 'Le fonctionnement de la préfecture urbaine', in: *La Rome impériale: démographie et logistique*, Rome 1997, 111–119.
Chausson, F., 'Une soeur de Constantin: Anastasia', in: J.-M. Carrié and R. Lizzi Testa (eds.), *Humana sapit. Études d'antiquité tardive offertes à Lellia Cracco Ruggini*, Turnhout 2002, 131–135.
Chauvot, A., *Opinions romaines face aux barbares au IVe siècle ap. J.-C.*, Paris 1998.
Chauvot, A., 'Ammien Marcellin, les clarissimes et la torture au IVe siècle', in: *Romanité et cité chrétienne. Permanences et mutations, intégration et exclusion du Ier au Ve siècle. Mélanges en l'honneur d'Yvette Duval*, Paris 2000, 65–76.
Chauvot, A., 'La détention chez Ammien Marcellin. Images littéraires et problèmes juridiques', in: C. Bertrand-Dagenbach e.a. (eds.), *Carcer II*.

Prison et privation de liberté dans l'empire romain et l'occident médiéval, Paris 2004, 33-40.
Christes, J., 'Lucilius [I 6]', *DNP* 7 (1999) 463-465.
Chrysos, E., 'Räumung und Aufgabe von Reichsterritorien. Der Vertrag von 363', *BJ* 193 (1993) 165-202.
Clauss, M., *Kaiser und Gott. Herrscherkult im römischen Reich*, Stuttgart-Leipzig 1999.
Clerc, J.-B., *Homines Magici. Étude sur la sorcellerie et la magie dans la société romaine impériale* (Europäische Hochschulschriften III, 673), Frankfurt am Main 1995.
Cleve, R.L., *Severus Alexander and the Severan Women*, Los Angeles 1982.
Cornelissen, J.J., 'Ad Ammianum Marcellinum adversaria critica', *Mnemosyne* 14 (1886) 234-304.
Coşkun, A., 'Die *Praefecti praesent(al)es* und die Regionalisierung der Praetorianerpraefecturen im vierten Jahrhundert', *Millennium* 1 (2004) 279-328.
Curran, J., 'From Jovian to Theodosius', in: Av. Cameron and P. Garnsey (eds.), *The Cambridge Ancient History* XIII. The Late Empire, A.D. 337-425, Cambridge 1998, 78-110.
Dagron, G., *Naissance d'une capitale: Constantinople et ses institutions de 330 à 451*, Paris 1974.
Damsté, P.H., 'Ad Ammianum Marcellinum', *Mnemosyne* 58 (1930) 1-12.
Davies, J.P., *Rome's Religious History. Livy, Tacitus and Ammianus on their Gods*, Cambridge 2004.
Delmaire, R., 'Les usurpateurs du Bas-Empire et le recrutement des fonctionnaires (Essai de réflexion sur les assises du pouvoir et leur limites)', in: F. Paschoud and J. Szidat (eds.), *Usurpationen in der Spätantike* (Historia Einzelschriften 111), Stuttgart 1997, 111-126.
Demandt, A., *Zeitkritik und Geschichtsbild im Werk Ammians*, Bonn 1965.
Demandt, A., 'Die Afrikanischen Unruhen unter Valentinian I.', in: J.H. Diesner, H. Barth and H.D. Zimmermann (eds.), *Afrika und Rom in der Antike*, Halle 1968, 277-292.
Demandt, A., 'Die Tripolitanischen Wirren unter Valentinian I.', *Byzantion* 38 (1968) 333-363.
Demandt, A., '*Magister militum*', *RE* Suppl. 12 (1970) 553-790.
Demandt, A., *Die Spätantike. Römische Geschichte von Diocletian bis Justinian 284-565 n. Chr.* (Handbuch der Altertumswissenschaft III.6), Munich 1989.
Demandt, A., *Das Privatleben der römischen Kaiser*, Munich 1997².
Demandt, A., 'Lebensweisheit bei Ammian', in: H. Heftner and K. Tomaschitz (eds.), Ad Fontes! *Festschrift für Gerhard Dobesch zum fünfundsechzigsten Geburtstag am 15. September 2004, dargebracht von Kollegen, Schülern und Freunden*, Vienna 2004, 805-808.
Dickie, M.W., *Magic and Magicians in the Greco-Roman World*, London-New York 2001.
Dietz, K., Senatus contra principem. *Untersuchungen zur senatorischen Opposition gegen Maximinus Thrax*, Munich 1980.

Dignas, B., see E. Winter.
Dixon, K.R., see P. Southern.
Dovere, E., '"*Oblatum imperium deprecatus es*": etica e "*recusatio imperii*" in età tardoantica', *SDHI* 62 (1996) 551–562.
Drew-Bear, T., 'A Fourth-Century Latin Soldier's Epitaph at Nakolea', *HSPh* 81 (1977) 257–274.
Drijvers, J.W., *Helena Augusta: The Mother of Constantine the Great and the Legend of her Finding of the True Cross*, Leiden 1992.
Drijvers, J.W., 'Ammianus on the Revolt of Firmus', in: J. den Boeft, J.W. Drijvers, D. den Hengst and H.C. Teitler (eds.), *Ammianus after Julian. The Reign of Valentinian and Valens in Books 26–31 of the* Res Gestae, Leiden 2007, 129–155.
Drinkwater, J.F., '"The Germanic Threat on the Rhine Frontier": A Romano-Gallic Artefact?', in: R.W. Mathisen and H. Sivan (eds.), *Shifting Frontiers in Late Antiquity*, Aldershot 1996, 20–30.
Drinkwater, J.F., *The Alamanni and Rome, 213–496. Caracalla to Clovis*, Oxford 2007.
Ducloux, A., Ad ecclesiam confugere. *Naissance du droit d'asile dans les églises (IVe – milieu du Ve s.)*, Paris 1994.
Dufraigne, P., 'Quelques remarques sur l'*adventus* chez Ammien Marcellin et les Panégyristes', in: L. Holtz and J.C. Fredouille (eds.), *De Tertullien aux Mozarabes. Mélanges offerts à Jacques Fontaine à l'occasion de son 70e anniversaire par ses élèves, amis et collègues*, I, Paris 1992, 497–509.
Duval, N., 'Les résidences impériales: leur rapport avec les problèmes de légitimité, les partages de l'empire et la chronologie des combinaisons dynastiques', in: F. Paschoud and J. Szidat (eds.), *Usurpationen in der Spätantike* (Historia Einzelschriften 111), Stuttgart 1997, 127–153.
Dzino, D., '*Sabaiarius*: Beer, wine and Ammianus Marcellinus', in: W. Mayer and S. Trzcionka (eds.), *Feast, Fast or Famine. Food and Drink in Byzantium* (Byzantina Australiensia 15), Brisbane 2005, 57–68.
Effenberger, A., see N. Asutay-Effenberger.
Ehrhardt, A., '*Tormenta*', *RE* 6A (1937) 1775–1794.
Ehrismann, H., *De temporum et modorum usu Ammianeo*, Diss. Strasbourg 1886.
Eichele, H., 'Zu *Aulaeum* als Theatervorhang, vornehmlich bei Ammian', *QC* 6 (1984) 145–160.
Elliott, T.G., *Ammianus Marcellinus and fourth-century History*, Sarasota–Toronto 1983.
Elton, H., *Warfare in Roman Europe, AD 350–425*, Oxford 1996.
Emmett, A., 'Introductions and Conclusions to Digressions in Ammianus Marcellinus', *MPhL* 5 (1981) 15–33.
Ensslin, W., *Zur Geschichtsschreibung und Weltanschauung des Ammianus Marcellinus* (Klio-Beiheft 16), Leipzig 1923 (repr. Aalen 1971).
Ensslin, W., 'Zum Heermeisteramt des spätrömischen Reiches, II. Die *magistri militum* des 4. Jahrhunderts', *Klio* 24 (1931) 102–147.
Ensslin, W., 'Der konstantinische Patriziat und seine Bedeutung im 4. Jahrhundert', in: *Mélanges Bidez* (Annuaire de l'Institut de Philologie et d'Histoire Orientales et Slaves 2), Brussels 1934, 361–376.

Ensslin, W., 'Germanen in römischen Diensten', *Gymnasium* 52 (1941) 5–25.
Ensslin, W., 'Zur Torqueskrönung und Schilderhebung bei der Kaiserwahl', *Klio* 35 (1942) 268–298.
Ensslin, W., '*Paedagogiani*', *RE* 18.1 (1942) 2204–2205.
Ensslin, W., 'Prokopios (Usurpator)', *RE* 23.1 (1957) 252–256.
Errington, R.M., *Roman Imperial Policy from Julian to Theodosius*, Chapel Hill 2006.
Fleer, C., see E. Wirbelauer.
Fletcher, G.B.A., 'Notes on Ammianus Marcellinus', *CQ* 24 (1930) 193–197.
Fletcher, G.B.A., 'Ammianea', *AJPh* 58 (1937) 392–402.
Fletcher, G.B.A., 'On Ammianus Marcellinus 21, 2, 4 and 26, 5, 2', *AJPh* 60 (1939) 242.
Flobert, P., *Les verbes déponents latins des origines à Charlemagne*, Paris 1975.
Fluss, M., 'Helvius 15a', *RE* Suppl. 3 (1918) 895–904.
Fögen, M.Th., *Die Enteignung der Wahrsager. Studien zum kaiserlichen Wissensmonopol in der Spätantike*, Frankfurt am Main 1997.
Folkerts, M., 'Archimedes 1', *DNP* 1 (1996) 997–1001.
Fornara, C.W., 'The Prefaces of Ammianus Marcellinus', in: M. Griffith and D.J. Mastronarde (eds.), *Cabinet of Muses. Essays on Classical and Comparative Literature in Honor of Thomas G. Rosenmeyer*, Atlanta 1990, 163–172.
Fornara, C.W., 'Studies in Ammianus Marcellinus, II: Ammianus' Knowledge and Use of Greek and Latin Literature', *Historia* 41 (1992) 420–438.
French, D., *Roman Roads and Milestones of Asia Minor. Fasc. I: The Pilgrim's Road* (BAR International Series 105), Oxford 1981.
Fuchs, K., e.a. (eds.), *Die Alamannen*, Stuttgart 1997.
Gager, J.G., *Curse Tablets and Binding Spells from the Ancient World*, Oxford–New York 1992.
Gaggiotti, M., 'L. Turcius Apronianus Asterius: un inedito *consularis Campaniae*', *AFLPer* 23 (1985–1986) 153–162.
Garnsey, P., *Social Status and Legal Privilege in the Roman Empire*, Oxford 1970.
Garnsey, P., 'Famine in History', in: P. Garnsey, *Cities, Peasants and Food in Classical Antiquity. Essays in Social and Economic History*, ed. by W. Scheidel, Cambridge 1998, 272–292.
Garnsey, P., and C. Humfress, *The Evolution of the Late Antique World*, Cambridge 2001.
Gärtner, H., 'Zu Ammianus Marcellinus', *Hermes* 97 (1969) 362–371.
Gatier, P.-L., see B. Cabouret.
Gilliam, J.F., 'Ammianus and the *Historia Augusta*: the Lost Books and the Period 117–285' (BHAC 1970), Bonn 1972, 125–147.
Grattarola, P., 'L'usurpazione di Procopio e la fine dei Costantinidi', *Aevum* 60 (1986) 82–105.
Green, P.M., *Alexander to Actium. The Historical Evolution of the Hellenistic Age*, Berkeley–Los Angeles 1990.
Gregory, T.E., 'Urban Violence in Late Antiquity', in: R.T. Marchese (ed.), *Aspects of Graeco-Roman Urbanism. Essays on the Classical City* (BAR International Series 188), Oxford 1983 (1984), 138–161.

Grodzynski, D., 'Tortures mortelles et catégories sociales. Les *summa supplicia* dans le droit romain aux IIIe et IVe siècles', in: *Du châtiment dans la cité. Supplices corporels et peine de mort dans le monde antique* (Collections de l'École Française de Rome 79), Rome 1984, 361–403.
Günther, O., *Quaestiones Ammianeae criticae*, Diss. Göttingen 1888.
Günther, O., 'Zur Textkritik des Ammianus Marcellinus', *Philologus* 50 (1891) 65–73.
Gušić, S., 'Mediana', in: D. Srejović (ed.), *Roman Imperial Towns and Places in Serbia*, Belgrade 1993, 169–177.
Gutmann, B., *Studien zur römischen Aussenpolitik in der Spätantike (364–395 n. Chr.)*, Bonn 1991.
Gutsfeld, A., 'Der Prätorianerpräfekt und der kaiserliche Hof im 4. Jahrhundert n. Chr.', in: A. Winterling (ed.), *Comitatus. Beiträge zur Erforschung des spätantiken Kaiserhofes*, Berlin 1998, 75–102.
Guzmán Armario, F.J., *Los bárbaros en Amiano Marcelino*, Madrid 2002.
Haack, M.-L., '*Haruspices* publics et privés: tentative d'une distinction', *REA* 104 (2002) 111–133.
Haas, C.J., *Alexandria in Late Antiquity. Topography and Social Conflict*, Baltimore–London 1997.
Haensch, R., 'La christianisation de l'armée romaine', in: Y. Le Bohec and C. Wolff (eds.), *L'armée romaine de Dioclétien à Valentinien Ier*, Lyon–Paris 2004, 525–531.
Hagendahl, H., *Studia Ammianea*, Diss. Uppsala 1921.
Hagendahl, H., 'De abundantia sermonis Ammianei', *Eranos* 22 (1924) 161–216.
Hahn, I., 'Zur Frage der sozialen Grundlagen der Usurpation des Procopius (in Russian, with a summary in German)', *AAntHung* 6 (1958) 199–211.
Hajnóczi, G. (ed.), *La Pannonia e l'impero Romano* (Atti del convegno internazionale 'La Pannonia e l'impero Romano', Accademia d'Ungheria e l'Istituto Austriaco di Cultura, Roma, 13–16 gennaio 1994), Rome 1995.
Hall, S.G., see Av. Cameron.
Hamilton, W., and A. Wallace-Hadrill, *Ammianus Marcellinus: the Later Roman Empire (A.D. 354–378)*, Harmondsworth 1986.
Hannah, R., *Greek and Roman Calendars. Constructions of Time in the Classical World*, London 2005.
Harmon, A.M., *The Clausula in Ammianus Marcellinus* (Transactions of the Connecticut Academy of Arts and Sciences 16, 117–245), New Haven 1910.
Harries, J., 'The Roman imperial *quaestor* from Constantine to Theodosius II', *JRS* 78 (1988) 148–172.
Harries, J., *Law and Empire in Late Antiquity*, Cambridge 1999.
Hasluck, F.W., *Cyzicus*, Cambridge 1910.
Haupt, M., 'De historiarum Ammiani Marcellini emendatione', in: M. Haupt, *Opuscula* II, Leipzig 1876, 371–394.
Haupt, M., 'Emendantur Ammiani Marcellini historiae', in: M. Haupt, *Opuscula* II, Leipzig 1876, 490–507.

Häussler, R., *Nachträge zu A. Otto, Sprichwörter und sprichwörtliche Redensarten der Römer*, Darmstadt 1968.
Heather, P., *Goths and Romans 332–489*, Oxford 1991.
Heather, P., 'Senators and Senates', in: Av. Cameron and P. Garnsey (eds.), *The Cambridge Ancient History* XIII. *The Late Empire, A.D. 337–425*, Cambridge 1998, 184–210.
Heather, P., 'Goths and Huns, c. 320–425', in: Av. Cameron and P. Garnsey (eds.), *The Cambridge Ancient History* XIII. *The Late Empire, A.D. 337–425*, Cambridge 1998, 487–515, cited as Heather, 1998b.
Heather, P., 'The Barbarian in Late Antiquity. Image, Reality and Transformation', in: R. Miles (ed.), *Constructing Identities in Late Antiquity*, London 1999, 234–258.
Heering, W., *Kaiser Valentinian I. (364–375 n. Chr.)* (Diss. Jena), Magdeburg 1927.
Heil, W., *Der konstantinische Patriziat* (Basler Studien zur Rechtswissenschaft 78), Basle 1966.
Heim, F., '*Vox exercitus, vox dei*. La désignation de l'empereur charismatique au IVe siècle', *REL* 68 (1990) 160–172.
Hekster, O.J., *Commodus. An Emperor at the Crossroads*, Amsterdam 2002.
Hengst, D. den, *The Prefaces in the* Historia Augusta, Amsterdam 1981.
Hengst, D. den, 'The scientific digressions in Ammianus' *Res Gestae*', in: J. den Boeft, D. den Hengst and H.C. Teitler (eds.), *Cognitio Gestorum. The Historiographic Art of Ammianus Marcellinus*, Amsterdam 1992, 39–46.
Hengst, D. den, 'Literary Aspects of Ammianus' Second Digression on Rome', in: J. den Boeft, J.W. Drijvers, D. den Hengst and H.C. Teitler (eds.), *Ammianus after Julian. The reign of Valentinian and Valens in Books 26–31 of the* Res Gestae, Leiden 2007, 159–179.
Henry, M., 'Le témoignage de Libanius et les phénomènes sismiques du IVe siècle de notre ère. Essai d'interprétation', *Phoenix* 39 (1985) 36–61.
Herkommer, E., *Die Topoi in den Proömien der römischen Geschichtsschreiber*, Diss. Tübingen 1968.
Herz, P., *Studien zur römischen Wirtschaftsgesetzgebung. Die Lebensmittelversorgung*, Stuttgart 1988.
Heumann, H.G., and E. Seckel, *Handlexikon zu den Quellen des römischen Rechts*, Graz 1958^{10}.
Hoffmann, D., *Das spätrömische Bewegungsheer und die* Notitia Dignitatum, 2 vols., Düsseldorf 1969–1970.
Hofmann, J.B., and A. Szantyr, *Lateinische Syntax und Stilistik*, Munich 1965 (repr. 1972), cited as Szantyr.
Hopwood, K., 'Ammianus on Isauria', in: J.W. Drijvers and D. Hunt (eds.), *The Late Roman World and its Historian. Interpreting Ammianus Marcellinus*, London–New York 1999, 224–235.
Hübner, W., 'Euktemon', *DNP* 4 (1998) 244.
Hübner, W., 'Hipparchos 6', *DNP* 5 (1998) 568–571, cited as Hübner, 1998a.
Hübner, W., 'Meton 2', *DNP* 8 (2000) 107–108.

Hübner, W., 'Tierkreis', *DNP* 12/1 (2002) 553–563.
Humfress, C., see P. Garnsey.
Hunt, D., 'Valentinian and the Bishops: Ammianus 30.9.5 in Context', in: J. den Boeft, J.W. Drijvers, D. den Hengst and H.C. Teitler (eds.), *Ammianus after Julian. The reign of Valentinian and Valens in Books 26–31 of the* Res Gestae, Leiden 2007, 71–93.
Huttner, U., Recusatio Imperii. *Ein politisches Ritual zwischen Ethik und Taktik* (Spudasmata 23), Hildesheim 2004.
Isaac, B., *The Limits of Empire. The Roman Army in the East*, Oxford 1992².
Jacques, F., and B. Bousquet, 'Le raz de marée du 21 juillet 365. Du cataclysme local à la catastrophe cosmique', *MEFR* 96 (1984) 423–461.
Jenkins, F.W., 'Theatrical Metaphors in Ammianus Marcellinus', *Eranos* 85 (1987) 55–63.
Jones, A.H.M., 'The Social Background of the Struggle between Paganism and Christianity', in: A. Momigliano (ed.), *The Conflict between Paganism and Christianity in the Fourth Century*, Oxford 1963, 17–37.
Jones, A.H.M., 'Collegiate Prefectures', *JRS* 54 (1964) 78–89 (repr. in A.H.M. Jones, *The Roman Economy*, ed. P.A. Brunt, London 1974, 375–395), cited as Jones, 1974.
Jones, A.H.M., *The Later Roman Empire 284–602. A Social Economic and Administrative Survey*, Oxford 1964 (repr. 1986), cited as Jones.
Jordan, D.R., 'A Survey of Greek *defixiones* not included in the Special Corpora', *GRBS* 26 (1985) 151–197.
Jordan, D.R., 'A Curse on Charioteers and Horses at Rome', *ZPE* 141 (2002) 141–147 (corrigendum: *ZPE* 144 [2003] 30).
Jouanaud, J.-L., '*Barbarus*, Malalas et le *bissextus*. Pistes de recherche', in: J. Beaucamp (ed.), *Recherches sur la Chronique de Jean Malalas*, Paris 2004, 165–180.
Kaerst, J., 'Aeropos 5', *RE* 1 (1894) 679.
Kellerbauer, A., 'Kritische Kleinigkeiten (zu Ammianus Marcellinus)', *Blätter für das Bayerische Gymnasialschulwesen* 7 (1871) 11–24; 9 (1873) 81–91, 127–141.
Kelly, Chr., *Ruling the Later Roman Empire*, Cambridge Mass. 2004.
Kelly, G., 'The New Rome and the Old: Ammianus Marcellinus' Silences on Constantinople', *CQ* 53 (2003) 588–607.
Kelly, G., 'Ammianus and the Great Tsunami', *JRS* 94 (2004) 141–167.
Kelly, G., 'The Sphragis and Closure of the *Res Gestae*', in: J. den Boeft, J.W. Drijvers, D. den Hengst and H.C. Teitler (eds.), *Ammianus after Julian. The reign of Valentinian and Valens in Books 26–31 of the* Res Gestae, Leiden 2007, 219–241.
Kent, J.P.C., '*Fel. Temp. Reparatio*', *NC* 7 (1967) 83–90.
Kettenhofen, E., *Die syrischen Augustae in der historischen Überlieferung: ein Beitrag zum Problem der Orientalisierung*, Bonn 1979.
Kienast, D., *Untersuchungen zu den Kriegsflotten der römischen Kaiserzeit*, Bonn 1966.
Kienast, D., *Römische Kaisertabelle. Grundzüge einer römischen Kaiserchronologie*, Darmstadt 1996².

Kneppe, A., *Untersuchungen zur städtischen Plebs des 4. Jahrhunderts n. Chr.*, Bonn 1979.
Kohns, H.P., *Versorgungskrisen und Hungerrevolten im spätantiken Rom*, Bonn 1961.
Kolendo, J., 'Les noms dynastiques de villes. Philippe l'Arabe et Philippopolis de Thrace et d'Arabie', *Index* 20 (1992) 51–55.
Konrad, C.F., *Plutarch's Sertorius. A Historical Commentary*, Chapel Hill–London 1994.
Koukouli-Chrysanthaki, Ch., 'Via Egnatia-Akontisma' (in Greek, with a summary in English), *AAA* 5 (1972) 474–485.
Krause, J.-U., *Gefängnisse im Römischen Reich* (Heidelberger Althistorische Beiträge und Epigraphische Studien 23), Stuttgart 1996.
Krebs, J.Ph., and J.H. Schmalz, *Antibarbarus der lateinischen Sprache*, Basle 1905–1907 (repr. Darmstadt 1984).
Krenkel, W.A., *Saturae Menippeae / Marcus Terentius Varro*, vol. 2, St. Katharinen 2002.
Kroon, C.H.M., *Discourse Particles in Latin. A Study of* nam, enim, autem, vero, *and* at, Amsterdam 1995.
Kübler, B., '*Patres, patricii*', *RE* 18.2 (1949) 2222–2232.
Kudlien, F., see W. Seyfarth.
Kühner, R., and B. Gerth, *Ausführliche Grammatik der griechischen Sprache (Satzlehre)*, 2 vols., Leverkusen 1955[4].
Kühner, R., and F. Holzweissig, *Ausführliche Grammatik der lateinischen Sprache*, I, *Elementar-, Formen- und Wortlehre*, Hannover 1912[2].
Kühner, R., and C. Stegmann, *Ausführliche Grammatik der lateinischen Sprache*, II, *Satzlehre*, 2 vols., Hannover 1955[4], 1976[5], cited as Kühner-Stegmann.
Lafond, Y., see E. Meyer.
Langenfeld, H., *Christianisierungspolitik und Sklavengesetzgebung der römischen Kaiser von Konstantin bis Theodosius II.* (Antiquitas 1, 26), Bonn 1977.
Latte, K., 'Todesstrafe', *RE* Suppl. 7 (1940) 1599–1619.
Lee, A.D., *Information and Frontiers. Roman Foreign Relations in Late Antiquity*, Cambridge 1993.
Lehnen, J., Adventus principis. *Untersuchungen zu Sinngehalt und Zeremoniell der Kaiserankunft in den Städten des Imperium Romanum*, Frankfurt am Main 1997.
Lendle, O., *Schildkröten. Antike Kriegsmaschinen in poliorketischen Texten* (Palingenesia 10), Wiesbaden 1975.
Lendon, J.E., *Empire of Honour. The Art of Government in the Roman World*, Oxford 1997.
Lenski, N., *Failure of Empire. Valens and the Roman State in the Fourth Century A.D.*, Berkeley–Los Angeles–London 2002.
Lenski, N., 'Were Valentinian, Valens and Jovian Confessors before Julian the Apostate?', *ZAC* 6 (2002) 253–276, cited as Lenski, 2002a.
Lepore, P., 'In margine ad Ammiano Marcellino 26.5.8–14', *Athenaeum* 88 (2000) 585–597.
Leppin, H., and W. Portmann, *Themistius, Staatsreden*. Übersetzung, Einführung und Erläuterungen, Stuttgart 1998.

Leppin, H., 'Der Reflex der Selbstdarstellung der valentinianischen Dynastie bei Ammianus Marcellinus und den Kirchenhistorikern', in: J. den Boeft, J.W. Drijvers, D. den Hengst and H.C. Teitler (eds.), *Ammianus after Julian. The reign of Valentinian and Valens in Books 26–31 of the* Res Gestae, Leiden 2007, 33–51.

Leumann, M., *Lateinische Laut- und Formenlehre*, Munich 1977, cited as Leumann.

Löfstedt, E., *Beiträge zur Kenntnis der späteren Latinität*, Diss. Uppsala 1907.

Löfstedt, E., *Philologischer Kommentar zur* Peregrinatio Aetheriae. *Untersuchungen zur Geschichte der lateinischen Sprache*, Uppsala 1911.

Loguercio, G., '*Quaestor sacri palatii*', *Euresis* (1986) 75–90.

Lorenz, S., Imperii fines erunt intacti. *Rom und die Alamannen 350–378* (Europäische Hochschulschriften III, 722), Frankfurt am Main 1995.

Lotz, A., *Der Magiekonflikt in der Spätantike*, Bonn 2005.

MacMullen, R., *Soldier and Civilian in the Later Roman Empire*, Cambridge Mass. 1963.

MacMullen, R., 'Judicial Savagery in the Roman Empire', *Chiron* 16 (1986) 147–166.

Madvig, J.N., *Adversaria critica ad scriptores Graecos et Latinos* III, Haunia (Copenhagen) 1884.

Manfredini, A.D., '"*Ad ecclesiam confugere*", "*ad statuas confugere*" nell'età di Teodosio I', *Accad. Costantiniana VI conv. intern.* (1986) 39–58.

Mango, C., *Le développement urbain de Constantinople (IVe–VIIe siècles)*, Paris 1985.

Mango, C., 'The Empress Helena, Helenopolis, Pylae', *T&MByz* 12 (1994) 143–158.

Marié, M.-A., *Ammien Marcellin, Histoire V (Livres XXVI–XXVIII)*, Paris 1984.

Martin, J., *Antike Rhetorik. Technik und Methode* (Handbuch der Altertumswissenschaft II.3), Munich 1974.

Mary, L., 'Reconnaissance par les gouffres: métaphysique des séismes et poétique de l'histoire chez Ammien Marcellin', in: E. Foulon (ed.), *Connaissance et représentations des volcans dans l'Antiquité* (Collection ERGA, Recherches sur l'Antiquité 5), Clermont-Ferrand 2004, 171–190.

Matthews, J.F., *The Roman Empire of Ammianus*, London 1989.

Maurice, J., 'La terreur de la Magie au IVe siècle', *RD* 6 (1927) 108–120.

Mazza, M., 'Cataclismi e calamità naturali: la documentazione letteraria', *Kokalos* 36–37 (1990–1991 [1994]) 307–330.

Mazza, M., 'Bisanzio e Persia nella tarda antichità: note su guerre e diplomazia nella seconda metà del IV secolo D.C.', in: U. Criscuolo (ed.), *Da Costantino a Teodosio il Grande. Cultura, società, diritto* (Atti Convegno Internazionale Napoli 26–28 Aprile 2001), Naples 2003, 405–440.

McCormick, M., *Eternal Victory. Triumphal Rulership in Late Antiquity, Byzantium, and the Early Medieval West*, Cambridge 1986.

McLynn, N., 'The Transformation of Imperial Churchgoing in the Fourth Century', in: S. Swain and M. Edwards (eds.), *Approaching Late Antiquity: the Transformation from Early to Late Empire*, Oxford 2004, 235–270.

Meurig-Davies, E.L.B., 'Notes on Ammianus Marcellinus', *C&M* 10 (1948 [1949]) 182–194.
Meyer, E., and Y. Lafond, 'Methone [1]', *DNP* 8 (2000) 98.
Michael, H., *De Ammiani Marcellini studiis Ciceronianis*, Diss. Breslau 1874.
Michael, H., 'Beiträge zur Charakteristik des Ammianus Marcellinus', *Philologische Abhandlungen Martin Hertz zum siebzigsten Geburtstage dargebracht von ehemaligen Schülern*, Berlin 1888, 229–239.
Michels, A.K., *The Calendar of the Roman Republic*, Princeton 1967.
Millar, F., *The Roman Near East, 31 BC – AD 337*, Cambridge Mass. 1993.
Miller, J., 'Bericht über die Literatur zu Ammianus Marcellinus aus den Jahren 1925–1932', *JAW* 247 (1935) 52–57.
Mirković, M., 'Ein Tribunus Batavorum in Mediana bei Naissus', in: G. Wirth (ed.), *Romanitas-Christianitas. Untersuchungen zur Geschichte und Literatur der römischen Kaiserzeit*. Johannes Straub zum 70. Geburtstag am 18. Oktober 1982 gewidmet, Berlin–New York 1982, 360–366.
Modéran, Y., *Les Maures et l'Afrique romaine (IV*^{e}*–VII*^{e} *siècle)*, Rome 2003.
Mommsen, Th., 'Die Scriptores Historiae Augustae', *Hermes* 25 (1890) 228–292.
Müller, C.F.W., 'Zu Ammianus Marcellinus', *Fleckeisens Jbb.* 19 [107] (1873) 341–365.
Münzer, F., 'Perperna 6', *RE* 19.1 (1937) 897–901.
Mutafian, C., *La Cilicie au carrefour des empires*, 2 vols., Paris 1988.
Naudé, C.P.T., 'The Date of the Later Books of Ammianus Marcellinus', *AJAH* 9 (1984) 70–94.
Nelis-Clément, J., 'Les *stationes* comme espace et transmission du pouvoir', in: A. Kolb (ed.), *Herrschaftsstrukturen und Herrschaftspraxis. Konzepte, Prinzipien und Strategien der Administration im römischen Kaiserreich*, Berlin 2006, 269–298.
Nellen, D., *Viri litterati. Gebildetes Beamtentum und spätrömisches Reich zwischen 284 und 395 n. Chr.*, Bochum 1981².
Nelson, M., *The Barbarian's Beverage. A History of Beer in Ancient Europe*, London–New York 2005.
Neri, V., 'Ammiano Marcellino e l'elezione di Valentiniano', *RSA* 15 (1985) 153–182.
Neri, V., 'L'Usurpatore come tiranno nel lessico politico della tarda antichità', in: F. Paschoud and J. Szidat (eds.), *Usurpationen in der Spätantike* (Historia Einzelschriften 111), Stuttgart 1997, 71–86.
Neue, F., *Formenlehre der lateinische Sprache*. Dritte, sehr vermehrte Auflage von C. Wagener, Leipzig 1892–1905 (repr. Hildesheim 1985).
Nicasie, M.J., *Twilight of Empire. The Roman Army from the Reign of Diocletian until the Battle of Adrianople*, Amsterdam 1998.
Nixon, C.V.E., 'The Early Career of Valentinian I', in: T.W. Hillard e.a. (eds.), *Ancient History in a Modern University*, II. *Early Christianity, Late Antiquity and Beyond*, Grand Rapids–Cambridge 1998, 294–304.
Noethlichs, K.L., 'Strukturen und Funktionen des spätantiken Kaiserhofes', in: A. Winterling (ed.), Comitatus. *Beiträge zur Erforschung des spätantiken Kaiserhofes*, Berlin 1998, 13–49.

Norman, A.F., *Libanius' Autobiography (Oration 1)*, Oxford 1965.
Nörr, D., see B. Bischoff.
Norren, J.J. van, *Plautianus. Commandant van de lijfwacht van keizer Septimius Severus*, Hilversum 1953.
Nuffelen, P. van, 'Earthquakes in A.D. 363-368 and the Date of Libanius, Oratio 18', *CQ* 56 (2006) 657-661.
Oberhummer, E., 'Haemimontus', *RE* 7 (1912) 2181-2182.
Olariu, C., 'Datianus, Valentinian and the Rise of the Pannonian Faction', *Historia* 54 (2005) 351-354.
Olshausen, E., and M. Wörrle, 'Nakoleia', *DNP* 8 (2000) 699-700.
Olshausen, E., and A. Wittke, 'Phryges, Phrygia', *DNP* 9 (2000) 965-967.
Otto, A., *Die Sprichwörter und sprichwörtlichen Redensarten der Römer*, Leipzig 1890 (repr. Hildesheim 1962).
Pabst, A., Divisio regni. *Der Zerfall des Imperium Romanum in der Sicht der Zeitgenossen*, Bonn 1986.
Pabst, A., *Quintus Aurelius Symmachus. Reden*, Darmstadt 1989.
Pabst, A., Comitia imperii. *Ideelle Grundlagen des römischen Kaisertums*, Darmstadt 1997.
Pack, R., 'Curiales in the Correspondence of Libanius', *TAPhA* 82 (1951) 176-192; repr. in: G. Fatouros and T. Krischer (eds.), *Libanios* (Wege der Forschung 621), Darmstadt 1983, 185-205, cited as Pack, 1983.
Palanque, J.-R., 'Famines à Rome à la fin du IVe siècle', *REA* 33 (1931) 346-356.
Paschoud, F., *Zosime, Histoire Nouvelle* II² (*Livre IV*), Paris 1979.
Paschoud, F., 'Valentinien travesti, ou: De la malignité d'Ammien', in: J. den Boeft, D. den Hengst and H.C. Teitler (eds.), *Cognitio Gestorum. The Historiographic Art of Ammianus Marcellinus*, Amsterdam 1992, 67-84.
Paschoud, F., 'Biographie und Panegyricus: Wie spricht man vom lebenden Kaiser?', in: K. Vössing (ed.), *Biographie und Prosopographie. Internationales Kolloquium zum 65. Geburtstag von Anthony R. Birley* (Historia Einzelschriften 178), Stuttgart 2005, 103-118.
Pearce, J.W.E., *The Roman Imperial Coinage, IX. Valentinian I—Theodosius I*, London 1951.
Pergami, F., *La legislazione di Valentiniano e Valente (364-375)*, Milan 1993.
Petit, P., *Les étudiants de Libanius. Un professeur de Faculté et ses élèves au bas empire*, Paris 1956.
Petit, P., 'Les Sénateurs de Constantinople dans l'oeuvre de Libanius', *AC* 26 (1957) 347-382 = 'Die Senatoren von Konstantinopel im Werk des Libanios', in: G. Fatouros and T. Krischer (eds.), *Libanios* (Wege der Forschung 621), Darmstadt 1983, 206-247, cited as Petit, 1983.
Petrović, P., 'Naissus, a Foundation of Emperor Constantine', in: D. Srejović (ed.), *Roman Imperial Towns and Places in Serbia*, Belgrade 1993, 54-81.
Petschenig, M., 'Bemerkungen zum Texte des Ammianus Marcellinus', *Philologus* 50 (1891) 336-354; 51 (1892) 519-529, 680-691.
Petschenig, M., 'Zu Ammian', *Philologus* 51 (1892) 360.
Petschenig, M., 'Zu Ammian', *Philologus* 52 (1893 [1894]) 117, 218, 317, 421, 495.

Petschenig, M., 'Zu Ammian', *Philologus* 56 (1897) 381-382.
Petschenig, M., 'Alliteration bei Ammianus Marcellinus', *Philologus* 56 (1897) 556-560.
Piganiol, A., and A. Chastagnol, *L'Empire Chrétien (325-395)*, Paris 1972².
Pighi, G.B., *Studia Ammianea. Annotationes criticae et grammaticae in Ammianum Marcellinum*, Milan 1935.
PLRE I, *The Prosopography of the Later Roman Empire, I, A.D. 260-395*, A.H.M. Jones, J.R. Martindale and J. Morris (eds.), Cambridge 1971.
PLRE II, *The Prosopography of the Later Roman Empire, II, A.D. 395-527*, J.R. Martindale (ed.), Cambridge 1980.
Popović, V., 'Sirmium, a Town of Emperors and Martyrs', in: D. Srejović (ed.), *Roman Imperial Towns and Places in Serbia*, Belgrade 1993, 12-27.
Portmann, W., see H. Leppin.
Price, S.R.F., *Rituals and Power. The Imperial Cult in Asia Minor*, Cambridge 1984.
Raimondi, M., *Valentiniano I e la scelta dell'Occidente*, Milan 2001.
Raimondi, M., 'Il *Breviarium* di Festo e il funzionariato cappadoce alla corte di Valente', *Historia* 55 (2006) 191-206.
Rance, P., 'Attacotti, Déisi and Magnus Maximus: the Case for Irish Federates in Late Roman Britain', *Britannia* 32 (2001) 243-270.
Reddé, M., Mare Nostrum. *Les infrastructures, le dispositif et l'histoire de la marine militaire sous l'empire romain*, Rome 1986.
Reiche, F., *Chronologie der letzten 6 Bücher des Ammianus Marcellinus* (Diss. Jena), Liegnitz 1889.
Reynolds, L.D., and N.G. Wilson, *Scribes and Scholars. A Guide to the Transmission of Greek and Latin Literature*, Oxford 1991³.
Riedl, P., *Faktoren des historischen Prozesses. Eine vergleichende Untersuchung zu Tacitus und Ammianus Marcellinus*, Tübingen 2002.
Rives, J.B., 'Magic, Religion, and Law: the Case of the *Lex Cornelia de sicariis et veneficiis*', in: C. Ando and J. Rüpke (eds.), *Religion and Law in Classical and Christian Rome* (Potsdamer Altertumswissenschaftliche Beiträge 15), Stuttgart 2006, 47-67.
Robinson, D.M., 'The Wheel of Fortune', *CPh* 41 (1946) 207-216.
Roda, S., 'Magistrature senatorie minori nel tardo impero Romano', *SDHI* 43 (1977) 23-112.
Rohrbacher, D., 'Ammianus Marcellinus and Valerius Maximus', *AHB* 19 (2005) 20-30.
Rolfe, J.C., *Ammianus Marcellinus*, with an English translation, 3 vols., London-Cambridge Mass. 1935-1939 (repr. 1971-1972).
Romanelli, P., *Storia delle province romane dell'Africa*, Rome 1959.
Rosen, K., *Ammianus Marcellinus* (Erträge der Forschung 183), Darmstadt 1982.
Ruge, W., 'Korykos 4', *RE* 11 (1922) 1451-1452.
Ruge, W., 'Midum', *RE* 15 (1932) 1548.
Ruge, W., 'Olympos 16', *RE* 18.1 (1939) 314.
Rugullis, S., *Die Barbaren in den spätrömischen Gesetzen: eine Untersuchung des Terminus barbarus*, Frankfurt am Main 1992.

Sabbah, G., *La méthode d'Ammien Marcellin. Recherches sur la construction du discours historique dans les* Res Gestae, Paris 1978.
Sabbah, G., and L. Angliviel de la Beaumelle, *Ammien Marcellin, Histoire VI (Livres XXIX–XXXI)*, Paris 1999.
Şahin, S., 'Studien über die Probleme der historischen Geographie des nordwestlichen Kleinasiens I: Strabon XII 3, 7 p. 543. Der Fluss Gallos, die Stadt Moder<en>e in Phrygia, Epiktetos und die Schiffbarkeit des Sangarios', *EA* 7 (1986) 125–152.
Saliou, C., see B. Cabouret.
Samartzidou, S., 'La via Egnatia entre Philippes et Néapolis' (in Greek, with a summary in French), *Mélanges D. Lazaridis*, Thessaloniki–Athens 1990, 559–587.
Samberger, C., 'Die "Kaiserbiographie" in den *Res Gestae* des Ammianus Marcellinus. Eine Untersuchung zur Komposition der ammianeischen Geschichtsschreibung', *Klio* 51 (1969) 349–482.
Sandwell, I., 'Outlawing "Magic" or Outlawing "Religion"? Libanius and the Theodosian Code as Evidence for Legislation against "Pagan" Practices', in: W.V. Harris (ed.), *The Spread of Christianity in the First Four Centuries. Essays in Explanation*, Leiden–Boston 2005, 87–123.
Scharf, R., *Comites und comitiva primi ordinis*, Stuttgart 1994.
Schlinkert, D., 'Dem Kaiser folgen. Kaiser, Senatsadel und höfische Funktionselite (*comites consistoriani*) von der "Tetrarchie" Diokletians bis zum Ende der konstantinischen Dynastie', in: A. Winterling (ed.), *Comitatus. Beiträge zur Erforschung des spätantiken Kaiserhofes*, Berlin 1998, 133–159.
Schmalz, J.H., see J.Ph. Krebs.
Schulten, A., 'Sertorius 3', *RE* 2A (1923) 1746–1753.
Seager, R., *Ammianus Marcellinus. Seven Studies in his Language and Thought*, Columbia 1986.
Seager, R., 'Ammianus and the Status of Armenia in the Peace of 363', *Chiron* 26 (1996) 275–284.
Seeck, O., *Die Briefe des Libanius zeitlich geordnet*, Leipzig 1906 (repr. Hildesheim 1966).
Seeck, O., 'Zur Chronologie und Quellenkritik des Ammianus Marcellinus', *Hermes* 41 (1906) 481–539, cited as Seeck, 1906a.
Seeck, O., *Geschichte des Untergangs der antiken Welt*, 6 vols., Stuttgart 1920–1923$^{2-4}$.
Seeck, O., *Regesten der Kaiser und Päpste für die Jahre 311 bis 476 n. Chr. Vorarbeit zu einer Prosopographie der christlichen Kaiserzeit*, Stuttgart 1919 (repr. 1964).
Seyfarth, W., and F. Kudlien, 'Medizinisches in lateinischen Inschriften', *Philologus* 104 (1960) 156–161.
Seyfarth, W., *Von der Bedeutung der Plebs in der Spätantike*, Berlin 1969.
Seyfarth, W., *Ammiani Marcellini rerum gestarum libri qui supersunt*, adiuvantibus L. Jacob-Karau et I. Ulmann, 2 vols., Leipzig 1978 (repr. 1999).
Seyfarth, W., *Ammianus Marcellinus, Römische Geschichte. Lateinisch und Deutsch und mit einem Kommentar versehen*, IV, Berlin 1986^3.

Sirks, A.J.B., *Food for Rome. The Legal Structure of the Transportation and Processing of Supplies for the Imperial Distributions in Rome and Constantinople*, Amsterdam 1991.
Solari, A., 'La rivolta procopiana a Constantinopoli', *Byzantion* 7 (1932) 143–148.
Solari, A., 'Strategia nella lotta tra Procopio e Valente', *RFIC* 61 (1933) 492–496.
Sommer, M., *Die Soldatenkaiser*, Darmstadt 2004.
Sordi, M., 'Come Milano divenne capitale', in: M. Sordi (ed.), *L'impero romano-cristiano. Problemi politici, religiosi, culturali*, Rome 1991, 33–45.
Southern, P., and K.R. Dixon, *The Late Roman Army*, London 1996.
Speidel, M.A., '*Militia*. Zu Sprachgebrauch und Militarisierung in der kaiserzeitlichen Verwaltung', in: A. Kolb (ed.), *Herrschaftsstrukturen und Herrschaftspraxis. Konzepte, Prinzipien und Strategien der Administration im römischen Kaiserreich*, Berlin 2006, 263–268
Stadter, P.A., *A Commentary on Plutarch's Pericles*, Chapel Hill–London 1989.
Steigerwald, G., 'Das kaiserliche Purpurprivileg in spätrömischer und frühbyzantinischer Zeit', *JbAC* 33 (1990) 209–239.
Stein, E., 'Fulvius 101', *RE* 7 (1912) 270–278.
Stertz, S.A., 'Ammianus Marcellinus' Attitudes toward Earlier Emperors', in: C. Deroux (ed.), *Studies in Latin Literature and Roman History*, II, Brussels 1980, 487–514.
Stiros, S.C., 'The AD 365 Crete Earthquake and possible Seismic Clustering during the Fourth to Sixth Centuries AD in the Eastern Mediterranean: a Review of Historical and Archaeological Data', *Journal of Structural Geology* 23 (2001) 545–562.
Straub, J.A., *Vom Herrscherideal in der Spätantike*, Stuttgart 1939 (repr. 1964).
Strobel, K., 'Pessinus', *DNP* 9 (2000) 658–660.
Strobel, K., 'Sangarios', *DNP* 11 (2001) 38–39.
Strobel, K., and A. Berger, 'Nikaia [5]', *DNP* 11 (2001) 895–896.
Stroheker, K.F., 'Alamannen im römischen Reichsdienst', in: J. Kroymann (ed.), *Eranion* (Festschrift für Hildebrecht Hommel), Tübingen 1961, 127–148 (= K.F. Stroheker, *Germanentum und Spätantike*, Zurich–Stuttgart 1965, 30–53).
Sulimirski, T., *The Sarmatians*, London–New York 1979.
Swain, S., *Hellenism and Empire. Language, Classicism and Power in the Greek World AD 50–250*, Oxford 1996.
Syme, R., *Ammianus and the* Historia Augusta, Oxford 1968.
Syme, R., 'The Date of Justin and the Discovery of Trogus', *Historia* 37 (1988) 358–371.
Szantyr, A., see J.B. Hofmann.
Szidat, J., '*Imperator legitime declaratus* (Ammian 30, 10, 5)', in: M. Piérart and O. Curty (eds.), *Historia testis. Mélanges d'épigraphie, d'histoire ancienne et de philologie offerts à Tadeusz Zawadzki*, Fribourg 1989, 175–188.
Talbert, R.J.A. (ed.), *Barrington Atlas of the Greek and Roman World*, Princeton 2000.

Teitler, H.C., Notarii *and* Exceptores. *An Inquiry into Role and Significance of Shorthand Writers in the Imperial and Ecclesiastical Bureaucracy of the Roman Empire (from the Early Principate to c. 450 A.D.)*, Amsterdam 1985.

Teitler, H.C., 'Raising on a Shield: Origin and Afterlife of a Coronation Ceremony', *IJCT* 8 (2002) 501–521.

Teitler, H.C., 'Ammianus on Valentinian. Some Observations', in: J. den Boeft, J.W. Drijvers, D. den Hengst and H.C. Teitler (eds.), *Ammianus after Julian. The reign of Valentinian and Valens in Books 26–31 of the* Res Gestae, Leiden 2007, 53–70.

Thompson, E.A., *The Historical Work of Ammianus Marcellinus*, Cambridge 1947 (repr. Groningen 1969).

Thompson, E.A., 'Ammianus Marcellinus', in: T.A. Dorey (ed.), *Latin Historians*, London 1966, 143–157.

Till, R., 'Die Kaiserproklamation des Usurpators Procopius (Ein Beitrag zu Ammian 26, 6, 15)', *Jahrbuch für fränkische Landesforschung* 34/35 (1974–1975) 75–83.

Tomlin, R.S.O., '*Seniores-iuniores* in the late-Roman Field Army', *AJPh* 93 (1972) 253–278.

Tomlin, R.S.O., *The Emperor Valentinian I*, Diss. Oxford 1973.

Tomlin, R.S.O., 'The Date of the "Barbarian Conspiracy"', *Britannia* 5 (1974) 303–309.

Tomlin, R.S.O., 'Ammianus Marcellinus 26.4.5–6', *CQ* 73 (1979) 470–478.

Tomlin, R.S.O., 'Christianity and the Late Roman Army', in: S.N.C. Lieu and D. Montserrat (eds.), *Constantine. History, Historiography and Legend*, London–New York 1998, 21–51.

Tritle, L.A., 'Whose Tool? Ammianus Marcellinus on the Emperor Valens', *AHB* 8 (1994) 141–153.

Vallejo Girvés, M., '*In insulam deportatio* en el siglo IV d.C. Aproximación a su comprensión a través de causas, personas y lugares', *Polis* 3 (1991) 153–167.

Vanderspoel, J., *Themistius and the Imperial Court. Oratory, Civic Duty, and* paideia *from Constantius to Theodosius*, Ann Arbor 1995.

Vera, D., 'Alcune note sul *quaestor sacri palatii*', in: *Hestiasis. Studi di tarda antichità offerti à S. Calderone*, I, Messina 1986, 27–53.

Vergote, J., 'Folterwerkzeuge', *RAC* 8 (1972) 112–141.

Viansino, G., *Ammiani Marcellini rerum gestarum Lexicon*, 2 vols., Hildesheim–Zurich–New York 1985.

Viansino, G., *Ammiano Marcellino. Storie*, 3 vols., Milan 2001–2002.

Vogt, J., 'Ammianus Marcellinus als erzählender Geschichtsschreiber der Spätzeit', *Akad. d. Wiss. u. d. Lit. Mainz*, Abh. d. geistes- u. sozialwiss. Kl. 8 (1963) 802–825.

Voisin, J.L., 'Les Romains, chasseurs de têtes', in: *Du châtiment dans la cité. Supplices corporels et peine de mort dans le monde antique* (Collections de l'École Française de Rome 79), Rome 1984, 241–293.

Waas, M., *Germanen im römischen Dienst im 4. Jh. n. Chr.*, Bonn 1971².

Waerden, B.L. van der, *Die Astronomie der Griechen. Eine Einführung*, Darmstadt 1988.

Waldherr, G., 'Die Geburt der "kosmischen Katastrophe". Das seismische Großereignis am 21. Juli 365 n. Chr.', *Orbis Terrarum* 3 (1997) 169-201.
Wallinga, H.T., *The Boarding-Bridge of the Romans. Its Construction and its Function in the Naval Tactics of the First Punic War*, Groningen 1956.
Watson, A., *Aurelian and the Third Century*, London-New York 1999.
Weber, G., *Kaiser, Träume und Visionen in Prinzipat und Spätantike* (Historia Einzelschriften 143), Stuttgart 2000.
Wenger, L., 'Asylrecht', *RAC* 1 (1950) 840-844.
Wiebe, F.J., *Kaiser Valens und die heidnische Opposition* (Antiquitas 1, 44), Bonn 1995.
Wiedemann, T.E.J., 'Between Men and Beasts: Barbarians in Ammianus Marcellinus', in: I.S. Moxon, J.D. Smart and A.J. Woodman (eds.), *Past Perspectives. Studies in Greek and Roman Historical Writings*, Cambridge 1986, 189-201.
Wiel, M.P. van de, *Hoofdstukken uit de geschiedenis van Rome in Ammianus Marcellinus Res Gestae*, Diss. Amsterdam 1989.
Williams, G., 'Some Aspects of Roman Marriage Ceremonies and Ideals', *JRS* 48 (1958) 16-29.
Winter, E., and B. Dignas, *Rom und das Perserreich. Zwei Weltmächte zwischen Konfrontation und Koexistenz*, Berlin 2001.
Winterbottom, M., *The Elder Seneca I, Controversiae I-VI*, London-Cambridge Mass. 1974.
Wintjes, J., *Das Leben des Libanius* (Diss. Würzburg 2003/2004), Rahden 2005.
Wirbelauer, E., and C. Fleer, '*Totius orbis Augustus*. Claudius Mamertinus als *praefectus praetorio* der Kaiser Julian und Valentinian', in: M. Weinmann-Walser (ed.), *Historische Interpretationen: Gerold Walser zum 75. Geburtstag dargebracht von Freunden, Kollegen und Schülern*, Stuttgart 1995, 191-201.
Wirz, H., 'Ammians Beziehungen zu seinen Vorbildern, Cicero, Sallustius, Livius, Tacitus', *Philologus* 36 (1877) 627-636.
Woods, D., 'A Note Concerning the Early Career of Valentinian I', *AncSoc* 26 (1995) 273-288.
Woods, D., 'Ammianus and Some *tribuni scholarum palatinarum* c. A.D. 353-64', *CQ* 47 (1997) 269-291.
Woods, D., 'Valens, Valentinian I, and the *Ioviani Cornuti*', in: C. Deroux (ed.), *Studies in Latin Literature and Roman History* IX, Brussels 1998, 462-486.
Woods, D., 'Ammianus Marcellinus and the *Rex Alamannorum* Vadomarius', *Mnemosyne* 53 (2000) 690-710.
Woods, D., 'On the Alleged Reburial of Julian the Apostate in Constantinople', *Byzantion* 76 (2006) 364-371.
Wörrle, M., see E. Olshausen.
Wotawa, A. von, 'Didius 8', *RE* 5 (1905) 412-424.
Ziegler, K., '*Palatium*', *RE* 18.2 (1949) 1-81.

INDICES

I. *Lexical (Latin)*

abruptus: 233
abscidere: 68
ac si: 249
accedere: 119, 286
accendere: 167
acceptus: 266, 281
acclamatio: 171
accursus: 252
acervus: 53
acquirere: 191
actitare: 124
actus: 14, 192
adlocutio: 169
adminiculum: 192
adultus: 242
adversus: 246
aeger: 278
aequatio: 283
aequitas: 54
aerumna: 89
affectare: 72, 116
agere: 116
agitare: 64
alienus: 223
altus: 31, 40, 128
ambigere: 53
ambitiosus: 57, 120
ancillaris: 164
anhelare: 128
anima: 198
animus: 198
annus: 107
aperire: 242
apex: 147
apparere: 179
apparitor: 83, 221
aptare: 166
apud: 10, 22
arctous: 202
ardere: 119

armatus: 25
asciscere: 52, 180, 214, 287
asperatus: 79
assumere: 147
astutia: 184
at: 75
atrox: 65
atterere: 151
attonitus: 207
auctoritas: 19
audax: 271
augere: 117
aulaeum: 163
auriga: 67
ausum: 191
autem: 114
avidus: 236
barritus: 210
bellator: 227
bissextus dies: 27
caecus: 194
callidus: 191, 246
campus: 41
capessere: 201
capitalis: 68, 283, 286
cardo: 29
castigatus: 127
castra: 181
caterva: 219
causari: 90, 235
causatio: 119
cautus: 131
cavillatio: 163
celsitudo: 11
celsus: 135, 221
cervix: 68
circulus: 66
circumclausus: 165
circumsaepire: 252
citus: 219

clarissimus: 172
claudere: 218
claustrum: 225
coercere: 10, 278
coetus: 180
cogitare: 49
cognatus: 128
cognitio: 14
coire: 156
collimitium: 151
comitatus: 109
comitia: 42
commentum: 190
communis: 131
compellare: 216
competens: 123
compingere: 186
complanare: 301
complere: 51
componere: 85
concinere: 82
concitare: 197
concors: 94
concrepare: 45, 267
condicere: 155
conectere: 300
conferre manus: 253
confidens: 184, 218
confidentia: 48
confinium: 3
conflagrare: 266
conflictare: 168
confundere: 145
confutare: 64
congruus: 200
coniectus: 229
consecratio: 154
consentire: 156
consideratio: 123, 126
consonus: 47
consortium: 77
conspirare: 151
conspiratio: 244
constipatio: 157
constrictus: 84
consumere: 149
consurgere: 209

contemplatio: 230
contiguus: 8
continens: 301
contorquere: 304
conturmalis: 154
convenire: 4
cruciabilis: 133
crudus: 143
cruentus: 282
cuppediae: 179
cura: 62, 184
curare: 17, 187
curia: 171
curiosus: 72
curriculus: 66
cursus: 181
decere: 11
decus: 83
dedere: 271
dedignari: 221
defendere a: 229
defensare: 198
defixus: 169
dehonestamentum: 164
densere: 228
densitas: 297
denuntiatio: 39
deportare: 279
deportatio: 279
despicabilis: 221
despondere: 204
destinare: 225
destinatio: 233
destinatus: 46
devius: 135
dextera: 207
diadema: 83
dicio: 90
diffidens: 203
digerere: 102, 123, 214
dignitas: 165, 249, 282
digredi: 101
dilabi: 181
dimensio: 30
diritas: 140, 275
dirus: 275
discurrere: 11

disparare: 96
dispendium: 107
displicere: 19
distinguere: 31
diu: 84
divus: 280
documentum: 118
domicilium: 34
dominatio: 158, 258
dominatus: 158
ductare: 194
ductus: 249
eculeus: 288
edicere: 24
educare: 126
effectus: 225
efficax: 64
effigiare: 201
effrenatus: 287
effundere: 236
egredi: 149
elabi: 37
elucere: 127
emercari: 47
en: 208
enim: 82, 100, 129
eous: 101
erectus: 165
erigere: 56
eruere: 236
erumpere: 48, 173
et quia: 185
et...quidem: 114
evanescere: 86
evehere: 174
evolvere: 298
ex: 137, 215
exambire: 192
examinator: 9
excandescere: 155
excursus: 118, 253
exinanire: 235
exordium: 158
expedire: 60
explicare: 60
exploratus: 134
exquisitus: 141

exsertus: 226
exstinguere: 230
exsultare: 49
extrudere: 303
exurere: 286
fabula: 296
facies: 302
facilis: 86
factio: 138, 194
faex: 194
fatum: 60
favorabilis: 185, 273
febris: 84
felix: 147
festinare: 117
fidelis: 123
fidens: 78, 218
fides: 117, 157
fidus: 274
figurare: 228
firmus: 194
flagitare: 275
flagrare: 141
fodicare: 272
formare: 26
formator: 51
fornicatus: 228
fors: 148
fortuna: 47, 289
fragilitas: 47
frumentum: 217
fundare: 35
funereus: 287
funus: 131, 275
furenter: 110
geminus: 267
genitalis: 266
genus: 70, 126
germen: 245
gladius: 253
gliscere: 257
globus: 225
gradatim: 228
gradus: 127
grassari: 282
grassator: 249
gratia: 46, 278

gravari: 301
gravis: 45
gregarius: 10
gubernaculum: 24
habitus: 141
haerere: 146
hastatus: 162
hinc inde: 207
honestus: 179
horror: 266
hostis: 245
iacere: 20, 70
iactare: 70
iam: 206, 250
iam inde: 255
idem: 81
igitur: 94, 178
ignotus: 139, 208
illicere: 198
illustris: 172
immanis: 69, 110
immunis: 289
impatientia: 53
impendio: 118, 142
impensus: 2
imperator: 46
imperium: 286
impius: 284
implacabilitas: 288
implicare: 176
implicatus: 170
impraepedite: 151
impropugnatus: 119
improtectus: 229
in commune: 52
in unum quaerere: 41
inaestimabilis: 235
incaute: 173
incautus: 266
incentivum: 140
incidere: 285
inconditus: 171
incruentus: 115, 262
indagare: 134
indemnatus: 132
indicium: 138
inducere: 70

inex(s)uperabilis: 224
infaustus: 283
inhiare: 198
inire: 52
iniungere: 131
iniuriosus: 216
inopinus: 243
inquirere: 85, 138
inscitia: 15
insidere: 303
insistere: 216
instare: 139, 228
institutio: 187
instrumentum: 203
insularis: 279
intactus: 150
integer: 61
intempestivus: 6
interdum: 185
intermeare: 137
internecivus: 119, 283
internus: 68
interpellare: 49
interturbare: 84
intervallare: 16
intervallum: 30
intimidus: 166
intrepidus: 143
involvere: 302
irrisivus: 216
itaque: 159, 255
iter: 219
itidem: 145
iucunditas: 168
iudex: 61, 268
iugiter: 73
labefactare: 209
labi: 68
labilis: 229
lapis: 96
laqueus: 176
latrocinium: 282
latus: 272
legitimus: 83
lenis: 72
levis: 19
libenter: 157

licenter: 300
licet: 46
licitari: 158
limatius: 2
limes: 109
linere: 285
locus: 154
luctuosus: 256
ludere: 218
ludibriosus: 164
lugubris: 165
machina: 228
maestus: 123
magicus: 68
magis...quam: 249
magnitudo: 37, 302
magus: 68
mappa: 163
maturare: 200
mature: 114
maturus: 214
memorare: 116
meridies: 30
miles: 137
militare: 128
militia (officialis): 137
mimicus: 163
moderamen: 50
moderator: 18
modo non: 70
moles: 270
moliri: 158
mollire: 119, 210
momentum: 236
monitus: 39
monumentum: 224
morem gerere: 250
morigerus: 83
mos: 211
mucro: 209
multiformis: 256
multiplex: 11, 294
mundus: 50
munire: 185
munitor: 218
munus: 109
nasci: 126

navis rostrata: 226
nebula: 168
nebulo: 250
necessitas: 135
necessitudo: 199, 269
negotio levi: 147
negotium: 247
novare: 25
novator: 294
novitas: 44, 236
novus: 133
noxa: 271
nudare: 141
numen: 35
numerus: 153
nunc usque: 71
nutare: 247
nutrire: 69
obmurmuratio: 45
obscurus: 116
obsidere: 157
obstare: 91
obtentus: 282
obtundere: 237
obumbrare: 32
occultus: 127
ocius: 22, 131
officium: 11
opimus: 70
opinari: 26, 299
opitulatio: 247
opportunus: 271
orbis Romanus: 50
ordinare: 100
ordo: 2
oriens: 60
oscitare: 244
pacare: 180
paedagogianus: 162
palatinus: 137
palatium: 105, 179, 265
pannulus: 163
parare: 151
pars: 54, 101, 253
particula: 29
partiri: 97, 104
parum: 37

patrare: 218
patricius: 140
paupertinus: 146
pedem referre: 4
pellicere: 154
pensare: 259
per: 156
perdere: 152
perduellis: 118, 203, 205, 213
perendinus: 76
perfidia: 249
permeare: 214
perquam: 198
perrumpere: 122
perspicax: 127
persuasio: 203
persultare: 88, 118
pertinax: 85
pertinere: 91
perturbatio: 128
pervadere: 151
pervidere: 223
pessimo pede: 172
petulanter: 185
petulantia: 201
phalera(e): 71
phaleratus: 71
piacularis: 70
pilum: 253
plebs: 45, 62, 205
pone: 271
possidere: 225
potestas: 17, 284
potior: 40, 105
potiri: 209
potissimus: 50
prae: 48
praecinere: 73
praedatorius: 89
praefectura: 62
praeire: 152
praelucere: 255
praemeditari: 44
praemium: 158, 193
praescius: 26
praesidere: 189
praesidium: 243

praestituere: 32
praestrigiae: 86
praesumptio: 271
praesumptor: 235
praetendere: 170, 199, 284
praetorium: 192, 265
praetumidus: 285
praevertere: 218
precari: 278
pridie: 101
primigenius: 300
primitus: 107
primores: 76
princeps: 185, 267
principatus: 267
pro: 211
probare: 35
probrum: 216
procedere: 40, 165, 222
procinctus: 153
procursatio: 206
prodere: 188
producere: 81, 207
profecto: 173
profundere: 289
progredi: 84
proinde ut: 301
proinde: 15, 35, 52
promovere: 64, 97
promptus: 271
pronuntiare: 82
prope: 111
properare: 90
propior: 4
propositum: 204
proprius: 3
prosapia: 209
proscriptio: 290
prosperitas: 213
prosperus: 48
prosternere: 218
proterere: 209
protervia: 230
provectus natu: 249
provehere: 98
providere: 130
proximus: 251

publicatio: 290
publicum: 165
quaeritare: 65
quaeso: 52
quaestio: 64, 282
quam: 77
quantum: 137
quasi: 76, 190, 290
quatere: 253
quidam: 110, 290
quisnam: 77
rabidus: 143
rapere: 271
rapidus: 84
raptim: 171
rarescere: 62
ratio: 152, 267
rebellis: 190
receptaculum: 136
recingere: 101, 188
reciprocus: 206
recogitare: 120
rector: 43
redimere: 70
regalis: 232
regia: 58, 179, 192, 265
regius: 161, 286
regnum: 32
relatio: 116, 150
repedare: 117
reperire: 86, 301
replicare: 121
repulsa: 301
reputare: 118
res novae: 112
reserare: 231, 270
residere: 285
reverendus: 15
revolvere: 298
rex: 268
ritus: 138
robustus: 243
rumusculus: 139
sabaia: 216
sabaiarius: 216
saevitia: 88
sagax: 247

saltem: 73
saltuatim: 124
sapiens: 55
scaena: 163
scrutari: 54
scutum: 166
secundissimus: 43
secundus: 206
sedes: 183
sepelire: 168
serius: 43
signifer: 29
signum: 165
simplex: 52
simulacrum: 163
siparium: 163
sociare: 102
societas: 214
solere: 256
solito: 109
sollemnis: 153
sollers: 138
sors: 60, 174
species: 42, 197
spectabilis: 172
speculatio: 270
sperare: 170, 302
spes: 146, 219, 254
squalere: 135
squalidus: 30
statio: 190
stipatus: 165
stipendium: 154
stips: 291
stoliditas: 201
strepere: 10
stringere: 135
studium: 156
stupor: 169
sub-: 159
subaquilus: 260
subcurvus: 261
subditivus: 184
subinde: 124
sublatus: 144
sublimis: 29
submisse: 228

subsidere: 147
substernere: 289
suburbanum: 96
succendere: 139, 252
suffragari: 192
suffragatio: 19
suffrago: 228
suffugium: 254
sulcare: 272
summa res: 132
summas: 128, 291
superare: 290
superesse: 266
superstes: 15, 294
superstitio: 26
suppar: 281
surgere: 112
suscipere: 110, 287
suscitare: 242
susurrare: 129
susurrus: 47
suus: 208
syngrapha: 70
tabidus: 160
taedium: 41
tamen: 73
tamquam: 86
tandem denique: 120
temptare: 202
tendere: 244
tenus: 30
terribilis: 58
testudo: 227
textus: 130, 183
trabea: 107
tractus: 101, 243
tradere: 67
tranquillus: 180
transire: 31
trepidus: 203
tribunal: 42, 81
tribunus: 227

tristitia: 223
truculentus: 247
trux: 247
tum etiam: 69
tumultuarius: 171, 224
tumultus: 48
turbamentum: 195
turbo: 123
tutus: 243
ultor: 146
umbra: 267
umere: 303
undatim: 66
usu venire: 193
usurpator: 203
ut: 139
valescere: 286
validus: 190
vanus: 203
vaporatus: 182
vastatorius: 230
vastitare: 115
vecordia: 144
velut: 128, 192
veneficium: 62
venenum: 63
venire: 24, 248
verbum: 132
vero: 114, 242
vertere: 286
vertigo: 302
verum: 68
vesper(a): 38
vetus: 258
vexillum: 254
via: 203
vilis: 179
virtus: 50
vis: 48
vivax: 181
volubilis: 60
vulgaris: 15

II. Lexical (Greek)

φάρμακον: 63
κάμον: 217
καθίζω: 303

κωμῳδία: 159
μετέωρα: 29
τετραπλῆ: 142

III. Syntax and Style

ab urbe condita-construction: 66, 258
abl. gerundii, equivalent of the part. praes: 97
abundantia sermonis: 200, 284
accusative of Goal: 183
adverbs, final position: 152
alliteration: 56, 161, 172, 299
alternation of subjunctive and indicative in dependent clauses: 197
anacolouthon: 22
anaphoric expressions: 32
antonomasia: 230
asyndeton: 51
brevitas: 6
comparative for metrical reasons: 94, 266
composita with more than one prefix: 192
compound verbs: 179
correctio: 283
cursus: 4, 152, 181, 191, 203, 243, 266
dative in -u: 229, 289
dative of the Agens: 133
deponentia, passive sense: 44
dum with imperf. indic.: 274
ellipsis of esse: 138
enallage: 18, 168
erga with gerundive: 236
evidentia: 13
focus: 225
frequentativa: 115
gen. identitatis: 246
gen. inversus: 11, 62, 168, 180, 261, 275, 297, 299, 302
gen. plural mensuum: 34

gerundive as a part. fut. pass.: 10, 97, 250, 287
Gesetz der wachsenden Glieder: 45
Grecism: 101, 131, 180
hendiadys: 71, 302
hic: 131, 159, 166
hic, cataphoric: 198
idem, anaphoric: 117, 169, 229, 267
indic. fut. in virtual indirect speech: 198
indicative in indirect questions: 207
indicative in subordinate clauses of oratio obliqua: 91
is, cataphoric: 28, 195
iubere with dative: 221
metaphor: 57, 132
ni 'de rupture': 145
nomine with genitive: 222
nouns, adjectival use: 145
oxymoron: 164
participles, frequent use: 190
perfect 3rd pers. pl. in -ere: 231, 303
perfect instead of pluperfect: 231
perfect, contracted forms: 51
periphrasis: 299
personification: 299, 301
pleonasm: 120
prosopopoeia: 160
providere, constructions: 130
quidam "steigernd": 138
quod with indic. fut.: 91, 148
quod-clauses instead of an a.c.i.: 234
relative combined with a demonstrative pronoun: 281

Sallustianism: 67, 266
subjunctive, paratactical use: 130
suffix -anus: 214
suffix -arius: 216
suffix -nam: 77
syllable-quantity: 304

Synonymenhäufung: 118, 146, 173
verba inchoativa: 62
vesper(a): 38
zeugma: 253

IV. *Geographical Names*

Acontisma: 202
Adrianople: 95, 150, 153, 157, 189, 271, 293, 303
Africa: 89, 122
Alexandria: 66, 226, 296, 304
Altinum: 105
Anastasianae balneae: 155
Ancyra: 2, 21, 22, 184, 205, 215, 219, 244
Antiochia: 149, 169, 174, 183, 203, 238
Aquileia: 105, 226
Aquitania: 161
Arelate: 185, 226
Armenia: 90
Asiana: 223, 225
Astacenus Sinus: 215
Bithynia: 75, 205, 225
Boana Lacus: 218
Bona Mansio: 95
Caesarea: 116, 132, 149, 182
Cappadocia: 174
Chalcedon: 102, 134, 135, 174, 184, 215, 217, 267, 271, 277
Cherronesus: 279
Cibala: 22
Cilicia: 126, 182
Constantinople: 17, 56, 78, 80, 83, 89, 95, 106, 107, 136, 149, 154, 165, 171, 181, 182, 201, 203, 226
Corycus: 126
Cyzicus: 201, 214, 222, 223, 265
Dacia mediterranea: 116, 202
Dacia ripensis: 202
Dadastana: 17, 179, 220
Divitia: 152
Drepanum: 215

Egnatia via: 81, 95
Emesa: 174
Emona: 105
Eumolpias: 270
Galatia: 184, 203, 243
Gallia(e): 108, 119
Gallograecia: 184, 203
Gallus: 218
Gaugamela: 238
Haemimontus: 271
Helenopolis: 215
Hellespontus: 223, 225
Heraclea: 201
Heracleum: 227
Illyricum: 18, 116, 117, 269
Isauria: 230
Issicus Sinus: 238
Lugdunensis: 119
Lydia: 244
Macedonia: 174
Mediana: 96, 97
Mediolanum: 105, 107, 111
Methone: 304
Misenum: 226
Moesia: 89
Mothone: 304
Mygdum: 205
Nacolia: 104, 248, 252, 254, 257, 271, 279
Naissus: 93, 95, 97, 104
Neapolis: 202
Nicaea: 2, 17, 18, 22, 26, 56, 58, 75, 205, 215, 254, 264, 296
Nice: 190
Nicomedia: 17, 79, 80, 184, 201, 215, 218
Nisibis: 174, 265

INDICES 337

Noricum: 152
Numidia: 175
Olbianus Sinus: 215
Olympus Mons: 243
Oriens: 98, 223
Pannonia: 88
Pannonia Secunda: 104
Paris: 111, 277
Perinthus: 105
Pessinus: 243
Philadelphia: 233
Philippopolis: 18, 95, 277
Phrygia: 100, 243, 248
Phrygia Salutaris: 257
Pontica: 223
Pontus: 182
Pydna: 174
Raetia: 88, 108

Ratiaria: 202
Ravenna: 226
Rheims: 277
Salabria/Selymbria: 22, 39
Sangarius: 205, 219
Sardis: 249
Serdica: 95, 202
Sicilia: 296
Sirmium: 58, 96, 104, 105, 140, 242
Siscia: 85
Succi-pass: 202, 270
Sunonensis Lacus: 218
Syria(e): 65, 182, 238
Tarsus: 17, 132, 133
Thracia: 89, 95, 189, 267, 271
Thyatira: 244, 248, 250
Verona: 105

V. *Names of Persons/Peoples*

Aeropus: 246
Agilo: 140, 188, 192, 194, 248, 253, 254, 259, 265, 279
Aginatius: 65
Agrippina: 66
Alamanni: 88, 107, 121, 128, 215
Albinus: 277
Alexander: 238
Aliso: 227
Anastasia: 156
Andriscus: 173
Androclus: 211
Andronicus: 136, 276
Anepsia: 65
Antonius: 116
Apollonius of Tyana: 25
Apronianus: 59, 61, 286
Aratus: 28
Araxius: 136, 194, 230, 276, 278
Arbitio: 204, 234, 247, 248, 250, 266, 275, 285
Archimedes: 29
Arintheus: 17, 21, 100, 102, 103, 220
Athanaricus: 150, 268

Attacotti: 89
Auchenius: 67
Aurelianus: 142
Aurelius Ampelius: 96
Ausonius: 119
Barbatio: 166
Barchalba: 180, 230, 255, 260, 265, 276
Basilina: 170
Bassianus: 156
Bucinobantes: 110
Caesarius: 21, 170, 182, 186
Capelianus: 175
Caracalla: 145, 174
Carosa: 156
Cassius: 284
Cato: 284
Censorinus: 2
Charietto: 112–114
Claudius: 279
Cleander: 144, 282
Commodus: 144, 157, 233, 238
Constantia: 199
Constantia Postuma: 245
Constantinus: 150, 156, 161, 199, 215, 268, 294

Constantius: 21, 49, 51, 52, 54, 63, 78, 80, 82, 85, 88, 105, 109, 115, 118, 122, 158, 186, 188, 192, 194, 211, 219, 231, 234, 245, 247, 250, 287
Crassus, M. Licinius: 261
Cretio: 122
Cyrillus: 66
Dagalaifus: 17, 21, 25, 78, 102, 103, 112, 114, 242
Darius III: 238
Datianus: 21
Demosthenes: 225
Didius Iulianus: 157, 166
Domnica: 140
Duil(l)ius: 71
Equitius: 18, 21, 25, 40, 101, 116, 202, 270
Eratosthenes: 28
Euctemon: 28
Eudoxus: 28
Eugenius: 136, 154, 180, 193
Eunomius: 136, 231
Euphrasius: 136, 187, 194, 230, 280
Eusebia: 20
Eusebius: 266
Faustina: 196, 200, 245, 269
Firmus: 161
Florentius: 230, 254, 260, 264, 276
Gaius Gracchus: 57
Gallienus: 210
Gallus: 82, 102, 140, 194, 266
Gaudentius: 123
Geiseric: 142
Germanianus: 106
Gomoarius: 136, 188, 194, 232, 244, 248, 250, 252, 254, 259, 265
Gordiani: 173, 175
Gordianus III: 138
Gothi: 89, 150, 267
Gratianus: 25, 83, 199, 208, 242, 245, 262
Gratianus, father of Valentinianus: 20

Grumbates: 265
Hadrianus: 223
Hecataeus: 28
Helena: 215
Heliodorus: 250
Heliogabalus: 173, 174, 184, 199
Helpidius: 136, 180, 193, 262, 276, 290
Heraclius: 136
Hilarinus: 67
Hipparchus: 28
Hormisdas iunior: 136, 231, 248
Hormisdas senior: 231
Hortarius: 109
Huni: 25
Hyperechius: 136, 179, 180, 220
Ianuarius: 19, 40
Iovianus: 2, 5, 16–18, 20, 22, 25, 39, 40, 45, 47, 75, 80, 81, 91, 97, 100, 133, 158, 160, 164, 220, 265, 267, 305
Iovinus: 97, 102, 103, 115
Iulia Domna: 145
Iulia Mamaea: 175
Iulianus: 20, 45, 47, 51, 54, 58, 76, 78, 80, 82, 87, 97, 100, 122, 137, 150, 153, 158, 162–164, 169, 170, 180, 184–186, 188, 189, 198, 199, 207, 215, 219, 232, 244, 250, 262, 280, 305
Iulius Caesar: 151
Iulius: 118, 189
Iustinianus: 96
Iuthungi: 110
Labienus: 14
Lampadius: 166
Lentienses: 110
Leo: 19, 21, 25
Leontius: 67
Libanius: 136
Lucilius: 262
Lupicinus: 100, 219, 243
Macrianus: 210
Macrinus: 173, 174, 277
Macrobius: 2
Magi: 68

INDICES

Magnentius: 272, 277
Mamertinus: 106, 117
Marcellus: 136, 225, 230, 264, 267, 269, 275, 276
Marcus Aurelius: 144
Marina Severa: 242
Marius Maximus: 12
Masaucio: 122
Maxentius: 277
Maximinus: 19, 134, 189
Maximinus Thrax: 173, 175, 277
Maximus: 59
Maximus of Ephesus: 86
Metellus, Q. Caecilius Macedonicus: 174
Meton: 28
Nebridius: 140, 170, 186
Neoterius: 122
Nero: 66
Nevitta: 17
Nicomachus Flavianus: 78
Orestes: 66
Otho: 207
Palladius: 222
Papa: 77, 163
Pentadius: 102
Perillus: 273
Perperna, M. Veiento: 258
Pertinax: 157, 277
Pescennius Niger: 238, 239, 277
Petronius: 19, 140, 167, 168, 186, 194, 282, 286
Petronius Probus: 261
Phalaris: 273
Philoromus: 67
Phronimius: 136, 182, 187, 194, 230, 276, 279
Picti: 89
Plato: 233
Plautianus: 145
Plautilla: 145
Plotinus: 28
Pompeius: 258, 259
Poppaea: 66
Praetextatus: 278
Probus: 106
Ptolemaeus: 28

Quadi: 88
Quartinus: 277
Remigius: 25, 110, 176
Rufinus: 160
Rumitalca: 193, 214, 218, 264
Sabinianus: 40, 283
Sallustius: 279
Salutius: 17, 18, 21, 37, 38, 40, 86, 103, 106, 186
Sapor: 5, 90, 140, 233
Saxons: 89
Scotti: 89
Sebastianus: 129
Seianus: 186
Septimius Severus: 145, 199, 238
Sequani: 119
Serenianus: 19, 101, 102, 224, 231, 265, 266, 274
Sertorius: 258
Severianus: 112–114, 153
Severus: 102
Severus Alexander: 173, 175
Silvanus: 46, 109, 138, 160, 272
Solinus: 2, 4
Sophronius: 167, 181
Strategius: 136, 180, 193
Strategius Musonianus: 136
Suetonius: 2
Sulpicianus: 157
Symmachus: 59, 61, 189
Tarracius Bassus: 67
Terentius: 261
Theodora: 156
Theodosius: 89
Theodosius senior: 9, 58, 89
Thervingi: 268
Traianus: 52
Tungri: 152
Ursatius: 19, 21, 85, 110, 112
Ursicinus: 40, 51, 128, 132, 134
Ursicinus: 46
Ursulus: 198
Vadomarius: 183, 215
Valentinianus II: 1, 5, 18, 203
Varronianus: 20
Venustus: 222
Vetiana: 192

Victor: 17, 21, 100, 102, 103
Visigoths: 233
Vitalianus: 207

Vitellius: 66
Viventius: 21, 85
Vulcacius Rufinus: 117

VI. *Military Matters*

actuarius: 20
annona: 222
auxilia: 112
barritus: 210
castra: 181
centuria: 45
centurio primi pili: 155
cingulum: 101
cohors: 45
comes domesticorum: 102
comes et tribunus cornutorum: 21
comes rei militaris: 20, 97, 101, 102, 117, 122, 189, 233
Cornuti: 104
division of the army: 104
Divitenses: 152, 154–156, 195, 205
donativum: 222
draconarius: 162
ducenarius: 104
fleets, Mediterranean: 226
fleets, river: 226
gladius: 253
Iovii: 195, 205, 207, 264
iuniores: 104, 153
legio comitatensis: 140
legio II Italica: 152
legio: 206
magister armorum: 98
magister equitum: 97, 100, 219
magister equitum per Gallias: 97
magister equitum praesentalis: 97
magister militum: 102, 117, 189

magister militum per Illyricum: 18
magister peditum: 98, 100
manipulus: 45
milites stationarii: 190
navis rostrata: 226
numerarius: 25
pilum: 253
praepositus militum: 140
praesidiorum magister: 264
praesidiorum praefectus: 264
praesidium: 243
procursator: 206
protector domesticus: 79, 225, 264
schola Scutariorum: 123
schola prima Scutariorum: 40
schola secunda Scutariorum: 22
scutum: 166
seniores: 104, 153
shields, clashing: 165
statio: 190
stipendium: 222
testudo: 227
tribunus: 116, 227, 255
tribuni scholarum: 19
tribunus Batavorum: 96
tribunus stabuli: 79
Tungricani: 152, 154–156, 205
turma: 197
vexillum: 254
Victores: 195, 205, 207, 264
warships: 226

VII. *Various Topics*

a pugione: 144
acclamatio: 26, 43, 171
adlocutio: 42
Adrastia/Nemesis: 24
adventus: 205
Alamanni, invasion: 108, 112

Ammianus
   animal images: 147
   and Ausonius: 94
   authorial presence, -9
   endorses legitimate power: 193

eyewitness, -9
fire metaphors: 252
freedom of speech: 9
Greekness: 14
personal preferences: 233
reading experience: 144
references to books 1–13: 144
references to his own time: 71
respect for Cicero: 15
sources, -13
theatre: 159
time of writing: 122
amphitheatre: 66
anticipation, -12: 85
Apollonius of Tyana: 28
apparitor: 221
Armenia, division in 387: 91
asylum: 68
Ausonius: 119
bad characters: 266
barbarian raids: 87
barbarians: 119
barbarians, fickleness: 25
barbarians, payments: 109
beer: 216
bissextus dies: 2, 23
campus Martius: 41
carriage, joining the emperor in: 83
castrensianus: 220
castrensis: 221
Censorinus: 2
chaos: 301
Cicero, letters to Nepos: 15
clarissimi: 172
coinage: 185, 192, 201, 222, 224
comes Africae: 20
comes Britanniae: 20
comes domesticorum: 102, 265
comes primi ordinis: 129
comes rei privatae: 21, 180, 187
comes sacrarum largitionum: 222
comitatus: 109
comites consistoriani: 128
commendatio: 26, 43
concordia: 94
consecration: 154, 281

consistorium: 78, 119, 129, 204
coronation ceremony: 44
correspondence between natural and historical disasters: 295
cubicularius: 193
cura palatii: 162, 214, 264
curia: 171
cursus publicus: 190
death penalty: 64, 68, 202
decapitation: 64, 277
defixio: 67
detention: 186
diadema: 83
dies imperii: 2
digna memoratu: 12, 13
divus: 280
donativum: 56
electio: 26, 43
elogium: 260
emperor, address to the troops: 211
emperor, attire: 43, 160
emperor, process of choosing: 26
Euctemon: 28
feminine virtues: 233
fides: 9
food, shortage: 62
Fortuna: 234, 256, 305
Fortune, ball: 234
Fortune, wheel: 234
geographical names, old and new: 270
Gothi, support for Procopius: 195
Gothi, treaty: 150
Gothi, wars: 89
haruspices: 25
henotheism: 35, 147
Hermes Termaximus: 28
Hipparchus: 28
Historia Augusta and Ammianus: 13
Holy Week: 81
honestiores: 272
illustres: 172
imperator: 46
intercalary day: 27, 37
interregnum: 22, 24

Iovianus, election: 20
Issus, battle: 238
iudex: 61
Iulianus
    Ammianus' view: 5
    consecration: 281
    posthumous presence, -10, -11: 118
    virtues: 281
Iustitia: 259
Labienus: 14
last books, final touches: 294
Latin: 207
law and order, maintenance: 62
leap year: 2, 27
lex Cornelia de sicariis et veneficis: 63
limes: 109
loyalty to the ruling dynasty: 199, 246, 264
Lucilius: 262
Macrobius: 2
Magi: 68
magical practices: 60, 63
magister officiorum: 21, 25, 110, 182, 187, 279
Marius Maximus: 12
Mars: 231
Meton: 28
ministerialis: 162
moral corruption, after Julian: 69
munus: 109
Mylae, battle: 72
Nicomachus Flavianus: 78
notarius: 25, 122, 128, 182
numen: 35
oath: 211
oath of allegiance: 208
orbis Romanus: 50, 88
Oriens: 98
paedagogianus: 162
palace, Constantinople: 172
palatium: 105, 179, 265
Palm Sunday: 81
Pannonians, cruelty: 19
Pannonians, rudeness: 19
patricius: 140

physiognomy: 260
pillory: 289
plebs: 62
Plotinus: 28
poena quadrupli: 142
praefectura: 62
praefectus praetorio: 38, 85, 106
praefectus praetorio Galliarum: 21
praefectus praetorio Orientis: 186
praefectus urbis Constantinopolitanae: 21, 181, 187, 279
praefectus urbis Romae: 21, 59, 61, 62, 73, 85, 181
praetor urbanus: 11
praetorium: 192, 265
princeps: 49, 185, 267
principatus: 267
proconsul: 232
Procopius
    pagan reaction: 136
    part of the integral plan of the Res Gestae: 7
    revolt, extension: 244
programmatic statements: 2, 11
prolepsis: 189
promotion: 140
protector: 272
provinces, well-being: 49
punishment: 202
quaestor (sacri) palatii: 85, 186
regia: 179, 192, 265
Regifugium: 27
regius minister: 161
relatio: 150
retirement: 180
Roma aeterna: 2, 35
rumours: 85
saevitia: 88
senate, Constantinople: 137, 171
shield, raising: 44
shields, clashing: 165
ship of state: 305
solar year: 2
soldiers, fickleness: 25
soldiers, unanimity: 211
solidus: 201

Solinus: 2, 4
spectabiles: 172
statutus: 220
Suetonius: 2, 27
supernumerarius: 220
Symmachus and Ammianus: 42
synchronization of solar year and lunar months: 28
tax arrears: 142
terminus post quem for Books 26–31: 5
Thyatira, battle: 248, 250
torture: 272
treaty of 363: 90
tribunal: 42, 81
tribunus: 128
tsunami, -13: 291
Typhon: 126
urbs aeterna: 61
Valens
    character: 19
    compared with Julian, -12: 281
    cruelty: 19, 266
    dies imperii: 81, 93
    hostility towards the memory of Julian: 86
    investiture: 83
Valentinianus
    character: 19
    compared with Julian, -11: 281
    cruelty: 19, 266
    date of birth: 22
    dies imperii: 23
    duration of his reign: 23
    family: 20
    hostility towards the memory of Julian: 86, 280
    inauguration: 76
    judgment of Ammianus: 20
    military experience: 21
    proclamation: 76
    qualities: 20
veneficium: 60, 62, 67
venenum: 63
vicarius: 106
wine, shortage: 62
zodiac: 34

VIII. *Passages referred to (Latin)*

Acro ad Hor. Ep. 1.1.6: 66
AE 1936.51 = 1993.1401: 202
AE 1989: 699, 249
AE 1995: 1465d, 249
AE 1998.1585: 65
Ambr. epist. 6.30.10: 203
Ambr. epist. extra coll. 14.40: 204
Ambr. Noe 21.75: 203
Ambr. in psalm. cxviii: 3, 273
Andr. trag. 3–4: 97
Anon. de mach. bell. 10.1: 267
Anon.Vales. 12.64: 271
Apul. apol. 45.6: 70
Apul. Met. 1.25: 190
Apul. Met. 2.13: 70
Apul. Met. 2.15: 120
Apul. Met. 3.22: 120, 169
Apul. Met. 4.18: 134
Apul. Met. 5.10: 190
Apul. Met. 5.16: 176
Apul. Met. 6.10: 132, 217
Apul. Met. 6.26: 172
Apul. Met. 9.11: 169
Apul. Met. 10.14: 120
Apul. Met. 11.14: 169
Apul. Mun. pr.: 32
Apul. Pl. 1.12: 60
Arnob. 1.43: 67
Arnob. 1.64: 290
August. adult. coniug. 1.7.7: 282
August. bon. coniug. 14.16: 262
August. c. Maximin.1.747: 203
August. C.D. 10.32: 14
August. Conf. 1.18.29: 65
August. cura mort. 9: 53
August. de nupt. et concup. 1.2.2: 193
August. doctr. 1.30.31: 236
August. Ep. 55.7: 27
August. Ep. 108.6: 69

August. Ep. 194.10: 285
August. gen. c. Manich. 1.5.9: 302
August. in psalm. 50.22: 270
August. serm. 239 (PL 38.1127): 281
August. Trin. 4.4: 27
Aur. Vict. Caes. 14.6: 265
Aur. Vict. Caes. 19.4: 265
Aur. Vict. Caes. 25.1: 175
Aur. Vict. Caes. 28.1: 77
Aur. Vict. Caes. 35.7: 142
Aur. Vict. Caes. 39.28: 188
Aur. Vict. Caes. 40.17: 19
Auson. 1.25–27: 265
Auson. Grat. act. 2.6: 79
Auson. Grat. act. 3.13: 94
Auson. Grat. act. 3.15: 41
Auson. Grat. act. 6.29: 79
Auson. Grat. act. 7.34: 164
Auson. Grat. act. 9.44: 42
Auson. Mos. 172: 230
Auson. Mos. 309: 285
Auson. Mos. 326: 270
Auson. Periocha Odussiae 22.12: 230
Auson. versus Paschales 6–23: 95
Caes. Civ. 3.9.2: 39
Caes. Gal. 1.1.2: 150
Caes. Gal. 3.23.2: 151
Caes. Gal. 4.34.2: 223
Caes. Gal. 6.42.1: 190
Caes. Gal. 7.76.5: 49
Cassian. inst. 8.11: 288
Cat. 64.140: 221
Cat. 80.5: 129
CE 1178.40: 236
CE 1604: 65
Cels. pr. p. 8, l. 22: 27
Cens. 20.1–10: 27
Cens. 20.10: 23
Chalcid. Comm. 2.310 (p. 310.17W): 267
Cic. Amic. 85: 55
Cic. Amic. 91: 285
Cic. Att. 2.5: 139
Cic. Att. 5.9.2: 33
Cic. Att. 7.11.1: 289

Cic. Att. 8.9.1: 154
Cic. Att. 10.2.2: 223
Cic. Att. 10.14.1: 236
Cic. Att. 11.6.2: 20
Cic. Att. 14.9.2: 289
Cic. Caec. 60: 291
Cic. Cael. 10: 107
Cic. Cael. 33: 160
Cic. Cael. 59: 170
Cic. Cat. 1.27: 194, 283
Cic. Cat. 4.22: 146
Cic. Clu. 10: 284
Cic. Clu. 39: 138
Cic. Clu. 49: 61
Cic. Clu. 77: 139
Cic. Clu. 147: 179
Cic. de Orat. 2.334: 154
Cic. de Orat. 3.93: 237
Cic. de Orat. 3.199: 285
Cic. de Orat. 3.220: 44
Cic. de Orat. 3.225: 57
Cic. Deiot. 8: 207
Cic. Div. 2.22: 4
Cic. Div. Caec. 11: 235
Cic. Dom. 61: 283
Cic. Dom. 80: 185
Cic. Dom. 107: 283
Cic. Fam. 6.18.4: 52
Cic. Fam. 7.2.4: 33
Cic. Fam. 7.3.2: 243
Cic. Fam. 8.6.5: 33
Cic. Fam. 9.16.7: 256
Cic. Fam. 10.8.5: 132
Cic. Fam. 11.21.4: 286
Cic. Fam. 12.27: 54
Cic. Fin. 1.17: 13
Cic. Fin. 2.54: 127
Cic. Fin. 2.58: 47
Cic. Fin. 5.92: 261
Cic. Flac. 94: 128
Cic. Inv. 1.32: 97
Cic. Inv. 2.10: 84
Cic. Inv. 2.27: 183
Cic. Leg. 2.29: 33
Cic. Leg. 3.35: 139
Cic. Man. 30: 258
Cic. Marc. 22: 47

INDICES 345

Cic. Marc. 31: 289
Cic. Mil. 11: 282
Cic. Mil. 56: 244
Cic. Mur. 3: 285
Cic. Mur. 45: 138
Cic. Mur. 84: 283
Cic. N.D. 1.25: 300
Cic. N.D. 1.95: 91
Cic. Off. 1.94: 285
Cic. Off. 1.131: 172
Cic. Off. 2.27: 288
Cic. Off. 2.73: 283
Cic. Off. 3.4: 255
Cic. Off. 3.100: 141
Cic. Orat. 34: 278
Cic. Phil. 1.29: 38
Cic. Phil. 2.64: 146
Cic. Phil. 4.15: 283
Cic. Phil. 7.3: 88
Cic. Phil. 11.7: 288
Cic. Phil. 11.27: 128
Cic. Phil. 11.32: 243
Cic. Phil. 14.33: 258
Cic. Pis. 20: 258
Cic. Pis. 22: 234
Cic. Planc. 12: 228
Cic. Q. fr. 1.1.19: 55
Cic. Q. fr. 1.1.38: 54, 55
Cic. Quinct. 83: 291
Cic. Quinct. 93: 285
Cic. Rab. Perd. 3: 209
Cic. Red. Pop. 7: 138
Cic. Red. Pop. 24: 199
Cic. Rep. 1.62: 84
Cic. Rep. 6.17: 297
Cic. Rep. 6.24: 28
Cic. S. Rosc. 61: 283
Cic. S. Rosc. 87: 156
Cic. Sen. 10: 249
Cic. Sen. 44: 72
Cic. Sest. 07: 20
Cic. Sest. 20: 24
Cic. Sest. 20: 132
Cic. Sest. 84: 157
Cic. Sest. 145: 145
Cic. Sul. 44: 256
Cic. Tusc. 3.29: 16

Cic. Tusc. 3.31: 261
Cic. Tusc. 5.3: 47, 176
Cic. Tusc. 5.19: 198
Cic. Ver. 1.30: 61
Cic. Ver. 1.41: 266
Cic. Ver. 2.129: 33
Cic. Ver. 2.152: 283
Cic. Ver. 3.24: 145
Cic. Ver. 3.47: 107
Cic. Ver. 3.49: 70
Cic. Ver. 3.141: 185
Cic. Ver. 4.73: 273
Cic. Ver. 4.101: 118
Cic. Ver. 5.88: 132
Cic. Ver. 5.129: 160
[Cic.] epist. ad Oct. 3: 118
CIL 06.1768: 61
CIL 06.1770: 73
CIL 06.1771: 73
CIL 08.2756: 65
CIL 09.2461: 61
CIL 10.6441: 61
Claud. carm. min. 30.46: 50
Claud. Cons. Stil. 3 pr. 17: 275
Claud. In Ruf. 2.177: 162
Claud. In Ruf. 2.349: 82
Claud. IV Cons. Hon. 243: 140
Claud. Rapt. Pros. 2.340: 272
Cod. Iust. 10.69.1: 137
Cod. Iust. 10.72.3: 142
Cod. Iust. 11.62 [61].3: 111
Cod. Theod. 1.6.2: 96
Cod. Theod. 1.6.2: 280
Cod. Theod. 1.16.6: 66
Cod. Theod. 1.29.1: 106
Cod. Theod. 2.1.1: 146
Cod. Theod. 2.33.2: 142
Cod. Theod. 3.5.11: 142
Cod. Theod. 3.10.1: 142
Cod. Theod. 4.6.3: 142
Cod. Theod. 5.13.3: 280
Cod. Theod. 5.15.15: 105
Cod. Theod. 5.15.17: 280
Cod. Theod. 6.24.2-3: 102
Cod. Theod. 6.37.1: 95
Cod. Theod. 7.1.4: 122
Cod. Theod. 7.1.5: 95

Cod. Theod. 7.1.10: 138
Cod. Theod. 7.4.3: 122
Cod. Theod. 7.4.10: 61
Cod. Theod. 7.4.12: 95
Cod. Theod. 7.4.17: 37
Cod. Theod. 7.6.1: 106
Cod. Theod. 7.7.2: 280
Cod. Theod. 7.22.7: 140, 183
Cod. Theod. 8.1.11: 280
Cod. Theod. 8.4.8: 95
Cod. Theod. 8.4.9: 280
Cod. Theod. 8.5.12: 106
Cod. Theod. 8.5.17: 96
Cod. Theod. 8.5.19: 95
Cod. Theod. 8.5.20: 280
Cod. Theod. 8.5.21: 105
Cod. Theod. 8.7.9: 122
Cod. Theod. 8.11.1: 106
Cod. Theod. 9.2.3: 186
Cod. Theod. 9.5.1: 272
Cod. Theod. 9.6.3: 146
Cod. Theod. 9.7.3: 146
Cod. Theod. 9.7.9: 146
Cod. Theod. 9.12.1: 290
Cod. Theod. 9.14.3.7: 260
Cod. Theod. 9.16.1: 63
Cod. Theod. 9.16.3: 63
Cod. Theod. 9.16.4: 63, 64, 146
Cod. Theod. 9.16.5: 63–65
Cod. Theod. 9.16.6: 63, 272
Cod. Theod. 9.16.7: 65
Cod. Theod. 9.16.7: 103
Cod. Theod. 9.16.11: 67
Cod. Theod. 9.30.1: 105
Cod. Theod. 9.34.10: 146
Cod. Theod. 9.42.2: 146
Cod. Theod. 9.42.20: 290
Cod. Theod. 9.45.1: 68
Cod. Theod. 10.1.8: 96
Cod. Theod. 10.4.2: 280
Cod. Theod. 10.19.3: 122
Cod. Theod. 10.24.1: 142
Cod. Theod. 11.1.8: 95
Cod. Theod. 11.1.13: 111, 142
Cod. Theod. 11.2.2: 105
Cod. Theod. 11.7.9: 95
Cod. Theod. 11.7.20: 142

Cod. Theod. 11.30.32: 96
Cod. Theod. 11.30.34: 105
Cod. Theod. 11.31.1: 105
Cod. Theod. 11.36.15: 96
Cod. Theod. 12.1.58: 95
Cod. Theod. 12.6.5: 103, 182
Cod. Theod. 12.6.10: 142
Cod. Theod. 12.12.3: 95
Cod. Theod. 12.12.4: 105
Cod. Theod. 12.13.2: 105
Cod. Theod. 13.1.5: 95, 103
Cod. Theod. 13.5.29: 142
Cod. Theod. 13.9.6: 37
Cod. Theod. 14.2.1: 95
Cod. Theod. 14.3.3: 95
Cod. Theod. 14.4.3: 73
Cod. Theod. 14.6.3: 69
Cod. Theod. 14.21.1: 105
Cod. Theod. 15.1.11: 95
Cod. Theod. 15.1.13: 96
Cod. Theod. 15.1.35: 265
Cod. Theod. 16.10.4: 146
Col. 1 pr. 3: 272
Comput. a. 452 chron. I p. 153: 69: 51
Consul. Constant. a 364: 81
Consul. Constant. a. 364.3: 82
Consul. Constant. a. 365: 155
Consul. Constant. a. 365: 295
Consul. Constant. a. 366: 252
Consul. Constant. a. 366: 257
Consul. Constant. a. 375: 23
Consult. 9.6: 96, 104
Curt. 3.5.1: 182
Curt. 4.2.7: 298
Curt. 5.12.18: 181
Curt. 6.10.10: 288
Cypr. epist. 03.1: 69
Cypr. epist. 58.11: 146
Dict. 6.14: 134
Dig. 36.1.38: 132
Dig. 50.16.98: 23
epit. 25.1: 175
epit. 26.1: 175
epit. 26.2: 175
epit. 32.1: 194
epit. 40.10: 19

epit. 40.10: 265
epit. 42.16: 82
epit. 45.1: 23
epit. 45.4: 83
Eutr. 10.18.3: 5
Eutr. pr.: 4
Flor. Epit. 2.6.9: 256
Flor. Epit. 3.16.2: 71
Fortunat. rhet. 1.30: 45
Fro. Amic. 2.3.3: 256
Fron. Aq. 4.2: 199
Fron. Str. 2.3.3: 243
Gaius Inst. 3.134: 70
Gaius Inst. 4.75: 271
Gaius, Inst. 4.4: 142
Gel. 1.6.4: 119
Gel. 1.11.10–16: 57
Gel. 2.28.11: 16
Gel. 4.13.1: 72
Gel. 5.2.4: 181
Gel. 5.14.9: 211
Gel. 5.14.26: 134
Gel. 6.3.7: 291
Gel. 8.10: 168
Gel. 10.22.1: 282
Gel. 12.5.2: 84
Gel. 12.15.2: 124
Gel. 13.17.1: 187
Gel. 13.25.10: 235
Gel. 15.18: 24
Gel. 17.7.7: 139
Gel. 17.12.5: 16
Gel. 18.10.2: 84
Gel. 20.1.26: 84
Greg. M. Dial. 1.5: 141
HA A 07.4: 257
HA A 39.3: 142
HA AC 10.10: 132
HA AC 12.5: 160
HA AS 05.3: 184
HA AS 59.7–8: 175
HA AS 61.4–7: 175
HA C 06.3: 144
HA C 06.9–10: 144
HA C 06.12–13: 144
HA C 07.1: 144
HA Car 06.2: 193

HA Car. 15.10: 5
HA Cc 01.7: 145
HA Cl 05.4: 164
HA Cl 10.6: 77
HA Dd. 9.4: 277
HA DI 02.6: 157
HA Gd 16.3: 176
HA Gd. 5.1: 175
HA Gd. 7.2: 175
HA Gd. 8.1–4: 175
HA Gd. 15–16: 175
HA Max. 7.4: 175
HA OM 02.1–3: 174
HA OM 02.1–5: 174
HA OM 04.7: 174
HA OM 08.1: 174
HA OM 08.4: 174
HA OM 10.1–3: 174
HA P 03.7: 144
HA PN 01.5: 238
HA PN 02.2: 238
HA PN 03.1: 47, 238
HA PN 05.8: 239
HA PN 11.6: 5
HA S 14.8: 145
HA S. 7.1: 254
HA T 07.4: 43
HA Tac. 7.2: 41
HA V 03.8: 77
Hier. adv. Rufin. 1.30: 262
Hier. adv. Rufin. 3.36: 53
Hier. Chron. a. 366: 257, 276, 295
Hier. Chron. pr. p. 7.3–9: 5
Hier. epist. 01.3: 272, 289
Hier. epist. 03.3: 182
Hier. epist. 07.5: 262
Hier. epist. 52.13: 139
Hier. epist. 130.13: 262
Hier. Hilar. 11: 67
Hier. Hilar. 29.1: 294, 302
Hier. in Is. 7.19: 217
Hier. Malchi 03: 65
Hirt. Gal. 8.23.2: 157
Hor. AP 169: 235
Hor. Carm. 1.1.24–25: 168
Hor. Carm. 1.22.1: 52
Hor. Carm. 2.1.6–8: 8

Hor. Carm. 2.1.18–20: 283
Hor. Carm. 3.6.36: 140
Hor. Carm. 3.9.15: 289
Hor. Ep. 1.18.21: 141
Hor. Epod. 1.5: 15
Hor. Epod. 9.37–38: 246
ILS 0055: 72
ILS 0056: 72
ILS 0730: 280
ILS 0755: 106
ILS 0762: 94, 117
ILS 0774: 117
ILS 1229: 61
ILS 1255: 103
ILS 1267: 106
ILS 1268: 106
ILS 1277: 281
ILS 2346: 152
ILS 2777: 152
ILS 4147: 18
ILS 4938: 280
ILS 5905: 190
ILS 8753–8754: 67
Inst. Iust. 4.6.25–27: 142
Iord. Rom. 307: 98
Isid. Orig. 6.17.25: 27
Itin. Burdig. 567: 95
Itin. Burdig. 571.11–575.6: 219
Itin. Burdig. 573.4–575.4: 22
Iulius Severianus 1 Halm 355: 203
Iust. 7.2.8–11: 246
Iust. 16.4.17: 186
Juv. 7.39–40: 140
Juv. 8.186: 164
Lact. Inst. 1.11.39: 203
Lact. Inst. 4.15.4: 86
Lact. Inst. 5.3.11: 86
Lact. mort. pers. 32.5: 42
Lact. mort. pers. 37.1: 285
Lex XII: 8.8–9, 63
Liv. 1 pr. 5: 8
Liv. 1.29.3: 169
Liv. 1.56.8: 282
Liv. 2.31.6: 229
Liv. 3.28.7: 44
Liv. 3.32.1: 107
Liv. 3.35.7: 119

Liv. 3.47.6: 169
Liv. 4.3.16: 132
Liv. 5.1.5: 301
Liv. 5.5.11: 57
Liv. 5.15.5: 70
Liv. 8.4.3: 283
Liv. 9.10.7: 68
Liv. 9.17.13: 229
Liv. 9.25.9: 283
Liv. 9.26.17: 181
Liv. 9.30.1: 278
Liv. 10.13.4: 208
Liv. 10.28.6–7: 197
Liv. 21.41.2: 270
Liv. 21.43.7: 70
Liv. 22.2.5: 298
Liv. 22.54.6: 197
Liv. 23.20.3: 129
Liv. 24.45.7: 57
Liv. 25.33.7: 165
Liv. 26.5.5: 236
Liv. 27.40.7: 107
Liv. 28.21.4: 46
Liv. 29.33.8: 218
Liv. 30.19.11: 129
Liv. 30.32.5: 259
Liv. 34.5.7: 165
Liv. 37.60.2: 216
Liv. 38.16.4: 225
Liv. 38.49.4: 229
Liv. 39.48.1: 286
Liv. 40.8.9: 290
Liv. 40.23.8: 284
Liv. 40.56.6: 160
Liv. 44.9.6: 227, 228
Liv. 44.34.8: 166, 253
Liv. 45.8.6: 234
Liv. per. 17.2: 72
Liv. per. 48–50: 174
Luc. 5.634–635: 301
Luc. 6.242–243: 210
Luc. 6.737: 160
Luc. 8.16-7: 303
Luc. 8.529: 168
Luc. 9.343/4: 298
Luc. 9.1046: 60
Luc. 10.187: 34

Lucr. 2.745: 285
Lucr. 5.728: 244
Lucr. 6.442: 301
Macr. comm. 2.11.13: 29
Macr. comm. 2.12.3: 118
Macr. Sat. 1.12.38–14.15: 27
Macr. Sat. 1.13.8: 34
Macr. Sat. 1.14 91: 34
Macr. Sat. 1.14.1: 33
Macr. Sat. 1.14.2: 32
Macr. Sat. 1.14.3: 34
Macr. Sat. 1.14.4: 28
Macr. Sat. 1.14.6: 23
Macr. Sat. 1.14.6: 27
Macr. Sat. 1.14.13–15: 34
Macr. Sat. 2.1.6: 262
Macr. Sat. 5.2.15: 270
Man. 4.156: 283
Mart. Cap. 5.543: 45
Mela 01.70: 238
Mela 02.26.: 304
Nep. Con. 2.2: 156
Nep. fr. 3: 15
Not. Dign. Occ. 5.147: 152
Not. Dign. Occ. 5.148: 152
Not. Dign. Occ. 38.8: 226
Not. Dign. Occ. 42.7: 226
Not. Dign. Occ.42.4: 226
Not. Dign. Occ.42.9: 226
Not. Dign. Occ.42.11: 226
Not. Dign. Occ.42.14: 226
Not. Dign. Or. 2.32: 225
Not. Dign. Or. 7.40: 140
Not. Dign. Or. 20: 232
Not. Urb. Const. 3.8: 171
Not. Urb. Const. 3.9: 169
Not. Urb. Const. 4.19: 171
Not. Urb. Const. 10.8: 156
Origo Const. 5.20: 265
Oros. hist. 1.20.3: 274
Oros. hist. 2.19.13: 254
Oros. hist. 6.21.13: 66
Oros. hist. 7.32.1: 43
Oros. hist. 7.32.2: 22
Oros. hist. 7.36.9–10: 210
Oros. hist. 7.36.10: 254
Oros. hist. 7.40.6: 160

Ov. Am. 1.8.83–84: 273
Ov. Am. 3.8.53: 237
Ov. Ars 1.227: 273
Ov. Ars 1.653–654: 273
Ov. Ars 2.69: 206
Ov. Fast. 2.685–686: 27
Ov. Fast. 4.89: 242
Ov. Fast. 5.188: 273
Ov. Met. 1.7–9: 301
Ov. Met. 1.290–291: 299
Ov. Met. 1.593–594: 254
Ov. Met. 2.263–264: 299
Ov. Met. 3.111–112: 164
Ov. Met. 3.395: 301
Ov. Met. 8.74: 140
Ov. Met. 9.338–339: 200
Ov. Met. 11.506: 299
Ov. Met. 12.7: 131
Ov. Rem. 665: 206
Ov. Tr. 1.9b.27–28: 251
Ov. Tr. 2.141: 185
Ov. Tr. 3.3.13: 20
Ov. Tr. 5.1.53–54: 273
Ov. Tr. 5.12.27–28: 305
Pac. trag. 184: 132
Pac. trag. 366–367: 234
Pac. trag. 416: 301
Pan. 2.36.3: 210
Pan. 3.3.1: 78
Pan. 4.4.5: 79
Pan. 4.9.5: 79
Pan. 4.16.4: 79
Pan. 4.20.1: 246
Pan. 4.31.4: 277
Pan. 7.2.5: 246
Pan. 12.18.3: 277
Pereg. Aeth. 5.9: 222
Pers. 3.59: 244
Petr. 117.5: 198
Petr. 117.7: 223
Pl. Rud. 422: 261
Pl. Rud. 741: 126
Pl. Stich. 492: 291
Plin. Ep. 5.8.12: 9
Plin. Ep. 5.13.10: 129
Plin. Ep. 7.27.13: 162
Plin. Ep. 9.26.2: 57

Plin. Ep. 10.1.1: 132
Plin. Ep. 10.97.2: 129
Plin. Nat. 2.200: 297
Plin. Nat. 6.11: 205
Plin. Nat. 7.79: 261
Plin. Nat. 13.96: 66
Plin. Nat. 15.125: 191
Plin. Nat. 18.151: 217
Plin. Nat. 18.211: 31, 34
Plin. Nat. 33.40: 162
Plin. Nat. 33.81: 267
Plin. Nat. 34.20: 72
Plin. Nat. 34.89: 274
Plin. Nat. pr. 20: 14
Plin. Pan. 4.4: 209
Plin. Pan. 4.7: 52
Plin. Pan. 7.4: 46
Prisc. gramm. II 105.5–6: 139
Prop. 1.20.15–16: 51
Prop. 2.25.11–12: 273
Prop. 3.5.4: 50, 51
Prud. c. Symm. 2.920: 129
Pub. C. 43: 191
Quad. hist. 12: 206
Quint. Decl. 276.10: 151
Quint. Decl. 314.17: 203
Quint. Inst. 1.7.12: 72
Quint. Inst. 2.2.12: 203
Quint. Inst. 3.8.15: 154
Quint. Inst. 3.8.54: 160
Quint. Inst. 5.10.42: 139
Quint. Inst. 6.5.5: 228
Quint. Inst. 10.6: 49
Quint. Inst. 11.3.84: 45
Quint. Inst. 11.3.89–120: 45
Quint. Inst. 12.5.1: 38
Quint. Inst. 12.10.61: 160
Quint. Inst. 12.10.62: 57
[Quint.] Decl. 10.19: 143
[Quint.] Decl. 12.14: 71
Rhet. Her. 1.3.4: 301
Rhet. Her. 2.8: 139
Ruf. Fest. 13: 98
Rufin. hist. 2.2: 22
Rufin. hist. 11.2: 83
Rut. Lup. 1.6: 55
Sal. Cat. 3.2: 8

Sal. Cat. 6.7: 286
Sal. Cat. 20.13: 146
Sal. Cat. 30.6: 260
Sal. Cat. 32.1: 80
Sal. Cat. 32.2: 271
Sal. Cat. 41.2: 77
Sal. Cat. 44.6: 132
Sal. Cat. 51.37: 91
Sal. Cat. 52.36: 67
Sal. Cat. 59.1: 283
Sal. Hist. 1.55.22: 164
Sal. Hist. 3.48.5: 193
Sal. Jug. 10.6: 53
Sal. Jug. 13.6: 191
Sal. Jug. 13.8: 193
Sal. Jug. 24.3: 157
Sal. Jug. 28.4: 185
Sal. Jug. 58.2: 232
Sal. Jug. 59.3: 256
Sal. Jug. 74.2: 151
Sal. Jug. 85.39: 266
Sal. Jug. 97.5: 246
Sal. Jug. 113.1: 80
Schol. Juv. 4.13: 216
Schol. Juv. 13.33: 216
Sen. Ben. 2.24.2: 228
Sen. clem. 1.10.2: 273
Sen. Contr. 10 pr. 8: 14
Sen. de vita beata 17.2: 162
Sen. Ep. 67.3: 289
Sen. Ep. 90.13: 261
Sen. Ep. 111.2: 49
Sen. Ep. 124: 162
Sen. Herc. Oet. 731–732: 298
Sen. Nat. 1 pr. 13: 205
Sen. Nat. 2.32.4: 60
Sen. Nat. 5.15.3: 237
Sen. Nat. 6.1.4: 297
Sen. Nat. 6.6.3: 298
Sen. Ot. 5.2: 134
Sen. Prov. 1.2: 297
Sen. Thy. 361–362: 303
Sen. Tranq. 3.1: 131
[Sen.] Oct. 523–524: 168
Serv. A. 12.850: 179
Sil. 2.650: 16
Sil. 6.358: 226

Sil. 15.237–238: 298
Sol. 1.34: 33
Sol. 1.34–47: 27
Sol. 1.39: 32
Sol. 1.42: 34
Sol. 1.43: 33, 35
Sol. 1.44: 31
Sol. 1.45: 32, 34
Sol. 1.46–47: 34
Sol. 1.47: 35
Sol. 1.82: 194
Sol. 1.95: 303
Sol. 5.13: 159
Sol. 7.21: 266
Sol. 53.26: 155
Sol. pr. 3: 4
Stat. Th. 2.489–490: 194
Stat. Th. 4.620: 275
Stat. Th. 9.756: 275
Suet. Aug. 31.2: 34
Suet. Aug. 44.2: 162
Suet. Aug. 51.1: 231
Suet. Cal. 23.3: 90
Suet. Cal. 28.1: 249
Suet. Dom. 10.5: 231
Suet. Jul. 32: 151
Suet. Jul. 40.1: 31, 33
Suet. Nero 28.1: 162
Suet. Nero 57.2: 199
Suet. Tib. 50.2: 185
Suet. Tib. 51.1: 143
Suet. Tib. 62.2: 141
Suet. Vesp. 8.1: 247
Suet. Vit. 18.1: 253
Sulp. Sev. Chron. 1.1.1: 4
Symm. Or. 1.3: 246
Symm. Or. 1.9: 42
Symm. Or. 1.10: 50
Symm. Or. 1.11: 83
Symm. Or. 1.12: 82
Symm. Or. 1.13: 94
Symm. Or. 1.14: 99
Symm. Or. 1.15: 99
Symm. Or. 1.16: 99
Symm. Or. 1.17: 114, 116
Symm. Or. 1.18: 121
Symm. Or. 1.19: 121

Symm. Or. 1.21: 276
Symm. Or. 1.22: 288
Symm. Or. 3.3: 42
Symm. Or. 3.5: 42
Symm. Or. 3.11: 99
Symm. Or. 4.2: 42
Symm. Or. 4.7: 42
Symm. Or. 4.10: 25
Symm. rel. 23.9: 66
Symm. rel. 30.3: 85
Tab. Peut. IX.2-IX.4: 22
Tab. Peut. VIII 3: 205
Tac. Agr. 6.1: 194
Tac. Agr. 33.6: 151
Tac. Ann. 1.7.7: 266
Tac. Ann. 1.17.1: 247
Tac. Ann. 1.28.4: 157
Tac. Ann. 1.40.1: 190
Tac. Ann. 1.42.2: 180
Tac. Ann. 1.57.1: 271
Tac. Ann. 1.58.2: 189
Tac. Ann. 1.65.1: 170
Tac. Ann. 2.20.1: 286
Tac. Ann. 2.21.2: 216
Tac. Ann. 2.64.3: 149
Tac. Ann. 3.34.3: 61
Tac. Ann. 3.56.2: 53
Tac. Ann. 3.61.1: 69
Tac. Ann. 4.15.1: 107
Tac. Ann. 4.17.3: 257
Tac. Ann. 4.18.1: 186
Tac. Ann. 4.22.3: 65
Tac. Ann. 4.33.4: 8
Tac. Ann. 4.52.2: 66
Tac. Ann. 4.52.3: 127
Tac. Ann. 6.15.3: 135
Tac. Ann. 6.31.1: 237
Tac. Ann. 6.45.1: 107
Tac. Ann. 11.18.3: 70
Tac. Ann. 11.29.2: 192
Tac. Ann. 11.35.3: 138
Tac. Ann. 11.37.1: 286
Tac. Ann. 12.27.2: 283
Tac. Ann. 13.4.2: 51
Tac. Ann. 13.46.2: 286
Tac. Ann. 14.11.1: 77
Tac. Ann. 14.61.2: 66

Tac. Ann. 15.36.4: 66
Tac. Ann. 15.61.4: 156
Tac. Dial. 21.7: 4
Tac. Dial. 23.1: 234
Tac. Ger. 6.4: 176
Tac. Hist. 1.1: 16
Tac. Hist. 1.15.4: 52
Tac. Hist. 1.36.3: 207
Tac. Hist. 1.37.5: 69
Tac. Hist. 1.43.2: 148
Tac. Hist. 1.48.4: 271
Tac. Hist. 2.12.1: 202, 225
Tac. Hist. 2.29.2: 290
Tac. Hist. 2.30.3: 253
Tac. Hist. 2.63.1: 66
Tac. Hist. 2.74.1: 190
Tac. Hist. 2.74.2: 270
Tac. Hist. 3.72.1: 256
Tac. Hist. 3.75.1: 154
Tac. Hist. 3.78.2: 46
Tac. Hist. 3.82.1: 197
Tac. Hist. 4.15.2: 201
Tac. Hist. 4.18.2: 246
Tac. Hist. 4.23.2: 228
Tac. Hist. 4.81.3: 185
Tert. anim. 52.3: 262
Tert. Apol. 13: 162
Tert. Apol. 17.6: 147
Tert. Apol. 20.3: 62
Tert. Apol. 34: 51
Tert. test. 2: 147
Tib. 1.5.70: 234
[Tib.] 3.7.72: 303
V. Fl. 1.668: 226
V. Fl. 6.412: 302
V. Max. 2.2.4: 179
V. Max. 2.2.7: 184
V. Max. 2.7.7: 289
V. Max. 3.6.4: 72
V. Max. 3.7.9: 49
V. Max. 3.8.2 ext.: 54
V. Max. 6.2.7: 161
V. Max. 6.8.1: 288
V. Max. 7.3.2: 237
V. Max. 7.6.6: 236
V. Max. 8.7 ext. 1: 225
Var. L. 6.4.33: 242

Var. L. 7.80: 206
Veg. mil. 2.21: 155
Veg. mil. 3.18.9: 211
Veg. mil. 4.8: 226
Veg. mil. 4.22.1: 225
Veg. mil. 4.29.1: 226
Veg. mil. 4.31: 226
Veg. mil. 4.46.9: 226
Vell. 1.4.3: 236
Vell. 2.30.1: 258
Vell. 2.61.2: 165
Vell. 2.85.5: 210
Vell. 2.94.2: 221
Vell. 2.101.2: 154
Vell. 2.129.4: 168
Verg. A. 1.123: 304
Verg. A. 1.291–293: 208
Verg. A. 1.567: 237
Verg. A. 2.84: 138
Verg. A. 2.629: 297
Verg. A. 3.411: 62
Verg. A. 4.172: 274
Verg. A. 4.346: 201
Verg. A. 5.143: 226
Verg. A. 5.320: 251
Verg. A. 5.720: 115
Verg. A. 6.336: 302
Verg. A. 6.602–603: 206
Verg. A. 7.113: 135
Verg. A. 7.201: 303
Verg. A. 7.496: 139
Verg. A. 7.529–530: 301
Verg. A. 8.524: 297
Verg. A. 8.580: 115
Verg. A. 9.219: 274
Verg. A. 9.462–463: 242
Verg. A. 9.749: 209
Verg. A. 10.221: 47
Verg. A. 11.627–628: 298
Verg. A. 11.727–728: 242
Verg. A. 12.584: 270
Verg. A. 12.729: 209
Verg. A. 12.849–850: 179
Verg. G. 1.458: 256
Verg. G. 1.461: 234
Verg. G. 2.159–160: 301
Verg. G. 2.161: 225

INDICES

Verg. G. 3.25: 164
Verg. G. 3.541-543: 298
Vir. ill. 1.2: 186
Vir. ill. 38.4: 72

Vitr. 9.1.6: 28-30
Vitr. 9.6.3: 28
Vulg. Luc. 3.16: 281

IX. Passages referred to (Greek, including Ephraem Syrus)

Acta Concilii Chalcedoniensis XIV.27-30: 17
Apollod. 1.6.3: 126
App. BC 01.115: 258
App. BC 02.6.42: 254
Art. pass. 70: 23, 81
Athan. Festal Letters, nr. 37: 295
Basil. Ep. 21: 141
Basil. Ep. 86.1: 278
Basil. Ep. 269.2: 221
Cedrenus Chron. 1.541: 78
Chron. Pasch. a. 364: 21, 39, 81
Chron. Pasch. a. 365: 295
Chron. Pasch. a. 366: 252, 257
Chrys. Hom. 1-67 in Gen. = PG. 53.33: 302
Chrys. oppugn. 1.7 = PG 47.328-329): 19
Chrys. pan. Ign. = PG 50.590: 289
Constantinus Porphyrogenitus Cer. 1.411 Reiske: 44
D.C. 49.30.3: 228
D.C. 49.36.3: 217
D.C. 72.10.2: 144
D.C. 72.12.1: 144
D.C. 72.12.3: 144
D.C. 72.12.5: 144
D.C. 73.1-10: 157
D.C. 73.10.2: 277
D.C. 74.8.3: 277
D.C. 74.11.3-6: 157
D.C. 74.13.5: 238
D.C. 75.7.1: 238
D.C. 75.7.3: 277
D.C. 75.14: 145
D.C. 75.14.1: 145
D.C. 75.14.5: 145
D.C. 75.15: 145
D.C. 75.15.2: 145
D.C. 76.2.5: 145

D.C. 78.13.1: 145
D.S. 5.1.3: 10
D.S. 12.36.2-3: 28
D.S. 31.40a: 174
Eun. fr. 15: 7
Eun. fr. 24: 76
Eun. fr. 27.1: 150
Eun. fr. 30: 8
Eun. fr. 31: 76
Eun. fr. 34.3: 128, 136
Eun. fr. 34.4: 204
Eun. fr. 34.6-7: 244
Eun. fr. 34.8: 232
Eun. fr. 34.9: 276
Eun. fr. 37: 268, 269
Eun. VS 07.5.2: 194
Eun. VS 07.5.9: 103
Eus. VC 04.5: 150
Eus. VC 04.58-60: 17
Eus. VC 04.61.1: 215
Gem. 8.50-56: 28
Georgius Monachus 560-561: 299
Greg. Nyss. Eun. 1.143: 98
Hdn. 1.12.3: 144
Hdn. 2.1-5: 157
Hdn. 2.6.13: 166, 167
Hdn. 2.7.8: 238
Hdn. 2.8.4: 238
Hdn. 2.12.2: 238
Hdn. 2.15.6-7: 11
Hdn. 3.4.2-3: 238
Hdn. 3.4.6: 239
Hdn. 3.4.7: 238
Hdn. 3.8.1: 277
Hdn. 3.10.5: 145
Hdn. 3.10.7: 145
Hdn. 3.12: 145
Hdn. 4.12.5-13.8: 174
Hdn. 4.13.3: 130
Hdn. 4.15.9: 174

Hdn. 5.4.11: 174, 277
Hdn. 6.8–9: 175
Hdn. 7.1.10: 277
Hdn. 7.5: 175
Hdn. 7.9.1–4: 175
Hdn. 8.6.5–6: 277
Hdt. 8.137.1: 246
Hdt. 8.139: 246
Hippol. Haer. 41.18: 29
J. Vit. 359–360: 14
Joh. Ant. fr. 179 Müller = 271 Roberto: 79
Joh. Ant. fr. 184 Müller = 277 Roberto: 273
Joh. Ant. fr. 184.1 Müller = 276 Roberto: 252, 257
Jul. Caes. Caes. 329 a: 109
Jul. Caes. Ep. ad Ath. 280a–b: 109
Jul. Caes. Ep. ad Ath. 286 a: 109
Jul. Caes. Or. 3.98 c–d: 109
Jul. Mis. 348c–d: 19
Leo Gramm. Chron. p. 97: 78, 99
Lib. Ep. 308: 220
Lib. Ep. 792: 220
Lib. Ep. 1186.1: 80
Lib. Ep. 1499: 183
Lib. Ep. 1505: 183
Lib. Or. 1.163–165: 136
Lib. Or. 1.171: 276
Lib. Or. 12.78: 150
Lib. Or. 17.30: 150
Lib. Or. 18.273: 130
Lib. Or. 18.290: 108
Lib. Or. 18.292: 296
Lib. Or. 19.15: 167, 276
Lib. Or. 20.25: 22
Lib. Or. 20.25–26: 276
Lib. Or. 24.13: 128, 132, 151
Lib. Or. 36.15: 65, 67
Lib. Or. 62.58–60: 136, 193
Lib. Or. 62.59: 276
Lucianus Hist. Conscr. 27: 12
Lyd. Mens. 1.27: 226
Malalas Chron. 11.279: 223
Malalas Chron. 13.337: 39
Malalas Chron. 13.338: 21, 22, 81, 103

Nic. Call. 11.4 = PG 146: 593, 257
Philost. HE 07.7: 21, 22
Philost. HE 07.10: 136, 193, 276
Philost. HE 08.5: 22
Philost. HE 08.8: 21, 38, 44, 48, 49, 51, 53, 83, 98, 100, 103, 105
Philost. HE 08.16: 22
Philost. HE 09.5: 127, 128, 130, 149, 151, 251, 254, 257, 262, 264
Philost. HE 09.6: 136, 231
Pi. P. 1.96: 273
Pl. Phd. 59 b: 179
Pl. Phdr. 248 a: 179
Plb. 6.11.3–7: 7
Plb. 20.5.7: 303
Plb. 28.11.2: 227
Plb. 36.10: 174
Plut. Alex. 43.6: 257
Plut. Caes. 47: 25
Plut. Per. 28.2: 289
Plut. Pomp. 20.3–4: 258
Plut. Pomp. 20.4: 259
Plut. Sert. 27.2–4: 258
PMag 4.2211–2216: 67
PMag 7.390–394: 67
Priscus fr. 11.2 (Blockley): 217
Procop. Aed. 4.4.3: 96
Procop. Aed. 5.1.2–5: 215
Procop. Vand. 2.8.25: 142
Socr. HE 01.39.1: 215
Socr. HE 04.1.1: 23
Socr. HE 04.1.4: 80, 81, 83
Socr. HE 04.1.8: 22, 79
Socr. HE 04.2.1: 99
Socr. HE 04.2.2.: 149
Socr. HE 04.2.4: 149
Socr. HE 04.3.1: 183, 194, 205
Socr. HE 04.3.2: 204
Socr. HE 04.5.2: 183, 252
Socr. HE 04.5.3: 257, 279
Socr. HE 04.5.4: 257
Socr. HE 04.8.1: 217, 277
Socr. HE 04.9.5: 156
Socr. HE 04.9.8: 257
Socr. HE 04.26.21: 140
Socr. HE 04.31.6: 23

INDICES

Socr. HE 05.1.3: 140
Socr. HE 07.13.6: 66
Soz. HE 02.2.5: 215
Soz. HE 05.15.7: 223
Soz. HE 06.2.13: 294
Soz. HE 06.6.2: 43
Soz. HE 06.6.3–6: 22
Soz. HE 06.6.8: 49, 51, 53
Soz. HE 06.6.9: 83, 99
Soz. HE 06.7.8: 105
Soz. HE 06.7.10: 149, 183
Soz. HE 06.8.2: 252, 257
Soz. HE 06.8.3: 257, 279
Soz. HE 06.9.3: 156
Soz. HE 06.39.4: 167
Soz. HE 07.1.2: 140
Str. 1.3.20 (61C): 304
Str. 2.5.18 (121C): 238
Str. 2.5.24 (125C): 238
Str. 12.3.7 (543C): 218
Str. 12.8.11 (575C): 226
Str. 14.5.19 (676C): 238
Synes. Ep. 66: 99
Th. 3.89.5: 297
Thdt. h. rel. 13.15: 183
Thdt. HE 03.16: 22
Thdt. HE 04.6.2: 49, 51, 53
Thdt. HE 04.6.3: 79, 83, 99
Thdt. HE 05.1.2: 99
Them. Or. 6.74 b: 99
Them. Or. 6.75 d: 94
Them. Or. 6.82a–b: 99
Them. Or. 6.82 d: 83
Them. Or. 6.83 a: 82
Them. Or. 7.86 b: 205
Them. Or. 7.86 c: 126
Them. Or. 7.87 b: 254
Them. Or. 7.90 b: 127, 261
Them. Or. 7.91 a: 159
Them. Or. 7.91 b: 186
Them. Or. 7.91 c–d: 201
Them. Or. 7.91 d: 181, 184
Them. Or. 7.91a–b: 155
Them. Or. 7.91c: 161
Them. Or. 7.91d–92a: 185
Them. Or. 7.92 a: 99
Them. Or. 7.92 b: 155

Them. Or. 7.92 c: 186
Them. Or. 7.93a–c: 276
Them. Or. 7.95 c–d: 276
Them. Or. 7.97 d: 194
Them. Or. 7.98 a: 276
Them. Or. 7.98 d: 290
Them. Or. 8.110d–111a: 276
Them. Or. 11.148 b: 276
Them. Or. 15.190d–191a: 269
Them. Or. 18.224 a: 101
Theoph. Chron. p. 54 De Boor: 83, 99
Theoph. Chron. p. 55 De Boor: 252, 257
Theoph. Chron. p. 56 De Boor: 296, 299
Theoph. Chron. p. 57 De Boor: 156
Zon. 1.13: 302
Zon. 12.24: 210
Zon. 12.26: 121
Zon. 13.14.15–16: 38
Zon. 13.14.16: 18
Zon. 13.14.18: 21
Zon. 13.15: 99
Zon. 13.15.4: 22
Zon. 13.16: 128, 257
Zos. 1.13.1–2: 175
Zos. 2.40.2: 140
Zos. 3.13.3: 100
Zos. 3.35.2: 128
Zos. 3.36.1: 38, 41
Zos. 3.36.1–2: 18, 40
Zos. 3.36.2: 22
Zos. 4.1.1: 84–86
Zos. 4.1.2: 46, 82
Zos. 4.2: 86
Zos. 4.2.2: 86
Zos. 4.2.3: 102, 106
Zos. 4.2.4: 103
Zos. 4.3.1: 98
Zos. 4.3.4: 87, 108
Zos. 4.4.1: 79, 149
Zos. 4.4.2: 128, 130
Zos. 4.4.3: 132
Zos. 4.5.1–2: 135
Zos. 4.5.3–4: 193, 195

Zos. 4.5.3: 136, 154, 180
Zos. 4.5.5: 155, 156, 159, 167, 170
Zos. 4.6.2–3: 170
Zos. 4.6.2: 103, 186, 187, 191
Zos. 4.6.3: 169, 181
Zos. 4.6.4: 194
Zos. 4.6.4–5: 224
Zos. 4.6.5: 265
Zos. 4.7.1: 128, 195, 205, 233, 265
Zos. 4.7.2: 267
Zos. 4.7.3: 116, 182, 204, 235
Zos. 4.7.4: 114, 121, 248
Zos. 4.8.1: 232
Zos. 4.8.1–2: 244, 248, 250
Zos. 4.8.3: 248, 252, 253, 257, 264
Zos. 4.8.4–5: 275
Zos. 4.8.4: 257, 267, 273
Zos. 4.10.1: 268
Zos. 4.10.4: 103
Zos. 4.19.1: 19
Zos. 4.20.1–2: 230
Zos. 4.30.5: 233